D1595843

CIVILIZATION IN THE UNITED STATES

AN INQUIRY BY THIRTY AMERICANS

EDITED BY HAROLD E. STEARNS

GREENWOOD PRESS, PUBLISHERS
WESTPORT, CONNECTICUT

Originally published in 1922
by Harcourt, Brace and Company, New York

First Greenwood Reprinting 1971

Library of Congress Catalogue Card Number 71-109977

SBN 8371-4483-3

Printed in the United States of America

PREFACE

THIS book has been an adventure in intellectual co-operation. If it were a mere collection of haphazard essays, gathered together to make the conventional symposium, it would have only slight significance. But it has been the deliberate and organized outgrowth of the common efforts of like-minded men and women to see the problem of modern American civilization as a whole, and to illuminate by careful criticism the special aspect of that civilization with which the individual is most familiar. Personal contact has served to correct overemphasis, and slow and careful selection of the members of a group which has now grown to some thirty-odd has given to this work a unity of approach and attack which it otherwise could not possibly have had.

The nucleus of this group was brought together by common work, common interests, and more or less common assumptions. As long ago as the autumn of last year Mr. Van Wyck Brooks and I discussed the possibility of several of us, who were engaged in much the same kind of critical examination of our civilization, coming together to exchange ideas, to clarify our individual fields, and to discover wherein they coincided, overlapped, or diverged. The original desire was the modest one of making it possible for us to avoid working at cross-purposes. I suggested that we meet at my home, which a few of us did, and since that time until the delivery of this volume to the publishers we have met every fortnight. Even at our first meeting we discovered our points of view to have so much in common that our desire for informal and pleasant discussions became the more serious wish to contribute a definite and tangible piece of work towards the advance of intellectual life in America. We wished to speak the truth about American civilization as we saw it, in order to do our share in making a real civilization possible—for I think with all of us there was a common assumption that a field cannot be

ploughed until it has first been cleared of rocks, and that constructive criticism can hardly exist until there is something
on which to construct.

Naturally the first problem to arise was the one of ways and
means. If the spirit and temper of the French encyclopædists
of the 18th century appealed strongly to us, certainly their
method for the advancement of knowledge was inapplicable in
our own century. The cultural phenomena we proposed to
survey were too complicated and extensive; besides, we wished
to make a definite contribution of some kind or another while,
so to speak, there was yet time. For the cohesiveness of the
group, the good-humoured tolerance and cheerful sacrifice of
time, were to some extent the consequence of the intellectual
collapse that came with the hysterical post-armistice days,
when it was easier than in normal times to get together intelligent and civilized men and women in common defence against
the common enemy of reaction. We wished to take advantage of this strategic situation for the furtherance of our co-
operative enterprise, and decided, finally, that the simplest plan
would be the best. Each of us was to write a single short
essay on the special topic we knew most thoroughly; we were
to continue our meetings in order to keep informed of the
progress of our work and to see that there was no duplication;
we were to extend the list of subjects to whatever legitimately
bore upon our cultural life and to select the authors by common agreement; we were to keep in touch with each other
so that the volume might have that inner consistency which
could come only from direct acquaintance with what each of
us was planning.

There were a few other simple rules which we laid down
in the beginning. Desirous of avoiding merely irrelevant criticism and of keeping attention upon our actual treatment of
our subjects rather than upon our personalities, we provided
that all contributors to the volume must be American citizens.
For the same reason, we likewise provided that in the list there
should be no professional propagandists—except as one is a
propagandist for one's own ideas—no martyrs, and no one who
was merely disgruntled. Since our object was to give an uncompromising, and consequently at some points necessarily

harsh, analysis, we desired the tone to be good-natured and
the temper urbane. At first, these larger points of policy were
decided by common agreement or, on occasion, by majority
vote, and to the end I settled no important question without
consultation with as many members of the group as I could
approach within the limited time we had agreed to have this
volume in the hands of the publisher. But with the extension
of the scope of the book, the negotiations with the publisher,
and the mass of complexities and details that are inevitable in
so difficult an enterprise, the authority to decide specific questions and the usual editorial powers were delegated as a matter
of convenience to me, aided by a committee of three. Hence
I was in a position constantly to see the book as a whole,
and to make suggestions for differentiation, where repetition
appeared to impend, or for unity, where the divergence
was sharp enough to be construed by some as contradictory.
In view both of the fact that every contributor has full liberty
of opinion and that the personalities and points of view finding
expression in the essays are all highly individualistic, the underlying unity which binds the volume together is really
surprising.

It may seem strange that a volume on civilization in the
United States does not include a specific article on religion,
and the omission is worth a paragraph of explanation. Outside the bigger cities, certainly no one can understand the social
structure of contemporary American life without careful study
of the organization and power of the church. Speaking generally, we are a church-going people, and at least on the surface the multiplicity of sects and creeds, the sheer immensity
of the physical apparatus by which the religious impulse is
articulated, would seem to prove that our interest in and
emotional craving for religious experience are enormous. But
the omission has not been due to any superciliousness on our
part towards the subject itself; on the contrary, I suppose I
have put more thought and energy into this essay, which has
not been written, than into any other problem connected with
the book. The bald truth is, it has been next to impossible
to get any one to write on the subject; most of the people I
approached shied off—it was really difficult to get them to talk

about it at all. Almost unanimously, when I did manage to procure an opinion from them, they said that real religious feeling in America had disappeared, that the church had become a purely social and political institution, that the country is in the grip of what Anatole France has aptly called Protestant clericalism, and that, finally, they weren't interested in the topic. The accuracy of these observations (except the last) I cannot, of course, vouch for, but it is rather striking that they were identical. In any event, the topic as a topic has had to be omitted; but it is not neglected, for in several essays directly—in particular, "Philosophy" and "Nerves"—and in many by implication the subject is discussed. At one time Mr. James Harvey Robinson consented to write the article —and it would have been an illuminating piece of work—but unfortunately ill health and the pressure of official duties made the task impossible for him within the most generous time limit that might be arranged.

I have spoken already of the unity which underlies the volume. When I remember all these essays, and try to summon together the chief themes that run through them, either by explicit statement or as a kind of underlying rhythm to all, in order to justify the strong impression of unity, I find three major contentions that may be said to be basic—contentions all the more significant inasmuch as they were unpremeditated and were arrived at, as it were, by accident rather than design. They are:

First, That in almost every branch of American life there is a sharp dichotomy between preaching and practice; we let not our right hand know what our left hand doeth. Curiously enough, no one regards this, and in fact no one consciously feels this as hypocrisy—there are certain abstractions and dogmas which are sacred to us, and if we fall short of these external standards in our private life, that is no reason for submitting them to a fresh examination; rather are we to worship them the more vociferously to show our sense of sin. Regardless, then, of the theoretical excellence or stupidity of these standards, in actual practice the moral code resolves itself into the one cardinal heresy of being found out, with the chief sanction enforcing it, the fear of what people will say.

Second, That whatever else American civilization is, it is not
Anglo-Saxon, and that we shall never achieve any genuine
nationalistic self-consciousness as long as we allow certain
financial and social minorities to persuade us that we are still
an English Colony. Until we begin seriously to appraise and
warmly to cherish the heterogeneous elements which make up
our life, and to see the common element running through all
of them, we shall make not even a step towards true unity;
we shall remain, in Roosevelt's class-conscious and bitter but
illuminating phrase, a polyglot boarding-house. It is curious
how a book on American civilization actually leads one back
to the conviction that we are, after all, Americans.

Third, That the most moving and pathetic fact in the social
life of America to-day is emotional and æsthetic starvation,
of which the mania for petty regulation, the driving, regimen-
tating, and drilling, the secret society and its grotesque regalia,
the firm grasp on the unessentials of material organization of
our pleasures and gaieties are all eloquent stigmata. We have
no heritages or traditions to which to cling except those that
have already withered in our hands and turned to dust. One
can feel the whole industrial and economic situation as so
maladjusted to the primary and simple needs of men and
women that the futility of a rationalistic attack on these in-
fantilisms of compensation becomes obvious. There must be
an entirely new deal of the cards in one sense; we must change
our hearts. For only so, unless through the humbling of
calamity or scourge, can true art and true religion and true
personality, with their native warmth and caprice and gaiety,
grow up in America to exorcise these painted devils we have
created to frighten us away from the acknowledgment of our
spiritual poverty.

If these main contentions seem severe or pessimistic, the
answer must be: we do not write to please; we strive only
to understand and to state as clearly as we can. For American civilization is still in the embryonic stage, with rich and
with disastrous possibilities of growth. But the first step in
growing up is self-conscious and deliberately critical examination of ourselves, without sentimentality and without fear. We
cannot even devise, much less control, the principles which are

to guide our future development until that preliminary understanding has come home with telling force to the consciousness
of the ordinary man.   To this self-understanding, this book is,
in our belief, a genuine and valuable contribution.   We may
not always have been wise; we have tried always to be honest.
And if our attempt will help to embolden others to an equally
frank expression of their beliefs, perhaps in time wisdom will
come.

I am glad that, however serious, we are never solemn in these
essays.   Often, in fact, we are quite gay, and it would be a
humourless person indeed who could not read many of them,
even when the thrusts are at himself, with that laughter which
Rabelais tells us is proper to the man.   For whatever our defects, we Americans, we have one virtue and perhaps a saving
virtue—we still know how to laugh at ourselves.

H. E. S.

New York City, July Fourth, 1921.

CONTENTS

CONTENTS

CIVILIZATION IN THE UNITED STATES

THE CITY

A ROUND us, in the city, each epoch in America has been concentrated and crystallized. In building our cities we deflowered a wilderness. To-day more than one-half the population of the United States lives in an environment which the jerry-builder, the real estate speculator, the paving contractor, and the industrialist have largely created. Have we begotten a civilization? That is a question which a survey of the American city will help us to answer.

If American history is viewed from the standpoint of the student of cities, it divides itself roughly into three parts. The first was a provincial period, which lasted from the foundation of Manhattan down to the opening up of ocean commerce after the War of 1812. This was followed by a commercial period, which began with the cutting of canals and ended with the extension of the railroad system across the continent, and an industrial period, that gathered force on the Atlantic seaboard in the 'thirties and is still the dominant economic phase of our civilization. These periods must not be looked upon as strictly successive or exclusive: the names merely express in a crude way the main aspect of each era. It is possible to telescope the story of America's colonial expansion and industrial exploitation by following the material growth and the cultural impoverishment of the American city during its transformations.

The momentum of the provincial city lasted well on to the Civil War. The economic basis of this period was agriculture and petty trade: its civic expression was, typically, the small New England town, with a central common around which were grouped a church—appropriately called a meeting-house—a school, and perhaps a town hall. Its main street would be lined with tall suave elms and bordered by reticent white houses of much the same design as those that dotted the countryside. In the growing towns of the seaboard this culture was

3

overthrown, before it had a chance to express itself adequately in either institutions or men, and it bloomed rather tardily, therefore, in the little towns of Concord and Cambridge, between 1820 and the Civil War. We know it to-day through a largely anonymous architecture, and through a literature created by the school of writers that bears the name of the chief city. Unfortunately for the further development of what we might call the Concord culture, the agricultural basis of this civilization shifted to the wheat-growing West; and therewith channels of trade were diverted from Boston to ports that tapped a richer, more imperial hinterland. What remained of the provincial town in New England was a mummy-case.

The civilization of the New England town spent itself in the settlement of the Ohio Valley and the great tracts beyond. None of the new centres had, *qua* provincial towns, any fresh contribution to make. It had taken the culture of New England more than three centuries before it had borne its Concord fruit, and the story of the Western movement is somehow summed up in the legend of Johnny Appleseed, who planted dry apple seeds, instead of slips from the living tree, and hedged the roads he travelled with wild apples, harsh and puny and inedible. Cincinnati and Pittsburgh jumped from a frustrate provincialism into the midst of the machine era; and so for a long time they remained destitute of the institutions that are necessary to carry on the processes of civilization.

West of the Alleghanies, the common, with its church and school, was not destined to dominate the urban landscape: the railroad station and the commercial hotel had come to take their place. This was indeed the universal mark of the new industrialism, as obvious in 19th-century Oxford as in Hoboken. The pioneer American city, however, had none of the cultural institutions that had been accumulated in Europe during the great outbursts of the Middle Age and the Renaissance, and as a result its destitution was naked and apparent. It is true that every town which was developed mainly during the 19th century—Manchester as well as Milwaukee—suffered from the absence of civic institutes. The peculiarity of the

New World was that the facilities for borrowing from the older centres were considerably more limited. London could export Madox Brown to Manchester to do the murals in the Town Hall: New York had still to create its schools of art before it had any Madox Browns that could be exported.

With the beginning of the 19th century, market centres which had at first tapped only their immediate region began to reach further back into the hinterland, and to stretch outward, not merely for freight but for immigrants, across the ocean. The silly game of counting heads became the fashion, and in the literature of the 'thirties one discovers that every commercial city had its statistical lawyer who was bold enough to predict its leadership in " population and wealth " before the century was out. The chief boast of the American city was its prospective size.

Now the New England town was a genuine community. In so far as the New England community had a common social and political and religious life, the town expressed it. The city which was representative of the second period, on the other hand, was in origin a trading fort, and the supreme occupation of its founders was with the goods life rather than the good life. New York, Pittsburgh, Chicago, and St. Louis have this common basis. They were not composed of corporate organizations on the march, as it were, towards a New Jerusalem: they were simply a rabble of individuals " on the make." With such a tradition to give it momentum it is small wonder that the adventurousness of the commercial period was exhausted on the fortuities and temptations of trade. A state of intellectual anæsthesia prevailed. One has only to compare Cist's *Cincinnati Miscellany* with Emerson's *Dial* to see at what a low level the towns of the Middle West were carrying on.

Since there was neither fellowship nor social stability nor security in the scramble of the inchoate commercial city, it remained for a particular institution to devote itself to the gospel of the " glad hand." Thus an historian of Pittsburgh records the foundation of a Masonic lodge as early as 1785, shortly after the building of the church, and in every Ameri-

can city, small or big, Odd Fellows, Mystic Shriners, Woodmen, Elks, Knights of Columbus, and other orders without
number in the course of time found for themselves a prominent place. (Their feminine counterparts were the D.A.R.
and the W.C.T.U., their juniors, the college Greek letter fraternities.) Whereas one will search American cities in vain
for the labour temples one discovers to-day in Europe from
Belgium to Italy, one finds that the fraternal lodge generally
occupies a site of dignity and importance. There were doubtless many excellent reasons for the strange proliferation of
professional fraternity in the American city, but perhaps the
strongest reason was the absence of any other kind of fraternity. The social centre and the community centre, which
in a singularly hard and consciously beatific way have sought
to organize fellowship and mutual aid on different terms, are
products of the last decade.

Perhaps the only other civic institution of importance that
the commercial towns fostered was the lyceum: forerunner
of the elephantine Chautauqua. The lyceum lecture, however,
was taken as a soporific rather than a stimulant, and if it
aroused any appetite for art, philosophy, or science there was
nothing in the environment of the commercial city that could
satisfy it. Just as church-going became a substitute for religion, so automatic lyceum attendance became a substitute for
thought. These were the prayer wheels of a preoccupied
commercialism.

The contrast between the provincial and the commercial
city in America was well summed up in their plans. Consider
the differences between Cambridge and New York. Up to the
beginning of the 19th century New York, at the tip of Manhattan Island, had the same diffident, rambling town plan that
characterizes Cambridge. In this old type of city layout the
streets lead nowhere, except to the buildings that give onto
them: outside the main roads the provisions for traffic are so
inadequate as to seem almost a provision against traffic. Quiet
streets, a pleasant aspect, ample domestic facilities were the
desiderata of the provincial town; traffic, realty speculation,
and expansion were those of the newer era. This became evident as soon as the Empire City started to realize its " mani-

fest destiny " by laying down, in 1808, a plan for its future development.

New York's city plan commissioners went about their work with a scarcely concealed purpose to increase traffic and raise realty values. The amenities of city life counted for little in their scheme of things: debating " whether they should confine themselves to rectilinear and rectangular streets, or whether they should adopt some of those supposed improvements, by circles, ovals, and stars," they decided, on grounds of economy, against any departure from the gridiron design. It was under the same stimulus that these admirable philistines had the complacency to plan the city's development up to 155th Street. Here we are concerned, however, with the results of the rectangular plan rather than with the motives that lay behind its adoption throughout the country.

The principal effect of the gridiron plan is that every street becomes a thoroughfare, and that every thoroughfare is potentially a commercial street. The tendency towards movement in such a city vastly outweighs the tendency towards settlement. As a result of progressive shifts in population, due to the changes to which commercial competition subjects the use of land, the main institutions of the city, instead of cohering naturally—as the museums, galleries, theatres, clubs, and public offices group themselves in the heart of Westminster—are dispersed in every direction. Neither Columbia University, New York University, the Astor Library, nor the National Academy of Design—to seize but a few examples—is on its original site. Yet had Columbia remained at Fiftieth Street it might have had some effective working relation with the great storehouse of books that now occupies part of Bryant Park at Forty-second Street; or, alternatively, had the Astor Library remained on its old site it might have had some connection with New York University—had that institution not in turn moved!

What was called the growth of the commercial city was really a manifestation of the absence of design in the gridiron plan. The rectangular parcelling of ground promoted speculation in land-units and the ready interchange of real property: it had no relation whatever to the essential purposes for which a city exists.   It is not a little significant that Chicago, Cincinnati, and St. Louis, each of which had space set aside for public purposes in their original plans, had given up these civic holdings to the realty gambler before half of the 19th century was over.   The common was not the centre of a well-rounded community life, as in New England, but the centre of land-speculation—which was at once the business, the recreation, and the religion of the commercial city.   Under the influence of New York the Scadders whom Martin Chuzzlewit encountered were laying down their New Edens throughout the country.

It was during the commercial period that the evolution of the Promenade, such as existed in New York at Battery Park, took place.   The new promenade was no longer a park but a shop-lined thoroughfare, Broadway.   Shopping became for the more domesticated half of the community an exciting, bewildering amusement; and out of a combination of Yankee "notions," Barnum-like advertisement, and magisterial organization arose that *omnium gatherum* of commerce, the department store.   It is scarcely possible to exaggerate the part that Broadway—I use the term generically—has played in the American town.   It is not merely the Agora but the Acropolis.   When the factory whistle closes the week, and the factory hands of Camden, or Pittsburgh, or Bridgeport pour out of the buildings and stockades in which they spend the more exhausting half of their lives, it is through Broadway that the greater part of their repressions seek an outlet.   Both the name and the institution extend across the continent from New York to Los Angeles.   Up and down these second-hand Broadways, from one in the afternoon until past ten at night, drifts a more or less aimless mass of human beings, bent upon extracting such joy as is possible from the sights in the windows, the contacts with other human beings, the occasional or systematic flirtations, and the risks and adventures of purchase.

In the early development of Broadway the amusements were adventitious· Even at present, in spite of the ubiquitous movie, the crowded street itself, at least in the smaller communities, is the main source of entertainment. Now, under normal conditions, for a great part of the population in a factory town one of the chief instincts to be repressed is that of acquisition (collection). It is not merely that the average factory worker cannot afford the luxuries of life: the worst is that he must think twice before purchasing the necessities. Out of this situation one of Broadway's happiest achievements has arisen: the five and ten cent store. In the five and ten cent store it is possible for the circumscribed factory operative to obtain the illusion of unmoderated expenditure—and even extravagance—without actually inflicting any irreparable rent in his purse. Broadway is thus, in more than one sense, the great compensatory device of the American city. The dazzle of white lights, the colour of electric signs, the alabaster architecture of the moving-picture palaces, the æsthetic appeals of the shop windows—these stand for elements that are left out of the drab perspectives of the industrial city. People who do not know how to spend their time must take what satisfaction they can in spending their money. That is why, although the five and ten cent store itself is perhaps mainly an institution for the proletariat, the habits and dispositions it encourages are universal. The chief amusement of Atlantic City, that opulent hostelry-annex of New York and Philadelphia, lies not in the beach and the ocean but in the shops which line the interminable Broadway known as the Boardwalk.

Broadway, in sum, is the façade of the American city: a false front. The highest achievements of our material civilization—and at their best our hotels, our department stores, and our Woolworth towers are achievements—count as so many symptoms of its spiritual failure. In order to cover up the vacancy of getting and spending in our cities, we have invented a thousand fresh devices for getting and spending. As a consequence our life is externalized. The principal institutions of the American city are merely distractions that take our eyes off the environment, instead of instruments which would help us to mould it creatively a little nearer to humane hopes and desires.

The birth of industrialism in America is announced in the

opening of the Crystal Palace in Bryant Park, Manhattan, in 1853. Between the Crystal Palace Exhibition and the Chicago World's Fair in 1893 lies a period whose defects were partly accentuated by the exhaustion that followed the Civil War. The debasement of the American city during this period can be read in almost every building that was erected. The influence of colonial architecture had waned to extinction during the first half of the century. There followed a period of eclectic experiment, in which all sorts of Egyptian, Byzantine, Gothic, and Arabesque ineptitudes were committed—a period whose absurdities we have only in recent years begun to escape. The domestic style, as the century progressed, became more limited. Little touches about the doors, mouldings, fanlights, and balustrades disappeared, and finally craftsmanship went out of style altogether and a pretentious architectural puffery took its place. The " era of good feeling " was an era of bad taste.

Pittsburgh, St. Louis, and Chicago give perhaps the most naked revelation of the industrial city's characteristics. There were two institutions that set their mark upon the early part of this period. One of them was the Mechanics' Hall. This was usually a building of red brick, structural iron, and glass, whose unique hideousness marks it as a typical product of the age of coal-industrialism, to be put alongside the " smoke-halls " of the railroad termini. The other institution was the German beer-garden—the one bright spot on the edge of an urban landscape that was steadily becoming more dingy, more dull, and more depressing. The cities that came to life in this period had scarcely any other civic apparatus to boast of. Conceive of Pittsburgh without Schenley Park, without the Carnegie Institute, without the Library or the Museum or the Concert Hall, and without the institutions that have grown up during the last generation around its sub-Acropolis —and one has a picture of Progress and Poverty that Henry George might have drawn on for illustration. The industrial city did not represent the creative values in civilization: it stood for a new form of human barbarism. In the coal towns of Pennsylvania, the steel towns of the Ohio and its tributaries, and the factory towns of Long Island Sound and Narragansett Bay was an environment much more harsh, antagonistic, and brutal than anything the pioneers had encountered. Even the fake exhilaration of the commercial city was lacking.

The reaction against the industrial city was expressed in various ways. The defect of these reactions was that they were formulated in terms of an escape from the environment rather than in a reconstruction of it. Symptomatic of this escape, along one particular alley, was the architecture of Richardson, and of his apprentices, McKim and White. No one who has an eye for the fine incidence of beautiful architecture can avoid a shock at discovering a monumental Romanesque building at the foot of Pittsburgh's dingy "Hump," or the hardly less monstrous beauty of Trinity Church, Boston, as one approaches it from a waste of railroad yards that lie on one side of it. It was no accident, one is inclined to believe, that Richardson should have returned to the Romanesque only a little time before Henry Adams was exploring Mont St. Michel and Chartres. Both men were searching for a specific against the fever of industrialism, and architects like Richardson were taking to archaic beauty as a man who was vaguely ill might have recourse to quinine, in the hope that his disease had sufficient similarity to malaria to be cured by it.

The truth is that the doses of exotic architecture which Richardson and his school sought to inject into the American city were anodynes rather than specifics. The Latin Renaissance models of McKim and White—the Boston Public Library and Madison Square Garden, for example—were perhaps a little better suited to the concrete demands of the new age; but they were still a long way from that perfect congruence with contemporary habits and modes of thought which was recorded in buildings like Independence Hall. Almost down to the last decade the best buildings of the industrial period have been anonymous, and scarcely ever recognized for their beauty. A grain elevator here, a warehouse there, an office building, a garage—there has been the promise of a stripped, athletic, classical style of architecture in these buildings which shall embody all that is good in the Machine Age:

its precision, its cleanliness, its hard illuminations, its unflinching logic. Dickens once poked fun at the architecture of Coketown because its infirmary looked like its jail and its jail like its town hall. But the joke had a sting to it only because these buildings were all plaintively destitute of æsthetic inspiration. In a place and an age that had achieved a well-rounded and balanced culture, we should expect to find the same spirit expressed in the simplest cottage and the grandest public building. So we find it, for instance, in the humble market towns of the Middle Age: there is not one type of architecture for 15th-century Shaftesbury and another for London; neither is there one style for public London and quite another for domestic London. Our architects in America have only just begun to cease regarding the Gothic style as especially fit for churches and schools, whilst they favour the Roman mode for courts, and the Byzantine, perhaps, for offices. Even the unique beauty of the Bush Terminal Tower is compromised by an antiquely " stylized " interior.

With the beginning of the second decade of this century there is some evidence of an attempt to make a genuine culture out of industrialism—instead of attempting to escape from industrialism into a culture which, though doubtless genuine enough, has the misfortune to be dead. The schoolhouses in Gary, Indiana, have some of the better qualities of a Gary steel plant. That symptom is all to the good. It points perhaps to a time when the Gary steel plant may have some of the educational virtues of a Gary school. One of the things that has made the industrial age a horror in America is the notion that there is something shameful in its manifestations. The idea that nobody would ever go near an industrial plant except under stress of starvation is in part responsible for the heaps of, rubbish and rusty metal, for the general disorder and vileness, that still characterize broad acres of our factory districts. There is nothing short of the Alkali Desert that compares with the desolateness of the common American industrial town. These qualities are indicative of the fact that we have centred attention not upon the process but upon the return; not upon the task but the emoluments; not upon what we can get out of our work but upon what we can achieve when we get away from our work. Our industrialism has been in the grip of business, and our industrial cities, and their institutions, have exhibited a major preoccupation with business. The coercive repression of an impersonal, mechanical technique was compensated by the pervasive will-to-power—or at least will-to-comfort—of commercialism.

We have shirked the problem of trying to live well in a régime that is devoted to the production of T-beams and toothbrushes and TNT. As a result, we have failed to react creatively upon the environment with anything like the inspiration that one might have found in a group of mediæval peasants building a cathedral. The urban worker escapes the mechanical routine of his daily job only to find an equally mechanical substitute for life and growth and experience in his amusements. The Gay White Way with its stupendous blaze of lights, and Coney Island, with its fear-stimulating roller coasters and chute-the-chutes, are characteristic by-products of an age that has renounced the task of actively humanizing the machine, and of creating an environment in which all the fruitful impulses of the community may be expressed. The movies, the White Ways, and the Coney Islands, which almost every American city boasts in some form or other, are means of giving jaded and throttled people the sensations of living without the direct experience of life—a sort of spiritual masturbation. In short, we have had the alternative of humanizing the industrial city or de-humanizing the population. So far we have de-humanized the population.

The external reactions against the industrial city came to a head in the World's Fair at Chicago. In that strange and giddy mixture of Parnassus and Coney Island was born a new conception of the city—a White City, spaciously designed, lighted by electricity, replete with monuments, crowned with public buildings, and dignified by a radiant architecture. The men who planned the exposition knew something about the better side of the spacious perspectives that Haussmann had designed for Napoleon III. Without taking into account the fundamental conditions of industrialism, or the salient facts of economics, they initiated what shortly came to be known as the City Beautiful movement. For a couple of decades Municipal Art societies were rampant. Their programme had the defects of the régime it attempted to combat. Its capital effort was to put on a front—to embellish Main Street and make it a more attractive thoroughfare. Here in æsthetics, as elsewhere in education, persisted the brahminical view of culture: the idea that beauty was something that could be acquired by any one who was willing to put up the cash; that it did not arise naturally out of the good life but was something which could be plastered on impoverished life; in short, that it was a cosmetic.

Until the Pittsburgh Survey of 1908 pricked a pin through superficial attempts at municipal improvement, those who sought to remake the American city overlooked the necessity for rectifying its economic basis. The meanness, the spotty development, and the congestion of the American city was at least in some degree an index of that deep disease of realty speculation which had, as already noted, caused cities like Chicago to forfeit land originally laid aside for public uses. Because facts like these were ignored for the sake of some small, immediate result, the developments that the early reformers were bold enough to outline still lie in the realms of hopeless fantasy—a fine play of the imagination, like Scadder's prospectus of Eden. Here as elsewhere there have been numerous signs of promise during the last decade; but it is doubtful whether they are yet numerous enough or profound enough to alter the general picture.

At best, the improvements that have been effected in the American city have not been central but subsidiary. They have been improvements, as Aristotle would have said, in the material bases of the good life: they have not been improvements in the art of living. The growth of the American city during the past century has meant the extension of paved streets and sewers and gas mains, and progressive heightening of office buildings and tenements. The outlay on pavements, sewers, electric lighting systems, and plumbing has been stupendous; but no matter what the Rotary Clubs and Chambers of Commerce may think of them, these mechanical ingenuities are not the indices of a civilization. There is a curious confusion in America between growth and improvement. We use the phrase " bigger and better " as if the conjunction were inevitable. As a matter of fact, there is little evidence to show that the vast increase of population in every urban area has been accompanied by anything like the necessary increase of schools, universities, theatres, meeting places, parks, and so forth. The fact that in 1920 we had sixty-four cities with more than 100,000 population, thirty-three with more than 200,000, and twelve with more than 500,000 does not mean that the resources of polity, culture, and art have been correspondingly on the increase. The growth of the American city has resulted less in the establishment of civilized standards of life than in the extension of Suburbia.

" Suburbia " is used here in both the accepted and in a more literal sense. On one hand I refer to the fact that the growth of the metropolis throws vast numbers of people into distant dormitories where, by and large, life is carried on without the discipline of rural occupations and without the cultural resources that the Central District of the city still retains in its art exhibitions, theatres, concerts, and the like. But our metropolises produce Suburbia not merely by reason of the fact that the people who work in the offices, bureaus, and factories live as citizens in a distant territory, perhaps in another state: they likewise foster Suburbia in another sense. I mean that the quality of life for the great mass of people who live within the political boundaries of the metropolis itself is inferior to that which a city with an adequate equipment and a thorough realization of the creative needs of the community is capable of producing. In this sense, the " suburb " called Brookline is a genuine city; while the greater part of the " city of Boston " is a suburb. We have scarcely begun to make an adequate distribution of libraries, meeting places, parks, gymnasia, and similar equipment, without which life in the city tends to be carried on at a low level of routine—physically as well as mentally. (The blatantly confidential advertisements of constipation remedies on all the hoardings tell a significant story.) At any reasonable allotment of park space, the Committee on Congestion in New York pointed out in 1911, a greater number of acres was needed for parks on the lower East Side than was occupied by the entire population. This case is extreme but representative.

It is the peculiarity of our metropolitan civilization, then, that in spite of vast resources drawn from the ends of the earth, it has an insufficient civic equipment, and what it does possess it uses only transiently. Those cities that have the beginnings of an adequate equipment, like New York—to choose no more invidious example—offer them chiefly to those engaged in travelling. As a traveller's city New York is near perfection. An association of cigar salesmen or an international congress of social scientists, meeting in one of the auditoriums of a big hotel, dining together, mixing in the lounge, and finding recreation in the theatres hard by, discovers an environment that is ordered, within its limits, to a nicety. It is this hotel and theatre district that we must charitably think of when we are tempted to speak about the triumphs of the American city. Despite manifold defects that arise from want of planning, this is the real civic centre of America's Metropolis. What we must overlook in this characterization are the long miles of slum that stretch in front and behind and on each side of this district—neighbourhoods where, in spite of the redoubtable efforts of settlement workers, block organizers, and neighbourhood associations, there is no permanent institution, other than the public school or the sectarian church, to remind the inhabitants that they have a common life and a common destiny.

Civic life, in fine, the life of intelligent association and common action, a life whose faded pattern still lingers in the old New England town, is not something that we daily enjoy, as we work in an office or a factory. It is rather a temporary state that we occasionally achieve with a great deal of time, bother, and expense. The city is not around us, in our little town, suburb, or neighbourhood: it lies beyond us, at the end of a subway ride or a railway journey. We are citizens occasionally: we are suburbanites (*denizens, idiots*) by regular routine. Small wonder that bathtubs and heating systems and similar apparatus play such a large part in our conception of the good life.

Metropolitanism in America represents, from the cultural

angle, a reaction against the uncouth and barren countryside
that was skinned, rather than cultivated, by the restless, individualistic, self-assertive American pioneer. The perpetual
drag to New York, and the endeavour of less favourably situated cities to imitate the virtues and defects of New York,
is explicable as nothing other than the desire to participate
in some measure in the benefits of city life. Since we have
failed up to the present to develop genuine regional cultures,
those who do not wish to remain barbarians must become
metropolitans. That means they must come to New York,
or ape the ways that are fashionable in New York. Here
opens the breach that has begun to widen between the metropolis and the countryside in America. The countryman,
who cannot enjoy the advantages of the metropolis, who has
no centre of his own to which he can point with pride, resents
the privileges that the metropolitan enjoys. Hence the periodical crusades of our State Legislatures, largely packed with
rural representatives, against the vices, corruptions, and follies
which the countryman enviously looks upon as the peculiar
property of the big city. Perhaps the envy and resentment
of the farming population is due to a genuine economic griev-
ance against the big cities—especially against their banks,
insurance companies, and speculative middlemen. Should the
concentration of power, glory, and privilege in the metropolis
continue, it is possible that the city will find itself subject to
an economic siege. If our cities cannot justify their existence
by their creative achievements, by their demonstration of the
efficacy and grace of corporate life, it is doubtful whether they
will be able to persuade the country to support them, once the
purely conventional arrangements by means of which the city
browbeats the countryside are upset. This, however, brings
us to the realm of social speculation; and he who would enter
it must abandon everything but hope.

Metropolitanism is of two orders. At its partial best it is
exhibited in New York, the literal mother city of America.
In its worst aspect it shows itself in the sub-metropolises which
have been spawning so prolifically since the 'eighties. If we
are to understand the capacities and limitations of the other

great cities in America, we must first weigh the significance of
New York.

The forces that have made New York dominant are inherent in our financial and industrial system; elsewhere those
same forces, working in slightly different ways, created London, Rome, Paris, Berlin, Vienna, Petrograd, and Moscow.
What happened in the industrial towns of America was that
the increments derived from land, capital, and association went,
not to the enrichment of the local community, but to those who
had a legal title to the land and the productive machinery. In
other words, the gains that were made in Pittsburgh, Springfield, Dayton, and a score of other towns that became important in the industrial era were realized largely in New York,
whose position had been established, before the turn of the
century, as the locus of trade and finance. (New York passed
the 500,000 mark in the 1850 census.) This is why, perhaps,
during the 'seventies and 'eighties, decades of miserable depression throughout the industrial centres, there were signs of
hope and promise in New York: the Museums of Art and
Natural History were built: *Life* and *Puck* and a batch of
newspapers were founded: the Metropolitan Opera House and
Carnegie Hall were established: and a dozen other evidences
of a vigorous civic life appeared. In a short time New York
became the glass of fashion and the mould of form, and through
the standardization, specialization, and centralization which
accompany the machine process the Metropolis became at
length the centre of advertising, the lender of farm mortgages, the distributor of boiler-plate news, the headquarters
of the popular magazine, the publishing centre, and finally the
chief disseminator of plays and motion pictures in America.
The educational foundations which the exploiter of the Kodak
has established at Rochester were not characteristic of the early
part of the industrial period—otherwise New York's eminence
might have been briskly challenged before it had become, after
its fashion, unchallengeable. The increment from Mr. Carnegie's steel works built a hall of music for New York long
before it created the Carnegie Institute in Pittsburgh. In
other words, the widespread effort of the American provincial
to leave his industrial city for New York comes to something

like an attempt to get back from New York what had been previously filched from the industrial city.

The future of our cities depends upon how permanent are the forces which drain money, energy, and brains from the various regions in America into the twelve great cities that now dominate the countryside, and in turn drain the best that is in these sub-metropolises to New York. To-day our cities are at a crossing of the ways. Since the 1910 census a new tendency has begun to manifest itself, and the cities that have grown the fastest are those of a population from 25,000 to 100,000. Quantitatively, that is perhaps a good sign. It may indicate the drift to Suburbia is on the wane. One finds it much harder, however, to gauge the qualitative capacities of the new régime; much more difficult to estimate the likelihood of building up, within the next generation or two, genuine regional cultures to take the place of pseudo-national culture which now mechanically emanates from New York. So far our provincial culture has been inbred and sterile: our provincial cities have substituted boosting for achievement, fanciful speculation for intelligent planning, and a zaniacal optimism for constructive thought. These habits have made them an easy prey to the metropolis, for at its lowest ebb there has always been a certain amount of organized intelligence and cultivated imagination in New York—if only because it is the chief point of contact between Europe and America. Gopher Prairie has yet to take to heart the fable about the frog that tried to inflate himself to the size of a bull. When Gopher Prairie learns its lessons from Bergen and Augsburg and Montpellier and Grenoble, the question of " metropolitanism versus regionalism " may become as active in America as it is now in Europe.

Those of us who are metropolitans may be tempted to think that the hope for civilization in America is bound up with the continuance of metropolitanism. That is essentially a cockney view of culture and society, however, and our survey of the development of the city in America should have done something to weaken its self-confident complacence. Our metropolitan civilization is not a success. It is a different kind of wilderness from that which we have deflowered—but the feral rather than the humane quality is dominant: it is still a wilderness. The cities of America must learn to remould our mechanical and financial régime; for if metropolitanism continues they are probably destined to fall by its weight.

LEWIS MUMFORD

POLITICS

No person shall be a Representative who . . . shall not, when elected, be an inhabitant of that State in which he shall be chosen. . . . No person shall be a Senator who . . . shall not, when elected, be an inhabitant of that State for which he shall be chosen.

SPECIALISTS in political archæology will recognize these sentences: they are from Article I, Sections 2 and 3, of the constitution of the United States. I have heard and forgotten how they got there; no doubt the cause lay in the fierce jealousy of the States. But whatever the fact, I have a notion that there are few provisions of the constitution that have had a more profound effect upon the character of practical politics in the Republic, or, indirectly, upon the general colour of American thinking in the political department. They have made steadily for parochialism in legislation, for the security and prosperity of petty local bosses and machines, for the multiplication of pocket and rotten boroughs of the worst sort, and, above all, for the progressive degeneration of the honesty and honour of representatives. They have greased the ways for the trashy and ignoble fellow who aspires to get into Congress, and they have blocked them for the man of sense, dignity, and self-respect. More, perhaps, than any other single influence they have been responsible for the present debauched and degraded condition of the two houses, and particularly of the lower one. Find me the worst ass in Congress, and I'll show you a man they have helped to get there and to stay there. Find me the most shameless scoundrel, and I'll show you another.

No such centripedal mandate, as far as I have been able to discover, is in the fundamental law of any other country practising the representative system. An Englishman, if ambition heads him toward St. Stephen's, may go hunting for a willing constituency wherever the hunting looks best, and if he fails in the Midlands he may try again in the South, or in the North, or in Scotland or Wales. A Frenchman of like dreams has the same privilege; the only condition, added after nineteen years of the Third Republic, is that he may not be a candidate in two or more *arrondissements* at once. And so with a German, an Italian, or a Spaniard. But not so with an American. He must be an actual inhabitant of the State he aspires to represent at Washington. More, he must be, in all save extraordinary cases, an actual inhabitant of the congressional district—for here, by a characteristic American process, the fundamental law is sharpened by custom. True enough, this last requirement is not laid down by the constitution. It would be perfectly legal for the thirty-fifth New York district, centring at Syracuse, to seek its congressman in Manhattan, or even at Sing Sing. In various iconoclastic States, in fact, the thing has been occasionally done. But not often; not often enough to produce any appreciable effect. The typical congressman remains a purely local magnifico, the gaudy cock of some small and usually far from appetizing barnyard. His rank and dignity as a man are measured by provincial standards of the most puerile sort, and his capacity to discharge the various and onerous duties of his office is reckoned almost exclusively in terms of his ability to hold his grip upon the local party machine.

If he has genuine ability, it is a sort of accident. If he is thoroughly honest, it is next door to a miracle. Of the 430-odd representatives who carry on so diligently and obscenely at Washington, making laws and determining policies for the largest free nation ever seen in the world, there are not two dozen whose views upon any subject under the sun carry any weight whatsoever outside their own bailiwicks, and there are not a dozen who rise to anything approaching unmistakable force and originality. They are, in the overwhelming main, shallow fellows, ignorant of the grave matters they deal with and too stupid to learn. If, as is often proposed, the United States should adopt the plan of parliamentary responsibility and the ministry should be recruited from the lower house, then it would be difficult, without a radical change in election methods, to fetch up even such pale talents and modest decencies as were assembled for their cabinets by Messrs. Wilson and Harding. The better sort of congressmen, to be sure, acquire after long service a good deal of technical proficiency. They know the traditions and precedents of the two houses; they can find their way in and out of every rathole in the Capitol; they may be trusted to carry on the legislative routine in a more or less shipshape manner. Of such sort are the specialists paraded in the newspapers—on the tariff, on military affairs, on foreign relations, and so on. They come to know, in time, almost as much as a Washington correspondent, or one of their own committee clerks. But the average congressman lifts himself to no such heights of sagacity. He is content to be led by the fugelmen and bellwethers. Examine him at leisure, and you will find that he is incompetent and imbecile, and not only incompetent and imbecile, but also incurably dishonest. The first principles of civilized law-making are quite beyond him; he ends, as he began, a local politician, interested only in jobs. His knowledge is that of a third-rate country lawyer—which he often is in fact. His intelligence is that of a country newspaper editor, or evangelical divine. His standards of honour are those of a country banker—which he also often is. To demand sense of such a man, or wide and accurate information, or a delicate feeling for the public and private proprieties, is to strain his parts beyond endurance.

The constitution, of course, stops with Congress, but its influence is naturally powerful within the States, and one finds proofs of the fact on all sides. It is taking an herculean effort everywhere to break down even the worst effects of this influence; the prevailing tendency is still to discover a mysterious virtue in the office-holder who was born and raised in the State, or county, or city, or ward. The judge must come from the bar of the court he is to adorn; the mayor must be part and parcel of the local machine; even technical officers, such as engineers and health commissioners, lie under the constitutional blight. The thing began as a belief in local self-government, the oldest of all the sure cures for despotism. But it has gradually taken on the character of government by local politicians, which is to say, by persons quite unable to comprehend the most elemental problems of State and nation, and unfitted by nature to deal with them honestly and patriotically, even if they could comprehend them. Just as prohibition was forced upon the civilized minorities collected in the great cities against their most vigorous and persistent opposition, so the same minorities, when it comes to intra-state affairs, are constantly at the mercy of predatory bands of rural politicians. If there is any large American city whose peculiar problems are dealt with competently and justly by its State legislature, then I must confess that twenty years in journalism have left me ignorant of it. An unending struggle for fairer dealing goes on in every State that has large cities, and every concession to their welfare is won only at the cost of gigantic effort. The State legislature is never intelligent; it represents only the average mind of the county bosses, whose sole concern is with jobs. The machines that they represent are wholly political, but they have no political principles in any rational sense. Their one purpose and function is to maintain their adherents in the public offices, or to obtain for them in some other way a share of the State funds. They are quite willing to embrace any new doctrine, however fantastic, or to abandon any old one, however long supported, if only the business will promote their trade and so secure their power.

This concentration of the ultimate governmental authority in the hands of small groups of narrow, ignorant, and unconscionable manipulators tends inevitably to degrade the actual office-holder, or, what is the same thing, to make office-holding prohibitive to all men not already degraded. It is almost impossible to imagine a man of genuine self-respect and dignity offering himself as a candidate for the lower house—or, since the direct primary and direct elections brought it down to the common level, for the upper house—in the average American constituency. His necessary dealings with the electors themselves, and with the idiots who try more or less honestly to lead them, would be revolting enough, but even worse would be his need of making terms with the professional politicians of his party—the bosses of the local machine. These bosses naturally make the most of the constitutional limitation; it works powerfully in their favour. A local notable, in open revolt against them, may occasionally beat them by appealing directly to the voters, but nine times out of ten, when there is any sign of such a catastrophe, they are prompt to perfume the ticket by bringing forth another local notable who is safe and sane, which is to say, subservient and reliable. The thing is done constantly; it is a matter of routine; it accounts for most of the country bankers, newspaper owners, railroad lawyers, proprietors of cement works, and other such village bigwigs in the lower house. Here everything runs to the advantage of the bosses. It is not often that the notable in rebellion is gaudy enough to blind the plain people to the high merits of his more docile opponent. They see him too closely and know him too well. He shows none of that exotic charm which accounts, on a different plane, for exogamy. There is no strangeness, no mysteriousness, above all, no novelty about him.

It is my contention that this strangle-hold of the local machines would be vastly less firm if it could be challenged, not only by rebels within the constituency, but also by salient men from outside. The presidential campaigns, indeed, offer plenty of direct proof of it. In these campaigns it is a commonplace for strange doctrines and strange men to force themselves upon the practical politicians in whole sections of the country, despite their constant effort to keep their followers faithful to the known. All changes, of whatever sort, whether in leaders or in ideas, are opposed by such politicians at the start, but time after time they are compelled to acquiesce and to hurrah. Bryan, as every one knows, forced himself upon the Democratic party by appealing directly to the people; the politicians, in the main, were bitterly against him until further resistance was seen to be useless, and they attacked him again the moment he began to weaken, and finally disposed of him. So with Wilson. It would be absurd to say that the politicians of his party—and especially the bosses of the old machines in the congressional districts—were in favour of him in 1912. They were actually against him almost unanimously. He got past their guard and broke down their resolution to nominate some more trustworthy candidate by operating directly upon the emotions of the voters. For some reason never sufficiently explained he became the heir of the spirit of rebellion raised by Bryan sixteen years before, and was given direct and very effective aid by Bryan himself. Roosevelt saddled himself upon the Republican party in exactly the same way. The bosses made heroic efforts to sidetrack him, to shelve him, to get rid of him by any means short of homicide, but his bold enterprises and picturesque personality enchanted the people, and if it had not been for the extravagant liberties that he took with his popularity in later years he might have retained it until his death.

The same possibility of unhorsing the machine politicians, I believe, exists in even the smallest electoral unit. All that is needed is the chance to bring in the man. Podunk cannot produce him herself, save by a sort of miracle. If she has actually hatched him, he is far away by the time he has come to his full stature and glitter—in the nearest big city, in Chicago or New York. Podunk is proud of him, and many other Podunks, perhaps, are stirred by his ideas, his attitudes, his fine phrases—but he lives, say, in some Manhattan congressional district which has the Hon. Patrick Googan as its representative by divine right, and so there is no way to get him into the halls of Congress. In his place goes the Hon. John P. Balderdash, State's attorney for five years, State senator for two terms, and county judge for a brief space—and always a snide and petty fellow, always on the best of terms with the local bosses, always eager for a job on any terms they lay down. The yokels vote for the Hon. Mr. Balderdash, not because they admire him, but because their only choice is between him and the Hon. James Bosh. If anything even remotely resembling a first-rate man could come into the contest, if it were lawful for them to rid themselves of their recurrent dilemma by soliciting the interest of such a man, then they would often enough rise in their might and compel their parish overlords, as the English put it, to adopt him. But the constitution protects these overlords in their business, and in the long run the voters resign all thought of deliverance. Thus the combat remains one between small men, and interest in it dies out. Most of the men who go to the lower house are third-raters, even in their own narrow bailiwicks. In my own congressional district, part of a large city, there has never been a candidate of any party, during the twenty years that I have voted, who was above the intellectual level of a corner grocer. No successful candidate of that district has ever made a speech in Congress (or out of it) worth hearing, or contributed a single sound idea otherwise to the solution of any public problem. One and all, they have confined themselves exclusively to the trade in jobs. One and all, they have been ciphers in the house and before the country.

Well, perhaps I labour my point too much. It is, after all, not important. The main thing is the simple fact that the average representative from my district is typical of Congress —that, if anything, he is superior to the normal congressman of these, our days. That normal congressman, as year chases year, tends to descend to such depths of puerility, to such abysses of petty shysterism, that he becomes offensive alike to the intelligence and to the nose. His outlook, when it is honest, is commonly childish—and it is very seldom honest. The product of a political system which puts all stress upon the rewards of public office, he is willing to make any sacrifice, of dignity, of principle, of honour, to hold and have those rewards. He has no courage, no intellectual *amour propre,* no ardent belief in anything save his job, and the jobs of his friends. It was easy for Wilson to beat him into line on the war issue; it was easy for the prohibitionists to intimidate and stampede him; it is easy for any resolute man or group of men to do likewise. I read the *Congressional Record* faithfully, and have done so for years. In the Senate debates, amid oceans of tosh, I occasionally encounter a flash of wit or a gleam of sense; direct elections have not yet done their work. But in the lower house there is seldom anything save a garrulous and intolerable imbecility. The discussion of measures of the utmost importance—bills upon which the security and prosperity of the whole nation depend—is carried on in the manner of the chautauqua and the rural stump. Entire days go by without a single congressman saying anything as intelligent, say, as the gleams that one sometimes finds in the New York *Herald,* or even in the New York *Times.* The newspapers, unfortunately, give no adequate picture of the business. No American journal reports the daily debates comprehensively, as the debates in the House of Commons are reported

by the London *Times, Daily Telegraph,* and *Morning Post.*
All one hears of, as a rule, is the action taken, and only too
often the action taken, even when it is reported fairly, is un-
intelligible without the antecedent discussion. If any one who
reads this wants to know what such a discussion is like, then
I counsel him to go to the nearest public library, ask for the
Record for 1918, and read the debate in the lower house on the
Volstead Act. It was, I believe, an average debate, and on a
subject of capital importance. It was, from first to last, almost
fabulous in its evasion of the plain issue, its incredible timorousness and stupidity, its gross mountebankery and dishonesty.
Not twenty men spoke in it as men of honour and self-respect.
Not ten brought any idea into it that was not a silly idea and
a stale one.

That debate deserves a great deal more study than it will
ever get from the historians of American politics, nearly all of
whom, whether they lean to the right or to the left, are be-
dazzled by the economic interpretation of history, and so seek
to account for all political phenomena in terms of crop movements, wage scales, and panics in Wall Street. It seems to me
that that obsession blinds them to a fact of the first importance,
to wit, the fact that political ideas, under a democracy as under
a monarchy, originate above quite as often as they originate
below, and that their popularity depends quite as much upon
the special class interests of professional politicians as it depends upon the underlying economic interests of the actual
voters. It is, of course, true, as I have argued, that the people
can force ideas upon the politicians, given powerful leaders of
a non-political (or, at all events, non-machine) sort, but it is
equally true that there are serious impediments to the process,
and that it is not successful very often. As a matter of everyday practice the rise and fall of political notions is determined
by the self-interest of the practical politicians of the country,
and though they naturally try to bring the business into harmony with any great popular movements that may be in progress spontaneously, they by no means wait and beg for man-
dates when none are vociferously forthcoming, but go ahead
bravely on their own account, hoping to drag public opinion
with them and so safeguard their jobs. Such is the origin of

many affecting issues, later held dear by millions of the plain people. Such was the process whereby prohibition was foisted upon the nation by constitutional amendment, to the dismay of the solid majority opposed to it and to the surprise of the minority in favour of it.

What lay under the sudden and melodramatic success of the prohibitionist agitators was simply their discovery of the incurable cowardice and venality of the normal American politician—their shrewd abandonment of logical and evidential propaganda for direct political action. For years their cause had languished. Now and then a State or part of a State went dry, but often it went wet again a few years later. Those were the placid days of white-ribbon rallies, of wholesale pledge-signings, of lectures by converted drunkards, of orgiastic meetings in remote Baptist and Methodist churches, of a childish reliance upon arguments that fetched only drunken men and their wives, and so grew progressively feebler as the country became more sober. The thing was scarcely even a nuisance; it tended steadily to descend to the level of a joke. The prohibitionist vote for President hung around a quarter of a million; it seemed impossible to pull it up to a formidable figure, despite the stupendous labours of thousands of eloquent dervishes, lay and clerical, male and female. But then, out of nowhere, came the Anti-Saloon League, and—sis! boom! ah! Then came the sudden shift of the fire from the people to the politicians—and at once there was rapid progress. The people could only be wooed and bamboozled, but the politicians could be threatened; their hold upon their jobs could be shaken; they could be converted at wholesale and by *force majeure*. The old prohibition weepers and gurglers were quite incapable of this enterprise, but the new janissaries of the Anti-Saloon League—sharp lawyers, ecclesiastics too ambitious to pound mere pulpits, outlaw politicians seeking a way back to the trough—were experts at every trick and dodge it demanded. They understood the soul of the American politician. To him they applied the economic interpretation of history, resolutely and with a great deal of genial humour. They knew that his whole politics, his whole philosophy, his whole concept of honesty and honour, was embraced in his single and insatiable yearning for a job, and they showed him how, by playing with them, he could get it and keep it, and how, by standing against them, he could lose it. Prohibition was rammed into the constitution by conquering the politicians; the people in general were amazed when the thing was accomplished; it may take years to reconcile them to it.

It was the party system that gave the Anti-Saloon League manipulators their chance, and they took advantage of it with great boldness and cleverness. The two great parties divide the country almost equally; it is difficult to predict, in a given year, whether the one or the other musters the most votes. This division goes down into the lowest electoral units; even in those backward areas where one party has divine grace and the other is of the devil there are factional differences that amount to the same thing. In other words, the average American politician is never quite sure of his job. An election (and, if not an election, then a primary) always exposes him to a definite hazard, and he is eager to diminish it by getting help from outside his own following, at whatever cost to the principles he commonly professes. Here lies the opportunity for minorities willing to trade on a realistic political basis. In the old days the prohibitionists refused to trade, and in consequence they were disregarded, for their fidelity to their own grotesque candidates protected the candidates of both the regular parties. But with the coming of the Anti-Saloon League they abandoned this fidelity and began to dicker in a forthright and unashamed manner, quickly comprehensible to all professional politicians. That is, they asked for a pledge on one specific issue, and were willing to swallow any commitment on other issues. If Beelzebub, running on one ticket, agreed to support prohibition, and the Archangel Gabriel, running on another, found himself entertaining conscientious doubts, they were instantly and solidly for Beelzebub, and they not only gave him the votes that they directly controlled, but they also gave him the benefit of a campaign support that was ruthless, pertinacious, extraordinarily ingenious, and overwhelmingly effective. Beelzebub, whatever his swinishness otherwise, was bathed in holy oils; Gabriel's name became a thing to scare children.

Obviously, the support thus offered was particularly tempting to a politician who found himself facing public suspicion for his general political practices—in brief, to the worst type of machine professional. Such a politician is always acutely aware that it is not positive merit that commonly gets a man into public office in the United States, but simply disvulnerability. Even when they come to nominate a President, the qualities the two great parties seek are chiefly the negative ones; they want, not a candidate of forceful and immovable ideas, but one whose ideas are vague and not too tenaciously held, and in whose personality there is nothing to alarm or affront the populace. Of two candidates, that one usually wins who least arouses the distrusts and suspicions of the great masses of undifferentiated men. This advantage of the safe and sane, the colourless and unprovocative, the apparently stodgy and commonplace man extends to the most trivial contests, and politicians are keen to make use of it. Thus the job-seeker with an aura of past political misdemeanour about him was eager to get the Christian immunity bath that the prohibitionists offered him so generously, and in the first years of their fight they dealt almost exclusively with such fellows. He, on his side, promised simply to vote for prohibition—not even, in most cases, to pretend to any personal belief in it. The prohibitionists, on their side, promised to deliver the votes of their followers to him on election day, to cry him up as one saved by a shining light, and, most important of all, to denounce his opponent as an agent of hell. He was free, by this agreement, to carry on his regular political business as usual. The prohibitionists asked no patronage of him. They didn't afflict him with projects for other reforms. All they demanded was that he cast his vote as agreed upon when the signal was given to him.

At the start, of course, such scoundrels frequently violated their agreements. In the South, in particular, dry legislature after dry legislature sold out to the liquor lobby, which, in those days, still had plenty of money. An assemblyman would be elected with the aid of the prohibitionists, make a few maudlin speeches against the curse of drink, and then, at the last minute, vote wet for some thin and specious reason, or for no

avowed reason at all.   But the prohibition manipulators, as I
have said, were excellent politicians, and so they knew how
to put down that sort of treason.   At the next election they
transferred their favour to the opposition candidate, and inasmuch as he had seen the traitor elected at the last election
he was commonly very eager to do business.   The punishment
for the treason was condign and merciless.   The dry rabble-
rousers, lay and clerical, trumpeted news of it from end to end
of the constituency.   What was a new and gratifying disvulnerability was transformed into a vulnerability of the worst
sort; the recreant one became the county Harry Thaw, Oscar
Wilde, Captain Boy-Ed, and Debs.   A few such salutary examples, and treason became rare.   The prohibitionists, indeed,
came to prefer dealing with such victims of their reprisals.
They could trust them perfectly, once the lesson had been
learned; they were actually more trustworthy than honest believers, for the latter usually had ideas of their own and interfered with the official plans of campaign.   Thus, in the end,
the professional politicians of both parties came under the yoke.
The final battle in Congress transcended all party lines; democrats and republicans fought alike for places on the band-
wagon.   The spectacle offered a searching and not unhumor-
ous commentary on the party system, and on the honour of
American politicians no less.   Two-thirds, at least, of the votes
for the amendment were cast by men who did not believe in it,
and who cherished a hearty hope, to the last moment, that some
act of God would bring about its defeat.

Such holocausts of frankness and decency are certainly not
rare in American politics; on the contrary, they glow with
normalcy.   The typical legislative situation among us—and
the typical administrative situation as well—is one in which
men wholly devoid of inner integrity, facing a minority that is
resolutely determined to get its will, yield up their ideas, their
freedom, and their honour in order to save their jobs.   I say
administrative situation as well; what I mean is that in these
later days the pusillanimity of the actual law-maker is fully
matched by the pusillanimity of the enforcing officer, whether
humble assistant district attorney or powerful judge.   The
war, with its obliteration of customary pretences and loosening

of fundamental forces, threw up the whole process into high
relief. For nearly two long years there was a complete abandonment of sense and self-respect. Rowelled and intimidated
by minorities that finally coalesced into a frantic majority,
legislators allowed themselves to be forced into imbecility after
imbecility, and administrative officers, including some of the
highest judges in the land, followed them helter-skelter. In
the lower house of Congress there was one man—already forgotten—who showed the stature of a man. He resigned his
seat and went home to his self-respect. The rest had no
self-respect to go home to. Eager beyond all to hold their
places, at whatever cost to principle, and uneasily conscious of
their vulnerability to attack, however frenzied and unjust, they
surrendered abjectly and repeatedly—to the White House, to
the newspapers, to any group enterprising enough to issue orders to them and resolute enough to flourish weapons before
them. It was a spectacle full of indecency—there are even
congressmen who blush when they think of it to-day—but
it was nevertheless a spectacle that was typical. The fortunes
of politics, as they now run, make it overwhelmingly probable
that every new recruit to public office will be just such a pol-
troon. The odds are enormously in favour of him, and enormously against the man of honour. Such a man of honour
may occasionally drift in, taken almost unawares by some
political accident, but it is the pushing, bumptious, unconscionable bounder who is constantly *fighting* to get in, and only
too often he succeeds. The rules of the game are made to fit
his taste and his talents. He can survive as a hog can survive
in the swill-yard.

Go to the Congressional Directory and investigate the origins
and past performances of the present members of the lower
house—our typical assemblage of typical politicians, the cor-
nerstone of our whole representative system, the symbol of our
democracy. You will find that well over half of them are
obscure lawyers, school-teachers, and mortgage-sharks out of
almost anonymous towns—men of common traditions, sordid
aspirations, and no attainments at all. One and all, the members of this majority—and it is constant, no matter what party
is in power—are plastered with the brass ornaments of the

more brummagem fraternal orders.   One and all, they are devoid of any contact with what passes for culture, even in their
remote bailiwicks.   One and all their careers are bare of
civilizing influences. . . . Such is the American *Witenagemot*
in this 146th year of the Republic.   Such are the men who
make the laws that all of us must obey, and who carry on our
dealings with the world.   Go to their debates, and you will
discover what equipment they bring to their high business.
What they know of sound literature is what one may get out of
McGuffey's Fifth Reader.   What they know of political science is the nonsense preached in the chautauquas and on the
stump.   What they know of history is the childish stuff taught
in grammar-schools. What they know of the arts and sciences—
of all the great body of knowledge that is the chief intellectual
baggage of modern man—is absolutely nothing.

                                        H. L. MENCKEN

JOURNALISM

ACCORDING to the *World Almanac* for 1921 the daily circulation of newspapers in the big cities of the United States in 1914 (evidently the most recent year for which the figures have been compiled) was more than forty million. For the six months ending April 1, 1920, the average daily circulation of five morning newspapers and eleven evening newspapers in Greater New York City was, as shown by sworn statements, more than three and a third million. These statistics cover only daily newspapers, not weekly or monthly journals; and the figures for New York do not include papers in languages other than English. The American certainly buys newspapers. To what extent he reads them it is impossible to determine. But we may fairly assume that the great majority of literate inhabitants of the United States of all ages are every day subjected in some measure to the influence of the newspaper. No other institution approaches the newspaper in universality, persistence, continuity of influence. Not the public school, with all other schools added to it, has such power over the national mind; for in the lives of most people formal schooling is of relatively short duration, ceasing with adolescence or earlier. The church? Millions of people never go to church, and the day when the clergy dominated human thought is gone for ever. If we add to the daily press the weekly and monthly periodicals, with a total circulation per issue of two hundred million (for the year 1914), we shall not be far wrong in saying that the journalist, with the powers behind him, has more to do, for good or for evil, than the member of any other profession, in creating and shaping the thoughts of the multitude. Compared with him the teacher, the preacher, the artist, the politician, the man of science, are restricted, interrupted, indirect in reaching the minds of their fellow-men.

So that in estimating the capacities and contents of the

American mind, which we have no means of lining up in its hundred million individual manifestations and examining directly, an analysis of the American newspaper is a fair rough-and-ready method. What everybody reads does not tell the whole story of what everybody is, but it tells a good deal. Moreover, it is not necessary to analyze any one newspaper or to separate its clientèle from that of any other newspaper. For though everybody knows that the New York *Tribune* and the New York *World* have distinct qualities which differentiate them from each other, that some papers are better and some are worse, yet on the whole the American newspaper is amazingly uniform from Portland, Maine, to Portland, Oregon. It is, indeed, a more or less unified institution fed by the same news services and dominated by kindred financial interests. If you travel much, as actors do, without interest in local affairs, when you go to the hotel news-stand in the morning, you cannot tell from the general aspect of the newspaper you pick up what city you are in; and in a small city it is likely to be a metropolitan paper that has come a hundred miles or more during the night. Indeed, this is the first thing to be learned about the American from a study of his newspapers, that he lacks individuality, is tediously uniform, and cut according to one intellectual pattern. He may have his " favourite " newspaper, and with no sense that his confession of habitude is shameful he may write the editor that he has read it constantly for forty years. But if it goes out of existence, like his favourite brand of chewing-gum or cigarettes, there is no aching void which cannot be comfortably filled by a surviving competitor. Editors, except those in charge of local news, move with perfect ease from one city to another; it is the same old job at a different desk.

The standardization of the newspaper reader and the standardization of the journalist are two aspects of the same thing. As a citizen, a workman, a human being, the journalist is simply one of us, a victim of the conformity which has overwhelmed the American. When we speak of the influence of the journalist, we are not speaking of an individual, but of " the powers behind him," of which he is nothing but the wage-earning servant, as impotent and unimportant, considered as an individual, as a mill-hand. Journalism in America is no longer a profession, through which a man can win to a place of real dignity among his neighbours. If we had a Horace Greeley to-day, he would not be editor of a newspaper. He would not wish to be, and he would not be allowed to be. Certainly his vigorous integrity would not be tolerated in the modern unworthy successor of the newspaper which he founded. The editor of a newspaper is no doubt often a man of intelligence and experience and he may be well paid, like the manager of a department store; but he is usually submerged in anonymity except that from time to time the law requires the newspaper to publish his name. His subordinates, assistant editors, newswriters, reporters, and the rest, are as nameless as floor-walkers, shipping clerks, salesladies, and ladies engaged in more ancient forms of commerce.

It is true that during the last generation there has been a tendency in the newspaper to " feature " individuals, such as cartoonists, conductors of columns, writers on sport, dramatic critics, and so on. But these men are artists, some of them very clever, who have nothing to do with the news but contribute to the paper its vaudeville entertainment. During the war there was a great increase in the amount of signed cable matter and correspondence. This was due to the necessity of the prosperous newspaper to show its enterprise and to cajole its readers into believing that it had men of special ability in close touch with diplomats and major-generals collecting and cabling at great expense intimate information and expert opinion. The circumstances were so difficult that the wisest and most honest man could not do much, except lose his position, and nobody will blame the correspondents. But it is significant that not a single American correspondent emerged from the conflict who is memorable, from the point of view of a more or less careful reader, as having been different from the rest. If from a miscellaneous collection of clippings we should cut off the dates, the alleged place of origin and the names of the correspondents, nobody but an editor with a long and detailed memory could tell t'other from which, or be sure whether the despatch was from Mr. Jones, the special correspondent of the *Christian Science Monitor* (copyright by the

Chicago *News*) or an anonymous cable from the London office
of the Associated Press. And even the editor, who may be
assumed to know the names of hundreds of his colleagues and
competitors, would begin his attempt at identification by examining the style of type to see if it looked like a column from
the *Sun* or from the *World*. Almost all the war news was a
hopeless confusion of impressions, of reports of what somebody said somebody else, " of unquestionable authority," had
heard from reliable sources, and of sheer mendacity adapted to
the momentary prejudices of the individual managing editor,
the American press as a whole, and the American people. And
this is a rough recipe for all the news even in times of peace,
for the war merely aggravated the prevalent diseases of the
newspapers.

Since the purpose of this book is to discuss peculiarly American characteristics, it should be said at once that the tendency
of the newspaper to obliterate the journalist as a person immediately responsible to the public is not confined to America.
Economic conditions in Europe and America are fundamentally
alike, and the modern newspaper in every country must be a
business institution, heavily capitalized, and conducted for
profit. In England the decline of journalism as a profession
and the rise of the " stunt " press has been noted and deplored
by Englishmen. Years ago it meant something to be editor
of the London *Times*, and the appointment of a new man to
the position was an event not less important than a change in
the cabinet. Who is editor of the *Times* now is a matter of no
consequence except to the man who receives the salary check.
English journalism is in almost as bad a case as American. In
England, however, there is at least one exception which
has no counterpart in America, the Manchester *Guardian;*
this admirable newspaper has the good fortune to be owned
by people who are so rich that they are not obliged, and so
honest that they are not willing, to sell out. It is this fact
which has afforded Mr. Scott, the editor-in-chief for nearly
half a century, an opportunity adequate to his courage and
ability. There are few such opportunities in England, and
none in America. Even the Springfield *Republican* has largely
lost its old character.

As for the continental papers, one who does not read any of them regularly is in no position to judge. In 1900 William James, a shrewd observer, wrote in a letter: " The Continental papers of course are ' nowhere.' As for our yellow papers— every country has its criminal classes, and with us and in France, they have simply got into journalism as part of their professional evolution, and they must be got out. Mr. Bosanquet somewhere says that so far from the ' dark ages ' being over, we are just at the beginning of a new dark-age period. He means that ignorance and unculture, which then were merely brutal, are now articulate and possessed of a literary voice, and the fight is transferred from fields and castles and town walls to ' organs of publicity.' " This is only a passing remark in an informal letter. But it is a partial explanation of American yellow journalism which in twenty years has swamped the whole press, including papers that pretend to be respectable, and it suggests what the state of things was, and is, in France.

It should be noted, however, that personal journalism has not entirely disappeared in France, that the editor can still be brought to account, sometimes at the point of a pistol, for lies and slander, and that a young French *littérateur*, before he has won his spurs in poetry, drama, or fiction, can regard journalism as an honourable occupation in which it is worth while to make a name.

With the decadence in all countries, certainly in America, of the journalist as a professional man in an honourable craft, there might conceivably have been a gain in objectivity, in the right sort of impersonality. Anonymity might have ensured a dispassionate fidelity to facts. But there has been no such gain. Responsibility has been transferred from the journalist to his employers, and he is on his mettle to please his employers, to cultivate whatever virtues are possible to journalism, accuracy, clearness of expression, zeal in searching out and interpreting facts, only in so far forth as his employers demand them, only as his livelihood and chances of promotion depend on them. The ordinary journalist, being an ordinary human being, must prefer to do honest work; for there is no pleasure in lying, though there is a temptation to fill space with unfounded or unverified statements.   And if his manager orders him to find a story where there is no story, or to find a story of a certain kind where the facts lead to a story of another kind, he will not come back empty-handed lest he go away empty-handed on pay-day.   Any one who has worked in a newspaper office knows that the older men are likely to be weary and cynical and that the younger men fall into two classes, those who are too stupid to be discontented with any aspect of their position except the size of their salaries, and those who hope either to rise to the better paid positions, or to " graduate," as they put it, from daily journalism to other kinds of literary work.

The journalist, then, should be acquitted of most of the faults of journalism.   Mr. Walter Lippmann says in his sane little book, " Liberty and the News ": " Resistance to the inertias of the profession, heresy to the institution, and willingness to be fired rather than write what you do not believe, these wait on nothing but personal courage."   That is a little like saying that the harlot can stop harlotry by refusing to ply her trade—which is indeed the attitude of some people in comfortable circumstances.   I doubt if Mr. Lippmann would have written just as he did if he had ever had to depend for his dinner on pleasing a managing editor, if he had not been from very early in his brilliant career editor of a liberal endowed journal in which he is free to express his beliefs.   Most newspaper men are poor and not brilliant.   The correspondents whom Mr. Lippmann mentions as " eminences on a rather flat plateau " are nearly all men who have succeeded in other work than newspaper correspondence, and if not a newspaper in the world would hire them, most of them could afford to thumb their noses at the Ochses, Reids, and Harmsworths. Personal courage is surely a personal matter, and it can seldom be effective in correcting the abuses of an institution, especially when the institution can hire plenty of men of adequate if not equal ability to take the place of the man of stubborn integrity. I know one journalist who lost his position as managing editor of two wealthy newspapers, one in Boston, the other in New York, in the first instance because he refused to print a false and cowardly retraction dictated by a stockholder whom the editor-in-chief desired to serve, in the second instance because he refused to distort war news. But what good did his single-handed rebellion do, except to make a few friends proud of him? Did either newspaper lose even one mournful subscriber? Did the advertising department suffer? Far from it. Another man took his place, a man not necessarily less honest, but of more conformable temperament. The muddy waters of journalism did not show a ripple. Paradoxically, the journalist is the one man who can do little or nothing to improve journalism. Mr. Lippmann's suggestion that our salvation lies " ultimately in the infusion of the news-structure by men with a new training and outlook," is, as he knows, the expression of a vague hope, too remotely ultimate to have practical bearing on the actual situation. The man of training and outlook, especially of outlook, is the unhappiest man in the employ of a newspaper. His salvation, if not ours, lies in getting out of newspaper work and applying his ability and vision in some occupation which does not discourage precisely the merits which an honest institution should foster. This is not merely the opinion of a critical layman but represents accurately if not literally the advice given to me by a successful editor and writer of special articles. " In this game," he said, " you lose your soul."

The stories of individuals who have tried to be decent in newspaper work and have been fired might be valuable if they were collated and if the better journalists would unite to lay the foundation in fact of more such stories. But a profession, a trade, which has so little sense of its own interest that it does not even make an effective union (to be sure, the organization of newspaper writers met with some success, especially in Boston, but to-day the organization has practically disappeared) to keep its wages up can never be expected to unite in the impersonal interests of truth and intellectual dignity. The individual who charges against an enormous unshakable institution with the weapons of his personal experience is too easily disposed of as a sore-head and is likely to be laughed at even by his fellow-journalists who know that in the main he is right.

This has happened to Mr. Upton Sinclair. I have studied " The Brass Check " carefully for the selfish purpose of getting enough material so that the writing of this chapter should be nothing but a lazy man's task of transcription, not to speak of the noble ethical purpose of reforming the newspaper by exposing its iniquities. I confess I am disappointed. " The Brass Check" is a mixture of autobiography, valuable in its way to those who admire Mr. Sinclair, as I do most sincerely, and of evidence which, though properly personal, ought to be handled in an objective manner. I am puzzled that a man of " training and outlook," who has shown in at least one of his novels an excellent sense of construction, could throw together such a hodge-podge of valid testimony, utterly damning to his opponents, and naïve trivialities, assertions insecurely founded and not important if they were well founded. I am so sure that Mr. Sinclair is on the whole right that I am reluctant to criticize him adversely, to lend a shadow of encouragement to the real adversary, who is unscrupulous and securely entrenched. But as a journalist of " training and outlook " I lament that another journalist of vastly more ability, experience, and information should not have done better work in selecting and constructing his material. As a lawyer said to his client, " You are a saint and you are right, but a courtroom is no place for a saint and you are a damn bad witness." Mr. Sinclair's evidence, however, is all there to be dug out by whoever has the will and the patience. If one-tenth of it is valid and nine-tenths of doubtful value, the one-tenth is sufficient to show the sinister forces behind the newspapers and to explain some of the reasons why the newspapers are untrustworthy, cowardly, and dishonest.

Though Mr. Sinclair tells some damaging stories about the sins of anonymous reporters and of the prostitution of writers like the late Elbert Hubbard, who had no excuse for being anything but honest and independent, yet Mr. Sinclair on the whole would agree with me that the chief responsibility for the evils of journalism does not rest upon the journalist. He tries to place it squarely where it belongs on the owners of the press and the owners of the owners. But it is difficult to determine how the weight of guilt is distributed, for the press is a monster with more than two legs.

Part of the responsibility rests upon the reader, if indeed

the reader is to blame for being a gullible fool and for buying shoddy goods. Mr. Lippmann says: " There is everywhere an increasingly angry disillusionment about the press, a growing sense of being baffled and misled." And Mr. Sinclair says: " The people want the news; the people clamour for the news." Both these statements may be true. But where do the learned doctors find the symptoms? A few of us who have some special interest in the press, in publicity, in political problems, are disillusioned and resentful. Probably everybody has said or heard somebody else say: " That's only a newspaper story," or " You cannot believe everything you read." But such mild scepticism shows no promise of swelling to an angry demand on the part of that vague aggregate, the People, for better, more honest newspapers, to such an angry demand as you can actually hear in any house you enter for cheaper clothes and lower taxes.

If we make a rough calculation of the number of papers sold and of the number of people in the main economic classes, it is evident that papers of large circulation must go by the million to the working-people. Well, is there any sign of growing wrath in the breasts of the honest toilers against the newspapers, against Mr. Hearst's papers, which throw them sops of hypocritical sympathy, not to speak of papers which are openly unfair in handling labour news? Or consider the more prosperous classes. In the smoking-car of any suburban train bound for New York some morning after eight o'clock, look at the men about you, business men, the kind that work, or do something, in offices. They are reading the *Times* and the *Tribune*. There may be some growls about something in the day's news, something that has happened on the stock-market, or a stupid throw to third base in yesterday's game. But is there any murmur of discontent with the newspaper itself? I fail to find any evidence of widespread disgust with the newspaper as it is and a concomitant hunger for something better. The Reader, the Public is mute, if not inglorious, and accepts uncritically what the daily press provides. The reader has not much opportunity to choose the better from the worse. If he gives up one paper he must take another that is just as bad. He is between the devil and the deep sea, as when he casts his ballot for Democrat or Republican. And if he votes Socialist he gets the admirable New York *Call*, which is less a newspaper than a vehicle of propaganda. When one paper is slightly more honest and intelligent than its rivals, the difference is so slight that only those especially interested in the problems of the press are aware of it. For example, in discussing these problems with newspaper men, with critical readers of the press, persons for any reason intelligently interested in the problems, I have never found one who did not have a good word to say for the New York *Globe*. It is so appreciably more decent than the other New York papers that I can almost forgive it for thrusting Dr. Frank Crane under my nose when I am looking at the amusing pictures of Mr. Fontaine Fox—the newspaper vaudeville has to supply stunts for all juvenile tastes. Yet the *Globe* does not find a clamorous multitude willing to reward it for its superiority to its neighbours, which I grant is too slight for duffers to discern. The American reader of newspapers, that is, almost everybody, is a duffer, so far as the newspaper is concerned, uncritical, docile, only meekly incredulous. It may be that " the people " get as good newspapers as they wish and deserve, just as they are said to get as good government as they wish and deserve. Certainly if the readers of newspapers seem to demand nothing better, the manufacturers of newspapers have no inducement to give them anything better. But this does not get us any nearer a solution of the problem or do more than indicate that some vaguely indeterminate part of the responsibility for the evils of the newspapers must rest on the people who buy them.

From the buyer to the seller is the shortest step. The newspaper is a manufacturing concern producing goods to sell at a profit; it is also a department store, and it has some characteristics that suggest the variety show and the brothel. But the newspaper differs from all other commodities in that it does not live by what it receives from the consumer who buys it. Three cents multiplied a million times does not support a newspaper. The valuable part of a newspaper from the manufacturer's point of view, and also to a great extent from the reader's point of view, is the advertisements. The columns of

" reading matter," so called, are little more than bait to attract enough readers to make the paper worth while as a vehicle for advertisements. It is of no importance to the management whether a given column contain news from Washington or Moscow, true or false, or a scandal or a funny story, as long as it leads some thousands of human eyes to look at it and so to look at adjacent columns in which are set forth the merits of a safety razor or an automobile tire or a fifty-dollar suit of clothes at thirty-nine dollars and a half. There has to be a good variety and a certain balance of interest in the columns of reading matter to secure the attention of all kinds of people. This accounts for two things, the great development in the newspaper of pure, or impure, entertainment, of more or less clever features, at the expense of space that might be devoted to news, and also the tendency to accentuate narrative interest above all other kinds of interest. A reporter is never sent out by his chief to get information, but always, in the lingo of the office, to get a " story." This is sound psychology. Everybody likes a story, and there are only a few souls in the world who yearn at breakfast for information. To attack the newspaper for being sensational is to forget that all the great stories of the world, from the amatory exploits of Helen of Troy and Cleopatra to the scandalous adventures of Mrs. Black, the banker's wife, are sensational and should be so treated. The newspaper manager is indifferent to every quality in his news columns except their power to attract the reader and so secure circulation and so please the advertiser. And the advertiser has as his primary interest only that of bringing to the attention of a certain number of people the virtues of his suspenders, shoes, and soothing syrup.

But the advertiser has a secondary interest. The newspaper willy-nilly deals with ideas, such as they are. No idea inimical to the advertiser's business or in general to the business system of which he is a dependent part must be allowed in the paper. Therefore all newspapers are controlled by the advertising department, that is, the counting-room. They are controlled negatively and positively. We are discussing general characteristics and have not space for detailed evidence. But one or two cases will suffice.

An example of the coercion of the newspaper by the advertiser was recently afforded by the Philadelphia press. The Gimbel Brothers, owners of a department store, were charged by United States Government officials with profiteering. The only Philadelphia paper that made anything of the story was the *Press*, which was owned by Mr. Wanamaker of the rival department store. The other papers ignored the story or put it in one edition and then withdrew it. If there is an elevator accident in a general office building, it is reported. If there is a similar accident in a department store, it is usually not reported. When the New York *Times* (April 25, 1921) prints a short account of the experience of four Wellesley college students who disguised their intellectual superiority and got jobs in department stores, the head-line tells us that they " Find They Can Live on Earnings," though the matter under the head-line does not bear this out. Perhaps it does no harm to suppress, or fail to publish, news of accidents and to make out a good case for the living and working conditions of shop-girls. These are minor matters in the news of the world and their importance would appear only if they were accumulated in their tediously voluminous mass.

The positive corruption of the newspaper by the advertiser goes deeper and proceeds from larger economic powers than individual merchants. There is all over the world a terrific economic contest between the employing classes and the wage-earning classes. The dramatic manifestation of this contest is the strike. Almost invariably the news of a strike is, if not falsified, so shaped as to be unfavourable to the workers. In the New York *Nation* of January 5, 1921, Mr. Charles G. Miller, formerly editor of the Cleveland *Plain Dealer*, exposes the lies of the Pittsburgh papers during the steel strike. In two weeks the Pittsburgh papers published more than thirty pages of paid advertisements denouncing the leadership of the strike and invoking " Americanism " against radicalism and syndicalism. The news and editorial attitude of the papers coincided with the advertisements and gave the impression that the strikers were disloyal, un-American, bolshevik. They were silent on the real questions at issue, hours, pay, working conditions. And not only the Pittsburgh press but the press of the entire country was poisoned. For the Associated Press and other news services are not independent organizations feeding news to their clients but simply interrelated newspapers swapping each other's lies. The Denver newspapers control all the news that is read in Boston about the Colorado coal mines. The Boston newspapers control all the news that is read in San Francisco about the New England textile mills. The head of a local bureau of the Associated Press is not a reporter; he is merely a more or less skilful compiler and extracter who sends to the nation, to the whole world, matter which is furnished him by the papers of his district. So that he can usually hold up his hand and swear to the honesty of his service; he is like an express agent who ships a case of what he thinks is canned corn, and it is not his fault if there is opium concealed in the case.

The power of the advertiser to make the newspaper servile and right in its opinions is not confined to the local department store or the special industry operating through a district press. Nor is it confined to the negative punishment of withdrawing advertising of commodities like hosiery, chewing gum, and banking service from papers that offend their masters. There is another method of exerting this power, and that is to buy advertising space in which to set forth ideas calculated to influence public opinion. Here is a full page from a New York paper containing a cartoon and text, the main idea of which is that Labour and Capital should pull together. It is signed by " 'America First' Publicity Association " and is Bulletin No. 115 in a series—" be sure to read them all." This full-page bulletin, of which there have already been more than a hundred, appeared in many newspapers—I do not know how many; and a full page costs a good deal of money. What is the object of this patriotic association?   The prevailing theme of the bulletins which I have seen is " Labour be good! Fight Bolshevism! Beware the Agitator! " Who is going to be influenced by these bulletins? Not the workingman. He knows what he wants, and if he is the dupe of agitators and false theories, these sermons can never rescue him. Not the capitalist. He knows what he wants, and gets it. Perhaps the little middle-class fellow may swallow such buncombe on his daily journey between his office and his home in the suburbs. But he is already an intellectually depraved servant of the employing classes, and it is not worth hundreds of thousands of dollars to complete and confirm his corruption. The primary object of the advertisement is to keep the newspaper " good," to encourage its editorial departments, through the advertising department, not to fall below 99 and 44/100% pure Americanism or admit ideas inimical to the general interests of chambers of commerce, manufacturers' associations, and other custodians of the commonweal. I suspect that some clever advertising man has stung the gentlemen who supply the money for this campaign of education, but what is a few million to them? The man who can best afford to laugh is the business manager of the newspaper when he looks at the check and meditates on the easy money of some of his advertising clients and the easy credulity of some of his reading clients.

It may be argued that the newspaper, which is a business, ought to be controlled, directly and indirectly, by business interests; and certainly if we allow the commercial powers to manage our food supply, transportation, and housing, it is a relatively minor matter if the same powers dominate our press. In like manner if we tolerate dishonest governments, we are only dealing with an epiphenomenon when we consider the dishonest and inefficient treatment by the press of public affairs, national and international. All the news of politics, diplomacy, war, world-trade emanates from government officials or from those who are interested in turning to their own advantage the actions of officials. Business is behind government, and government is behind business; which comes first is unimportant like the problem of the chicken and the egg. It is a partnership of swindle, and though the details of the relation are infinitely complicated, the relation in itself is easy to understand and accounts quite simply for the fact that world news is the most viciously polluted of all the many kinds of news. The efforts of a merchant to keep up the good name of his department store, or of a group of manufacturers to break a strike are feeble and even reasonable, so far as they use the newspapers, compared to the audacious perversion of truth by the combination of arch criminals, government and international business.

The star example in modern times is the current newspaper history of Russia. The New York *Nation* of March 6, 1920, published an article showing that in the columns of the New York *Times* Lenin had died once, been almost killed three times, and had fallen and fled innumerable times. The *New Republic* published August 4, 1920, a supplement by Lippmann and Merz summarizing the news which the *Times* printed about Russia during the three years preceding March 1920. The analysis shows an almost unbroken daily misrepresentation of the programme, purposes and strength of the Russian government and continuous false " optimism," as the writers gently call it, about the military exploits of Russia's enemies, the " white hopes," Kolchak and Denekin. The writers expressly state that they did not select the *Times* because it is worse than other papers but, on the contrary, because it " is one of the really great newspapers of the world." " Rich " or " powerful " would have been a better word than " great." The sources of error in the *Times* were the Associated Press, the special correspondents of the *Times,* government officials and political factions hostile to the present Russian régime. Among the offenders was the United States Government or the journalistic fake-factory in or adjacent to the Department of State. At this writing the article in the *New Republic* has been out nearly a year, that in the *Nation* more than a year. It is fair to assume that they have been seen by the managers of the *Times* and other powerful journalists, that if there was any misstatement the weekly journals would have been forced to recant, which they have not done, and that if the Ochses of the newspaper world had any conscience they would have been at least more careful after such devastating exposures. But the game of " Lying about Lenin " goes merrily on.

The American government and the American press have not been more mendacious in their treatment of Russia than the governments and the press of other nations, but they have been more persistently stupid and unteachable in the face of facts. The British government has been engaged in an agile zigzag retreat from its first position of no intercourse with

Russia, and when the London *Labour Herald* exposed the trick
of Lloyd George which consisted of printing and sending out
from Russia propaganda against the Soviet government, the
prince of political liars was obliged to stop that fraud.   On
the other hand one of the first acts of our new administration
was Mr. Hughes's idiotic confirmation of the attitude held by
the old administration, and he furnished the newspapers real
news, since the Secretary's opinions, however stupid, are real
news, to add to their previous accumulation of ignorance and
lies, and thereby encouraged them in their evil ways.   If a
government is composed of noodles and rogues, the press
which reports the activities of the government and the opinions
of its officials is only secondarily responsible for deceiving the
public.   The editors might be more critical in sifting the true
from the false.   But the newspaper has no motive for trying
to correct the inherent vices of business and government; it
does not originate those vices but merely concurs in them and
reflects them.   The newspaper is primarily responsible only
for the stupidity and mendacity of its correspondents and
editors.   It is not an independent institution with its own ethic,
with either will or full opportunity to serve the truth, but is
only the symptom and expression of the vast corruption that
lies behind it and of the dense popular ignorance that stands
gaping before it.

The *Dunciad* of the Press does not end in quite universal
darkness.   There is a little light over the horizon.   A new
organization called The Federated Press, which endeavours to
" get the news in spite of the newspapers and the great news
agencies," announces that already two hundred editors all over
the world are using its service.   It is too soon to tell how successful this enterprise will be, but it is a ray of promise, because it is an association of working journalists and not a
vague aspiration of reformers and uplifters.   Until some such
organization does become powerful and by practical labour
make an impression on the daily paper, we shall have to depend for enlightenment on a few weekly and monthly periodicals of relatively small circulation.   Most of the popular
weeklies and monthlies are as bad in their way as the newspapers, but they aim chiefly at entertainment; their treatment

of the news in special articles and editorials is a subordinate matter, and their chief sin is not dishonesty but banality. The periodicals which do handle the news, always honestly, usually with intelligence, the *Nation*, the *New Republic*, the *Freeman* and one or two others, must have an influence greater than can be measured by their circulation; for though the giant press laughs at the cranky little Davids with their vicious radical ideas, and though it is too strong to be slain or even severely wounded, yet it cannot be quite insensible to the stones that fly from those valorous slings. It is, however, an indication of the low mental level of America that the combined circulation of these journals, which are, moreover, largely subscribed for by the same readers, is less than that of a newspaper in a second-rate city. Two of them are endowed or subsidized by liberal men of means and none of them is shiningly prosperous. An intelligent populace would buy them by the million. So we leave the responsibility where, after all, it belongs. The American press is an accurate gauge of the American mind.

JOHN MACY

THE LAW

"THE first thing we do, let's kill all the lawyers." This outcry of Jack Cade's followers that the disappearance of the whole profession was the initial step in man's progress toward a better world would be echoed in the United States by the revolutionists of to-day, and also by not a few solid business men who have nothing else in common with the mediæval agitator except perhaps the desire to see the fountains run wine and make it a felony to drink near-beer. Indeed almost every one takes his fling at the law. Doctors and ministers can be avoided if we dislike them, but the judge has a sure grip upon us all. He drags us before him against our will; no power in the land can overturn his decision, but defeated litigants, disappointed sociologists, and unsuccessful primary candidates all join in a prolonged yell, " Kill the umpire."

Where there is smoke, there is fire. Underneath all this agitation is a deep-seated suspicion and dissatisfaction aroused by the legal profession and the whole machinery of justice. It exists despite the fact observed by Bryce, that our system of written constitutions has created a strongly marked legal spirit in the people and accustomed them to look at all questions in a legal way—a characteristic exemplified when other peoples judged the Covenant of the League of Nations as an expression of broad policies and the aspirations of a hundred years, while we went at it word by word with a dissecting knife and a microscope as if it had been a millionaire's will or an Income Tax Act. Moreover, although lawyers as a class are unpopular, they are elected to half the seats in the legislatures and in Congress. The profession which cannot boast a single English Prime Minister in the century between Perceval and Asquith, has trained every President who was not a general, except Harding. Perhaps this very fact that lawyers receive public positions out of all proportion to their numbers partially accounts for the prejudice felt against them by men in other professions and occupations.

Hostility to lawyers and case-law is no new phenomenon in this country. Puritans and Quakers arrived with unpleasant memories of the English bench and bar, who had harried them out of their homes. To them, law meant heresy trials, and the impression that these left on the minds of their victims has been set down forever by Bunyan in the prosecution of Faithful at Vanity Fair. The Colonists were no more anxious to transplant some Lord Hate-good, his counsellors, and his law books to our shores, than Eugene V. Debs would strive to set up injunctions and sedition statutes if he were founding a socialistic commonwealth in the South Seas. The popular attitude toward lawyers was re-inforced by the clergy who were naturally reluctant to have their great moral and intellectual influence disputed by men who would hire themselves out to argue either side of any question. The ministers who ruled Massachusetts and Connecticut by the Law of Moses, wanted no rivals to challenge their decisions upon the authority of Bracton and Coke. And everywhere, except perhaps on the Southern plantations, the complicated structure of feudal doctrines, which constituted such a large part of English law well into the 18th century, was as unsuited to Colonial ways and needs as a Gothic cathedral in the wilderness. Life was so pressing, time was so short, labour so scarce, that the only law which could receive acceptance must be so simple that the settlers could apply it themselves. Although Justice Story has spread wide the belief that our ancestors brought the Common Law to New England on the *Mayflower*, the truth is that only a few fragments got across. These were rapidly supplemented by rules based on pioneer conditions. Much the same phenomenon occurred as in the California of 1849, where the miners ignored the water-law of the Atlantic seaboard which gave each person bordering on a stream some share of the vater, and adopted instead the custom better suited to a new country of first come, first served. Almost the earliest task of the founders of a Colony was the regulation of the disputes which arise in a primitive civilization by a brief legislative code concerning crimes, torts, and the simplest contracts, in many ways like the dooms of the Anglo-Saxon kings. Gaps in these codes were not filled from the Common Law, as would be the case to-day, but by the discretion of the magistrate, or in some Colonies, in the early days, from the Bible. Land laws and conveyances were simple,—the underlying English principle of primogeniture was abolished outright by several Colonial charters, and disputes of title were lessened by the admirable system of registering deeds. Such law did not require lawyers, and it is not surprising that even the magistrates were usually laymen. The chief justice of Rhode Island as late as 1818 was a blacksmith. Oftentimes a controversy was taken away from the court by the legislature and settled by a special statute. Thus, instead of the English and modern American judge-made law, the Colonists received for the most part executive and legislative justice, and lived under a protoplasmic popular law, with the Common Law only one of its many ingredients.

The training of the few Colonists who did become lawyers may be judged from that of an early attorney general of Rhode Island:

" When he made up his mind to study law, he went into the garden to exercise his talents in addressing the court and jury. He then selected five cabbages in one row for judges, and twelve in another row for jurors. After trying his hand there a while, he went boldly into court and took upon himself the duties of an advocate, and a little observation and experience there convinced him that the same cabbages were in the court house which he thought he had left in the garden,—five in one row and twelve in another."

The natural alienation of such attorneys from the intricacies of English law was increased by occasional conflicts between that system and Colonial statutes or conceptions of justice. An excellent Connecticut act for the disposal of a decedent's land was declared void by the Privy Council in London as contrary to the laws of England, and the attempt of the New York governor and judges to enforce the obnoxious English law of libel in the prosecution of Peter Zenger in order to throttle the criticism of public officials by the press, would have succeeded if the jury had not deliberately rejected the legal definitions given by the court.

The Common Law became somewhat more popular when the principles of individual rights which had blocked Stuart oppression were used against George III. After the Revolution, however, it suffered with all things English. Many lawyers had been Loyalists. The commercial depression turned the bar into debt collectors. The great decisions of Lord Mansfield which laid the foundations of modern business law were rejected by Jefferson and many other Americans because of that judge's reactionary policy towards the Colonies. Many States actually passed legislation forbidding the use of English cases as authorities in our courts. The enforcement of the Common Law of sedition and criminal libel by judges, many of whom had been educated in England, identified the Common Law with the suppression of freedom of speech. Nevertheless, the old simple Colonial rules were insufficient to decide the complex commercial questions which were constantly arising, especially in maritime transactions. Aid had to be obtained from some mature system of law.

At this moment a rival to the Common Law presented itself in the Napoleonic code of 1804, attractive to the populace just because it was French, and to many of the bar because of its logical arrangement and because unlike English lawyers they were widely read in Roman and modern Continental law. For a time it was actually doubtful whether the legal assistance which American judges needed would be drawn from England or France. French writers were cited in the courts and Livingston drafted a code on the Napoleonic model for Louisiana. The English law had, however, one great advantage. It was written in our own language. Furthermore, a group of exceptionally able judges such as Joseph Story and James Kent, by their decisions and writings, virtually imported the great bulk of the Common Law into this country and reworked it to meet American conditions. Nevertheless, this law was something that came from outside and had not grown up altogether from the lives and thoughts of our own people, so that it has never meant to Americans what English law means to Englishmen,

for whom it is as much a product of their own land as parliamentary government or the plays of Shakespeare.

Another reason for American hostility to law was found at
the frontier. The pioneer, imbued with the conviction that he
was entitled to the land which he had cleared, ploughed and
sown, often thrown by crop failures into debt to the tradesmen
in the town, resented law as something which was forced upon
him by people who led easy lives, who took his land away
for some technical defect of title, foreclosed mortgages, compelled him to pay for goods of high prices and low quality,
suppressed hereditary feuds, and substituted a mass of book
learning which he was too ignorant or too busy to read, for
the simple principles of fair play which seemed sufficient to
him. Habitual obedience to law was a spirit which could not
develop in men who were largely squatters, and who, from
the outset of our national history, disregarded the Congressional statutes which required that public lands must be surveyed before they were settled. Sometimes, as in this instance,
the settler's resistance to law was successful. More often they
were overpowered by the strength of civilization and submitted
to the law sullen and unconvinced.

The old frontier is gone, a new frontier has arisen. The
meeting place of unfriendly races has moved Eastward from
the Missouri to the Merrimac. The pioneers of to-day came
often from autocratic lands where law was something imposed
on them from above, and they were slow to regard our law
as different in kind. It was not a part of themselves. Moreover, they did not find in America the energetic police organization which had compelled their obedience in Europe. The
men who framed our system of laws were taught by Puritanism that duties declared by those lawfully in authority
should be voluntarily performed. A statute once on the books
got much vitality from this spirit and from the social pressure
of the homogeneous settled communities, whatever the difficulties of enforcement at the frontier. These forces behind law
became weaker when the population was split into numerous
and diverse races by the great tide of immigration. Obedience
to law, never automatic among us, now became liable to cease

altogether whenever a person thought the law unreasonable or felt fairly certain that he would not be found out.

This belief that a law ceases to have obligation when it becomes inexpedient to obey it, extends far beyond the recently arrived elements in our population. For instance, a wealthy man with several American generations behind him, who was serving on the jury in an accident case, stood up on a chair as soon as the jury got into the consultation-room and urged them to disregard everything which the judge had instructed them about the inability of the plaintiff to recover if he, as well as the defendant, was negligent. " This doctrine of contributory negligence," said this educated juryman, " is not the law of France or Germany or any country on the Continent of Europe. A number of eminent writers agree that it is a thoroughly bad law. Let's have nothing to do with it." Needless to say, the plaintiff recovered. This conception of a higher law than that on the books may owe something to the Abolitionists' belief that they were not bound by the laws protecting the inhuman institution of slavery. Many conscientious persons still hold that a man ought not to be punished for disobeying a law which he believes to be morally wrong. Fortunately, a corrective to this dangerous doctrine of the inner legal light is found in the words of a leading Abolitionist, Judge Ebenezer Rockwood Hoar, in charging the Grand Jury on riotous resistance to the fugitive slave law, although he himself regarded it as vicious legislation:

" A man whose private conscience leads him to disobey a law recognized by the community must take the consequences of that disobedience. It is a matter solely between him and his Maker. He should take good care that he is not mistaken, that his private opinion does not result from passion or prejudice, but, if he believes it to be his duty to disobey, he must be prepared to abide by the result; and the laws as they are enacted and settled by the constituted authorities to be constitutional and valid, must be enforced, although it may be to his grievous harm. It will not do for the public authorities to recognize his private opinion as a justification of his acts."

Disrespect for law has been aggravated by the changing

function of the lawyer since the Civil War. In the forties and fifties, he stood out as a leader in his community, lifted by education above the mass of citizens, often before the public gaze in the court-room and chosen because of his forensic eloquence to deliver many of those set orations which Americans constantly demand, brought forward by the litigation of those days as the avenger of crime, the defender of those unjustly imprisoned, the liberator of the escaping slave, or upholding some great public right on behalf of his city or State—the construction of a toll-free bridge across the Charles, the maintenance of the charter of Dartmouth College. After 1870, this pre-eminence was challenged by the new captains of industry, and their appearance was accompanied by an alteration in the work of many an able lawyer, which soon obscured him to the popular imagination. The formation of large businesses required more and more the skill which he possessed. Rewards for drafting and consultation became greater than for litigation, which was growing tedious and costly, so that his clients avoided it whenever possible. Consequently, he changed from an advocate into a " client care-taker," seldom visible to the people and often associated in their minds with the powerful and detested corporations which he represented. Much of the prejudice against " corporation lawyers " was unjust, and the business development of to-day would have been impossible without the skill in organization and reorganization of great enterprises which they displayed during the last half century. However, popular opinion of a class is inevitably based, not on all its members, but on a conspicuous few, and the kind of legal career described in Winston Churchill's " Far Country" was common enough to furnish data for damaging generalizations. In any case, the decline in the public influence of the bar was inevitable, especially as certain businesses retained the exclusive legal services of a staff of men, so that it could be said: " Lawyers used to have clients; now, clients have lawyers."

Of course, during this period there were many lawyers who made a notable success by conducting cases against corporations. These accident lawyers were, however, no more popular than their opponents, even with the workingmen whom they represented. The small means of their clients made any remuneration from them improbable unless damages were recovered. Consequently, the lawyer agreed to take nothing if defeated, but to even matters up insisted on a large fraction of the amount awarded, usually one-third or even more, if he won. Therefore, he fought not merely for justice and his client, but for his own fee, and the temptation to win by every possible means was great. Business men were quick to label him unscrupulous, while working-men resented it when a large slice of the money which the jury gave to them as a just measure for suffering a lifelong disability vanished into some lawyer's pockets.

No satisfactory substitute for the contingent fee was suggested, but the prejudice created by the system and by the dislike of corporation lawyers was too great to be dispelled by the many members of the bar whose practice lay in neither of these two fields. And indeed, the profession as a whole cannot free itself from blame for some very definite evils, soon to be discussed. Unfortunately, the long-standing antagonism between lawyers and laymen has distracted the thoughts of both sides from wrongs which ought to be and can be cured, and turned them to never-ending disputes on problems of relatively small importance. For instance, almost any layman will open a discussion of the function of the lawyer by condemning the profession because it defends criminals who are known to be guilty. The solution of this problem is not easy, but it is not worth a hundredth of the attention it receives, for it hardly ever arises. The criminal law is a small part of the whole law, and lawyers who have spent their whole lives in that field have declared that they were not certain of the guilt of a single client. A far more important problem is whether a lawyer should advocate the passage of legislation which he personally considers vicious. Indeed, the underlying question, to which lawyers and laymen ought to be devoting themselves, is this. How far can the State ascertain the proper course of action by limiting itself to hearing paid representatives of the persons directly interested, financially or otherwise; or should the State also call in and pay trained men to investigate the question independently? The solution of this question will affect not only lawyers, but other professions as well. Medical experts, for instance, might cease to be hired by millionaires to prove them insane, or by the prosecuting attorney with the opposite purpose, but might be employed by the court to make an impartial inquiry into the mental condition of a prisoner. In short, it may be that we have carried the notion of litigation as a contest of wits between two sides so far that the interests of society have not been adequately safeguarded.

If laymen have erred in concentrating on minor points, lawyers have been far too ready to deny laymen any right to discuss law at all. It is just as if school-teachers should maintain that parents and citizens in general have no concern in the problems of education. The time has come to close the gulf in American life between the legal profession and the people who are ruled by laws. Law is the surface of contact where the pressure of society bears upon the individual. Doubtless, he attributes to the law many of the features in this pressure to which he objects, whereas they actually result from the social structure itself. The man who feels wronged by a prosecution for bigamy, or for stealing bread when he is starving for lack of employment, cannot expect to change the law without also changing the views of the community on monogamous marriage and the organization of industry. These institutions of society show themselves in the law just as the veins in a block of marble show themselves at the surface, but it is as futile for him to blame the law for " capitalism," private property, or our present semi-permanent marriages as to try to get rid of the veins by scraping the surface of the marble. On the other hand, there are aspects of law which do not correspond to any existing social requirements or demands, and the layman has good cause to offer his opinion. And it may be worth listening to. The onlooker often sees most of the game. Although the layman may lack technical knowledge, he can appreciate the relation of law to his own department of human activity—business, social service, health— in ways that are difficult for the lawyer who is absorbed in the pressing tasks of each day. Moreover, the lawyer's habitual and necessary obligation to conform to existing laws naturally

inclines him to overlook their defects, which are obvious to
those who can spend in detached criticism the same time which
he requires for practical application. Modern medicine was
created by Pasteur, who was not a doctor; modern English
law by Bentham, who was a lawyer to the extent of arguing
one case and who was edited by Mill, a philosopher and
economist.

Knowledge is no longer a matter of water-tight compart-
ments. "All good work is one," says Wells in "Joan and
Peter." Law touches psychology in its treatment of the defective and insane, medicine and surgery in industrial accidents and disease, political science in municipal corporations,
economics in taxation, philosophy in its selection of the purposes it should strive to accomplish. And this is a meagre list.
The greatest need of American law is the establishment of
means for intelligent mutual understanding and effective co-operation, not merely between lawyers and experts in such other
fields as those mentioned, but between lawyers and the mass of
our population, who fill the jails, pay the taxes, drink city
water, get hurt in factories, buy, sell, invest, build homes, and
leave it all to their children when they die.

For these men and women have a right to complain of our
law. Its evils are not those commonly decried, lawyers to defend the guilty, reliance on precedents instead of common
sense, bribed judges. The real defect is failure to keep up to
date. Many existing legal rules have the same fault as New
York surface-cars before the subway or Hoboken Ferries
before the tubes. They were good in their day, but it has
gone by and they cannot handle the traffic. The system
formulated by Story and Kent worked well for the farms,
small factories, and small banks of their time, but the great
development of national resources and crowded cities presented new situations unsuited to the old legal rules, and kept
men too busy for the constructive leisure necessary for thinking out a new system. The law became a hand-to-mouth
affair, deciding each isolated problem as it arose, and often
deciding it wrong. Yet lawyers were satisfied with law, just
as business men with business. Then came the agitation of
the last fifteen years, which has at least made us discontented

about many things. The next task is to stop calling each other names, sit down together, think matters through to a finish, and work together to complete the process which is farther along than we realize, of making over the common law system of an agricultural population a century ago to meet the needs of the city-dwelling America of to-day.

A first step toward co-operation would be more discussion of law in the press. Several years ago Charles E. Hughes in a public address said that one reason why courts and lawyers were so unpopular in this country was the unfamiliarity of the people with what they were doing. Outside of criminal prosecutions, divorces, and large constitutional cases, newspapers give very little attention to legal questions, and even these cases are presented fragmentarily with almost no attempt to present their historical background and the general principles at issue. There is nothing to compare with the resumé of trials and decisions which appears from day to day in the London *Times,* no popular exposition of legal problems such as Woods Hutchinson has done for medicine or numerous writers for the achievements of Einstein. Surely law can be made as intelligible and interesting to the ordinary educated reader as relativity. It enters so intimately into human relationships that some knowledge of it is very important, not as a guide in specific transactions as to which a lawyer ought to be consulted, but as part of the mental stock-in-trade of the well-informed citizen. Wider realization of the difficulties of the work of judges and lawyers would bring about a friendlier and more helpful popular attitude.

The public might understand, for example, why law does not progress so conspicuously and rapidly as medicine or engineering. Part of the blame rests, no doubt, upon lawyers, who have been less active than other professions in discussing and applying new ideas, but the very nature of the subject is an obstacle to quick change. In law, progress requires group action; the individual can accomplish little. The physician who discovers a new antitoxin, the surgeon who invents a new method of operating for gastric ulcer, can always, if his reputation be established, find some patient upon whom to test his conception. Its excellence or its faults can be rapidly proved to his own mind and that of any skilled onlooker. And new ideas, if sound, mean a larger practice and money in his pocket. The lawyer gets no such rewards for improving the law, and has no such opportunities for experiment. If he is convinced by observation, wide reading, and long thinking, that arrest for debt should be abolished, or the property of a spendthrift protected by law from his creditors, or trial by jury abandoned except in criminal trials, he cannot try out these theories upon some client. He must sacrifice days from his regular work to persuade a whole legislature to test his idea upon thousands of citizens, and if the idea is a bad one, the experiment will be a widespread disaster. Consequently law reform always faces an instinctive and discouraging legislative opposition. Even after every State except two had adopted the Uniform Negotiable Instruments Law, the Georgia legislature refused to do so because the Act abolished days of grace, the old custom allowing a debtor three days beyond the time of payment named in his note. They said that when a man had promised to pay a debt on May 1, it was un-American not to let him wait till May 4. Again, a committee of very able New York lawyers recently drew a short Practice Act setting forth the main requirements for the conduct of a law-suit, and leaving the details to the judges, who may be supposed to know more about their own work than the legislature. Similar laws have long been in successful operation in England, Massachusetts, and Connecticut, whereas the existing New York Code of Civil Procedure with its thousands of sections has been a vexatious source of delay and disputes in the press of urban litigation. The new measure was an admirable and thorough piece of work, endorsed by the Bar Associations of New York City and the State. Yet it was killed by the age-long opposition of the country to the town. Upstate lawyers, less harassed by the old Code because of uncrowded rural dockets, objected to throwing over their knowledge of the existing system and spending time to learn a new and better one. The legislature hated to give more power to the courts. As a result, the new bill was scrapped, and nothing has been done after years of agitation except to renumber the sections of the old Code with a few improvements.

Another factor in law reform is the existence of fifty legal systems in one nation. Even if the law is modernized in one State, the objectionable old rule will remain in the other forty-seven until their legislatures are persuaded by the same tedious process. On the other hand, this diversity has its merits. Some of the progressive Western States serve as experiment stations for testing new legal and governmental schemes. Still more important, the limitations on legal experimentation are somewhat offset by the opportunities for observation of the workings of different legal rules in neighbouring States. The possibilities of this comparative method for judging the best solution of a legal problem have not yet been fully utilized. For example, a dispute has long raged whether it is desirable to compel a doctor to disclose professional secrets on the witness-stand without the patient's consent. About half the States require him to keep silent. The reasons given are, that patients will seek medical aid less freely if their confidences may be disclosed; doctors would lie to shield their patients; some doctors are hired by employers to treat workmen injured in accidents and will try to get evidence on behalf of the employers if they are allowed to testify. So far, the discussion has turned on the probability or improbability that these arguments represent the facts, and neither side has collected the facts. The discussion could be brought down to earth by an investigation in New York which has the privilege, and Massachusetts, where secrecy is not maintained. Are doctors less consulted in Massachusetts, do they perjure themselves, do they ingratiate themselves with workmen to defeat subsequent accident suits? Statistics, personal interviews with judges and physicians, and examination of the stenographic records of trials ought to give valuable assistance in determining which half of the States has the better rule.

Since law reform requires highly organized group action, some individual should be charged with the responsibility of organization. At present, it is everybody's business. Judges are hearing cases all day and writing opinions at night, and they have no legislative position as in England, where they can draft bills and present them in the House of Lords. Individual lawyers carry little weight. The Bar Associations have accomplished much, but the work of their members is done without pay in the intervals of practice, and they have no official standing. The Attorney General is necessarily a partisan, representing the State's side in litigation, with neither the time nor the duty to improve the law in general. The United States and the larger States badly need a Minister of Justice. All complaints of legal inefficiency would come to him, and he would be constantly collecting statistics of the cases in the courts and their social consequences, observing procedure personally, or through a corps of expert assistants, conferring with the judges and the Bar Associations, drafting or examining measures affecting the administration of justice and giving his opinion about them to the legislature, and charged with the general duty of ascertaining whether every person can find a certain remedy from the laws for all injuries or wrongs, obtaining right and justice freely and without purchase, completely and without denial, promptly and without delay.

Until we establish such an official, we can rely on three instruments of legal advance, each of which may be a point of cooperation between lawyers and laymen. Of the first, the Bar Associations, something has already been said. The second is the judiciary. Unfortunately, the tendency of the American antagonism to law to concentrate on personal topics has warped the prolonged discussion of this branch of our government during the last ten years, and, indeed, since 1789. Charges of corruption and incompetency against individual judges, and methods of getting a bad judge off the bench, have entirely obscured the problem of getting good judges on the bench. The power of judges to declare statutes unconstitutional and void makes them the controlling factor in our government, yet there is no country where less attention is paid to their selection and training. It is of no use to recall a poor judge by popular vote if the people are eager to put one of the same type in his place. Nothing need be added to the estimate in Bryce's " Modern Democracies " of the unevenness of judicial personnel. The most obvious need, if the inferior judges are to be brought up to the level of the best men, is for higher salaries. But that alone is not enough to induce leaders of the bar to become judges. No salary could be so high as the income of successful metropolitan lawyers. The time has come for greater willingness on their part to retire from a large practice in middle life and devote their talents to judicial work. And even this will be useless, unless selection is based on merit. Our system of an elective judiciary is probably too deeply rooted to be entirely abandoned, though it is clear that legal talent is not a quality, like executive ability, readily capable of being appraised by the electorate. On the other hand, it is not altogether certain that State governors would appoint judges without regard to partisan considerations. An interesting compromise plan has been suggested, that there should be a Chief Justice, elected by the people, who should be in effect the Minister of Justice already described. All the other judges would be appointed by him, for life or for long terms, while his responsibility for wise selections would be secured by a short term or even by the recall. A governor does so many tasks that his judicial appointments do not play a large part in the popular judgment of his record, but the Chief Justice would stand or fall on the merits of the administration of law under his management.

Moreover, we do not deal fairly by the judges chosen under existing systems. After they have been selected, they should have more opportunity to study the special duties of their position before beginning work, and more leisure amid trials and opinions for general legal reading and for observation of the complexities of modern life which are inevitably involved in their decisions, especially on constitutional questions. Most litigation grows out of urban and industrial conditions, with which State supreme court judges may easily get out of touch, if they remain continuously in the State House in a small upstate city like Springfield, Albany, or Sacramento, with little opportunity to visit the factories and tenements of Chicago, New York, and San Francisco. It may also be doubted whether our usual system which restricts some judges to trials and others to appellate work is wise; an occasional change from one to the other is both refreshing and instructive. Judges frequently complain of the monotony of their work, cooped up with a few associates of similar mental interests, so that the atmosphere may acquire the irritability of a boarding-house. It is not generally understood how much judges are cut off from other men. Close intimacy with their former friends at the bar or with wealthy business men who may have cases before them, is sure to cause talk. Graham Wallas's suggestion of an occasional transfer to active work of a semi-judicial character, like Judge Sankey's chairmanship of the English Coal Commission, seems valuable. Our Interstate Commerce Commission would provide such an opportunity. Finally, the existing gulf between courts and law schools might be narrowed by summer conferences on growing-points in the law, where each side could give much out of its experience to the other.

The remaining instrument of progress is the law schools. " Legal education," says Bryce, " is probably nowhere so thorough as in the United States." The chief reasons for this success are two, the professional law teacher, who has replaced the retired judge and the practising lawyer who lectured in his spare hours; and the case-system of instruction. This method is not, as is popularly believed, the memorization by the students of the facts of innumerable cases. It imparts legal principles, not on the say-so of a text-book or a professor, but by study and discussion of the actual sources of those principles, the decisions of the courts. The same method in the Continental Law would result in a class-room discussion of codes and commentators, which are there the sources. One of the most interesting signs of its success is its spread from law into other sciences such as medicine. Books based on the study of concrete situations are used in public schools for the study of geography and hygiene, and charitable societies work out the general needs of the community from the problems of individual families. This system has superseded in all the leading law schools the old methods of lecturing and reading treatises. Its most conspicuous service is, of course, vocational, the training of men whose advice a client can safely accept. Already some States have required a law-school degree as a condition of admission to the bar, and the old haphazard law-office apprenticeship will eventually disappear, although the question of how far a man who is earning his living should be allowed to study law in his spare hours at a night law school whose standards must usually be lower than a full-time school remains as a difficult problem in a democratic country. Efficiency of training conflicts with equality of opportunity. A second service of the leading law schools is the modernization of the law through the production of books. A great example of this is the " Treatise on Evidence," by John H. Wigmore, dean of Northwestern Law School, which is every day influencing courts and renovating the most antiquated portion of the common law.

Of late years, the need for fresh changes in method has become plain. Christopher Columbus Langdell, the inventor of the case-system, laid down ,two fundamental propositions: " First, that law is a science; second, that all the available materials of that science are contained in printed books." Experience has proved that he was right in believing that attendance in a lawyer's office or at the proceedings of courts was not essential to a legal education. But the scope of legal study must now extend beyond printed books, certainly beyond law books. Since law is not an isolated department of knowledge, but a system of rules for the regulation of human life, the truth of those rules must be tested by many facts outside the past proceedings of courts and legislatures. Not only law in books but law in action has to be considered, and after learning the principles evolved by a process of inclusion and exclusion in the decisions or by intermittent legislative action, the scholar must find how those principles actually work in the bank, the factory, the street, and the jail. The problem is still debated, whether this can better be done in the pre-legal college course or by the use of non-legal experts in the law schools, or whether the necessary material should be assimilated and presented by the law teachers themselves. Yet this widening of the content of legal study does not in the least impair the validity of Langdell's method, the systematic investigation of the sources of law at first hand, whether those sources be found in the reports and statutes which he had in mind, or in the economic, social, and psychological facts which have demanded attention in recent years.

Something must be said in closing of those portions of the law where change has been most necessary. Of these our criminal law is easily the most disgraceful. Its complete inability to perform its task has been exhaustively demonstrated by the opening chapter of Raymond Fosdick's "American Police Systems." The lawyers and judges are only partly to blame, for their work forms only the middle of three stages in the suppression of crime. The initial stage of arrest and the final stage of punishment are in the hands of administrative officials, beyond the control of the bench and bar. Many criminals are never caught, and the loss of public confidence in the justice or effectiveness of prisons makes juries reluctant to convict. Yet the legal profession is sorely at fault for what takes place while the prisoner is in the dock. The whole problem calls for that co-operation between lawyers, other experts, and laymen, of which I have already spoken. Unless something is soon done, we may find crime ceasing to be a legal matter at all. Even now, many large department stores have so little belief in the criminal courts and prisons that they are trying embezzlers and shoplifters in tribunals of their own, and administering a private system of probation and restitution. The initial step is a reformulation of the purpose of punishment. Twenty-five years ago, Justice Holmes asked, " What have we better than a blind guess to show that the criminal law in its present form does more good than harm? "

One serious reason for its breakdown has been the creation of innumerable minor offences, which are repeatedly committed and almost impossible to suppress. The police are diverted from murders and burglaries to gambling and sexual delinquencies, while the frequent winking at such breaches of law destroys the essential popular conviction that a law ought to be obeyed just because it is law. The Chief of Police of New Orleans told Raymond Fosdick, " If I should enforce the law against selling tobacco on Sunday, I would be run out of office in twenty-four hours. But I am in constant danger of being run out of office because I don't enforce it." So they were hanging green curtains, which served the double purpose of advertising the location of the stands and of protecting the virtue of the citizens from visions of evil.

At the present time we have thrown a new strain on the

criminal law by the enactment of nation-wide prohibition. The future will show whether the main effect of this measure will be an increase in disrespect and antagonism for law, or the ultimate removal of one of the chief causes of lawlessness and waste. Unfortunately, the perpetual discussion of home-brew receipts and hidden sources of supply has prevented a general realization that we are witnessing one of the most far-reaching legislative experiments of all time. What we ought to be talking about is the consequences of prohibition to health, poverty, crime, earning-power, and general happiness. It is possible, for instance, that total abstinence for the working classes coupled with apparently unlimited supplies of liquor for their employers may have the double consequence of in-creasing the resentful desire of the former to wrest the con-trol of wealth from those who are monopolizing a time-honoured source of pleasure, and of weakening the ability of the heavy-drinking sons of our captains of industry to stand up in the struggle against the sober brains of the labour leaders of the future. Prohibition may thus bring about a striking shift of economic power.

The delays, expense, and intricacies of legal procedure de-mand reform. The possession of a legal right is worthless to a poor man if he cannot afford to enforce it through the courts. The means of removing such obstacles have been set forth by Reginald H. Smith in " Justice and the Poor." For instance, much has already been accomplished by Small Claims Courts, where relief is given without lawyers in a very simple manner. When a Cleveland landlady was sued by a boarder because she had detained his trunk, she told the judge that he had set fire to his mattress while smoking in bed and refused to pay her twenty-five dollars for the damage. The judge, instead of calling expert witnesses to prove the value of the mattress, telephoned the nearest department store, found he could buy another for eight dollars, and the parties agreed to settle on that basis. Again, family troubles are now scattered through numerous courts. A father deserts, and the mother goes to work. The neglected children get into the Juvenile Court. She asks for a separation in the Probate Court. A grocer sues her husband for food she has bought, before a jury. She prosecutes him before a criminal court for non-support, and finally secures a divorce in equity. One Court of Domestic Relations should handle all the difficulties of the family, which ought to be considered together. Much of the injustice to the poor has been lessened by legal aid societies, which have not only conducted litigation for individuals but have also fought test-cases up to the highest courts, and drafted statutes in order to protect large groups of victims of injustice. The injury done to the poor by antiquated legal machinery is receiving wide attention, but it is also a tax on large business transactions which is ultimately paid by the consumer. Reform is needed to secure justice to the rich.

The substantive law which determines the scope of rights and duties has been more completely overhauled, and many great improvements have been accomplished. Relations between the public and the great corporations which furnish transportation and other essential services are no longer left to the arbitrary decisions of corporate officers or the slow process of isolated litigation. Public service commissions do not yet operate perfectly, but any one who doubts their desirability should read a contemporary Commission Report and then turn to the history of the Erie Railroad under Jim Fiske and Jay Gould as related in " The Book of Daniel Drew." The old fellow-servant rule which threw the burden of an industrial accident upon the victim has been changed by workmen's compensation acts which place the risk upon the employer. He pays for the injured workman as for a broken machine and shifts the expense to his customers as part of the costs of the business. The burden is distributed through society and litigation is rapid and inexpensive. Unfortunately, no such satisfactory solution has been reached in the law of labour organizations, but its chaotic condition only corresponds to the general American uncertainty on the proper treatment of such organizations. It is possible that just as the King, in the Middle Ages, insisted on dragging the Barons into his courts to fight out their boundary disputes there, instead of with swords and battleaxes on the highway, so society which is the victim of every great industrial dispute will force employers and workmen alike to settle their differences before a tribunal while production goes on. The Australian Courts of Conciliation have lately been imitated in Kansas, an experiment which will be watched with close interest.

Less importance must be attached, however, to the development of particular branches of the law than to the change in legal attitude. The difference between the old and the new is exemplified by two extracts from judicial decisions which were almost contemporaneous. Judge Werner, in holding the first New York Workmen's Compensation Act unconstitutional, limited the scope of law as follows:

" This quoted summary of the report of the commission to the legislature, which clearly and fairly epitomizes what is more fully set forth in the body of the report, is based upon a most voluminous array of statistical tables, extracts from the works of philosophical writers and the industrial laws of many countries, all of which are designed to show that our own system of dealing with industrial accidents is economically, morally, and legally unsound. Under our form of government, however, courts must regard all economical, philosophical and moral theories, attractive and desirable though they may be, as subordinate to the primary question whether they can be moulded into statutes without infringing upon the letter or spirit of our written constitutions. . . . With these considerations in mind we turn to the purely legal phases of the controversy." (Ives *v.* South Buffalo Ry. Co., 201 N. Y. 271, 287, 1911.)

A different attitude was shown by the Supreme Court of the United States in its reception of the brief filed by Mr. Louis D. Brandeis on behalf of the constitutionality of an Oregon statute limiting woman's work to ten hours a day. Besides decisions, he included the legislation of many States and of European countries. Then follow extracts from over ninety reports of committees, bureaus of statistics, commissioners of hygiene, inspectors of factories, both in this country and in Europe, to the effect that long hours of labour are dangerous for women, primarily because of their special physical organization. Following them are extracts from similar reports discussing the general benefits of shorter hours from the economic aspect of the question. Justice Brewer said:

" The legislation and opinions referred to in the margin may not be, technically speaking, authorities, and in them is little or no discussion of the constitutional question presented to us for determination, yet they are significant of a widespread belief that woman's physical structure, and the functions she performs in consequence thereof, justify special legislation restricting or qualifying the conditions under which she should be permitted to toil. Constitutional questions, it is true, are not settled by even a consensus of present public opinion, for it is a peculiar value of a written constitution that it places in unchanging form limitations upon legislative action, and thus gives a permanence and stability to popular government which otherwise would be lacking. At the same time, when a question of fact is debated and debatable, and the extent to which a special constitutional limitation goes is affected by the truth in respect to that fact, a widespread and long continued belief concerning it is worthy of consideration. We take judicial cognizance of all matters of general knowledge." (Muller *v.* Oregon, 208 U. S. 412, 420, 1907.)

The decision displays two qualities which are characteristic of the winning counsel since his elevation to the bench; it keeps its eye on the object instead of devoting itself to abstract conceptions, and it emphasizes the interest of society in new forms of protection against poverty, disease, and other evils. To these social interests, the property of the individual must often be partly sacrificed and in recent years we have seen the courts upholding the guarantee of bank deposits, State regulation of insurance rates, and suspension of the right of landlords to recover unreasonable rents or dispossess their tenants. All this would have been regarded as impossible fifty years ago.

These extensions of governmental power over property have been accompanied by legislation severely restricting freedom of discussion of still more radical types of State control. It is argued that the right of free speech must face limitation like the right of the landlord. The true policy is exactly the opposite. Not only is it unjust for the State to carry out one form of confiscation while severely punishing the discussion of another form, but in an age of new social devices the widest liberty for the expression of opinion is essential, so that the merits and demerits of any proposed plan may be thoroughly known and comparisons made between it and alternative schemes, no matter how radical these alternatives may be. A body of law that was determined to stand still might discourage thought with no serious damage; but law which is determined to move needs the utmost possible light so that it may be sure of moving forward.

No one has expressed so well the new importance of social interests, and the value of freedom of speech; no one, indeed, has expressed so nobly the task and hopes of American Law, as the man of whom it is said that among the long list of American judges, he seems " the only one who has framed for himself a system of legal ideas and general truths of life, and composed his opinions in harmony with the system already framed." (John H. Wigmore, " Justice Holmes and the Law of Torts," 29 Harv. L. Rev. 601.) Yet no one has been more cautious than Justice Holmes in warning us not to expect too much from law.

" The law, so far as it depends on learning, is indeed, as it has been called, the government of the living by the dead. It cannot be helped, it is as it should be, that the law is behind the times. As law embodies beliefs that have triumphed in the battle of ideas and then have translated themselves into action, while there is still doubt, while opposite convictions still keep a battle front against each other, the time for law has not come; the notion destined to prevail is not yet entitled to the field." " Collected Legal Papers," 138, 294.)

It is the work of the present generation of American lawyers to be sure that the right side wins in the many conflicts now waging. We cannot be certain that the law will make itself rational, while we remain as inactive as in the past, absorbed in our own routine, and occasionally pausing to say, " All's right with the world "; for, to quote Holmes once more, " The mode in which the inevitable comes to pass is through effort."

ZECHARIAH CHAFEE, JR.

EDUCATION

IF Henry Adams had lived in the 13th century he would have
found the centre of a world of unity in the most powerful
doctrine of the church, the cult of the Virgin Mary. Living
in the 19th century he sums up his experience in a world of
multiplicity as the attempt to realize for himself the saving
faith of that world in what is called education. Adams was
not the first to be struck with the similarity of the faiths of
the mediæval and the modern world. This comparison is the
subject of an article by Professor Barrett Wendell published
in the *North American Review* for 1904 and entitled " The
Great American Superstition ":

" Undefined and indefinite as it is, the word education is
just now a magic one; from the Atlantic to the Pacific, it is
the most potent with which you can conjure money out of
public chests or private pockets. Let social troubles declare
themselves anywhere, lynchings, strikes, trusts, immigration,
racial controversies, whatever you chance to hold most threat-
ening, and we are gravely assured on every side that education is the only thing which can preserve our coming generations from destruction. What is more, as a people we listen
credulously to these assurances. We are told, and we believe
and evince magnificent faith in our belief, that our na†ional
salvation must depend on education."

Professor Wendell goes on trenchantly to compare this reign-
ing modern faith with that in the mediæval church. He calls
attention to the fact that whereas the dominant architectural
monuments of the Old World are great cathedrals and religious houses, implying the faith that salvation could be assured
by unstinted gifts to the church, in our modern times the most
stately and impressive structures are our schools, colleges, and
public libraries, many of them, like the cathedrals, erected

by sinners of wealth in the pursuit of individual atonement and social salvation. "Ask any American what we shall do to be saved, and if he speak his mind he will probably bid us educate our fellow-men." He might have extended his comparison to the personal hierarchy of the two institutions, for at the time of his article the President of Harvard spoke to the people of the United States with the voice of Innocent III, surrounded by his advisers among university presidents and superintendents gathered like Cardinal Archbishops, in the conclave of the National Education Association, of which the Committee of Ten was a sort of papal curia. Although the educational papacy has fallen into schism, the cities are still ruled by superintendents like bishops, the colleges by president and deans, like abbots and priors, and the whole structure rests on a vast population of teachers holding their precarious livings like the parish priests at the will of their superiors, tempered by public opinion. Indeed, Professor Wendell is struck by the probability that as European society was encumbered by the itinerant friars, so America will have "its mendicant orders of scholars—the male and female doctors of philosophy." But it is his main theme which concerns us here, that "the present mood of our country concerning education is neither more nor less than a mood of blind, mediæval superstition."

The difference between faith as religion and as superstition may be hard to define, the terms having become somewhat interchangeable through controversy, but in general we should doubtless use the pragmatic test. A vital and saving faith which actually justifies itself by results is religion; a faith which is without constructive effect on character and society, and is merely fanciful, fantastic, or degrading we call superstition. The old education which America brought from England and inherited from the Renaissance was a reasonable faith. It consisted of mathematics, classics, and theology, and while it produced, except in rare instances, no mathematicians, classical scholars, or theologians, it trained minds for the learned professions of those days and it gave the possessors of it intellectual distinction, and admitted them to the society of cultivated men everywhere. Its authority was largely traditional, but it worked in the world of that day much as the thirty-three Masonic degrees do in the world of Masonry. It may properly be called a religion, and in its rigid, prescribed, dogmatic creed it may be compared to the mediæval theology. At any rate, it suffered the same fate and from the same cause. Its system was too narrow for the expanding knowledge and the multiplying phenomena of the advancing hour. It failed to take account of too many things. The authority of tradition, by which it maintained its position, was challenged and overthrown, and private judgment was set in its place.

Private judgment in education is represented by the elective system; President Eliot was the Luther of this movement and Harvard College his Wittenberg. Exactly as after the Reformation, however, the attitudes of assertion and subservience in spiritual matters continued to manifest themselves where the pope had been deposed, in Geneva and Dort and Westminster, so in spite of the anarchy of the elective system the educational function continues to impose itself in its traditional robes of authority, and to be received with the reverence due to long custom. And in this way education in America from being a saving faith has become an illusion. The old education, its authority challenged, its sway limited, and nobody caring whether its followers can quote Latin or not, is in the position of the Church of Rome; the so-called new education, uncertain in regard to material and method, direction and destination, is like the anarchic Protestant sects. Neither possesses authority; the old system has lost it, and the new ones have never had it. They are alike in depending upon the blindness of the masses which is superstition.

Although the generalization remains true that the mood of America toward education is a mood of superstition, there are certain forms of education operative in America to-day which approve themselves by performance and justify the reasonable faith in which they are held. The argument in favour of the elective system, by force of which it displaced the prescribed classical course, was that it was necessary to give opportunity for specialization. This opportunity it has given, and in certain directions the results produced by American institutions are of high value. Our scientific education is the most advanced, and in the professions which depend upon it, engineering and medicine, our product doubtless "compares favourably" with that of Europe. These facts cannot be cited, however, as a valid reason for the American faith in education as a whole. It is recognized to-day that progress in natural science has far outrun that in politics, social life, culture—therein lies the tragedy of the world. A few men of science have a knowledge of the means by which the human race can be destroyed in a brief space—and no statesmen, philosophers, or apostles of culture have the power to persuade the human race not to permit it to be done.

In another direction a great increase of specialization has taken place—in the preparation for business. Our colleges of business administration rival our scientific schools in the exactness of their aim, and the precision of their effort. Here again, however, it may be questioned whether their success is one to justify belief in the educational process as a whole. The result of such specialization upon the business organization of society can hardly be to arouse a critical, and hence truly constructive, attitude in regard to the whole economic problem; it is nearly certain to promote a disposition to take advantage of the manifest shortcomings of that organization for individual successful achievement. Whether society as a whole will profit by the efforts of such experts as our business colleges are turning out remains to be seen. Whether we are wise in strengthening the predatory elements which put a strain on the social organization, at a time when the whole structure is trembling, is open to question. Here again the faith of America in education as social salvation is not justified by individual results, however brilliant and fortunate.

The value of the specialist to society is unquestionable, but he alone will not save it. Such salvation must come from the diffusion and validity of the educational process as a whole, from the men and women of active intelligence, broad view, wide sympathy, and resolute character who are fitted as a result of it to see life steadily and see it whole, reason soundly to firm conclusions in regard to it, and hold those decisions in the face of death. The specialist indeed may be considered a necessary subtraction from the general social army, a person set apart for special duty, whose energies are concentrated and loyalties narrowed. We expect him to die, if need be, in maintaining that the world moves, but not for freedom of thought in the abstract. It is by the generally trained, all-round product of our education that the system must be judged. And what do we find?

The general student, it appears, tends to be the product of as narrow a process as the specialist, but not as deep. As the demands of specialization become more exacting, its requirements reach farther and farther back into the field of general education, and more and more of the area is restricted to its uses. The general student in consequence becomes a specialist in what is left over. Moreover, he exercises his right of private judgment and free election along the path of least resistance. Laboratory science he abhors as belonging to a course of specialization which he has renounced. The classics and mathematics, to which a good share of our educational machinery is still by hereditary right devoted, he scorns as having no *raison d'être* except an outworn tradition. With the decline of the classics has gone the preliminary training for modern languages, which the general student usually finds too exacting and burdensome, and from the obligation of which colleges and secondary institutions also are now rapidly relieving him. We boasted in the late war that we had no quarrel with the German language, and yet by our behaviour we recognized that one of the fruits of victory was the annihilation of at least one foreign speech within our borders. The general student is thus confined, by right of private judgment of course, to his own language and literature, and such superficial studies in history and social science as he can accomplish with that instrument alone. His view is therefore narrow and insular. His penetration is slight. He is, in short, a specialist in the obvious.

Not only does the general student tend to be as restricted in subject-matter as the specialist, but he lacks the training in investigation, reasoning, and concentration which the latter's responsibility for independent research imposes. The definition of the aim of general education on which Professor Wendell rested his case for the old curriculum in the article quoted above, is "such training as shall enable a man to devote his faculties intently to matters which of themselves do not interest him." Now clearly if the student persistently chooses only the subjects which interest him, and follows them only as far as his interest extends, he escapes all training in voluntary attention and concentration. In his natural disposition to avoid mental work he finds ready accomplices in his instructors and text-book writers. They realize that they are on trial, and that interest alone is the basis of the verdict. Accordingly they cheerfully assume the burden of preliminary digestion of material, leaving to the student the assimilation of so much as his queasy stomach can bear. One way in which the study of English literature or history can be made a matter of training in criticism and reasoning is to send the student to the sources, the original material, and hold him responsible for his conclusions. He may gain a wrong or inadequate view, but at any rate it is his own, and it affords him a solid basis for enlargement or correction. Instead of this the student is invited to a set of criticisms and summaries already made, and is usually discouraged if by chance he attempts a verification on his own account. The actual reading of Shakespeare, Bacon, Milton, Swift, Burke will give the student at least a certain training in concentration; but this is hard, slow, and dry work. It is much easier and more comprehensive, instead of reading one play of Shakespeare, to read *about* all the plays, including the life of the author, his dramatic art, and some speculations in regard to the Elizabethan stage. It was William James who pointed out the difference between *knowledge about* and *acquaintance with* an author. The extent to which we have substituted for the direct vision, with its stimulating appeal to individual reaction, the conventional summary and accepted criticism, the official formula and the stereotyped view, is the chief reason for the ready-made uniformity of our educated product.

The pioneer democracy of America itself is responsible for a method of instruction typically American. The superstitious faith in education was the basis of a system whereby many busy, middle-aged persons whose early advantages had been limited, by means of attractive summaries, outlines, and hand-books, could acquaint themselves with the names of men, books, and events which form the Binet-Simon test of culture, and enable the initiate to hold up his head in circles where the best that has been thought or said in the world is habitu-ally referred to. This method is carried out in hundreds of cultural camp-meetings every summer, by thousands of popu-lar lectures, in countless programmes of study for women's clubs. Unfortunately it is coming to be not only the typical but the only method of general education in America. Chau-tauqua has penetrated the college and the university. Better that our fathers had died, their intellectual thirst unsatisfied, than that they had left this legacy of mental soft drinks for their children.

Thus far I have had the college chiefly in mind, but the same observations apply equally to the secondary school. The elective system has made its way thither, and indeed one of the chief difficulties of organizing a college curriculum for the general student which shall represent something in the way of finding things out, of reasoning from facts to conclusions, and of training in voluntary attention, is that of determining any common ground on the basis of previous attainment. Not only the elective system but the Chautauqua method has largely permeated our high schools. The teachers, often on annual appointment, more than the college instructors, with compara-tive security of tenure, are dependent on the favour of pupils, a favour to be maintained in competition with dances, movies, and *The Saturday Evening Post*, by interesting them. It is therefore a common thing for teachers to repeat in diluted form the courses which they took in college—and which in the original were at best no saturate solutions of the subject. The other day, on visiting a class in Shakespeare at a Y.M.C.A. school, I ventured to suggest to the teacher that the method used was rather advanced. " Ah, but my daughter at high school," he said, " is having Professor Blank's course in the mediæval drama." Now such a course intended for graduate students investigating sources, influences, and variations among saints' plays and mystery plays, could have no educational value in material or method for a high-school pupil, but it was, no doubt, as interesting as a Persian tale.

Inasmuch as the colleges and the secondary schools are both uncertain as regards the meaning and aim of general education, it is not surprising to find the grade schools also at sea, their pupils the victims both of meaningless tradition and reckless experiment. The tradition of our grade schools, educational experts tell us, was brought by Horace Mann from Prussia. There the *Volkschule* was designed for the children of the people, who should be trained with a view to remaining in the station in which they had been born. At least, it may be conceded, the German designers of the system had a purpose in mind, and knew the means to attain it; but both purpose and means are strangely at variance with American conditions and ideals. Other experts have pointed out the extraordinary retarding of the educational process after the first years, when the child learns by a natural objective method some of the most difficult processes of physical life, accomplishing extraordinary feats of understanding and control; and some of the most hopeful experiments in primary education look toward continuing this natural method for a longer time. At present the principle of regimentation seems to be the most important one in the grade school, and as the pace is necessarily that of the slowest, the pupils in general have a large amount of slack rope which it is the problem of principals and teachers to draw in and coil up. Altogether the grade school represents a degree of waste and misdirection which would in itself account for the tendencies toward mental caprice or stagnation which are evident in the pupils who proceed from it.

Thus the parallel which Professor Wendell established between our educational system and the mediæval church would seem to have a certain foundation. In the colleges, as in the monasteries, we have a group of ascetic specialists, sustained in their labours by an apocalyptic vision of a world which they can set on fire, and in which no flesh can live; and a mass of idle, pleasure-loving youth of both sexes, except where some Abbot Samson arises, with strong-arm methods momentarily to reduce them to order and industry. In the high schools, as in the cathedrals, we have great congregations inspired by the music, the lights, the incense, assisting at a ceremony of which the meaning is as little understood as the miracle of the mass. In the grade schools, as in the parish churches, we have the humble workers, like Chaucer's poor parson of the town, trying with pathetic endeavour to meet the needs and satisfy the desires of their flocks, under conditions of an educational and political tyranny no less galling than was the ecclesiastical.

But, we may well enquire, whence does this system draw its power to impose itself upon the masses?—for even superstition must have a sign which the blind can read, and a source of appeal to human nature. The answer bears out still further Professor Wendell's parallel. The mediæval church drew its authority from God, and to impose that authority upon the masses it invented the method of propaganda. It claimed to be able to release men from the burden which oppressed them most heavily, their sins, and in conjunction with the secular power it enforced its claims against all gainsayers, treating the obstinate among them with a series of penalties, penance, excommunication, the stake. Education finds its authority in the human reason, and likewise imposes that authority by propaganda. It too claims the power of salvation from the evils which oppress men most sorely to-day—the social maladjustments, " lynchings, strikes, trusts, immigration, racial controversies "—and it is in alliance with the secular power to preserve its monopoly of social remedies from the competition of anything like direct action. Now it is clear that in the religion of Christ in its pure form the church had a basis for its claims to possess a power against sin, and a means of salvation. Similarly it may be maintained that human reason, allowed to act freely and disinterestedly, would be sufficient to cope with the evils of our time and bring about a social salvation. Indeed, it is curious to remark how nearly the intellectual conclusions of reason have come to coincide with the intuitive wisdom of Jesus. The church was faithless to its mission by alliance with temporal power, by substituting its own advancement for the will of God, by becoming an end in itself. Education likewise is by way of being faithless to itself, by alliance with secular power, political and financial, by the substitution of its own institutional advancement for disinterested service of truth, by becoming likewise an end in itself.

In one of the most remarkable pronouncements of the present commencement season, President Hopkins of Dartmouth College summarized the influences which make against what he calls Verihood. They are first, Insufficiency of mentality, or over-professionalization of point of view; second, Inertia of mentality or closed mindedness; and third, False emphasis of mentality or propaganda. The late war and its evil aftermath have put in high relief the extent of this third influence. President Hopkins speaks as one of the Cardinal Archbishops of Education, and I quote his words with the authority which his personality and position give them:

" Now that the war is passed, the spirit of propaganda still remains in the reluctance with which is returned to an impatient people the ancient right of access to knowledge of the truth, the right of free assembly, and the right of freedom of speech. Meanwhile the hesitancy with which these are returned breeds in large groups vague suspicion and acrimonious distrust of that which is published as truth, and which actually is true, so that on all sides we hear the query whether we are being indulged with what is considered good for us, or with that which constitutes the facts. Thus we impair the validity of truth and open the door and give opportunity for authority which is not justly theirs to be ascribed to falsehood and deceit."

The war was a test which showed how feeble was the hold of American education upon the principle which alone can give it validity. Nowhere was the suppression of freedom of mind, of truth, so energetic, so vindictive as in the schools. Instances crowd upon the mind. I remember attending the trial of a teacher before a committee of the New York School Board, the point being whether his reasons for not entering with his class upon a discussion of the Soviet government concealed a latent sympathy with that form of social organization. The pupils were ranged in two groups, Jews and Gentiles, and were summoned in turn to give their testimony—they had previously been educated in the important functions of modern American society, espionage, and mass action. Another occasion is commemorated by the New York *Evening Post,* the teacher being on trial for disloyalty and the chief count in his indictment that he desired an early peace; and his accuser, one Dr. John Tildsley, an Archdeacon or superintendent of the diocese of New York under Bishop Ettinger:

" Are you interested in having this man discharged? "

" I am," said Dr. Tildsley.

" Do you know of any act that would condemn him as a teacher? "

" Yes," said Dr. Tildsley, " he favoured an early peace."

" Don't you want an early, victorious peace? "

" Why ask me a question like that? "

" Because I want to show you how unfair you have been to this teacher."

" But Mr. Mufson wanted an early peace without victory," said Dr. Tildsley.

" He didn't say that, did he? He did not say an early peace without victory? "

" No."

" Then you don't want an early peace, do you? "

" No."

" You want a prolongation of all this world misery? "

" To a certain extent, yes," said Dr. Tildsley.

Nor did the sabotage of truth stop with school boards and superintendents. A colleague of mine writing a chapter of a text-book in modern history made the statement that the British government entered the war because of an understanding with France, the invasion of Belgium being the pretext which appealed to popular enthusiasm—to which a great publishing house responded that this statement would arouse much indignation among the American people, and must therefore be suppressed.

We need not be surprised that since the war education has not shown a disinterested and impartial attitude toward the phenomena of human affairs, a reliance on the method of trial and error, of experiment and testimony, which it has evolved. Teachers who are openly, or even latently, in sympathy with a form of social organization other than the régime of private control of capital are banned from schools and colleges with candle, with book, and with bell. Text-books which do not agree with the convenient view of international relations are barred. Superintendents like Ettinger and Tildsley in New York are the devoted apologists for the system to which they owe their greatness. To its position among the vested interests of the world, to the prosperity of its higher clergy, education has sacrificed its loyalty to that which alone can give it authority.

The prevention of freedom of thought and enquiry is of course necessary so long as the purpose of education is to produce belief rather than to stimulate thought. The belief which it is the function of education to propagate is that in the existing order. Hence we find the vast effort known as " Americanization," which is for the most part a perfect example of American education at the present day. The spirit of " Americanization " is to consider the individual not with reference to his inward growth of mind and spirit, but solely with a view to his worldly success, and his relation to the existing order of society, to which it is considered that the individual will find his highest happiness and usefulness in contributing. This programme naturally enough finds a sponsor in the American Legion, but it is truly disconcerting to find the National Education Association entering into alliance with this super-legal body, appointing a standing committee to act in co-operation with the Legion throughout the year, accepting the offer of the Legion to give lectures in the schools, and endorsing the principle of the Lusk Law in New York, which imposes the test of an oath of allegiance to the Government as a requirement for a teacher's certificate.

We have now the chief reason why education remains the dominant superstition of our time; but one may still wonder how an institution which is apparently so uncertain of its purpose and methods can continue to exercise such influence on the minds and hearts of men. The answer is, of course, that education is not in the least doubtful of its purpose and methods. Though the humble and obscure teacher, like the Lollard parson, may puzzle his brains about the why and how and purpose of his being here, his superiors, the bishops, the papal curia, know the reason. Education is the propaganda department of the State, and the existing social system. Its resolute insistence upon the essential rightness of things as they are, coupled with its modest promise to reform them if necessary, is the basis of the touching confidence with which it is received. It further imposes itself upon the credulity of the people by the magnificence of its establishment. The academic splendour of the commencement season when the hierarchs bestow their favours, and honour each other and their patrons by higher degrees, is of enormous value in impressing the public. Especially to the uneducated does this majesty appeal. That an institution which holds so fair an outlook on society, which is on such easy and sympathetic terms with all that is important in the nation, which commands the avenues by which men go forward in the world, should be able to guarantee success in life to its worshippers is nothing at which to be surprised. Hence we find the poor of different grades making every sacrifice to send sons and daughters through high school, through college, in the same pathetic faith with which they once burned candles to win respite for the souls of their dead.

There are reasons, however, for thinking that the superstition is passing. In the first place, nowhere do we find more scepticism in regard to the pretensions of education than among those who have been educated, and this number is rapidly increasing. In the second place, the alliance between education and a social system depending on private capital is too obvious, and the abrogation of the true functions of the former is too complete. The so-called Americanization campaign is so crude an attempt to put something over that even the unsophisticated foreigner whom it is intended to impress watches the pictures or reads the pamphlets which set forth the happy estate of the American workman, with his tongue in his cheek.

The social groups which feel aggrieved under the present order are marking their defection by seceding from the educational system and setting up labour universities of their own. So serious is this secession that New York has passed the Lusk Law, designed to bring the independent movement under State control. In the third place, the claim of education to be an open sesame to success in life is contradicted by the position of its most constant votaries, the teachers. The prestige which used to attach to the priests of learning and which placed them above the lure of riches has vanished; their economic station has declined until even college professors have fallen into the servantless class, which means the proletariat. Truly for such as they to declare that education means success in life is a dismal paradox.

Another sign of approaching reformation in the educational system is to be found in the frankly corrupt practices which infest it. Here the parallel to the mediæval church is not exact, for in the latter it was the monasteries and religious houses that were the chief sources of offence, while the colleges and private institutions of higher learning which correspond to them are singularly free from anything worse than wasteful internal politics. It is the public educational system which by reason of its contact with political government partakes most palpably of the corruption that attends the democratic State. It is unnecessary to mention the forms which this corruption takes where a school board of trustees by political appointment is given the exploitation of the schools— the favouritism in appointments and promotions, the graft in text-books and equipment, the speculation in real estate and building contracts, the alienation of school property. There is scarcely a large city in the country in which pupils and teachers alike are not shamefully and scandalously defrauded by action of school trustees which can be characterized in the mildest terms as wilful mismanagement conducing to private profit.

There are two things necessary to the reform of education. One is democratic control, that is, management of institutions of teaching by the teachers. It is to be noted that this is the demand everywhere of labour which respects itself —control of the means of production and responsibility for the result. Surely the teachers should be one of the first groups of toilers to be so trusted. Under democratic control the spoliation of the schools by politicians, the sacrifice of education to propaganda, the tyranny of the hierarchy can be successfully resisted. Once the teachers are released from servile bondage to the public through the political masters who control appointments and promotions, they will deal with their problems with more authority, and be independent of the suffrage of the pupils. Through joint responsibility of the workers for the product they will arrive at that *esprit de corps* which consists in thinking in terms of the enterprise rather than of the job, and from which we may expect a true method of education. Already the movement toward democratic control of teaching is taking form in school systems and colleges. There are a hundred and fifty unions of teachers affiliated with the American Federation of Labour. But the true analogy is not between teachers and labour, but between education and other professions. To quote Dr. H. M. Kallen:

" To the discoverers and creators of Knowledge, and to its transmitters and distributors, to these and to no one else beside belongs the control of education. It is as absurd that any but teachers and investigators should govern the art of education as that any but medical practitioners and investigators should govern the art of medicine."

The other thing needful to restore education to health and usefulness is that it should surrender its hold upon the superstitious adoration of the public, by giving up its pretensions to individual or social salvation, by ceasing its flattery of nationalistic and capitalistic ambitions, and by laying aside its pomps and ceremonies which conduce mainly to sycophancy and cant. Education has shown in special lines that it can be thoroughly scientific, disinterested, devoted. It is its task to translate these virtues of the specialist into the general field. It is not the business of education to humbug the people in the interest of what any person may think to be for their or for his advantage. It is its business to deal frankly and honestly with them, accepting in the most literal sense the responsibility and the promise contained in the text: " Ye shall know the truth, and the truth shall make you free."

ROBERT MORSS LOVETT

SCHOLARSHIP AND CRITICISM

IT is natural for the musician to think any land barbarous if it has produced no great composers, the painter if it has produced no great painters, the critic or the scholar if it has produced no great scholars and critics, and so on for all the other arts and sciences. But it is idle to insist that every race should express itself in the same way, or to assume that the genius of a nation can be tested by its deficiencies in any single field of the higher life. Great critics are rare in every age and country; and even if they were not, what consolation is there for the clash and diversity of races and nations except the special and diverse gifts which each may furnish to the spiritual whole? England has achieved greatness without great music, Germany without great sculpture, ancient Rome without great science or philosophy, Judæa with little but poetry and religion; and it is not necessary to lay too much stress on our own lack of great scholars and great critics—yes, even on our lack of great poets and great painters. They may come to-day or to-morrow, or we may be destined never to have them. The idea that great national energy must inevitably flower in a great literature, and that our wide-flung power must certainly find expression in an immortal poem or in the " great American novel," is merely another example of our mechanical optimism. The vision of great empires that have been both strong and silent, Assyria, Babylonia, Egypt, haunts all history; Virgil or Camoens only fitfully expresses the power that is summed up in Cæsar or Magellan.

But without insisting on impossible aims or illusory standards of greatness, it is fair to ask some flow of spiritual activity, some general spirit of diffused culture,—in a word, the presence of a soul. For though we must eat (and common sense will cook better dinners than philosophy), though we must work (and the captain of industry can organize trade better than the poet), though we must play (and the athlete can win more games than the scholar), the civilization that has no higher outlets for its intellect and imagination will show at least some marks of spiritual starvation. You may see the signs of its restless gnawing on the face of almost any American woman beyond the first flush of youth; you may see some shadow of its hopeless craving on the face of almost any mature American man.

The same signs are to be seen in American scholarship and American criticism. If scholarship were what most people think it, the dull learning of pedants, and criticism merely the carping and bickering of fault-finders, the fact would hardly be worth recording. But since they are instruments which the mind of man uses for some of its keenest questionings, their absence or their weakness must indicate something at least in the national life and character which it is not unimportant to understand.

I

The tradition of scholarship, like so many other things, comes to us from what used to be called the Renaissance, the period (it may not be ironical to be reminded) in which the Americas were discovered and explored; and whatever savour of distinction inheres in the idea of "the gentleman and the scholar" was created then. Scholarship at first meant merely a knowledge of the classics, and though it has since widened its scope, even then the diversity of its problems was apparent, for the classical writers had tilled many fields of human knowledge, and the student of Homer and Virgil was really faced with a different problem from the student of Plato or Thucydides. Scholarship has never been a reality, a field that could be bounded and defined in the sense in which poetry, philosophy, and history can be. It is a point of view, an attitude, a method of approach, and, so far as its meaning and purpose can be captured, it may be said to be the discipline and illumination that come from the intellectual mastery of a definite problem involved in the growth of the human spirit.

Scholarship, conceived in this sense, has no history (though dull and learned hodge-podges have served as such), for it is a spirit diffused over various fields of study; and in America this spirit has scarcely even come into existence. American Universities seem to have been created for the special purpose of ignoring or destroying it. The chief monuments of American scholarship have seldom if ever come from men who have been willing to live their whole lives in an academic atmosphere. The men whom we think of as our foremost literary scholars, Gildersleeve, Norton, and the rest, acquired their fame rather through their personalities than their scholarly achievements. The historians, Motley, Prescott, Bancroft, Parkman, Rhodes, Lea, Fiske, Mahan, were not professors; books like Taylor's " Mediæval Mind," Henry Adams's " Mont Saint Michel and Chartres," Thayer's " Cavour," Villard's " John Brown," and Beveridge's " John Marshall," even Ticknor's " History of Spanish Literature," were not written within University walls, though Ticknor's sixteen years of teaching tamed the work of a brilliant man of the world until there is little left save the characteristic juiceless virtue of an intelligent ordering of laborious research. It would seem as if in the atmosphere of our Universities personality could not find fruitage in scholarly achievement worthy of it, and learning can only thrive when it gives no hostages to the enemy, personality.

Of the typical products of this academic system, the lowest is perhaps the literary dissertation and the highest the historical manual or text-book. It may be because history is not my own special field of study that I seem to find its practitioners more vigorous intellectually than the literary scholars. Certainly our historians seem to have a special aptitude for compiling careful summaries of historical periods, and some of these have an ordered reasonableness and impersonal efficiency not unlike that of the financial accounting system of our large trusts or the budgets of our large universities. To me most of them seem feats of historical engineering rather than of historical scholarship; and if they represent a scholarly " advance " on older and less accurate work, written before Clio became a peon of the professors, it can only be said that history has not yet recovered from the advance. Nor am I as much impressed as the historians themselves by the more recent clash between the " old " school and the " new," for both seem to me equally lacking in a truly philosophic conception of the meaning of history. Yet there is among the younger breed a certain freshness of mind and an openness to new ideas, though less to the problems of human personality or to the emotional and spiritual values of man's life. This deficiency is especially irritating in the field of biography. Not even an American opera (*corruptio optimi*) is as wooden as the biographies of our statesmen and national heroes; and if American lives written by Englishmen have been received with enthusiasm, it was less because of any inherent excellence than because they at least conceived of Hamilton or Lincoln as a man and not as an historical document or a political platitude.

But literary scholarship is in far worse plight in our Universities. No great work of classical learning has ever been achieved by an American scholar. It may be unfair to suggest comparison with men like Gilbert Murray, Croiset, or Wilamowitz; but how can we be persuaded by the professors or even by a dean that all culture will die if we forget Greek and Latin, until they satisfy us by their own work that they themselves are alive? Asia beckons to us with the hand of Fate, but Oriental scholarship is a desert through which a few nomadic professors wander aimlessly. As to the literatures in the modern European tongues, Dante scholarship has perhaps the oldest and most respectable tradition, but on examination dwindles into its proper proportions: an essay by Lowell and translations by Longfellow and Norton pointed the way; a Dante Society has nursed it; and its modern fruits, with one or two honourable exceptions, are a few unilluminating articles and text-books. Ticknor's pioneer work in the Spanish field has had no successors, though Spanish America is at our doors; the generous subsidies of rich men have resulted as usual in buildings but not in scholarship. Of the general level of our French and German studies I prefer to say nothing; and silence is also wisest in the case of English. This field fairly teems with professors; Harvard has twice as many as Oxford and Cambridge combined, and the University of Chicago almost as many as the whole of England. Whether this plethora of professors has justified itself, either by distinguished works of scholarship or by helping young America to love literature and to write good English, I shall not decide, but leave entirely to their own conscience. This at least may be said, that the mole is not allowed to burrow in his hole without disturbance; for in this atmosphere, as a protest and counterfoil, or as a token of submission to the idols of the marketplace, there has arisen a very characteristic academic product, —the professor who writes popular articles, sometimes clever, sometimes precious, sometimes genteel and refined, sometimes merely commonplace, but almost always devoid of real knowledge or stimulating thought. Even the sober pedant is a more humane creature than the professorial smart-Aleck.

Whence arises this inhibition of mediocrity, this fear of personality and intellect, this deep antinomy of pedant and dilettante? The " fear-of-giving-themselves-away disease " which affected the professors of the Colleges of Unreason in " Erewhon " is mildly endemic in every University in the world, and to a certain degree in every profession; but nowhere else does it give the tone to the intellectual life of a whole people. If I were a sociologist, confident that the proper search would unearth an external cause for every spiritual defect, I might point to any one of a dozen or more damning facts as the origin and source of all our trouble,—to the materialism of a national life directed solely toward practical ends, to the levelling and standardizing influences of democracy, to Anglo-Saxon " Colonialism," to the influence of German scholarship, or to the inadequate economic rewards of the academic life. I should probably make much of that favourite theme of critical fantasy, the habits derived from the " age of the pioneers," a period in which life, with its mere physical discomforts and its mere demands on physical energy and endurance, was really so easy and simple that Americans attempt to reproduce it on all their holidays.

But in so far as they have any reality, all these are merely symptoms of the same disease of the soul. The modern sanatorium may be likened to the mediæval monastery without its spiritual faith; the American University to a University without its inner illumination. It is an intellectual refuge without the integration of a central soul,—crassly material because it has no inner standards to redeem it from the idols of the marketplace, or timid and anæmic because it lacks that quixotic fire which inheres in every act of faith. It is at one and the same time our greatest practical achievement and our greatest spiritual failure. To call it a compound of sanatorium and machine-shop may seem grossly unfair to an institution which has more than its share of earnest and high-minded men; but though the phrase may not describe the reality, it does indicate the danger. When we find that in such a place education does not educate, we cry for help to the only gods we know, the restless gods of Administration and Organization; but scholarship cannot be organized or administered into existence, even by Americans.

What can we say (though it seem to evade the question) save that America has no scholarship because as yet it has a body but no soul? The scholar goes through all the proper motions,—collects facts, organizes research, delivers lectures, writes articles and sometimes books,—but under this outer seeming there is no inner reality. Under all the great works of culture there broods the quivering soul of tradition, a burden sometimes disturbing and heavy to bear, but more often helping the soul to soar on wings not of its own making. We think hungrily that the freshness of outlook of a young people should be more than compensation; but the freshness is not there. Bad habits long persisted in, or new vices painfully acquired, may pass for traditions among some spokesmen of " Americanism," but will not breathe the breath of life into a national culture. All is shell, mask, and a deep inner emptiness. We have scholars without scholarship, as there are churches without religion.

Until there comes a change of heart or a new faith or a deep inner searching, scholarship must continue to live this thwarted and frustrated life. Only a profound realization of its high purpose and special function, and the pride that comes from this realization, can give the scholar his true place in an American world. For this special function is none other than to act as the devoted servant of thought and imagination and to champion their claims as the twin pillars that support all the spiritual activities of human life,—art, philosophy, religion, science; and these it must champion against all the materialists under whatever name they disguise their purpose. What matter whether they be scientists who decry " dialectics," or sociologists who sneer at " mere belles-lettres," or practical men who have no use for the " higher life "? Whether they be called bourgeois or radical, conservative or intellectual, —all who would reduce life to a problem of practical activity and physical satisfaction, all who would reduce intellect and imagination to mere instruments of practical usefulness, all who worship dead idols instead of living gods, all who grasp at every flitting will-o'-the-wisp of theory or sensation,—all these alike scholarship must forever recognize as its enemies and its chief tempters.

II

Scholarship, so conceived, is the basis of criticism. When a few years ago I published a volume which bore the subtitle of " Essays on the Unity of Genius and Taste," the pedants and the professors were in the ascendant, and it seemed necessary to emphasize the side of criticism which was then in danger, the side that is closest to the art of the creator. But the professors have been temporarily routed by the dilettanti, the amateurs, and the journalists, who treat a work of the imagination as if they were describing fireworks or a bull-fight (to use a phrase of Zola's about Gautier); and so it is necessary now to insist on the discipline and illumination of scholarship, —in other words, to write an " Essay on the Divergence of Criticism and Creation."

American criticism, like that of England, but to an even greater extent, suffers from a want of philosophic insight and precision. It has neither inherited nor created a tradition of æsthetic thought. For it every critical problem is a separate problem, a problem in a philosophic vacuum, and so open for discussion to any astute mind with a taste for letters. Realism, classicism, romanticism, imagism, impressionism, expressionism, and other terms or movements as they spring up, seem ultimate realities instead of matters of very subordinate concern to any philosophy of art,—mere practical programmes which bear somewhat the same relation to æsthetic truth that the platform of the Republican Party bears to Aristotle's " Politics " or Marx's " Capital." As a result, critics are constantly carrying on a guerilla warfare of their own in favour of some vague literary shibboleth or sociological abstraction, and discovering anew the virtues or vices of individuality, modernity, Puritanism, the romantic spirit or the spirit of the Middle West, the traditions of the pioneer, and so on ad infinitum. This holds true of every school of American criticism, " conservative " or " radical "; for all of them a disconnected body of literary theories takes the place of a real philosophy of art. " Find an idea and then write about it " sums up the American conception of criticism. Now, while the critic must approach a work of literature without preconceived notion of what that individual work should attempt, he cannot criticize it without some understanding of what all literature attempts. The critic without an æsthetic is a mariner without chart, compass, or knowledge of navigation; for the question is not where the ship should go or what cargo it should carry, but whether it is going to arrive at any port at all without sinking.

Criticism is essentially an expression of taste, or that faculty of imaginative sympathy by which the reader or spectator is able to re-live the vision created by the artist. This is the soil without which it cannot flourish; but it attains its end and becomes criticism in the highest sense only when taste is guided by knowledge and thought. Of these three elements, implicit in all real criticism, the professors have made light of taste, and have made thought itself subservient to knowledge, while the dilettanti have considered it possible to dispense with both knowledge and thought. But even dilettante criticism is preferable to the dogmatic and intellectualist criticism of the professors, on the same grounds that Sainte-Beuve is superior to Brunetière, or Hazlitt to Francis Jeffrey; for the dilettante at least meets the mind of the artist on the plane of imagination and taste, while the intellectualist or moralist is precluded by his temperament and his theories from ever understanding the primal thrill and purpose of the creative act.

Back of any philosophy of art there must be a philosophy of life, and all æsthetic formulæ seem empty unless there is richness of content behind them. The critic, like the poet or the philosopher, has the whole world to range in, and the farther he ranges in it, the better his work will be. Yet this does not mean that criticism should focus its attention on morals, history, life, instead of on the forms into which the artist transforms them. Art has something else to give us; and to seek morals, or economic theories, or the national spirit in it is to seek morals, economic theories, the national spirit, but not art. Indeed, the United States is the only civilized country where morals are still in controversy so far as creative literature is concerned; France, Germany, and Italy liberated themselves from this faded obsession long ago; even in England critics of authority hesitate to judge a work of art by moral standards. Yet this is precisely what divides the two chief schools of American criticism, the moralists and the anti-moralists, though even among the latter masquerade some whose only quarrel with the moralists is the nature of the moral standards employed.

Disregarding the Coleridgean tradition, which seems to have come to an end with Mr. Woodberry, and the influence of the " new psychology," which has not yet taken a definite form, the main forces that have influenced the present clashes in the American attitude toward literature seem to be three. There is first of all the conception of literature as a moral influence, a conception which goes back to the Græco-Roman rhetoricians and moralists, and after pervading English thought from Sidney to Matthew Arnold, finds its last stronghold to-day among the American descendants of the Puritans. There is, secondly, the Shavian conception of literature as the most effective vehicle for a new *Weltanschauung,* to be judged by the novelty and freshness of its ideas, a conception particularly attractive to the school of young reformers, radicals, and intellectuals whose interest in the creative imagination is secondary, and whose training in æsthetic thought has been negligible; this is merely an obverse of the Puritan moralism, and is tainted by the same fundamental misconception of the meaning of the creative imagination. And there is finally the conception of literature as an external thing, a complex of rhythms, charm, beauty without inner content, or mere theatrical effectiveness, which goes back through the English 'nineties to the French 'seventies, when the idea of the independence of art from moral and intellectual standards was distorted into the merely mechanical theory of " art for art's sake "; the French have a special talent for narrowing æsthetic truths into hard-and-fast formulæ, devoid of their original nucleus of philosophic reality, but all the more effective on this account for universal conquest as practical programmes.

The apparent paradox which none of these critics face is that the *Weltanschauung* of the creative artist, his moral convictions, his views on intellectual, economic, and other subjects, furnish the content of his work and are at the same time the chief obstacles to his artistic achievement. Out of morals or philosophy he has to make, not morals or philosophy, but poetry; for morals and philosophy are only a part, and a small part, of the whole reality which his imagination has to encompass. The man who is overwhelmed with moral theories and convictions would naturally find it easiest to become a moralist, and moralists are prosaic, not poetic. A man who has strong economic convictions would find it easiest to become an economist or economic reformer, and economics too is the prose of life, not the poetry. A man with a strong philosophic bias would find it easiest to become a pure thinker, and the poet's visionary world topples when laid open to the cold scrutiny of logic. A poet is a human being, and therefore likely to have convictions, prejudices, preconceptions, like other men; but the deeper his interest in them is, the easier it is for him to become a moralist, economist, philosopher, or what not, and the harder for him to transcend them and to become a poet. But if the genius of the poet (and by poet I mean any writer of imaginative literature) is strong enough, it will transcend them, pass over them by the power of the imagination, which leaves them behind without knowing it. It has been well said that morals are one reality, a poem is another reality, and the illusion consists in thinking them one and the same. The poet's conscience as a man may be satisfied by the illusion, but woe to him if it is not an illusion, for that is what we tell him when we say, " He is a moralist, not a poet." Such a man has really expressed his moral convictions, instead of leaping over and beyond them into that world of the imagination where moral ideas must be interpreted from the standpoint of poetry, or the artistic needs of the characters portrayed, and not by the logical or reality value of morals.

This " leaping over " is the test of all art; it is inherent in the very nature of the creative imagination. It explains, for example, how Milton the moralist started out to make Satan a demon and how Milton the poet ended by making him a hero. It explains the blindness of the American critic who recently objected to the " loose thinking " of a poem of Carl Sandburg in which steel is conceived of as made of smoke and blood, and who propounded this question to the Walrus and the Carpenter: " How can smoke, the lighter refuse of steel, be one of its constituents, and how can the smoke which drifts away from the chimney and the blood which flows in the steelmaker's veins be correlates in their relation to steel? " Where shall we match this precious gem? Over two centuries ago, Othello's cry after the death of Desdemona,

> " O heavy hour,
> Methinks it should now be a huge eclipse
> Of sun and moon! "

provoked another intellectualist critic to enquire whether " the sun and moon can both together be so hugely eclipsed in any one heavy hour whatsoever; " but Rymer has been called " the worst critic that ever lived " for applying tests like these to the poetry of Shakespeare. Over a century ago a certain Abbé Morellet, unmoved by the music of Chateaubriand's description of the moon,—

> " She pours forth in the wooas this great secret of melancholy which she loves to recount to the old oaks and the ancient shores of the sea,"—

asked his readers: " How can the melancholy of night be called a secret; and if the moon recounts it, how is it still a secret; and how does she manage to recount it to the old oaks and the ancient shores of the sea rather than to the deep valleys, the mountains, and the rivers? "

These are simply exaggerations of the inevitable consequence of carrying over the mood of actual life into the world of the imagination. "Sense, sense, nothing but sense!" cried a great Austrian poet, "as if poetry in contrast with prose were not always a kind of divine nonsense. Every poetic image bears within itself its own certain demonstration that logic is not the arbitress of art." And Alfieri spoke for every poet in the world when he said of himself, "Reasoning and judging are for me only pure and generous forms of feeling." The trained economist, philosopher, or moralist, examining the ideas of a poet, is always likely to say: "These are not clearly thought out or logical ideas; they are just a poet's fancy or inspiration;" and that is the final praise of the poet. If the expert finds a closely reasoned treatise we may be sure that we shall find no poetry. It is a vision of reality, and not reality, imagination and not thought or morals, that the artist gives us; and his spiritual world, with all that it means for the soaring life of man, fades and disappears when we bring to it no other test than the test of reality.

These are some of the elementary reasons why those who demand of the poet a definite code of morals or manners— "American ideals," or "Puritanism," or on the other side, "radical ideas"—seem to me to show their incompetence as critics. How can we expect illumination from those who share the "typical American business man's" inherent inability to live in the world of fantasy which the poets have created, without the business man's ability to face the external facts of life and mould them to his will? These men are schoolmasters, pedants, moralists, policemen, but neither critics nor true lovers of the spiritual food that art provides. To the creative writers of America I should give a wholly different message from theirs. I should say to them: "Express what is in you, all that serene or turbulent vision of multitudinous life which is yours by right of imagination, trusting in your own power to achieve discipline and mastery, and leave the discussion of 'American ideals' to statesmen, historians, and philosophers, with the certainty that if you truly express the vision that is in you, the statesmen, historians, and philosophers of the future· will point to your work as a fine expression of the 'American ideals' you have helped to create."

But it is no part of the critic's duty to lay down laws for

the guidance of the creator, though he may have insight enough
to foresee some of the directions which literature is likely to
take. He may even point out new material for the imagination of poets to feed on,—the beautiful folklore of our native
Indians, the unplumbed depths of the Negro's soul, the poetry
and wisdom of Asia (which it may be our chief destiny to interpret for the nations of Europe), the myth and story of the
hundred races that are to make up the new America, and all
the undiscovered coigns and crannies of our national life. I
shall not say that these services are extraneous and unimportant, like furnishing the fountain-pen with which a great poem
is written; but incursions into the geography of the imagination are incidental to the critic's main duty of interpreting
literature and making its meaning and purpose clear to all who
wish to love and understand it.

The first need of American criticism to-day is education in
æsthetic thinking. It needs above all the cleansing and stimulating power of an intellectual bath. Only the drenching discipline that comes from intellectual mastery of the problems of
æsthetic thought can train us for the duty of interpreting the
American literature of the future. The anarchy of impressionism is a natural reaction against the mechanical theories
and jejune text-books of the professors, but it is a temporary
haven and not a home. The haphazard empiricism of English
criticism and the faded moralism of our own will serve us no
more. We must desert these muddy waters, and seek purer
and deeper streams. In a country where philosophers urge men
to cease thinking, it may be the task of the critic to revivify
and reorganize thought. Only in this way can we gain what
America lacks, the brain-illumined soul.

The second need of American criticism can be summed up
in the word scholarship—that discipline of knowledge which
will give us at one and the same time a wider international outlook and a deeper national insight. One will spring from the
other, for the timid Colonial spirit finds no place in the heart
of the citizen of the world; and respect for native talent, born
of a surer knowledge, will prevent us alike from overrating its
merits and from holding it too cheap. Half-knowledge is either
too timid or too cocksure; and only out of this spiritual

discipline can come a true independence or judgment and taste.

For taste is after all both the point of departure and the goal; and the third and greatest need of American criticism is a deeper sensibility, a more complete submission to the imaginative will of the artist, before attempting to rise above it into the realm of judgment. If there is anything that American life can be said to give least of all, it is training in taste. There is a deadness of artistic feeling, which is sometimes replaced or disguised by a fervour of sociological obsession, but this is no substitute for the faculty of imaginative sympathy which is at the heart of all criticism. When the social historian is born, the critic dies; for taste, or æsthetic enjoyment, is the only gateway to the critic's judgment, and over it is a flaming signpost, " Critic, abandon all hope when this gate is shut."

> " To ravish Beauty with dividing powers
>   Is to let exquisite essences escape."

Only out of the fusion of these three elements of taste, intellect, and knowledge can American criticism gain what in one of its manifestations is called " personality " and in another " style." Only in this way can it win in the battle against the benumbing chaos and the benumbing monotony of American art and life.

We are all cocksure but bewildered children in a world we cannot understand. We are all parvenus—parvenus on a new continent, on the fringes of which some have lived a little longer than others, but the whole of which has been encompassed by none of us for more than two or three generations; parvenus in a new world of steam and electricity, wireless and aeroplane machinery and industry, which none of us has yet been able to subdue to a mould that satisfies our deepest cravings; parvenus in our culture, which still seems like a borrowed garment instead of flesh of our flesh and bone of our bone. What is the good of all the instruments that our hands have moulded if we have neither the will nor the imagination to wield them for the uses of the soul? Not in this fashion shall we justify our old dream of an America that is the hope of the world. Here are hundreds of colleges and universities; why not fill these empty barracks with scholars and thinkers?   Here are a hundred races; why not say to them: " America can give you generous opportunity and the most superb instruments that the undisciplined energy of practical life has ever created, but in the spiritual fields of art, poetry, religion, culture, it has little or nothing to give you; let us all work together, learning and creating these high things side by side "?   Here are more hearts empty and unfulfilled and more restless minds than the world has ever before gathered together; why not lead them out of their corrals, and find a fitting pasture for their brains and souls?

J. E. SPINGARN

GLOSSARY

The English language, extraordinarily rich and expressive in everything that concerns the practical or the imaginative life, suffers from the poverty and lack of precision of English æsthetic thought. It may therefore be useful to indicate briefly the special sense in which certain terms are used in this essay.

" *Spectator:* I should say that you have advanced a subtlety that is little more than a play on words.
" *Friend:* And I maintain that when we are speaking of the operations of the soul, no words can be delicate and subtle enough."—GOETHE.

Art—Any creation of the imagination, whether in the form of imaginative literature or of painting, sculpture, music, etc.

Artist—The creator of a work of art in any of its forms; not used in this essay in the narrower sense of painter or sculptor.

Poetry—All literature in which reality has been transfigured by the imagination, including poetry in its narrower sense, the novel, the drama, etc.; used instead of " imaginative literaure," not merely for the sake of brevity, but as implying a special emphasis on creative power.

Poet—A writer of imaginative literature in any of its forms; not used in this essay in the narrower sense of a writer of verse.

Taste—The faculty of imaginative sympathy by which the reader or spectator is able to re-live the vision of the artist, and therefore the essential pre-requisite to all criticism.

Criticism—Any expression of taste guided by knowledge and

thought. (The critic's training in knowledge is scholarship, and his special field of thought æsthetics.)

Æsthetics—An ordered and reasoned conception of the meaning and purpose of art, intended for the guidance of the critic and not of the artist.

A Literary Theory—An isolated " idea " or theory in regard to imaginative literature, without reference to any ordered and reasoned conception of its meaning and purpose.

Impressionist Criticism—Any expression of taste without adequate guidance of knowledge or thought.

Intellectualist (or dogmatic) criticism—Criticism based on the conception that art is a product of thought rather than of imagination, and that the creative fantasy of the artist can be limited and judged by the critic's pre-conceived theories; or in the more ornate words of Francis Thompson, criticism that is " for ever shearing the wild tresses of poetry between rusty rules."

The Intellectuals—All who lay undue stress on the place of intellect in life, and assume that the turbulent flux of reality can be tied up in neat parcels of intellectual formulæ.

Learning—The accumulation of certain forms of knowledge as a basis for scholarship, but no more the main purpose of scholarship than his preparatory training is the sole object of the athlete or soldier.

Scholarship—The discipline and illumination that come from the intellectual mastery of a definite problem in the spiritual (as opposed to the practical) life of man.

Pedant—Any one who thinks that learning is the whole of scholarship.

J. E. S.

SCHOOL AND COLLEGE LIFE

SHOULD we ever entertain an intelligent explorer from Mars, we should of course importune him, in season and out, for his impressions of America. And if he were candid as well as intelligent, he might ultimately be interviewed somewhat as follows:

" At first I thought the most striking fact about you was your passion for education. While I have been enjoying your so thorough hospitality I have met a minority of Americans who express themselves less complacently than the rest about your material blessings; I have talked with a few dissidents from your political theory; and I have even heard complaints that it is possible to carry moral enthusiasm too far. But I have yet to meet that American who is sceptical about education as such, though on the other hand I have found few of your citizens quite content with the working of every part of your educational establishment. And this very discontent was what clinched my first impression that schooling is the most vital of your passionate interests.

" Yet as I have travelled from one to another of your cities, a second fact about you has struck me so forcibly as to contest the supremacy of the first. You Americans more and more seem to me to be essentially alike. Your cities are only less identical than the trains that ply between them. Nearly any congregation could worship just as comfortably in nearly any other church. The casts of almost any two plays, the staffs of almost any two newspapers, even the faculties of almost any two colleges could exchange ' vehicles ' with about the same results that would attend their exchanging clothes.

" And in nothing are you so alike as in your universal desire to be alike—to be inconspicuous, to put on straw hats on the same day, to change your clothes in Texas in accordance with the seasons in New York, to read the books everybody else is reading, to adopt the opinions a weekly digests for you from the almost uniform opinions of the whole of the daily press, in war and peace to be incontestably and entirely American.

"Now, I should scarcely make bold to be so frank about these observations if some of my new friends had not reassured me with the information that they are not novel, that a distinguished Englishman has put them into what you have considered the most representative and have made the most popular book about your commonwealth, that in fact you rather enjoy having outsiders recognize the success of your efforts in uniformity. There is, of course, no reason why you should not be as similar to each other as you choose, and you must not interpret my surprise to mean that I am shocked by anything except the contradiction I find between this essential similarity and what I have called your passion for education.

"On Mars it has for a long time been our idea that the function of the school is to put our youth in touch with what all sorts of Martians have thought and are thinking, have felt and are feeling. I say 'put in touch' rather than 'teach,' because it is not so much our notion to pack their minds and hearts as to proffer samples of our various cultures and supply keys to the storehouses—not unlike your libraries, museums, and laboratories—that contain our records. We prefer to think of schooling as a kind of thoroughfare between our past and our present, an avenue to the recovery and appreciation of as many as possible of those innumerable differences between Martian and Martian, those conflicting speculations and cogitations, myths and hypotheses regarding our planet and ourselves that have gone into the warp and woof of our mental history. Thus we have hoped not only to preserve and add to the body of Martian knowledge, but also to understand better and utilize more variously our present minds. So it seems to us perfectly natural, and has rather pleased than distressed us, that our students should emerge from their studies with a multitude of differing sympathies, beliefs, tastes, and ambitions. We have thought that such an education enriched the lives of all of us, lives that ignorance could not fail to constrict and subject to hum-drum monotony.

"So when I return to Mars and report that I found Earth's most favourable continent inhabited by its most literate great

people, a people that has carried the use of print and other
means of communication to a point we Martians have never
dared dream about; that this people has at once the most
widely diffused enthusiasm for education and the most comprehensive school equipment on Earth; and finally that this people
is at the same time the most uniform in its life—well, I fear
I shall not be believed."

On subsequent visits the Martian might, as a wise man does
who is confronted by a logical impasse, re-examine the terms
of his paradox.

As regards our uniformity, fresh evidence could only endorse
his first impressions. The vestigial remnants of what regional
cultures we have had are rapidly being effaced by our un-
thinking standardization in every department of life. The
railroad, the telephone and telegraph, the newspaper, the Ford,
the movies, advertising—all have scarcely standardized themselves before they have set about standardizing everything
within their reach. Not even our provinces of the picturesque
are immune, the places and things we like to think of as " different " (word that betrays our standard sameness!) and glam-
orous of our romantic golden age. In the Old South, Birmingham loves to call herself the Pittsburgh of the South; our railroads have all but hounded the packets from the Mississippi;
it is notorious that our apostles to the Indians, whether political, religious, or pedagogic, wage relentless war on the very
customs and traditions we cherish in legend; the beautiful Missions that a kindlier evangelism bequeathed to them are repeated and cheapened in every suburb and village of the land,
under every harsher sky; those once spontaneous fêtes of the
plains, the " Stampede " and the " Round-Up," have been made
so spurious that the natives abandon them for a moth-eaten
Wild West Show made in the East; and in only a year or two
even New Orleans' Mardi Gras will be indistinguishable from
its counterfeits in St. Louis and elsewhere.

As with these adventitious and perhaps not very important
regional differentiations, so with the one fundamental demarca-
tion our people have all along recognized as conditioning the
give-and-take of American life. The line between the East
and the West, advancing from the Alleghanies to the Rockies

and then part of the way back, has never stayed long enough in one zone to be precisely drawn, but it has always been sharply felt. Since Colonial times the East has meant many things—wealth, stability, contacts with Europe, refinement, industry, centralized finance—and the West has meant many things—hardship and adventure, El Dorado, outlawry, self-reliance, agriculture, vast enterprise; but they have never been so close to meaning the same things as to-day. To-morrow they will merge. Even now the geographical line between them may be drawn anywhere in a belt two thousand miles wide, in which it will be fixed according to the nativity of the critic rather than by any pronounced social stigmata. East or West, there is a greater gulf between the intelligent and the unintelligent of the same parish than divides the intelligent of different parishes. East or West, Americans think pretty much the same thoughts, feel about the same emotions, and express themselves in the American tongue—that is, in slang. If the slang, the accent, the manner differ noticeably, as they still do, there are not wanting signs that another generation will obliterate these differences too. Publishing, to be sure, tends to concentrate in the East, though without impoverishing the West, since all notable circulations have to be national to survive. The very fact that the country's publishing can be done from New York, Philadelphia, and Boston demonstrates our national unanimity of opinion and expression.

Before it overleapt the geographical walls, this national unanimity had wiped out every class distinction but one, which it has steadily tended to entrench—the money line. Families may continue to hold their place only on the condition that they keep their money or get more; and a moderate fortune, no matter how quickly come by, has only to make a few correct strokes, avoid a few obvious bunkers, and it will found a family by inadvertence. The process is so simple that clerks practise it during their vacations at the shore.

Besides money, there is one other qualification—personal charm. Its chief function, perhaps, is to disguise the essentially monetary character of American social life. At any rate, Americans are almost as uniformly charming as they are uniformly acquisitive. For the most part it is a negative charm, a careful skirting of certain national taboos: it eschews frank egoism, unfavourable criticism, intellectual subtlety, unique expressions of temperament, humour that is no respecter of persons, anything that might disturb the *status quo* of reciprocal kindliness and complacent optimism. The unpopular American is unpopular not because he is a duffer or a bore, but because he is " conceited," a " knocker," a " highbrow," a " nut," a " grouch," or something of that ilk. We do not choose, as the Martian suggested, to be as similar as possible; we choose *not* to be dissimilar. If our convictions about America and what is American sprang from real knowledge of ourselves and of our capacities, we should relish egoists, disinterested critics, intellectuals, artists, and irreverent humourists, instead of suppressing them when we cannot mould them. That we do not relish them, that we protect ourselves from them, is evidence that we fear them. What reason should we have to fear them save a secret distrust of our asseverated convictions? Our unanimity, then, would seem to the Martian to be an artificial substitute for some natural background we lack but should like to have; and a most dangerous wish-fulfilment it is, for it masks our ignorance of what we are and what we may reasonably become. Far from being self-knowledge, Americanism would seem to him to be a hallucination, an article of faith supported only by our determination to believe it, and to coerce others into believing it. The secret of our uniformity would be a stubborn ignorance.

At which point our critic would have to re-examine his earlier impressions about our " passion for education," and strive to understand the uses to which we actually put our educational establishment, to appraise its function in our life.

Beginning with the kindergarten, it provides us a few hours' relief from our responsibility toward our youngsters. Curiously, the Americans most given to this evasion are the Americans most inveterately sentimental about the " kiddies " and most loath to employ the nursery system, holding it somehow an undemocratic invasion of the child's rights. Then somewhere in the primary grades we begin to feel that we are purchasing relief from the burden of fundamental instruction. Ourselves mentally lazy, abstracted, and genuinely bewildered by the flow of questions from only one mouth, we blithely refer that awakening curiosity to a harassed young woman, probably less well informed than we are, who has to answer, or silence, the questions of from a score to three score mouths. So begins that long throttling of curiosity which later on will baffle the college instructor, who will sometimes write a clever magazine essay about the complacent ignorance of his pupils.

A few years, and our expectation has shifted to the main chance. We begin worrying over grade reports and knotting our brows over problems in arithmetic by way of assisting our offspring to the practical advantages of education. For the child, we now demand of his teachers solid and lasting preparation in the things whose monetary value our office or domestic payroll keeps sharply before us—figures, penmanship, spelling, home economics. For us, the vicarious glory of his " brightness." But we want this brightness to count, to be in the direct avenue to his career; so we reinforce the environment that gently discourages him from the primrose paths of knowledge. Nothing " practical " is too good for the boy at this moment—tool chests, bicycles, wireless, what not. Thank God, we can give him a better start than we had. As for arts and letters, well, we guess what was good enough for his dad is good enough for him. Meanwhile we are rather pleased than not at the athletics and the other activities in which the grammar school apes the high school that apes the college.

The long spiral of repetitive schooling in study and sport has now commenced its climb: year by year reviews and adds its fresh increment to last year's subject-matter in the classroom and on the field. Is it so strange that when the boy meets his college professors he is cock-sure of knowing to a hair the limits of what is normal and important in life, beyond which lie the abnormal interests of the grinds? That mediocre C is a gentleman's mark? Not his to question the system that, in season and out, has borne down on passing instead of on training, and that ends somewhere, soon or late, with a diploma and, amid family plaudits, graduation from family control.

The high schools are expected to fit ninety-five per cent. of their charges for life and five per cent. for college. If our boy and girl are of the ninety and five, we demand very early specialization toward their precious careers, wax enthusiastic over the school's model mercantile and banking establishment, expand to know our children are being dosed with a course in "Civics," generously admire the history note-books in which they have spread much tinted ink over a little stereotyped information, and in what we fool ourselves into believing are the margins to all these matters proudly watch them capture a class numeral or a school letter, grumblingly pay for real estate signs that have gone up in flame to celebrate some epochal victory, and bear with their antics during hazings and initiations. It's a democratic country, and if the poor man's son cannot go to college, why the college must come to him. Nor are we without a certain undemocratic satisfaction in the thought that he has stolen a four years' march into business over the rich man's son, who spends his college hours, we assure ourselves, acquiring habits that will leave him weak in the hour of competition.

Meanwhile the straddling masters are cramming the other five with all the dates and rules and verbs and prose passages which long and bitter experience has demonstrated to be likeliest on entrance examinations. From the classrooms, as term follows term with its endless iteration of short advances and long reviews, there rises the bruit of rivalry: masters decorously put forward the claims of their own colleges; pupils rejoice when their future alma mater notches another athletic victory to the well-remembered tally; the weak of heart are urging upon their bewildered parents the superior merits of the "back-door" route to some exacting university—by certificate to a small college and transfer at the end of the first year.

There are high schools in whose cases all this is understatement; and of course there are innumerable others, especially in these days when the most rigorous colleges have lost a little of their faith in entrance examinations, where it is absurd overstatement. Nevertheless your son, if he goes to a representative Eastern college from a representative high school, goes as a man steals second in the seventh. And his subsequent instructors marvel at the airy nonchalance with which he ignores "the finer things of life"!

The private secondary schools, save those that are frankly

designed to relieve parents of recalcitrant boys when the public schools will have no more of them, are pretty much without the ninety-five per cent. of non-college men. Frequently they have their charges for longer periods. So they are free to specialize in cramming with more singleness of mind and at the same time to soften the process as their endowments and atmospheres permit. But at bottom the demand you make of the " prep school " is the same demand your bookkeeper puts on his son's high school: you want your boy launched into college with the minimum of trouble for yourself and the maximum of practical advantage for him; your bookkeeper wants his boy launched into business with a minimum of frippery and a maximum of marketable skill. One boy is experted into college, the other is experted into business. You are both among those passionate believers in education who impressed the Martian on his first visit.

Some educator has announced that the college course should not only provide preparation for life but should itself be a satisfactory portion of life. What college student so dull as not to know that? For the most part, he trusts the faculty to provide the preparation—sometimes it would seem that he dares it to—but he takes jolly good care that the four years shall give him life more abundantly. He has looked forward to them with an impatience not even the indignity of entrance examinations could balk; he will live them to the top of his bent; and he will look back on them tenderly, even sentimentally, as the purplest patch of his days. So the American undergraduate is representative of the American temper at its best. He is the flower of our youth at its moment of perfect bloom, its ideals not yet corrupted, its aspirations unwithered. As he thinks and feels, all America would think and feel if it dared and could.

At this point, therefore, the Martian's inquiry into what we expect from our educational establishment would have to shift its point of view from the older to the younger generation. The Martian would be much in demand at our colleges, both as a sure-fire lecturer and as a shining target for degrees certain to attract wide publicity to the donors. Let us imagine him setting aside a page in his notebook for a scheme of undergraduate emphases, grouped and amended as his triumphant progress permitted him to check up on his observations.

Athletics would of course head the list. Regarded as play—that is, as they affect the spectator—college sports proffer a series of thrilling Roman holidays extending from the first week or so of term-time to the final base-ball game and crew race of Commencement week the next June, and for some colleges there may be transatlantic sequels in midsummer or later. It is by no means all play for the spectator, whose loyalty to his institution makes it his duty to watch the teams practise, follow the histories of the gladiators who are at once his representatives and his entertainers, and drill himself in songs and yells at noisy mass meetings; to bet on his college according to his purse and without any niggardly regard for his sober judgment as to the event; then to deck himself in the colours, march to the field, and watch the fray from the cheering section, where his attention will be perpetually interrupted by the orders and the abuse of a file of insatiable marionettes who are there to dictate when he may and when he may not give throat to his enthusiasm; and finally, if Providence please, to be one of the snake-dancing celebrants of victory. If he have the right physique or talent for one of the sports, he will find himself conscripted by public opinion to enter upon the long and arduous regimen that turns out the annual handful of athletic heroes—to slave on freshman squads, class teams, scrub and third and second teams, and finally perhaps, if he has been faithful, to play a dull minute or two of a big game that is already decided and so receive his coveted letter and side-line privilege as a charity. Or at the dizziest pinnacle of success, a " star," to endure the unremitting discipline of summer practice, incessant training, eating with his fellow-stars at the training table, in season and out to be the butt of instruction and exhortation from all the experts of the entourage. As they affect the participant, then, college sports are to be regarded as work that differs from the work of professional sportsmen chiefly by being unremunerated.

The student's next most vivid concern is the organization of the social life in the academic commonwealth of which he is a citizen. Every American college has, or fancies it has, its

own tone, its ideal type of man; and good citizenship prescribes conformity to the spirit of the place and observance of
the letter of its unwritten code. For the type is defined by a
body of obligations and taboos transmitted from generation to
generation, sometimes through the mouthpiece of the faculty,
sometimes by way of the college " Bible " (to use the slang
name for those handy manuals of what to do and what to avoid
which the college Y.M.C.A. issues for the guidance of newcomers), but most often by a rough process of trial and error
which very speedily convinces the freshman that the Fence is
for seniors only, or that it is impracticable to smoke his pipe
in the Yard, or that it is much healthier to take the air in a
class cap than bareheaded. The cherished " traditions " of a
college are for the most part a composite of just such privileges
and prohibitions as these, clustering round the notion of the
type and symbolizing it; and, curiously, the younger the institution, the more insistent it is likely to be about the sanctity
of its traditions—a college feels the need of a type in much
the same degree that a factory needs a trademark.

Conformity thus becomes an article in loyalty. Sometimes
the mere conformity is the desiderate virtue, as used (at least)
to be the case in Yale. Sometimes the type will go in for
individualism, as at Harvard a decade ago, where the thing to
conform to was non-conformity. One tradition is probably
universal: is there anywhere in America a college which does
not boast that it is more " democratic " than others? Democracy undergoes some engaging redefinition in support of these
conflicting claims, but at bottom it refers to an absence of
snobs, arrogant critics, incomprehensible intellectuals, bouncing
wits, uncomfortable pessimists—in short, the discouragement
of just such individual tastes and energies as the Martian
found discouraged in our social life at large. The money line
remains. Theoretically, the poor may compete in athletics
and in other student enterprises and reap the same social rewards as the rich: practically, they may compete and go socially unrewarded, precisely as in the outside world. It is
natural and seemly that this should be the case, for the poor
cannot afford the avenues of association ·hich are the breath
of society to the rich. There have been football heroes whom

the well-to-do have put in the way of acquiring wealth after they left college, but this is patronage, not democracy. There are also colleges proud to be known as poor men's colleges, and for that very reason devoid of the democracy they boast. Not long ago the president of Valparaiso had to resign, and it developed that among the counts against him were the deadly facts that he had attended the annual alumni dinner in dress clothes and had countenanced " dances, athletics, fraternities, and such." No, all that we really mean by democracy in college is the equal opportunity to invest one's inoffensive charm and perfectly good money in a transient society, to be neighbourly across geographical and family lines, to cultivate the local twist of the universal ideal—to be a " regular fellow." Which is very much what we mean by democracy outside. Whatever the precise type of man a college exalts, its characteristic virtues are those that reflect a uniform people— hearty acceptance of unexamined ideals, loyal conformity to traditional standards and taboos, unassuming modesty in " playing the game," and a wholesome optimism withal.

But as for genuine democracy, the unrestricted interplay of free spirits against a common background, what college can boast that its social organization approaches even the measure of equality enjoyed by its disinterested scholars? There was a modicum of it in the free elective system that obtained in Dr. Eliot's Harvard. There was an indifference to seniority that sorely puzzled the graduates of other colleges. Alas, freshman dormitories descended upon it, treacherously carrying the banners of " democracy "; and a " group system " of courses began to externalize intellectual interests to which the elective system, abused as it was, had offered every opportunity for spontaneity. It may be that the Amherst of Dr. Meiklejohn's experiments, or the Smith that President Neilson envisages, will recapture opportunities now fled from Cambridge. These cases, after all, are exceptional. For the typical American college, private or public, marshals its students in two caste systems so universal and so familiar that it never occurs to us to scrutinize the one and we are liable to criticize the other only when its excesses betray its decadence.

The former, the divisioning and tagging of every recruit with the year of his graduation, looks to be an innocent convenience until you have surveyed its regimental effect. Freshmen are green; so we clap ridiculous caps on them, dub them " Frosh " or " Fish," haze them, confine them to a York Street of their kind or impound them in freshman dormitories, where we bid them save themselves, the which they do in their sophomore year at the expense of the next crop of recruits. It is not so much the occasional brutality of hazing parties and " rushes " that should arrest us here, nor yet such infrequent accidents as the probably insane despair of that Harvard freshman whose phobia for eggs drove him to suicide to escape the inflexible diet of his class commons, as it is the remorseless mob invasion of personality and privacy which either leaves the impressionable boy a victim of his ingrowing sensibility or else converts him into a martinet who in his turn will cripple others. In the case of the Cornell freshman who was ducked for stubbornly refusing to wear the class cap and was saved from more duckings by an acting president who advised him—" in all friendliness," said the newspapers!—to submit or to withdraw from college for a year, it is not necessary to applaud what may have been pig-headedness in the victim, or to flay what may have been wisdom in the executive, in order to admire the single professor who stood ready to resign in order to rebuke his college for her bigotry. What was really significant here, however, and what is everywhere characteristic of this sort of benevolent assimilation, was the tone of the university daily's editorial apologia:

" Complete liberty of action has never been recognized by any but avowed anarchists; granted the validity of the law, there can be no charge of intolerance in the enforcement of it."

The legal " validity " of an arbitrary tradition! No " intolerance " in its enforcement by Judge Lynch! The editor of the *Cornell Sun* went on to say that the existence of the " law " in question is " no secret from the prospective Cornellian," implying, no doubt, that to offer oneself for matriculation at Cornell is *ipso facto* to accept the whole body of Ithacan tradition and taboos, along with their interpretation and enforcement according to the momentary caprice of the majority, as a *contrat social*. Small wonder he called the refractory freshman a " red." The young editor's reasoning should recommend his early appointment to a place in the greater *Sun*.

The caste system of academic seniority, like all caste systems, is worst at its base. Such customs as the sequestering of the upper classes in their private quads or ovals, the jealous protection of senior privileges, and the calendrical elaboration of the alumni programme serve to import a picturesque if rather forced variety into our drab monotony. That men should choose to organize themselves to protect some more or less irrelevant distinction is of no special importance to outsiders so long as they do not use their organization to dragoon minorities or to bully individuals. Yet, speak out against the exploitation, and you will be accused of attacking the fellowship. Criticize the shackling of freshmen, and there will not be wanting college editors to call you a fanatic who cannot bear the jolly sight of cap and gown.

The other system of caste, to which we give sharp attention when it goes badly wrong, is of course the club hierarchy. Wherever there are clubs their social capital will necessarily fluctuate with the quality of the members they take in. The reformers who deplore the institution of " rushing " have of course exaggerated its evils, but the evils are there. In young colleges, and wherever clubs are insecure, the candidates are liable to be spoiled for any club purposes before their destination is settled; wherever the candidates must do the courting, either brazenly or subtly, they tend to debauch the club. The dilemma holds, in one form or another, all the way from the opposed " literary " societies of the back-woods college to the most powerful chapters of the national fraternities; and it is particularly acute where the clubhouse is also the student's residence. Any remedy thus far advanced by the reformers is worse than the disease.

In many of the older colleges the equilibrium has been stabilized by a device similar to the gentlemen's agreement in industry. The important clubs have gradually adjusted themselves into a series through which the clubman passes, or into which he penetrates as far as his personality and money will carry him. So the initial competition for untried material is done away with or greatly simplified; one or two large freshman or sophomore clubs take in all the likely candidates; the junior clubs do most of their choosing from among this number; and the senior clubs in turn draw on the junior. Meanwhile the member turnover is perhaps trebled, and initiations and other gay functions multiply.

It is to be remembered, however, that not all the brethren shift onward and upward year by year. Many have to content themselves with clubs already won, and those who pass on are a narrowing band, whose depleted ranks are by no means restored in the eleventh hour recruiting of " elections at large," deathbed gestures of democracy after a career of ballotting to exclude candidates who had not taken all the earlier degrees. Thus increasing distinction is purchased through the tried and true method of decreasing numbers. To be sure, the same end could be served if all would remain in one club and periodically drop groups of the least likely members. Initiations might be reversed, and punches be given to celebrate the lightening of the ship: it would be no more fantastic than a good part of the existing ceremonial. But—it would be undemocratic! And, too, the celebrations might be fatally hilarious. The present pre-initiation discipline is one that tests for regularity and bestows the accolade on the inconspicuous, so that the initiates turn out pretty much of a piece and the entertainment they provide is safely conventional. But reverse the process, assemble in one squad all the hands suspected of being exceptional—all the queer fish and odd sticks—and there's no predicting what capers they might cut as they walked the plank.

The real evil of the club caste is its taste for predictability, its standardization of contacts, its faintly cynical sophistication where life might be a riot of adventures and experiments and self-discoveries—in one word, its respectability. Not that it does not provide much good fellowship and a great deal of fun (including the varieties that have distressed its moral critics). But that everything it provides is so definitely provided *for*, so institutionalized, and so protected from the enrichment different types and conditions of men could bring to it that it is exclusive in a more sinister sense than the one intended by the critics of its alleged snobbery.

Normally the club system is by no means so snobbish as it is thought to be; it dislikes, and is apt to punish with the black ball, the currying of social favour and the parade of special privilege. For youth is youth, and in the last analysis the enemy of caste. It is the glory of college life that the most unexpected friendships will overleap the fences run by class and club regimentation. It is its pity that the fences, which yield so easily to irregular friendships once they have discovered themselves, should nevertheless be stout enough to herd their victims past so many unrecognized opportunities for spontaneous association. The graduate who looks back fondly on his halcyon days is very likely passing over the Senior Picnic and his row of shingles to recall haze-hung October afternoons of tobacco and lazy reminiscence on the window-seat of somebody who got nowhere in class or club, or is wistful for the midnight arguments he had with that grind who lived in his entry freshman year—nights alive with darting speculation and warm with generous combat. Of these clandestine sweets he will say nothing; he is a regular fellow; but he affords one of the proofs that the well-worn social channels are not deep enough to carry off all the wine of free fellowship. And that even the moderate caste of college, securely established as it seems, must defend itself from youth (even from its own youth!) is demonstrated by two phenomena not to be explained satisfactorily on any other hypothesis. What is all the solemn mummery, the preposterous ritual, the pompous processions to and from temples of nightmare architecture, the whole sacrosanct edifice of the secret fraternities, if it be not an embroidery wherewith to disguise from present and future devotees the naked matter-of-factness of the cult? And, on the other hand, what are the too early maturity, the atmosphere of politely blasé languor, the ubiquitous paraphernalia for comfort and casual hospitality that characterize the non-secret and citified clubs of the " indifferent " college but so many disarming confessions of the predictability of everything—the predictability, and the necessity for quiet acceptance? Under all the encouraging variations and exceptions runs the regimental command of our unanimity: if you are to belong, you must conform; you must accept the limits of the conventional world for the bounds of your reality; and then, according to the caprice of your *genius loci,* you will play the game as if everything, even the minutiæ of the ritual your club has inherited from freer spirits, were of tremendous moment, or you will play it no less thoroughly but with the air of one who knows that nothing is of any moment at all. The clubs, that have so often been criticized for their un-American treason to democracy, are only too loyally American.

The third emphasis would be corollary to these two—the political management of athletic and class and club affairs. The politics are those of personal popularity, the management is that of administration rather than legislation, the spirit is the American flair for petty regulation. Where issues are in question the tone is almost certain to be propagandist, conservatives and radicals dividing a field littered with hard names. College life has accumulated an abundance of machinery for the expression of the managing instinct, and most of it works. Nowadays the lines of representation finally knot in a Student Council, which is at once the Cabinet, the Senate, and the Supreme Court of the undergraduate commonwealth. The routine of its work is heavily sumptuary, and such matters as the sizes and colours and seasons for hatband insignia, the length of time students may take off to attend a distant game, the marshalling of parades, are decided with taste and tact. Then, abruptly, it is a tribunal for major cases, just if severe: a class at Yale fails to observe the honour rule, and upon the Council's recommendation twenty-one students are expelled or suspended; it was the Student Council at Valparaiso that secured the president's withdrawal; and at Cornell it was the Student Council that came to the rescue of tradition when a freshman refused to wear the freshman cap. Invariably, one concludes, its edicts and verdicts will support righteousness, as its constituents understand righteousness.

The constituents themselves are ordinarily on the side of light, as they see the light. Not so long ago the faculty of a small New England college decided to dispense with compulsory chapel: the students voted it back. Moral crusades spring up like mushrooms and command the allegiance of all but the recalcitrant " rough-necks," whom student opinion is sometimes tempted to feel are beating their way through an education for which they make no equivalent return in public spirit. A typical campaign of the sort was recently put in motion by the student daily at Brown: the editors discovered that " the modern age of girls and young men is intensely immoral"; they penned sensational editorials that evoked column-long echoes in the metropolitan press; they raised a crusade against such abominations as petting parties, the toddle (" Rome," they wrote, " toddled before it fell "), and " parties continued until after breakfast time "; almost immediately they won a victory—the Mothers' Club of Providence resolved that dances for children must end by eleven o'clock. . . .

And now the undergraduate will emphasize study. But a sharp line must be drawn between study that looks forward merely to the A.B. degree as the end of schooling and the beginning of business, and study that is a part of professional training, that looks forward to some professional degree at Commencement or to matriculation in a graduate school. Both come under the head of preparation for life; but in the former case the degree itself is the preparation, whereas in the latter case it is recognized that one must master and retain at least a working modicum of the subject-matter of the professional courses and of the liberal courses preliminary to them.

The arts man, then, recognizes only the same necessity he has faced all the way up the school ladder—to pass. If he have entrance conditions, they are mortgages that must be paid off, perhaps in the Summer School; he must keep off probation to protect his athletic or political or other activity status; beyond this, he must garner enough courses and half-courses, semester hours or points, to purchase the indispensable sheepskin. Further effort is supererogatory so far as concerns study *per se:* prizes and distinctions fall in the category of " student activities," hobbies, and belong of right to the " sharks "; scholarships, which in America are for the poor only, have to do with still another matter—earning one's way through— and are mostly reserved for the " paid marks men," professional studiers, grinds.

Upon his programme of courses the student will often expend as much mental energy as would carry him through an ordinary examination: he will pore over the catalogue, be zealous to avoid nine o'clocks and afternoon hours liable to conflict with games, make an elaborate survey of the comparative competence of instructors, both as graders and as entertainers and even (quaintly enough) as experts in their fields, and enquire diligently after snap courses. Enrolled in a course, he will speedily estimate the minimum effort that will produce a safe pass, unless the subject happens to be one that commends itself to his interest independently of academic necessity. In that case he will exceed not only the moderate stint calculated to earn a C, but sometimes even the instructor's extravagant requirements. There is, in fact, scarcely a student but has at least one pet course in which he will " eat up " all the required reading and more, take gratuitous notes, ask endless questions, and perhaps make private sallies into research. The fact that he holds most of this labour to be self-indulgence will not temper his indignation if he fails to " pull " an A or B, though it is a question whether, when the grade has sealed the course, he will be much the wiser for it than for the others.

On the evils of the course system there is probably no new thing to be said. Such devices as the " group system " at Harvard interfere with liberty of election without appreciably correcting the graduate's ignorance of the courses he has passed and cashed in for his degree. Recognizing this fact, certain faculties have latterly inaugurated general examinations in the whole subject-matter studied under one department, as notably in History, Government, and Economics; but thus far the general examination affects professional preparation, as notably for the Law School, much more than it affects the straight arts career, where it provides just one more obstacle to " pass."

This business of passing is a seasonal nuisance. The early weeks of term-time are an Arcady of fetching lectures, more or less interesting assigned reading, and abundant " cuts." Across the smiling sky float minatory wisps of cloud—exercises, quizzes, tests. Then up from the horizon blow the " hour exams," first breath of the academic weather that later on will rock the earth with " mid-years " and " finals." But to be forewarned is, for the prudent student, to get armed, and Heaven knows he is amply warned by instructor, registrar, and dean. So he hies himself to the armourer, the tutor, one of the brotherhood of experts who saw him through the entrance examinations; he provides himself with bought or leased notebooks and summaries; he crams through a few febrile nights of cloistral deprivations and flagellations; and the sun shines again on his harvest of gentlemen's C's, the proud though superfluous A or B, and maybe a D that bespeaks better armour against the next onset. Or, of course, he may have slipped into " probation," limbo that outrageously handicaps his athletic or political ambitions. Only if he have been a hapless probationer before the examinations is there any real risk of his having to join the exceedingly small company of living sacrifices whom a suddenly austere college now " rusticates." (For in America suspensions and expulsions are the penalties rather of irregular conduct than of mental incompetence or sloth.) In four years, after he has weathered a score of these storms and concocted a few theses, the president hands him a diploma to frame, he sells his other furniture, puts mothballs in his cap and gown, and plunges into business to overtake his non-college competitors.

Student opinion recognizes that the man enrolled in professional courses or headed for a graduate school faces more stringent necessities. He may devote himself to his more specific training without the imputation of being a " grind," and if he pursues honours it will be in the line of business rather than of indoor sport. He will be charier of cuts, more painstaking as regards his notes and reading, and the professional manner will settle on him early. In every college commons you can find a table where the talk is largely shop—hypothetical cases, laboratory experiments, new inventions, devices for circumventing the income tax. All this, however, is really a quantitative difference, not a qualitative. Of disinterested intellectual activity he is if anything more innocent than his fellow in the arts school.

So much for the four great necessities of average student life —in order of acknowledged importance: athletics, social life, politics, study. Deans and other official but theoretical folk will tell our Martian that the business of college is study and that all the undergraduate's other functions are marginal matters; but their own conduct will already have betrayed them to him, for he will not have missed the fact that most of their labour is devoted to making study as dignified and popular as the students have made sports and clubs and elections. These four majors hold their places at the head of the list of student emphases because no representative undergraduate quite escapes any of them; the next ones may be stressed more variously, according rather to the student's capricious private inclinations than to his simpler group reactions.

Now, for instance, he is free to " go in for " some of the innumerable " student activities," avocations as opposed to the preceding vocations. There are the minor sports which are not so established in popularity that they may conscript players—lacrosse, association football, trap shooting, swimming, and so on. There are the other intercollegiate competitions—chess and debating and what not. The musical clubs, the dramatic clubs, the magazines, and many semi-professional and semi-social organizations offer in their degree more or less opportunity to visit rival institutions. Then, too, there is in the larger colleges a club for almost every religious cult, from Catholic to Theosophist, whose devotees may crave a closer warmth of communion than they realize in the chapel, which is ordinarily non-sectarian; a club apiece for some of the great fraternal orders; a similar club for each of the political parties, to say nothing of a branch of the Intercollegiate Socialist Society, with another organization forming to supply the colleges with associated Liberal Clubs. Moreover, all the important preparatory schools, private and public, are certain to be represented by clubs of their alumni, some of which maintain scholarships but all of which do yeoman service scouting for athletes. Frequently there is a Cosmopolitan Club for foreign students and travelled Americans. And, finally, there are clubs to represent the various provinces of knowledge—the classics, philosophy, mathematics, the various sciences, and so on indefinitely. Then, in colleges in or near cities, there are well-organized opportunities for students who care to make a hobby of the Uplift and go in for social service. While, for amateur and professional sharks and grinds, there is the honour roll of prizes, scholarships, fellowships, distinctions, and other academic honours. Verily a paradise for the joiner. Day by day, the calendar of meetings and events printed in the university paper resembles nothing so much as the bulletin board of a metropolitan hotel which caters to conventions.

If at first glance all this welter of endeavour looks to be anything but evidence of uniformity, at second will appear its significant principle. Every part of it is cemented together by a universal institutionalizing of impulses and values. There is scarcely a college activity which can serve for a hobby but has its shingle and ribbon and certificated niche in the undergraduate régime.

Even the undergraduate's extra-collegiate social life, which would probably stand next on the Martian's list, is thoroughly regimented. Speaking broadly, it is incorrect to call on girls at the nearest girls' college; and, speaking still more broadly, there is usually one correct college whereat it is socially incumbent to pay devoirs. In coeducational institutions the sex line is an exacting but astonishingly innocent consumer of time and energy, of which the greater part is invested in the sheer maintenance of convention. Along both these social avenues the student practises a mimicry of what seems to him to be the forms regnant in secular society and, intent on the forms, tends to miss by a little what neighbourly ease really exists there, so that he out-conventionalizes the conventional world. The non-college American youth, of both sexes, would scarcely tolerate the amount of formalism, chaperonage, and constraint that our college youth voluntarily assumes.

The word " fussing " is the perfect tag for the visiting, the taking to games and dances, the cherishing at house-parties, and the incessant letter-writing that are the approved communications across the sex line. You make a fuss over a girl, and there it ends; or you make a fuss over a girl and get engaged, and there it ends; or—and this is frequent only in the large Western universities where well-nigh all the personable youths of the State's society are in college together—you make a fuss over a girl, you get engaged, and in due time you get married. So far as fussing is concerned, sex is far more decorous among collegians than among their non-collegiate fellows of the same ages and social levels. There is a place, of course, where it is indecorous enough; but that place is next on the Martian's list.

Which now shifts its weakening emphasis to recreation. You will have thought that most of the foregoing attached to recreation and that all play and no work is the undergraduate rule. You will have erred. Above this point almost everything on the list is recognized by the student to be in some sort an obligation, a serious concern, a plough on which he finds his hand gently laid by custom but which he cannot decently relinquish till he has gained the end of the furrow.

"Nobody could be busier than the normal undergraduate. His team, his paper, his club, show, or other activity, sometimes several at once, occupy every spare moment which he can persuade the office to let him take from the more formal part of college instruction."

The quotation is not from a baccalaureate sermon: it is from the Harvard class oration of 1921.

The prime relaxation is talk, infinite talk—within its local range, full of tang, flicking with deft satire the rumps of pompous asses, burlesquing the comic (that is, the abnormal) in campus situations, making of gossip a staccato criticism—and beyond that range, a rather desultory patter about professional sport, shows, shallow books, the froth of fashion, all treated lightly but taken with what a gravity! For the other relaxations there are, according to taste, the theatre of girls and music, the novel, bath-robed sessions at poker and bridge, late afternoon tennis or golf or handball (very nearly the only sports left to play for their own sake), and the bouts with Bacchus and Venus which, though they attract fewer college men than non-college men, are everywhere the moral holidays that insure our over-driven Puritanism against collapse.

A favourite subject for college debates and Freshman themes argues the case for and against going to college. You could listen to scores of such debates, read thousands of such themes, without once meeting a clear brief for education as a satisfaction of human curiosity. Everywhere below the level of disinterested scholarship, education is regarded as access to that body of common and practical information without which one's hands and tongue will be tied in the company of one's natural peers. " Institutions of learning," as the National Security League lately advised the Vice-President of the United States, " are established primarily for the dissemination of knowledge, which is acquaintance with fact and not with theory." Consequently the universal expectation of the educational establishment has little to do with any wakening of appropriate if differing personalities, and has everything to do with a standard patina, varying only in its lustre, its brighter or duller reflection of the established scene.

Nevertheless, the essential Adam does break through and quiz the scene. Though it come lowest in his scale of emphasis, the typical underclassman knows the qualms and hungers of curiosity, experiments a little with forbidden fruit, at some time fraternizes with a man of richer if disreputable experience, perhaps strikes up a wistful friendship with a sympathetic instructor. Then the world of normal duties and rewards and certainties closes round him, and security in it becomes his first concern. Sometime he intends really to read, to think long thoughts again, to go to the bottom of things. Meanwhile he falls into the easy habit of applying such words as " radical " or " highbrow " to those infrequent hardier spirits who continue restless and unappeased. Later in life you will catch him explaining that radicalism is a perfectly natural manifestation of adolescence and the soundest foundation for mature conservatism. Wise churchmen still talk that way about religious doubt, and bide their time, and later refer to the " death of doubt "—which has really been buried alive. The Martian would conclude that the function of terrestrial education is to bury curiosity alive.

But could he now feel that this educational establishment, this going machine of assimilation, is responsible for our uniformity? Will not American school and college life now seem too perfect a reflection of American adult life to be its parent? Everything in that scale of college values, from the vicarious excitements of football to what Santayana has called the " deprivations of disbelief " has its exact ana-

logue in our life at large; and neither any college tradition nor
yet the " genteel tradition " is of so much significance as the
will to tradition that both reveal. The Martian will long since
have suspected himself guilty of a very human error, that of
getting the cart before the horse.

For we have made our schools in our own image. They
are not our prisons, but our homes. Every now and again
we discipline a rash instructor who carries too far his private
taste for developing originality; we pass acts that require
teachers to sink their own differences in our unanimity; and
our fatuous faith in the public school system as the " cradle of
liberty " rests on the political control we exercise over it. Far
from being the dupes of education, we ourselves dupe the educated; and that college men do not rebel is due to the fact
that inside a world our uniformity dominates as easily as it
dominates the school, the regimen works, college men really
do get ahead, and the " queer " really are frustrate.

Then, what is the origin of our " desperate need to agree "?
There is a possible answer in our history, if only we can be
persuaded to give our history a little attention. When we became a nation we were not a folk. We were, in fact, so far
from being alike that there were only our common grievances
and a few propositions on which we could be got together at
all, and the propositions were more like stubborn articles of
faith than like tested observations: " We hold these truths to
be self-evident, that all men are created equal . . . certain
inalienable Rights . . . Life, Liberty, and the Pursuit of Happiness . . . the consent of the governed . . . are, and of
Right ought to be, Free and Independent States." That is not
the tone of men who are partakers in a common tradition and
who share reasonable and familiar convictions. Thus under
the spur of our first national necessity we gave the first evidence of our capacity to substitute an arbitrary and not too
exacting lowest common denominator to which men can subscribe, for the natural and rigorous highest common multiple
that expresses their genuine community of interest. The device succeeded because we succeeded, but it was the propositions that got the credit. The device has continued to succeed ever since for the same reason that tradition succeeds in

the modern college—nobody who has had any reason to challenge the propositions has been able to get at us.

Our proper job was to create a people, to get acquainted with each other and develop a common background. But the almost miraculous success of our lowest common denominator stood in the way of our working out any highest common multiple. Instead of developing a common background, we went on assimilating subscribers to the Declaration, our arbitrary tradition, "Americanism." We have been so increasingly beset by aliens who had to be assimilated that their Americanization has prevented our own.

We now believe our national job was the Conquest of the West, as if scattering people over a continent were any substitute for creating a People. But we have never been seriously challenged. If our good luck should hold, the second or third generation after us will believe our job was the subjugation of a hemisphere, including the assimilation of genuine peoples who have done us less harm even than the Indians did. But, whatever our practice, we shall never admit that our theory has altered. Still lacking any common background, we shall still enclose ourselves against the void in the painted scene of our tradition.

But our luck may not hold. We may be challenged yet.

CLARENCE BRITTEN

THE INTELLECTUAL LIFE

WHEN Professor Einstein roused the ire of the women's clubs by stating that "women dominate the entire life of America," and that "there are cities with a million population, but cities suffering from terrible poverty—the poverty of intellectual things," he was but repeating a criticism of our life now old enough to be almost a *cliché*. Hardly any intelligent foreigner has failed to observe and comment upon the extraordinary feminization of American social life, and oftenest he has coupled this observation with a few biting remarks concerning the intellectual anæmia or torpor that seems to accompany it. Naturally this attitude is resented, and the indiscreet visitor is told that he has been rendered astigmatic by too limited observation. He is further informed that he should travel in our country more extensively, see more people, and live among us longer. The inference is that this chastening process will in due time acquaint him with a beauty and a thrilling intellectual vitality coyly hidden from the superficial impressionist.

Now the thesis of this paper is that the spontaneous judgment of the perceptive foreigner is to a remarkable degree correct. But it is a judgment which has to be modified in certain respects rather sharply. Moreover, even long residence in the United States is not likely to give a visitor as vivid a sense of the historical background that has so largely contributed to the present situation as is aroused in the native American, who in his own family hears the folklore of the two generations preceding him and to whom the pioneer tradition is a reality more imaginatively plausible than, say, the emanations of glory from English fields or the aura of ancient pomp enwrapping an Italian castle. The foreigner is too likely to forget that in a young country, precisely because it is young, traditions have a social sanction unknown in an older country where memory of the past goes so far back as to become shadowy and unreal. It is a paradox of history that from ancient cultures usually come those who " were born too soon," whereas from young and groping civilizations spring the panoplied defenders of conventions. It is usually when a tradition is fresh that it is respected most; it is only when it has been followed for years sufficient to make it meaningless that it can create its repudiators. America is a very young country—and in no respect younger than that of all Western nations it has the oldest form of established government; our naïve respect for the fathers is surest proof that we are still in the cultural awkward age. We have not sufficiently grown up but that we must still cling to our father and mother. In a word, we still *think* in pioneer terms, whatever the material and economic facts of a day that has already outgrown their applicability.

And it is the pioneer point of view, once thoroughly understood, which will most satisfactorily explain the peculiar development of the intellectual life in the United States. For the life of the mind is no fine flower of impoverishment, and if the beginnings of human reflection were the wayward reveries of seamen in the long watches of the night or of a shepherd lying on his back idly watching the summer clouds float past, as surely have the considered intellectual achievements of modern men been due to the commercial and industrial organization which, whether or not conducive to the general happiness, has at least made leisure possible for the few. But in the pioneer community leisure cannot exist, even for the few; the struggle is too merciless, the stake—life itself, possibly— too high. The pioneer must almost of necessity hate the thinker, even when he does not despise thought in itself, because the thinker is a liability to a community that can afford only assets; he is non-productive in himself and a dangerously subversive example to others. Of course, the pioneer will tolerate the minister, exactly as primitive tribes tolerated medicine men—and largely for the same reasons. The minister, if he cannot bring rain or ward off pestilence as the medicine man at least pretended he could, can soften the hardness of the human lot and can show the road to a future kingdom that will amply compensate for the drudgery of the present world. He has, in brief, considerable utilitarian value. The thinker *per se*, however, has none; not only that, he is a reproach and a challenge to the man who must labour by the sweat of his brow—it is as if he said, " For what end, all this turmoil and effort, merely to live? But do you know if life is worth while on such terms? " Questions like these the pioneer must cast far from him, and for the very good reason that if they were tolerated, new communities might never become settled. Scepticism is an expensive luxury possible only to men in cities living off the fruit of others' toil. Certainly America, up to the end of the reconstruction period following the Civil War, had little practical opportunity and less native impulse for the cultivation of this tolerant attitude towards ultimate values, an atmosphere which is a talisman that a true intellectual life is flourishing.

Consider the terrible hardness of the pioneer's physical life. I can think of no better description of it than in one of Sherwood Anderson's stories, " Godliness," in his book, " Winesburg, Ohio."   He is writing of the Bentley brothers just before the Civil War: " They clung to old traditions and worked like driven animals. They lived as practically all of the farming people of the time lived. In the spring and through most of the winter the highways leading into the town of Winesburg were a sea of mud. The four young men of the family worked hard all day in the fields, they ate heavily of coarse, greasy food, and at night slept like tired beasts on beds of straw. Into their lives came little that was not coarse and brutal, and outwardly they were themselves coarse and brutal." Naturally, this intense concentration upon work is not the whole of the picture; there was gaiety and often there was romance in the early days of pioneering, it ran like a coloured thread through all the story of our *Drang nach Westen*. But on the whole the period from our confederation into a Union until the expanding industrial era following the Civil War— roughly the century from 1783 to 1883—was a period in which the cardinal command was, " Be active, be bold, and above all, work."   In that century we subdued and populated a continent. There was no time for the distractions of art or the amenities of literature.

To be sure, a short-range perspective seems to belie this last generalization. The colonial times and the first part of the 19th century witnessed a valid and momentous literary and intellectual efflorescence, and it was then we contributed many names to the biography of greatness. Yet it was a culture centred almost wholly in New England and wholly East of the Alleghanies; it had its vitality because it was not self-conscious, it was frankly derivative from England and Europe, it made no pretensions to being intrinsically American. The great current of our national life went irresistibly along, ploughing, and tilling, and cutting down the trees and brush, making roads and bridges as it filled the valleys and the plains. That was the real America, a mighty river of life, compared with which, for instance, Emerson and the Transcendentalists seemed a mere backwater—not a stagnant or brackish one to be sure, often a pool of quietude in which the stars, like Emerson's sentences, might be reflected. But the real America was still in the heart of the pioneer. And in one sense, it still is to-day.

The "real America," I say, because I mean the America of mind and attitude, the inner truth, not the outer actuality. That outer actuality has made the fact of the pioneer almost grotesque. The frontier is closed; the nation is the most prosperous among the harassed ones of the earth; there is no need for the old perpetual preoccupation with material existence. In spite of trade depressions and wars and their aftermaths, we have conquered that problem. But we have not conquered ourselves. We must still go on in the old terms, as if the purpose of making money in order to make more money were as important as the purpose of raising bread in order to support life. The facts have changed, but we have not changed, only deflected our interests. Where the pioneer cleared a wilderness, the modern financier subdues a forest of competitors. He puts the same amount of energy and essentially the same quality of thought into his task to-day, although the practical consequences can hardly be described as identical.

And what have been those practical consequences? As the industrial revolution expanded, coincidently with the filling up of the country, the surplus began to grow. That surplus was expended not towards the enrichment of our life—if one omit the perfunctory bequests for education—but towards the most obvious of unnecessary luxuries, the grandiose maintenance of our women. The daughters of pioneer mothers found themselves without a real job, often, indeed, the chief instrument for advertising their husbands' incomes. For years the Victorian conception of women as ornaments dominated what we were pleased to call our " better elements "—those years, to put it brutally, which coincided with that early prosperity that made the conception possible. If the leisure of the landed gentry class of colonial times had been other than a direct importation, if there had ever been a genuine *salon* in our cultural history, or if our early moneyed aristocracy had ever felt itself really secure from the constant challenge of immigrant newcomers, this surplus might have gone towards the deepening and widening of what we could have felt to be an indigenous tradition. Or if, indeed, the Cavalier traditions of the South (the only offshoot of the Renaissance in America) had not been drained of all vitality by the Civil War and its economic and intellectual consequences, this surplus might have enhanced the more gracious aspects of those traditions. None of these possibilities existed; and when prosperity smiled on us we were embarrassed. We were parvenus—even to this day the comic series, " Bringing Up Father," has a native tang. We know exactly how Mr. Jiggs feels when Mrs. Jiggs drags him away to a concert and makes him dress for a stiff, formal dinner, when all his heart desires is to smoke his pipe and play poker with Dinty and the boys. Indeed, this series, which appears regularly in all the newspapers controlled by Mr. Hearst, will repay the social historian all the attention he gives it. It symbolises better than most of us appreciate the normal relationship of American men and women to cultural and intellectual values. Its very grotesqueness and vulgarity are revealing.

In no country as in the United States have the tragic consequences of the lack of any common concept of the good life been so strikingly exemplified, and in no country has the break with those common concepts been so sharp. After all, when other colonies have been founded, when other peoples have roved from the homeland and settled in distant parts, they have carried with them more than mere scraps of tradition. Oftenest they have carried the most precious human asset of all, a heritage of common feeling, which enabled them to cling to the substance of the old forms even while they adapted them to the new conditions of life. But with us the repudiation of the old heritages was complete; we deliberately sought a new way of life, for in the circumstances under which we came into national being, breaking with the past was synonymous with casting off oppression. The hopefulness, the eagerness, the enthusiasm of that conscious attempt to adjudge all things afresh found its classic expression in the eloquent if vague Declaration of Independence, not even the abstract phraseology of which could hide the revolutionary fervour beneath. Yet a few short years and that early high mood of adventure had almost evaporated, and men were distracted from the former vision by the prospect of limitless economic expansion, both for the individual and the nation as a whole. The Declaration symbolized only a short interlude in the pioneer spirit which brought us here and then led us forth to conquer the riches nature, with her fine contempt of human values, so generously spread before us. The end of the revolutionary mood came as soon as the signing of the Constitution by the States, that admirable working compromise in government which made no attempt to underscore democracy, as we understand it to-day, but rather to hold it in proper check and balance. Free, then, of any common heritage or tradition which might question his values, free, also, of the troublesome idealism of the older revolutionary mood, the ordinary man could go forth into the wilderness with singleness of purpose. He could be, as he still is to-day, the pioneer *toujours*.

Now when his success in his half-chosen rôle made it unnecessary for him to play it, it was precisely the lack of a common concept of the good life which made it impossible for him to be anything else. It is not that Americans make money because they love to do so, but because there is nothing else to do; oddly enough, it is not even that the possessive instincts are especially strong with us (I think the French, for instance, are naturally more avaricious than we), but that we have no notion of a definite type of life for which a small income is enough, and no notion of any type of life from which work has been consciously eliminated. Never in any national sense having had leisure, as individuals we do not know what to do with it when good fortune gives it to us. Unlike a real game, we must go on playing *our* game even after we have won.

But if the successful pioneer did not know what to do with his own leisure, he had naïve faith in the capacity of his women to know what to do with theirs. With the chivalric sentimentality that often accompanies the prosperity of the primitive, the pioneer determined that his good luck should bestow upon his wife and sisters and mother and aunts a gift, the possession of which slightly embarrassed himself. He gave them leisure exactly as the typical business man of to-day gives them a blank check signed with his name. It disposed of them, kept them out of his world, and salved his conscience—like a check to charity. Unluckily for him, his mother, his wife, his sisters, and his aunts were of his own blood and breeding; they were the daughters of pioneers like himself, and the daughters of mothers who had contributed share and share alike to those foundations which had made his success possible. Although a few developed latent qualities of parasitism, the majority were strangely discontented (strangely, that is, from his point of view) with the job of mere Victorian ornament. What more natural under the circumstances than that the unimportant things of life—art, music, religion, literature, the intellectual life—should be handed over to them to keep them busy and contented, while he confined himself to the real man's job of making money and getting on in the world? Was it not a happy and sensible adaptation of function?

Happy or not, it was exactly what took place. To an extent almost incomprehensible to the peoples of older cultures, the things of the mind and the spirit have been given over, in America, into the almost exclusive custody of women. This has been true certainly of art, certainly of music, certainly of education. The spinster school-marm has settled in the impressionable, adolescent minds of boys the conviction that the cultural interests are largely an affair of the other sex;

the intellectual life can have no connection with native gaiety, with sexual curiosity, with play, with creative dreaming, or with adventure. These more genuine impulses, he is made to feel, are not merely distinguishable from the intellectual life, but actually at war with it. In my own day at Harvard the Westerners in my class looked with considerable suspicion upon those who specialized in literature, the classics, or philosophy—a man's education should be science, economics, engineering. Only " sissies," I was informed, took courses in poetry out in that virile West. And to this day for a boy to be taught to play the piano, for example, is regarded as " queer," whereas for a girl to be so taught is entirely in the nature of things. That is, natural aptitude has nothing to do with it; some interests are proper for women, others for men. Of course there are exceptions enough to make even the boldest hesitate at generalizations, yet assuredly the contempt, as measured in the only terms we thoroughly understand, money, with which male teachers, male professors (secretly), male ministers, and male artists are universally held should convince the most prejudiced that, speaking broadly, this generalization is in substance correct.

In fact, when we try to survey the currents of our entire national life, to assess these vagrant winds of doctrine free from the ingenuousness that our own academic experience or training may give us, the more shall we perceive that the dichotomy between the cultural and intellectual life of men and women in this country has been carried farther than anywhere else in the world. We need only recall the older women's clubs of the comic papers—in truth, the actual women's clubs of to-day as revealed by small-town newspaper reports of their meetings—the now deliquescent Browning Clubs, the Chautauquas, the church festivals, the rural normal schools for teachers, the women's magazines, the countless national organizations for improving, elevating, uplifting this, that, or the other. One shudders slightly and turns to the impeccable style, the slightly tired and sensuous irony of Anatole France (not yet censored, if we read him in French) for relief. Or if we are so fortunate as to be " regular " Americans instead of unhappy intellectuals educated beyond our environment, we go gratefully back to our work at the office. Beside the stilted artificiality of this world of higher ethical values the business world, where men haggle, cheat, and steal with whole-hearted devotion is at least real. And it is this world, the world of making money, in which alone the American man can feel thoroughly at home. If the French romanticists of the 18th century invented the phrase *la femme mécomprise*, a modern Gallic visitor would be tempted to observe that in this 20th century the United States was the land of *l'homme mécompris*.

These, then, are the cruder historical forces that have led directly to the present remarkable situation, a situation, of course, which I attempt to depict only in its larger outlines. For the surface of the contemporary social structure shows us suffrage, the new insights into the world of industry which the war gave so many women for the first time, the widening of professional opportunity, co-education, and, in the life which perhaps those of us who have contributed to this volume know best, a genuine intellectual camaraderie. Nevertheless, I believe the underlying thesis cannot be successfully challenged. Where men and women in America to-day share their intellectual life on terms of equality and perfect understanding, closer examination reveals that the phenomenon is not a sharing but a capitulation. The men have been feminized.

Thus far through this essay I have by implication rather than direct statement contrasted genuine interest in intellectual things with the kind of intellectual life led by women. Let me say now that no intention is less mine than to contribute to the old controversy concerning the respective intellectual capacities of the two sexes. If I use the adjective " masculine " to denote a more valid type of intellectual impulse than is expressed by the adjective " feminine," it is not to belittle the quality of the second impulse; it is a matter of definition. Further, the relative degree of " masculine " and " feminine " traits possessed by an individual are almost as much the result of acquired training as of native inheritance. The young, independent college girl of to-day is in fact more likely to possess " masculine " intellectual habits than is the average

Y.M.C.A. director. I use the adjectives to express broad, general characteristics as they are commonly understood.

For a direct examination of the intellectual life of women —which, I repeat, is practically the intellectual life of the nation—in the United States shows the necessity of terms being defined more sharply. Interest in intellectual things is first, last, and all the time *disinterested;* it is the love of truth, if not exclusively for its own sake, at least without fear of consequences, in fact with precious little thought about consequences. This does not mean that such exercise of the native disposition to think, such slaking of the natural metaphysical curiosity in all of us, is not a process enwrapped—as truly as the disposition to make love or to get angry—with an emotional aura of its own, a passion as distinctive as any other. It merely means that the occasions which stimulate this innate intellectual disposition are of a different sort than those which stimulate our other dispositions. An imaginative picture of one's enlarged social self will arouse our instincts of ambition or a desire to found a family, whereas curiosity or wonder about the mystery of life, the meaning of death, the ultimate nature of God (objects of desire as truly as other objects) will arouse our intellectual disposition. These occasions, objects, hypotheses are of necessity without moral significance. The values inherent in them are the values of satisfied contemplation and not of practical result. Their immediate utility—although their ultimate, by the paradox that is constantly making mere common sense inadequate, may be very great—is only subjective. In this sense, they seem wayward and masculine; and, cardinal sin of all, useless.

Perhaps the meaning of the " feminine " approach to the intellectual life may be made somewhat clearer by this preliminary definition. The basic assumption of such an approach is that ideas are measured for their value by terms outside the ideas themselves, or, as Mrs. Mary Austin recently said in a magazine article, by " her [woman's] deep sense of social applicability as the test of value." Fundamentally, in a word, the intellectual life is an instrument of moral reform; the real test of ideas lies in their utilitarian success.

Hence it is hardly surprising that the intellectual life, as I have defined it, of women in America turns out on examination not to be an intellectual life at all, but sociological activity. The best of modern women thinkers in the United States—and there are many—are oftenest technical experts, keen to apply knowledge and skill to the formulation of a technique for the better solution of problems *the answers to which are already assumed.* The question of fundamental ends is seldom if ever raised: for example, the desirability of the modern family, the desirability of children glowing with health, the desirability of monogamy are not challenged. They are assumed as ends desirable in themselves, and what women usually understand by the intellectual life is the application of modern scientific methods to a sort of enlarged and subtler course in domestic science.

This attitude of contempt for mere intellectual values has of course been strengthened by the native pioneer suspicion of all thought that does not issue immediately in successful action. The remarkable growth of pragmatism, and its sturdy offspring instrumentalism, where ideas become but the lowly handmaidens of " getting on," has been possible to the extent to which we see it to-day precisely because the intellectual atmosphere has been surcharged with this feminized utilitarianism. We are deeply uncomfortable before introspection, contemplation, or scrupulous adherence to logical sequence. Women do not hesitate to call these activities cold, impersonal, indirect—I believe they have a phrase for them, " the poobah tradition of learning." With us the concept of the intellect as a soulless machine operating in a rather clammy void has acquired the force of folklore because we have so much wished to strip it of warmth and colour. We have wanted to discredit it in itself; we have respected it only for what it could do. If its operations lead to better sanitation, better milk for babies, and larger bridges over which, in Matthew Arnold's phrase, we might cross more rapidly from one dismal, illiberal city to another dismal, illiberal city, then those operations have been justified. That the life of the mind might have an emotional drive, a sting or vibrancy of its own, constituting as valuable a contribution to human happiness as, say, the satisfied marital felicity of the bacteria-less suburbanite in his concrete villa has been incomprehensible. Every science must be an *applied* science, the intellect must be *applied* intellect before we thoroughly understand it. We have created an environment in which the intellectual impulses must become fundamentally social in quality and mood, whereas the truth of the matter is that these impulses, like the religious impulse, in their pristine spontaneity are basically individualistic and capricious rather than disciplined.

But such individualism in thought, unless mellowed by contact with institutions that assume and cherish it and thus can, without patronizing, correct its wildnesses, inevitably turns into eccentricity. And such, unfortunately, has too often been the history of American intellectuals. The institutional structure that might sustain them and keep them on the main track of the humanistic tradition has been too fragile and too slight. The university and college life, the educational institutions, even the discipline of scholarship, as other essays in this volume show us, have been of very little assistance. Even the church has provoked recalcitrance rather than any real reorientation of religious viewpoint, and our atheists—recall Ingersoll—have ordinarily been quite conventional in their intellectual outlook. With educated Englishmen, for example, whatever their religious, economic, or political views, there has been a certain common tradition or point of departure and understanding, i.e., the classics. Mr. Balfour can speak the same language as Mr. Bertrand Russell, even when he is a member of a government that puts Mr. Russell in gaol for his political opposition to the late war. But it really is a strain on the imagination to picture Mr. Denby quoting Hume to refute Mr. Weeks, or Vice-President Coolidge engaging in an epistemological controversy with Postmaster-General Hays. There is no intellectual background common to President Harding and Convict Debs or to any one person and possibly as many as a hundred others—there are only common social or geographical backgrounds, in which the absence of a real community of interests is pathetically emphasized by grotesque emphasis upon fraternal solidarity, as when Mr. Harding discovered that he and his chauffeur belonged to the same lodge, regarding this purely fortuitous fact as a symbol of the healing power of the Fathers and of American Democracy!

In such an atmosphere of shadowy spiritual relationships, where the thinness of contact of mind with mind is childishly disguised under the banner of good fellowship, it might be expected that the intellectual life must be led not only with that degree of individualistic isolation which is naturally necessary for its existence, but likewise in a hostile and unintelligent environment of almost enforced " difference " from the general social type. Such an atmosphere will become as infested with cranks, fanatics, mushroom religious enthusiasts, moral prigs with new schemes of perfectability, inventors of perpetual motion, illiterate novelists, and oratorical cretins, as a swamp with mosquitoes. They seem to breed almost overnight; we have no standard to which the wise and the foolish may equally repair, no criterion by which spontaneously to appraise them and thus, by robbing them of the breath of their life, recognition, reduce their numbers. On the contrary, we welcome them all with a kind of Jamesian gusto, as if every fool, like every citizen, must have his right to vote. It is a kind of intellectual enfranchisement that produces the same sort of leadership which, in the political field of complete suffrage, we suffer under from Washington and our various State capitals. Our intellectual life, when we judge it objectively on the side of vigour and diversity, too often seems like a democracy of mountebanks.

Yet when we turn from the more naïve and popular experiments for finding expression for the baulked disposition to think, the more sophisticated *jeunesse dorée* of our cultural life are equally crippled and sterile. They suffer not so much from being thought and being " queer "—in fact, inwardly deeply uncomfortable at not being successful business men, they are scrupulously conventional in manner and appearance —but from what Professor Santayana has called, with his usual felicity, " the genteel tradition." It is a blight that falls on the just and the unjust; like George Bernard Shaw, they are tolerant before the caprices of the mind, and intolerant before the caprices of the body. They acquire their disability from the essentially American (and essentially feminine) timorousness before life itself; they seem to want to confine, as do all good husbands and providers, adventure to mental adventure and tragedy to an error in ratiocination. They will discant generously about liberty of opinion—although, strictly speaking, *opinion* is always free; all that is restricted is the right to put it into words—yet seem singularly silent concerning liberty of action. If this were a mere temperamental defect, it would of course have no importance. But it cuts much deeper. Thought, like mist, arises from the earth, and to it must eventually return, if it is not to be dissipated into the ether. The genteel tradition, which has stolen from the intellectual life its own proper possessions, gaiety and laughter, has left it sour and *déraciné*. It has lost its earthy roots, its sensuous fulness, its bodily *mise-en-scène*. One has the feeling, when one talks to our correct intellectuals, that they are somehow brittle and might be cracked with a pun, a low story, or an animal grotesquerie as an eggshell might be cracked. Yet whatever else thought may be in itself, surely we know that it has a biological history and an animal setting; it can reach its own proper dignity and effectiveness only when it functions in some kind of rational relationship with the more clamorous instincts of the body. The adjustment must be one of harmony and welcome; real thinkers do not make this ascetic divorce between the passions and the intellect, the emotions and the reason, which is the central characteristic of the genteel tradition. Thought is nourished by the soil it feeds on, and in America to-day that soil is choked with the feckless weeds of correctness. Our sanitary perfection, our material organization of goods, our muffling of emotion, our deprecation of curiosity, our fear of idle adventure, our horror of disease and death, our denial of suffering— what kind of soil of life is that?

Surely not an over-gracious or thrilling one; small wonder that our intellectual plants wither in this carefully aseptic sunlight.

Nevertheless, though I was tempted to give the sub-title " A Study in Sterility " to this essay, I do not believe that our soil is wholly sterile. Beneath the surface barrenness stirs a germinal energy that may yet push its way through the weeds and the tin-cans of those who are afraid of life.   If the genteel tradition did not succumb to the broad challenge of Whitman, his invitations have not been wholly rejected by the second generation following him.   The most hopeful thing of intellectual promise in America to-day is the contempt of the younger people for their elders; they are restless, uneasy, disaffected.   It is not a disciplined contempt; it is not yet kindled by any real love of intellectual values—how could it be?   Yet it is a genuine and moving attempt to create a way of life free from the bondage of an authority that has lost all meaning, even to those who wield it.   Some it drives in futile and pathetic expatriotism from the country; others it makes headstrong and reckless; many it forces underground, where, much as in Russia before the revolution of 1905, the *intelligentsia* meet their own kind and share the difficulties of their common struggle against an environment that is out to destroy them.   But whatever its crudeness and headiness, it is a yeast composed always of those who *will not* conform.   The more the pressure of standardization is applied to them the sharper and keener—if often the wilder—becomes their rebellion against it.   Just now these non-conformists constitute a spiritual fellowship which is disorganized and with few points of contact.   It may be ground out of existence, for history is merciless and every humanistic interlude resembles a perilous equipoise of barbaric forces.   Only arrogance and self-complacency give warrant for assuming that we may not be facing a new kind of dark age.   On the other hand, if the more amiable and civilized of the generation now growing up can somehow consolidate their scattered powers, what may they not accomplish?   For we have a vitality and nervous alertness which, properly channelled and directed, might cut through the rocks of stupidity with the precision and spaciousness with which our mechanical inventions have seized on our natural resources and turned them into material goods.   Our cup of life is full to the brim.

I like to think that this cup will not all be poured upon the sandy deltas of industrialism . . . we have so much to spare!   Climb to the top of the Palisades and watch the great city in the deepening dusk as light after light, and rows of lights after rows, topped by towers of radiance at the end of the island, shine through the shadows across the river. Think, then, of the miles of rolling plains, fertile and dotted with cities, stretching behind one to that other ocean which washes a civilization that was old before we were born and yet to-day gratefully accepts our pitiful doles to keep it from starvation, of the millions of human aspirations and hopes and youthful eagernesses contained in the great sprawling, uneasy entity we call our country—must all the hidden beauty and magic and laughter we know is ours be quenched because we lack the courage to make it proud and defiant? Or walk down the Avenue some late October morning when the sun sparkles in a clear and electric air such as can be found nowhere else in the world. The flashing beauty of form, the rising step of confident animalism, the quick smile of fertile minds—must all these things, too, be reduced to a drab uniformity because we lack the courage to proclaim their sheer physical loveliness? Has not the magic of America been hidden under a fog of ugliness by those who never really loved it, who never knew our natural gaiety and high spirits and eagerness for knowledge? They have the upper hand now—but who would dare to prophesy that they can keep it?

Perhaps this is only a day-dream, but surely one can hope that the America of our natural affections rather than the present one of enforced dull standardization may some day snap the shackles of those who to-day keep it a spiritual prison. And as surely will it be the rebellious and disaffected who accomplish the miracle, if it is ever accomplished. Because at bottom their revolt, unlike the aggressions of the standardizers, is founded not on hate of what they cannot understand, but on love of what they wish all to share.

HAROLD E. STEARNS

SCIENCE

THE scientific work of our countrymen has probably evoked less scepticism on the part of foreign judges than their achievements in other departments of cultural activity. There is one obvious reason for this difference. When our letters, our art, our music are criticized with disdainfully faint commendation, it is because they have failed to attain the higher reaches of creative effort. Supreme accomplishment in art certainly presupposes a graduated series of lesser strivings, yet from what might be called the consumer's angle, mediocrity is worthless and incapable of giving inspiration to genius. But in science it is otherwise. Here every bit of sound work—however commonplace—counts as a contribution to the stock of knowledge; and, what is more, on labours of this lesser order the superior mind is frequently dependent for its own syntheses. A combination of intelligence, technical efficiency, and application may not by itself suffice to read the riddles of the universe; but, to change the metaphor, it may well provide the foundation for the epoch-makers' structure. So while it is derogatory to American literature to be considered a mere reflection of English letters, it is no reflection on American scientists that they have gone to Europe to acquire that craftsmanship which is an indispensable prerequisite to fruitful research. And when we find Alexander von Humboldt praising in conversation with Silliman the geographical results of Maury and Frémont, there is no reason to suspect him of perfunctory politeness to a transatlantic visitor; the veteran scholar might well rejoice in the ever widening application of methods he had himself aided in perfecting.

Thus even seventy years ago and more the United States had by honest, painstaking labour made worthwhile additions to human knowledge and these contributions have naturally multiplied a hundredfold with the lapse of years. Yet it would be quite misleading to make it appear as if the total represented merely a vast accumulation of uninspired routine jobs. Some years ago, to be sure, an American writer rather sensationally voiced his discontent with the paucity of celebrated *savants* among our countrymen. But he forgot that in science fame is a very inadequate index of merit. The precise contribution made by one man's individual ability is one of the most tantalizingly difficult things to determine—so much so that scholars are still debating in what measure Galileo's predecessors paved the way for his discoveries in dynamics. For a layman, then, to appraise the relative significance of this or that intellectual worthy on the basis of current gossip is rather absurd. Certainly the lack of a popular reputation is a poor reason for denying greatness to a contemporary or even near-contemporary scientific thinker. Two remarkable instances at once come to mind of Americans who have won the highest distinction abroad yet remain unknown by name to many of their most cultivated compatriots. Who has ever heard of Willard Gibbs? Yet he was the recipient of the Copley medal, British learning's highest honour, and his phase rule is said to mark an epoch in the progress of physical chemistry. Again, prior to the Nobel prize award, who outside academic bowers had ever heard of the crucial experiment by which a Chicago physicist showed, to quote Poincaré, " that the physical procedures are powerless to put in evidence absolute motion "? Michelson's name is linked with all the recent speculations on relativity, and he shares with Einstein the fate of finding himself famous one fine morning through the force of purely external circumstances.

In even the briefest and most random enumeration of towering native sons it is impossible to ignore the name of William James. Here for once the suffrage of town and gown, of domestic and alien judges, is unanimous. Naturally James can never mean quite the same to the European world that he means to us, because in the United States he is far more than a great psychologist, philosopher, or literary man. Owing to our peculiar spiritual history, he occupies in our milieu an altogether unique position. His is the solitary example of an American pre-eminent in a branch of science who at the same time succeeded in deeply affecting the cultural life of a whole generation. Further, he is probably the only one of our genuinely original men to be thoroughly saturated with the essense of old world civilization. On the other side of the Atlantic, of course, neither of these characteristics would confer a patent of distinction. Foreign judgment of James's psychological achievement was consequently not coloured by external considerations, and it is all the more remarkable that the " Principles of Psychology" was so widely and by such competent critics acclaimed as a synthesis of the first order.

Without attempting to exhaust the roster of great names, I must mention Simon Newcomb and his fellow-astronomer, George W. Hill, both Copley medallists. Newcomb, in particular, stood out as the foremost representative of his science in this country, honoured here and abroad alike for his abstruse original researches into the motion of the moon and the planetary system and for his effective popularization. Henry Augustus Rowland, the physicist, was another of our outstanding men—one, incidentally, whose measure was taken in Europe long before his greatness dawned upon his colleagues at home. He is celebrated, among other things, for perfecting an instrument of precision and for a new and more accurate determination of the mechanical equivalent of heat. Among geologists Grove Karl Gilbert, famous for his exploration of Lake Bonneville—the major forerunner of Great Salt Lake—and his investigations of mountain structure, stands forth as one of our pre-eminent savants. Even those who, like the present writer, enjoyed merely casual contact with that grand old man could not fail to gain the impression that now they knew what a great scientist looked like in the flesh and to feel that such a one would be a fit member of any intellectual galaxy anywhere.

If from single individuals we turn to consider currents of scientific thought, the United States again stands the trial with flying colours. It can hardly be denied that in a number of branches our countrymen are marching in the vanguard. " Experimental biology," said a German zoologist some time before the War, " is pre-eminently an American science."

Certainly one need merely glance at German or British manuals to learn how deeply interpretations of basic evolutionary phenomena have been affected by the work of Professor T. H. Morgan and his followers. In psychology it is true that no one wears the mantle of William James, but there is effective advancement along a number of distinct lines. Thorndike's tests marked an era in the annals of animal psychology, supplanting with a saner technique the slovenly work of earlier investigators. Experimental investigation of mental phenomena generally, of individual variability and behaviour in particular, flourishes in a number of academic centres. In anthropology the writings of Lewis H. Morgan have proved a tremendous stimulus to sociological speculation the world over and still retain their hold on many European thinkers. They were not, in my opinion, the product of a great intellect and the scheme of evolution traced by Morgan is doomed to abandonment. Yet his theories have suggested a vast amount of thought and to his lasting credit it must be said that he opened up an entirely new and fruitful field of recondite research through his painstaking accumulation and discussion of primitive kinship terminologies.

More recently the anthropological school headed by Professor Boas has led to a transvaluation of theoretical values in the study of cultural development, supplanting with a sounder historical insight the cruder evolutionary speculation of the past. Above all, its founder has succeeded in perfecting the methodology of every division of the vast subject, and remains probably the only anthropologist in the world who has both directly and indirectly furthered ethnological, linguistic, somatological and archæological investigation. Finally, the active part played by pathologists like Dr. Simon Flexner in the experimental study of disease is too well known to require more than brief mention.

Either in its individual or collective results, American research is thus very far from being a negligible factor in the scientific life of the world. Nevertheless, the medal has a reverse side, and he would be a bold optimist who should sincerely voice complete contentment either with the status of science in the cultural polity of the nation or with the work achieved by the average American investigator. Let us, then, try to face the less flattering facts in the case.

The fundamental difficulty can be briefly summarized by applying the sociologist's concept of maladjustment. American science, notwithstanding its notable achievements, is not an organic product of our soil; it is an epiphenomenon, a hothouse growth. It is still the prerogative of a caste, not a treasure in which the nation glories. We have at best only a nascent class of cultivated laymen who relish scientific books requiring concentrated thought or supplying large bodies of fact. This is shown most clearly by the rarity of articles of this type even in our serious magazines. Our physicians, lawyers, clergymen and journalists—in short, our educated classes—do not encourage the publication of reading-matter which is issued in Europe as a profitable business venture. It is hard to conceive of a book like Mach's " Analyse der Empfindungen " running through eight editions in the United States. Conversely, it is not strange that hardly any of our first-rate men find it an alluring task to seek an understanding with a larger audience. Newcomb and James are of course remarkable exceptions, but they *are* exceptions. Here again the contrast with European conditions is glaring. Not to mention the classic popularizers of the past, England, e.g., can boast even to-day of such men as Pearson, Soddy, Joly, Hinks—all of them competent or even distinguished in their professional work yet at the same time skilful interpreters of their field to a wider public. But for a healthy cultural life a rapport of this sort between creator and appreciator is an indispensable prerequisite, and it is not a whit less important in science than in music or poetry.

The estrangement of science from its social environment has produced anomalies almost inconceivable in the riper civilizations of the Old World. Either the scientist loses contact with his surroundings or in the struggle for survival he adapts himself by a surrender of his individuality, that is, by more or less disingenuously parading as a lowbrow and representing himself as a dispenser of worldly goods. It is quite true that, historically, empirical knowledge linked with practical needs is earlier than rational science; it is also true that applied and pure science can be and have been mutual benefactors. **This** lesson is an important one and in a country with a scholastic tradition like Germany it was one that men like Mach and Ostwald did well to emphasize. But in an age and country where philosophers pique themselves on ignoring philosophical problems and psychologists have become experts in advertising technique, the emphasis ought surely to be in quite the opposite direction, and that, even if one inclines in general to a utilitarian point of view. For nothing is more certain than that a penny-wise Gradgrind policy is a pound-foolish one. A friend teaching in one of our engineering colleges tells me that owing to the "practical" training received there the graduates are indeed able to apply formulæ by rote but flounder helplessly when confronted by a new situation, which drives them to seek counsel with the despised and underpaid "theoretical" professor. The plea for pure science offered by Rowland in 1883 is not yet altogether antiquated in 1921: "To have the applications of a science, the science itself must exist . . . we have taken the science of the Old World, and applied it to all our uses, accepting it like the rain of heaven, without asking whence it came, or even acknowledging the debt of gratitude we owe to the great and unselfish workers who have given it to us. . . . To a civilized nation of the present day, the applications of science are a necessity, and our country has hitherto succeeded in this line, only for the reason that there are certain countries in the world where pure science has been and is cultivated, and where the study of nature is considered a noble pursuit."

The Bœotian disdain for research as a desirable pursuit is naturally reflected in the mediocre encouragement doled out to investigators, who are obliged to do their work by hook or by crook and to raise funds by the undignified cajolery of wealthy patrons and a disingenuous *argumentum ad hominem*. Heaven forbid that money be appropriated to attack a problem which, in the opinion of the best experts, calls for solution; effort must rather be diverted to please an ignorant benefactor bent on establishing a pet theory or fired with the zeal to astound the world by a sensational discovery.

Another aspect of scientific life in the United States that reflects the general cultural conditions is the stress placed on organization and administration as opposed to individual effort. It is quite true that for the prosecution of elaborate investigations careful allotment of individual tasks contributory to the general end is important and sometimes even indispensable. But some of the greatest work in the history of science has been achieved without regard for the principles of business efficiency; and whatever advantage may accrue in the future from administrative devices is negligible in comparison with the creative thought of scientific men. These, and only these, can lend value to the machinery of organization, which independently of them must remain a soulless instrument. The overweighting of efficiency schemes as compared to creative personalities is only a symptom of a general maladjustment. Intimately related with this feature is that cynical flouting of intellectual values that appears in the customary attitude of trustees and university presidents towards those who shed lustre on our academic life. The professional pre-eminence of a scientist may be admitted by the administrative officials but it is regarded as irrelevant since the standard of values accepted by them is only remotely, if at all, connected with originality or learning.

There are, of course, scientists to whom deference is paid even by trustees, nay, by the wives of trustees; but it will be usually found that they are men of independent means or social prestige. It is, in other words, their wealth and position, not their creative work, that raises them above their fellows. One of the most lamentable results of this contempt for higher values is the failure to provide for ample leisure that might be devoted to research. The majority of our scientists, like those abroad, gain a livelihood by teaching, but few foreign observers fail to be shocked by the way the energies of their American colleagues are frittered away on administrative routine and elementary instruction till neither time nor strength remains for the advancement of knowledge. But even this does not tell the whole story, for we must remember that the younger scientists are as a rule miserably underpaid and are obliged to eke out a living by popular writing or lecturing, so that research becomes a sheer impossibility. If Ostwald and Cattell are right in associating the highest productivity with the earlier years of maturity, the tragic effects of such conditions as I have just described are manifest.

In justice, however, mention must be made of a number of institutions permitting scientific work without imposing any obligation to teach or onerous administrative duties. The U. S. Geological Survey, the Carnegie Institution, the Rockefeller Institute may serve as examples. We must likewise remember that different individuals react quite differently to the necessity for teaching. Some of the most noted investigators—Rowland, for instance—find a moderate amount of lecturing positively stimulating. In a utopian republic of learning such individual variations would be carefully considered in the allotment of tasks. The association of the Lick Observatory with the University of California seems to approximate to ideal conditions, inasmuch as its highly trained astronomers are relieved of all academic duties but enjoy the privilege of lecturing to the students when the spirit moves them.

To return to the main question, the maladjustment between the specific scientific phase of our civilization and the general cultural life produces certain effects even more serious than those due to penury, administrative tyranny, and popular indifference, for they are less potent and do not so readily evoke defence-mechanisms on the victims' part. There is, first of all, a curtailment of potential scientific achievement through the general deficiencies of the cultural environment.

Much has been said by both propagandists and detractors of German scholarship about the effects of intensive specialization. But an important feature commonly ignored in this connection is that in the country of its origin specialization is a concomitant and successor of a liberal education. Whatever strictures may be levelled at the traditional form of this preparatory training—and I have seen it criticized as severely by German writers as by any—the fact remains that the German university student has a broad cultural background such as his American counterpart too frequently lacks; and what is true of Germany holds with minor qualifications for other European countries.

A trivial example will serve to illustrate the possible advantages of a cultural foundation for very specialized research.

Music is notoriously one of the salient features of German culture, not merely because Germany has produced great composers but because of the wide appreciation and quite general study of music. Artistically the knowledge of the piano or violin acquired by the average child in the typical German home may count for naught, yet in at least two branches of inquiry it may assume importance. The psychological aspect of acoustics is likely to attract and to be fruitfully cultivated by those conversant with musical technique, and they alone will be capable of grappling with the comparative problems presented by the study of primitive music—problems that would never occur to the average Anglo-Saxon field ethnologist, yet to which the German would apply his knowledge as spontaneously as he applies the multiplication table to a practical matter of everyday purchase.

As a matter of fact, all the phenomena of the universe are interrelated and, accordingly, the most important advances may be expected from a revelation of the less patent connections. For this purpose a diversity of interests with corresponding variety of information may be not only a favourable condition but a prerequisite. Helmholtz may have made an indifferent physician; but because he combined a medical practitioner's knowledge with that of a physicist he was enabled to devise the ophthalmoscope. So it may be that not one out of ten thousand men who might apply themselves to higher mathematics would ever be able to advance mathematical theory, but it is certainly true that the manipulatory skill acquired would stand them in good stead not only in the exact sciences but in biology, psychology, and anthropometry, in all of which the theory of probability can be effectively applied to the phenomenon of variability.

I do not mean to assert that the average European student is an Admirable Crichton utilizing with multidexterity the most diverse methods of research and groups of fact. But I am convinced that many European workers produce more valuable work than equally able Americans for the sole reason that the European's social heritage provides him with agencies ready-made for detecting correlations that must inevitably elude a vision narrower because deprived of the same artificial aid. The remedy lies in enriching the cultural atmosphere and in insisting on a broad educational training over and above that devoted to the specialist's craftsmanship.

Important, however, as variety of information and interests doubtless are, one factor must take precedence in the scientist's equipment—the spirit in which he approaches his scientific work as a whole. In this respect the point that would probably strike most European or, at all events, Continental scientists is the rarity in America of philosophical inquiries into the foundations of one's scientific position. The contrast with German culture is of course sharp, and in many Teutonic works the national bent for epistemological discussion is undoubtedly carried to a point where it ceases to be palatable to those not to the manner born. Yet this tendency has a salutary effect in stimulating that contempt for mere authority which is indispensable for scientific progress. What our average American student should acquire above all is a stout faith in the virtues of *reasoned nonconformism,* and in this phrase adjective and noun are equally significant. On one hand, we must condemn the blind deference with which too many of our investigators accept the judgments of acknowledged greatness. What can be more ridiculous, e.g., than to make dogmas of the *obiter dicta* of a man like William James, the chief lesson of whose life is a resentment of academic traditionalism? Or, what shall we think of a celebrated biologist who decides the problem of Lamarckianism by a careful weighing not of arguments but of authorities? No one can approve of the grim ferocity, reminiscent of the literary feuds of Alexander Pope, with which German savants sometimes debate problems of theoretic interest. Yet even such billingsgate as Dührring levelled at Helmholtz is preferable to obsequious discipleship. It testifies, at all events, to the glorious belief that in the republic of learning fame and position count for naught, that the most illustrious scientist shall not be free from the criticism of the meanest *Privatdozent.* But the nonconformism should be rational. It is infantile to cling to leading-strings but it is no less childish to thrust out one's tongue at doctrines that happen to disagree with those of one's own clique. Indeed, frequently both forms of puerility are combined: it is easy to sneer with James at Wundt or to assault the selectionists under cover of De Vries's mutationism. A mature thinker will forego the short and easy but misleading road. Following Fechner, he will be cautious in his belief but equally cautious in his disbelief.

It is only such spiritual freedom that makes the insistence on academic freedom a matter worth fighting for. After all, what is the use of a man's teaching what he pleases, if he quite sincerely retails the current folk-lore? In one of the most remarkable chapters of the " Mechanik " Ernst Mach points out that the detriment to natural philosophy due to the political power of the Church is easily exaggerated. Science was retarded primarily not because scientists were driven by outward compulsion to spread such and such views but because they uncritically swallowed the cud of folk-belief. *Voilà l'ennemi!* In the insidious influence of group opinions, whether countenanced by Church, State or a scientific hierarchy, lies the basic peril. The philosophic habit of unremitting criticism of one's basic assumptions is naturally repugnant to a young and naïve culture, and it cannot be expected to spring up spontaneously and flower luxuriantly in science while other departments of life fail to yield it nurture. Every phase of our civilization must be saturated with that spirit of positive scepticism which Goethe and Huxley taught before science can reap a full harvest in her own field. But her votaries, looking back upon the history of science, may well be emboldened to lead in the battle, and if the pioneers in the movement should fail they may well console themselves with Milton's hero: ". . . and that strife was not inglorious, though the event was dire! "

ROBERT H. LOWIE

PHILOSOPHY

PHILOSOPHY is at once a product of civilization and a stimulus to its development. It is the solvent in which the inarticulate and conflicting aspirations of a people become clarified and from which they derive directing force. Since, however, philosophers are likely to clothe their thoughts in highly technical language, there is need of a class of middle-men-interpreters through whom philosophy penetrates the masses. By American tradition, the philosophers have been professors; the interpreters, clergymen. Professors are likely to be deflected by the ideas embodied in the institutions with which they associate themselves. The American college, in its foundations, was designated a protector of orthodoxy and still echoes what Santayana has so aptly called the " genteel tradition," the tradition that the teacher must defend the faith. Some of the most liberal New England colleges even now demand attendance at daily chapel and Sunday church. Less than a quarter of a century ago, one could still find, among major non-sectarian institutions, the clergyman-president, himself a teacher, crowning the curriculum with a senior requirement, Christian Evidences, in support of the Faith.

The nineteenth century organized a vigorous war against this genteel tradition. Not only were the attacks of rationalism on dogma reinforced by the ever-mounting tide of scientific discovery within our institutions of learning, but also the news of these scientific discoveries began to stir the imagination of the public, and to carry the conflict of science and theology beyond the control of the church-college. The greatest leaven was Darwin's " Origin of Species," of which two American editions were announced as early as 1860, one year after its publication in England. The dogma of science came publicly to confront the dogma of theology. Howsoever conservative the college, it had to yield to the new intellectual temper and the capitulation was facilitated by the army of young professors whom cheapened transportation and the rumour of great achievements led to the universities of Germany.

From the point of view of popular interest, the immediate effects of these pilgrimages were not wholly advantageous to philosophy. In losing something of their American provincialism, these pilgrims also lost their hold on American interests. The problems that they brought back were rooted in a foreign soil and tradition. To students they appeared artificial and barren displays of technical skill. Thus an academic philosophy of professordom arose, the more lonely through the loss of the ecclesiastical mediators of the earlier tradition. But here and there American vitality showed through its foreign clothes and gradually an assimilation took place, the more easily, perhaps, since German idealism naturally sustains the genteel tradition and thrives amid the modes of thought that Emerson had developed independently and for which his literary gifts had obtained a following.

Wherever New England has constituted the skeletal muscles of philosophic culture, its temper has remained unchanged. Calvinism was brought to America because it suited this temper, and the history of idealism in America is the history of its preservation by adaptation to a changing environment of ideas. Its marks are a sense of the presence of the Divine in experience and a no less strong sense of inevitable evil. Jonathan Edwards writes, " When we behold the light and brightness of the sun, the golden edges of an evening cloud, or the beauteous bow, we behold the adumbrations of His glory and goodness; and in the blue sky, of his mildness and gentleness. There are also many things wherein we may behold His awful majesty: in the sun in his strength, in comets, in thunder, with the lowering thunder-clouds, in ragged rocks and the brows of mountains." Emerson's version is: " Nature is always consistent, though she feigns to contravene her own laws. . . . She arms and equips an animal to find it place and living in the earth, and at the same time she arms and equips another animal to destroy it. Space exists to divide creatures; but by clothing the sides of a bird with a few feathers she gives him a petty omnipresence. . . . Nature is the incarnation of a thought, and turns to a thought again, as ice becomes water and gas. Every moment instructs and every object; for wisdom is infused into every form." And Royce's: "When they told us in childhood that we could not see God just *because* he was everywhere, just because his omnipresence gave us no chance to discern him and to fix our eyes upon him, they told us a deep truth in allegorical fashion. . . . The Self is so little a thing merely guessed at as the unknown source of experience, that already, in the very least of daily experiences, you unconsciously know him as something present."

In its darker aspect this temper gives us Edwards's "Sinners in the Hands of an Angry God," whose choices we may not fathom. But Emerson is not far behind: "Great men, great nations, have not been boasters and buffoons, but perceivers of the terror of life, and have manned themselves to face it. . . . At Lisbon, an earthquake killed men like flies. At Naples, three years ago, ten thousand persons were crushed in a few minutes. Etc. . . . Providence has a wild, rough, incalculable road to its end, and it is of no use to try to whitewash its huge, mixed instrumentalities, or to dress up that terrific benefactor in the clean shirt and white neckcloth of a student of divinity." For Royce, "the worst tragedy of the world is the tragedy of the brute chance to which everything spiritual seems to be subject amongst us—the tragedy of the diabolical irrationality of so many among the foes of whatever is significant."

Emersonian philosophy fails in two respects to satisfy the demands of the puritanical temperament upon contemporary thought. In building altars to the "Beautiful Necessity," it neglects to assimilate the discoveries of science, and it detaches itself from the Christian tradition within which alone this spirit feels at home. Both of these defects are met by the greatest of American idealists, Professor Royce.

In character and thought Royce is the great reconciler of contradictions. Irrational in his affections, and at his best in the society of children, he stands for the absolute authority of reason; filled with indignation at wrong and injustice, he explains the presence of evil as an essential condition for the good; keenly critical and not optimistic as to the concrete characters of men, he presents man as the image of God, a part of the self-representative system through which the Divine nature unfolds itself. Never was there a better illustration of Pascal's dictum that we use our reasons to support what we already believe, not to attain conclusions. And never was there greater self-deception as to the presence of this process.

What man not already convinced of an Absolute could find in error the proof of a deeper self that knows in unity all truth? Who else could accept the dilemma "*either* . . . your real world yonder is through and through a world of ideas, an outer mind that you are more or less comprehending through your experience, *or else,* in so far as it is real and outer, it is unknowable, an inscrutable X, an absolute mystery"? Without the congeniality of belief, where is the thrill in assimilating self-consciousness as infinite to a greater Infinite, as the infinite systems of even numbers, or of odd numbers, or an infinity of other infinite series can be assimilated to the greater infinity of the whole number series as proper parts? Yet Royce has been able to clothe these doctrines with vast erudition and flashes of quaint humour, helped out by a prolix and somewhat desultory memory, and give them life.

By virtue of the obscurantist logic inherent in this as in other transcendental idealisms, there is a genuine attachment to a certain aspect of Christianity. The identification of the Absolute with the Logos of John in his "Spirit of Modern Philosophy" and the frequent lapses into Scriptural language are not mere tricks to inspire abstractions with the breath of life. By such logic "selves" are never wholly distinct. If we make classifications, they are all *secundum quid.* Absolute ontological sundering is as mythical as the Snark. The individual is essentially a member of a community of selves that establishes duties for him under the demands of Loyalty. This is the basis of Royce's ethics. But the fellowship in this community is also a participation in the "beloved community" within which sin, atonement, and the dogma of Pauline Christianity unfold themselves naturally in the guise of social psychology. In such treatment of the "Problem of Christianity" there is at most only a slight shifting of emphasis from the somewhat too self-conscious individualism of his earliest philosophy.

Royce used to tell a story on himself that illustrates a reaction of a part of the public to idealistic philosophy. At the close of a lecture before a certain woman's organization, one of his auditors approached him with the words: " Oh, my dear Professor Royce, I *did* enjoy your lectures *so* much! Of course, I didn't understand one word of it, but it was so evident *you* understood it all, that it made it *very* enjoyable! " The lady, though more frank in her confession, was probably not intellectually inferior to a considerable portion of the idealist's public. James notes the fascination of hearing high things talked about, even if one cannot understand. But time is, alas, productive of comparative understanding, and it may be with Royce, as with Emerson before him, that growth of understanding contributes to narrowing the circle of his readers. The imported mysteries of Eucken and Bergson offer newer thrills, and a fuller sense of keeping up to date.

If Royce's philosophy of religion has not the success that might have been anticipated among those seeking a freer religion, it is probably, as Professor Hocking suggests, because " idealism does not do the work of religious truth." Royce has no interest in churches or sects. Christ is for him little more than a shadow. Prayer and worship find no place in his discussion. The mantle of the genteel tradition must then fall on other shoulders, probably those of Hocking himself. His " Meaning of God in Human Experience " is an effort to unite realism, mysticism, and idealism to establish Christianity as " organically rooted in passion, fact, and institutional life." Where idealism has destroyed the fear of Hell, this new interpretation " restores the sense of infinite hazard, a wrath to come, a heavenly city to be gained or lost in the process of time and by the use of our freedom "!

In this philosophy, we ask, what has religion done for humanity and how has it operated? Its effects appear in " the basis of such certainties as we have, our self-respect, our belief in human worth, our faith in the soul's stability through all catastrophes of physical nature, and in the integrity of history." But if we accept this " mass of actual deed, once and

for all accomplished under the assurance of historic religion "
and through the medium of religious dogma and practice, does
this guarantee the future importance of religion? Much has
been accomplished under the conception that the earth was
flat, but the conception is nevertheless not valid.

It is too soon to estimate the depth of impression that this
philosophy will make on American culture. Professor Hocking warns us against hastening to judge that the world is
becoming irreligious. He believes that the current distaste
for the language of orthodoxy may spring from the opposite
reason, that man is becoming potentially more religious. If
so, this fact may conspire with the American tradition of the
church-college to verify Professor Cohen's assertion that " the
idealistic tradition still is and perhaps will long continue to be
the prevailing basis of philosophic instruction in America."
But there are signs that point to an opposite conclusion and
the means of emancipation are at hand both in a change of
popular spirit and within philosophy itself.

The economic and social conditions that scattered the more
adventurous of the New Englanders through the developing
West, and the tides of immigration of the 19th century, have
weakened the hold of the Calvinistic spirit. These events, and
scientific education, are producing a generation that can look
upon the beauties of nature, be moved to enjoyment, admiration, and wonder by them without, on that account, feeling
themselves in the presence of a supernatural Divine principle.
Success in mastering nature has overcome the feeling of help-
lessness in the presence of misfortune. It breeds optimists of
intelligence. To a cataclysm such as the San Francisco earthquake, it replies with organized relief and reconstruction in
reinforced concrete. If pestilence appears, it seeks the germ,
an antitoxin, and sanitary measures. There are no longer
altars built to the Beautiful Necessity.

Within philosophy, the most radical expression of this attitude appears in the New Realism, and in the instrumentalism of
Dewey. In 1910, six of the younger American philosophers
issued in the *Journal of Philosophy, Psychology and Scientific Method* " The Programme and First Platform of Six
Realists," followed shortly by a co-operative volume of studies

to elaborate the doctrine. Their deepest bond of union is a distaste for the romantic spirit and obscurantist logic of Absolute Idealism. Hence their dominant idea is to cut at the very foundations of this system, the theory of relations in general, and the relation of idea and object in particular. Young America is not fond of the subtleties of history, hence these realists take their stand upon the " unimpeachable truth of the accredited results of science " at a time when, by the irony of history, science herself has begun to doubt.

To thwart idealism, psychology must be rewritten. While consciousness exists there is always the chance that our world of facts may fade into subjective presentations. Seizing a fruitful suggestion of James', they introduce us to a world of objects that exists quite independently of being known. The relations of these objects are external to them and independent of their character. Sometimes, however, there arise relations between our organisms and other objects that can best be described by asserting that these objects have entered into our consciousness. How then can we fall into error? Only as nature makes mistakes, by reacting in a way that brings conflict with unnoted conditions. Perhaps the greatest contribution of Realism as yet to American thought is the contribution of some of its apostles to its implicit psychology, already independently established as behaviourism, the most vital movement in contemporary psychology.

The highly technical form of the Six Realists' co-operative volume has kept their doctrine from any great reading public. But in its critical echoes, the busy American finds a sympathetic note in the assertion of the independent reality of the objects with which he works and the world in which he has to make his way. His also is practical faith in science, and he is glad to escape an inevitable type of religion and moral theory to be swallowed along with philosophy. Until the New Realists, however, develop further implications of their theory, or at least present congenial religious, moral, and social attitudes, their philosophy has only the negative significance of release. If it is going to take a deep hold on life, it must also be creative, not replacing dogma by dogma, but elaborating some new world vision. As yet it has told us little more than that truth, goodness, and beauty are independent realities, eternal subsistencies that await our discovery.

Professor Perry has outlined a realistic morality. For him a right action is any that conduces to goodness and whatever fulfils an interest is good. But a good action is not necessarily moral. Morality requires the fulfilment of the greatest possible number of interests, under the given circumstances; the highest good, if attainable, would be an action fulfilling all possible interests. This doctrine, though intelligible, is hard to apply in specific instances. In it realism dissolves into pragmatism, and its significance can best be seen in connection with that philosophy, where it has received fuller development and concrete applications.

Pragmatism obtained its initial impulse through a mind in temper between the sturdy common sense of the New Realists and the emotionalistic romanticism of the Idealists, or rather comprehending both within itself. This mind is that of William James, the last heir of the line of pure New England culture, made cosmopolitan by travel and intellectual contacts. Of Swedenborgian family, skilled alike in science and art, James lived the mystical thrills of the unknown but could handle them with the shrewdness of a Yankee trader. With young America, his gaze is directed toward the future, and with it, he is impatient of dogma and restraint. He is free from conventions of thought and action with the freedom of those who have lived them all in their ancestry and dare to face realities without fear of social or intellectual *faux pas*. With such new-found freedom goes a vast craving for experience. For him, the deepest realities are the personal experiences of individual men.

James' greatest contribution is his " Psychology." In it he places himself in the stream of human experience, ruthlessly cutting the gordian knots of psychological dogma and conventions. The mind that he reports is the mind each of us sees in himself. It is not so much a science of psychology as the materials for such a science, a science in its descriptive stage, constantly interrupted by shrewd homilies wherein habit appears as the fly-wheel of society, or our many selves enlarge the scope of sympathetic living. Nor is it congenial to this adventurer in experience that his explorations should constrain human nature within a scientist's map. Not only must the stream of consciousness flow between the boundaries of our concepts, but also in the human will there is a point, be it ever so small, where a " we," too real ever to be comprehended by science or philosophy, can dip down into the stream of consciousness and delay some fleeting idea, be it only for the twinkling of an eye, and thereby change the whole course and significance of our overt action. Freedom must not unequivocally surrender to scientific determinism, or chance to necessity.

James is a Parsifal to whom the Grail is never quite revealed. His pragmatism and radical empiricism are but methods of exploration and no adventure is too puny or mean for the quest. We must make our ideas clear and test them by the revelation they produce. Thoughts that make no difference to us in living are not real thoughts, but imaginings. The way is always open and perhaps there is a guiding truth, a working value, in the operations of even the deranged mind. We must entertain the ecstatic visions of saints, the alleged communications of spiritualists, mystical contacts with sources of some higher power, and even the thought-systems of cranks, that nothing be lost or untried. Not that we need share such beliefs, but they are genuine experiences and who can foretell where in experiences some fruitful vision may arise!

As a psychologist, James knew that the significance of a belief lies not so much in its content as in its power to direct the energies it releases. His catholic interests are not equivalent to uncritical credulity. Santayana, the wisest of his critics, is right in his assertion that James never lost his agnosticism: " He did not really believe; he merely believed in the right of believing that you might be right if you believed." As for Pascal, the wager on immortality might be worth the making for if one won there was the blessedness of Heaven, and if one lost—at least there should have been a sustaining optimism through the trials of this life. Communion with the infinite might open new sources of power. If so, the power was there. If not, no harm had been done by the trial. Yet there is no evidence in James' philosophy that he himself drew inspiration from any of such sources.

If James has drawn to himself the greatest reading public of all American philosophers, it is because in him each man can find the sanction for himself. Without dogmatism or pedantry, James is the voice of all individual human experiences. In him, each man can find a sympathetic auditor, and words vivid with the language of the street, encouraging his endeavours or at least pointing out the significance of his experiences for the great business of living. Sometimes James listens to human confessions with a suppressed cry of pain and recalls wistfully " A Certain Blindness in Human Beings," or asks " Is Life Worth Living? " Once with indignation at " the delicate intellectualities and subtleties and scrupulosities " of philosophy he confronts " the host of guileless thoroughfed thinkers " with the radical realities of Morrison I. Swift, only to partially retract a few pages later with the admission, for him grudgingly given, that the Absolute may afford its believers a certain comfort and is " in so far forth " true. We live after all in an open universe, the lid is off and time relentlessly operates for the production of novelties. No empiricist can give a decision until the evidence is all in, and in the nature of the case this can never happen.

Such openness of interest forefends the possibility of James' founding a school of philosophy. It also renders all his younger contemporaries in some measure his disciples. Popularly he is the refuge of the mystics and heterodox, the spiritualists and the cranks who seek the sanction of academic scholarship and certified dignity. There are more things in the philosophies of these who call him master than are dreamed of in his philosophy. In academic philosophy there is a dual descent of the James tradition. As a principle of negative criticism, it may be turned into its opposite, as with Hocking, who enunciates the extreme form of the pragmatic principle, If a theory is not interesting, it is false—and utilizes it for his realistic, mystic, idealistic absolutism. The philosophy of Henri Bergson, that has been widely read in this country, reinforces this mystical spiritual side, but American mysticism has popularly tended to degenerate into the occultisms of second-rate credulous minds.

On the other hand, for those in whom the conflict of science and religion is settling itself on the side of science, the principle of pragmatism lends itself to the interpretation originally intended by Charles Peirce, the author of the term, as an experimentalism, a search for verifiable hypotheses after the manner of the sciences. But this side of the doctrine is the one that has been developed by John Dewey.

Professor Dewey is without question the leading American philosopher, both from the thoroughness of his analyses and the vigour of his appeal to the American public. In discarding the Hegelian Idealism in which he was trained, he is thoroughly aligned with the New America. In him science has wholly won, and although of New England, Vermont, ancestry, there remains not a trace of the New Englander's romantic spiritual longings for contact with a vast unknown. His dogmatic faiths, and no man is without such faiths, relate to evolution, democracy, and the all-decisive authority of experience.

For Dewey, as for the Realists, psychology is the study of human behaviour. For him mind is the instrument by which we overcome obstacles and thinking takes place only when action is checked. Hence in the conventional sense there are no abstractions. Our concepts are instruments by which we take hold of reality. If we need instruments to manufacture instruments, or to facilitate their use, these instruments are also concepts. We may call them abstract, but they are not thereby removed from the realm of experienced fact. Since, therefore, our real interest is not in things as they are in themselves, but in what we can do with them, our judgments are judgments of value, and value is determined by practice. Such judgments imply an incomplete physical situation and look toward its completion. But the will to believe is gone. There is no shadow of James' faith in the practicality of emotional satisfactions, or in his voluntaristic psychology. Our " sensations are not the elements out of which perceptions are composed, constituted, or constructed; they are the finest, most carefully discriminated objects of perception." Early critics, particularly among the realists, have accused Dewey of subjectivism, but except in the sense that an individual must be recognized as one term in the reaction to a situation, and the realists themselves do this, there is no ground for the charge.

Such a philosophy as Dewey's is nothing if it is not put to work. And here is his greatest hold on American life. Like most Americans, he has no sympathy for the lazy, and even the over-reflective may suffer from the contamination of sloth; the true American wants to see results, and here is a philosophy in which results are the supreme end. Reform is, for America, a sort of sport and this philosophy involves nothing but reform. Metaphysical subtleties and visions leave the busy man cold; here they are taboo.

Professor Dewey puts his philosophy to work in the fields of ethics and education. Perhaps his ethics is the least satisfactory, howsoever promising its beginnings. Moral codes become the expression of group-approval. But they easily pass into tradition, get out of touch with fact, are superannuated. The highest virtue is intelligence and with intelligence one can recognize the uniqueness of every moral situation and develop from it its own criteria of judgment. Progress in morals consists in raising the general level of intelligence and extending the group whose approvals are significant from a social class to the nation, a notion of highest appeal to Democracy, with its faith in the individual man. But with Dewey the limit of group expansion is humanity, and this may verge on dangerous (unfortunately) radicalism. Dewey's weapon against conventional ethics is two-edged. For the intelligent man perhaps there is no better actual moral standard than that springing from intelligent specific judgments, but for the uneducated, it is only too easy to identify intelligence with sentimental opinion and to let practice degenerate into legislative repression.

After all, judgments of practice do face incomplete situations and the problem is not only to complete but also to determine the manner in which the completion shall be brought about. What men transform is not merely the world, but themselves, and the ethics is incomplete without some further consideration of such questions as what are human natures, and what do we want them to become. But perhaps such questions are too dangerously near metaphysics to have appealed to Dewey's powers of analysis. At any rate, the general effectiveness of his ethics is weakened by his neglect of attention to principles in some sense at least ultimate.

In education Dewey's philosophy has its most complete vitality, for here he is dealing with concrete needs and the means of satisfying them. The problem of education is to integrate knowledge and life. He finds no joy in information for information's sake. Curiosity may be the gift of the child, but it must be utilized to equip the man to hold his own in a world of industrialism and democracy. Yet Dewey's sympathies are with spontaneity. He is a Rousseau with a new methodology. Connected with the Laboratory School at Chicago from 1896 to 1903, he has since followed with sympathetic interest all radical experimentation from the methods of Madame Montessori to those of the Gary Schools. The vast erudition amassed in this field, and his careful and unprejudiced study of children, has made him competent above all men to speak critically of methods and results.

In regard to education, he has given a fuller consideration of the ends to be attained than in the case of ethics. The end is seen as continued growth, springing from the existing conditions, freeing activity, and flexible in its adaptation to circumstances. The educational result is social efficiency and culture. This efficiency does not, however, imply accepting existing economic conditions as final, and its cultural aspect, good citizenship, includes with the more specific positive virtues, those characteristics that make a man a good companion. Culture is a complete ripening of the personality. " What is termed spiritual culture has usually been futile, with something rotten about it, just because it has been conceived as a thing which a man might have internally—and therefore exclusively." The antithesis between sacrificing oneself for others, or others for oneself, is an unreal figment of the imagination, a tragic product of certain spiritual and religious thinking.

Professor Dewey well understands the dangers that lurk behind such terms as *social efficiency* and *good citizenship*. To him sympathy is much more than a mere feeling: it is, as he says it should be, " a cultivated imagination for what men have in common and a rebellion at whatever unnecessarily divides them." But his very gift of clear vision, his penetration of the shams of dogma, economic and social, leads him to treat these things with scant respect. In consequence his fellow-philosophers, the educators over whom his influence is profound, and the public suspect him of radicalism. Only too often, to avoid suspicion of themselves, they turn his doctrine to the very uses that he condemns: industrial efficiency for them becomes identical with business expedience; the school, a trade school; culture, a detached æstheticism to be condemned; and democracy, the privilege of thinking and acting like everybody else.

The greatest weakness of Dewey's philosophy, and it is serious, for Dewey as no other American philosopher grasps principles through which American civilization might be transformed for the better—lies in its lack of a metaphysics. Not, of course, a transcendentalism or a religious mysticism, but above all an interpretation of human nature. Emotionality represents a phase of the behaviour process too real to deny, yet it has no place in Dewey's philosophy of man. Human longings and aspirations are facts as real as the materials of industry. Most men remain religious. Must they rest with quack mystics or unintelligent dogmatists? What is religion giving them that they crave? Is it a form of art, an attitude toward the ideal, or some interpretation of the forces of nature that they seek to grasp? Professor Dewey is himself a lover of art, but what place has art in his philosophy? If it is an instrument of education, what end does it serve, and how is it to be utilized? The pragmatic ethics gives no guarantee that the moral criteria developed by specific situations will always be the same even for two men equally intelligent. Perhaps, in spite of the paradox, there may be several best solutions. If so, this fact has some significance rooted in man's nature and his relations to the world that philosophy should disclose. Such supplementation need not change the character of the results, but it might forefend them from misinterpretation and abuse.

With all its incompleteness, Dewey's philosophy is undeniably that of the America of to-day. What shall we say of the future? No nation in the world has more abused its philosophies than ours. The inspirational elements of our idealisms have become the panderings of sentimentalists. The vitalizing forces of our pragmatisms threaten to congeal into the dogmata of cash-success. The war has intensified our national self-satisfaction. We tend to condemn all vision as radical, hence unsound, hence evil, hence to be put down. Philosophy thrives in the atmosphere of the Bacchæ:

> " What else is Wisdom? What of man's endeavour
> Or God's high grace, so lovely and so great?
> To stand from fear set free, to breathe and wait;
> To hold a hand uplifted over Hate;
> And shall not loveliness be loved for ever? "

But what have we now of this atmosphere?

At Christmas-time, the American Philosophical Association devoted three sessions to the discussion of the Rôle of the Philosopher in Modern Life. From report, opinion was divided between those who would have him a social reformer, to the exclusion of contemplative background, and those with a greater sense of playing safe, who would have him turn to history, of any sort, or contemplation quite detached from social consequences. Let us hope these opinions are not to be taken seriously. Our social reformers are not all like Dewey, whose neglect of basic reflection is probably not as great as the omission of such reflections from his published works would indicate. Nor is an academic chair generally suited to the specific contacts with life from which successful reforms must be shaped. On the other hand, abstract contemplation with the pedagogic reinforcements advocated, will confirm the popular American sentiment against reflection, if it is true, as Dewey asserts, that education must be an outgrowth of existing conditions. Fortunately genius, if such there be amongst us, will not submit to the opinions of the American Philosophic Association. If philosophy can find freedom, perhaps America can yet find philosophy.

HAROLD CHAPMAN BROWN

THE LITERARY LIFE

AMONG all the figures which, in Mrs. Wharton's " The Age of Innocence," make up the pallid little social foreground, the still more pallid middle distance, of the New York of forty years ago, there is none more pallid than the figure of Ned Winsett, the " man of letters untimely born in a world that had no need of letters." Winsett, we are told, " had published one volume of brief and exquisite literary appreciations," of which one hundred and twenty copies had been sold, and had then abandoned his calling and taken an obscure post on a women's weekly. " On the subject of *Hearth-fires* (as the paper was called) he was inexhaustibly entertaining," says Mrs. Wharton; " but beneath his fun lurked the sterile bitterness of the still young man who has tried and given up." Sterile bitterness, a bright futility, a beginning without a future: that is the story of Ned Winsett.

One feels, as one turns Mrs. Wharton's pages, how symbolic this is of the literary life in America. I shall say nothing of the other arts, though the vital conditions of all the arts have surely much in common; I shall say nothing of America before the Civil War, for the America that New England dominated was a different nation from ours. But what immediately strikes one, as one surveys the history of our literature during the last half century, is the singular impotence of its creative spirit. That we have and have always had an abundance of talent is, I think, no less evident: what I mean is that so little of this talent succeeds in effectuating itself. Of how many of our modern writers can it be said that their work reveals a continuous growth, or indeed any growth, that they hold their ground tenaciously and preserve their sap from one decade to another? Where, to speak relatively, the characteristic evolution of the European writer is one of an ever-increasing differentiation, a progress toward the creation, the possession of a world absolutely his own (the world of Shaw, the world of

Hardy, the world of Hamsun, of Gorky, of Anatole France),
the American writer, having struck out with his new note,
becomes—how often!—progressively less and less himself.
The blighted career, the arrested career, the diverted career
are, with us, the rule. The chronic state of our literature is
that of a youthful promise which is never redeemed.

The great writer, the *grand écrivain*, has at the best of times
appeared but once or twice in America: that is another matter. I am speaking, as I say, of the last half century, and I
am speaking of the rank and file. There are those who will
deny this characterization of our literature, pointing to what
they consider the robust and wholesome corpus of our "normal" fiction. But this fiction, in its way, precisely corrobo-
rates my point. What is the quality of the spirit behind it?
How much does it contain of that creative element the character of which consists in dominating life instead of being
dominated by it? Have these novelists of ours any world of
their own as distinguished from the world they observe and
reflect, the world they share with their neighbours? Is it a
personal vision that informs them, or a mob-vision? The
Danish writer, Johannes V. Jensen, has described their work
as "journalism under exceptionally fortunate conditions."
Journalism, on the whole, it assuredly is, and the chief of these
fortunate conditions (fortunate for journalism!) has been the
general failure of the writers in question to establish and develop themselves as individuals; as they have rendered unto
Cæsar what was intended for God, is it any wonder that Cæsar
has waxed so fat? "The unfortunate thing," writes Mr. Mon-
trose J. Moses, "is that the American drama "—but the observation is equally true of this fiction of ours—"has had many
brilliant promises which have finally thinned out and never
materialized." And again: "The American dramatist has
always taken his logic second-hand; he has always allowed his
theatrical sense to be a slave to managerial circumstance." The
two statements are complementary, and they apply, as I say, to
the whole of this "normal" literature of ours. Managerial
circumstance? Let us call it local patriotism, the spirit of the
times, the hunger of the public for this, that, or the other:
to some one of these demands, these promptings from without,

the " normal " American writer always allows himself to become a slave. It is the fact, indeed, of his being a slave to some demand from without that makes him " normal "—and something else than an artist.

The flourishing exterior of the main body of our contemporary literature, in short, represents anything but the integrity of an inner well-being. But even aside from this, one can count on one's two hands the American writers who are able to carry on the development and unfolding of their individualities, year in, year out, as every competent man of affairs carries on his business. What fate overtakes the rest? Shall I begin to run over some of those names, familiar to us all, names that have signified so much promise and are lost in what Gautier calls " the limbo where moan (in the company of babes) still-born vocations, abortive attempts, larvæ of ideas that have won neither wings nor shapes "? Shall I mention the writers—but they are countless!—who have lapsed into silence, or have involved themselves in barren eccentricities, or have been turned into machines? The poets who, at the very outset of their careers, find themselves extinguished like so many candles? The novelists who have been unable to grow up, and remain withered boys of seventeen? The critics who find themselves overtaken in mid-career by a hardening of the spiritual arteries? Our writers all but universally lack the power of growth, the endurance that enables one to continue to produce personal work after the freshness of youth has gone. Weeds and wild flowers! Weeds without beauty or fragrance, and wild flowers that cannot survive the heat of the day.

Such is the aspect of our contemporary literature; beside that of almost any European country, it is indeed one long list of spiritual casualties. For it is not that the talent is wanting, but that somehow this talent fails to fulfil itself.

This being so, how much one would like to assume, with certain of our critics, that the American writer is a sort of Samson bound with the brass fetters of the Philistines and requiring only to have those fetters cast off in order to be able to conquer the world! That, as I understand it, is the position of Mr. Dreiser, who recently remarked of certain of our novel-

ists: "They succeeded in writing but one book before the
iron hand of convention took hold of them." There is this
to be said for the argument, that if the American writer as a
type shows less resistance than the European writer it is plainly
because he has been insufficiently equipped, stimulated, nourished by the society into which he has been born. In this sense
the American environment is answerable for the literature it
has produced. But what is significant is that the American
writer *does* show less resistance; as literature is nothing but the
expression of power, of the creative will, of "free will," in
short, is it not more accurate to say, not that the "iron hand
of convention" takes hold of our writers, but that our writers
yield to the "iron hand of convention"? Samson had lost his
virility before the Philistines bound him; it was because he
had lost his virility that the Philistines were able to bind him.
The American writer who "goes wrong" is in a similar case.
"I have read," says Mr. Dreiser, of Jack London, "several
short stories which proved what he could do. But he did not
feel that he cared for want and public indifference. Hence his
many excellent romances." *He did not feel that he cared for
want and public indifference.* Even Mr. Dreiser, as we observe, determinist that he is, admits a margin of free will,
for he represents Jack London as having made a choice. What
concerns us now, however, is not a theoretical but a practical
question, the fact, namely, that the American writer as a rule
is actuated not by faith but by fear, that he cannot meet the
obstacles of "want and public indifference" as the European
writer meets them, that he is, indeed, and as if by nature, a
journeyman and a hireling.

As we see, then, the creative will in this country is a very
weak and sickly plant. Of the innumerable talents that are
always emerging about us there are few that come to any sort
of fruition: the rest wither early; they are transformed into
those neuroses that flourish on our soil as orchids flourish in
the green jungle. The sense of this failure is written all over
our literature. Do we not know what depths of disappoint-
ment underlay the cynicism of Mark Twain and Henry Adams
and Ambrose Bierce? Have we failed to recognize, in the
surly contempt with which the author of "The Story of a

Country Town " habitually speaks of writers and writing, the unconscious cry of sour grapes of a man whose creative life was arrested in youth? Are we unaware of the bitterness with which, in certain letters of his later years, Jack London regretted the miscarriage of his gift? There is no denying that for half a century the American writer as a type has gone down in defeat.

Now why is this so? Why does the American writer, relatively speaking, show less resistance than the European writer? Plainly, as I have just said, because he has been insufficiently equipped, stimulated, nourished by the society into which he has been born. If our creative spirits are unable to grow and mature, it is a sign that there is something wanting in the soil from which they spring and in the conditions that surround them. Is it not, for that matter, a sign of some more general failure in our life?

" At the present moment," wrote Mr. Chesterton in one of his early essays (" The Fallacy of the Young Nation "), struck by the curious anæmia of those few artists of ours who have succeeded in developing themselves, usually by escaping from the American environment; " at the present moment the matter which America has very seriously to consider is not how near it is to its birth and beginning, but how near it may be to its end. . . . The English colonies have produced no great artists, and that fact may prove that they are still full of silent possibilities and reserve force. But America has produced great artists and that fact most certainly means that she is full of a fine futility and the end of all things. Whatever the American men of genius are, they are not young gods making a young world. Is the art of Whistler a brave, barbaric art, happy and headlong? Does Mr. Henry James infect us with the spirit of a school-boy? No, the colonies have not spoken, and they are safe. Their silence may be the silence of the unborn. But out of America has come a sweet and startling cry, as unmistakable as the cry of a dying man." That there is truth behind this, that the soil of our society is at least arid and impoverished, is indicated by the testimony of our own poets; one has only to consider what George Cabot Lodge wrote in 1904, in one of his letters: " We are a dying race, as every race must be of which the men are, as men and not accumulators, third-rate "; one has only to consider the writings of Messrs. Frost, Robinson, and Masters, in whose presentation of our life, in the West as well as in the East, the individual as a spiritual unit invariably suffers defeat. Fifty years ago J. A. Froude, on a visit to this country, wrote to one of his friends: "From what I see of the Eastern states I do not anticipate any very great things as likely to come out of the Americans. . . . They are generous with their money, have much tenderness and quiet good humour; but the Anglo-Saxon power is running to seed and I don't think will revive." When we consider the general colourlessness and insipidity of our latter-day life (faithfully reflected in the novels of Howells and his successors), the absence from it of profound passions and intense convictions, of any representative individuals who can be compared in spiritual force with Emerson, Thoreau, and so many of their contemporaries, its uniformity and its uniform tepidity, then the familiar saying, "Our age has been an age of management, not of ideas or of men," assumes indeed a very sinister import. I go back to the poet Lodge's letters. "Was there ever," he writes, "such an anomaly as the American man? In practical affairs his cynicism, energy, and capacity are simply stupefying, and in every other respect he is a sentimental idiot possessing neither the interest, the capacity, nor the desire for even the most elementary processes of independent thought. . . . His wife finds him so sexually inapt that she refuses to bear him children and so drivelling in every way except as a money-getter that she compels him to expend his energies solely in that direction while she leads a discontented, sterile, stunted life. . . ." Is this to be denied? And does it not in part explain that extraordinary lovelessness of the American scene which has bred the note of a universal resentment in so much of our contemporary fiction? As well expect figs from thistles as any considerable number of men from such a soil who are robust enough to prefer spiritual to material victories and who are capable of achieving them.

It is unnecessary to go back to Taine in order to realize that here we have a matrix as unpropitious as possible for literature and art. If our writers wither early, if they are too generally pliant, passive, acquiescent, anæmic, how much is this not due to the heritage of pioneering, with its burden of isolation, nervous strain, excessive work and all the racial habits that these have engendered?

Certainly, for example, if there is anything that counts in the formation of the creative spirit it is that long infancy to which John Fiske, rightly or wrongly, attributed the emergence of man from the lower species. In the childhood of almost every great writer one finds this protracted incubation, this slow stretch of years in which the unresisting organism opens itself to the influences of life. It was so with Hawthorne, it was so with Whitman in the pastoral America of a century ago: they were able to mature, these brooding spirits, because they had given themselves for so long to life before they began to react upon it. That is the old-world childhood still, in a measure; how different it is from the modern American childhood may be seen if one compares, for example, the first book (" Boyhood ") of " Pelle the Conqueror " with any of those innumerable tales in which our novelists show us that in order to succeed in life one cannot be up and doing too soon. The whole temper of our society, if one is to judge from these documents, is to hustle the American out of his childhood, teaching him at no age at all how to repel life and get the best of it and build up the defences behind which he is going to fight for his place in the sun. Who can deny that this racial habit succeeds in its unconscious aim, which is to produce sharp-witted men of business? But could anything be deadlier to the poet, the artist, the writer?

Everything in such an environment, it goes without saying, tends to repress the creative and to stimulate the competitive impulses. A certain Irish poet has observed that all he ever learned of poetry he got from talking with peasants along the road. Whitman might have said almost as much, even of New York, the New York of seventy years ago. But what nourishment do they offer the receptive spirit to-day, the harassed, inhibited mob of our fellow-countrymen, eaten up with the " itch of ill-advised activity," what encouragement to become anything but an automaton like themselves? And what direction, in such a society, does the instinct of emulation receive, that powerful instinct of adolescence? A certain visitor of Whitman's has described him as living in a house " as cheerless as an ash-barrel," a house indeed " like that in which a very destitute mechanic " might have lived. Is it not symbolic, that picture, of the esteem in which our democracy holds the poet? If to-day the man of many dollars is no longer the hero of the editorial page and the baccalaureate address, still, or rather more than ever, it is the " aggressive " type that overshadows every corner of our civilization; the intellectual man who has gone his own way and refused to flatter the majority was never less the hero or even the subject of intelligent interest; at best ignored, at worst (and usually) pointed out as a crank, he is only a " warning " to youth, which is exceedingly susceptible in these matters. But how can one begin to enumerate the elements in our society that contribute to form a selection constantly working against the survival of the creative type? By cutting off the sources that nourish it, by lending prestige to the acquisitive and destroying the glamour of the creative career, everything in America conspires to divert the spirit from its natural course, seizing upon the instincts of youth and turning them into a single narrow channel.

Here, of course, I touch upon the main fact of American history. That traditional drag, if one may so express it, in the direction of the practical, which has been the law of our civilization, would alone explain why our literature and art have never been more than half-hearted. To abandon the unpopular and unremunerative career of painting for the useful and lucrative career of invention must have seemed natural and inevitable to Robert Fulton and Samuel Morse. So strong is this racial compulsion, so feeble is the hold which Americans have upon ultimate values, that one can scarcely find to-day a scientist or a scholar who, for the sake of science or scholarship, will refuse an opportunity to become the money-gathering president of some insignificant university. Thus our intellectual life has always been ancillary to the life of business and organization: have we forgotten that the good Washington Irving himself, the father of American letters, thought it by no means beneath his dignity to serve as a sort of glorified press-agent for John Jacob Astor?

It is certainly true that none of these unfavourable factors of American life could have had such a baleful effect upon our literature if there had been others to counteract them. An aristocratic tradition, if we had ever had it, would have kept open among us the right of way of the free individual, would have preserved the claims of mere living. " It is curious to observe," writes Nietzsche in one of his letters, " how any one who soon leaves the traditional highway in order to travel on his own proper path always has more or less the sense of being an exile, a condemned criminal, a fugitive from mankind." If that is true in the old world, where society is so much more complex and offers the individual so much more latitude, how few could ever have had the strength in a society like ours, which has always placed such an enormous premium on conformity, to become and to remain themselves? Is it fanciful indeed to see in the famous " remorse " of Poe the traces left by this dereliction of the tribal law upon the unconscious mind of an artist of unique force and courage? Similarly, a tradition of voluntary poverty would have provided us with an escape from the importunities of bourgeois custom. But aside from the fact that even so simple a principle as this depends largely for its life on precedent (Whitman and the painter Ryder are almost alone among latter-day Americans in having discovered it for themselves), aside from the fact that to secede from the bourgeois system is, in America, to subject oneself to peculiar penalties (did it ever occur to Mark Twain that he *could* be honourably poor?)—aside from all this, poverty in the new world is by no means the same thing as poverty in the old: one has only to think of Charles Lamb and all the riches that London freely gave him, all the public resources he had at his disposal, to appreciate the difference. With us poverty means in the end an almost inevitable intellectual starvation. Consider such a plaint as Sidney Lanier's: " I could never describe to you " (he writes to Bayard Taylor) " what a mere drought and famine my life has been, as regards that multitude of matters which I fancy one absorbs when one is in an atmosphere of art, or when one is in conversational relationship with men of letters, with travellers, with persons who have either seen, or written, or done large things. Perhaps you know that, with us of the younger generation in the South since the war, pretty much the whole of life has been merely not dying." That is what poverty means in America, poverty and isolation, for Lanier, whose talent, as we can see to-day, was hopelessly crippled by it, was mistaken if he supposed that there was anything peculiar to the South in that plight of his: it has been the plight of the sensitive man everywhere in America and at all times. Add to poverty the want of a society devoted to intellectual things and we have such a fate as Herman Melville's in New York. "What he lacked," wrote Mr. Frank Jewett Mather the other day, explaining the singular evaporation of Melville's talent, "was possibly only health and nerve, but perhaps even more, companionship of a friendly, critical, understanding sort. In London, where he must have been hounded out of his corner, I can imagine Melville carrying the reflective vein to literary completion." Truly Samuel Butler was right when he jotted down the following observation in his note-book: "America will have her geniuses, as every other country has, in fact she has already had one in Walt Whitman, but I do not think America is a good place in which to be a genius. A genius can never expect to have a good time anywhere, if he is a genuine article, but America is about the last place in which life will be endurable at all for an inspired writer of any kind."

To such circumstances as these, I say, the weakness of our literary life is due. If we had lacked nothing else indeed, the lack of great leaders, of a strong and self-respecting literary guild, even of an enlightened publishing system would have sufficed to account for much of it. To consider the last point first: in the philosophy of American publishing, popularity has been regarded not only as a practical advantage but as a virtue as well. Thanks to the peculiar character of our democracy, our publishers have been able to persuade themselves that a book which fails to appeal to the ordinary citizen cannot be good on other grounds. Thus, if we had had to depend on the established system, the present revival in our letters, tentative as it is, would have been still more sadly handicapped. The history of Mr. Dreiser's "Sister Carrie" is enough to suggest what may well have been the fate of many an incipient author less persistent than he. It is certain, in any case, that many another, at a critical moment, has drifted away from literature because of the lack in our publishing world of those opportunities for a semi-creative hack-work which have provided countless European writers with a foothold and even a guideway. The Grub Street of London and Paris is a purgatory, but as long as it exists, with its humble instrumentalities, translating, editing, reviewing, one can at least survive until one has either lost or found oneself: it scarcely needs to be pointed out that the American magazine, with its mechanical exactions, which levy such a terrible toll upon one's individuality, is anything but an advantageous substitute. Till one has found oneself, the less one is subjected to such powerful, such essentially depolarizing influences, the better; the most mediocre institutions, if they enable one at the same time to maintain one's contact with literature and to keep body and soul together, are as life is to death beside them. How many English writers owe their ultimate salvation to such trivial agencies as *T. P.'s Weekly?* In America, where nothing of the kind has existed until lately, or nothing adequate to the number of those who might have benefitted by it, the literary aspirant is lost unless his powers mature at once.

But the lack of great leaders, of a strong and self-respecting literary guild (the one results from the other)—is not this our chief misfortune? In the best of circumstances, and considering all the devils that beset the creative spirit, a strong impulse is scarcely enough to carry one through: one must feel not only that one is doing what one wishes to do but that what one is doing *matters.* If dozens of American writers have fallen by the wayside because they have met with insuperable obstacles, dozens of others have fallen, with all their gifts, because they have lost interest in their work, because they have ceased to "see the necessity" of it. This is just the point where the presence of a leader, of a local tradition, a school, a guild makes all the difference. "With the masters I converse," writes Gauguin in his journal. "Their example fortifies me. When I am tempted to falter I blush before them." If that could have been true of Gauguin, the " Wolf," who walked by himself as few have walked, what shall we say of other men whose artistic integrity, whose faith in themselves, is exposed every day to the corroding influences of a third-rate civilization? It would be all very well if literature were merely a mode of " having a good time;" I am speaking of those, the real artists, who, with Nietzsche, make a distinction (illusory perhaps) between " happiness " and " work," and I say that these men have always fed on the thought of greatness and on the propinquity of greatness. It was not for nothing that Turgeniev bore in his memory, as a talisman, the image of Pushkin; that Gorky, having seen Tolstoy once, sitting among the boulders on the seashore, felt everything in him blending in one happy thought, " I am not an orphan on the earth, so long as this man lives on it." The presence of such men immeasurably raises the morale of the literary life: that is what Chekhov meant when he said, " I am afraid of Tolstoy's death," and is it not true that the whole contemporary literature of England has drawn virtue from Thomas Hardy? The sense that one is *working in a great line:* this, more than anything else perhaps, renews one's confidence in the " quaint mania of passing one's life· wearing oneself out over words," as Flaubert called it, in the still greater folly of pursuing one's ego when everything in life combines to punish one for doing so. The successful pursuit of the ego is what makes literature; this requires not only a certain inner intensity but a certain courage, and it is doubtful whether, in any nation, any considerable number of men can summon up that courage and maintain it unless they have *seen the thing done.* The very notion that such a life is either possible or desirable, the notion that such a life exists even, can hardly occur to the rank and file: some individual has to start the ball rolling, some individual of extraordinary force and audacity, and where is that individual to be found in our modern American literature? Whitman is the unique instance, for Henry James, with all his admirable conscience, was at once an exile and a man of singularly low vitality; and Whitman was not only essentially of an earlier generation, he was an invalid who folded his hands in mid-career.

Of those others what can we say, those others whose gifts have fitted them to be our leaders? Mr. Howells once observed of the American drama of the last few decades that "mainly it has been gay as our prevalent mood is, mainly it has been honest, as our habit is, in cases where we believe we can afford it." In this gently ironical pleasantry one seems to discern the true spirit of modern American letters. But it was Howells himself who, in order to arrive at the doctrine that "the more smiling aspects of life are the more American," deliberately, as he has told us, and professed realist that he was, averted his eyes from the darker side of life. And Mark Twain suppressed his real beliefs about man and the universe. And Henry Adams refused to sponsor in public the novels that revealed what he considered to be the truth about American society. Thus spake Zarathustra: "There is no harsher misfortune in all the fate of man than when the mighty ones of earth are not also the most excellent." At its very headwaters, as we see, this modern literature of ours has failed to flow clear: the creative impulse in these men, richly endowed as they were, was checked and compromised by too many other impulses, social and commercial. If one is to blame anything for this it is the immense insecurity of our life, which is due to its chaotic nature; for one is not entitled to expect greatness even of those who have the greatest gifts, and of these men Henry Adams was alone secure; of Howells and Mark Twain, Westerners as they were, it may be said that they were obliged to compromise, consciously or unconsciously, in order to gain a foothold in the only corner of the country where men could exist as writers at all. But if these men were unable to establish their independence (one has only to recall the notorious Gorky dinner in order to perceive the full ignominy of their position), what must one expect to find in the rank and file? Great men form a sort of wind shield behind which the rest of their profession are able to build up their own defences; they establish a right of way for the others; they command a respect for their profession, they arouse in the public a concern for it, an interest in it, from which the others benefit. As things are, the literary guild in America is not respected, nor does it respect itself. In " My Literary Passions " Howells,

after saying that his early reading gave him no standing among
other boys, observes: " I have since found that literature gives
one no more certain station in the world of men's activities,
either idle or useful. We literary folk try to believe that it
does, but that is all nonsense. At every period of life among
boys or men we are accepted when they are at leisure and
want to be amused, and at best we are tolerated rather than
accepted." Pathetic? Pusillanimous? Abject? Pathetic, I
suppose. Imagine Maxim Gorky or Knut Hamsun or Bernard
Shaw " trying to believe " that literature gives him a certain
station in the world of men's activities, conceiving for a moment that any activity could exceed his in dignity! Howells,
we observe, conscientious craftsman as he was, instinctively
shared, in regard to the significance of his vocation, the feeling of our pragmatic philosophers, who have been obliged to
justify the intellectual life by showing how useful it is—not to
mention Mr. R. W. Chambers, who has remarked that writers
" are not held in excessive esteem by really busy people, the
general idea being—which is usually true—that literature is a
godsend to those unfitted for real work." After this one can
easily understand why our novelists take such pains to be mistaken for business men and succeed so admirably in their effort. One can easily understand why Jack London preferred
the glory of his model ranch and his hygienic pigsties to the
approval of his artistic conscience.

So much for the conditions, or at least a few of them, that
have prevented our literature from getting its head above
water. If America is littered with extinct talents, the halt, the
maimed and the blind, it is for reasons with which we are all
too familiar; and we to whom the creative life is nothing less
than the principle of human movement, and its welfare the true
sign of human health, look upon this wreckage of everything
that is most precious to society and ask ourselves what our
fathers meant when they extolled the progress of our civilization. But let us look facts in the face. Mr. Sinclair Lewis
asserts that we are in the midst of a revival and that we are
too humble in supposing that our contemporary literature is
inferior to that of England. That we are in the midst of a
revival I have no doubt, but it is the sustained career that

makes a literature; without the evidence of this we can hope much but we can affirm nothing. What we can see is that, with all its hope, the morale of the literary profession in this country is just what its antecedents have made it. I am reminded of the observation of a friend who has reason to know, that the Catholic Church in America, great as it is in numbers and organization, still depends on the old world for its models, its task-masters and its inspiration; for the American priest, as a rule, does not feel the vocation as the European feels it. I am reminded of the American labour movement which, prosperous as it is in comparison with the labour movements of Europe, is unparalleled for the feebleness of its representatives. I am reminded of certain brief experiences in the American university world which have led me to believe that the professors who radiate a genuine light and warmth are far more likely to be Russians, Germans, Englishmen, Irishmen, Dutchmen, Swedes and Finns than the children of '76. That old hostility of the pioneers to the special career still operates to prevent in the American mind the powerful, concentrated pursuit of any non-utilitarian way of life: meanwhile everything else in our society tends to check the growth of the spirit and to shatter the confidence of the individual in himself. Considered with reference to its higher manifestations, life itself has been thus far, in modern America, a failure. Of this the failure of our literature is merely emblematic.

Mr. Mencken, who shares this belief, urges that the only hope of a change for the better lies in the development of a native aristocracy that will stand between the writer and the public, supporting him, appreciating him, forming as it were a *cordon sanitaire* between the individual and the mob. That no change can come without the development of an aristocracy of some sort, some nucleus of the more gifted, energetic and determined, one can hardly doubt. But how can one expect the emergence of an aristocracy outside of the creative class, and devoted to its welfare, unless and until the creative class itself reveals the sort of pride that can alone attract its ministrations? " The notion that a people can run itself and its affairs anonymously is now well known to be the silliest of absurdities." Thus William James, in defence of the aristocratic principle; and what he says is as applicable to literature as to every other department of social life. But he continues: " Mankind does nothing save through initiatives on the part of inventors, great and small, and imitation by the rest of us— these are the sole factors alive in human progress. Individuals of genius show the way, and set the patterns, which common people then adopt and follow." In other words, as I understand it, and so far as literature is concerned, the burden of proof lies on the writer himself—which brings one back to a truism: it is not for the public or any aristocratic minority within the public to understand the writer, it is for the writer to create the taste by which he is understood. Is it not by this indeed (in a measure, at least) that we recognize the creator?

Certainly if our contemporary literature is not respected, if it has not been able to rally to its support the sensitive public that already exists in this country, it is partly because this literature has not respected itself. That there has been every reason for it makes no difference; that it has begun to respect itself again makes no difference either, for when a people has lost confidence in its literature, and has had grounds for losing confidence in it, one cannot be surprised if it insists a little cynically upon being " shown." The public supported Mark Twain and Howells and the men of their generation, it admired them for what was admirable in them, but it was aware, if only unconsciously, that there was a difference between them and the men of the generation before them; and in consequence of this the whole stock of American literature fell. But those who insist in our day that America prefers European writers to its own, because America is still a colony of Europe, cannot ignore the significant fact that at a time when America was still more truly colonial than it is now American writers had all the prestige in this country that European writers have at present; and it is not entirely because at that time the country was more homogeneous. Poe and Thoreau found little support in the generation of which I speak, as Whitman found little support in the generation that followed it. On the other hand, there were no European writers (and it was an age of great writers in Europe) who were held in higher esteem in this country than Hawthorne, Emerson, Motley, and one or two others almost equally distinguished, as well from a European as from an American point of view; there were few, if any, European writers, in fact, who were esteemed in this country as highly as they. How can one explain it? How can one explain why, at a time when America, in every other department of life, was more distinctly colonial than it is now, American literature commanded the full respect of Americans, while to-day, when the colonial tradition is vanishing all about us, it so little commands their respect that they go after any strange god from England? The problem is not a simple one, but among the many explanations of it one can hardly deny that there were in that period a number of writers of unusual power, who made the most (who were able to make the most) of their power, who followed their artistic conscience (who were able to follow it) and who by this fact built up a public confidence in themselves and in the literature they represented. Does it matter at all whether to-day we enjoy these writers or not? They were men of spiritual force, three or four of them: that is the important point. If the emerging writers of our epoch find themselves handicapped by the scepticism of the public, which has ceased to believe that any good thing can come out of Nazareth, let them remember not only that they are themselves for the most part in the formative stage, but that they have to live down the recent past of their profession.

Meanwhile, what constitutes a literature is the spiritual force of the individuals who compose it. If our literature is ever to be regenerated, therefore, it can only be through the development of a sense of " free will " (and of the responsibility that this entails) on the part of our writers themselves. To be, to feel oneself, a " victim " is in itself not to be an artist, for it is the nature of the artist to live, not in the world of which he is an effect, but in the world of which he is the cause, the world of his own creation. For this reason, the pessimistic determinism of the present age is, from the point of view of literature, of a piece with the optimistic determinism of the age that is passing. What this pessimistic determinism reveals, however, is a *consciousness of the situation*: to that extent it represents a gain, and one may even say that to be conscious of the situation is half the battle. If we owed nothing else to Mr. Dreiser, for instance, we should owe him enough for the tragic sense of the waste and futility of American life, as we know it, which his books communicate. It remains true that in so far as we resent this life it is a sign of our own weakness, of the harm not only that our civilization has done us but that we have permitted it to do us, of our own imperfectly realized freedom; for to the creative spirit in its free state the external world is merely an impersonal point of departure. Thus it is certain that as long as the American writer shares what James Bryce calls the "mass fatalism" of the American people, our literature will remain the sterile, supine, and inferior phenomenon which, on the whole, it is.

"What we want," wrote Henry Adams in 1862 to his brother Charles, "is a *school*. We want a national set of young men like ourselves or better, to start new influences not only in politics, but in literature, in law, in society, and throughout the whole social organism of the country—a national school of our own generation. And that is what America has no power to create. . . . It's all random, insulated work, for special and temporary and personal purposes. And we have no means, power or hope of combined action for any unselfish end." *That is what America has no power to create.* But can it be said that any nation has ever created a school? Here we have the perfect illustration of that mass fatalism of which I have spoken, and Henry Adams himself, in his passivity, is the type of it. Secure as he was, uniquely secure, why did he refuse to accept the responsibility of those novels in which he expressed the contempt of a powerful and cultivated mind for the meanness, the baseness, the vulgarity of the guiding element in American society? In the darkest and most chaotic hours of our spiritual history the individual has possessed a measure of free will only to renounce it: if Henry Adams had merely signed his work and accepted the consequences of it, he might by that very fact have become the founder, the centre, of the school that he desired. But it is true that in that generation the impulses of youth were, with an extraordinary unanimity, focused upon a single end, the exploitation of the continent; the material opportunities that American life offered were too great and too all-engrossing, and it is unlikely that any considerable minority could have been rallied for any non-utilitarian cause. Sixty years later this school remains, and quite particularly as regards our literature, the one thing necessary; the reforestation of our spiritual territory depends on it. And in more than one sense the times are favourable. The closing of the frontier seems to promise for this country an intenser life than it has known before; a large element of the younger generation, estranged from the present order, exists in a state of ferment that renders it highly susceptible to new ideas; the country literally swarms with half-artists, as one may call them, men and women, that is to say, who have ceased to conform to the law of the tribe but who have not accepted the discipline of their own individual spirits. "What I chiefly desire for you," wrote Ibsen to Brandes at the outset of his career, "is a genuine, full-blooded egoism, which shall force you for a time to regard what concerns you yourself as the only thing of any consequence, and everything else as non-existent. . . . There is no way in which you can benefit society more than by coining the metal you have in yourself." The second half of this rather blunt counsel of perfection is implied in the first, and it connotes a world of things merely to name which would be to throw into relief the essential infantility of the American writer as we know the type. By what prodigies of alert self-adaptation, of discriminating self-scrutiny, of conscious effort does the creative will come into its own! As for us, weak as too many of us are, ignorant, isolated, all too easily satisfied, and scarcely as yet immune from the solicitations of the mob, we still have this advantage, that an age of reaction is an age that stirs the few into a consciousness of themselves.

VAN WYCK BROOKS

MUSIC

WE spend more money upon music than does any other nation on earth; some of our orchestras, notably those of Boston, Chicago, and Philadelphia, are worthy to rank among the world's best; in the Metropolitan Opera House we give performances of grand opera that for consistent excellence of playing, singing, and *mise-en-scène* are surpassed probably nowhere. Yet there has never been a successful opera by an American offered at that opera house, and the number of viable American orchestral works is small enough to be counted almost upon one's fingers. We squander millions every year upon an art that we cannot produce.

There are apologists for the American composer who will say that we do produce it, but that it is strangled at birth. According to their stock argument, there are numberless greatly gifted native composers whose works never get a hearing, (a) because Americans are prejudiced against American music and in favour of foreign music, and (b) because the foreigners who largely control the musical situation in this country jealously refuse to allow American works to be performed. This would be impressive if it were consistent or true. As far as concerns the Jealous Foreigner myth—he does not dominate the musical situation—I have never noticed that the average European in this country is deficient either in self-interest or tact. He is generally anxious, if only for diplomatic reasons, to find American music that is worth singing or playing. Even when he fails to find any that is worth performing, he often performs some that isn't, in order to satisfy local pride. Moreover, Americans are no more prejudiced against American musicians than they are against other kinds. As a matter of fact, if intensive boosting campaigns produced creative artists, the American composer during the past decade should have expanded like a hot-house strawberry. We have had prize contests of all kinds, offering substantial sums for everything from

grand operas to string quartettes, we have had societies formed
to publish his chamber-music scores; publishers have rushed to
print his smaller works; we have had concerts of American
compositions; we have had all-American festivals. Meanwhile
the American composer has, with a few lonely exceptions, ob-
stinately refused to produce anything above the level of what
it would be flattering to call mediocrity.

No. If he is not heard oftener in concert halls and upon recital platforms, it is because he is not good enough. There is,
in the music of even the second-rate Continental composers, a
surety of touch, a quality of evident confidence in their material and ease in its handling that is rarely present in the work
of Americans. Most American symphonic and chamber music
lacks structure and clarity. The workmanship is faulty, the
utterance stammers and halts. Listening to an average American symphonic poem, you get the impression that the composer was so amazed and delighted at being able to write a
symphonic poem at all that the fact that it might be a dull
one seemed of minor importance to him. When he isn't
being almost entirely formless he is generally safely conventional, preferring to stick to what a statesman would call the
Ways of the Fathers rather than risk some structural innovation what might or might not be effective. Tschaikovsky's
variation of the traditional sequence of movements in the
Pathétique symphony, for example—ending with the slow
movement instead of the march—would scandalize and terrify
the average American.

This feebleness and uncertainty in the handling of material
makes American music sound more sterile and commonplace
than it really is. The American composer never seems certain
just what, if anything, he wants to say. His themes, his fundamental ideas, are often of real significance, but he has no
control over that very essence of the language of music, mood.
He lacks taste. The fact that an American composition may
begin in a genuinely impressive mood is no guarantee at all that
inside of twenty-four bars it may not fall into the most appalling banalities. We start with lyric beauty and finish in
stickiness. The curse of bathos is upon us. We lack staying
power. Just as so many American dramatists can write two

good acts of a three-act play, so many American novelists can write superb opening chapters, so do American composers devise eloquent opening themes. But we all fail when it comes to development. The train is laid, the match is applied, and the spectators crowd back in delighted terror amid tremendous hissings and sputterings. But when the awaited detonation comes, it is too often only a pop.

Such failure to make adequate use of his ideas is partially attributable to the American musician's pathetically inadequate technical equipment. Generally speaking, he doesn't know his business. He has been unable, or hasn't bothered, to learn his trade. Imagine if you can a successful dramatist who can neither read nor write, but has to dictate his plays, or a painter who can only draw the outlines of his pictures, hiring some one else to lay in the colours, and you have something analogous to many an American " composer " whose music is taken seriously by Americans, and who cannot write out a playable piano part, arrange a song for choral performance, or transcribe a hymn tune for a string quartette. Such elementary work he has to have done for him, whenever it is necessary, by some hack. This, to say nothing of the more advanced branches of musical science, like counterpoint, fugue, orchestration. Though it is risky to generalize, it is probably safe to say that among Americans who write music, the man who can construct a respectable fugue or canon or score a piece for full orchestra is decidedly the exception. In Europe, of course, any man who did not have these technical resources at his fingertips would have to be a Moussorgsky to be taken seriously as a composer at all.

It is not entirely the American's fault that he is so ill-equipped. Much of his comparative musical illiteracy, true, is the result of his own laziness and his traditional American contempt for theory and passion for results. On the other hand, the young American who honestly desires a good theoretical training in music must either undertake the expensive adventure of journeying to one of the few cities that contain a first-class conservatory, or the equally expensive one of going to Europe. If he can do neither, he must to a great extent educate himself. Some kinds of training it is nearly impossible for him to obtain here at any price. Orchestration, for instance, a tremendously complex and difficult science, can be mastered only by the time-honoured trial and error method, i.e., by writing out scores and hearing them played. How is our young American to manage this? Granted that there is a symphony orchestra near him, how can he get his scores played? The conductor cannot be blamed for refusing. He is hired to play the works of masters, not to try out the apprentice efforts of unskilled aspirants. What we need so badly here are not more first-class orchestras, but more second-rate ones, small-town orchestras that could afford to give the tyro a chance.

Because of their lack of technical skill many composers in this country never venture into the broader fields of composition at all. As a class, we write short piano and violin pieces, or songs. We write them because we do earnestly desire to write something and because they do not demand the technical resourcefulness and sustained inspiration that we lack. Parenthetically, I don't for a moment mean to imply that clumsy workmanship and sterility are unknown in Europe, that we are all mediocrities and they are all *Uebermenschen*. As a matter of fact, we have to-day probably much more creative musical talent, if less brains, than Europe; but, talent for talent, the European is infinitely better trained. This, at least in part, because he respects theory and has a desire for technical proficiency that we almost totally lack. Then too, the European has some cultural background. There is a curious lack of inter-communication among the arts in this country. The painter seems to feel that literature has nothing direct to give him, the writer, that music and painting are not in his line, and the musician—decidedly the worst of the three in this respect—that his own art has no connection with anything.

The American composer's most complete failure is intellectual. The fact that he writes music seldom warrants the assumption that he has the artist's point of view at all. He is likely to be a much less interesting person than one's iceman. Ten to one, he never visits a picture gallery or a sculpture exhibition, his taste in the theatre is probably that of the tired business man, and what little reading he does is likely to be confined to trade papers, *Snappy Stories*, and best-sellers. He takes no interest in politics, economics, or sociology, either national or international (how could they possibly concern him?), and probably cannot discuss even music with pleasure or profit to anybody.

The natural inference that might be drawn from this diatribe —that the composing of music in this country is confined exclusively to the idiot classes—is not strictly true. Plenty of American musicians are intelligent and cultured men as well; but that is not America's fault. She is just as cordial to the stupid ones. And the widespread impotence and technical sloppiness of American music is the inevitable result of the American attitude toward music and to the anomalous position the art occupies in this country.

Let me be platitudinous in the interest of clarity and point out what we so often forget: that our nation, unlike most of the others, is not a race as well. We have common wellsprings of thought, but—and this is significant and ominous—none of feeling. Sheer environment may teach people to think alike within a generation; but it takes centuries of common emotional experiences to make them feel alike. Any average American, even of the National-Security-League-one-hundred-percentum variety, may have in his veins the blood of English, French, Italian, and Russian ancestors, and there is no saying that his emotional nature is going to find many heart-beats in common with some equally average neighbour, whose ancestry may be, say, Irish, Danish, and Hungarian. What national spirit we have has been determined, first, by the fact that the ancestors of every one of us, whether they came here twenty years ago or two hundred, were pioneers. Every one of them left a civilization whose cultural background had been established for centuries, to come to a land where the problem of mere existence was of prime importance. Again, many of them were religious fanatics. In the life of the pioneer there was little room for art of any sort, and least for music. What he demanded of music, when he had time to spare for it, was that above all things it distract him from the fatigue and worry of everyday life, either by amusing him or by furnishing a sentimental reminder of old ways. To the Puritan, music, both for its own sake and as entertainment, was anathema. As sensuous beauty it was popish, and as entertainment it was worldly pleasure, and therefore wicked. To be tolerated at all, it must be practical, i.e., perform some moral service by being a hymn tune. And what the American pioneer and the American Puritan asked a few generations back, the average American asks to-day whenever he is confronted with any work of art: Does it point a moral? If not, will it help me to kill time without boring me?

Instruction, release, or amusement: that, in general, is all we want of art. The American's favourite picture is one that tells a story, or shows the features of some famous person, or the topography of some historic spot. Fantastic pictures he likes, because they show him people and places far removed from his own rather tedious environment, but they must be a gaudy, literal, solid sort of fantasy—Maxfield Parrish rather than Aubrey Beardsley. If he can't have these, he wants pretty girls or comics. Purely decorative or frankly meaningless pictures—Hokusai and Whistler (except, of course, the portraits of Carlyle and his mother)—do not exist for him. Sculpture—which he does not understand—is probably his favourite art-form, for it is tangible, three-dimensionable, stable. He doesn't mind poetry, for it, too, gives him release. He likes novels, especially " glad " ones or mystery stories. He even tolerates realism if, as in " Main Street," it gives him release by showing him a set of consistently contemptible and uncultured characters to whom even he must feel superior. His architecture he likes either ornate to imbecility or utilitarian to hideousness.

In other words, the typical American goes to an art-work either frankly to have his senses tickled or for the sake of a definite thing that it says or a series of extraneous images or thoughts that it evokes—never for the *Ding an sich*. Of pure æsthetic emotion he exhibits very little. To him, beauty is emphatically not its own excuse for being. He does not want it for its own sake, and distrusts and fears it when it appears before him unclothed in moral lessons or associated ideas. In such a civilization music can occupy but a very unimportant place. For music is, morally or intellectually, the most meaningless of arts: it teaches no lesson, it offers no definite escape from life to the literal-minded, and aside from the primitive and obvious associations of patriotic airs and " mother " songs, it evokes no associated images or ideas. To love music you must be willing to enjoy beauty pretty largely for its own sake, without asking it to mean anything definite in words or pictures. This the American hates to do. Since he cannot be edified, he refuses to be stirred. There is nothing left for him, therefore, in music, except such enjoyment as he can get out of a pretty tune or an infectious rhythm.

And that, despite our admirable symphony orchestras and our two superb permanent opera companies (all run at a loss, by the way), is about all that music means to the average American—amusement. He simply does not see how an art that doesn't teach him anything, that is a shameless assault upon his emotions (he makes no distinction between emotions and senses), can possibly play any significant part in his life. So, as a nation, he does what he generally does in other matters of art, delegates its serious cultivation to women.

Women constitute ninety per cent. of those who support music in this country. It is women who attend song and instrumental recitals; it is women who force reluctant husbands and fathers to subscribe for opera seats and symphony concerts; the National Federation of Musical Clubs, which works throughout the country to foster the appreciation of music, is composed entirely of women; at least two-thirds of the choral organizations in the United States contain women's voices only. It is no disparagement of their activities to say that such a state of affairs is unhealthy. This well-nigh complete feminization of music is bad for it. After all, art, to be alive, must like any other living thing be the result of collaboration. Women have undertaken to be the moral guardians of the race, and no one can deny that they guard, upon the whole, as well as men could; but their guardianship is a bit too zealous at times, and their predominance in our musical life aggravates our already exaggerated tendency to demand that art be edifying. One of the conditions of the opera contest conducted by the National Federation in 1914 was that the libretto must contain nothing immoral or suggestive (I paraphrase). Now music is, after all, an adult occupation, and it might be assumed that a composer competent to write an opera score might have taste and intelligence enough not to be vulgar—for, surely, vulgarity was all they wanted to guard against. If the clause were to be interpreted literally, it would bar the librettos of *Tristan, Walküre, Carmen, Pelléas et Mélisande,* and *L'Amore dei Tre Re*—a supposition quite too unthinkable. The feminine influence helps to increase the insularity of our musicians. Women are more chauvinistic in art matters—if possible—than men, and among the women's clubs that are trying to encourage the American composer there is a tendency to insist rather that he be American than that he be a composer. Since it is women who support our recitals and concerts it is they who must assume responsibility for our excessive cult of the performer. This land is certainly the happy hunting-ground of the virtuoso, be he singer, player, or conductor. What he chooses to sing, play, or conduct is comparatively unimportant to us. Our audiences seem to gather not so much to listen as to look; or if they do listen, it is to the voice or the instrument rather than to the music. The announcement, " Farrar in *Carmen* " will pack the Metropolitan to the doors; but if the bill be changed, and *Zaza* be substituted at the last moment, who cares? Indeed the ticket agencies, knowing what people really attend opera for, frankly advertise " tickets for Farrar to-night." Rachmaninoff is a great pianist, and Rachmaninoff playing an all-Chopin programme could fill Carnegie Hall at any time. But Rachmaninoff playing a programme of Czerny's " Exercises for the Beginner " could fill it just as well. Announce an all-Chopin programme without naming the pianist, and see how much of an audience you draw. The people who go to hear Galli-Curci sing the shadow-song from *Dinora* do not go to hear music at all. They go as they would go to see Bird Millman walk a slack wire; they go to hear a woman prove that, given a phenomenal development of the vocal cords, she can, after years of practice, perform scales and trills *in altissimo* very nearly as well as the union flute-player who furnishes her obligato. All this is to a certain extent true elsewhere, of course. It is natural that if one person can sing or play better than another, audiences should prefer to hear him rather than another. But this worship of the performance rather than the thing performed, this blind adoration of skill for its own sake, is cultivated in America to a degree that is quite unparalleled.

Many American cities and large towns hold annual musical festivals, lasting from two days to a week or more, and these are often mentioned as evidence of the existence of a genuine musical culture among us. Are they? What happens at them? For one thing, the local choral society performs a cantata or oratorio. This is more than likely to be either *The Messiah* or *Elijah*, works which through long association have taken on less the character of musical compositions than of devotional exercises. Edification again. Soloists are engaged, as expensive and famous as the local budget allows, and these give recitals during the remaining sessions of the festival. The audiences come largely to see these marvels rather than to hear music, for after the annual spree of culture is over they return home contentedly enough to another year void of any music whatever. Hearing a little music is better than hearing none, but the test of genuine culture is whether or not it is an integral part of life rather than a vacation from it. By this test the annual festival would seem to exert about as much permanent cultural influence as a clambake.

The total unconsciousness on the part of his fellow-countrymen that art is related to life, a sense of futility and unreality, is what makes the lot of the musician in America a hard one, and is responsible for his failure as an artist. If people get the kind of government they deserve, they most certainly get the kind of art they demand; and if, comparatively speaking, there is no American composer, it is because America doesn't want him, doesn't see where he fits in.

Suppose most American music is trivial and superficial? How many Americans would know the difference if it were profound? The composer here lives in an atmosphere that is, at the worst, good-natured contempt. Contempt, mind you, not for himself—that wouldn't matter—but for his very art. In the minds of many of his compatriots it ranks only as an entertainment and a diversion, slightly above embroidery and unthinkably below baseball. At best, what he gets is unintelligent admiration, not as an artist, but as a freak. Blind Tom, the negro pianist, is still a remembered and admired figure in

American musical history; and Blind Tom was an idiot. To an American, the process of musical composition is a mysterious and incomprehensible trick—like sword-swallowing or levitation—and as such he admires it; but he does not respect it. He cannot understand how any normal he-man can spend his life thinking up tunes and putting them down on paper. Tunes are pleasant things, of course, especially when they make your feet go or take you back to the days when you went straw-riding; but as for taking them seriously, and calling it work—man's work—to think them up . . . any one who thinks that can be dismissed as a crank.

If the crank could make money, it might be different. The respect accorded to artists in our country is pretty sharply graded in accordance with their earning power. Novelists and playwrights come first, since literature and the stage are known to furnish a " good living." Sculptors have a certain standing, on account of the rumoured prices paid for statues and public memorials, though scenario writers are beginning to rank higher. Painters are eyed with a certain suspicion, though there is always the comfortable belief that the painter probably pursues a prosperous career of advertising art on the side. But poets and composers are decidedly men not to be taken seriously. This system of evaluation is not quite as crass as it sounds. America has so long been the land of opportunity, we have so long gloried in her supremacy as the place to make a living, that we have an instinctive conviction that if a man is really doing a good job he must inevitably make money at it. Only, poetry and music have the bad luck to be arts wherein a man may be both great and successful and still be unable to look the landlord in the eye. Since such trades are so unprofitable, we argue, those who pursue them are presumably incompetent. The one class of composer whom the American does take seriously is the writer of musical comedy and popular songs, not only because he can make money, but because he provides honest, understandable entertainment for man and beast. That, perhaps, is why our light music is the best of its kind in the world.

The self-styled music-lover in this country too often brings little more genuine comprehension to music. He is likely to be a highbrow (defined as a person educated beyond his intelligence), with all the mental obtuseness and snobbishness of his class. He divides music into " popular "—meaning light— and " classical "—meaning pretentious. Now there is good music and bad, and the composer's pretensions have little to do with the case. Compare, for example, the first-act finale of Victor Herbert's *Mlle. Modiste* with such vulgar rubbish as *Donna è mobile*. Yet because the latter is sung by tenors, at the Metropolitan, the highbrow solemnly catalogues it as " classical," abolishing the work of Herbert, Berlin, and Kern, three greatly gifted men, with the adjective " popular." In general, he is the faithful guardian of the Puritan tradition, always sniffing the air for a definite " message " or moral, seeking sermons in tones, books in running arpeggios. It never occurs to him that just as words are the language of intellect, so is music the language of emotion, that its whole excuse for existence is its perfection in saying what lies just beyond and above words, and that if you can reduce a composer's message to words, you automatically render it meaningless.

Music criticism in America is amazingly good in the cities. The system under which the critics must work, however, whereby they are supposed to " cover " everything (in New York this theoretically entails making some sort of critical comment upon every one of three or four hundred events in a single season) is so impossible that much of their work is inevitably scamped and perfunctory. Elsewhere throughout the country criticism is handed over to reporters, who generally avoid trouble by approving of everything. There is a tendency toward the double standard—holding the stranger strictly to account, especially the foreigner, and being " nice " to the native—that produces demoralizing results.

Of real musical journalism we have none. There is *The Musical Quarterly*, good of its kind, but rather ponderous and making no pretence to timeliness. The monthlies are chiefly for the teacher. The weeklies are in general frankly " shop " organs, devoted to the activities of the performer and filled with his advertisements, portraits, and press notices. There is no medium for the exchange of contemporary thought, for the discussion of topics having a non-professional cultural interest. Music publishing here is an industry, conducted like any other industry. The Continental type of publisher, who is a scholar and a musician, and a gentleman who is conscious of a duty to music as well as to the stockholders, is almost unknown here. To our publishers music is a commodity, to be bought cheap and sold dear, and most of them will publish anything that looks profitable, regardless of its quality. Their typographical standards are higher than those anywhere in the world, except Germany.

So the American composer in America works more or less in a vacuum. He is out of things, and he knows it. If he attempts to say something, through his art, that will be intelligible to his countrymen, he is baffled by the realization that his countrymen don't understand his language. This particular difficulty, this sense of inarticulateness, probably weighed less heavily upon the last two generations of American composers; for they were, most of them, virtually German composers. In their time a thorough technical education in music was so nearly unobtainable here that it was simpler to go abroad for it. So, from Paine to MacDowell, they went to Germany. There they learned their trade, and at least learned it thoroughly; but they learned to write, not only music, but German music. To them, German music *was* music. Their songs were *Lieder;* their symphonies and overtures were little sinister sons of Beethoven, Raff, and Brahms. So completely Teutonized did our musical speech become that we still find it hard to believe that French music, Spanish music, Russian music is anything but an imperfect translation from the German. A few went to Paris and learned to write with a French accent. MacDowell was, and remains, our best: a first-rank composer, who died before his work was done. His earlier music was all written, performed, and published in Germany, and it is as *echt Deutsch* as that of Raff, his master. Not until he approached middle life did he evolve a musical idiom that was wholly of MacDowell, the American. Most of the rest came back to spend their days fashioning good, honest, square-toed *Kapellmeistermusik* that had about as much genuine relation to their America as the Declaration of Independence has to ours. They might feel this lack of contact, but at least they had the consolation of knowing that there were people in the world to whom what they said was at least intelligible.

The American of the present generation has no such consolation. He has probably not been trained abroad. He wants to write music, and being human, he wants it understood. But the minute he tries to express himself he betrays the fact that he does not know what he wants to express. Any significant work of art is inevitably based on the artist's relation and reaction to life. But the American composer's relation to the common life is unreal. His activities strike his fellows as unimportant and slightly irrational. He can't lay his finger upon the great, throbbing, common pulse of America because for him there is none. So he tries this, that, and the other, hoping by luck to stumble upon the thing he wants to say. He tries desperately to be American. Knowing that the great national schools of music in other countries are based upon folksong, he tries to find the American folksong, so as to base his music upon that. He utilizes Negro tunes, and when they fail to strike the common chord he devises themes based upon Indian melodies. What he fails to see is that the folksongs of Europe express the common *racial* emotions of a nation, not its geographical accidents. When a Frenchman hears *Malbrouck* he is moved by what moved generations of long-dead Frenchmen; when a Russian hears *Dubinushka* he is stirred by what has stirred Russians for centuries. But even if some melody did stir the pulse of Geronimo, the mere fact that he was a former resident of my country is no proof that it is going to stir mine. If you insist that Negro music is the proper basis for an American school of composition, try telling a Southerner that when he hears *Swing Low, Sweet Chariot*, he is hearkening to the voices of his ancestors!

A curious symptom of this feeling of disinheritance is the tendency of so many Americans to write what might be called the music of escape, music that far from attempting to affirm the composer's relation to his day and age is a deliberate attempt to liberate himself by evoking alien and exotic moods and atmosphere. The publishers' catalogues are full of Arab meditations, Persian dances, Hindu serenades, and countless similar attempts to get "anywhere out of the world." The best work of Charles Griffes, whose untimely death last year robbed us of a true creative talent, was his symphonic poem, "The Pleasure Dome of Kubla Khan," and his settings of Chinese and Japanese lyrics in Oriental rhythms and timbres. Not that the mere choice of subject is important; it is the actual mood and idiom of so much of this music that is significant evidence of the impulse to give up and forget America, to create a dream-world wherein one can find refuge from the land of chewing gum and victrolas.

These same victrolas, by the way, with their cousin, the player-piano, which so outrage the sensibilities of many a musician of the elder day, are a very real force in helping to civilize this country musically. The American is by no means as unmusical as he thinks he is. His indifference to art is only the result of his purely industrial civilization, and his tendency to mix morals with æsthetics is a habit of thought engendered by his ancestry. The Puritan tradition makes him fearful and suspicious of any sort of sensuous or emotional response, but it has not rendered him incapable of it. Catch him off his guard, get him away from the fear of being bored, and he is far from insensitive to music. He buys victrola records because he is a hero-worshipper, because he wants to hear the expensive Caruso and Kreisler and McCormack; but inevitably he is bound to take some notice of what they play and sing, and to recognize it when he hears it again. In spite of himself he begins to acquire a rudimentary sort of musical background. He begins by buying jazz rolls for his player-piano, and is likely in the long run, if only out of curiosity, to progress from "blues" to Chopin, via Moszkovski and Grainger.

But the greatest present-day force for good, musically, in this country, is the large motion-picture house. Music has always been a necessary accompaniment to motion pictures, in order to compensate for the uncanny silence in which these photographic wraiths unfold their dramas. Starting with a modest ensemble of piano and glass crash, the motion-picture orchestra has gradually increased in size and quality, the pipe organ has been introduced to augment and alternate it, so that the larger houses to-day can boast a musical equipment that is amazingly good. A few years ago S. L. Rothafel devised a glorified type of entertainment that was a sort of combination picture-show and "pop" concert. He built a theatre, the Rialto, especially to house it, containing a stage that was little more than a picture frame, a large pipe organ, and an orchestra platform large enough to hold seventy or eighty players. He recruited a permanent orchestra large enough to play symphonic works, and put Hugo Riesenfeld, an excellent violinist and conductor, who had been trained under Arthur Nikisch, in charge of the performances. These, besides the usual film presentations, comprised vocal and instrumental solos and detached numbers by the orchestra. All the music played at these entertainments was good—in what is known in this country as "classical." Riesenfeld devised a running accompaniment to the films, assembled from the best orchestral music obtainable—a sort of synthetic symphonic poem that fitted the mood and action of the film presented, and was, of course, much too good for it.

This new entertainment form was instantly successful, and is rapidly becoming the standard offering at all the larger picture houses. It is a significant step in our musical life, for it is the first entirely successful attempt in this country to adapt art to popular wants. At last the average man is going of his own accord into a public hall and hearing music—real music —and discovering that he likes it. The picture house allows him to pretend that he is going solely to see the films, and needn't listen unless he wants to. He finds that "classical" music is not nearly so boresome as many of its admirers. Freed from the highbrow's condescension, unconscious of uplift, he listens and responds to music like the prelude to *Tristan,* the *Walkürenritt,* the *New World* symphony, Tschaikovsky's *Fourth,* and the *Eroica.* Theodore Thomas rendered no more valuable service to music in America than have Samuel Rothafel and Hugo Riesenfeld.

We are still far from utopia, however. In one of his essays upon communal art Henry Caro-Delvaille speaks of "the true Mediterranean *esprit,* the viable art philosophy of the French race, which is essentially plastic, accepting and delineating life, free alike from dogmatism and mysticism." Try to frame a sentence like that about America. Try to make any generalization about the American spirit without using "liberty," "free institutions," "resourcefulness," "opportunity," or other politico-economic terms, if you would know what confronts the American artist, above all the American musician, when he attempts to become articulate to his countrymen. We simply have no common æsthetic emotions. No wonder our music flounders and stammers, and trails off into incoherence!

Wagner wrote *Die Meistersinger* in a deliberate effort to express the German artistic creed; Verdi wrote consciously as an Italian; Glinka founded an entire school of composers whose sole aim was to express Russia. Such a task is beyond the American. The others were spokesmen for a race: he has no race to speak for, and the moment he pretends that he has, and tries to speak for it, he becomes conscious and futile. To speak of American music, in any ethnic sense, is naïve; you might as well speak of Baptist music. No. The American must accept his lot. There is but one audience he can write for, and that is himself. John Smith, American composer, dare not say: "I write to express America." He can only say: "I write to express John Smith. I accept my life because, after all, it is mine, and I interpret my life because it is the only life I know." And because John Smith is an American, and because somewhere, remote and inarticulate, there must be an American soul, then perhaps, if he does honest work and is true to himself, he may succeed in saying something that is of America, and of nowhere else, and that other Americans will hear and understand.

DEEMS TAYLOR

POETRY

THERE are many fashions, among contemporary critics, of regarding American poetry, each of them perhaps of equal helpfulness, since each is one facet of an imaginable whole. There is the view of Mr. John Middleton Murry, an English critic, that it depends perhaps a shade too much on narrative or dramatic interest, on bizarrerie (if I may very freely elaborate his notion) or, in general, on a kind of sensationalism, a use of superficially intriguing elements which are not specifically the right—or at all events the best—elements of poetry. There is the view of Mr. Louis Untermeyer, one of the ablest of our own critics and also one of the most versatile of our parodists and poets, that our contemporary poetry is good in measure as it comes in the direct line from Whitman: good, that is to say, when it is the voice of the poet who accepts, accepts joyously and largely, even loosely, this new world environment, these new customs, social and industrial, above all, it may be, the new sense of freedom which he might, if pressed, trace back to Karl Marx on one hand and Sigmund Freud on the other. There is again the view of Miss Amy Lowell that our poetry is good, or tends to be, precisely in proportion as it represents an outgrowing, by the poet, of his acute awareness of a social or ethical " here and now," and the attainment of a relatively pure pre-occupation with beauty— the sense of freedom here exercising itself principally, if not altogether, with regard to literary tradition, especially the English: once more, I dilate the view to make it the more broadly representative. And there is, finally, the view of the conservative, by no means silent even in this era, that what is good in contemporary American poetry is what is for the moment least conspicuous—the traditional, seen as it appears inevitably in America to be seen, as something graceful, sentimental, rightly ethical, gently idealistic.

What will be fairly obvious is that if we follow a little way any particular one of these critics, we shall find him attempting to urge our poetry in a particular direction, a direction which he prefers to any other direction, and analysing its origins in such a way, if he analyses at all, as to make plausible its (postulated) growth in that direction. This is the natural, even perhaps the best thing, for a participant critic to do—it contributes, certainly, an interest and an energy. But if in some freak of disinterestedness, we wish if for only a moment to see American poetry with no concern save that of inordinate and intelligent curiosity, then it is to all of these views that we must turn, rather than to any one, and to the obverse of each, as well as to the face. For if one thing is apparent to-day in a study of American letters, it is that we must heroically resist any temptation to simplify, to look in only one direction for origins or in only one direction for growth. Despite our national motto, American civilization is not so much one in many as many in one. We have not, as England has and as France has, a single literary heart; our literary capitals and countries are many, each with its own vigorous people, its own self-interest, its own virtues and provincialisms. We may attribute this to the mere matter of our size, and the consequent geographical sequestration of this or that group—that is no doubt a factor, but of equal importance is the fact that in a new country, of rapid and chaotic material growth, we must inevitably have, according to the locality, marked variations in the rapidity of growth of the vague thing we call civilization. Chicago is younger than Boston, older than San Francisco. And what applies to the large unit applies also to the small—if the country in general has not yet reached anything remotely like a cultural homogeneity (as far, that is, as we ever in viewing a great nation expect such a thing) neither has any section of it, nor any city of it. It is no longer possible, if indeed it ever was, to regard a section like New England, for example, as a definite environmental factor, say "y," and to conclude, as some critics are so fond of doing, that any poet who matures there will inevitably be representable as "yp." This is among the commonest and falsest of false simplifications. Our critics, frantically determined to find an

American poetry that is autochthonous, will see rocky pastures, mountains and birches in the poetry of a New Englander,
or skyscrapers in the poetry of a New Yorker, or stockyards
in the poetry of a Chicagoan, as easily as a conjurer takes
a rabbit from a hat.

What refuge we have from a critical basis so naïve is in
assuming from the outset, toward contemporary American
poetry, an attitude guardedly pluralistic—we begin by observing merely that American poetry is certainly, at the moment,
if quantitative production and public interest are any measure,
extraordinarily healthy and vigorous. We are accustomed to
hearing it called a renaissance. The term is admissible if we
carefully exclude, in using it, any implication of a revival of
classicism. What we mean by it is simply that the moment is
one of quite remarkable energy, productiveness, range, colour,
and anarchy. What we do not mean by it is that we can trace
with accuracy where this outburst comes from. The origins of
the thing are obscure. It was audible in 1914—Mr. Edwin
Arlington Robinson and Mr. Ezra Pound were audible before
that; it burst into full chorus in 1915; and ever since there
has been, with an occasional dying fall, a lusty corybantic
cacophony. Just where this amazing procession started nobody
clearly knows. Mr. Untermeyer would have us believe that
Walt Whitman was, as it were, the organizer of it, Miss Monroe tries to persuade us that it was *Poetry: a Magazine of
Verse*. But the facts, I think, wave aside either postulate.
If one thing is remarkable it is that in this spate of poetry the
influence of Walt Whitman—an influence, one would suppose,
as toxic for the young as Swinburne—is so inconsiderable: if
another is even more remarkable, it is that in all this chorus
one so seldom hears a voice of which any previous American
voice was the clear prototype. We have had, of course, our
voices—of the sort, I mean, rich enough in character to make
imitation an easy and tempting thing. Longfellow, Lowell,
Bryant, Sill, Lanier are not in this regard considerable,—but
what of Poe, whose influence we have seen in French poetry
on Baudelaire, and in contemporary English poetry on Mr.
Walter de la Mare? No trace of him is discoverable, unless
perhaps we find the ghostliest of his shadows now and then

across the work of Mr. John Gould Fletcher, or Mr. Maxwell Bodenheim, or Mr. Wallace Stevens, a shadow cast, in all these cases, amid much else, from a technical and colouristic standpoint, which would have filled Poe with alarm. And there is another American poet, perhaps as great as Poe, perhaps greater (as he in turn is perhaps greater than Whitman —as poet, though not as personality)—Emily Dickinson. Of that quietist and mystic, who walked with tranquillity midway between Blake and Emerson, making of her wilful imperfections a kind of perfectionism, why do we hear so little? Do we catch now and again the fleetingest glimpse of her in the early work of Mr. Robert Frost? If so, it is certainly nowhere else. Yet it would be hard to prove that she has no right to a place with Poe and Whitman, or indeed among the best poets in the language.

But nowhere in America can we find, for contemporary poetry, any clear precursive signal. Little as it may comfort our fuglemen of the autochthonous, we must, I think, look to Europe for its origins. This is not, as some imagine, a disgrace—it would be a melancholy thing, of course, if we merely imitated the European, without alteration. But Browning would hardly recognize himself, even if he cared to, in the "Domesday Book" of Mr. Edgar Lee Masters, Mallarmé and Rimbaud would find Mr. Fletcher a mirror with an odd trick of distortion, Laforgue would have to look twice at Mr. T. S. Eliot's "Prufrock" (for all its Hamletism), M. Paul Fort would scarcely feel at home in Miss Amy Lowell's "Can Grande's Castle," Mr. Thomas Hardy and the ghost of Tennyson would not quarrel much for the possession of Mr. Robinson's work, nor Mr. Chesterton and the author of "The Ingoldsby Legends" for the lively sonorities of Mr. Vachel Lindsay. In such cases we have not so much "influence" as fertilization. It is something of Mr. Masters that "The Ring and the Book" reveals to Mr. Masters: something of Miss Lowell to which M. Paul Fort offers her the key. Was it a calamity for Baudelaire that he lived only by a transfusion of blood from an American? Is Becquer the less Becquer or Spanish for having fed upon the "Buch der Lieder"? . . . Culture is bartered, nowadays, at open frontiers, and if to-day a new theme, chord, or colour-scheme is French, German, or American, to-morrow it is international.

If we differ in this respect from any other country it is only that we are freer to exploit, really exhaust, the new, because we hold, less than any other, to any classical traditions: for traditions our poets seldom look back further than the 19th century. We have the courage, often indistinguishable from folly, of our lack of convictions. Thus it comes about that as America is the melting-pot for races, so she is in a fair way to become a melting-pot for cultures: we have the energy, the curiosity, the intelligence, above all the lack of affiliations with the past, which admirably adapt us to a task—so precisely demanding complete self-surrender—of æsthetic experiment. Ignorance has some compensations—I mean, of course, a partial ignorance. If Mr. Lindsay had been brought up exclusively on Aristotle, Plato, Æschylus, and Euripides, and had been taken out of the shadow of the church by Voltaire and Darwin, perhaps he would not have been so " free " to experiment with the " higher vaudeville." It will be observed that this is an odd kind of " freedom," for it amounts in some ways to little more than the " freedom " of the prison. For if too severe a training in the classics unfits one somewhat for bold experiment, too little of it is as likely, on the other hand, to leave one with an æsthetic perceptiveness, a sensibility, in short, relatively rudimentary.

This, then, is something of the cultural *mise en scène* for our contemporary poetry. We have repeated waves of European suggestion breaking Westward over our continent, foaming rather more in Chicago than in New York; and we have our lusty young company of swimmers, confident that they are strong enough to ride these waves farther than any one in Europe rode them and with a more native grace. What is most conspicuously American in most of these swimmers is the fact that they rely not so much on skill and long training as on sheer energy, vitality, and confidence. They rely, indeed, in most cases, on a kind of exuberance or superabundance. Do we not feel this in the work of Mr. Edgar Lee Masters—does he not try, in these many full books of his, where the good is so inextricably enmeshed with the bad, simply to beat us down as under a cataract? " Domesday Book " is, rather, an avalanche. He never knows what to exclude, where to stop. Miss Lowell, Mr. Fletcher, Mr. Carl Sandburg, and Mr. Lindsay are not far behind him, either—they are all copious. I do not mean to imply that this is a bad thing, at the moment—at the moment I am not sure that this sheer exuberance is not, for us, the very *best* thing. Energy is the first requisite of a " renaissance," and supplies its material, or, in another light, its richness of colour. Not the beginning, but the end, of a renaissance is in refinement; and I think we are certainly within bounds in postulating that the last five years have given us at the least a superb beginning, and enough more than that, perhaps, to make one wonder whether we have not already cast Poe and Whitman, Sidney Lanier, and Emily Dickinson, our strange little quartette, into a shadow.

All that our wonder can hope for is at best a very speculative answer. If parallels were not so dangerous, we might look with encouragement at that spangled rhetorical torrent which we call Elizabethan literature. Ben Jonson did not consider Shakespeare much of an artist, nor did Milton, and classicists ever since have followed them in that opinion. If one can be the greatest of poets and yet not much of an artist, we may here keep clear of the quarrel: what we get at is the fact that Shakespeare and the other Elizabethans participated in a literary movement which, like ours, began in energy, violence, and extravagance, was at its best excessively rhetorical and given to unpruned copiousness, and perished as it refined. Will a future generation see us in a somewhat similar light— will it like us for our vitality, for the reckless adventurousness of our literature, our extravagances, and forgive us, if it does not precisely enjoy as something with a foreign flavour, our artistic innocence? That is conceivable, certainly. Yet the view *is* speculative and we dare not take it too seriously. For if we have kept hopefully and intelligently abreast of the contemporary we have kept, none the less, our own very sufficient aloofness, our own tactilism and awareness, in the light of which we are bound to have our own scepticisms and self-distrust. I do not mean that we would perhaps prefer some-

thing more classical or severe than " Spoon River Anthology "
or " The Congo " or the colour symphonies of Mr. Fletcher,
merely on the ground that it is the intrinsically classical and
severe which we most desire.   What we seem to see in contemporary American poetry is a transition from the more to
the less exuberant, from the less to the more severe; and what
we most *desire* to see is the attainment of *that point*, in this
transition, which will give us our parallel to the Shakespearean,
if we may hope for anything even approximately so high; a
point of equipoise.

This hope gives us a convenient vantage from which to
survey the situation, if we also keep in mind our perception of
American cultural heterogeneity and the rashness of any attempt to generalize about it.   The most exact but least divert-
ing method would be the merely enumerative, the mere roll-
call which would put before us Mr. Edwin Arlington Robinson and Mr. Ezra Pound as the two of our poets whose public
literary activities extend farthest back, and after them the
group who made themselves known in the interval between
1914 and 1920: Mr. Robert Frost, Mr. Fletcher, Mr. Masters,
Mr. Sandburg, Miss Lowell, Mr. Lindsay, Mr. Alfred Kreymborg, Mr. Maxwell Bodenheim, Mr. Wallace Stevens, " H. D.,"
Mr. T. S. Eliot, and Miss Sara Teasdale.   These poets, with
few exceptions, have little enough in common—nothing, perhaps, save the fact that they were all a good deal actuated at
the outset by a disgust with the dead level of sentimentality
and prettiness and moralism to which American poetry had
fallen between 1890 and 1910.   From that point they diverge
like so many radii.   One cannot say, as Miss Lowell has tried
to persuade us, that they have all followed one radius, and
that the differences between them are occasioned by the fact
that some have gone farther than others.   We may, for convenience, classify them, if we do not attach too much importance to the bounds of our classes.   We may say that Mr.
Robinson, Mr. Frost, and Mr. Masters bring back to our
poetry a strong sense of reality; that Mr. Fletcher, Mr. Pound,
Miss Lowell, " H. D.," and Mr. Bodenheim bring to it a sharpened consciousness of colour; that Mr. Eliot, Mr. Kreymborg,
and Mr. Stevens bring to it a refinement of psychological

subtlety; Mr. Sandburg, a grim sense of social responsibility;
Mr. Lindsay, a rhythmic abandon mixed with evangelism; Miss
Teasdale, a grace. The range here indicated is extraordinary.
The existence side by side in one generation and in one country of such poets as Mr. Masters and Mr. Fletcher, or Mr.
Eliot and Miss Lowell, is anomalous. Clearly we are past
that time when a nation will have at a given moment a single
direct literary current. There is as yet no sign that to any
one of these groups will fall anything like undivided sway.
Mr. Frost's " North of Boston " and Mr. Fletcher's " Irradiations " came out in the same year; " Spoon River Anthology "
and the first " Imagist Anthology "; Mr. Robinson's " Lancelot " and Mr. Bodenheim's " Advice." And what gulfs even
between members of any one of our arbitrary " classes "! Mr.
Frost's actualism is seldom far from the dramatic or lyric,
that of Mr. Masters seldom far from the physiological. Mr.
Masters is bitter-minded, tediously explanatory, and his passionate enquiries fall upon life like so many heavy blows;
his delvings appear morbid as well as searching. Mr. Frost
is gentle, whether in irony, humour, or sense of pain: if it is
the pathos of decay which most moves him, he sees it, none
the less, at dewfall and moonrise, in a dark tree, a birdsong.
The inflections of the human voice, as he hears them, are as
tender as in the hearing of Mr. Masters they are harsh. And
can Mr. Robinson be thought a commensal of either? His
again is a prolonged enquiry into the why of human behaviour,
but how bared of colour, how muffled with reserves and dimmed
with reticence! Here, indeed, is a step toward romanticism.
For Mr. Robinson, though a realist in the sense that his preoccupation is with motive, turns down the light in the presence
of his protagonist that in the gloom he may take on the air
of something larger and more mysterious than the garishly
actual. Gleams convey the dimensions—hints suggest a depth.
We are not always too precisely aware of what is going on in
this twilight of uncertainties, but Mr. Robinson seems to whisper that the implications are tremendous. Not least, moreover, of these implications are the moral—the mirror that Mr.
Robinson holds up to nature gives us back the true, no doubt,
but increasingly in his later work (as in " Merlin " and

"Lancelot," particularly the latter) with a slight trick of re-fraction that makes of the true the exemplary.

We cross a chasm, from these sombre psycho-realists, to the colourists. To these, one finds, what is human in behaviour or motive is of importance only in so far as it affords colour or offers possibilities of pattern. Mr. Fletcher is the most brilliant of this group, and the most " uncontrolled ": his colourism, at its best, is a pure, an astonishingly absolute thing. The " human " element he wisely leaves alone—it baffles and escapes him. One is aware that this kaleidoscopic whirl of colour is " wrung out " of Mr. Fletcher, that it conveys what is for him an intense personal drama, but this does not make his work "human." The note of " personal drama " is more complete in the poetry of " H. D.," but this too is, in the last analysis, a nearly pure colourism, as static and fragmentary, however, as Mr. Fletcher's is dynamic. Mr. Bodenheim is more detached, cooler, has a more conscious eye for correspondences between colour and mood: perhaps we should call him a symbolist. Even here, however, the " human," the whim of tenderness, the psychological gleam, are swerved so that they may fall into a fantastic design. Miss Lowell, finally, more conscious, deliberate and energetic than any of these, brilliantly versatile, utterly detached, while she " sees " more of the objective world (and has farther-ranging interests), sees it more completely than any of them simply as raw colour or incipient pattern. If the literary pulse is here often feverishly high, the empathic and sympathetic temperature is as often absolute zero.

Mr. Pound shares with Miss Lowell this immersion in the " literary "—he is intensely aware of the literary past, rifles it for odds and ends of colour, atmosphere, and attitude, is perpetually adding bright new bits, from such sources, to his Joseph's coat: but if a traditionalist in this, a curio-hunter, he is an experimentalist in prosody; he has come far from the sentimental literary affectedness of his early work and at his best has written lyrics of a singular beauty and transparent clarity. The psychological factor has from time to time intrigued him, moreover, and we see him as a kind of link between the colourists and such poets as Mr. T. S. Eliot, Mr. Alfred Kreymborg, and Mr. Wallace Stevens. These poets are alike in achieving, by a kind of alchemy, the lyric in terms of the analytic: introspection is made to shine, to the subtly seen is given a delicate air of false simplicity. Mr. Stevens is closest to the colourists. His drift has been away from the analytic and towards the mere capture of a "tone." Mr. Kreymborg is a melodist and a mathematician. He takes a pleasure in making of his poems and plays charming diagrams of the emotions. Mr. Eliot has more of an eye for the sharp dramatic gesture, more of an ear for the trenchant dramatic phrase—he looks now at Laforgue, now at John Webster. His technical skill is remarkable, his perception of effect is precise, his range narrow, perhaps increasingly narrow.

Even so rapid and superficial a survey cannot but impress us with the essential anarchy of this poetic community. Lawlessness has seemed at times to be the prevailing note; no poetic principle has remained unchallenged, and we have only to look in the less prosperous suburbs and corners of this city to see to what lengths the bolder rebels, whether of the "Others" group or elsewhere, have gone. Ugliness and shapelessness have had their adherents among those whom æsthetic fatigue had rendered momentarily insensitive to the wellshaped; the fragmentary has had its adherents among those whom cynicism had rendered incapable of any service, too prolonged, to one idea. But the fetichists of the ugly and the fragmentary have exerted, none the less, a wholesome and fructifying influence. Whatever we feel about the ephemerality of the specifically ugly or fragmentary, we cannot escape a feeling that these, almost as importantly as the new realism or the new colourism, have enlarged what we might term the general "poetic consciousness" of the time. If there was a moment when the vogue of the disordered seemed to threaten, or predict, a widespread and rapid poetic decadence, that moment is safely past. The tendency is now in the other direction, and not the least interesting sign is the fact that many of the former apostles of the disordered are to-day experimenting with the things they yesterday despised—rhyme, metre, and the architecture of theme.

We have our affections, in all this, for the fragmentary and ugly as for the abrupt small hideousness—oddly akin to virility

—of gargoyles. We have our affections, too, for the rawest of our very raw realisms—for the maddest of our colourisms, the most idiosyncratic subtleties of our first introspectionists. Do we hesitate a little to ask something more of any of the poets whom we thus designate? What we fear is that in attempting to give us our something more, they will give us something less. What we want more of, what we see our contemporary poets as for the most part sadly deficient in, is " art." What we are afraid they will lose, if we urge them in this direction, is their young sharp brilliance. Urge them, however, we must. What our poets need most to learn is that poetry is not merely a matter of outpouring, of confession. It must be serious: it must be, if simple in appearance, none the less highly wrought: it must be packed. It must be beautifully elaborate rather than elaborately beautiful. It must be detached from dogma—we must keep it away from the all too prevalent lecture platform.

What we should like to see, in short, is a fusion, of the extraordinary range of poetic virtues with which our contemporary poets confront us, into one poetic consciousness. Do we cavil too much in assuming that no one of our poets offers us quite enough? Should we rather take comfort in the hope that many of their individual " personalities " are vivid enough to offset their onesidedness, and in that way to have a considerable guarantee of survival? We have mentioned that possibility before, and certainly it cannot be flatly dismissed. But I think it cannot be contested that many of these poets already feel, themselves, a sharper responsibility, a need for a greater comprehensiveness, for a finer and richer tactile equipment, a steadier view of what it is that constitutes beauty of form. They are immeasurably distant from any dry, cold perfectionism, however; and if we cheer them in taking the path that leads thither, it is in the hope of seeing them reach the halfway house rather than the summit. For to go all the way is to arrive exhausted; to go half way is to arrive with vigour. . . . That, however, is to interpose our own view and to lose our detachment. We return to a reiteration of our conclusion that American poetry is at the moment extraordinarily healthy. Its virtues are the virtues of all good poetry, and they are sufficient to persuade us that the future of English poetry lies as much in America as in England. Its faults are the faults of a culture that is immature. But again, we reiterate that we have here many cultures, and if some are immature, some are not. Let those who are too prone to diagnose us culturally from " Spoon River Anthology " or " Smoke and Steel " keep in mind also Mr. Robinson's " Merlin " and Mr. Frost's " North of Boston"; Mr. Fletcher's " Goblins and Pagodas " and Miss Lowell's " Can Grande's Castle."

CONRAD AIKEN

ART

THE problem of American Art is unlike that of any other country of the present or the past. We have not here the racial and historical foundation on which, until now, every art has been built and so our striving (it is far too soon to speak of success or failure) must be judged from another standpoint than the one to be taken in viewing an art that originates with its people or is directly transmitted from an older race. Egypt and ancient Mexico furnish examples of the first case, Italy and France of the second. When the latter countries were colonized by the Greeks, Phœnicians and others, they received a culture which could take on fresh vigour when grasped by a new race.

We did not start as a new race, but as Europeans possessing the same intellectual heritage as the men who stayed in the parent countries. Our problem was not one of receiving the ancient tradition from an invading or colonizing people who brought with them an art already formed. Ourselves the invaders and colonizers, our problem was to keep alive the ideas that we had had in Europe, or to take over those of our new home, or to evolve an art of our own.

To begin with the second possibility, the question of our relation to the ideas of the Indians may obviously be disposed of very briefly. The tribes encountered by the early settlers were in a state of savagery, and this fact, together with the constant warfare between the two races, is a sufficient explanation why we find no influence from the red men. Even where the Europeans encountered culture of a very high order, as in Mexico and Peru, the remoteness of the native ideas from those of the invading race prevented for centuries a just appreciation of the earliest and unquestionably the greatest art produced in the Western Hemisphere. It is only in quite recent years that we have realized its merit, and it is unlikely that even our present-day interest in the exotic arts will bring about any important influence from the Indians, although in regions such as our Southwest and the parts of Mexico where " Americanizing " has not yet killed their art-instinct, they are still producing beautiful work.

We have, of course, retained European ideals, but they have been conditioned by circumstances and we have not kept pace with Europe or even followed the course of the great art-movements until they were almost or quite superseded abroad. Our distance from the centres of ancient and modern culture on one hand, and the needs of building up the new continent on the other, combined to make our people lose interest in art, which, indeed, had never found a propitious soil among our British forebears. The case of literature is different. The love of it is an abiding one with the Anglo-Saxon race, and as Shakespeare and the Bible could be read in the frontier cabin almost as well as in London or Dublin, there was not the loss of knowledge of literature, the break in the production of it that we find in the case of the plastic arts.

It is easy to exaggerate on this score, however, forgetting that the art-instinct accumulated in a race for centuries is not to be lost by a period of neglect. When he goes to the museum, the American recognizes the same masters as does the European, but the smaller opportunity here to know the classic past has the double effect of keeping art-lovers in America in a far more reduced minority and at the same time of weakening the authority of tradition.

Not to speak of 17th or 18th century conditions, nor even of those of the 19th century, one need only consider the America of to-day to realize how little opportunity our people has to know art. In all but a few cities, Americans can learn only from reproductions and books, though even these are an immeasurably safer guide than the bad original works which are usually the first to arrive. When one thinks of the European countryside and the numberless small towns of all the old countries where there is no museum, one may be tempted to ask whether art conditions are so very different there. But they are different. There will be an old church, or some houses of a good period, or some objects in the houses, or—on the walls of the inn—some old prints handing on the tradition

of the great religious pictures (such things were made quite
commonly until recent times and have not entirely ceased to be
produced); a tradition of construction and of colour makes the
modern houses fit in quite acceptably with those of the past.
The centuries have built up a sense of fitness and beauty in
the making and wearing of costume; there will be some form
of folk-singing or other collective action of an artistic character, and thus the exceptional individual, born with a strong
instinct toward art, has surroundings and a foundation that are
lacking here. A striking proof of the difference between the
two continents is the effect of the war on art-interest: whereas
in America public attention has been turned away from art to
a most marked degree, Europe is producing and buying art
with a fervour that can only be explained by the desire to get
back to essentials after the years in which people were deprived of them.

Another phenomenon to be noted at this point is the dominance of women in American art-matters. It is unknown in
any other country. The vast majority of American men are
engrossed in the drive of work, their leisure goes to sport and
to the forms of entertainment that call for the smallest amount
of mental effort. The women, with their quicker sensibility
and their recognition of art as one of the things that mark the
higher orders of life, take over the furnishing of the home and
through this and the study that their greater leisure permits
them, exert a strong influence on the purchase of art-works
for private collections and even museums. The production
of the American painter and sculptor is also much affected as
a consequence, and in the direction of conventionality. I do
not claim that the level of art in America would be greatly
improved at present if it were the men instead of the women
who took the lead; perhaps, in view of the state of appreciation in our people, it would be lowered; but I maintain that
the fact that art is so much in the hands of women and the
suspicion among men that it carries with it some implication
of effeminacy are among the indications of American imma-
turity in art-appreciation. We cannot expect an art really
representative of America until there is a foundation of regard
for his work that the artist can build on. In the old civili-

zations the artist was meeting an active demand on the part of his people; in America, he has to seek desperately for a living. Albrecht Dürer summed up the difference between the two states of civilization when he wrote from Venice to a friend in the young Germany of his day: " Oh, how I shall freeze for this sun when I get home; here I am a gentleman, at home a parasite."

It will seem to many that even such famous words should not be repeated in a country where art is so often mentioned in the papers, where museums are springing up in large numbers, where unheard-of prices are paid for the work of famous men, and where even those who take no interest in art will accord it a sort of halo. But the very fact that it is relegated to the class of Sunday things instead of entering into everyday life shows that our colonial period—in the cultural sense of the word—is not yet passed. This should not be looked on as discouraging; it is natural that the formation of character and ideas should require time and I shall endeavour to show that the development is really a rapid and healthy one. The mistake Americans are most prone to, that of imagining the country to have reached a mature character and a valid expression, shows their eagerness to advance, and explains their readiness to tear down or to build up.

In the presence of such a spirit, one must see the mistakes of conservatism or of ignorance in due perspective. However trying to those who suffer from them at the time, they cannot fatally warp the growth that is going on. For years we retained a tariff that obstructed the coming into the country of works of art. That is a thing of the past, and as one of the reasons used to defend it was that it protected American artists against the foreigner, so, with the abolition of the tariff, there has been more of a tendency to judge works of art for their own qualities, without question of their nationality and without the puerile idea of nurturing the American product by keeping out work from abroad. How far this mistake had gone may be judged from the fact that in a certain city of our Far West a group of painters made a protest against the attention given by a newspaper to an exhibition sent out from New York, raising no question of the quality of the work, but merely demanding that local men be spoken of when art was discussed in the paper—which promptly acquiesced, and removed the critic from his position. The case may seem an extreme one, yet it illustrates the attitude of many of our collectors and even our museum authorities who, in the name of Americanism, are " helping to fame many, the sight of whose painting is a miseducation," to use a phrase that Mr. Berenson has applied to another matter.

There is no question to-day but that America must evolve along the lines of contemporary thought throughout the civilized world. There will be a local tang to our art. Certain enthusiasms and characteristics, as we develop them, may give emphasis to special phases of our production, but there is no longer the possibility of an isolated, autochthonic growth, such as seemed to be forecast up to about the time of the Revolution. The 18th century in America with its beautiful architecture, its fine craftsmen, and its painting, is only less far from the America of to-day than is the art of the Indians. We still put up buildings and make furniture in what is called the Colonial style, but so do we follow the even more remote Mission style of architecture in our Western States, and attempt to use Indian designs in decoration. The usual fate of attempted continuings of a bygone style overtakes all these efforts. Our materials are different, our needs are different, our time is different. A glance at two houses, as one speeds by in an automobile, tells us which is the real Colonial architecture, which the imitation. At the Jumel Mansion in New York it is easy to see which are the old parts, which the restorations, although enough time has passed since the latter were made to weather them to the tone of the original places.

In painting, the change that occurred after we became a republic is even more unmistakable. The English School underwent considerable modification when its representatives here began to work for themselves. Where Reynolds, Gainsborough, and Lawrence were consulting the old masters with such studious solicitude, Sir Joshua especially pursuing his enquiry into the processes of Titian, men like Copley and Blackburn were thrown back on such technical resources as they could find here and had to depend for progress on tightening their hold on character. Copley has the true note of the primitive in the intensity with which he studies his people, and must be reckoned with portraitists of almost the highest order.

What a change in the next generation! The more independent we are politically the more we come out of the isolation that gave us quiet and freedom to build up the admirable style of pre-Revolutionary days. And then there was so much to be done in getting our new institutions to work and our new land under cultivation, there was so much money to be made and so much to import from Europe. It is significant that the best painter of the period is John Vanderlyn, who had been sent to Paris to study under Ingres. Fine artist that Vanderlyn was, and informed by a greater tradition than Copley knew, he never reached the impressiveness of the latter.

I shall not attempt to describe at any length the various steps by which we rose from the artistic poverty which was ours in the earlier decades of the 19th century. My purpose is not to write even a short history of American art, but to enquire into its character and accomplishment. The test of these is evidently not what each period or school meant to the American artists before or after it, but how it compares with the rest of the world's art at its time. The thought occurs to one forcibly on hearing of the wildly exaggerated esteem— whether measured by words or by money—in which the more celebrated of American artists are held; one asks oneself how the given work would be considered in Europe by competent men. Few indeed are the reputations that will stand the test; and we do not need to go abroad to apply it, for the galleries of our large cities supply ample opportunity for the comparison.

Beginning with the landscape artists who are the earliest of the modern Americans to be looked on as our possible contribution to art, one's most impersonal observation is that in point of time, they, like their successors in this country, follow the Europeans of the school to which they belong by something like a generation. Now, art-ideas moved very rapidly in the 19th century, and—however mechanical an indication it may appear at first sight—it is almost a sure condemnation of a European painter to find him in one period trying to work with the formula of the generation before him. In America this test does not apply so well, for we must allow for the effect of distance and compare the American with his immediate contemporaries abroad only in proportion to the advance of time—which is to say in proportion to the convenience of travel to Europe and the possibility of seeing contemporary work here.

Thus when we consider that Inness, Wyant, and Martin were born about a generation after the Barbizon men and very nearly at the time of the French Impressionists, we shall not say that it was to the latter school that the Americans should have belonged. Whereas the European followers of Corot and Rousseau were merely *retardataires* who had not the intellectual power to seize on the ideas of their own day, the Americans could feel a little of the joy of discoverers through having themselves worked out some of the ideas of naturalism in their evolution from the earlier landscape painting in this country. And so if they add nothing to what the Frenchmen had done already—with an incomparably greater tradition to uphold them—our trio of nature-lovers expressed genuine sentiment, and Homer Martin pushed on to a quality of painting that often places him within hailing distance of the classic line which, in France, kept out of the swamps of sentimentality that engulfed the followers of Wyant and Inness here.

The cases of Winslow Homer and Albert P. Ryder have an interest aside from the actual works of the two painters. They are doubtless the strongest Americans of their time—and the ones who owe the least to Europe. It must be men of such a breed who will make real American art when we are ready to produce it. In any case their work must rank among our permanently valuable achievements: Homer's for the renewal of the sturdy self-reliance that we noted in Copley, Ryder's for the really noble design he so often obtained and for the grand and moving fidelity to a vision.

If their independence is so valuable a factor in both men's work, there is also to be noted the heavy price that each paid for having been reared in a provincial school. With a boldness of character that recalls Courbet, Winslow Homer fails utterly to hold a place in art analogous to that of the French realist, because all the power and ability that went into his work were unequal to compensating for his lack of the knowledge of form, of structure, of optical effect that Ingres and Delacroix, among others, furnished, ready to the hand, of Courbet. Thus Homer's painting goes on throughout his lifetime quite innocent of any real concern with the central problems of European picture-making and owes most of its strength to the second-rate quality of illustration. One hesitates to say that Ryder would have gone farther had he been born in France, yet the fact of his labouring for ten or fifteen years on many a small canvas, the very limited number of his works which has resulted from the difficulty he had in saying the thing that was in him, are marks of a bad training. His range is not a wide one, but the deep beauty he infused into his pictures is one of our chief reasons for confidence in the art-instinct that lies dormant in our people.

None of the men in the next group we must consider, the artists who enter fully into European painting, have the foundation of talent that Ryder had. Whistler is, of course, the painter to whom most Americans pin their faith in searching among their compatriots for an essential figure in 19th-century art. But take the first opportunity to see him with the great Frenchmen of his time: beside Degas his drawing is of a sickly weakness but slightly relieved by his sense of rhythm in line and form; beside Manet his colour and painting seem even more etiolated, and to save one's feeling for him from utter demolition one hastens to the usual American refuge of the sentiment and—in the etchings—to the Yankee excellence of the craftsmanship. The nocturnes really do have a felicity in their rendering of the poetry of the night that would make us regret their loss, and when the unhappy Whistlerian school has been forgotten (an artist must take *some* responsibility for his followers) we shall have more satisfaction in the butterfly that Whistler knew himself to be, since he adopted it as his signature. It is merit of no such slightness that we love in Ryder, and yet when we reach Chase and Sargent we find even less of basic talent, for which their immersion in the current of European painting could have furnished a finely tempered instrument of expression. Both men show the natural bent for painting that is often a valuable asset and often—as in their case—a source of danger. They do not enrich our annals by any great works, but they do the country an immense service when they cause its students and collectors to take one of the final steps in the direction of the live tradition of Europe. They never appreciated what was greatest among their contemporaries, and failing to have this grasp of the creative impulse and of the new principles that were at work in Paris, they offered clever manipulations of the material as a substitute. Feeling the insufficience of this, Sargent has tried the grave style of the early Italians in his decorations at the Public Library in Boston. But his Biblical personages get him no nearer to the essentials of art than the society people of whom he has done so many likenesses. In Boston, it is Chavannes who shows which is the great tradition of the period and how it accords with the classic past. Sargent is perhaps most American in his unreadiness to perceive the immense things that Europe, modern and ancient, had to offer him.

Even so, with Chase and Sargent we find ourselves far nearer the period when American artists shall partake in art-ideas during their moment of full fertility. Our Impressionists are only a decade or two behind the Frenchman, and while one must not slip into a too easy trick of rating talent by the time of its appearance, one cannot fail to be struck by the fact that John H. Twachtman and J. Alden Weir approached the quality of their French preceptors with far greater closeness than that with which the Inness-Wyant group followed the Barbizon men. Much as there is of charm and sound pictorial knowledge in Twachtman's work and Weir's, one feels that they are not yet deep enough in the great tradition to go on to an art of their own creation, and we have to content ourselves with giving them a place among the Impressionists of secondary rank.

An interesting case among the Americans who made the serious study of European art that began soon after the middle of the 19th century, is that of John La Farge. We know the history of his seeking, his copying, his associations, speculations, and travels. All his life he is the man from the new country asking the dead and the living representatives of the classic tradition for help. How little we see of the man himself in the mosaic of charming things that make up his art. Winslow Homer exists as a personality, ill-educated and crude, but affirmative and arresting. La Farge disappears in the smoke of the incense that he burns before the various shrines to which his eclecticism led him.

If not to be admired as a great artist, he was a man of great gifts and a genuine appreciator of the masters. Therefore, he is not to be confused for a moment with the ignoble *pasticheurs* who achieve office and honours in the anæmic institutions with which we imitate the academies and salons of Europe. These are among the youthful errors I mentioned on an earlier page —depressing enough when one sees the acres of " decorative " abominations which fill our state-houses, courts, and libraries, but in reality of no great importance as a detriment to our culture. Like the soldiers' monuments, the dead architecture, the tasteless manufactured articles of common use, they sink so far below any level of art that the public is scarcely affected by them. Only the persons trained in schools to admire the painting of a Mr. E. H. Blashfield or the sculpture of a Mr. Daniel C. French ever try to think of them as beautiful; the rest of the public takes them on faith as something that goes with the building, like the " frescoed " cupids to be found in the halls of apartment houses or the tin cupolas and minarets on the roof. The popular magazine-illustrators, poor as they are, have more power to mislead than our quasi-official nonentities.

Between the pseudo-classic decorators and the frankly " lowbrow " artists of the commercial publications, the posters, and the advertisements, there is the large class of men whose work is seen at the annual exhibitions, the dealers' galleries, and the American sections of the museums. They partake of the vice of each of the other two classes: the easily learned formula for their product being a more or less thorough schooling in some style derived from the past, plus an optimistic or " redblooded " or else gently melancholy attitude toward the subject. Velasquez has been the main victim of their caricature in the later years, but a little Chinese, Florentine, Impressionist, or even Cubist style will often be added to give a look of " modernity " to the work. As long as there is a recognizable proficiency in drawing and painting (it is of course only for the cheaper trade that the picture has to be guaranteed as done by hand), the erudite patron or museum trustee is assured of the seriousness of the artist's intentions, while to make the thing take with the general buyer, the most important matter is judgment as to the type of American girl, the virile male, or the romantic or homely landscape that our public likes to live with.

The only excuse for mentioning such things in an essay on American art is that they help to define it by contrast—for these pictures are neither art nor American. The disease of which they are an outward sign infects Europe almost as much as it does our own country, and there is hardly a distinguishing mark to tell whether the Salon picture was done in Madrid, Berlin, or Indianapolis. A sentence from an eminent American critic, Russell Sturgis, gives the key to the situation. He said, " The power of abstract design is lost to the modern world,—we must paint pictures or carve expressional groups when we wish to adorn." In the half generation that has passed since these words were spoken, the French have proven by several arts based entirely on abstract design that the power for it was not lost to the world and that men still know the difference between expression by form and colour and expression by concrete ideas.

Throughout this survey I have taken painting as the index to the art-instinct of America, and as we glance again at even our best painters we see that it is on concrete ideas that they have built: on character in portraiture with Copley, on romantic vision with Ryder, on observation of appearances with Homer. Precisely the reason for Whistler's great success among his countrymen was the promise of release he afforded by his reaching out for the design and colour of the Orient, with which one associates also his spoken words, offering us " harmonies " and " symphonies " in place of the art built on intellectual elements that we had had before. The fact that Whistler himself was not strong enough in his grasp of tradition, or of a nature to achieve an important result along the lines he pointed to, does not change the issue. We had begun to be aware of the repression of instinct that was marking American life. We had recognized that the satisfaction of the senses, quite as much as intellectual pleasure, is to be demanded of art. Puritan morality and Quaker drabness had turned us away from any such conception, and when they took notice of art at all, it was for its educational value, either to inculcate religious or patriotic ideas, or for its connection with the classic past.

Add to this the utilitarian needs of a country that had to build rapidly, caring for cheapness more than for permanence (so little of the building, in fact, was intended to be permanent), and one has an explanation of the absence of architectural quality in the American houses of the last hundred years. The characteristic of building in the time is seen in the lifeless blocks of " brownstone fronts," in the apartments that have so little of the home about them that in the restlessness of his search for a place to live satisfactorily, the American of the cities has earned the name of the " van-dweller,"—one sees the thing again in the abject monotony of farm-houses and country residences. Their spirit, or lack of it, is continued in furniture and decoration. One understands why Europe has been the magic word for countless thousands of Americans. Perhaps it was the palaces and museums that they set out to see and that they told about on their return, but more impressive to them—because more satisfying to their hunger for a beauty near to their daily lives—was the sight of an Italian village built with love for hillsides and with understanding of the forms of the hill and of the type of construction that would suit it. Or was it the cheeriness of the solid Dutch houses whose clear reds and blacks look out so robustly through the green of the trees that border the canals? The bright-coloured clothing of the peasants became delightful to the traveller, even if he still gave it a pitying smile when he saw it again on the immigrant here; and the humble foreigner, anxious to fit in to his new surroundings, hastened to tone down the vivacity of his native costume to the colourlessness of the American farmer's or workman's garb. In place of the gay pink or green stucco of his cottage at home, the immigrant got more or less of sanitary plumbing, higher wages, and other material benefits, to recompense him for the life he had left behind.

The life! That was the magic that Europe held for our visitors. They might return to the big enterprises, the big problems here, and feel that America was home because they had a share in its growth, but their nostalgia for the old countries continued to grow in the measure that they came to appreciate the wisdom with which life was ordered there—as they realized how the stable institutions, the old religions, festivals, traditions, all the things that flower into art, had resisted the terrific change that the industrial revolution had brought into the 19th century. Behind all questions of the coming of objects of art into this country or the appearance of new artists or new schools here, lies this most pivotal matter of the elements of art in American life. They need not be, they cannot be the same as those in European life, but it is futile to think of having an art here if we deny ourselves the ideas and feelings of which art has been made—the joy and awe of life that the Greek responded to in his marbles, the Italian in his frescoes, the Spaniard, the Fleming, the Dutchman, and the Frenchman in his canvases. Copying the externals of their work without again living their lives can result only in academism—bad sculpture and bad pictures.

It was not as a protest against bad art, local or foreign, that the International Exhibition of 1913 was organized, and it is very solidly to the credit of our public that it did not regard the event in that negative fashion—but as a positive thing, a revelation of the later schools of European painting of which it had been kept in ignorance by the will of the academies here and abroad. The " Armory Show," as it was called, drew forth a storm of ridicule, but it also attracted such hundreds of thousands of visitors as no current exhibition had ever gathered in this country before. The first contact of our public with the arts that have succeeded Impressionism—with the painting of Cézanne, Redon, Gauguin, van Gogh, Matisse, the Cubists, and others—was made at this epoch-marking show. With the jeers that it received there were not a few hosannas, and even the vast majority of visitors—doubtful as to the exact value of the various exhibits, knew that qualities existed in the new schools that had never been seen here and that were needed. Some three hundred works went from the walls of the Armory to form a vanguard for the far more important purchases of modern art that have since been building up our collections; so that at the moment of this writing an exhibition can be opened at the Metropolitan Museum which, while representing a mere fraction of the wealth of such pictures in American possession, gives a superb idea of the great schools of the later 19th century and the 20th century in France. It is worthy of note that in its response to the great show of 1913 and to the smaller ones that followed, America was only giving, in a stronger form, the measure of a power of appreciation it had shown before. Earlier examples of this are to be found in the great collections of Barbizon and Impressionist pictures here. A thing that should weigh against many a discouraging feature of our art-conditions is the fact that an American museum was the first in the world, and the only one during the lifetime of Manet, to hang works by that master.

Returning now to our own painting, one man in this country resisted with complete success the test of an exhibition with the greatest of recent painters from abroad. It was Mr. Maurice B. Prendergast, who for thirty years had been joyously labouring at an art which showed its derivation from the best French painting of his day, its admirable acceptances of the teaching of Cézanne (scarcely a name even in Europe when Mr. Prendergast first studied him), and its humorous and affectionate appreciation of the American scenes that the artist had known from his youth. In original and logical design, in brilliant colour that yet had the mellowness of a splendid wine, he expresses the modern faith in the world we see and makes it lovable. At last we welcome an art in accord with the finest of the ancient-modern tradition, as European critics have since declared; yet it remains American in provenance and in the air of unconscious honesty that has always been a characteristic of the good work of this country.

The latest wave of influence to come over American art has almost been the most far-reaching and invigorating. To go further than this assertion, at least in the matter of individuals, would be to forego the support of too large a part of that body of opinion that I know to be behind my statements throughout this essay. Art-matters must, in the final analysis, be stated dogmatically, but I am unwilling to speak of the schools now developing save in a general way, especially as the most interesting men in them have still to reach a definitive point in their evolution. They are abreast or nearly abreast of the ideas of Europe, and there is an admirable vigour in the work that some individuals are producing with those ideas. But the changes brought about by the International are still too recent for us to expect the most important results from them for a number of years. The general condition here has probably never been as good before.

I have, till now, spoken only of the more traditional aspects of art—the kind one finds in museums—and that last word calls for at least a mention of the great wealth of art-objects that are heaping up in our public collections, and in the private galleries which so often come to the aid of the museums.

There is, however, another phase of our subject that demands comment, if only as a point of departure for the study that will one day be given to the American art that is not yet recognized by its public or its makers as one of our main expressions. The steel bridges, the steel buildings, the newly designed machines, and utensils of all kinds we are bringing forth show an adaptation to function that is recognized as one of the great elements of art. Perhaps the process has not yet gone far enough for us to look on these things as fully developed works of art, perhaps we shall still need some influence from Europe to make us see the possibilities we have here, or again, it may be in America that the impetus to creation along such lines will be the stronger. At all events we may feel sure that the study of the classics, ancient and modern, which is spreading throughout the country has, in some men, reached a point of saturation which permits the going on to new discovery, and we may be confident of the ability of our artists to make good use of their advantage.

WALTER PACH

THE THEATRE

OF the perceptible gradual improvement in the American popular taste so far as the arts are concerned, the theatre as we currently engage it offers, comparatively, the least evidence. The best-selling E. Phillips Oppenheims, Robert W. Chamberses, and Eleanor H. Porters of yesterday have given considerable ground to Wharton and Bennett, to Hergesheimer and Wells. The audiences in support of Stokowski, the Flonzaley Quartette, the Philharmonic, the great piano and violin virtuosos, and the recognized singers, are yearly augmented. Fine painting and fine sculpture find an increasing sober appreciation. The circulation of *Munsey's Magazine* falls, and that of the *Atlantic Monthly* rises. But the best play of an American theatrical season, say a " Beyond the Horizon," has still to struggle for full breath, while across the street the receipts of some " Ladies' Night," " Gold Diggers," or " Bat," running on without end, mount to the half-million mark.

If one speaks of the New York theatre as the American theatre, one speaks with an exaggerated degree of critical charity, for the New York theatre—so far as there is any taste in the American theatre—is the native theatre at its fullest flower. Persons insufficiently acquainted with the theatre have a fondness for controverting this, but the bookkeeping departments offer concrete testimony that, if good drama is supported at all, it is supported in the metropolitan theatre, not in the so-called " road " theatre. The New York theatre supports an American playwright like Booth Tarkington when he does his best in " Clarence," where the road theatre supports him only when he does his worst, as in " Mister Antonio." The New York theatre, these same financial records prove, supports Shaw, O'Neill, Galsworthy, Bahr, and others of their kind, at least in sufficient degree to permit them to pay their way, where the theatre of Philadelphia, Boston, Cleveland, Chicago, St. Louis, Baltimore, and Pittsburgh spells failure for them. Save it be played by an actor or actress of great popular favour, a first-rate piece of dramatic writing has to-day hardly a chance for success outside of New York. These other cities of America, though they are gradually reading better books and patronizing better music and finer musicians, are almost drama-deaf. " There is, in New York," the experienced Mr. William A. Brady has said to me, " an audience of at least fifteen thousand for any really good play. That isn't a large audience; it won't turn the play into a profitable theatrical venture; but it is a damned sight larger audience than you'll be able to find in any other American city." Let the native sons of the cities thus cruelly maligned, before they emit their habitual bellows of protest, consider, once they fared forth from New York, the fate of nine-tenths of the first-rate plays produced in the American theatre without the hocus-pocus of fancy box-office " stars " during the last ten years.

The theatrical taste of America at the present time, outside of the metropolis, is demonstrated by the box-office returns to be one that venerates the wall-motto *opera* of Mr. William Hodge and the spectacular imbecilities of Mr. Richard Walton Tully above the finest work of the best of its native dramatists like O'Neill, and above the finest work of the best of the modern Europeans. In the metropolis, an O'Neill's " Beyond the Horizon," a Galsworthy's " Justice," a Shaw's " Androcles," at least can live; sometimes, indeed, live and prosper. But for one respectable piece of dramatic writing that succeeds outside of New York, there are twenty that fail miserably. The theatrical culture of the American countryside is in the main of a piece with that of the French countryside, and to the nature of the latter the statistics of the French provincial theatres offer a brilliant and dismaying attestation. Save a good play first obtain the endorsement of New York, it is to-day impossible to get a paying audience for it in any American city of size after the first curiosity-provoking performance. These audiences buy, not good drama, but notoriety. Were all communication with the city of New York suddenly to be cut off for six months, the only theatrical ventures that could earn their way outside would be the Ziegfeld " Follies," the Winter Garden shows, " Ben Hur," and the hack dramatizations of the

trashier best-sellers like " Pollyanna " and " Daddy Longlegs."
This is not postured for sensational effect. It is literally true.
So true, in fact, that there is to-day not a single producer in
the American theatre who can afford to, or who will, risk the
loss of a mere four weeks' preliminary " road " trial of a first-
class play. If he cannot get a New York theatre for his production, he places it in the storehouse temporarily until he
can obtain a metropolitan booking rather than hazard the financial loss that, nine times in ten, is certain to come to him.

More and more, the better producing managers—men like
Hopkins, William Harris, Jr., Ames, *et al.*—are coming to open
their plays in New York " cold," that is, without the former
experimental performances in thitherward cities. And more
and more, they are coming to realize to their sorrow that, unless New York supports these plays of the better sort, they can
look for no support elsewhere. Chicago, boasting of its hospitality to sound artistic endeavour, spent thirty-five hundred
dollars on a drama by Eugene O'Neill in the same week that it
spent forty-five thousand dollars on Al Jolson's Winter Garden show. Boston, one of the first cities to rush frantically
forward with proofs of its old New England culture, has turned
into a prompt and disastrous failure every first-rate play presented in its theatres without a widely advertised star actor
during the last five years, and at the same time has made a
fortune for the astute Mr. A. H. Woods, who, gauging its culture accurately, has sent it " Up in Mabel's Room," " Getting
Gertie's Garter," and similar spicy boudoir and hay-mow
farces, together with Miss Theda Bara in " The Blue Flame."
(It is no secret among the theatrical managers that the only
way to bring the culture of Boston to the box-office window is
through a campaign of raw advertising: the rawer the better.
Thus the Boston Sunday newspaper advertisements of " Up in
Mabel's Room " were made to display a girl lying on a bed,
with the suggestive catch-lines, " 10,000 Visitors Weekly " and
" Such a Funny Feeling." Thus, the advertisements of another exhibit presented a rear view of a nude female with the
title of the show, " Oh, Mommer," printed across the ample
buttocks. Thus, the advertisements of a Winter Garden music
show, alluding to the runway used in these exhibitions, chris-

tened it " The Bridge of Thighs.")   No play presented in
Philadelphia since " The Girl with the Whooping Cough "
(subsequently suppressed by the New York police authorities
on the ground of indecency) has been patronized to the extent
where it has been found necessary to call out the police reserves to maintain order, as was the case when the play in point
was produced.   Washington is a cultural wilderness; I have
personally attended the premières of ten highly meritorious
dramas in the national capital in the last six years and can
report accurately on the quality of the receptions accorded to
them.   Washington would seem still to be what it was some
fifteen years or so ago when, upon the initial revelation of
Barrie's " Peter Pan," it essayed to boo it into permanent discard.   Baltimore, Detroit (save during the height of the war
prosperity when the poor bohicks, wops, and Greeks in the
automobile works found themselves suddenly able to buy theatre seats regularly), Cleveland, St. Louis, San Francisco—
the story is the same.   Honourable drama spells ruin; legs,
lewdness and sentimentality spell riches.

In comparison with the taste of the great American cultural
prairie whereon these cities are situated, the city of New
York, as I have written, looms up an æsthetic Athens.   In
New York, too, there is prosperity for bare knees, bed hu-
mours, and " Peg o' My Heart " bathos, but not alone for
these.   Side by side with the audiences that crowd into the
leg shows, the couch farces, and the uplift sermons are audiences of considerable bulk that make profitable the production
of such more estimable things as Shaw's " Heartbreak House,"
O'Neill's " Emperor Jones," the plays of St. John Ervine and
Dunsany, of Tolstoy and Hauptmann, of Bahr and Benavente
and Guitry.   True enough, in order to get to the theatres in
which certain of these plays are revealed, one is compelled to
travel in a taxicab several miles from Broadway—and at times
has to sit with the chauffeur in order to pilot him to far streets
and alleyways that are not within his sophisticated ken—
but, once one gets to the theatres, one finds them full, and
their audiences enthusiastic and responsive.   The culture of
the American theatre—in so far as it exists—may be said, in
fact, to be an alleyway culture.   Almost without exception in

the last dozen years and more have the best dramatists of Europe and of our own country been driven up alleyways and side-streets for their first American hearing. Up these dark alleys and in these remote malls alone have they been able to find a sufficient intelligence for their warés. Hervieu, Shaw, Echegaray, Strindberg, Björnson, Dunsany, Masefield, Ervine, Bergström, Chekhov, Andreyev, Benavente, O'Neill— hese and many others of eminence owe their New York introduction to the side-street American who, in the majority of cases, is found upon analysis to be of fifty per cent. foreign blood. And what thus holds true of New York holds equally true in most of the other cities. In most of such cities, that is, as have arrived at a degree of theatrical polish sufficient to boast a little playhouse up an ulterior mews.

The more general American theatrical taste, reflected perhaps most fairly in such things as the idiotic endorsements of the Drama League and the various " white lists " of the different religious organizations, is—for all the undeniable fact that it seems gradually to be improving—still in the playing-blocks and tin choo-choo-car stage. Satire, unless it be of the most obvious sort and approach easily assimilable burlesque, spells failure for a producer. A point of view that does not effect a compromise with sentimentality spells failure for a dramatist. Sex, save it be presented in terms of a seltzer-siphon, " Abendstern," or the *Police Gazette,* spells failure for both. The leaders in the propagation of this low taste are not the American managers and producers, as is commonly maintained, but the American playwrights. During the seventeen years of my active critical interest in the theatre, I have not encountered a single honest piece of dramatic writing from an American hand that could not get a hearing—and an intelligent hearing—from one or another of these regularly abused managers and producers. And during these years I have, by virtue of my joint professional duties as critic and co-editor of a sympathetic literary periodical, read perhaps nine-tenths of the dramatic manuscripts which aspiring young America has confected. This young America, loud in its inveighing against the managers and producers, has in the space of time indicated produced very, very little that was worth producing, and that little has promptly found a market. A bad workman is always indignant. But I know of no good American play that either has not already been produced, or has not been bought for future production. Any good play by an American will find its producer readily enough. The first manager who read "Beyond the Horizon" bought it immediately he laid the manuscript down, and this, recall, was its professionally unknown author's first three-act play. The American theatre has altered in this department; the last fifteen years have wrought a tonic change.

No, the fault is not with the managers and producers, but with the playwrights. The latter, where they are not mere parrots, are cowards. Young and old, new and experienced, talented and talentless alike, they are in the mass so many *Saturday Evening Post* souls, alone dreaming of and intent upon achieving a sufficient financial gain to transmute the Ford into a Rolls-Royce and the Hudson Bay seal collar into Russian sable. A baby cannot be nourished and developed physically upon water; a theatrical public, for all its potential willingness, cannot be developed æsthetically upon a diet of snide writing. In the American theatre of the present time there are not more than two, or at most three, playwrights out of all the hundreds, who retain in their hearts a determined and uncorrupted purpose. Take away young O'Neill, and give a bit of ground to Miss Rita Wellman (whose accomplishment is still too vague for fixed appraisal), and there is next to nothing left. Flashes of talent, yes, but only flashes. Craven's "Too Many Cooks" and "The First Year" are observant, highly skilful depictions of the American scene, but they are dramatic literature only in the degree that "Main Street" and "This Side of Paradise" are literature. With the extraordinary "Papa," Miss Zoë Akins gave up and surrendered—at least temporarily—to the box-office skull and cross-bones. Until Tarkington proves that "Clarence" was not a happy accident in the long and unbroken line of "Up from Nowhere," "Mister Antonio," "The Country Cousin," "The Man from Home," "Cameo Kirby," "Your Humble Servant," "Springtime," "Getting a Polish," "The Gibson Upright," and "Poldekin," we shall have to hold up our decision on him. George Ade, the great promise of authentic American drama, is no more; he pulled in his oars, alas, in mid-stream. Joseph Medill Patterson, an honest dramatist, fell through the bridge while not yet half way across. The rest? Well, the rest are the Augustus Thomases, left-overs from the last generation, proficient technicians with empty heads, or youngsters still dramatically wet behind the ears. The rest of the rest? Ticket salesmen.

In no civilized country in the world to-day is there among playwrights so little fervour for sound drama as in the United States. In England, they at least try, in a measure, to write well; in Germany, to experiment bravely in new forms; in France, to philosophize either seriously or lightly upon life as they find it; in Russia, to treat soberly of problems physical and spiritual; in Spain, to depict the Spanish heart and conscience and atmosphere; in Ireland, to reflect the life and thoughts, the humour and tragedy and encompassing aspirations, of a people. And in the United States—what? In the United States, with hardly more than two exceptions, there is at the moment not a playwright who isn't thinking of " success " above honest work. Good and bad craftsmen alike, they all think the same. Gold, silver, copper. And the result is an endless procession of revamped crook plays, detective plays, Cinderella plays, boudoir plays, bucolic plays: fodder for doodles. The cowardice before the golden snake's eye spreads to the highest as well as to the lowest. Integrity is thrown overboard as the ship is steered unswervingly into the Golden Gate. The unquestionable talent of an Avery Hopwood—a George M. Cohan—a George Bronson-Howard—is deliberately self-corrupted.

The American professional theatre is to-day at once the richest theatre in the world, and the poorest. Financially, it reaches to the stars; culturally, with exception so small as to be negligible, it reaches to the drains. For both of these reaches, the American newspaper stands largely responsible. The American newspaper, in general, regards the theatre with contempt. My early years, upon leaving the university, were spent on the staff of one of them—the leading daily journal of America, it was in those days—and I shall never forget its attitude toward the theatre: cheap, hollow, debased. If a play was produced by a manager who advertised extensively in the paper, it was praised out of all reason. If a play was produced by a manager who happened to be *persona non grata* in the office, it was dismissed with a brief reportorial notice. If a play was produced by a new and enterprising manager on the night of another production in a theatre patronized by fashionable audiences—the Empire, say—the former play, however worthy an effort it might be, was let down with a stick or two that there might be room to print the names of the fashionables who were in the Empire seats. The surface of things has changed somewhat since then, but the situation at bottom is much the same. A talented young reviewer writes honestly of a tawdry play in the *Evening Sun;* the producer of the play, an office favourite, complains; and the young reviewer is promptly discharged. A moving picture producer takes half-page advertisements of his forthcoming *opus* in the New York newspapers, and the screen exhibit, a piece of trash, is hailed as a master work. Let a new drama by Gerhart Hauptmann be presented in the Park Theatre to-night and let Mr. John Barrymore also appear at eight-thirty in a play by some obscure hack at the Empire, and there will not be a single newspaper in the whole of New York City that will not review the latter flashy affair at the expense of the former.

It is not that the newspapers, in New York as elsewhere, are dishonest—few of them are actually dishonest; it is that they are suburban, shoddy, cheap. With only four exceptions that I can think of, the American newspaper, wherever you find it, treats the theatre as if it were of very much less importance than baseball and of but a shade more importance than a rape in Perth Amboy, New Jersey. Two columns are given freely to the latest development in bootlegging in Harlem, and a begrudged half-column to a play by John Galsworthy. A society woman is accused by her husband of having been guilty of adultery with a half-breed Indian, and the allotment is four columns. On the same day, a Shakespearean production is mounted by the most artistic producer in the American theatre, and the allotment of space is two-thirds of a column. The reply of the newspapers is, " Well, we give the public what it wants! And it is more greatly interested in scandal than in Shakespeare." Have not then the theatrical managers the right to reply in the same terms? And when they do, some of them, disgustedly reply in the same terms, what is the hypo-critical appraisal of their offerings that the selfsame newspapers vouchsafe to them? If the New York *Times* devotes three columns to a dirty divorce case, I fail to see how it can with justice or reason permit its theatrical reviewer indignantly to denounce Mr. A. H. Woods in the same issue for devoting three hours to a dirty farce.

The American drama, like the American audience, lacks re-pose. This is ever logically true of a new civilization. Time must mellow the mind and heart before drama may achieve depth and richness; time must mellow the mind and heart be-fore an audience may achieve the mood of calm deliberation. Youth is a rare and precious attribute, but youth, for all its fine courage and derring-do, is inclined to be superficial. Its emotions and its reactions are respectively of and to the pri-mary colours; the pastels it is impatient of. The American theatre, drama, and audience are the theatre, drama, and audi-ence of the metaphysical and emotional primary colours: sub-stantial, vivid, but all too obvious and glaring. I speak, of course, generally. For there are a few notable exceptions to the rule, and these exceptions portend in the American theatre the first signs of the coming dawn. A producer like Arthur Hopkins, perhaps the first American man of the theatre gifted with a genuine passion for fine and beautiful things and the talent with which to do—or at least try to do—them; a drama-tist like young O'Neill, permitting no compromise or equivoke in the upward sweep of his dynamic imagination; an actor like Arnold Daly and an actress like Margaret Anglin to whom failure in the service of honest drama means absolutely nothing—these are they who inspire our faith in the future. Nor do they stand alone. Hume and Moeller, Jones, Peters, Simonson and Bel-Geddes, Glaspell, Wellman and Pottle—such youngsters, too, are dreaming their dreams, some of them, true enough, still silly dreams, but yet dreams. And the dreaming spreads, spreads. . . .

But in its slow and brave ascent, the American theatre is

still heavily retarded by the insular forces that, as in no other theatre save the English, operate in the Republic. The fight against outworn convention is a brave and bitter fight, but victory still rests mainly on the banners of the Philistines. The drama that dismisses sentimentality for truth, that seeks to face squarely the tragedy and comedy of love and life, that declines to pigeon-hole itself, and that hazards to view the American scene with cosmopolitan eyes, is confronted at every turn by the native Puritanism (as often shammed as inborn), and by the native parochialism and hypocrisy. The production that derides all stereotype—all the ridiculous and mossy rubber-stamps—is in turn derided. The actor or actress who essays to filter a rôle through the mind of a human being instead of through the mind of a rouged marionette is made mock of. Here, the playgoing public finds its leaders in three-fourths of the newspaper reviewing chairs, chairs influenced, directly or indirectly, by an intrinsic inexperience and ignorance, or by an extrinsic suggestion of " policy."

The American theatre and drama have long suffered from being slaves to the national hypocrisy. Only on rare occasions have they been successful in casting off the shackles, and then but momentarily. The pull against them is stubborn, strong. Cracking the black snake across their backs are a hundred padrones: newspapers trembling at the thought of offending their advertisers, religious orders poking their noses into what should not concern them, corrupt moral uplift organizations and lecherous anti-vice societies itching for the gauds of publicity, meddling college professors augmenting their humble wage by writing twenty-dollar articles on subjects they know nothing about for the Sunday supplements, ex-real estate reporters and divorcée interviewers become " dramatic critics," notoriety seeking clergymen, snide producers trying to protect their snide enterprises from the dangers of the invasion of truth and beauty. Let a group of drama-loving and theatre-loving young men, resourceful, skilful, and successful, come upon the scene, as the Washington Square Players came, let them bring flashes of authentic dramatic art into their native theatre, and against them is promptly hurled the jealous irony of the Old Guard that is dead, but never surrenders. Let

a young playwright like Zoë Akins write an admirable fantastic comedy (" Papa "), and against her are brought all the
weapons of the morals-in-art mountebanks. Let a producer
like Hopkins break away from the mantel-leaning histrionism
and palm-pot investiture, and against him is brought up the
curt dismissal of freakishness.

The native theatre, for all the fact that it is on the way,
is not yet ready for such things as demand a degree of civilization for receptive and remunerative appreciation. The " Pegs
o' My Heart " and " Pollyannas," the " Turn to the Rights "
and " Lightnin's " still make millions, while the bulk of finer
things languish and perish. I speak, remember, not of the
theatre of one city, but of the theatre of the land. This theatre, considering it in so far as possible as a unit, is still not
much above the Midway Plaisance, the honk-a-tonk, the Sunday School charade. That one, or maybe two, foreign national
theatres may not be much better is no apology. Such foreign
theatres—the French, say—are less national theatres than one-
city theatres, for Paris is France. But the American theatre
spreads from coast to coast. What it spreads, I have herein
tried to suggest.

GEORGE JEAN NATHAN

ECONOMIC OPINION

IF there were conscious restriction upon the expression of
opinion in America, this essay would possess the pompous
certainty of an official document. Instead of threading its
hazardous way through a mass of confused thought, it would
record in formal terms acceptable utterance. In fact, the very
restrictions upon thought and speech, with the aid of scissors
and a license to speech, could easily be turned into a statement of the reputable theory of the welfare of the community.

Unluckily, however, American life has not been arranged to
make matters easy for the interpreter of economic opinion.
Every American is conscious of a right to his own opinion
about " why all of us taken together are as well off as we are "
and " why some of us are better off and others of us worse off
than the average of us." Whether this privilege comes from
the Bill of Rights, the constitution of the United States, or his
Simian ancestry, he could not say; but he is fully assured that
it is " inalienable " and " indefeasible." No restriction of
birth, breeding, position, or wealth limits his right to an
opinion or persuades him to esteem his more fortunate neighbour's more highly than his own. Nor do intellectual limitations check the flow of words and of ideas. No one is examined upon the growth of industrialism, the institutions which
make up the economic order, or the nature of an industrial
problem before he is allowed to speak. In fact, the idea that
a knowledge of the facts about the subject under discussion, or
of the principles to be applied to it, is essential to the right
to an opinion is a strange notion little understood here. Even
if occasionally some potentate attempts a mild restriction upon
the spoken or the written word, it checks only those who talk
directly and therefore clumsily. Its principal effect is through
provocation to add mightily to the volume of opinion.

The result is a conglomerate mass of opinion that sprawls
through the known realm of economics and into regions un-

charted. The mighty men of finance spin a theory of national welfare in terms of foreign concessions no more glibly than the knights of the road in solemn convention solve with words the riddle of unemployment. The newly enfranchised women compete with the members of the Dynamite Club in proposals for setting the industrial cosmos in order. Economic opinion bobs up in the financial journals, " the labour press," the periodicals of the " learned " societies, and in all the " Christian " advocates. It shows itself boldly in political speeches, in directors' reports, in public hearings, and in propagandist sheets. It lurks craftily in editorials, moving pictures, drawing-room lectures, poems, cartoons, and hymns. It ranges from the sonorous apologies for the existing order voiced by the Aaron Baal Professor of Christian Homiletics in the Midas Theological Seminary to the staccato denunciation of what is by the Sons of Martha Professor of Proletarian Tactics in the Karl Marx College for Workers.

A mere semblance of order is given to this heterogeneous mass of opinion by the conditions which make it. A common system of legal, business, and social usages is to be found the country over. This has left its impress too firmly in the assumptions which underlie thought to allow this material to be separate bits from so many mental universes. The prevailing scheme of economic life is so definitely established as to force its imprint upon the opinion that moves about it. Acceptable opinion is created in its likeness, and unacceptable opinion becomes acceptable opinion when the negatives are skilfully extracted. Protestants are concerned rather with eliminating the " evils " of " capitalism " than with eradicating it root and branch. Protestantism is rather a variant of orthodox doctrine than an independent system of thought. Radical opinion that is likely to pass the decent bounds of negation is kept small in volume by a press which allows it little upon which to feed. Accordingly, varied doctrines wear the semblance of unity.

Such elements, however, do not free this adventure into speculation from its perils. They merely make the hazards mortal. In the paragraphs below the economic opinion in America is recklessly resolved into four main classes. These are the *laissez-faire* opinion of the mid-19th century, the conventional " case for capitalism," the protestant demand for " control," and the academic insistence upon conscious " direction " of industrial change. Radical opinion gets a competent judgment elsewhere in this volume. Even in this bold outline the opinions of small minorities are lost to sight, and views and doctrines, seemingly alien to the authors who know their subtle differences, are often blurred into a single picture. To avoid the charge that the lion and the lamb have been pictured as one, no names have been called. Here as elsewhere particulars will rise up to curse their generalizations, and the whole will be found to be entirely too scanty to be disbursed into its parts. But the chance must be taken, and, after all, truth does not reside in copy-book mottoes.

I

The current types of economic opinion in this country all have a common origin. The men who express them are but a scant generation or two removed from the country or the small town. The opinions are so many variants of a stream of thought which goes back to a mid-19th century America of small towns and open country. This primitive economic opinion was formed out of the dust of the ground in the likeness of an exploitative America. The conditions which shaped it might be set forth in two lines of a school history thus: First, abundant natural resources; second, a scanty population; and third, the principle of letting the individual alone.

It was a chance at an economic opportunity which made America of the 19th century the " land of promise." The raw materials of personal wealth were here in soil, stream, and mine. The equipment necessary to the crude exploitative farming of the time was easy to possess. Since there was an abundance, the resources essential to a chance at a living were to be had for the asking. One with enterprise enough to " go it alone " lived upon what he himself and his wealth in wife and children produced. He did not have to drive a shrewd bargain for the sale of his labour nor purchase the wherewithal to be fed and clothed in a market. There was no confusing scheme of prices to break the connection between effort and reward;

opportunity and responsibility went hand in hand; success or failure was of one's own fashioning. Where nature does most, man claims all; and in rural America men were quite disposed to claim personal credit for nature's accomplishments. Since ample resources smothered even mediocre effort in plenty, the voice of chronic failure which blamed circumstance, fate, or "the system" was unheard. A freedom to have and to hold economic resources plentiful enough to supply all was the condition of material prosperity.

Even when the lure of natural resources drew men from agriculture to industrial exploitation conditions did not change materially. The population of the new towns for a while kept at least one foot upon the soil. When at last the city possessed its people, aliens came out of Southeastern Europe to do the "dirty work," and the native born passed up into administrative, clerical, or professional positions. The alternative of farm employment and the rapid expansion of industry fixed a rough minimum beneath which wages could not fall. The expanding machine technique with large scale production by quantity methods turned out an abundance of goods evidenced alike in lower prices and in higher standards of living. The "captains of industry" were regarded by the community as the creators of the jobs which they dispensed and as the efficient cause of the prosperity of the neighbourhood. The trickle of immigration that swelled to a "stream" and rose to a "tide" is an eloquent testimonial of the time paid by the peasantry of Europe to the success of the American system of letting the individual alone in his business.

These conditions brought forth the lay economic theory acceptable to the national community. Its precepts came from experience, rather than from books; by intuition, rather than by reason. The welfare of the individual and the wealth of the nation were alike due to free institutions. In business and industry the individual was to be free to do as he pleased unless specifically forbidden by the State. The State was powerless to interfere with the individual unless granted specific "constitutional" authority to do so. Each knew what he wanted and was able to take care of himself. The interests of all were an aggregate of the interests of individuals. The prevailing scheme of institutions was accepted as a part of the immutable world of nature. Private property, if defended at all, was good because it gave the individual security and enabled him to enjoy the fruits of his own labour. The right of contract, exercised in a market characterized by "higgling," gave one an occasional adventure beyond the horizon of a household economy. If perchance the individual stumbled into a bad bargain occasionally, so much the better. The mistake was a useful exercise in the development of the cardinal virtue of self-reliance. When the coming of industrialism made contract the basis of all industrial relations, the older justification was still used. Competition, with which it was always associated, was regarded as the prime agency in the organization of industry. It forced the elements of production into order and exercised a moral restraint over them. Under its régime men were rewarded in accordance with their deserts. In general, it was true beyond peradventure that " opportunity " knocked once " at every gate "; that there was " plenty of room at the top "; that each built the ladder by which he rose; and that even the humblest was "master of his fate."

Out of such raw materials there was fashioned a body of professional economic theory. In a sense it was an imported product; for its earlier statement was that of English " classical " economics. But in reality it was the return of an earlier export, for accepted theory had been made from crude individualistic notions which England had got from America. In addition, at the hands of American economists it received a far more elaborate and articulate statement than had been given it overseas. These theorists used subtle analysis, ponderous logic, and circumlocution; but their decorous processes brought them to much the same conclusions that practical men gained from their limited experiences. Its strength and its acceptability were wholly due to the precision and verbiage with which it reduced to formal terms the common-sense economics of the day.

In its terms the economic order is made up of individuals. Each of these is actuated by the motive of self-interest. Each has for disposal personal services, goods, or property rights.

Each must live upon goods and services purchased from others. Each must compete with his fellows in the sale of his wares and the purchase of his articles of livelihood. Because of the competition of sellers the wages of labour, the profits of capital, and the prices of goods cannot be forced to untoward heights. Because of the competition of buyers they cannot be driven too low. The equilibrium of this double competitive process assures to each a return which represents the just value of the service, the property right, or the good. Prices, by moving up and down in response to changing conditions, stimulate and retard consumption and production. Their very movement constantly reallocates resources to the production of a variety of goods and services in just the proportion which the consumers demand. In this theory the institutions which comprise the framework of the economic order are taken for granted. It has no place for an interference by the State with " private business." It regards monopoly as a thing to be abjured, whether appearing as a capitalistic combine or as a union of workingmen. In the Eden of free enterprise the community's resources yield all they have and competition rewards justly all the faithful who by serving themselves serve society. It is small wonder that sermons were preached upon " The Relation of Political Economy to Natural Theology."

II

The conditions which made the economic opinion of the America of small towns and open country are gone. With their passing the older theories have been reshaped to new purposes. There are no longer free economic opportunities for all comers. Natural resources have been appropriated, and the natural differences between men have been enhanced by the artificial ones of ownership and inheritance. Wealth and control have alike been stripped from the many and concentrated in the few. The prevailing unit in business is the corporation. Establishments have been gathered into industries, and these have been articulated into a mighty industrial system, with its established rights, its customary ways of doing things, and its compulsions upon those who serve it. The older personal relation of "master" and "servant" abides only in indices of the records of the law courts. The contract of employment is now between a "soulless" but "legal entity" and a mere creature of flesh and blood. The more human individual, the survival of a less mechanical age, no longer lives upon the fruit of his individual toil. His welfare is pent in between his wages and the prices which he must pay for his necessities. Beyond this immediate bargain lies a mysterious economic system filled with unknown causes which threaten his income and even his employment. Those who possess have come into succession to those who ventured. In short, free enterprise has given way to an established system.

These events have left their mark upon economic opinion. It is altogether fitting that those who fell heir to the wealth piled up by free enterprise should gain its outer defences of theory and dialectic. So the older economics, with its logic and its blessing, has come as a legacy to those who have. Its newer statement, because of its well-known objective, may be called "the case for capitalism." In its revision the adventurous militarism bent upon exploitation has given way to a pacifistic defence of security, possession, and things as they are.

In outward form few changes were necessary to convert the older theory of *laissez-faire* into a presentable case for capitalism. A more rigid and absolute statement of the classical doctrine was almost enough. In its terms the economic order is independent of other social arrangements. It is an automatic, self-regulating mechanism. Over it there rules an immutable and natural "law of supply and demand." This maintains just prices, prevents exploitation, adjusts production and consumption to each other, secures the maximum of goods and services from the resources at hand, and disburses incomes in accordance with the merits of men and the verity of things. So just and impartial is the operation of this law that interference by the State amounts to meddlesome muddling. It cannot override natural law; therefore it should not.

It differs most from the older economics in the more explicit statement of the function of institutions. The growing inequality of income, of control, and of opportunity have presented facts that have to be faced. But even here, instead of contriving new defences, the advocates of capitalism have refurbished the older ones. The thing that is finds its justification in that which was. Property rights are to be preserved intact, because private property is essential to personal opportunity; just as if the propertyless did not exist and each was to win his living from his own acres or his own shop. The right of contract is not to be abridged, because the interests of both parties are advanced by a bargain between equals; just as if the corporate employer and the individual employé were alike in their freedom, their capacity to wait, and their power to shape the terms of the bargain. Prices are to be self-determined in open market, because competition will best reconcile the conflicting interests of buyers and sellers; just as if there was no semblance of monopoly among producers, no open price agreements, and no informal understandings. Individual initiative is not to be abridged, because it creates the wealth of the nation; just as if routine had no value for efficiency and the masses of men still had discretion in economic matters. The arrangements which make up the economic order find their validity in the symbolic language of ritual rather than in a prosaic recital of current fact.

This defence crosses the frontier which separates the economic from the political order only to appropriate the prestige of democracy. Its real concern is the preservation of the prevailing system wherein business controls industry for purposes of profit. Its formal solicitation is lest " the form of government " be changed. This concern finds expression in veneration for the work of the " fathers " (rather young men, by the way), not of machine technology and business enterprise, but of " representative government " and of " constitutional authority." Its creed becomes propaganda, not for the defence of business, the security of corporations, or the preservation of managerial immunities, but for the defence of the nation, the security of America, and the preservation of " constitutional " rights. The newer economic arrangements are masked behind political rights and given the values of the political institutions which antedate them by many decades. In short, the staunchest defenders of the prevailing economic system believe that "their economic preferences are shared by the constitution of the United States."

If we may borrow a term from its advocates, this body of opinion must be pronounced "theoretical." In their speech a "theory" is a generalization which goes much further than its particulars warrant. In that sense their conclusions are not "practical." The essential question with which this body of opinion is concerned is whether the scheme of institutions which focus upon profit-making make the members of the community, severally and collectively, as well off as they ought to be. It seems offhand that a realistic defence of the prevailing order might be convincingly formulated. At any rate, "the case for capitalism" is good enough to get into the records. Instead, its advocates have confused their own pecuniary success with the well-being of the community and have argued that because profits have been made the system is good. Like the classical economists they vindicate the system by assumption.

III

In the wake of the new industrialism there has come an economic opinion of protest. It is being gradually formulated by professional men, by farmers, by trade unionists, and by the younger business men who have escaped being "self-made." Its hesitating and confused statement is due to the disturbed conditions out of which it comes. The varied interests of its many authors prevents unity of words or of principles. Its origin in the contact of minds steeped in the older individualism with the arresting facts of the newer economic order explains its current inarticulate expression. It can be set forth briefly only by subordinating the reality of variety to the tendencies which are clearly inherent within it.

The objective of this newer opinion is a modification of the prevailing order, rather than its overthrow. It is quite conscious of defects in its arrangements and knows that its fruits are not all good. It has never considered the question of the efficiency or inefficiency of the system as a whole. The older individualistic notions are strong enough to give an intuitive belief that the theory of the control of industry by business for profit is essentially sound. But it would eliminate the bad, patch up the indifferent, and retain the good. It would set up in the government an external authority which through regulation and repression would make business interests serve the community. Its faith is in private enterprise compelled by the State to promote "public welfare." Its detail can best be suggested by typical illustrations.

There is, first of all, the attitude of the protestants towards freedom of contract. They accept the prevailing theory that the relations of buyer and seller, employer and employé, owner and agent, can safely be left to the free choice of all concerned. But they point out that in practice the principle does not give its assumed results. For, whereas the theory assumes the parties to be equal in their power to determine the terms of the contract, it is a matter of common knowledge that employers and labourers occupy unequal bargaining positions. They would leave relations to be determined by free bargaining; but, as a preliminary, they would attempt to establish equality of bargaining power. To that end they would have the contract made by "collective bargaining" between employers and employés "through representatives" chosen by each. Moreover, they would use the State to better the position of the weaker party. Thus legislation has been passed depriving employers of their right of requiring employés, as a condition of employment, not to remain members of labour unions. Although the courts have found such legislation to be "an arbitrary interference with the liberty of contract which no government can justify in a free land," its advocates will insist that their aim has been only "to establish that equality in position between the parties in which liberty of contract begins."

There is, in the next place, a growing opinion among the protestants that the State is "a moral agent" and should determine the rules under which business is to be carried on. They point out that in business there are bad as well as good conditions, that business men engage in proper as well as in improper practices, and that some activities harm while others help the community. In many instances the employer finds it to his advantage to establish conditions which the interests of the workers and of the consumers require. In others, the elevation of standards waits upon the pleasure of the most inconsiderate employer. The prohibition of child labour, the shortening of the working day, and the payment of a minimum wage may be advantageous alike to labourers and to the community; yet these innovations involve an increase in cost and cannot be made against the competition of the producer who will not establish them. In such cases it is the duty of the State to establish minimum conditions which must be met by all employers. The imposition of such standards in no way affects the system under which business is carried on; for the competition of rival sellers can be just as acute and just as considerate of the public, if all of them are forced to pay their employés a living wage, as if they are all free to force wages down to starvation. Upon this theory the State has established uniform weights and measures, prohibited the use of deleterious chemicals, stopped the sale of impure food, provided compensation for the human wear and tear of industry, and established minimum standards of safety, health, and service.

There is, finally, a growing opinion that in some industries the profit-making motive must be superseded by some other. In the railway industry it has been repeatedly shown that the pecuniary interest of the management fails to coincide with that of either the owners or of the shippers. Long ago the determination of charges for service was put beyond the discretion of the officials. Of late there has been an increasing tendency to make accounts, services, expenditures, valuations, and other matters meet standards of public service. When this has been effected, as it will be, the officials of the roads will become mere subordinates responsible to a public authority. Then profit-making as a guide to administration will have given way to an official judgment of results in terms of established standards. Then it will be discovered that public control formally rejected has been achieved by indirection. But many times ere this American opinion has come by devious paths to goals which its individualism has not allowed it to regard as quite desirable.

For the moment the medley of opinion here roughly characterized as a demand for control is dominant. Its proponents are almost as naïve as the advocates of capitalism in a belief in the essential goodness of a mythical system of " free enterprise." They differ from them in placing greater emphasis upon voluntary associations and in demanding that the State from without compel business to serve the common good. As yet they have formulated no consistent theory of economics and no articulate programme for achieving their ends. Without a clear understanding of the development of industry and of the structure of the economic order, they are content to face specific problems when they meet them. They are far from ready to surrender an inherited belief in an individualistic theory of the common good.

IV

The changes of the last four decades, which make up " The Industrial Revolution in America," have left their mark upon the economics of the schools. If there was a time when the thought of the professed economists was a thing apart from the common sense of the age, it ended with the coming of industrialism. Differ as it may in phrase, in method, and in statement, the economics in solid and dull treatises reflects, as it has always reflected, the opinions of the laity. If there were agreement among the sorts of men who gather at ball games and in smoking cars, the books on economics would all read alike. But when the plumber differs from the banker and the scrub woman refuses to take her ideas from the coupon clipper, it is futile to expect mere economists to agree. To some, the classical doctrine still serves as a sabbatical refuge from modern problems. Others, who " specialize " in trusts, tariffs, and labour are too busy being " scientific " to formulate general opinions. Still others insist upon creating a new economics concerned with the problem of directing industrial development to appointed ends. Each of these schools has a membership large enough to allow dissension within the ranks.

The revolt against the classical economics began when it encountered modern fact. Beyond the pale of doctrine taught by certified theorists appeared studies upon corporations, international trade, railway rates, craft unionism, and other matters of the newer fact. For a time those who studied these subjects were content to describe in superficial terms the results of their observations. But as facts accumulated they provoked generalizations at variance with the accepted principles of the older competitive theory. At the same time the rise of a newer history concerned with development rather than chronology, a new ethics that recognized the existence of a social order, and a new psychology that taught that the content of men's behaviour is poured in by the environment, together made the foundations of the older economics very insecure.

For a time this protest found expression only in critical work. The picture of an economic order as a self-regulating mechanism, peopled with folk who could not but serve the community in serving themselves became very unreal. The complexity of industrialism made it hard to believe that the individual had knowledge enough to choose best for himself. The suspicion that frequently thought follows action made it hard to continue to believe in man's complete rationality. The idea that incomes are different because opportunities are different led to a questioning of the justice of the ratings of men in the market. The unequal division of income made impossible pecuniary calculations in which each man counted for one and only for one. With these assumptions of 19th-century economics passed " the economic man," " the Crusoe economy," and the last of the divine theories, that of " enlightened self-interest." It was no longer possible to build a defence of the existing order upon " the hedonistic conception of man " as " a lightning calculator of pleasures and pains, who oscillates like a homogeneous globule of desire of happiness under the impulse of stimuli that shift him about the area, but leave him inert."

The most immediate effect of this criticism was a change in method. The older process of juggling economic laws out of assumptions about human nature, human motives, and the beneficence of competition lost prestige. It was evident that if the system was to be appraised the facts must be had. Accordingly a veritable multitude of facts, good, bad, and mostly indifferent were treasured up. This process of garnering information soon made it evident that the facts about the relationship of industry to the welfare of the community were too varied and too numerous to be separately catalogued. Since only totals could be used, economics came to rely upon facts presented in the quantitative language of statistics.

But since facts are not possessed of the virtue of self-determination, they did not yield an opinion which was very relevant or very truthful. Their use was for the moment nothing more than a substitution of the superstition of facts for that of logic. The facts were of value, because when properly interpreted they gave the story of what the economic system had done. But without the aid of standards it was impossible to determine whether it had worked well or ill, whether it had much or little to give in return for the solicitous concern about it. It was evident that modern industrialism was developing without conscious guidance. As long as no goal was fixed it was impossible to tell whether industrial development was proceeding in the right direction. As long as we were unmindful of the kind of society we wished ours to be, we could not appraise its accomplishments. Without standards all that could be said was that the system had worked as well as it had worked and that we were as well off as we were well off. The problem, therefore, became one of judging the system on the basis of the facts by means of standards.

Thus the newer economics has been of service in stating the problem with which opinion must be concerned. The " prevailing " economic order is one of many schemes of arrangements for making industry serve the purposes of the community. The system has been slowly evolved out of the institutions of the past, is constantly being affected by circumstances, and for the future is capable of conscious modification. How well it has served its purpose cannot be attested by an abstract argument proceeding from assumptions about human nature and the cosmos. A judgment upon its relative goodness or badness requires an appraisal of the facts in terms of standards. These standards must be obtained from our notions of the kind of society we want this to be. These notions must proceed from a scientific study of the properties of things and the needs of human beings. That judgment will be one not of goodness or badness, but of the relative merits of a very human scheme of arrangements compared with its alternatives.

The economists are reluctant to pass a judgment upon the prevailing order. The relevant facts are too scanty and the standards too inexact to warrant an appraisal of the virtues and the vices of " capitalism." They distrust the eulogies of apologists because they do not square with the known facts. They are not convinced by the reformers, because they fear that they know as little about their own schemes as they do about current arrangements. They insist that a general judgment must be a progressive affair. The system will change through gradual modification; the larger problem will be solved by attention to an endless succession of minor problems. Each of these must be met with the facts and with an ideal of what our society should be. They have too little faith in the rationality of the collect to believe that problems can be faced in battalions or that a new order can emerge as a work of creation. They have little fear for " the future of the nation," if only problems can be intelligently handled as they emerge. Their attitude towards the present system is one, neither of acceptance nor of rejection, but of doubt and of honest inquiry. Their faith is neither in the existing order nor in a hand-me-down substitute, but in a conscious direction of the process of change.

This tedious narrative has failed entirely in its purpose, if it has not revealed the strength and the weakness of economic opinion in America. Its merits stand out boldly in the preceding paragraphs; its defects are too striking to be concealed. The reader has already been informed; but the writer must inform himself. The essay, therefore, will close with an explicit statement of some three of the more obvious characteristics.

First, its most striking characteristic is its volume. In quantity it contains enough verbal and intellectual ammunition to justify or to wreck a dozen contradictory economic orders. If, in an orderly way, opinion became judgment and judgment ripened into the society of to-morrow, it would stand condemned. For little of it has a practical consequence and our ways of expression are very wasteful. But it also affords a harmless outlet for the dangerous emotions aroused by the wear and tear of everyday work in a humdrum universe. And, if it is true that we are, all of us, Simians by lineage, this is by far the most important function it serves.

Second, it is grounded none too well in information and principles. The ordinary mortal is busied with his own affairs. He lacks the time, the patience, and the equipment necessary to get at the facts about the material welfare of the nation. In the most casual way he makes up his mind, using for the purpose a few superficial facts, a number of prejudices, and a bit of experience. He has little idea of where we are in the course of social development, of the forces which have brought us here, or of where we ought to be going. Since the opinions of groups and of the nation are aggregates of individual opinion, the ideas of those who have an intellectual right to speak are not a large part of the compound.

Third, despite its crudeness and variety, it possesses elements of real value. Its very volume creates at least a statistical probability that some of it is of high quality. The waste of much of it gives the rest a real chance of expression in social policy. The common features of industrialism are giving to men something of a common experience out of which there will come a more or less common-sense appreciation of problems and of ideals. This will dictate the larger features of a future social policy. The particularized opinion which finds expression in the detailed formulation of programmes must be left to the experts. The great masses of men must learn that these problems are technical and must trust the judgment of those who know. Despite the record of halting development and of confused statement, the pages above indicate that the economic opinion in America is coming slowly to an appreciation of the factors upon which " the good life for all " really rests.

But enough. Opinion by being economic does not cease to be opinion, and an essay about it is only more opinion.

WALTON H. HAMILTON

RADICALISM

THE first obstacle to an assessment of radicalism in America is the difficulty of discovering precisely what American radicalism is. According to his enemies, a radical is a person whose opinions need not be considered and whose rights need not be respected. As a people we do not wish to understand him, or to deal with what he represents, but only to get him out of sight. We deport him and imprison him. If he writes a book, we keep it out of the schools and libraries. If he publishes a paper, we debar it from the mails. If he makes a speech, we drive him out of the hall and shoo him away from the street-corner. If by hook or crook he multiplies himself to considerable numbers, we expel his representatives from legislative chambers, break up his parades, and disperse his strikes with well-armed soldiery.

These being the associations which cluster about the word, it has naturally become less a definition than a weapon. Statisticians in the Federal Trade Commission publish certain figures dealing with the business of the packing-houses—a Senator loudly calls these devoted civil servants " radicals," and they are allowed to resign. A labour leader, following the precedent of federal law established for over a half a century, espouses the eight-hour day, but because he has the bad taste to do so in connection with the steel industry, he becomes a " radical," and is soundly berated in the press. If one were to ask the typical American Legion member how he would describe a radical—aside from the fact that a radical is a person to be suppressed—he would probably answer that a radical is (a) a pro-German, (b) a Russian or other foreigner, (c) a person who sends bombs through the mail, (d) a believer in free love, (e) a writer of free verse, (f) a painter of cubist pictures, (g) a member of the I.W.W., (h) a Socialist, (i) a Bolshevist, (j) a believer in labour unions and an opponent of the open shop, and (k) any one who would be looked upon with disapproval by a committee consisting of Judge Gary, Archibald Stevenson, and Brander Matthews.

There is scarcely more light to be had from the radicals themselves. Any one who feels a natural distaste for the censorious crowd of suppressors is likely to class himself with the free spirits whom they oppose. To call oneself a radical is in such circumstances a necessary accompaniment of self-respect. The content of the radicalism is of minor importance. There is an adventurous tendency to espouse anything that is forbidden, and so to include among one's affirmations the most contradictory systems—such as Nietzscheanism and Communism, Christianity of the mystical sort and rebellion. And when these rebels really begin to think, the confusion is increased. Each pours his whole ardour into some exclusive creed, which makes him scorn other earnest souls who happen to disagree about abstruse technical points. Among economic radicals, terms like " counter-revolutionary " and " bourgeois " are bandied about in a most unpleasant fashion. If, for instance, you happen to believe that Socialism may be brought about through the ballot rather than through the general strike, numbers of radicals will believe you more dangerous than the Czar himself; it is certain that when the time comes you will be found fighting on the wrong side of the barricade. Creeds have innumerable subdivisions, and on the exact acceptance of the creed depends your eternal salvation. Calvinists, Wesleyans, Lutherans, and the rest in their most exigent days could not rival the logical hair-splitting which has lately taken place among the sectarian economic dissenters, nor has any religious quarrel ever surpassed in bitterness the dogmatic dissidence with which the numerous schools of authoritarian rebellion rebel against authority.

There is a brilliant magazine published in New York which takes pride in edging a little to the left of the leftmost radical, wherever for the moment that may be. Its editor is a poet, and he writes eloquently of the proletariat and the worker. Not long ago I was speaking of this editor to an actual leader of labour—a man who is a radical, and who also takes a daily part in the workers' struggles. " Yes," he said, " he certainly can write. He is one of the best writers living." And he went on wistfully, " If the labour movement only had a writer like that! "

There is another brilliant magazine published in New York which takes exquisite pains to inform the reader that it is radical. In precise columns of elegant type, Puritan in its scorn of passion or sensation, it weekly derides the sentimental liberal for ignorance of " fundamental economics." Not long ago it made the startling discovery that Socialists favour taking natural resources out of private ownership. And its " fundamental economics," whenever they appear in language simple enough for the common reader to understand, turn out to be nothing more dangerous than that respectable and ancient heresy, the single tax.

Another method of definition is now in common use—a method which seems easy because of its mechanical simplicity. People are arranged in a row from left to right, according to their attitude toward the existing order. At the extreme right are the reactionaries, who want to restore the discarded. Next to them are the conservatives, who wish to keep most of what exists. At their elbow are the liberals, who are ready to examine new ideas, but who are not eager or dogmatic about change. And at the extreme left are the radicals, who want to change nearly everything for something totally new. Such an arrangement is a confusing misuse of words based on a misconception of social forces. Society is not a car on a track, along which it may move in either direction, or on which it may stand still. Society is a complex, with many of the characteristics of an organism. Its change is continuous, although by no means constant. It passes through long periods of quiescence, and comparatively brief periods of rapid mutation. It may collect itself into a close order, or again become dispersed into a nebula. There is much in its development that is cyclical; it has yet undiscovered rhythms, and many vagaries. The radical and the reactionary may be agreed on essentials; they may both wish sudden change and closer organization. The conservative may be liberal because he wishes to preserve an order in which liberal virtues may exist. Or a liberal may be so cribbed and confined by an unpleasant constriction of social tissue that he becomes radical in his struggle for immediate release. The terms are not of the same class and should not be arranged in parallel columns.

The dictionary definition is enlightening. " Radical—Going to the root or origin; touching or acting upon what is essential or fundamental; thorough. . . . *Radical reform*, a thorough reform. . . . Hence Radical Reformer equals Radical " (New English Dictionary). In this sense radicalism is an historic American tradition. The revolt of the Colonies against England and the formation of the Republic were, indeed, far from the complete break with the past which the schoolboy assumes them to have been, but what lives in the minds of the American people is, nevertheless, not the series of counterchecks which men like Hamilton and Madison wrote into the Constitution, but rather the daring affirmations of Jefferson which have a real kinship with the radical spirit of the French Revolution. Talk of " inalienable rights " such as life, liberty, and the pursuit of happiness was genuine radical talk; it searched out the bases of human relationship, proclaimed them against authority, and sought to found on them a system of government.

So strongly has this conception seized the imagination of Americans that it largely accounts for their almost instinctive hostility to new kinds of political change. The roots of politics have been uncovered, the change has in fact been made once for all—so they reason. To admit that any new fundamental alteration is necessary is to be disloyal to the historical liberation. Because the conservative American believes himself a complete democrat, because for him the " new order " was achieved in 1776, he is intolerant of modern radicals. Suggestions of new revolution touch him closely on his pride. In this sense Jefferson has been less a spur to future generations than an obstacle. If his fine frenzy about rights had been less eloquently expressed, if it had not obscured in a cloud of glory the true nature of the foundation of our government—a highly practical compromise which embodied a few moderate advances and many hesitancies—we should have a different temper about change to-day. We should not assume that all desirable fundamental modification of social and political structure had been completed nearly a century and a half ago.

The greatest historic expression of American radicalism has thus become the altar of the conservatives. To the unlettered man it may seem strange that a Supreme Court of elderly radicals will not allow Congress to forbid child-labour because of their loyalty to an 18th-century limitation of the federal government, presumably in the interest of freedom and humanity. To workmen voting for the eight-hour day the language of Jefferson did not seem hostile—they were struggling to pursue happiness in a way that he must have approved. And yet it is the sacred " right " of contract which deprived them, as voters, of the right to legislate for shorter hours. Workmen using their collective economic power to gain industrial freedom are met by a shower of injunctive denials, based chiefly on that same right of contract. In order to stay any further liberation of the human body and spirit, judges and officials and industrial barons have only to invoke the phrases of freedom thrown out against an ancient despotism. They have only to point out that freedom as defined abstractly over a hundred years ago forbids practical freedom to-day. Frozen radicalism of the past chills and destroys the new roots of American life.

Some appreciation of this state of affairs underlies the prevailing tendency to believe that all new radicalism has a foreign origin. It is, indeed, part of the best nationalistic tradition to attribute subversive doctrines to foreigners. This is the habit in every country. But in the United States the habit is perhaps more deep-seated than elsewhere. Americans are by definition free and equal; if then any one talks or acts as if he were not free and equal, he must have been born somewhere else. The American Government, being not a faulty product of human growth, but a new creation sprung perfect out of the ineffable minds of the Fathers, is unassailable; if any one assails it, he cannot know it, and must be subjected to courses in English and Civics (Americanization) until he recognizes its perfection. Treason in this country is not simple treason to a ruler, to a class, or to a system as elsewhere; it is an act of sacrilege, by one uninitiated, upon a religious mystery.

Of course there are and have been Americans whose radicalism is less crust and more meat. The spirit of Jefferson still lives, after all, to confute the interpretation put upon his words. And imported doctrine has actually had less to do with most of the radical movements in America than has American tradition itself. It is an easy step from the conception of political liberty to the conception of economic liberty, and the step has been made here as readily as in Europe. In a country which for so long offered extraordinary opportunities to the individual business man, it is only natural that economic liberty should have been conceived as a means of protecting his enterprise; and as a matter of fact our economic legislation for many years has been sprinkled with victories of the small business men and farmers over the interests which had already become large enough to seem to them oppressive. The regulation of the railroads, the succession of popular financial doctrines, and the anti-trust legislation, were all initiated by the interpretation of economic democracy naturally arising in the vigorous class of the small entrepreneurs. With the slow weakening of this class by its disintegration, on one hand into captains and lieutenants of the great principalities of industry, and on the other into permanently salaried or waged members of the rank and file, comes a corresponding tendency to change the prevailing conception of economic democracy. The radicalism of workmen in the United States has often been no less sweeping or assertive than the radicalism of workmen anywhere—witness the I.W.W. Even violence in the labour struggle has been practised chiefly by one hundred per cent. Americans—the steel workers in Homestead in 1892 and the West Virginia miners in Mingo County in 1921 were of old American stock. And the moment the predominating group in American thought and activity is composed of those who expect to live by their daily work rather than of those who expect to accumulate property, we are likely to see the rise of an economic radicalism more akin to that which exists in Europe, and one which, because of its sanction in our tradition, will be twice as militant and convinced.

For, after all, economic radicalism arises neither from a merely stupid desire for more material goods, nor from an intellectual adherence to a particular formula of industrial organization. It arises from a desire to be free, to achieve dignity and independence. Poverty is distressful not so much because of its physical hardships as because of its spiritual bondage. To be poor because one chooses to be poor is less annoying than to be moderately paid while the man who fixes one's wages rides in a Rolls-Royce. The most modest aspects of the labour movement are attempts of the workmen to gain some voice in determining the conditions under which they must work—in other words, to extend democracy into industry. And when the workman wakes up to the fact that industrial policies are governed by a comparatively small class of owners, and that the visible result of those policies seems to be a large class of underemployed, undernourished, and underhoused families on one hand, and a small class of abundantly supplied families on the other, he feels that he is suffering an indignity. You may challenge him to prove that any other system would work better. You may argue that if all the wealth of the rich were distributed equally, he would receive but a trifle. Such reasoning will affect him little. If every one must be miserable, he at least wants to share and exercise whatever power exists to alter that misery. Kings have argued that the people could rule no better than they, but that has not prevented peoples from demanding representative government. The American tradition is sure to be as subversive a motive in industry as it has been in the State. The technical problem of how industry may be better organized, important as it is, is subordinate to this cry of the personality. Essentially, this sort of radicalism arises from the instinct of the workman to achieve an adult relationship to the industrial world.

The impact of the war upon industry, and the reverberation of its social results abroad, for some time stimulated this latent feeling in American workmen. For the first time in decades the competition of the unemployed and the immigrant was virtually removed, and the wage-earner began to feel secure enough to assert his personality. He was necessary to the community in an immediate way. The policy of the government was to recognize this fact, and to prevent an unduly rapid increase in wages and in the power of organized labour by compromising with it on certain simple issues like collective bargaining and the eight-hour day. But larger aspirations arose in the rank and file, and when the Russian Revolution sent a word of emancipation around the world, they were ready to listen. In spite of the crushing force of the whole ruling propaganda machinery, which had been so successful in arousing hatred against Germany, countless American workmen sensed the approach of a new order as a result of the success of the Bolsheviki. A secondary impulse of the same sort, felt even more strongly in some quarters, arose from the Nottingham programme of the British Labour Party. But affairs moved slowly, hope was deferred, and at length the new spirit lost much of its freshness and power. The very acrimoniousness and volume of the controversy over what had or had not been done in Russia wearied most people of the whole matter. The many expected revolutions in other countries, which missed fire so many times, caused disillusionment. The doctrinaire and even religious adherents of the Russian Communists began to make trouble for every radical organization in the country by their quarrels and divisions. At length, the war being over, the American labour movement itself began to display a weakness in the face of renewed attack on the part of its opponents, which showed how illusory had been many of its recent gains and how seriously its morale had been injured.

Economic radicalism never looked—on the surface—weaker than it does in the United States to-day. On the strength of statements by Mr. Gompers and some other leaders of the trade unions, we are likely to assume that organized labour will have nothing to do with it. The professed radicals themselves have been weakened by dissensions and scattered by persecution. Yet a brief survey of the formal groups which now profess radical theories will indicate why the future of American radicalism should not be assessed on the evidence of their present low estate.

The Socialist Party, even more than the Socialist Parties in other countries, was placed by the war in a difficult situation.

With its roots not yet firmly in the soil, except in a few localities and among diverse national elements, it was faced with
the necessity, in accordance with its principles and tradition,
of denouncing the entrance of the United States into hostilities.
But this decision could command no effective support from
the workers organized on the economic field, who under a
different leadership adopted a different attitude.   Nor was the
party strong enough among any other element of the population to make its decision respected.   The only immediate
result of the gesture was therefore to place this unarmed little
force in the most exposed position possible, where it drew the
fire of all those who were nervously afraid the people would
not sanction the war.   Socialism was not judged on the basis
of its economic tenets, but was condemned as disloyal and
pro-German; and the effect was to render the party even more
sectarian and unrepresentative than ever before.   It had
adopted a position in which it could not expect recruits except
from moral heroes, and no nation nourishes a large proportion
of these.   Such episodes make good legend, but they do not
lead to prompt victories.   Even those who later have come to
believe that the Socialists were right about the war are likely
to express their belief in some other form than joining the
party.

In this weakened condition, the Socialist Party after the war
developed internal fissures.   Many bitter words have been
exchanged as to whether the " Left Wingers " were or were not
a majority of the party, whether they were or were not more
orthodox than those in control of the party machinery, and
whether, if they were more orthodox, their orthodoxy was wise.
At any rate, they broke away and formed two new parties of
their own, a fact which is the chief point of interest to one
who is more concerned with the larger issues of American
radicalism than with the minutiæ of Socialist politics.   The
Communist Party and the Communist Labour Party, whatever may have been the legitimacy of their gestation in the
bowels of Socialism, certainly found their reason for being
chiefly in logic which originated in Moscow and Berlin rather
than in the American situation.   At once selected for perse-

cution by government officials, they burrowed underground, doubtless followed by a band of spies at least as numerous as they. From these subterranean regions have come rumours of a fourth party—the United Communist, which swallowed most of the Communist Labourites and some of the Communists. At last accounts the Communists and the United Communists were each attempting to prove the other counter-revolutionary by reference to the latest documents from international revolutionary headquarters.

It is hazardous in the extreme for an outsider to speak of the differences in doctrine among these groups. It is probably fair to say, however, that the Communist parties are chiefly distinguished by their total lack of interest in anything save a complete revolution, because this is the only kind they believe possible. They reject as " compromises " partial gains of all sorts; piecemeal progress by evolutionary methods rather offends them than otherwise. Their eyes are turned always toward some future revolutionary situation; for this their organization and their theories are being prepared. This being the case, the validity of their position will be tested by the event. If, as the milder Socialists believe, economic changes may come gradually by process of growth and smaller shocks, the Communists are likely to remain a nearly functionless and tiny minority, even in the labour movement. If, as the Communists believe, the present order in the normal course of its development is destined to experience a sudden collapse similar to that which occurred in Russia near the end of the war, they will become the true prophets, and their mode of thought and action will presumably have fitted them to assume leadership.

The Farmer-Labour Party is a recent growth far less doctrinaire than either the Socialist or the Communist groups. It has neither prophet nor Bible, but is based rather on the principle of gathering certain categories of people together for political action, trusting that as they become organized they will work out their own programme in relation to the situation, and that that programme will develop as time goes on. The categories to which it appeals are chiefly the industrial workers and the small farmers, who have in general common economic interests as opposed to the large owners of land and capital. It hopes that other elements in the population, realizing that their major interests are much the same as those of the unionists and the farmers, will join forces with them to produce a majority. As an illustration of the operation of such tactics, the Farmer-Labourites point to the success of the Independent Labour Party of Great Britain, first in aiding the foundation of the British Labour Party, and second in building up for that party an increasingly coherent radical programme.

In all these cases, however, not much confidence is placed in the actual political machinery of elections. There is a widespread scepticism about the ability to accomplish industrial changes by the ballot, on account of experience with political corruption, broken election promises, adverse court decisions, and political buncombe in general. These parties are formed as much for the purpose of propagating ideas and creating centres of activity as for mobilizing votes. All radical parties lay great stress on the industrial power of the organized labour movement. This is not to say that they do not recognize the importance of the State in industrial matters. All agree that control of political machinery will in the long run be necessary, if only to prevent it from checking the advance of the people through the courts and police. But they also agree that control of the State is not held and cannot be attained by political machinery alone. The present influence of the proprietors of industry on politics is due, they see, chiefly to economic power, and the workers consequently must not neglect the development of their own economic organization. The Communists are completely hopeless of attaining results through the present election machinery; the Socialists and Farmer-Labourites believe it possible to secure a majority at the polls, which may then execute its will, if the workers are well enough organized for industrial action.

Outwardly the most successful of the radical movements is the least doctrinaire of all. It is unnecessary to repeat the history and achievements of the Nonpartisan League—an attempt on the part of organized farmers to use the machinery of the State in order to gain economic independence from the banking, milling, and packing interests. Other groups of farmers have aimed at a similar result through co-operation, with varying success.

In the industrial labour movement proper there have been numerous radical minorities. The most uncompromising of these, as well as the most characteristically American, was the Industrial Workers of the World, who aspired to build up a consciously revolutionary body to rival the unions composing the American Federation of Labour. This decline is due not so much to suppression as to their previous failure to enlist the continued support of the industrial workers themselves. Like the Communists, the I.W.W. predicated their success on a revolutionary situation, and lacking that situation they could not build a labour movement on an abstract idea. Over long periods not enough people are moved by a philosophy of salvation to give staying power to such an organization in the daily struggle with the employers. Other similar attempts, such as the W.I.I.U., and the more recent One Big Union, have encountered similar difficulties. They grow rapidly in crises, but fail under the strain of continued performance.

The failure of American radicals to build up a strong movement is in part due, of course, to the natural difficulties of the social and economic situation, but it is also due to the mental traits which usually accompany remoteness from reality. This is illustrated in the history of the I.W.W., if we accept William Z. Foster's acute analysis. The regular trade-union movement, slowly evolving towards a goal but half consciously realized, overcoming practical obstacles painfully and clumsily, as such obstacles usually are overcome, was too halting for these impatient radicals. They withdrew, and set up rival, perfectionist unions, founded in uncompromising revolutionary ardour. These organizations were often unable to serve the rank and file in their practical difficulties, and consequently could not supplant the historic labour movement. But they did draw out of that movement many of its most sincere and ardent spirits, thus depriving it of the ferment which was necessary to its growth. The I.W.W., for their part, failing to secure any large grip on reality, regressed into quarrels about theory, suffered divisions of their social personality, and at length—except in the far West—became little more than economic anchorites. As Foster says, " The I.W.W. were absolutely against results."

Too much of American radicalism has been diverted to the easy emotional satisfaction which is substituted for the arduous process of dealing with reality. We suffer a restriction of the personality, we cry out against the oppressor, we invent slogans and doctrines, we fill our minds with day dreams, with intricate mechanisms of some imaginary revolution. At the same time we withdraw from the actual next step. Here is the trade-union movement, built up painfully for over a century, a great army with many divisions which function every day in the industrial struggle. How many radicals know it in any detail? How many have paid the slightest attention to the technique of its organization, or have devoted any time to a working out of the smaller problems which must be worked out before it can achieve this or that victory? Here are our great industries, our complex systems of exchange. How many radicals really know the technique of even the smallest section of them? Radicals wish to reorganize the industrial system; would they know how to organize a factory?

If radicalism arises from the instinct for economic maturity, then it can find its place in the world only by learning its function, only by expressing its emotion in terms of the actual with which it has to deal. A period of adolescence was to be expected, but to prolong the characteristics of that period is to invite futility. And as a matter of fact American radicalism now exhibits a tendency to establish more contacts with reality. Instead of withdrawing from established unions to start a new and spotless labour movement, radicals are beginning to visualize and to carry out the difficult but possible task of improving the organization of the existing unions, and of charging them with new energy and ideas. Unions which were founded by radicals—such as the Amalgamated Clothing Workers of America—are devoting their efforts not to talking of a future revolution, but to organizing the workers more firmly in the present, to establishing constitutional government in industry through which tangible advances may be made and safeguarded, and to improving the productivity of industry itself. Engineers, encouraged by labour organizations, and in some cases actually paid by them, are investigating the problem of economic waste, and are demonstrating by line upon line and precept upon precept how the chaos of competition, industrial autocracy, and a controlling profit motive are reflected in idle hours, low wages, high prices, and inferior products. The co-operative movement is slowly providing a new and more efficient machinery of distribution, while co-operative banks are building up a reserve of credit for those who wish to experiment with undertakings conducted for other purposes than the profit of the proprietor. Such functional use of the labour movement is more dangerous to the existing disorder than volumes of phrases or a whole battalion of " natural rights."

Extremists call such activities compromise. They are compromise in the sense that any hypothesis must be changed to fit the facts, but they involve no compromise with scientific truth. The alchemist compromised when he gave up the search for the philosopher's stone and began to learn from the elements. He surrendered a sterile dogma for a fruitful science. In proportion as radicals learn how to put their emotions to work, in proportion as they devise ways to function in the world in which we live, will they make possible not only unity among themselves, but a rapprochement with other Americans. A man who believes there is no real possibility of change short of complete revolution can unite with a man who has no theory about the matter at all so long as they do not discuss abstract doctrine, but concentrate upon the problem of how to bring about a particular effect at a particular time. The most radical theories, if expressed in terms of concrete situations, will be accepted by those who are wary of generalities, or do not understand them. The theories will be tested in the fact. The operation of such a process may be blocked by those who dogmatically oppose all experiment, but in that case the forces of reason and of nature will be so clearly on the side of the radical that there can be no doubt about his ultimate fruitfulness.

GEORGE SOULE

THE SMALL TOWN

AMERICA is a nation of villagers, once remarked George Bernard Shaw in a moment of his most exclusive scorn for what he believed was our crude and naïve susceptibility to the modes and moods, to say nothing of the manners, of the professional patriots during that hectic period when Wilhelm was training to become the woodman of Amerongen. Now Shaw is the oracle of the Occident, and when he speaks there is no docile dog this side of Adelphi Terrace presumptuous enough to bark. At least there should not be; and in any event, neither history nor H. G. Wells records any spirited protest on America's part to the Shavian accusation. It was allowed to stand invulnerable and irrefutable. Of course, in our hearts we know Shaw is right. We may for the moment be signifying *rus in urbe,* but between you and me and the chief copy-reader of the Marion (Ohio) *Star, in urbe* is a superfluous detail.

Show me a native New Yorker and I will show you something as extinct as a bar-tender. There are no native New Yorkers. All New Yorkers come from small towns and farms. Ask Dad, ask the Sunday editor, ask the census-taker—they know. And what is true of New York is true of Boston and Chicago. The big men, the notable men of the big cities, hail from the small towns, the Springfields, the Jacksons, the Jamestowns, Georgetowns, Charlestowns—yes, and from the Elizabeths and Charlottes—of the nation.

Under the circumstances any back-to-the-land movement in this country seems futile if not ridiculous. The land is still confident and capable of taking care of itself. It needs no aid from the city chaps and asks none. The Freudians are not deceived for a moment over the basis of a return-to-the-farm enterprise. They recognize it for what it is—a sentimental complex superinduced by the nervous hysteria of the city. But even the amazingly small proportion of the population that is not Freudian refuses to become influenced by the cry of the sentimentalists. Because it is keenly, though unpretentiously, aware of the genuinely rural state of its culture and civilization.

The civilization of America is predominantly the civilization of the small town. The few libertarians and cosmopolites who continue to profess to see a broader culture developing along the Atlantic seaboard resent this fact, though they scarcely deny it. They are too intelligent, too widened in vision to deny it. They cannot watch the tremendous growth and power and influence of secret societies, of chambers of commerce, of boosters' clubs, of the Ford car, of moving pictures, of talking-machines, of evangelists, of nerve tonics, of the *Saturday Evening Post*, of Browning societies, of circuses, of church socials, of parades and pageants of every kind and description, of family reunions, of pioneer picnics, of county fairs, of firemen's conventions without secretly acknowledging it. And they know, if they have obtained a true perspective of America, that there is no section of this vast political unit that does not possess—and even frequently boast—these unmistakably provincial signs and symbols.

I do not mean to imply that such aspects make America an unfit place in which to live. On the contrary, America's very possession of them brings colour and rugged picturesqueness, if not a little pathos, to the individual with imagination sufficient to find them. Mr. Dreiser found them and shed a triumphant tear. "Dear, crude America" is to him a sweet and melancholy reality. It is a reality that has been expressed with a good deal of prophecy—and some profit—by the young novelists. Small-town realism with a vengeance, rather than a joy, has been the keynote of their remarkable success during the past year. However, they pulled the pendulum of cultural life too far in one direction. They failed, for the most part, of appreciating the similarity of human nature in city as in country, with the result that their triumph is ephemeral. Already the reaction has set in. There are now going on in the workrooms of the novelists attempts to immortalize Riverside Drive, Fifth Avenue, Beacon Street, Michigan Boulevard, and Pennsylvania Avenue.

Unless they penetrate into the soul of these avenues, unless they perceive that these avenues are not spiritually different from Main Street, though they may be clothed in the habiliments of metropolitan taste and fancy, they will fail to symbolize correctly America. They will be writing merely for money and controversial space in the literary supplements.

For the soul of these avenues is a soul with an *i* substituted for *u*. It is the soul of the land. It is a homely, wholesome provincialism, typifying human nature as it is found throughout the United States. We may herd in a large centre of population, assume the superficialities of cosmopolitan culture and genuinely believe ourselves devils of fellows. It takes all the force of a prohibition law to make us realize that we are more sinned against than sinning. Then are we confronted sharply by the fact that the herd is appallingly inefficient and inarticulate in a conflict with isolated individualism.

The prohibition movement originated in farming communities and villages where the evils of alcohol are ridiculously insignificant. No self-respecting or neighbour-respecting villager could afford to be known as a drinking man. His business or his livelihood was at stake. Then why did he foster prohibition? Why did he seek to fasten it upon the city resident who, if he drank, did not lose apparently his own or his neighbour's respect? Chiefly because of his very isolation. Because he was geographically deprived of the enjoyments which the city man shared. I can well imagine a farmer in the long sweating hours of harvest time or a small town storekeeper forced to currying favour with his friends and neighbours 365 days in a year, resolutely declaring that what he cannot have the man in the city shall not have. The hatching of all kinds of prohibitory plots can be traced to just such apparent injustices of life. Dr. Freud would correctly explain it under the heading of inferiority-complex.

City men have marvelled at the remarkable organization of the reformers. It is not so much organization, however, as it is a national feeling perceived and expressed simultaneously. Cities may conduct the most efficient propaganda against such a feeling, they may assemble their largest voting strength to assail it. All in vain. The country districts roll up the majorities and the cities are left unmistakably high and dry.

So it is with most of the laws and movements of America. The rural sections have but to will them and they become in due time established facts. An idea merely has to take root in the mind of some socially oppressed individual. He talks it over with his friends at lodge meeting or during an informal hour at a board of trade meeting. He receives encouragement. He imparts the idea to his wife, who carries it to her literary club, where it is given further airing. It spreads to the volunteer firemen's clubrooms, to the grange picnics and the church socials. It is discussed in the pulpits. Finally it reaches the ears of the village and county politicians who, impressed by its appeal to the moral force of the community, decide after hours in the back room of the post-office or the national bank to interest the congressman or assemblyman from their district in its merits as a possible law upon the statute books. The congressman and assemblyman, acutely aware of the side on which their bread is buttered, agree to do " everything within their power " to put the measure through. Having the assistance of other congressmen and assemblymen, most of whom are from rural districts, their tasks assuredly are not difficult.

Before the appearance of the automobile and the movie upon the national horizon, the small town was chiefly characterized by a distinctly rural and often melancholy peacefulness. A gentle air of depression hung over it, destructive of the ambitious spirit of youth and yet, by very reason of its existence, influencing this spirit to seek adventure and livelihood in wider fields. Amusements were few and far between. It was the day of the quilting party, of the Sunday promenade in the cemetery, of buggy-riding, of the ice-cream festival and the spelling bee. The bucolic note was ever present.

Such an environment, while joyous to the small boy, became hopelessly dull and lifeless to the youth of vitality and imagination. Restlessness with it tormented him day and night until it grew into an obsession. Especially did he dislike Sunday, its funeral quiet with stores closed and other possible avenues of excitement and adventure forbidden. He began to cherish dreams of a life strange and teeming in distant cities.

As he grew older and a measure of independence came to him he fled, provided there was no business established by a patient and hard-working ancestry which might lure him into remaining home. And even that did not always attract him. He was compelled to go by his very nature—a nature that desired a change from the pall of confining and circumscribed realism, the masks of respectability everywhere about him, the ridiculous display of caste, that saw a rainbow of fulfilled ideals over the hills, that demanded, in a word, romance.

He, who did not feel this urge, departed because of lack of business opportunities. Occasionally he returned disillusioned and exhausted by the city and eager to re-establish himself in a line of work which promised spiritual contentment. But more often he stayed away, struggling with the crowd in the city, returning home only for short vacation periods for rest and reminiscence, to see his people and renew boyhood friendships. At such times he was likely to be impressed by the seeming prosperity of those boys he left behind, of the apparent enjoyment they found in the narrow environment. The thought may have occurred to him that the life of the small town had undergone a marked change, that it had adopted awkward, self-conscious urban airs.

Suddenly he realizes that the automobile and the movie and to some extent the topical magazine are mainly responsible for the contrast. The motor-car has given the small town man an ever-increasing contact with the city, with life at formerly inaccessible resorts, with the country at large. And the movie and the magazine have brought him news and pictures of the outside world. He has patronized them and grown wiser.

The basis, the underlying motive, of all cultural life in the small town is social. The intellectual never enters. It may try to get in but the doors are usually barred. There is practically no demand for the so-called intellectual magazines. Therefore, they are seldom placed on sale. But few daily papers outside of a radius of fifty miles are read. Plays which have exclusive appeal to the imagination or the intellect are presented to rows of empty seats. On the other hand, dramas teeming with primitive emotions and the familiar devices of hokum attract large audiences, provided the producing managers care to abide by the present excessive transportation rates. There is but little interest manifested in great world movements, such as the economic upheaval in Eastern Europe. Normalcy is, indeed, the watchword so far as intellectual development is concerned.

It is in the social atmosphere that the American village has its real *raison d'être*. Therein do we meet the characteristics that have stamped themselves indelibly upon American life. The thousand and one secret societies that flourish here have particularly fertile soil in the small towns. Count all the loyal legionaries of all the chapters of all the secret societies between the Atlantic and Pacific oceans and you have a job suited only to the most irrepressible statistician. And the most loyal live in the small towns and villages of the United States. The choice is not limited. There are societies enough to suit all kinds of personalities and purses.

The Knights of Pythias, the Knights of the Maccabees, the Odd Fellows, the Elks, the Eagles, the Loyal Order of the Moose, the Modern Woodmen, the Masons with their elaborate subdivisions of Shriners and Knights Templar—all count their membership throughout the nation. And the women, jealous of their husbands' loyalty to various and complex forms of hocus-pocus, have organized auxiliary societies which, while not maintaining the secrecy that veils the fraternal orders, nevertheless build up a pretentious mystery intriguing to the male mind.

No town is a self-respecting town unless it can boast half a dozen of these societies. They are the fabric of which the basis of the social structure is built. They are the very essence of America. They dot the national landscape. Every city, as if to prove conclusively its provincial nature, displays one or more temples devoted to the rituals of fraternal organization.

Recently the South has revived the order of the Ku Klux Klan which flourished after the Civil War as a means of improving upon the orderly course of the law in dealing with the Negro race. Here is the apotheosis of the secret society, with its magnificent concealment of identity in a unique form of dress, its pretensions to 100 per cent. Americanism, its blatant proclamations of perpetuating the great and glorious traditions of the republic. The Negro has already organized to offset this propaganda. He knew that unless he could show secret orders of imposing strength he had no right even to the questionable heritage of habitation here. He would be outside the spirit of the times. He owed it to America, to " dear, crude America," to organize lodges and secret societies; and he has done so.

Undoubtedly the secret society plays a large part in the greatness of America. It has made the American class-conscious. It has made him recognize his own importance, his own right to the national distinction of good-fellowship. It provides him temporary surcease from domestic and business details, though there are countless numbers of men who join these orders to make business details, so far as they affect them, more significant.

The amazing prevalence of conventions in America is an outgrowth of the secret societies. Life to many 100 per cent. Americans is just one lodge convention after another. Held in a different city each year, a distinction that is industriously competed for, the convention has become a fixed fact in American cultural life. Here is the one occasion of the year when the serious diddle-daddle is laid aside, and refuge and freedom are sought in such amusements as the convention city can offer. The secret order convention has inspired the assembly of all kinds and descriptions of conventions—trade conventions, religious conventions, educational conventions—until there is no city in the land boasting a first-class hotel that does not at one time or another during the year house delegates with elaborate insignia and badges.

Probably the first parade held in America was that of a class-conscious fraternal organization eager to display its high standard of membership as well as a unique resplendence in elaborate regalia. The parade has continued an integral part of American life ever since. There is something of the vigour, the gusto and crudeness of America in a parade. It has come to represent life here in all its curious phases.

The parade had become an event of colourful significance

when P. T. Barnum organized the " greatest show on earth." He decided to glorify it—in his dictionary " to glorify " really meant " to commercialize "—and once and for all time associate it chiefly with the circus. He succeeded, mainly because the residents of the villages were receptive to the idea. They saw a bizarre relief from the monotony of existence. The farmers rolled down from the hills in their lumber-wagons and found an inarticulate joy, storekeepers closed shop and experienced a tumultuous freedom from the petty bickerings of trade, men and women renewed their youth, children were suddenly thrown into a very ecstasy of delight. Thus, the circus parade became part and parcel of American civilization.

And the precious and unique spirit created by the circus parade has been carried on in innumerable representations. To-day America shelters parades of every conceivable enterprise. Firemen have a day in every small town of the land on which they joyously pull flower-laden hose-carts for the entertainment of their fellow-citizens. Bearing such labels as Alerts, Rescues and Champion Hook and Ladder No. 1, they march proudly down Main Street—and the world goes hang. The volunteer firemen's organization is an institution peculiar to the American small town,—an institution, too, that is not without class-consciousness. The rough-and-ready, comparatively illiterate young men form one group. The clerks, men engaged in the professions and social favourites compose another. This class is usually endowed by the wealthiest resident of the town, and its gratitude is expressed usually by naming the organization for the local Crœsus.

The Elks parade, the Knights of Pythias parade, veterans of various wars parade, the Shriners and Knights Templar parade, prohibitionists parade, anti-prohibitionists parade, politicians parade, women parade, babies parade—everybody parades in America. Indeed, America can be divided into two classes, those who parade and those who watch the parade. The parade is indelibly identified with the small town. It is also inalienably associated with the large city, composed, as it is, of small-town men.

There has lately taken place in the villages throughout the country a new movement that has civic pride as its basis.

It is the formation of boosters' clubs. Everybody is boosting his home town, at least publicly, though in the privacy of the front porch he may be justly depressed by its narrowness of opportunity, its subservience to social snobbery, its intellectual aridity. " Come to Our Town. Free Sites Furnished for Factories," read the signs along the railroad tracks. " Boost Our Town " shout banners stretched across Main Street.

Is there not something vitally poignant in such a proud provincialism? Is not America endeavouring to lift itself up by its boot-straps, to make life more comfortable and interesting? The groping, though crude, is commendable. It is badly directed because there is no inspiration back of it, because its organizers are only remotely aware how to make life here more interesting. However, there is the effort and it is welcome.

Perhaps, when the towns—and for that matter the cities— realize that artistic sensitiveness is necessary to achieve comfort and interest we shall have boosters who are as enthusiastic on the front porch as in the board of trade meeting. When will our towns take artistic advantage of their river-fronts? The place for the most beautiful walk and drive and park presents usually unsightly piers, factories and sheds. Railroad tracks are often laid in the very heart of the town. For many years the leading hotels in practically all of our towns and cities were built in close proximity to the railroad station. In seeking to save a traveller time and convenience hotel proprietors subjected him to the bodily and mental discomforts that are related to the vicinity of a railroad station. Of late there is a marked tendency to erect hotels in quiet residential streets away from the noise and confusion of shops and railroad yards.

The billboard menace, while diminishing, is still imposing. It is to the everlasting shame of the towns and cities that in an era of prohibitions no legislative effort has been made to stop the evil of desecrating our finest streets with advertising signs. Such commercial greed is inconceivable to the foreign visitor. It is one of his first impressions, though he charitably takes refuge in public in attributing it to the high tension of our existence.

While the first symptoms of artistic appreciation are beginning to be faintly discerned upon the American horizon, the old and familiar phases of social life in the country are still being observed. The picnic of first settlers, the family reunion, the church supper, the sewing circle, the Browning society—all have national expression. The introduction of such modern industrial devices as the automobile has not affected them in the least. It can truly be asserted that the flivver has even added to their popularity. It has brought people of the country districts into closer contact than ever before. It has given a new prestige to the picnics and the reunions.

What offers more rustic charm and simplicity than a family reunion? Practically every family in the farming districts that claims an ancestral residence in this country of more than fifty years holds one annually. It is attended by the great and the near-great from the cities, by the unaffected relatives back home. Babies jostle great-grandparents. Large and perspiring women bake for days the cakes and pies to be consumed. The men of the house are foolishly helping in making the rooms and the front lawn ready. At last the reunion is at hand—a sentimental debauch, a grand gorging. Everybody present feels the poignancy of age. But while the heart throbs the stomach is working overtime. The law of compensation is satisfied. " A good time was had by all " finds another expression in the weekly paper, and the reunion becomes a memory.

At pioneer picnics one finds the family reunion on a larger scale. The whole township and county has for the time become related. It is the day of days, a sentimental tournament with handshaking as the most popular pastime. Organized in the rugged primitiveness of the early part of the 19th century by men who were first to settle in the vicinity, the pioneer picnic has been perpetuated, until to-day it is linked inalterably with America's development. It has weathered the passing of the nation from an agricultural to a great industrial commonwealth. It has stood the gaff of time. And so it goes on for ever, a tradition of the small town and the farming community. While it has been divested almost entirely of its original purpose, it serves to bring the politicians in touch

with the " peepul." Grandiloquent promises are made for a
day from the rostrum by a battalion of " Honourables "—and
forgotten both by the " Honourables " and the public intent
upon dancing and walking aimlessly about the grounds. The
politicians smile as they continue to preserve their heroic pose,
and the " peepul," satisfied that all is well with the world, turn
to various gambling devices that operate under the hypocritical
eye of the sheriff and to the strange dances that have crept
up from the jungle, for it is a day filled with the eternal spirit
of youth. There is ingenuous appeal in the fair samples of
the yokelry present. There is a quiet force beneath the bovine
expressions of the boys. The soul of America—an America
glad to be alive—is being wonderfully and pathetically manifested. No shams, no superficialities, no self-conscious sophistication are met. Merely the sturdy quality of the true American civilization, picturesque and haunting in its primitiveness.

The county fair belongs in the same classification as the first-
settler picnic. It is the annual relaxation by farmers and
merchants from the tedious tasks of seeing and talking to the
same people day after day. It offers them a measure of
equality with the people in the city with their excursion boats,
their baseball games, their park sports. And they make the
most of their opportunity. They come to see and to be seen,
to risk a few dollars on a horse race, to admire the free exhibitions in front of the side-shows, to watch with wide eyes the
acrobatic stunts before the grandstand, to hear the " Poet and
the Peasant " overture by the band, proud and serious in a
stand of its own.

Three or four days given to such pleasures naturally bestow
a fine sense of illusion upon the visitors. They begin to believe that life has been specially ordered for them. They see
through a glass lightly. They care not a whiff about the
crowded excitements of the city. They have something infinitely more enjoyable than a professional baseball game or an
excursion ride down the river. They have days of endless
variety, of new adventures, of new thoughts. They, too, know
that America cannot go wrong so long as they continue to find
illusion. And they are correct. They may not suspect that

American culture is crude. They do know, however, that it is dear. They should worry.

Against such a background have the flavour and essence of American life been compounded. Their influence has extended in all directions, in all walks of industry. They have left their impress upon the character of the country, upon the mob and the individual. Sentimental attachment to the old ties, to boyhood ideals and traditions remains potent though a little concealed by the mask, be it affected or real, of sophistication. It is the voice of a new land, of a vigorous and curious nationalism that is being exerted. There obviously cannot be among such a naturally healthy people a supercilious contempt for sentiment. We may laugh a little haughtily at the amazing susceptibility of folks to the extravagant eloquence of itinerant evangelists. We may look on an "old home week" with a touch of urban disdain. We may listen to the band concert on a Saturday night in the Court House Square with a studied indifference. We may assume an attractive weariness in watching the promenaders on Main Street visit one ice-cream emporium after another. But deep down in our hearts is a feeling of invincible pride in the charming homeliness, the youthful vitality, the fine simplicity, yes, and the sweeping pathos of these aspects of small-town civilization.

LOUIS RAYMOND REID

HISTORY

" Nescire autem quid antea quam natus sis
acciderit id est semper puerum esse."
Cicero.

"History is bunk."
Henry Ford

THE burghers of Holland, being (like the Chinese) inclined
towards a certain conservatism of both manners and
habits, continued the tradition of the " front parlour "—
the so-called " good-room "—well into the 20th century.
Every farmer had his " front parlour " filled with stuffy air,
stuffy furniture, and an engraving of the Eiffel Tower facing
the lithographic representation of a lady in mid-seas clinging
desperately to a somewhat ramshackle granite cross.

But the custom was not restricted to the bucolic districts.
His late Majesty, William III (whose funeral was the most
useful event of his long life), had been married to an estimable
lady of Victorian proclivities, who loved a " tidy " and an
" antimacassar " better than life itself.   An aristocracy, recruited from the descendants of East India Directors and West
India sugar planters, followed the Royal Example.   They
owned modest homes which the more imaginative Latin would
have called " Palazzi."   Most of the ground floor was taken
up by an immense " front parlour."   For the greater part of
the year it was kept under lock and key while the family clus-
tered around the oil lamp of the " back parlour " where they
lived in the happy cacophony of young daughters practising
Czerny and young sons trying to master the intricacies of
" paideuo—paideueis—paideuei."

As for the " front parlour " (which will form the main part
of my text), it was opened once or twice a twelve-month for
high family functions.   A week beforehand, the cleaning
woman (who received six cents per hour in those blessed

Neanderthal days) would arrive with many mops and many brooms. The covers would be removed from the antique furniture, the frames of the pictures would be duly scrubbed. The carpets were submitted to a process which resembled indoor ploughing and for fully half an hour each afternoon the windows were opened to the extent of three or four inches.

Then came the day of the reception—the birthday party of the grandfather—the betrothal of the young daughter. All the relatives were there in their best silks and satins. The guests were there in ditto. There was light and there was music. There was enough food and drink to keep an entire Chinese province from starving. Yet the party was a failure. The old family portraits—excellent pieces by Rembrandt or Terborch—looked down upon grandchildren whom they did not know. The grandchildren, on the other hand, were quite uncomfortable in the presence of this past glory. Sometimes, when the guests had expressed a sincere admiration of these works of art, they hired a hungry Ph.D. to write a critical essay upon their collection for the benefit of the " Studio " or the " Connoisseur." Then they ordered a hundred copies, which they sent to their friends that they might admire (and perhaps envy) the ancient lineage of their neighbours. Thereafter, darkness and denim covers and oblivion.

The history of our great Republic suffers from a fate similar to that of these heirlooms. It lives in the " front parlour " of the national consciousness. It is brought out upon a few grand occasions when it merely adds to the general discomfort of the assisting multitude. For the rest of the time it lies forgotten in the half dark of those Washington cellars which for lack of National Archives serve as a receptacle for the written record of our past.

Our popular estimate of history and the value of a general historical background was defined a few years ago by Henry Ford. Mr. Ford, having made a dozen flivvers go where none went before and having gained untold wealth out of the motor-car industry, had been appointed an ex-officio and highly esteemed member of our national Council of Wise Men. His opinion was eagerly asked upon such subjects as child-raising, irrigation, the future of the human race, and the plausibility of the Einstein theory. During a now memorable trial the subject of history came up for discussion, and Mr. Ford (if we are to believe the newspaper accounts) delivered himself of the heartfelt sentiment that " history is bunk." A grateful country sang Amen!

When asked to elucidate this regrettable expression of dislike, the average citizen will fall back upon reminiscences of his early childhood and in terms both contrite and unflattering he will thereupon describe the hours of misery which he has spent reciting " dreary facts about useless kings," winding up with a wholesale denunciation of American history as something dull beyond words.

We cannot say much in favour of late Stuarts, Romanoffs, and Wasa's, but we confess to a sincere affection for the history of these United States. It is true there are few women in it and no little children. This, to us, seems an advantage. " Famous women of history " usually meant " infamous trouble " for their much perturbed contemporaries. As for the ever-popular children motif, the little princes of the Tower would have given a great deal had they been allowed to whitewash part of Tom Sawyer's famous fence, instead of waiting in silken splendour for Uncle Richard's murder squad.

No, the trouble is not with the history of this land of endless plains and a limitless sky. The difficulty lies with the reader. He is the victim of an unfortunate circumstance. The Muses did not reach these shores in the first-class cabin of the *Aquitania*. They were almost held up at Ellis Island and deported because they did not have the necessary fifty dollars. They were allowed to sneak in after they had given a solemn promise that they would try to become self-supporting and would turn their white hands to something useful.

Clio, our revered mistress, has tried hard to live up to this vow. But she simply is not that sort of woman. An excellent counsellor, the most charming and trusted of friends, she has absolutely no gift for the practical sides of life. She was forced to open a little gift-shop where she sold flags and bunting and pictures of Pocahontas and Paul Revere. The venture was not a success. A few people took pity on her and tried to help. She was asked to recite poetry at patriotic gatherings and do selections from the " Founding Fathers." She did not like this, being a person of shy and unassuming character. And so she is back in the little shop. When last I saw her, she was trying to learn the Russian alphabet. That is always a dangerous sign.

And now, lest we continue to jumble our metaphors, let us state the case with no more prejudice than is strictly necessary.

The earliest settlers of this country brought their history with them. Little Snorri, son of Gudrid and Thorfinn Karlsefni, playing amidst the vines of his father's Labradorian garden, undoubtedly listened to the selfsame sagas that were being told at the court of good King Olaf Tryggvason in distant Norway. The children of San Domingo shared the glories of the Cid with the boys and girls who visited the schools of Moukkadir's ancient capital. And the long-suffering infants of the early New England villages merely finished an historical education that had begun at Scrooby and had been continued at No. 21 of the *Kloksteeg* in Leyden.

During the 17th century, the greater part of the Atlantic coast became English. The Dutch and the French, the Spanish and Swedish traditions disappeared. The history of the British Kingdom became the universal history of the territory situated between the thirtieth and the fiftieth degree of latitude. Even the American Revolution was a quarrel between two conflicting versions of certain identical principles of history. Lord North and George Washington had learned their lessons from the same text-book. His Lordship, of course, never cut the pages that told of Runymede, and George undoubtedly covered the printed sheets which told of the fate of rebels with strange geometrical figures. But the historical inheritance of the men who fought on the left bank of the Fish Kill and those who surrendered on the right shore was a common one, and Burgoyne and Gates might have spent a profitable evening sharing a bottle of rum and complimenting each other upon the glorious deeds of their respective but identical ancestors.

But during the 'twenties and 'thirties of the 19th century, the men of the " old régime "—the founder and fighters of the young Republic—descended into the grave and they took their

traditions, their hopes, and their beliefs with them. The curtain rose upon a new time and upon a new people. The acquisition of the Northwestern Territory in 1787 and the purchase of Napoleon's American real-estate in the year 1803 had
changed a little commonwealth of struggling Colonies into a
vast empire of endless plains and unlimited forests. It was
necessary to populate this new land. The history of the
Coast came to an end. The history of the Frontier began.
English traditions rarely crossed the Alleghanies. The long
struggle for representative government took on a new aspect in
a land where no king had ever set foot and where man was
sovereign by the good right of his own energy.

It is true that the first fifty years of the last century witnessed the arrival upon these shores of millions of men and
women from Europe who had enjoyed a grammar school education in the land of their birth. But dukes do not emigrate.
Those sturdy fellows who risked the terrors and horrors of the
Atlantic in the leaky tubs of the early forties came to the
country of their future that they might forget the nightmare
of the past. That nightmare included the biography of Might
which was then the main feature of the European text-book.
They threw it overboard as soon as they were well outside of
the mouth of the Elbe or the Mersey. Settled upon the farms
of Michigan and Wisconsin, they sometimes taught their children the songs of the old Fatherland but its history never.
After two generations, this migration—the greatest of all
" treks " since the 4th century—came to an end. Roads had
been made, canals had been dug, railroads had been constructed, forests had been turned into pastures, the Indian was
gone, the buffalo was gone, free land was gone, cities had been
built, and the scene had been made ready for the final
apotheosis of all human accomplishment—civilization.

The schoolmaster has ever followed in the wake of the full
dinner-pail. He now made his appearance and began to teach.
Considering the circumstances he did remarkably well. But
he too worked under a disadvantage. He was obliged to go
to New England for his learning and for his text-books. And
the historian of the Boston school, while industrious and patient, was not entirely a fair witness. The recollection of

British red-coats drilling on the Common was still fresh in the minds of many good citizens. The wickedness of George III was more than a myth to those good men and women whose own fathers had watched Major Pitcairn as he marched forth to arrest Adams and Hancock. They sincerely hated their former rulers, while they could not deny their love for the old mother country. Hence there arose a conflict of grave consequence. With one hand the New England chronicler twisted the tail of the British lion. With the other he fed the creature little bits of sugar.

Again the scene changed. The little red school-house had marched across the plains. It had followed the pioneer through the passes of the Rocky Mountains. It had reached the shores of the Pacific Ocean. The time of hacking and building and frying with lard came to a definite end. The little red school-house gave way for the academy of learning. College and University arose wherever a thousand people happened to be together. History became a part of the curriculum. The schoolmaster, jack of all learned trades and master of many practical pursuits, became extinct. The professional historian made his appearance. And thereby hangs a sad tale which takes us to the barren banks of the Spree.

Ever since the Thirty Years War, Germany had been the battlefield of Europe. The ambitions of the Napoleon who was four feet tall and smooth shaven and the prospective ambitions of the Napoleon who was five feet tall and who waxed his moustachios, had given and were actually giving that country very little rest. The intelligentsia of the defunct Holy Roman Empire saw but a single road which could lead to salvation. The old German State must be re-established and the kings of Prussia must become heirs to the traditions of Charlemagne. To prove this point it was necessary that the obedient subjects of half a hundred little potentates be filled with certain definite historical notions about the glorious past of Heinrich the Fat and Konrad the Lean. The patient historical camels of the Teutonic universities were driven into the heart of *Historia Deserta* and brought back those stupendous bricks of learning out of which the rulers of the land could build their monuments to the glorious memory of the Ancestors.

Whatever their faults and however misguided the ambition of these faithful beasts of burden, they knew how to work. The whole world looked on with admiration. Here, at last, in this country of scientific precision, history had been elevated to the rank of a "*Wissenschaft.*" Carrying high their banners, "For God, for Country, *und wie es eigentlich dagewesen*," all good historians went upon a crusade to save the Holy Land of the Past from the Ignorance of the Present.

That was in the blessed days when a first-class passage to Hamburg and Bremen cost forty-six dollars and seventy-five cents. Henry Adams and John Lothrop Motley were among the first of the pilgrims. They drank a good deal of beer, listened to many excellent concerts, and assisted, "privatissime and gratis," at the colloquia docta of many highly learned *Geheimräte*, and departed before they had suffered serious damage. Others did not fare as well. Three—four—five years they spent in the company of the Carolingians and the Hohenstaufens. After they had soaked themselves sufficiently in Ploetz and Bernheim to survive the *Examen Rigorosum* of the *Hochgelehrte Facultät*, they returned to their native shore to spread the gospel of true *Wissenschaftlichkeit*.

There was nothing typically American in this. It happened to the students of every country of the globe.

Of course, in making this point, we feel that we expose ourselves to the accusation of a slight exaggeration. "How now," the industrious reader exclaims, "would you advocate a return to the uncritical days of the Middle Ages?" To which we answer, "By no means." But history, like cooking or fiddling, is primarily an art. It embellishes life. It broadens our tolerance. It makes us patient of bores and fools. It is without the slightest utilitarian value. A handbook of chemistry or higher mathematics has a right to be dull. A history, never. And the professional product of the Teutonic school resembled those later-day divines who tried to console the dying by a recital of the Hebrew verb *abhar*.

This system of preaching the gospel of the past filled the pulpits but it emptied the pews. The congregation went elsewhere for its historical enlightenment. Those who were seriously interested turned to the works of a few laymen (hardware manufacturers, diplomats, coal-dealers, engineers) who devoted their leisure hours to the writing of history, or imported the necessary intellectual pabulum from abroad. Others took to the movies and since those temples of democratic delight do not open before the hour of noon, they spent the early morning perusing the endless volumes of reminiscences, memoirs, intimate biographies, and recollections which flood the land with the energy of an intellectual *cloaca maxima*.

But all this, let us state it once more, did not matter very much. When all is peace and happiness—when the hospitals are empty of patients—when the weather is fine and people are dying at the usual rate—it matters little whether the world at large takes a deep interest in the work of the Board of Health. The public knows that somewhere, somehow, someway, there exists a Board of Health composed of highly trained medical experts. They also appreciate from past experiences that these watchful gentlemen " know their job " and that no ordinary microbe can hope to move from Warsaw to Chicago without prompt interference on the part of the delousing squad. But when an epidemic threatens the safety of the community, then the public hastens to the nearest telephone booth—calls up the Health Commissioners and follows their instructions with implicit faith. It demands that these public servants shall spend the days of undisturbed health to prepare for the hour of sickness when there is no time for meditation and experiment.

The public at large had a right to expect a similar service from its historians. But unfortunately, when the crisis came, the scientific historical machine collapsed completely.

In Germany, the home country of the system of *historische Wissenschaftlichkeit,* the historian became the barker outside the Hohenzollern main tent, shouting himself hoarse for the benefit of half-hearted fellow citizens and hostile neutrals, extolling the ancestral Teutonic virtues until the whole world turned away in disgust. In France, they arrange those things better. Even the most unhealthy mess of nationalistic scraps can be turned into a palatable dish by a competent cook of the Parisian school. In England, the historian turned propagandist, and for three years, the surprised citizens of Copenhagen, Bern, and Madrid found their mail boxes cluttered with mysterious bundles of state documents duly stamped, beautifully illustrated, and presented (as the enclosed card showed) with the compliments of Professor So-and-so of Such-and-such College, Oxford, England. In Russia, a far-seeing government had taken its measures many years before. Those historians who had refused to be used as *cheval de bataille* for the glory of the house of Romanoff, were either botanising along the banks of the Lena or had long since found a refuge in the universities of Sofia and Geneva. I do not know what happened in Japan, but I have a suspicion that it was the same thing, the entire world over.

The historian turned apologist. He was as useful as a doctor who would show a partiality to the native streptococcus on the grounds of loyalty to the land of his birth.

What happened on this side of the ocean after the first three years of " peace without victory " had given place to " force to the uttermost " is too well known to demand repetition. Long before the first American destroyer reached Plymouth, the staunch old vessel of history had been *spurlos versenkt* in the *mare clausum* of the Western hemisphere. Text-books were recalled, rehashed, and revamped to suit the needs of the hour. Long and most deservedly forgotten treatises were called back to life and with the help of publishers' blurbs and reviews by members of the self-appointed guardians of national righteousness they were sent forth to preach the gospel of domestic virtue. Strange encyclopædias of current information were concocted by volunteers from eager faculties. The public mind was a blank. For a hundred years the little children had learned to dislike history and grown-ups had revaluated this indifference into actual hate. This situation had been created to maintain on high the principles of scientific historical investigation. Let popular interest perish as long as the Truth stand firm. But in the hour of need, the guardians of the Truth turned gendarmes, the doors of Clio's temple were closed, and the public was invited to watch the continuation of the performance in the next moving-picture house. At Versailles the curtain went down upon the ghastly performance.

After the first outbreak of applause the enthusiasm waned. Who had been responsible for this terrible tragedy? The supposed authors were branded as enemies of mankind. Nations tottered and ancient Empires crumbled to dust and were hastily carried to the nearest historical scrapheap. The ambitious monarch, who for thirty years had masqueraded as a second Charlemagne, made his exit amidst properties borrowed from the late King Louis Philippe. The gay young leader of the Death Head Hussars developed into the amateur bicycle-repairer of the island of Wieringen. International reputations retailed at a price which could only be expressed in Soviet rubles and Polish marks and no takers. The saviour of the world became the invalid of the White House. But not a word was said about those inconspicuous authors of very conspicuous historical works who had been the henchmen of the *Oberste* and *Unterste Kriegsherren*. They went back to the archives to prepare the necessary post-mortem statements. These are now being published at a price which fortunately keeps them well out of reach of the former soldiers.

In certain dramas and comedies of an older day it was customary to interrupt the action while the Chorus of moralising Villagers reviewed what had gone before and drew the necessary conclusions. It is time for the " goat-singers " to make their appearance.

" Are you, O Author," so they speak, " quite fair when you pronounce these bitter words? Are we not all human— too human? Is it reasonable to demand of our historians that they shall possess such qualities of detached judgment as have not been seen on this earth since the last of the Mighty Gods departed from High Olympus? Has a historian no heart? Do you expect him to stand by and discuss the virtues of vague political questions, when all the world is doing its bit—while his children are risking their lives for the safety of the common land? "

And when we are approached in this way, we find it difficult to answer " no." For we too are an animated compound of prejudice and unreasonable preferences and even more unreasoning dislikes, and we do not like to assume the rôle of both judge and jury.

The evidence, however, gives us no chance to decide otherwise. What was done in the heat of battle—what was done under the stress of great and sincere emotions—what was written in the agony of a thousand fears—all that will be forgotten within a few years. But enough will remain to convince our grandchildren that the historian was among those most guilty of creating that " state of mind " without which modern warfare would be an impossibility.

Here the music of the flutes grows silent. The Chorus steps back and the main action of our little play continues. The time is " the present " and the problem is " the future." The children who are now in the second grade will be called upon to bear the burden of a very long period of reconstruction. America, their home, has been compared to an exceedingly powerful and influential woman who is not very popular but who must not be offended on account of her eminent social position. The folk who live along our international Main Street are not very well disposed towards a neighbour who holds all the mortgages and lives in the only house that has managed to survive the recent catastrophe. It will not be an easy thing to maintain the peace in the neurasthenic community of the great post-war period. It has been suggested that the Ten Commandments, when rightly applied, may help us through the coming difficulties. We beg to suggest that a thorough knowledge of the past will prove to be quite as useful as the Decalogue. We do not make this statement hastily. Furthermore, we qualify it by the observation that both History and the Decalogue will be only two of a great many other remedies that will have to be applied if the world is to be set free from its present nightmare of poison gas and high-velocity shells. But we insist that History be included. And we do so upon the statement of a learned and famous colleague who passed through a most disastrous war and yet managed to keep a cool head. We mean Thucydides. In his foreword to the History of the Peloponnesian War he wrote: " The absence of romance in my history will, I fear, detract somewhat from its interest; but if it be judged by those inquirers who desire an exact knowledge of the past as an aid to the interpretation of the future, which in the course of human things, must resemble, if it does not reflect it, I shall be content."

When we measure out achievements in the light of this ancient Greek ideal, we have accomplished very little indeed. An enormous amount of work has been done and much of it is excellent. The great wilderness of the past has been explored with diligent care and the material lies, carefully classified, in those literary museums which we call libraries. But the public refuses to go in. No one has ever been able to convince the man in the street that time employed upon historical reading is not merely time wasted. He carries with him certain hazy notions about a few names, Cæsar and Joan of Arc (since the war) and Magna Charta and George Washington and Abraham Lincoln. He remembers that Paul Revere took a ride, but whither and for what purpose he neither knows nor cares to investigate. The historical tie which binds him to the past and which alone can make him understand his own position in relation to the future, is non-existent. Upon special occasions the multitude is given the benefit of a grand historical pyrotechnic display, paid for by the local Chamber of Commerce, and a few disjointed facts flash by amidst the fine roar of rockets and the blaring of a brass band. But this sort of historical evangelising has as little value as the slapstick vespers which delight the congregation of Billy Sunday's circus tent.

We live in an age of patent medicines. The short-cut to success is the modern *pons asinorum* which leads to happiness. And remedies which are " guaranteed to cure " are advertised down the highways and byways of our economic and social world. But no such cure exists for the sad neglect of an historical background. History can never be detached from life. It will continue to reflect the current tendencies of our modern world until that happy day when we shall discontinue the pursuit of a non-essential greatness and devote our energies towards the acquisition of those qualities of the spirit without which human existence (at its best) resembles the proverbial dog-kennel.

For the coming of that day we must be as patient as Nature.

HENDRIK WILLEM VAN LOON

SEX

"The sin I impute to each frustrate ghost
Is the unlit lamp and the ungirt loin."

IN one of the popular plays of last season, a melodrama toned up with snatches of satire and farce, the wife was portrayed as a beaten dog heeling her master after he has crushed her down across the table the better to rowel off her nose. Not until the would-be mutilator was finally disposed of by an untrammelled Mexican did the woman feel free to go to her lover, and even then she took little or no satisfaction in the venture. As for the lover, he had to be robbed of his pistol by the husband and shot at, and then—the husband out of the way—threatened by the bandit with the loss of the woman, before he felt free to take her. The two New Englanders were made happy in spite of themselves—and in accordance with the traditions or conventions of the audience.

To leave a husband for a lover is in theory un-American, unless the husband gives a legal ground for divorce and the divorce is secured. In several States cruelty is a legal ground, and so the conjugal fidelity of the stage-heroine was perhaps overdrawn. But the feeling that she was presumed to share with the audience—that the initiative towards freedom in love should not come from her—is a characteristic trait of American morality. If your husband is unrestrainedly a brute or a villain, you may leave him, in fact it behooves you to leave him, but if he is merely a bore, or perhaps a man you like well enough as a friend, but only as a friend, you must stay on with him in an intimacy where boredom readily becomes aversion and mere friendliness, disgust. The fact that you do not love a person is no reason at all, in American opinion, for not living as if you did.

This opinion or attitude is explicit in American divorce law. In none of the States is divorce granted either by mutual consent or at the desire, the overt desire, of either person. In fact collusion, as mutual consent is called, is accounted a reason against granting divorce, and desire for divorce on the part of one remains ineffectual until the other has been forced into entertaining it. He or she must be given due ground. Disinclination to intimacy is not of itself due ground. You must express disinclination in a way so disagreeable that he or she will want to get rid of you. The law sets a premium on being hateful, declares indeed that in this case it is an indispensable condition to not being miserable.

The grotesqueness, from either a social or psychological point of view, would be too obvious to emphasize, if the implications of this attitude towards divorce were not so significant of American attitudes at large towards sex—attitudes of repression or deception. Of deception or camouflage towards divorce there is one other conspicuous point I should like to note. "Strictness of divorce" is commonly argued to be protection of marriage for the sake of children, since brittle marriage is destructive of the family life. It is safe to say that from no contemporary discussion of divorce will this argument be omitted; and it is equally safe to say that the rejoinder that divorce laws should therefore discriminate between parents and non-parents will, by the opponents of divorce, pass unheeded. That this distinction should be so persistently ignored is accountable only, it seems to me, on the ground of emotional self-deception. What else but a covert emotional attitude could make tenable the irrationality, and what else is that attitude but that joy in mating is of negligible value, that sex emotion, if not a necessary evil, is at any rate a negligible good, deserving merely of what surplus of attention may be available from the real business of life? Indifference towards sex emotion is masked by concern for offspring.

In France, we may note, this confusion between parenthood and mating does not exist. The parental relation in both law and custom is highly regulated, much more regulated than among English-speaking peoples, but it is unlikely that it would be argued in France that mating and parenthood were inseparable concepts. Unlikely, because the French attitude towards sex differs so radically from the Anglo-Saxon.

To the French, as to many of the Continental peoples of Europe, sexual interest is normally to be kept stimulated, neither covered over nor suppressed. And in this case stimulation is seen to depend largely upon the factor of interrelation. Sex-facts are to be related to other facts of life, not rigidly or *a priori,* as in the American view that mating is inseparable from parenthood, but fluently and realistically, as life itself moves and finds expression. And sex-facts in European opinion are to be interrelated in a philosophy of sex. Failure to make these interrelations, together with the attitude of suppression, seem to me to be the outstanding aspects of the characteristically American attitude towards sex.

There is no need in this post-Freudian day of dwelling upon the effects of suppression of sex instinct or impulse. Suppression leads, we are told, either to sublimation, in which case it is diversion, rather than suppression, or it leads to perversion or disease. Unfortunately sex-pathology in the United States has been given little or no study, statistically. We have no statistical data of health or disease in relation to the expression or suppression of sex instinct, and no data on the extent or the effects of homosexuality or of the direction of the sex impulses towards self. Opinion therefore becomes merely a matter of personal observation and conclusion, observation of individuals or small groups. My own conclusion or guess in regard to perversion in this country is that part of the commonly observed spirit of isolation or antagonism between the sexes, and part of the spirit of competition between individuals, are associated with homosexual or masturbatory tendencies which get expressed in varying degrees according to varying circumstances. More particularly the lack of warmth in personal intercourse which makes alike for American bad manners and, in the more intellectual circles, for cheerlessness and aridity is due, I think, to failure of one kind or another in sex relations. I mean cultural failure, not merely individual failure.

May not some such theory of sex failure account also for that herd sense which is so familiar a part of Americanism, and which is not incompatible with the type of self-seeking or pseudo-individualism of which American individualism appears to be an expression? It is a tenable hypothesis that

sexually isolated individuals become dependent upon the group
for stimulus, whether of emotion or will, whereas persons in
normal sex relations, although they may contribute to the group
or co-operate with it, remain comparatively independent of it,
finding stimulus in sex and its sublimations.

If this theory is valid, we may expect to find a comparatively large number of sex failures in those circles which are
characterized by what Everett Dean Martin has recently
called crowd behaviour, reform circles intolerant of other
mindedness and obsessed by belief in the paramountcy of their
own dogma.

> " Leur printemps sans jeunesse exige des folies,
> Leur sang brûlant leur dicte des propos amers,
> L'émeute est un remède à la mélancolie,
> Et nous aurions la paix si leurs yeux étaient clairs,
> Ou leur femme jolie."

Were a set of tests for sex failure or sex fulfilment applied to
the more outstanding propagandists of this country, likewise,
of course, for comparative purposes, to an adequate number
of non-propagandists, the results might be of considerable
significance. I recommend the undertaking to the National
Research Council in co-operation with some organization for
social hygiene.

Meanwhile in what measure propagandism of various sorts
may be a perversion of sex or a sublimation remains speculative; and in applying theory one should be thoroughly aware
that from the day of Sappho and before to the day of Elizabeth Blackwell and after, even to the Russian Revolution, sex
failure of one kind or another, the kind considered at the time
most despicable, has commonly been imputed to persons or
groups disapproved of on other grounds or reprobated. Some
sublimation of sex in the United States there must be, of course,
not only in propaganda movements, but in other expressions
of American culture, in American art and letters and science,
in philanthropy, in politics, finance, and business. By and
large, however, in all·these cultural expressions does one see
any conspicuous measure of sex sublimation? Is not the concern practical rather than devotional, a matter of getting

rather than giving, of self-advancement or family support
rather than of interest in ideas and their forms or in the values
of taste or of faith?

Interest in impersonal subjects in general is not an American trait. Personal concrete terms are the terms commonly
used. Americans, as we say, are not given to abstract thought
or philosophy. They are interested in facts as facts, not as
related to other facts. How expect of Americans, therefore,
that kind of curiosity about sex which leads to a philosophy of
sex? Sex curiosity in American life does not lead past curiosity
about isolated facts, and that means that it leads not to philosophy but to gossip and pruriency. Not long ago I was talking
with a woman about a common acquaintance to whom I referred as singularly free through sophistication and circumstance to please any man she liked. "What do you mean?
Have you heard any scandal about her?" snapped out my
companion, not at all interested in the general reflection, but
avid of information about illicit affairs.

Facts which are not held together through theory call for
labels. People who do not think in terms of relations are
likely to be insistent upon names. Labels or names for sex
disposition or acts are, as a matter of fact, very definite in the
American vernacular. "Engaged," "attentive," "devoted,"
"a married man," "a man of family," "a grass widow," "a
good woman," "a *bad* woman"—there is no end to such tags.
Again, intimacy between a man and a woman is referred definitely to the act of consummation, a sex relation is strictly
classified according to whether or not it is physically consummated. In this attitude towards sex boundaries or captions
may lie the explanation, incidentally, of what is a constant
puzzle to the European visitor—the freedom of social intercourse allowed to the youth of opposite sexes. Since consummation only constitutes sexual intimacy in American opinion,
and since consummation, it is assumed, is utterly out of the
question, why raise barriers between boys and girls? The
assumption that consummation is out of the question is, by and
large, correct, which is still another puzzzle. To this some clue
may be found, I think, in our concluding discussion.

Fondness for captions and for the sort of classification that is so likely to paralyze perception of the finer distinctions and to arrest thought, are natural enough in a child, learning language and so pressed upon by the multiplicity of phenomena that in self-protection he must make rough classifications and remain unaware of much. The old who are dying to life are also exclusive, and they, too, cling to formulas. Is American culture in the matter of sex childish and immature, as Americans imply when they refer to their " young country," or is the culture representative of the aged; are Americans born old, as now and again a European critic asserts?

Such terms of age are figurative, of course, unless we take them in a historical sense, meaning either that a new culture was developed in this country—or rather that there were fresh developments of an old culture—or that an old culture was introduced and maintained without significant change. This is not the place to discuss the cultural aspects of Colonial America, but it is important to bear in mind in any discussion of merely contemporaneous sex attitudes in this country the contributions of European, and more particularly, English morality. Without recalling the traditions of early Christianity or of English Puritanism, those attitudes of ignoring or suppressing the satisfactions of the impulses of sex to which we have referred were indeed incomprehensible and bewildering— mere psychological interpretation seems inadequate. But viewed as consequences of the sense of sin in connection with sex, which was a legacy from Paul and his successors in English Puritanism, interpretation is less difficult, and the American attitude toward sex becomes comparatively intelligible—the attitude seen in divorce and in the melodramas, and in the standardizing of sex relations, in accordance with that most significant of Pauline dogmas that marriage is the lesser of two evils, that it is better to marry than to burn. Without the key of Paul and of the obscenities of the early Christian Fathers how explain the recent legislation in Virginia making it a crime to pay attention to a married man or woman, or such a sermon as was recently preached somewhere in the Middle West urging a crusade against the practice of taking another man's wife in to dinner or dancing round dances? " At a dinner of friends let every man take his own wife on his arm and walk in to their seats side by side at the dinner table to the inspiring music of 'Onward Christian Soldiers,'" urged the minister. As to dancing, whenever a man is seen to put his arm around a woman who is not his wife, the band should cease playing. I do not quote the words of the latter injunction, as they are rather too indecent.

Turning from the historical back to the psychological point of view—in one of those circles of cause and effect that are composed now of cultural inheritance or tradition, now of psychological trend or disposition—the American case of sex, whether a case of adolescence or of senescence, may be said to present symptoms of arrested development. Together with the non-realism of childish or senile formula, there is here the kind of emotionalism which checks emotional vitality and which is fed upon the sense of crisis; we may call it crisis-emotion. Life at large, the sex life in particular, is presented as a series of crises preceded and followed by a static condition, and in these conventional times of crisis only, the times when the labels are being attached, are the emotions aroused. In the intervals, in the stretches between betrothal, marriage, birth, christening, or divorce, there is little or no sense of change—none of the emotions that correspond to changing relations and are expressions of personal adjustment. The emotions of crisis are statutory, pre-determined, conventionalized; neither for oneself nor for others do they make any demands upon imagination, or insight, or spiritual concern.

Here in this psychology of crisis is the clue—before mentioned—to an understanding of the freedom allowed our youth, of " bundling," as the Colonials termed it, or, in current phrase, " petting." In general, " keeping company " is accounted one kind of a relationship, marriage, another—one characterized by courtship without consummation, the other by consummation without courtship. Between the two kinds of relationship there is no transition, it is assumed, except by convention or ritual. So inrooted is this social attitude that the young cannot escape adopting it, at least the very young to whom, at any rate, uncritical conservatism seems to be natural. Indeed the taboo on unritualized consummation partakes enough of the absolutism of the taboo, shall we say, on incest, to preclude any risk of individual youthful experimentation or venture across the boundary lines set by the Elders.

Given these boundary lines, given a psychology of crisis, all too readily the sex relations, in marriage or out, become stale, flat, colourless, or of the nature of debauch, which is only another aspect of crisis-psychology. Sex relations perforce become limited to two conventions, marriage and prostitution. Prostitute or wife, the conjugal or the disorderly house, these are the alternatives. In formulaic crisis-psychology there may be no other station of emotional experiment or range of emotional expression.

That a man should " sow his wild oats " before marriage, and after marriage " settle down," is becoming throughout the country a somewhat archaic formula, at least in so far as wild oats means exposure to venereal disease; but there has been no change, so far as I am aware, in the attitude towards the second part of the formula on settling down—in conjugal segregation. The married are as obtrusively married as ever, and their attitude towards persons of the opposite sex as dull and forbidding. Few " happily married " women but refer incessantly in their conversation to their husband's opinion or stand; and what devoted husband will fail to mention his wife in one way or another as a notice of his immunity against the appeal of sex in any degree by any other woman? Shortly after the war, a certain American woman of my acquaintance who was travelling in France found herself without money and in danger of being put off her train before reaching Paris and her banker's. She found a fellow-countryman and told him her predicament. He was quite willing to pay her fare; she was an American and a woman, but she was informed firmly and repeatedly that her knight was a married man, and besides, he was travelling with his business partner. Soon after I heard this anecdote I happened to repeat it to a Chicago lawyer who promptly joined in the laugh over the American man's timidity. " Still, a married man travelling can't be too prudent," he finished off.

Circumspection towards women, in travel or elsewhere, or, better still, indifference towards women, is the standardized attitude of American husbands. In marriage, too, a relationship of status rather than of attention to the fluctuations of personality, indifference to psychical experience, is a not uncommon marital trait. American men in general, as Europeans have noted, are peculiarly indifferent to the psychology of women. They are also peculiarly sentimental about women, a trait quite consistent with indifference or ignorance, but one which, in view of American prostitution and the persistent exclusion of many women from equal opportunities for education and for life, gives an ugly look of hypocrisy to the trumpeters of American chivalry.

And yet subject the American concept of chivalry to a little scrutiny and the taunt, at least of hypocrisy, will miss the mark. For the concept is, both actually and historically, a part of the already noted classification of women as more or less sequestered, on the one hand, and unsequestered or loose on the other, as inexperienced and over-experienced or, more accurately, partially over-experienced. In this classification the claims of both classes of women are settled by men on an economic basis, with a few sentimentalities about womanhood, pure or impure, thrown in for good measure. The personality of the woman a man feels that he is supporting, whether as wife or prostitute, may, theoretically, be disregarded and, along with her personality, her capacity for sexual response. Whether as a creature of sin or as an object of chivalry, a woman becomes a depersonalized, and, sexually, an unresponsive being.

People sometimes forget this when they discuss the relations between men and women in this country, and especially the sexlessness or coldness of American women. They forget it in arguing against the feminizing of education, the theatre, literature, etc., meaning, not that women run the schools or are market for the arts, but that immature, sexless women are in these ways too much to the fore. In part at least it is thanks to chivalry or to her " good and considerate husband " that the American woman, the non-wage earner at least, does not grow up, and that it is possible for so many women to marry without having any but the social consequences of marriage in mind. One surmises that there are numbers, very large numbers, of American women, married as well as unmarried, who have felt either no stirring of sex at all or at most only the generalized sex stir of pre-adolescence. What proportion of women marry " for a home " or to escape from a home, or a job, and what proportion marry for love? After marriage, with the advent of children, what of these proportions?

Marriage for a home or for the sake of children, chivalry, " consideration " for the wife, all these attitudes are matters of status, not of personality, and to personality, not to status, love must look, since love is an art, not a formula. It often seems that in American culture, whether in marriage or out, little or no place is open to this patient, ardent, and discerning art, and that lovers are invariably put to flight. Even if they make good their escape, their adventure is without social significance, since it is perforce surreptitious. Only when adventurers and artists in love are tolerated enough to be able to come out from under cover, and to be at least allowed to live, if only as variants from the commonplace, may they contribute of their spirit or art to the general culture.

ELSIE CLEWS PARSONS

THE FAMILY

THE American family is the scapegoat of the nations. Foreign critics visit us and report that children are forward and incorrigible, that wives are pampered and extravagant, and that husbands are henpecked and cultureless. Nor is this the worst. It only skims the surface by comparison with the strictures of home-grown criticism. Our domestic arbiters of every school have a deeper fault to find: they see the family as a crumbling institution, a swiftly falling bulwark. Catholic pulpits call upon St. Joseph to save the ruins and Puritan moralists invoke Will Carlton, believing in common with most of our public guardians that only saints and sentimentalism can help in such a crisis. Meanwhile the American family shows the usual tenacity of form, beneath much superficial change, uniting in various disguises the most ancient and the newest modes of living. In American family life, if anywhere, the Neolithic meets the modern and one needs to be very rash or very wise to undertake the nice job of finding out which is which. But one at least refuses to defeat one's normal curiosity by joining in the game of blind-man's buff, by means of which public opinion about the family secures a maximum of activity along with a minimum of knowledge.

A little science would be of great help. But popular opinion does not encourage scientific probing of the family. In this field, not honesty but evasion is held to be the best policy. Rather than venture where taboo is so rife and the material so sensitive, American science would much rather promote domestic dyes and seedless oranges. It is true that we have the Federal Census with its valuable though restrained statistics. But even the census has always taken less interest in family status and family composition, within the population, than in the classification of property and occupation and the fascinating game of "watching Tulsa grow." In no country is the collection of vital statistics so neglected and sporadic and the total yield of grab-bag facts so unamenable to correlation. Through the persistent effort of the Children's Bureau, this situation has been considerably improved during the past ten years; so that now there exist the so-called " registration areas " where births, marriages, and deaths are actually recorded. For the country as a whole, these vital facts still go unregistered. The prevailing sketchiness in the matter of vital statistics is in distinct contrast to the energy and thoroughness with which American political machinery manages to keep track of the individual who has passed the age of twenty-one.

One of the tendencies, statistically verified, of the native family is its reduction in size. In the first place the circumference of the family circle has grown definitely smaller through the loss of those adventitious members, the maiden aunt and the faithful servant. The average number of adult females in the typical household is nowadays just one. The odd women are out in the world on their own; they no longer live " under the roofs " of their brothers-in-law. Miss Lulu Bett is almost an anachronism in 1920. The faithful servant has been replaced by the faithless one, who never by any chance remains long enough to become a familial appendage, or else she has not been replaced at all. Even " Grandma " has begun to manifest symptoms of preferring to be on her own. Thus the glory of the patriarchal household has visibly departed, leaving only the biological minimum in its stead.

In the dwindling of this ultimate group lies the crux of the matter. The American grows less and less prolific, and panicky theorists can already foresee a possible day when the last 100 per cent. American Adam and the last 100 per cent. American Eve will take their departure from our immigrationized stage. It is providentially arranged—the maxim tells us—that the trees shall not grow and grow until they pierce the heavens; but is there any power on the job of preventing the progressive decline of the original Anglo-Saxon stock even to the point of final extinction? This is a poignant doubt in a country where the Anglo-Saxon strain enjoys a prestige out of all proportion to its population quota. The strain may derive what comfort it can from the reflection that the exit of the Indian was probably not due to birth control.

Still, birth control is not new. If it did not originate with the Indians, it did at least with the Puritans. As the census books and genealogy books show, every succeeding American generation has manifested a tendency to reduce the birth-rate. The new aspects of the situation are the acceleration of the tendency and the propaganda for family limitation by artificial methods. In the birth registration area, which includes twenty-three States, the number of births for the year 1919 compared with those for 1918 showed a slump of seven per cent. Also the current assumption that children are more numerous on farms, where they are an economic asset, than they are in cities, where they became an economic handicap, has recently received a startling correction through a survey made by the Department of Agriculture. Among the surprises of the study, says the report, was the small number of children in farm homes:—" Child life is at a premium in rural districts." The farm is not the national child reserve it has been supposed to be. As far as the salaried class is concerned, it has stood out as the national pace-setter in family limitation. The editorial writer of the New York *Times,* who may be trusted for a fairly accurate statement of the standards of this group, justifies its conduct thus: " Unless the brain-worker is willing to disclass his children, to subject them to humiliation, he must be willing to feed, clothe, and educate them during many years. In such circumstances, to refuse parenthood is only human." It therefore remains for the manual worker, who cannot obtain from his Church the same absolution that the suburban resident can obtain from his *Times,* to produce the bulk of the population. This, as a whole, is not yet stationary; the recent census estimates an annual excess of births over deaths throughout the United States amounting to about one per cent. What will the next decade do with it?

A peculiar feature of the American propaganda for birth control is its specific advocacy of artificial methods. The defenders of this cause have been compelled, it appears, to define a position which would be self-evident in any society not incorrigibly Puritan. People who regard celibacy as a state of grace and celibacy within marriage as a supreme moral victory are still growing, it would seem, on every bush. This unwholesome belief must have its effect upon the birth control methods of the married population. It is a matter of speculation how many marriages succumb to its influence, especially after the birth of a second or third child; but there is reason to believe that the ascetic method is by no means uncommon. You cannot hold up an ideal before people steadily for forty years without expecting some of them to try to follow it. This kind of rigorous negativism passes for morality in America and finds its strongest devotees among the middle-aged and the heads of families. Such people are greatly shocked at the wild conduct of the young who are certainly out of bounds since the war; but the most striking feature of the current wave of so-called immorality is the exposure of the bankruptcy of ideals among the older generation. There are thirty million families in the United States; presumably there are at least sixty million adults who have experimented with the sexual relationship with the sanction of society. But experience has taught them nothing if one may judge by the patented and soulless concepts which still pass for sexual morality among people who are surely old enough to have learned about life from living it.

The population policies of the government are confined to the supply through immigration. A few years ago, an American president enunciated population policies of his own and conducted an energetic though solitary campaign against " race suicide." But no faction rallied to his standard, no organization rose up to speed his message. His bugle-call was politely disregarded as the personal idiosyncrasy of a popular president who happened to be the proud father of six children. Mr. Roosevelt was evidently out of tune with his own generation, as, no doubt, Mr. Washington was with his, for exactly the opposite reason. But the more retiring nature of our first president saved him from the egoistic error of regarding his own familial situation as the only proper and desirable example. The complete failure of Mr. Roosevelt's crusade is significant. There are clerical influences in America which actively fight race suicide, but with these obscurantist allies the doughty son of a Dutch Reform family had too little else in common. Among the men of his own class he stirred not an echo. Is it because the American husband is too uxorious or too indifferent? I have heard a married man say, " It is too much to expect of any woman;" and still another one explain, " The Missis said it was my turn next and so we stopped with one." Or is there any explanation in the fact that the American father tends more and more to spend his life in a salaried job and has little land or business to bequeath? Whatever the reason, the Business Man is in accord with the Club Woman on the subject of birth control, in practice if not in theory.

So far as relative distribution of income is concerned, the families of the United States fare much as those in the industrial countries of Europe. In 1910, the same relative inequality of wealth and income existed in feudal Prussia and democratic America. The richest fifth of the families in each country claimed about half the income while the poorest two-thirds of the families were thankful for about one-third. The same law of economic relativity falls alike on the just American and the unjust Prussian. But the American family, it appears, is in every case two or three times better off than the corresponding family in Prussia. You must multiply Herr Stinnes by two to get a Judge Gary and the wealth of a Silesian child labourer is only half that of a Georgia mill-child. This economic advantage of our American rich and poor alike is measured chiefly in dollars and marks and not in actual standards of living. It is apparently difficult to get real standards of living out into the open; otherwise the superior fortune of American families of every estate might be less evident. Some of us who may have visited middle-class Prussian people only half as well off as ourselves probably did not commiserate the poor things as they deserved. My hostess, I recall, had eight hundred dollars a year on which she maintained an apartment of two rooms, bath, and kitchen; kept a part-time maid; bought two new suits a year; drove out in a hired carriage on Sunday; and contributed generously to a society which stirred up women to call themselves Frau instead of Fräulein. Any " single woman " in an American city of equal size who could have managed as much in those days on fifteen hundred a year would certainly have deserved a thumping thrift-prize. . . . And then there were all those poor little children in a Black Forest village, who had to put up with rye bread six days in the week and white bread only on Sundays. Transported to America, they might have had package crackers every day and ice-cream sandwiches on Sunday. One wonders whether the larger income of the American family is not largely spent on things of doubtful value and pinchbeck quality.

According to theory, the income of the family normally belongs to the man of the house. According to theory, he has earned it or derived it from some lawful business enterprise. " The head of the family ordinarily divides income between himself and his various dependents in the proportion that he deems best," says Mr. Willford King. The American husband has a peculiarly unblemished reputation as a provider—and probably deserves it. Certainly few husbands in the world are so thoughtful of their widows; they invest extensively in life insurance but rarely in annuities against a period of retirement. Trust Companies remind them through advertisements every day to make their wills, and cemetery corporations nag them incessantly to buy their graves. " Statistics show that women outlive men! " says the promoter of America's Burial Park. "They show that the man who puts off the selection of a burial place leaves the task to the widow in her grief. For the man it is easy now—for the woman an ordeal then." The chivalry of the business man leads him to contrive all sorts of financial mechanisms for his widow's convenience and protection. His will, like his insurance policy, is in her favour. Unlike the European husband, he hates to leave the man's world of business and to spend his declining years in the society of his wife. After he is dead, she is welcome to his all, but so long as he lives he keeps business between them.

Though in life and death a generous provider, he is not a systematic one. Financial arrangements between husband and wife are extremely casual. As the dowry hardly exists, so a regular cash allowance is very rare. He loves to hold the purse-strings and let her run the bills. This tendency is known in the outside business world, and the American wife, therefore, enjoys a command of credit which would amaze any solvent foreign housekeeper. She has accounts on every hand. She orders food by telephone or through the grocer's boy and " charges it." The department store expects her to have a charge account, and gives her better service if she does. For instance, the self-supporting woman who is, for obvious reasons, more inclined to pay as she goes, finds herself discriminated against in the matter of returning or exchanging goods. In numerous ways, the charge account has the inside track. This would not seem strange if credit were limited to the richest fraction. But that is not the case; almost every housewife in the country has credit, from the Newport ladies to the miners' wives who " trade at the company store." The only difference is that, in the case of these two extremes—Newport and the company store—longer credit than uusal seems to be the rule. In the meantime, the preaching of thrift to the American housewife goes on incessantly by apostles from a business world which is largely organized on the assumption that she does not possess it and which would be highly disconcerted if she actually developed it. American business loves the house-wife for the same reason that it loves China—that is, for her economic backwardness.

The record of the American husband as a provider is not uniform for all classes. In Congress it is now and then as-serted with appropriate oratory that there are no classes in America. This is more or less true from the point of view of a Cabin Creek vote-getter, who lives in a factitious political world, where economic realities fail to penetrate; to him middle-class and working-class are much the same since they have equal rights not to " scratch the ticket." But the econo-mist finds it convenient, as has been said, to classify the totality of American families in definite income-groups corresponding to the Prussian classes. As one descends the income scale one finds that the American husband no longer fulfils his reputation for being sole provider for his family. According to Edgar Sydenstricker, " less than half of the wage-earners' families in the United States, whose heads are at work, have been found to be supported by the earnings of the husband or father." The earnings of the mother and the children are a necessary supplement to bring the family income up to the subsistence level. Half the workingmen, who have dutifully " founded " families, cannot support them. According to the latest figures published, it costs $2,334 a year to keep a family

of five in New York. Have the young Lochinvars of the tenements never heard of those appalling figures? Very likely they
have a premonition, if not an actual picture of the digits. In
any case they have their mothers to warn them. "Henry's
brought it on himself," said the janitress. "He had a right
not to get married. He had his mother to take care of him."
If he had only chosen bachelorhood, he might have lived at
home in comfort and peace on his twenty-five a week. But
having chosen, or been chosen by, Mrs. Henry instead, it is
now up to the latter to go out office-cleaning or operating,
which she very extensively does. It is estimated that since
the war fully one-third of all American women in industry are
married.

Going back up the scale to the middle-class wife, we find
new influences at work upon her situation. Custom has re-
laxed its condemnation of the economically independent wife,
and perhaps it is just as well that it has done so. For this is
the class which has suffered the greatest comparative loss of
fortune, during the last fifteen years. "If all estimates cited
are correct," writes Mr. Willford King, "it indicates that, since
1896, there has occurred a marked concentration of income in
the hands of the very rich; that the poor have relatively lost
but little; but that the middle class has been the principal sufferer." It is, then, through the sacrifices of our middle-class
families that our very richest families have been able to improve their standard of living. The poor, of course, have had
no margin on which to practise such benevolence, but the generous middle-class has given till it hurts. The deficit had to
be relieved, the only possible way being through the economic
utilization of the women. At first daughters became self-supporting, while wives still tarried in the odour of domestic sanctity; then wives came to be sporadically self-supporting. The
war, like peace still bearing hardest on the middle-class, enhanced all this. Nine months after the armistice, fifty per
cent. more women were employed in industry than there were
in the year before the war.

In America, we have no surplus women. The countries of
western Europe are each encumbered with a million or two,
and their existence is regarded as the source of acute social

problems. What shall be done with them is a matter of earnest consideration and anxious statecraft. America has been spared all this. She has also no surplus men—or none that anybody has ever heard of. It is true that the population in 1910 consisted of ninety-one millions, of whom forty-seven millions were men and forty-four were women. There were three million more men than women, but for some reason they were not surplus or " odd " men and they have never been a " problem." The population figures for 1920,—one hundred and five millions,—have not yet been divided by sexes, but the chances are that there is still a man for every woman in the country, and two men apiece for a great number of them. However, no one seems to fear polyandry for America as polygamy is now feared in Europe.

The situation is exceptional in New England where the typical European condition is duplicated. Beyond the Berkshire Hills, all the surplus women of America are concentrated. In the United States as a whole there are a hundred and five men for each one hundred women, but in New England the balance shifts suddenly to the other side. Within the present century, a gradual increase has taken place in the masculine contingent owing to immigration. But the chances of marriage have not correspondingly improved, for matches are rarely made between New England spinsters and Armenian weavers or Neapolitan bootblacks.

In America only the very rich and the very poor marry early. Factory girls and heiresses are, as a rule, the youngest brides. It is generally assumed that twenty-four for women and twenty-nine for men are the usual ages for marriage the country over. Custom varies enormously, of course, in so polyglot a population. Now and then an Italian daughter acquires a husband before the compulsory education law is through with her. In such cases, however, there is apparently a gentleman's agreement between the truant officer and the lady's husband which solves the dilemma. At the opposite extreme from these little working-class Juliets are the mature brides of Boston. As the result of a survey covering the last ten years, the registrar of marriage licenses discovered that the women married between twenty-seven and thirty-three and the men between thirty and forty. Boston's average marriage age for both sexes is over thirty. This does not represent an inordinate advance upon the practice of the primitive Bostonians. According to certain American genealogists, the Puritans of the 17th century were in no great haste to wed —the average age of the bride being twenty-one and of the bridegroom twenty-five. The marriage age in the oldest American city has moved up about ten years in a couple of centuries. The change is usually ascribed to increasing economic obstacles, and nobody questions its desirability. Provided that celibacy is all that it seems to be, the public stands ready to admire every further postponement of the marriage age as evidence of an ever-growing self-control and the triumphant march of civilization.

In the majority of marriages, the American wife outlives her husband. This is partly because he is several years older than she and partly because she tends to be longer-lived than he. Americans of the second and third generation are characterized by great longevity,—the American woman of American descent being the longest-lived human being on earth. Consequently the survivors of marriage are more likely to be widows than widowers. In the census of 1910, there were about two million and a half widows of forty-five or over as compared with about one million widowers of corresponding age. Nor do they sit by the fire and knit as once upon a time; they too must " hustle." Among the working women of the country are a million and a quarter who are more than forty-five and who are probably to a very large extent— though the census provides no data on the subject—economically independent widows. As was said before, " Grandma " too is on her own nowadays.

The widow enjoys great honour in American public life, although it usually turns out to be rather a spurious and sentimental homage. Political orators easily grow tearful over her misfortunes. For generations after the Civil War, the Republican Party throve on a pension-system which gathered in the youngest widow of the oldest veteran, and Tammany has always understood how to profit from its ostentatious alms-giving to widows and orphans. From my earliest childhood, I can recollect how the town-beautifiers, who wanted to take down the crazy board fences, were utterly routed by the aldermen who said the widow's cow must range and people must therefore keep up their fences. Similarly, the Southern States have never been able to put through adequate child labour laws because the widow's child had to be allowed to earn in order to support his mother. All this sentimentalism proved to be in time an excellent springboard for a genuine economic reform—the widow's pension systems of the several states which would be more accurately described as children's pensions. The legislatures were in no position to resist an appeal on behalf of the poor widow and so nicely narcotized were they by their traditional tender-heartedness that they failed to perceive the socialistic basis of this new kind of widow's pensions. Consequently America has achieved the curious honour of leading in a socialistic innovation which European States are now only just beginning to copy. Maternity insurance, on the other hand, has made no headway in America although adopted years and even decades ago in European countries. With us the obstacle seems to be prudishness rather than capitalism—it makes a legislator blush to hear childbirth spoken of in public while it only makes him cry to hear of widowhood.

One aspect of widowhood is seldom touched upon and that is its prevention. Aged widows, on the whole, in spite of their soap-boxing and their wage-earning, are a very lonely race. Why must they bring it on themselves by marrying men whose expectation of life is so much less than theirs? And yet so anxious are the marrying people to observe this conventional disparity of age, that if the bride happens to be but by three months the senior of the bridegroom, they conceal it henceforth as a sort of family disgrace. Even if this convention should prove to be immutable, is there nothing to be done about the lesser longevity of the American male? There is a life extension institute with an ex-president at the head but, as far as I am aware, it has never enlisted the support of the millions reported by the census as widows, who surely, if anybody, should realize the importance of such a movement. It is commonly assumed that the earlier demise of husbands is due to the hazardous life they lead in business and in industry; but domestic life is not without its hazards, and child-bearing is an especially dangerous trade in the United States, which has the highest maternal death-rate of seventeen civilized countries. If American husbands were less philosophical about the hardships of child-bed—the judgment of Eve and all that sort of thing—and American wives were less philosophical about burying their husbands—the Lord hath given and the Lord hath taken away and so on—it might result in greater health and happiness for all concerned.

But the main trouble with American marriage, as all the world knows, is that divorce so often separates the twain before death has any chance to discriminate between them. The growing prevalence of divorce is statistically set forth in a series of census investigations. In 1890, there was one divorce to every sixteen marriages; in 1900, there was one to every twelve marriages; and in 1916, there was one to every nine marriages. The number of marriages in proportion to the population has also increased during the same period, though not at a rate equal to that of divorce. But divorce, being so much younger than marriage, has had more room to grow from its first humble scared beginnings of fifty years ago. Queen Victoria's frown had a very discouraging effect on divorce in America; and Mrs. Humphry Ward, studying the question among us in the early 20th century, lent her personal influence towards the arrest of the American evil. We also have raised up on this side of the water our own apostles against divorce, among whom Mr. Horace Greeley perhaps occupies the first and most distinguished place. But in spite of all heroic crusades, divorce has continued to grow. One even suspects that the marked increase in the marriage rate is partly—perhaps largely—due to the remarriage of the divorced. At any rate, they constitute new and eligible material for marriage which formerly was lacking.

The true cause of the increase of divorce in America is not easy to come by. Commissions and investigations have worried the question to no profitable end, and have triumphantly come out by the same door by which they went in. That seems to be the test of a successful divorce inquiry; and no wonder,

for the real quest means a conflict with hypocrisy and prejudice, fear and taboo, which only the intrepid spirit of a John
Milton or a Susan B. Anthony is able to sustain. The people
who want divorces and who can pay for them seem to be able
to get them nowadays, and since it is the truth only that suffers the situation has grown more tolerable.

In the meantime, there are popular impressions and assumptions which do not tally with the known facts. It is assumed
that divorce is frequent in America because it is easy, and
that the logical way to reduce it would be to make it difficult.
Certain States of the West have lenient divorce laws but other
States have stringent laws, while South Carolina abolished divorce entirely in 1878. On the whole, our laws are not so
lenient as those of Scandinavia, whose divorce rate is still far
behind that of the United States. Neither is divorce cheap in
America; it is enormously expensive. Therefore for the poor
it is practically inaccessible. The Domestic Relations Courts do
not grant divorce and the Legal Aid Societies will not touch it.
The wage-earning class, like the inhabitants of South Carolina,
just have to learn to get along without it. Then there is another belief, hardly justified by the facts, that most divorced
wives get alimony. Among all the divorces granted in 1916,
alimony was not even asked for by 73 per cent. of the wives
and it was received altogether by less than 20 per cent. of them.
The statistics do not tell us whether the actual recipients of
alimony were the mothers of young children or whether they
were able-bodied ladies without offspring. The average American divorce court could not be trusted to see any difference
between them.

The war has naturally multiplied the actions for divorce in
every country. It was not for nothing that the British government called the stipends paid to soldiers' wives " separation
allowances." The war-time conditions had a tendency to
unmake marriages as well as to make them. The momentary
spread of divorce has revived again the idea of a uniform divorce law embodied in an amendment to the Federal Constitution. As no reasonable law can possibly be hoped for, the
present state of confusion is infinitely to be preferred as af-
fording at least some choice of resources to the individual who

is seeking relief. If there were any tendency to take divorce cases out of the hands of the lawyers, as has been done with industrial accidents, and to put it into domestic relations courts where it belongs; if there were the least possibility of curbing the vested interest of the newspapers in divorce news; if there were any dawning appreciation of the absurdity of penalizing as connivance the most unanswerable reason for divorce, that is, mutual consent; if there were any likelihood that the lying and spying upon which divorce action must usually depend for its success would be viewed as the grossest immorality in the whole situation; if there were any hope whatever that a statesman might rise up in Congress and, like Johan Castberg of Norway, defend a legal measure which would help ordinary men and women to speak the truth in their personal relationships—if there were any prospect that any of these influences would have any weight in the deliberations of Congress, one might regard the possibilities of Federal action with a gleam of hope. But since nothing of the kind can be expected, the best that can happen in regard to divorce in the near future is for Congress to leave it alone. There is a strong tradition in the historical suffrage movement of America which favours liberal divorce laws and which makes it improbable that a reactionary measure could gain sufficient support from the feminine electorate. Since the majority of those who seek divorce in this country are women, it seems to put them logically on the side of dissoluble marriage.

Though home is a sacred word in America, it is a portable affair. Migration is a national habit, handed down and still retained from the days when each generation went out to break new ground. The disasters of the Civil War sent Southern families and New England families scurrying to the far West. The development of the railway and express systems produced as a by-product a type of family life that was necessarily nomadic. The men of the railway " Brotherhoods " have always been marrying men, and their families acquired the art of living on wheels, as it were. Rich farmers of the Middle West retire to spend their old age in a California cottage surrounded by an orange grove—and the young farmers move to the city. The American family travels on any and every excuse. The neurotic pursuit of health has built up large communities in Colorado, Arizona, and other points West. Whole families " picked up," as the saying goes, and set out for the miraculous climate that was to save one of its members from the dreaded tuberculosis—and then later had to move again because somebody's heart couldn't stand the " altitude." The extreme examples of this nomadic habit are found among the families of the very poor and the very rich, who have regular seasonal migrations. The oyster canners and strawberry-pickers have a mobility which is only equalled by that of the Palm Beachers. And finally there is the curious practice of New England which keeps boarders in the summer-time in order that it may be boarded by Florida in the winter-time.

By contrast with all this geographical instability, the stable sway of convention and custom stands out impressively. With each change of environment, family tradition became more sacred. Unitarians who moved to Kansas were more zealous in the faith than ever, and F.F.V.'s who settled in Texas were fiercely and undyingly loyal to the memory of Pocahontas. Families that were always losing their background, tried to fixate in some form the ancestral prestige which threatened always to evaporate. Organizations composed of the Sons and Daughters of the Revolution, of the descendants of the Pilgrims, of Civil War Veterans, of the Scions of the Confederacy, and so on, sprang up and flourished on the abundant soil of family pride. All of which means that pioneering brought no spiritual independence or intellectual rebirth, and that new conditions were anxiously reformulated under the sanction of the old. Above all, sanction was important. That incredible institution, the " society column " of the local newspaper, took up the responsibility where the Past laid it down. Stereotyped values of yesterday gave way to stereotyped values of to-day. This was the commercial opportunity of a multitude of home journals and women's magazines which undertook—by means of stories, pictures, and advertisements—to regiment the last detail of home life. But the perforated patterns, the foods " shot from guns," and all the rest of the labour-saving ingenuities which came pouring into the home and which were supposed to mean emancipation for mothers and their families, brought little of the real spirit of freedom in their wake. Our materialistic civilization finds it hard to understand that liberty is not achieved through time-saving devices but only through the love of it.

But the notorious spoiling of the American child—some one says—is not that a proper cradle of liberty for the personality? A spoilt child may be a nuisance, but if he is on the way towards becoming a self-reliant, self-expressive adult, the " American way " of bringing up children may have its peculiar advantages. But a spoilt child is really a babyish child, and by that token he is on the way towards becoming a childish adult. Neither is his case disposed of simply by adjudging him a nuisance; the consequence of his spoiling carry much further than that. They are seen, for instance, in malnutrition of the children of the American rich—a fact which has but recently been discovered and which came as a great surprise to the experts. " In Chicago," one of them tells us, " it was found that a group of foreign children near the stockyards were only 17 per cent. underweight, while in the all-American group near the University of Chicago they were 57 per cent. below normal." The same condition of things was found in a select and expensive boarding school in the neighbourhood of Boston. A pathetic commentary—is it not?—on a country which leads the world in food-packing and food-profits, that it should contain so many parents who, with all the resources of the earth at their command, do not know how to feed their own children. Surely, the famous American spoiling has something to do with this. Whether it may not also be behind the vast amount of mental disturbance in the population may well be considered. The asylums are suddenly over-crowded. The National Committee for Mental Hygiene suggests for our consolation that this may be because the asylums are so much more humane than they used to be and the families of the sufferers are more willing than formerly to consign them to institutions.

It is the fashion to attribute all these mental tragedies to the strain of business life and industry, and more recently to war-shock. But if we are to accept the results of the latest psychological research, the family must receive the lion's share of blame. The groundwork for fatal ruptures in the adult personality is laid in childhood and in the home which produced the victim. For many years the discussion of American nerves has hinged on the hectic haste of business and industrial life, on the noise and bustle and lack of repose in the national atmosphere. But we have neglected to accuse the family to its face of failing to protect the child against the cataclysms of the future while it had the chance.

The tremendous influence of the family on the individuals, old and young, composing it is not merely a pious belief. We are, alas, what our families make us. This is not a pleasant thought to many individuals who have learned through bitter experience to look on family relationships as a form of soul imprisonment. Yet it seems to be an incontestable fact that personality is first formed—or deformed—in the family constellation. The home really does the job for which the school, the press, the church, and the State later get the credit. It is a smoothly articulated course from the cradle onward, however, in which the subjugated parent produces a subjugated child, not so much by the rod of discipline—which figures very little in American family life—but by the more powerful and pervasive force of habit and attitude. Parents allow themselves to be a medium for transmitting the incessant pressure of standards which allow no room for impulse and initiative; they become the willing instrument of a public mania for standardization which tries to make every human soul into the image of a folded pattern. The babe is moulded in his cradle into the man who will drop a sentimental tear, wear a white carnation, and send a telegram on Mother's Day—that travesty of a family festival which shames affection and puts spontaneous feeling to the blush.

As the family itself grows smaller, this pressure of mechanistic and conventional standards encroaches more closely upon the child. A sizeable group of brothers and sisters create for themselves a savage world which is their best protection against the civilization that awaits them. But with one or two children, or a widely scattered series, this natural protection is lost. The youngster is prematurely assimilated to the adult world of parents who are nowadays, owing to later marriage, not even quite so young as formerly they were. It is a peculiarity of parents, especially of mothers, that they never entertain a modest doubt as to whether they might be the best of all possible company for their children. And obviously the tired business man cannot properly substitute in the evenings for a roistering, shouting brother who never came into the world at all; nor can all the concentrated care of the most devoted mother take the place of the companionship and discipline which children get from other children. These considerations deserve more attention than they usually receive in connection with the falling birth-rate. The figures mean that the environment of the young child is being altered in a fundamental respect. Parents of small families need to take effective steps to counteract the loss. Practical things, like nursery schools, would be a help. But, chiefly, if parents will insist on being companions of their children, they need themselves to understand and practise the art of common joy and happiness.

KATHARINE ANTHONY

THE ALIEN

THE immigrant alien has been discussed by the Anglo-Saxon as though he were an Anglo-Saxon "problem." He has been discussed by labour as though he were a labour "problem"; by interpreters of American institutions as though man existed for institutions and for institutions which the class interpreting them found advantageous to its class. Occasionally the alien has been discussed from the point of view of the alien and but rarely from the point of view of democracy. The "problem" of the alien is largely a problem of setting our own house in order. It is the "problem" of Americanizing America. The outstanding fact of three centuries of immigration is that the immigrant alien ceases to be an alien when economic conditions are such as properly to assimilate him.

There is something rather humorous about the way America discusses "the alien." For we are all aliens. And what is less to our liking we are almost all descended from the peasant classes of Europe. We are here because our forebears were poor. They did not rule over there. They were oppressed; they were often owned. And with but few exceptions they came because of their poverty. For the rich rarely emigrate. And in the 17th and 18th centuries there was probably a smaller percentage of immigrants who could pass the literacy test than there are to-day. Moreover, in the early days only suffering could drive the poor of Europe from their poverty. For the conditions of travel were hazardous. The death toll from disease was very high. It required more fortitude to cross the Atlantic and pass by the ring of settlers out onto the unbroken frontier than it does to pass Ellis Island and the exploiters round about it to-day.

The immigration question has arisen because America, too, has created a master class, a class which owns and employs and rules. And the alien in America is faced by a class opinion, born of the change which has come over America rather than any change in the alien himself. America has changed. The alien remains much the same. And the most significant phase of the immigration problem is the way we treat the alien and the hypocrisy of our discussion of the subject.

Sociologists have given us a classification of the immigrant alien. They speak of the "old immigration" and the "new immigration." The former is the immigration of the 17th and 18th and the first three-quarters of the 19th centuries. It was English, Scotch, Irish, German, Scandinavian with a sprinkling of French, Swiss, and other nationalities. From the beginning, the preponderance was British. During the 18th century there was a heavy Scotch inflow and during the first half of the 19th a heavy Irish and German immigration. The Irish came because of the famine of 1848, the Scotch in large part because of the enclosure acts and the driving of the people from the land to make way for deer preserves and grazing lands for the British aristocracy. Most of the British immigration was the result of oppressive land laws of one kind or another. The population of Ireland was reduced from eight million to slightly over four million in three-quarters of a century. The British immigrant of the 17th century, like the recent Russian immigration, was driven from home by economic oppression. Only a handful came to escape religious oppression or to secure political liberty. The cause of immigration has remained the same from the beginning until now.

The "old immigration" was from the North of Europe. It was of Germanic stock. It was predominantly Protestant. But the most important fact of all and the fact most usually ignored is an economic fact. The early immigrant found a broad continent awaiting him, peopled only by Indians. He became a free man. He took up a homestead. He ceased to belong to any one else. He built for himself. He paid no rent, he took no orders, he kept what he produced, and was inspired by hope and ambition to develop his powers. It was economic, not political, freedom that distinguishes the "old immigration" from the "new."

The "new immigration" is from Southern and Central Europe. It is Latin and Slavic. It is largely Catholic. It, too, is poor. It, too, is driven out by oppression, mostly economic and for the most part landed. Almost every wave of immigration has been in some way related to changes for the worse in the landed systems of Europe. Wherever the poverty has been the most distressing, there the impulse to move has been the strongest. It has been the poverty of Europe that has determined our immigration from the 17th century until now.

The ethnic difference is secondary. So is the religious. The fundamental fact that distinguishes the " old immigration " from the " new " is economic. The " new immigration " works for the " old." It found the free land all taken up. The public domain had passed into the hand of the Pacific railroads, into great manorial estates. Land thieves had repeated the acts of the British Parliament of the 18th century. The Westward movement of peoples that had been going on from the beginning of time came to an end when the pioneer of the 80's and 90's found only the bad lands left for settlement. That ended an era. It closed the land to settlement and sent the immigrant to the city. The peasant of Europe has become the miner and the mill worker. He left one kind of serfdom to take up another. It is this that distinguishes the " old immigrant " from the " new." It is this that distinguishes the old America from the Amercia of to-day. And the problem of immigration, like the problem of America, is the re-establishment of economic democracy. The protective tariff bred exotic industry. The employer wanted cheap labour. The mine owners and mill owners combined with the steamship companies to stimulate immigration. They sent agents abroad. They brought in gangs from Southern and Central Europe. They herded them in mining camps, in mill towns, in the tenements. The closing of the public domain and the rise of monopoly industry marks the turning point in immigration. It marks the beginning of the immigration " problem." It is partly ethnic, but largely economic.

The " new immigration " from Southern and Central Europe began to increase in volume about 1890. It came from Southern rather than Northern Italy, from Poland, Hungary, Bohemia, Russia, the Balkans, and the Levant. There was a sprinkling of Spanish and Portuguese immigrants. In 1914 South and Central European immigration amounted to 683,000, while the North European immigration was but 220,000. Of the former 296,000 came from Italy, 123,000 from Poland, 45,000 from Russia, and 45,000 from Hungary. These figures do not include Jewish immigrants, who numbered 138,000. Of the North European immigrants 105,000 came from the British Isles, 80,000 came from Germany, and 36,000 from the Scandinavian countries.

Of the 14,000,000 persons of foreign birth now in the country, a very large percentage is of South and Central European stock.

We are accustomed to think of the old immigration and the new immigration in terms of races and religions. And much of the present-day hostility to immigration comes from the inexplicable prejudice which has recently sprung up against persons of differing races and religions. It is assumed that the new immigration is poor and ignorant because it is ethnically unfitted for anything different and that it prefers the tenement and the mining camp to American standards of living and culture. But the newly arrived immigrant goes to the mines and the crowded city not from choice but from necessity. He lives in colonies with his fellows largely because the employing class prefers that he be segregated and has no interest in his physical comfort or welfare. The alien has been a commodity, not a human being; he has been far cheaper than a machine because he provided his own capital cost and makes provision for his own depreciation and decay. He has been bought in the slums of Europe for his passage money and he can be left to starve when bad times or industrial power throws him on his own resources. The important difference between the " old immigration " and the " new immigration " is not ethnic. It is not religious. It is economic. The " old immigration " has become the owning and employing class, while the " new immigration " is the servile and dependent class. This is the real, the important difference between the " old immigration " and the " new." The former owns the resources of America. The economic division coincides roughly with the race division.

When economic privilege becomes ascendant fear is born. It is born of a subconscious realization on the part of the privileged classes that their privileges rest on an unjust if not an

unstable foundation.   Fear is the parent of hate, and back of
other explanations of the present demand for exclusion of the
alien is fear.   It is fear that gave birth to the persecution
and ruthless official and semi-official activity first against all
aliens under the White Slave Act and similar laws, next against
the Germans, and later against the " reds."   An economic psychology born of injustice explains our present attitude toward
the alien just as a different economic psychology explained our
attitude during the first two and a half centuries of our life
when it was the consuming desire of statesmen, real-estate spec-
ulators, and exploiters to people the continent and develop our
industries and resources as rapidly as possible.

The " immigration problem," so called, has always been and
always will be an economic problem.   There are many people
who feel that there is an inherent superiority in the Anglo-
Saxon race; that it has a better mind, greater virtue, and a
better reason for existence and expansion than any other race.
They insist there are eugenic reasons for excluding immigration from South and Central Europe; they would preserve
America for people of Anglo-Saxon stock.   As an immigration
official I presided over Ellis Island for five years.   During this
time probably a million immigrants arrived at the port of New
York.   They were for the most part poor.   They had that in
common with the early immigrant.   They had other qualities
in common.   They were ambitious and filled with hope.   They
were for the most part kindly and moved by the same human
and domestic virtues as other peoples.   And it is to me an
open question whether the " new immigration," if given a virgin continent, and the hope and stimulus which springs from
such opportunity, would not develop the same qualities of mind
and of character that we assume to be the more or less exclusive characteristics of the Anglo-Saxon race.   There is also
reason for believing that the warmer temperament, the emotional qualities, and the love of the arts that characterize the
South and Central European would produce a race blend,
under proper economic conditions, that would result in a better
race than one of pure Northern extraction.   For it is to be
remembered that it was not political liberty, religious liberty,
or personal liberty that changed the early immigrant of North-

ern Europe into the American of to-day. His qualities were born of economic conditions, of a free continent, of land to be had for the asking, of equal opportunity with his fellows to make his life what he would have it to be. The old immigrant recognized no master but himself. He was the equal of his neighbours in every respect. He knew no inferiority complex born of a servile relationship. It was this rather than our constitutions and laws that made the American of the first three centuries what he was. It was this alchemy that changed the serf of Northern Europe into the self-reliant freeman of America.

The immigration problem was born when this early economic opportunity came to an end. When the free land was all gone, the immigrant had to work for somebody else. He went to the mines and the city tenement not from the choice but from necessity. He took the first job that offered. When established he sent for his brother, his neighbour, or his friend. He, too, went to the mining camp or the slum. Colonies appeared. The alien became segregated. He lived by himself. And he developed the qualities that would be developed by any race under similar conditions. He, too, feared. He was known as a Dago, Wop, Hunkie. To him government meant a policeman, a health officer, and an immigration inspector—all agencies to be feared. He slowly learned to unionize. He came to understand group action. He found in his craft organization the only protection against the employers, and in the political boss the only protection against agencies that interfered with his personal and domestic life. The immigrant soon learned that our immigration laws were shaped by economic motives. He learned that he was in danger of being deported if he did not work. The menace which hangs over the immigrant during his early years is the phrase " likely to become a public charge." And this alleged reason for deportation covers a multitude of other excuses which can be used as it is used—as a drag-net accusation. So the immigrant feels and justly feels that what we want of him is to work, to work for some one else, and to accept what is offered and be content. For within the last few years the doctrine has become accepted by him and by the nation as well that the alien must not complain, he must not be an agitator, he must not protest against the established industrial order or the place which he occupies within it. This has heightened his fear complex. It has tended to establish his inferiority relationship.

Our legislative attitude toward the alien has mirrored the economic conditions of the country. Up to about the middle of the last century we had no restrictive laws of any kind. America was free to all comers. We wanted population. Western States pleaded for settlers. They drew them from the East as they drew them from Europe. We were hospitable to the oppressed. We opened our arms to revolutionary leaders. We had no fears. Experience had shown that the poorest of Europe, even the classified criminals of Europe, would quickly Americanize themselves under the stimulus of new opportunity in a virgin land where all men were potentially equal. For generations there was fear that the American continent could never be fully peopled.

But the free lands were all gone about 1890. The Western drift of peoples, which had been in movement since the earliest times, came to an end. Population closed in on the Pacific. Cities grew with unprecedented rapidity. Factories needed men. Employers looked to Europe. They sent agents abroad who employed them in gangs. Often they were used to displace American-born workers. They were used to break up labour organizations. The aliens were mixed to prevent them organizing. Wages were temporarily at least forced down. For some years our immigration policy was shaped by the big industrials who combined with the steamship companies to induce immigration.

Organized labour began to protest. It, too, was moved by economic motives. It secured the passage of the contract labour law, which prevents the landing of any worker for whom employment has been provided in advance by an employer. Organized labour began to demand restrictive legislation to protect its standard of living. But the country was not ready for restrictive legislation. Congress instead adopted a selective policy. We excluded paupers, the insane and diseased, criminals, immoral persons, and those who were likely to become a public charge. Later we extended the selective idea to persons who did not believe in organized government, to anarchists, and to persons of revolutionary beliefs. We now exclude and deport for opinions as well as for physical and mental conditions. The percentage of rejections under these selective laws was not great. Of the 1,200,000 aliens who came to the country in 1914 only one and one-third per cent. were denied admission by the immigration authorities.

The war stimulated the anti-alien feeling. It provided an opportunity for crusades. The press aided the hue and cry. In 1915 there was a nation-wide round-up of immoral cases. Thousands of prostitutes, of procurers, and of persons guilty of some personal irregularity were arrested all over the country. Many of them were deported. The demand for restrictive legislation was supported by many different groups. It had the backing of organized labour, of the Southern States, of many protestant organization and churches. It was strongly supported in the West.

The " literacy test," which went into effect in 1917, requiring of the alien an ability to read some language selected by him, was the first restrictive measure enacted. Its purpose was to check the South and Central European inflow. For in these countries illiteracy is very high. It rises as high as sixty and seventy per cent. in the Central European states. With the test of literacy applied it was felt that the old immigration from Northern Europe would reassert itself. Our industrial needs would be supplied from Great Britain, from Germany and from the Scandinavian countries. The same motive underlies the recently enacted law which arbitrarily fixes the number who may come in any one year from any one country to three per cent. of the aliens already here from that country. This will still further shift the immigration to the Northern countries, and if continued as the permanent policy of the Government will insure a predominant Anglo-Saxon-Germanic-Scandinavian stock as the racial stock of America.

Despite all of the Congressional concern over the alien and the recent nation-wide movement for his Americanization, there has never been any official concern for the alien, for his protection from exploitation and abuse, or any attempt to work out a policy of real Americanization. Not that the task is impossible. Not that it is even experimental. Australia, Brazil, and Canada have more or less well-developed agencies for aiding the alien on landing, for protecting him until he is able to protect himself, and for adjusting him as speedily as possible to new conditions of life. In all of these countries the aim of the government is to give the immigrant a stake in the land, to bring about his permanent residence in the country, and, if possible, to induce him to become a farmer rather than an industrial worker. This has not been done by agencies of distribution alone, but by conscious selection in the country from which the immigrant comes, by grants of land to those who are ready to take up land holdings, and by the extension of credit from state agencies to enable the settlers to stock and equip their farms. The policy of Brazil has been so successful that many colonies of Northern Italians have been induced to settle there who have become prosperous and contented farmers. In other words, these countries have consciously aimed to work out a continuing policy similar to that which prevailed in this country up to about 1890 when the immigrant drifted naturally to the land as a means of securing the freedom from the exploiting class that had driven him from Europe.

It is not to be inferred that our policy of hands off the alien after his landing has worked only evil. Viewed in the perspective of two centuries, it has worked amazingly well. The rapidity with which practically all immigrants rise in the world in spite of the obstacles of poverty, illiteracy, and unfamiliarity with our language is little short of a miracle. This is true of the older generation as it is of the younger. It is most true in the cities, least true in the mining camps and smaller industrial centres about the steel mills and slaughter houses where the tyranny of the employing class is most pronounced. For the newcomer speedily acquires the wants of those with whom he associates. He becomes dissatisfied with his shack. He demands more and better food and clothes. He almost always wants his children to have a schooling and to rise in the scale, which to him means getting out of the hod-carrying, day-labour, or even artisan class. And the next generation does rise. It rises only less rapidly than did the early immigrant. It increases its wants and demands. It finds the trades union a weapon with which it can combat the employer who seeks to bring about a confusion of tongues, a confusion of religion, and a confusion of races as a means of maintaining the open shop. As an evidence of this, the Amalgamated Clothing Workers of America is almost exclusively Jewish, Italian, and Latin in its membership. It is the most intelligent, the most social-minded, and the most highly developed labour organization in the country. The coal miners are largely men of foreign birth. They, too, have adopted an advanced social programme. The alien has found the trades union the most efficient if not the only agency through which he can Americanize himself. And in Americanizing himself he is merely doing what the aliens of earlier centuries who preceded him have done—he is seeking for economic freedom from a master class.

America is a marvellous demonstration of the economic foundations of all life. It is a demonstration of what happens to men when economic opportunities call forth their resourcefulness and latent ability on one hand and when the State, on the other, keeps its hands off them in their personal relationships. For the alien quickly adopts a higher standard of culture as he rises in the industrial scale, while his morals, whatever they may have been, quickly take on the colour of his new environment, whatever that may be. And if all of the elements which should enter into a consideration of the subject were included, I am of the opinion it would be found that the morals, the prevalence of vice and crime among the alien population is substantially that of the economic class in which he is found rather than the race from which he springs. In other words, the alleged prevalence of crime among the alien population is traceable to poverty and bad conditions of living rather than to ethnic causes, and in so far as it exists it tends disappear as the conditions which breed it pass away.

Despite the fact that our hands-off policy of the past has worked amazingly well, the time has come when it must be changed. Not because of any change in the character of the alien, but because of the change which has taken place in our own internal life. Economic conditions make it impossible for the alien, as it does for the native born, to become a farmer.

Exploiting agencies are making it difficult and often impossible for the farmer to make a living. Land speculation has shot up the price of farm land to prohibitive figures. The railroads and middle men and banking agencies are putting the American farmer into a semi-servile status. He is unable to market his crop after it is produced or he markets it at a figure that ultimately reduces him to bankruptcy. The immigration problem remains an economic problem. It has become an American problem. The policy we should adopt for Americanizing the alien is a policy we should adopt for our own people as well, for when economic opportunity came to an end for our own people, it created not only an immigration problem, but a domestic problem. The solution of one is the solution of the other.

The alien will Americanize himself if he is given the opportunity to do so. The bird of passage will cease to migrate when he possesses a stake in the land of his adoption. The best cure for Bolshevism is not deportation but a home, a farm, a governmental policy of land settlement. A constructive immigration policy and Americanization policy is one that will:

1. Direct the alien as well as the native born to opportunities of employment and especially to agencies that will enable them to become home owners and farm owners;

2. Provide government grants, as is done in Australia, Denmark, and some of the South American countries, to which the would-be farmer or home owner can go for financial assistance. In Denmark and Australia any man who shows aptitude and desire for farming and who is able to satisfy a local commission of his abilities, can secure a small farm in a farm colony, fully equipped for planting. The grant includes a house and barn, some cattle and machinery, and sufficient capital to carry the settler over the first season. The applicant must provide a certain portion of the initial outlay himself. He is aided by experts from the colony, he is advised as to what to plant and how to care for his cattle. His produce is marketed co-operatively, while much of the machinery is owned either by the community or by co-operative agencies identified with the community. The land is purchased in large tracts by the State in advance of settlement to prevent speculation, while settlers are required to develop their holdings. They may

not purchase for speculative purposes. The State of Denmark has planted thousands of home-owning farmers in this way and has all but ended farm tenancy in a generation's time. The farm tenant and farm labourer have become owners. A similar policy has been developed in Australia, where millions of dollars have been advanced by the State to settlers. In both of these countries the land settlement colonies have been a great success. There have been few failures and no losses to the State.

3. The savings of the alien should be used for the benefit of the alien. Hundreds of millions of dollars leave this country annually in the form of remittances. Much of it goes abroad because of fear of American banks. Many millions more are in 'hiding for the same reason. The deposits in the Postal Savings banks are largely the deposits of the immigrant. They are turned over to the National banks and find their way into commercial activities. If these funds were mobilized in cooperative banks, as is done all over Europe, or if the Government would dedicate them to a revolving fund for aiding persons to build homes, to buy farms, and to aid the alien with credit, which he now has no means of securing; he would be lured from the city to the land, he would become a home and farm owner rather than an industrial worker, and would rapidly develop those qualities of mind and character that are associated in our minds with the early Anglo-Saxon settler but which are rather the qualities which spring up of themselves when the economic conditions encourage them.

4. Our deportation laws are a disgrace to any country. They are an adaptation of the fugitive slave laws. The offending alien is subject to lynch law sanctioned by the State. He is arrested on complaint by an inspector. He is then tried by the man who arrests him. His friends and relatives are excluded from the trial. The judge who made the arrest is often the interpreter and the clerk who transcribes the testimony. He also is his jailer. He can and does hold the alien incommunicado. Often the alien scarcely knows why he has been arrested. Often he does not understand the testimony. The local findings have to be approved at Washington by the Department of Labour. But the approval is by a clerk who, like

the inspector, often wants to make a record. The opportunity for collusion with police, with crusaders, with employers, with Chambers of Commerce, and with organization bent on " ridding the country of disturbers " is manifest. Often men are arrested, tried, convicted, and possibly placed on ships for their home countries before their families are aware of what has happened to them.

The alien is denied every protection of our constitution. The Bill of Rights does not apply to him. He has no presentment before a Grand Jury, there is no jury trial, he rarely has counsel, and he is often held incommunicado by the official who has taken him into custody and who wants to justify his arrest. The only recourse the alien has is the writ of habeas corpus. But this is of practically no avail. For the courts have held that if there is a scintilla of evidence on which the inspector could act the court will not review the finding. And a scintilla is any evidence at all. When to this is added the fact that the charge " likely to become a public charge " has come to cover almost any condition that might arise, and as this charge is usually added to the others as a recourse on which the inspector may fall back, the chance of relief in the court is practically nil. Under the laws as they now exist the alien is a man without a country. He has no protection from the constitution and little protection under the laws. The alien knows this. He feels that he is defenceless. American liberty to him means the liberty of a policeman, a health or school official, an immigration inspector, and agents of the department of justice to invade his home, to seize his papers, to arrest without warrant, to hold incommunicado, and to deport on a charge that is often as foreign to the facts as anything could be.

It is this more than anything else that has embittered the alien towards America during the last few years. It is this that makes him feel that he is not wanted here. It is this that is sending hundreds of thousands back to Europe, many of them among the best of the aliens and many of them worthy in every way of our confidence and welcome.

A proper immigration policy should be a national policy. Not something for the alien alone but for our own people. For the immigration problem is merely another form of the domestic problem. When we are ready to settle the one we will settle the other. A cross section of one branch of our political State is a cross section of another. The alien of to-day is not very different from the alien of yesterday. He has the same instincts and desires as did those who came in the *Mayflower*. Only those who came in the *Mayflower* made their own laws and their own fortunes. Those who come to-day have their laws made for them by the class that employs them and they make their own fortunes only as those aliens who came first permit them to do so.

FREDERIC C. HOWE

RACIAL MINORITIES

" . . . not to laugh at the actions of men, nor yet to deplore or detest them, but simply to understand them."—*Spinoza.*

IN America, the race-problem is not only without answer; thus far it is even without formulation. In the face of ordinary economic, political, and religious difficulties, people habitually formulate creeds which give a kind of rhyme and reason to their actions; but where inter-racial relations are concerned, the leaders go pussy-footing all around the fundamental question, while the emotions of the masses translate themselves into action, and action back again into emotion, with less consideration of means and ends than one expects of the maddest bomb-thrower. Everybody has some notion of the millennial aims of the Communist Party, the National Association of Manufacturers, the W.C.T.U., the Holy Rollers; but what are the Southerners getting at, when they educate the Negro, and refuse him the ballot; what ultimate result does the North expect from the granting of the franchise and the denial of social equality? Do both the North and the South hope to maintain a permanent racial division of the country's population? If so, are the Indians, the Jews and the Asiatics to be classed with the Negroes, as unassimilable minorities? How is the conduct of the American majority suited to this aim, if it is an aim? How can permanent division be maintained, except by permanent prejudice? What do the racial liberators, ameliorators, uplifters, and general optimists think about it; or do they think about it at all?

From the moment of initial contact between the mass of the American population and the country's most important racial minorities—the Indian, the Jew, the Oriental, and the Negro—the self-congratulatory feelings of the majority have always found a partial or complete counterpart everywhere except among the slaves and the children of the slaves. The long delay in the inception of All-Africanism in America, and the groping uncertainty which still characterizes its manifestations, are due in large part to the cultural youthfulness of the American Negro. Biologically, the black race was matured in Africa; culturally it had made considerable advances there, before the days of the slave-trade. The process of enslavement could not strip away the physical characteristics of the race, but in all that has to do with cultural life and social inheritance, the Negro was re-born naked in the new world.

When one compares the condition of the Negro with that of the other three racial minorities at the moment of contact with the miscellaneous white population, the Indian seems closer to the Jew and the Oriental than to the slave. In a general way, the condition of the Indian tribes resembled that of the Negroes in Africa, but the Indians were left in possession of most of the elements of savage culture and were never entirely deprived of the means of maintaining themselves in this stage of development. Needless to say, the Jews and the Orientals were in still better case than the Indians, for their imported cultural equipment was far more elaborate and substantial, and their economic position much better.

The four racial minorities thus varied widely in the degree of their self-sufficiency, and likewise, inversely, in the degree of their need for absorption into the current of American life. Quite obviously the Negro was least independent and most in need of assimilation. However, the necessity of the alien group has not been the only factor of importance in this matter of assimilation. Each of the minorities has been from the beginning subjected to the prejudice of the majority, and that group which first lost all life of its own through contact with the whites has been signalled out for the maximum amount of persecution.

The standard explanation or excuse for race-prejudice is the theory of the inequality of racial stocks. However, for all their eagerness to bolster up a foregone conclusion, the race-patriots have not been able to prove by any sort of evidence, historical, biological, or psychological, that racial differences are not simply indications of unlikeness, rather than of inherent superiority or inferiority. The anthropologists are pretty well agreed that physical differences divide mankind into three major groups, European (including the Jews), Mongoloid (including the American Indians), and Negroid; but science has set no definite limit to the respective potentialities of these groups. In other words, it has remained for race-prejudice to assume an unproved inferiority, and to devise all possible measures for making the life of the objectionable races exactly what it would be, in the absence of interference, if the assumed inferiority were real.

To accept the term " race-prejudice " as accurately descriptive of the feelings to which it is usually applied, is to assume that these feelings originate in race-differences, if not in the inequality of races. This, however, is still to be proved. Race-differences are a factor of the situation wherever two races are in contact, but it is a matter of common knowledge that the members of two or more racial groups sometimes intermingle on terms of greatest friendliness. To attribute " race-prejudice " to race-difference, and to leave race-friendliness entirely unexplained, is to blind oneself deliberately to the existence of variable causes which alone can account for the variable results that appear in the presence of racial constants. Racial inequality of intelligence, if it actually exists, is simply one of a number of ever-present race-differences, and in all these differences taken together one can find no adequate explanation of the variable phenomenon commonly called " race-prejudice," but so designated here only for the sake of convenience.

Any serious attempt to get at the non-racial causes of " race-prejudice " in America would necessarily involve the comparison, point by point, of economic, social, political, and intellectual conditions in various localities in the United States with corresponding local conditions in other countries where the races here in conflict are more nearly at peace. In the present state of knowledge, the racial theory of race-prejudice is demonstrably inadequate, while the non-racial theory is an hypothesis which can neither be proved nor disproved. Such being the case, the haphazard speculations which follow are not offered as a proof of this hypothesis, or as an explanation of the existence of race-prejudice in America, but simply as a stimulus to inquiry.

Beginning with these speculations, it may be said that the goods and opportunities of the material life, unlike those of the intellectual life, are frequently incapable of division without loss to the original possessor. On this account, competition is likely to be particularly keen and vindictive where material interests are given the foremost place. It is also perhaps safe to say that the long preoccupation of the American majority with the development of its material inheritance has brought to the majority a heavy heritage of materialism. One may hazard the statement that the prejudice of America's native white majority against the Negroes, the Indians, the Jews and the Asiatics, is now and has always been in some sense attributable and proportional to the majority's fear of some action on the part of the minority which might injure the material interests of the majority; while the only race-differences which have had any real importance are those superficial ones which serve to make the members of the minorities recognizable at sight. At any rate, an examination of some of the facts that come most easily to hand shows an interesting coincidence between the prejudice of the majority and the power of the minority.

Before the Civil War, the structure of Southern society was bottomed on slavery, and the fear of any humanization of the Negro which would make him appear worthy of emancipation was strong enough to arouse any degree of prejudice, and any amount of repression. The prejudice of the Southern white populace as a whole reached its maximum intensity when emancipation threatened to place the blacks in permanent political and economic control of certain portions of the South. Even to-day, fear of the political power of the Negroes, and perhaps also the over-emphasized fear of black " outrages," still acts upon the white population as a unifying force; but in spite of this fact, class-interests have become plainly visible. When Black Republicanism had once been driven to cover, the masters set about rebuilding their privileges upon the foundation of Negro labour which is still their chief support. Only a few Negroes have been able to compete directly for a share in these privileges, and accordingly most of the fears of the well-to-do people of the South are anticipatory rather than immediate.

With the "poor whites," the case is altogether different. Here there is no question of keeping the Negro in his place, for ever since the Emancipation the place of the Negro has been very much that of the poor white himself, at least in so far as economic status is concerned. In the view of the white labourer, the Negro rises too high the moment he becomes a competitor for a job, and every Negro is potentially just that. Accordingly, the prejudice of the poorer whites is bitter and indiscriminate, and is certainly not tending to decrease with the cityward drift of the Negro population.

With the appearance of Negro workers in large numbers in Northern industrial centres, race-prejudice has begun to manifest itself strongly among the white workers. The Northern masters have, however, shown little tendency to reproduce the sentiments of their Southern peers, for in the North there is no fear of political dominance by the blacks, and a supply of cheap labour is as much appreciated as it is south of the Line.

In spite of the fact that the proportion of Negroes in the total population of the United States has declined steadily from 15.7 per cent. in 1850 to 9.9 per cent. in 1920, the attitude of both Northerners and Southerners is somewhat coloured by the fear that the blacks will eventually overrun the country. If prejudice had no other basis than this, there would perhaps be no great difficulty in effecting its cure. As a matter of course, immigration accounts in part for the increasing predominance of the white population; but this hardly disposes of the fact that throughout the South, during the years 1890-1910, the percentage of native whites of native parentage advanced in both urban and rural communities. Discussion of comparative birth-rates also gives rise to numerous alarums and excursions, but the figures scarcely justify the fears expressed. Statistics show that, in spite of the best efforts of the people who attempt to hold the black man down, and then fear him all the more because he breeds too generously, the improvement in the material condition of the Negro is operating inevitably to check the process of multiplication.

If the case of the Negro is complicated in the extreme, that of the Indian is comparatively simple. Here race-prejudice has always followed the frontier. As long as the Indian interfered with the exploitation of the country, the pioneers feared him, and disliked him cordially. Their feelings worked themselves out in all manner of personal cruelty, as well as in a process of wholesale expropriation, but as soon as the tribes had been cooped up on reservations, the white man's dislike for the Indian began to cool off perceptibly. From the beginning, the Indian interfered with expansion, not as an economic competitor, but as a military enemy; when the dread of him as a fighter disappeared, there was no new fear to take its place. During the years 1910 to 1920 the Indian population actually decreased 8.6 per cent.

If the Indian has neither shared the privileges nor paid the price of a generous participation in American life, the Jew has certainly done both. In every important field of activity, the members of this minority have proved themselves quite able to compete with the native majority, and accordingly the prejudice against them is not confined to any one social class, but is concentrated rather in those regions where the presence of Jews in considerable numbers predicates their competitive contact with individuals of all classes. Although as a member of one branch of the European racial family, the Jew is by no means so definitely distinguished by physical characteristics as are the members of the other minorities here under discussion, it is nevertheless true that when the Jew has been identified by his appearance, or has chosen to identify himself, the anti-Semite takes on most of the airs of superiority which characterize the manifestations of prejudice towards the other minorities. Nevertheless, the ordinary run of anti-Semitic talk contains frequent admissions of jealousy and fear, and it is safe to say that one must look chiefly to such emotions, as intensified by the rapid increase of the Jewish population from 1,500,000 in 1906 to 3,300,000 in 1918, rather than to the heritage of European prejudice, for an explanation of the growth of anti-Semitism in America. The inclusion of anti-Semitism with the other types of race-prejudice here under discussion follows naturally enough from the fact that the Jew is thought of as primarily a Jew, whatever the country of his origin may have been, while the Slav, for instance, is popularly regarded as a Russian, a Pole, a Serb —a *national* rather than a *racial* alien.

Like the Jew, the Oriental has come into the United States as a " foreigner," as well as a member of an alien race. The absence of this special disqualification has not particularly benefitted the Negro and the Indian, but its presence in the case of the Japanese has been of considerable service to the agitators. The prevalent dislike and fear of the new Japan as a world-power has naturally coloured the attitude of the American majority toward the Japanese settlers in this country; but this in itself hardly explains why the Californians, who were burning Chinamen out of house and home in the 'seventies, are now centring their prejudice upon the Japanese agriculturist. The fact is that since the passage of the Exclusion Laws the Chinese population of the United States has fallen off more than 40 per cent., and the importance of Chinese competition has decreased accordingly, while on the other hand the number of Japanese increased 53.9 per cent. between 1910 and 1920, and the new competitors are showing themselves more than a match for the white farmers. With a frankness that neither Negrophobia nor anti-Semitism has made us familiar with, many of the Californians have rested their case against the Japanese on an economic foundation, and have confessed that they are unable to compete with the Japanese on even terms. As a matter of course, there is the usual flow of talk about the inferiority of the alien race, but the fear of competition, here so frankly admitted, would be enough in itself to account for this new outbreak of " race-prejudice."

When one considers thus the course that prejudice has taken in the case of the Negro, the Indian, the Jew, and the Oriental, it begins to appear that this sentiment may wax and wane and change about astonishingly in the presence of racial factors that remain always the same. Such being the case, one is led to wonder what the attitude of the native majority would be, if the minorities were recognizable simply as groups, but *not* as *racial* groups. In other words, what would be the result if the racial factor were reduced simply to recognizability? The question has a more than speculative interest.

If the causes of race-prejudice lie quite beyond the reach of any simple explanation, the manifestation of this prejudice on the part of the American majority are perhaps capable of an analysis which will render the whole situation somewhat more comprehensible. By and large, and with all due allowance for exceptions, it may be said that, in its more familiar manifestations, race-prejudice takes a direction exactly opposite to that taken by prejudice against the ordinary immigrant of European stock; in the former case, a conscious effort is made to magnify the differences between the majority and the minority, while in the latter, a vast amount of energy is expended in the obliteration of these differences. Thus race-prejudice aspires to preserve and even to increase that degree of unlikeness which is its excuse for being, while alien-prejudice works itself out of a job, by " Americanizing " the immigrant and making him over into an unrecognizable member of the majority. On one hand, enforced diversity remains as a source of friction, while on the other, enforced uniformity is demanded as the price of peace.

Although no purpose can be served by cataloguing here all the means employed in the South to keep the black man in his place, a few examples may be cited, in order to show the scope of these measures of repression. In the economic field, there is a pronounced tendency to restrict Negro workers to the humblest occupations, and in the agricultural areas the system of peonage or debt-slavery is widely employed for the purpose of attaching Negro families to the soil. Residence-districts are regularly segregated, Jim Crow regulations are everywhere in force, and inter-racial marriages are prohibited by law in all the States of the South. The administration of justice is in the hands of white judges and white juries, and the Negro's chances in such company are notoriously small. In nearly one-fourth of the counties of the South, the population is half, or more than half black, but the denial of the ballot excludes the Negroes from local, State, and national political activities. In religious organizations, segregation is the invariable rule. Theatres and even public libraries are regularly closed to the Negro, and in every State in the South segregation in schools is prescribed by law. Some idea of the significance of the latter provision may be drawn from O. G. Ferguson's study of white and Negro schools in Virginia. In this comparatively progressive State, the general rating of the white schools is 40.8, as against 22.3 for the coloured schools, the latter figure being seven points lower than the lowest general rating for any State in the Union.

Such are some of the legal, extra-legal, and illegal manifestations of that prejudice which finds its supreme expression in the activities of the lynching-mob and the Ku Klux Klan. There is still a considerable annual output of lynchings in this country (in 1920 the victims numbered sixty-five, of whom fifty were Negroes done to death in the South), but the casualty-list for the South and for the country as a whole has decreased steadily and markedly since 1889, and the proportion of Negro victims who were accused of rape or attacks on women has also decreased, from 31.8 per cent. in 1889-1893 to 19.8 per cent. in 1914-1918.

On the other hand, the Ku Klux Klan has now re-commenced its ghost-walking activities under the command of an " Imperial Wizard " who claims that he has already enlisted 100,000 followers in the fight to maintain the " God-ordained " pre-eminence of the Anglo-Saxon race in America. Other statements from the lips of the Wizard seem to indicate that his organization is not only anti-African, but anti-Semitic, anti-Catholic, and anti-Bolshevik as well. Indeed, the bearers of the fiery cross seem bent upon organizing an all-American hate society, and the expansion of the Klan in the North is already under way.

However, the Klansmen might have succeeded in carrying the war into the enemy's country even without adding new prejudices to their platform. There has always been some feeling against the Negro in the North, and the war-time migration of the blacks to Northern industrial centres certainly has not resulted in any diminution of existing prejudice. The

National Urban League estimates that the recent exodus from Dixie has produced a net increase of a quarter of a million in the coloured population of twelve cities above the Line. This movement has brought black and white workers into competition in many industries where Negroes have hitherto been entirely unknown, and frequently the relations between the two groups have been anything but friendly. Since about half the " internationals " affiliated with the American Federation of Labour still refuse to accept Negro members, the unions themselves are in no small part to blame for the use that employers have made of Negro workers as strike-breakers.

In twelve Northern and Western States there are laws on the statute-books prohibiting marriage between whites and blacks. Jim Crow regulations are not in force north of Maryland, but in most of the cities there has been a continuous effort to maintain residential segregation, and the practice of discrimination in hotels and restaurants is the rule rather than the exception. Lynchings are infrequent, but the great riots of Washington and Chicago were not exactly indicative of good feeling between the races. One situation which revealed a remarkable similarity of temper between the North and the South was that which arose in the army during the war. It is notorious that Northerners in uniform fell in easily with the Southern spirit, and gave all possible assistance in an energetic Jim-Crowing of the Negroes of Michigan and the Negroes of Mississippi, from the first day of their service right through to the last.

The treatment of the Negro in literature and on the stage also reveals an unconscious but all the more important unanimity of opinion. It is true the North has produced no Thomas Dixons, but it is also true that the gentle and unassuming Uncle Tom of Northern song and story is none other than the Uncle Remus whom the South loves so much. In Boston, as in Baton Rouge, the Negro who is best liked is the loyal, humble, and not too able mammie or uncle of the good old days before the war. If an exception be made in the case of Eugene O'Neill's " Emperor Jones," it may be said that American literature has not yet cast a strong, upstanding black man for any other rôle than that of beast and villain.

And yet all these forms of discrimination and repression are not fully expressive of the attitude of the white population. The people of the South are fully sensible of the necessity of keeping the Negro in his place; still they do not keep him from attending school. Educational facilities, of a sort, are provided, however reluctantly, and in half the States of the South school attendance is even made compulsory by laws (which may or may not be enforced). The schooling is not of a kind that will fit the Negroes for the permanent and contented occupancy of a servile position. Generally speaking, the coloured children do not receive a vocational education that will keep them in their place, but an old-style three-R training that prepares for nothing but unrest. If unrest leads to urbanization, the half-hearted education of the Negro perhaps serves the interests of the new industrialists; but these industrial employers are so few in number that their influence cannot outweigh that of the planters who lose their peons, and the poor whites who find the Negro with one grain of knowledge a somewhat more dangerous competitor than the Negro with none. Hence there is every reason to believe that if the white South had rationalized this situation, the Negro would be as ruthlessly excluded from the school as he now is from the ballot-box. In fact, the education of the Negro seems quite inconsistent with race-prejudice as it is generally preached and practised in the South.

In the North there is no discrimination in the schools, and black children and white are put through the same mill. In the industrial field, prejudice cannot effectually close to the Negroes all those openings which are created by general economic conditions, and in politics the Northern Negro also finds some outlet for his energies.

While it would be quite impossible to show that the existence of these miscellaneous educational, industrial, and political opportunities is due to any general desire upon the part of the members of the white majority to minimize the differences between themselves and the Negroes, it is certainly true that this desire exists in a limited section of the white population. At the present time, white friends of the Negro are actively engaged in efforts to eliminate certain legal and illegal forms of discrimination and persecution, and are giving financial support to much of the religious work and most of the private educational institutions among the blacks. The Inter-racial Committee of the War Work Council of the Y.M.C.A. has listed thirty-three social and economic agencies, and twenty-three religious agencies, in which members of both races are working co-operatively. It must be admitted, however, that many, if not most, of the white participants in work of this sort are affected by race-prejudice to the extent that they desire simply to ameliorate the lowly condition of the Negro, without altogether doing away with a certain wholesome degree of racial segregation. For the complete elimination of the flavour of condescension, one must usually seek out those extreme socialist and syndicalist agitators who preach political or non-political class-organization, as a substitute for the familiar national and racial groupings.

In the case of the American Indian, the prejudice and self-interest of the white majority have placed the emphasis on geographic rather than social segregation. Here the demand of the whites has been for land rather than for labour, and by consequence servility has never been regarded as a prime virtue of Indian character.

If the early white settlers had so desired, they of course could have enslaved a considerable portion of the Indian population, just as the Spaniards did, in regions farther to the southward. However, the Americans chose to drive the Indians inland, and to replace them in certain regions with African tribesmen who in their native state had been perhaps as war-like as the Indians themselves. Thus in the natural course of events the African warrior was lost in the slave, while the Indian chief continued to be the military opponent rather than the economic servant of exploitation, and eventually gained romantic interest by virtue of this fact. The nature of this operation of debasement on one hand, and ennoblement on the other, is plainly revealed in American literature. The latter phase of the work is carried forward to-day with great enthusiasm by the Camp Fire Girls and the Boy Scouts, whose devotion to the romantic ideal of Indian life is nowhere paralleled by a similar interest in African tribal lore.

If the Indian has been glorified by remote admirers, he has

also been cordially disliked by some of his nearest neighbours, and indeed the treatment he has received at the hands of the Government seems to reflect the latter attitude rather than the former. In theory, most of the Indian reservations are still regarded as subject principalities, and the Indians confined within their boundaries are almost entirely cut off from the economic, social, and political life of the neighbouring white communities. Many of the tribes still receive yearly governmental grants of food, clothing, arms, and ammunition, but these allowances only serve to maintain them in a condition of dependence, without providing any means of exit from it. In justice it should be said, however, that the Government has declared an intention to make the Indian self-supporting, and accordingly it restricts the grants, in principle, to the old and the destitute. Several States have shown their complete sympathy with the system of segregation by enacting laws prohibiting the inter-marriage of Indians and whites.

On the other hand, the mental and moral Americanization of the red man has been undertaken by Protestant and Catholic missions, and more recently by Government schools. The agencies of the latter sort are especially systematic in their work of depriving the Indian of most of the qualities for which he has been glorified in romance, as well as those for which he has been disliked by his neighbours. Many a Western town enjoys several times each year the spectacle of Indian schoolboys in blue uniforms and Indian school-girls in pigtails and pinafores, marching in military formation through its streets. As long as these marchers are destined for a return to the reservation, the townsmen can afford to look upon them with mild curiosity. The time for a new adjustment of inter-racial relations will not come until the procession turns towards the white man's job on the farm and in the factory—if it ever does turn that way.

Attention has already been called to the fact that the Jewish immigrant normally marches from the dock directly to the arena of economic competition. Accordingly his progress is not likely to be at any time the object of mere curiosity. On the other hand, the manifestations of prejudice against the Jew have been less aggressive and much less systematic than those repressive activities which affect the other minorities. Where anti-Semitism is present in America, it seems to express itself almost entirely in social discrimination, in the narrow sense. On the other hand, economic, political, and educational opportunities are opened to the Jews with a certain amount of reluctance. A major exception to this rule of discrimination must be made in the case of those socialists, syndicalists and trade-unionists who have diligently sought the support of the Jewish workers.

The Chinaman has also some friends now among the people who once regarded him as the blackest of villains. Indeed, the Californian's attitude toward the Orientals has in it an element of unconscious irony which somewhat illuminates the character of the race-problem. The average Easterner will perhaps be surprised to learn that in Western eyes the Chinaman is an inferior, of course, but nevertheless an honest man, noted for square dealing and the prompt payment of his debts, while the Jap is a tricky person whom one should never trust on any account.

In California the baiting of the Japanese is now almost as much a part of political electioneering as is the abuse of the Negro in the South. The Native Sons of the Golden West and the American Legion have gone on record in determined opposition to any expansion of Japanese interests in California, while the Japanese Exclusion League is particularly active in trouble-making propaganda. Economic discrimination has taken statutory form in the Alien Land Laws of 1913 and 1920; discriminatory legislation of the same general type has been proposed in Texas and Oregon; a bill providing for educational segregation has been presented for a second time at Sacramento; Congress has been urged to replace the " gentlemen's agreement " with an absolute prohibition of Japanese immigration; and there is even a demand for a constitutional amendment which will deny citizenship to the American-born children of aliens who are themselves ineligible for naturalization. The method of legislation is perhaps preferable to the method of force and violence, but if the previous history of race-prejudice means anything, it means that force will be resorted to if legislation fails. At bottom, the spirit of the

California Land Laws is more than a little like that of a Georgia lynching; in the one case as in the other, the dominant race attempts to maintain its position, not by a man-to-man contest, with fair chances all around, but by depositing itself bodily and *en masse* on top of the subject people and crushing them.

If in the realm of individual conduct this sort of behaviour works injury to the oppressor, as well as to the oppressed, it is not otherwise where masses of men are concerned. Stephen Graham, in his recent book, " The Soul of John Brown," says that " in America to-day, and especially in the South, there is a hereditary taint left by slavery, and it is to be observed in the descendants of the masters as much as in the descendants of the slaves. It would be a mistake to think of this American problem as exclusively a Negro problem." Indeed, it is true that in every case the race-problem is the problem of the majority as well as of the minority, for the former can no more escape the reaction of prejudice than the latter can escape its direct effects.

To-day the white South is still under the influence of a system of life and thought that is far more enduring than the one institution which gave it most complete expression. The Emancipation abolished slavery, but it did not rid the master of the idea that it is his right to live by the labour of the slave. The black man is not yet relieved of the duty of supporting a certain proportion of the white population in leisure; nor does it appear that the leisured Southerner of to-day makes a better use of his time than his ancestors did before him. Indeed, an historian who judged the peoples chiefly by their contribution to science and the arts would still be obliged to condemn the white South, not for enslaving the Negro, but for dissipating in the practices of a barren gentility the leisure that Negro labour created, and still creates, so abundantly. It is notorious also that in the South the airs of gentility have been more widely broadcast among the white population than the leisure necessary for their practice, with the result that much honest work which could not be imposed upon the black man has been passed on to posterity, and still remains undone.

Any one who seeks to discover the cause of the mental lethargy that has converted the leisure of the South so largely into mere laziness must take some account of a factor that is always present where race-prejudice exists. The race which pretends to superiority may not always succeed in superimposing itself economically upon the inferior group; and yet the pride and self-satisfaction of the members of the " superior " race will pretty surely make for indolence and the deadening of the creative spirit. This will almost inevitably be true where the superiority of the one race is acknowledged by the other, and where no contest of wits is necessary for the maintenance of the *status quo*. This is the condition that has always obtained, and still obtains in most of the old slave territory. In Dixie it is a career simply to go through life inside of a white skin. However ignorant and worthless the white man may be, it is still his privilege to proclaim on any street corner that he is in all respects a finer creature than any one of several million human beings whom he classes all together as " good-for-nothin' niggers." If the mere statement of this fact is not enough to bring warm applause from all the blacks in the neighbourhood, the white man is often more than willing to use fire and sword to demonstrate a superiority which he seldom stoops to prove in any other fashion. Naturally this feeling of God-given primacy tends to make its possessors indolent, immune to new ideas of every sort, and quite willing to apply " the short way with the nigger " to any one who threatens the established order of the universe.

It would be foolish indeed to suppose that the general intolerance, bigotry, and backwardness which grow out of race-prejudice have affected the South alone. The North and the West have their prejudices too, their consciousness of a full-blooded American superiority that does not have to be proved, their lazy-mindedness, their righteous anger, their own short way with what is new and strange. No sane man will attribute the origin of all these evils to race-prejudice alone, but no honest man will deny that the practice of discrimination against the racial minorities has helped to infect the whole life and thought of the country with a cocky and stupefying provincialism.

Perhaps the most interesting phase of the whole racial situation in America is the attitude which the minorities themselves have maintained in the presence of a dominant prejudice which has constantly emphasized and magnified the differences between the minorities and majority, and has even maintained the spirit of condescension, and the principle of segregation in such assimilative activities as education and Christian mission work. One would naturally expect that such an attitude on the part of the majority would stimulate a counter race-prejudice in each of the minorities, which would render them also intent upon the maintenance of differentiation.

Although such a counter prejudice has existed from the beginning among the Indians, the Jews, and the Asiatics, it is only now beginning to take form among the Negroes. The conditions of the contact between the black minority and the white majority have thus been substantially different from those which existed in the other cases, and the results of this contact seem to justify the statement that, so long as it remains *one-sided*, the strongest race-prejudice cannot prevent the cultural and even the biological assimilation of one race to another. In other words, prejudice defeats itself, in a measure, just so long as one of the parties accepts an inferior position; in fact, it becomes fully effective only when the despised group denies its own inferiority, and throws the reproach back upon those with whom it originated. Thus the new racial self-consciousness of a small section of the Negro population gives the prejudiced whites a full measure of the differentiation they desire, coupled with an absolute denial of the inferiority which is supposed to justify segregation.

It has already been pointed out that the enslavement of the Negroes deprived them of practically everything to which racial pride might attach itself, and left them with no foundation of their own on which to build. Thus they could make no advances of any sort except in so far as they were permitted to assimilate the culture of the white man. In the natural course of events, the adoption of the English language came first, and then shortly the Negro was granted such a share in the white man's heaven as he has never yet received of the white man's earth. As the only available means of self-expression, religion took a tremendous hold upon the slaves, and from that day to this, the black South has wailed its heart out in appeals to the white man's God for deliverance from the white man's burden. The Negro " spirituals " are not the songs of African tribesmen, the chants of free warriors. Indeed, the white man may claim full credit for the sadness that darkens the Negro's music, and put such words as these into the mouth of the Lord:

> Go down, Moses,
>> Way down in Egyp' lan'
>>> Tell ole Pharaoh
>>> Le' ma people go!
> Israel was in Egyp' lan'
>> Oppres' so hard dey could not stan',
>>> Le' ma people go!

When casual observers say that the black man is naturally more religious than the white, they lose sight of the fact that the number of church-members per thousand individuals in the Negro population is about the same as the average for the United States as a whole; and they forget also the more important fact that the Negro has never had all he wanted of anything except religion—and in segregated churches at that. It is more true of the black men than of Engel's proletarians, that they have been put off for a very long time with checks on the bank of Heaven.

Emancipation and the Fourteenth Amendment seemed to open the path to an earthly paradise; but this vision was soon eclipsed by a second Civil War that resulted in a substantial victory for the white South. Economic repression could not be made entirely effective, however, and in the fifty-three years from 1866 to 1919 the number of American Negro home-owners increased from 12,000 to 600,000 and the number of Negroes operating farms from 20,000 to 1,000,000. In 1910 the Negro population still remained 72.6 per cent. rural, but the cityward movement of the blacks during the years 1890 to 1910 was more rapid than that of the whites. Education has directly facilitated economic progress, and has resulted in an increase of literacy among the Negroes from ten per cent. in 1866 to eighty per cent. in 1919. During the period 1900 to

1910, the *rate* of increase of literacy among the blacks was much more rapid than that among the whites. Thus from the day he was cut off from his own inheritance, the American Negro has reached out eagerly for an alien substitute, until to-day, in practically everything that has to do with culture, he is not black but white—and artificially retarded.

Since America has deprived the Negro of the opportunity to grow up as an African, and at the same time has denied him the right to grow up as a white man, it is not surprising that a few daring spirits among the Negroes have been driven at last to the conclusion that there is no hope for their race except in an exodus from the white man's culture and the white man's continent. The war did a great deal to prepare the way for this new movement; the Negroes of America heard much talk of democracy not meant for their ears; their list of wrongs was lengthened, but at the same time their economic power increased; and many of them learned for the first time what it meant to fight back. Some of them armed themselves, and began to talk of taking two lives for one when the lynching-mob came. Then trouble broke in Chicago and Washington—and the casualties were not all of one sort. Out of this welter of unrest and rebellion new voices arose, some of them calling upon the Negro workers to join forces with their white brothers; some fierce and vengeful, as bitterly denunciatory of socialism and syndicalism as of everything else that had felt the touch of the white man's hand; some intoxicated, ecstatic with a new religion, preaching the glory of the black race and the hope of the black exodus.

With much travail, there finally came forth, as an embodiment of the extreme of race-consciousness, an organization called the Universal Negro Improvement Association and African Communities League. This clan lays claim to a million members in the United States, the West Indies, South America and South Africa, and announces as its final object the establishment of a black empire in Africa. Connected with the U.N.I.A. are the Black Star Line, capitalized at $10,000,000, and the Negro Factories Corporation, capitalized at $2,000,000. Just what these astonishing figures mean in actual cash it is impossible to say, but this much is certain: the Black Star Line already owns three of the many vessels which—say the prophets of the movement—will some day ply among the Negro lands of the world.

To cap the climax, the U.N.I.A. held in New York City during the month of August, 1920, "the first International Negro Convention," which drew up a Negro Declaration of Independence, adopted a national flag and a national anthem, and elected "a Provisional President of Africa, a leader for the American Negroes, and two leaders for the Negroes of the West Indies, Central and South America."

The best testimony of the nature of this new movement is to be found in an astonishing pamphlet called the "Universal Negro Catechism," and issued "by authority of the High Executive Council of the Universal Negro Improvement Association." In this catechism one discovers such items as the following, under the head of "Religious Knowledge":

Q. Did God make any group or race of men superior to another?
A. No; He created all races equal, and of one blood, to dwell on all the face of the earth.

Q. What is the colour of God?
A. A spirit has neither colour, nor other natural parts, nor qualities.

Q. If . . . you had to think or speak of the colour of God, how would you describe it?
A. As black; since we are created in His image and likeness.

Q. What did Jesus Christ teach as the essential principle of true religion?
A. The universal brotherhood of man growing out of the universal Fatherhood of God.

Q. Who is responsible for the colour of the Ethiopians?
A. The Creator; and what He has done cannot be changed. Read Jeremiah 13: 23.

Q. What prediction made in the 68th Psalm and the 31st Verse is now being fulfilled?
A. "Princes shall come out of Egypt, Ethiopia shall soon stretch out her hands unto God."

Q. What does this verse prove?
A. That Negroes will set up their own government in Africa with rulers of their own race.

Q. Will Negroes ever be given equal opportunity and treatment in countries ruled by white men?
A. No; they will enjoy the full rights of manhood and liberty only when they establish their own nation and government in Africa.

Perhaps enough has already been said to make it clear that there exists in America no distinctive black culture which could spontaneously give rise to such a movement as this. Culturally the black man is American; biologically he is African. It is solely and entirely the prejudice of the American majority that has forced this group of Negroes to attempt to reconstruct a cultural and sentimental connection that was destroyed long ago. The task which faces the leaders of the new movement is one of almost insurmountable difficulty, for in spite of every sort of persecution, the general life and thought of America are still far more easily accessible to the Negro than is anything distinctively his own.

The cultural shipwreck of the Negro on the American shore has thus placed him more completely at the mercy of the majority than the other minorities have ever been. In the case of the Indians, the Jews, and the Orientals, the race-name has not stood simply for an incomplete Americanism, but for a positive cultural quality which has persisted in the face of all misfortune. These races were provisioned, so to speak, for a long siege, while the Negro had no choice but to eat out of the white man's hand, or starve.

The reservation-system has reduced many of the Indian tribes to a state of economic dependence, but it has also helped to preserve their cultural autonomy. In most cases the isolated communities on the reservations are distinctly Indian communities. The non-material inheritance of the past has come down to the present generation in a fairly complete form, with the result that the Indian of to-day may usually take his choice between Indian culture and white. Under these conditions the labours of missionaries and educators have not been phenomenally successful, as is witnessed by the fact that the number of Protestant Christians per thousand Indians is still only about one-seventh as large as that for the Negroes, while the percentage of illiterates is much larger among the Indians. However, school attendance is increasing at a more rapid rate than among the whites, and the prospect is that the Government schools will eventually deprive the country of all that is attractive in Indian life.

Toward the close of the 19th century, the Indian's resentment of the white man's overbearing actions found expression in a religious movement which originated in Nevada and spread eastward till it numbered among its adherents nearly all the natives between the Rocky Mountains and the Missouri River. This messianic faith bore the name of a ceremonial connected with it, the Ghost Dance, and was based upon a divine revelation which promised the complete restoration of the Indian's inheritance. Such doctrines have, of course, been preached in many forms and in many lands, but it is no great compliment to the amiability of American civilization that the gospel of deliverance has found so many followers among the Negroes, the Indians, and the Jews who dwell within the borders of the country.

It does not seem likely that the Zionist version of this gospel will produce any general exodus of the last-named minority from this country, for in spite of prejudice, the Jews have been able to make a large place for themselves in the United States. Since the movements of the Jews have not been systematically restricted, as those of the Negroes and the Indians have been, the great concentration of the Jewish population in the cities of the East would seem to be due in large measure to the choice of the Jews themselves. At the present time they dominate the clothing industry, the management of the theatre, and the production of motion-pictures. Approximately one-tenth of the trade-unionists in the United States are Jews, and the adherence of a considerable number of Jews to the doctrines of socialism and syndicalism has unquestionably been one of the causes of prejudice against the race.

In matters that pertain more directly to the intellectual life, the Jews have exhibited every degree of eagerness for, and opposition to, assimilation. There are among them many schools for the teaching of the Hebrew language, and some other schools—private and expensive ones—in which only non-Jewish, "all-American" teachers are employed. Of the seventy-eight Jewish periodicals published in the United States, forty-eight are printed in English. In every Jewish centre, Yiddish theatres have been established for the amusement of the people; but Jewish managers, producers, actors, and playrights have also had a large part in the general dramatic activities of the country. Finally, in the matter of religion, the response of the Jews to Christian missionary work has been very slight indeed, while, on the other hand, the number of synagogue-members per thousand Jews is only about one-fourth the general average of religious affiliation for the United States as a whole. When one considers the fact that in some fields the Jews have thus made advances in spite of opposition, while in others they have refused opportunities offered to them, it seems at least probable that the incompleteness of their cultural assimilation is due as much to their own racial pride as to the prejudice of the majority.

Similarly in the case of the Orientals, the pride and self-sufficiency of the minority has helped to preserve for it a measure of cultural autonomy. In the absence of such a disposition on the part of the Chinese, it would be difficult to account for the fact that their native costume has not disappeared during the thirty-nine years since the stoppage of immigration. San Francisco's Chinatown still remains very markedly Chinese in dress largely because the Chinese themselves have chosen to keep it so. The Japanese have taken much more kindly to the conventional American costume, but one is hardly justified in inferring from this that they are more desirous for general assimilation. Indeed, one would expect the opposite to be the case, for most of the Japanese in America had felt the impress of the nationalistic revival in Japan before their departure from that country. In a measure this accounts for the fact that Japanese settlers have established a number of Buddhist temples and Japanese-language schools in the United States. However, figures furnished by the " Joint Committee on Foreign Language Publications," which represents a number of Evangelical denominations, seem to indicate that the Japanese in the United States are much more easily Christianized than the Chinese, and are even less attached to Buddhism than are the Jews to their native faith. In the nature of things, the domestic practice of Shinto-worship among the Japanese is incapable of statistical treatment.

Thus the combination of all the internal and external forces that affect the racial minorities in America has produced a partial, but by no means a complete, remodelling of minority-life in accordance with standards set by the majority. Prejudice and counter-prejudice have not prevented this change, and there is no accounting for the condition of the American minorities to-day without due attention to the positive factor of cultural assimilation, as well as to the negative factor of ' prejudice.

Since it has already been implied that a greater or less assimilation by the minorities of the culture of the majority is inevitable, it is apparent that the relation of this assimilative change to the biological fusion of the groups is a matter of ultimate and absolute importance. Wherever friction exists between racial groups, the mere mention of biological fusion is likely to stir up so much fire and smoke that all facts are completely lost to sight; and yet it is quite obvious that the forces of attraction and repulsion which play upon the several races in America have produced biological as well as cultural results.

The mulatto population of the United States is the physical embodiment of a one-sided race-prejudice. By law, by custom, even by the visitation of sudden and violent death, the master-class of the South expresses a disapproval of relations between white women and coloured men, which does not apply in any forcible way to similar relations between white men and coloured women. The white male is in fact the go-between for the races. The Negroes have not the power, and sometimes not even the will, to protect themselves against his advances, and the result is that illegitimate mulatto children in great numbers are born of Negro mothers and left to share the lot of the coloured race.

If the infusion of white blood were stopped entirely, the proportion of mulattoes in the Negro race would nevertheless go on increasing, since the children of a mulatto are usually mulattoes, whether the other parent be mulatto or black. There is, however, no reason for supposing that under such conditions the proportion of mulattoes to blacks would increase *more* rapidly in one geographic area than in another. The fact is that during the period 1890 to 1910 the number of mulattoes per 1,000 blacks *decreased* in the North from 390 to 363, and *increased* in the South from 159 to 252; the inference as to white parenthood is obvious. During the same period the black population of the entire United States increased 22.7 per cent., while the mulatto population increased 81.1 per cent. The mulatto group is thus growing far more rapidly than either the black or the white, and the male white population of the South is largely responsible for the present expansion of this class, as well as for its historical origin.

Thus the South couples a maximum of repression with a maximum of racial intermixture; indeed, the one is naturally and intimately associated with the other. The white population as a whole employs all manner of devices to keep the Negro in the social and economic status most favourable to sexual promiscuity, and aggressive white males take full advantage of the situation thus created.

While it is not generally admitted in the South that the progressive whitening of the black race is a natural result of the maintenance of a system of slavery and subjection, the converse of this proposition is stated and defended with all possible ardour. That is to say, it is argued that any general improvement in the condition of the Negro will increase the likelihood of racial intermixture on a higher level, through inter-marriage. The Southerners who put forth this argument know very well that inter-marriage is not likely to take place in the presence of strong race-prejudice, and they know, too, that the Negro who most arouses their animosity is the " improved " Negro who will not keep his place. They are unwilling to admit that this increase in prejudice is due largely, if not wholly, to the greater competitive strength of the improved Negro; and likewise they prefer to disregard the fact that such a Negro resents white prejudice keenly, and tends to exhibit on his own part a counter prejudice which in itself acts as an additional obstacle to inter-marriage.

In the absence of such factors as Negro self-consciousness and inter-racial competition, it would be difficult to account for the extreme rarity of marriages between blacks and whites in the Northern States. No comprehensive study of this subject has been made, but an investigation conducted by Julius Drachsler has shown that of all the marriages contracted by

Negroes in New York City during the years 1908 to 1912, only c.93 per cent. were mixed. The same investigation revealed the fact that Negro men contracted mixed marriages about four times as frequently as Negro women.

Marriages between whites and Indians have not been so vigorously condemned by the American majority as those between whites and Negroes, and the presumption is that the former have been much more frequent. However, it appears that no systematic investigation of Indian mixed marriages has been made, and certainly no census previous to that of 1910 gives any data of value on the subject of mixed blood among the Indians. The enumeration of 1910 showed that 56.5 per cent of the Indians were full-blooded, 35.2 per cent. were of mixed blood, and 8.4 per cent. were unclassified. Although it is impossible to fix the responsibility as definitely here as in the case of the Negro, it is obvious that an infusion of white blood half again as great as that among the Negroes cannot be accounted for in any large part by racial inter-marriages. Without question, it is chiefly due to the same sort of promiscuity that has been so common in the South, and the present and potential checks upon the process of infusion are similar to those already discussed.

In the case of the Jews and the Asiatics, it seems that the only figures available are those gathered by Drachsler. He found that only 1.17 per cent. of the marriages contracted by Jews in New York City during the years 1908 to 1912 were classifiable as "mixed," while the corresponding percentages for the Chinese and the Japanese were 55.56 and 72.41 respectively. The largeness of the figures in the case of Orientals is accounted for in part by the fact that there are comparatively few women of Mongolian race in New York City. Besides this, it must be remembered that, whatever the degree of their cultural assimilation, the Chinese and Japanese residents of the metropolis are not sufficiently numerous to form important competitive groups, while the Jews constitute one-quarter of the entire population of the city. Does any one doubt that the situation in regard to mixed marriages would be partially reversed in San Francisco?

When due allowance is made for special conditions,

Drachsler's figures do not seem to run contrary to the general proposition that an improvement in the economic and social condition of one of the minorities, and a partial or complete adoption by the minority of the culture of the majority, does not necessarily prepare the way for racial fusion, but seems to produce exactly the opposite effect by increasing the competitive power of the minority, the majority's fear of its rivals, and the prejudice of each against the other.

In spite of all that prejudice can do to prevent it, the economic, social, and intellectual condition of the minorities is becoming increasingly like that of the majority; and yet it is not to be expected that as long as the minorities remain physically recognizable this change will result in the elimination of prejudice, nor is it likely that the cultural assimilation which checks the process of racial intermixture through promiscuous intercourse will result automatically in intermixture on a higher level, and the consequent disappearance of the recognizability of the minorities. Prejudice does not altogether prevent cultural assimilation; cultural assimilation increases competitive strength without eliminating recognizability; competitive strength *plus* recognizability produces more prejudice; and so on . . . and so on. . . . Thus it seems probable that race-prejudice will persist in America as long as the general economic, social, political, and intellectual system which has nurtured it endures. No direct attack upon the race-problem, as such, can alter this system in any essential way.

Is this conception sound, or not? It stands very high upon a slim scaffolding of facts, put together in pure contrariness after it had been stated that no adequate foundation for such a structure could be found anywhere. But, after all, it is no great matter what happens to the notion that race-prejudice can be remedied only incidentally. If the conditions which surround race-prejudice are only studied comparatively, this notion and others like it will get all the attention they deserve.

RACE PROBLEMS

(The answers are merely by way of suggestion, but the questions may prove to be worthy of serious attention.)

Q. Has the inherent inferiority of any human race been established by historical, biological or psychological evidence?
A. No.

Q. Does the theory of the inequality of human races offer a satisfactory explanation of the existence of race-prejudice?
A. No.

Q. Do physical characteristics make the members of the several races recognizable?
A. Yes.

Q. Is race-prejudice inherent and inevitable, in the sense that it always exists where two recognizably different races are in contact?
A. No.

Q. How does it happen that in the presence of *racial* factors which remain constant, race-prejudice exists in some localities, and is absent in others?
A. No satisfactory explanation of these local variations in interracial feeling has yet been given; however, the existence of the variations themselves would seem to indicate that the primary causes of race-prejudice are *not racial* but *regional*.

Q. What study will lead most directly to an understanding of race-prejudice—that of universal racial differences, or that of regional environmental differences which are associated with the existence and non-existence of racial prejudice?
A. The latter.

Q. Does the systematic study of regional environmental differences in the United States, in their relation to race-prejudice, yield any results of importance?
A. No such systematic study has ever been made; a casual glance seems to reveal an interesting coincidence between race-prejudice and the fear of competition.

Q. Is competition more likely to produce race-prejudice in the United States than elsewhere?
A. Because of the general preoccupation of the American people with material affairs, *economic* competition is likely to produce unusually sharp antagonisms.

Q. Does the coincidence between race-prejudice and the fear of competition offer a complete explanation of the existence and strength of race-prejudice in the United States?
A. No; no such claim has been advanced.

Q. Is the assimilation by the minorities of the culture of the majority talking place continuously, in spite of the prejudice of the majority and the counter-prejudice of three of the minorities?
A. Yes.

Q. Does this cultural assimilation make for better inter-racial feeling?
A. Probably not, because as long as physical race-differences remain, cultural assimilation increases the strength of the minority as a *recognizable* competitive group, and hence it also increases the keenness of the rivalry between the minorities and the majority.

Q. How can the recognizability of the minorities be eliminated?
A. By blood-fusion with the majority.

Q. How can blood-fusion come about if cultural assimilation increases rivalry and prejudice?
A. ....

Q. Is it then true that, as things stand, the future of inter-racial relations in the United States depends upon the ratio beween cultural assimilation, which seems inevitable, and biological assimilation, which seems unlikely?
A. It so appears.

Q. Does the race-problem in the United States then seem practically insoluble as a separate problem?
A. It does.

Q. Has the race-problem ever been solved anywhere by direct attack upon it as a *race* problem?
A. Probably not.

Q. Does not this conclusion involve a return to the assumption that race-prejudice is inevitable wherever race-differences exist; and has this not been emphatically denied?
A. On the contrary, the implication is that race-prejudice is inevitable where *race-prejudice* exists. The conclusion in regard to the United States is based on the single assumption that the *non-racial* conditions under which race prejudice has arisen will remain practically unchanged.

Q. Is it then conceivable that a complete alteration of non-racial conditions—as, for instance, an economic revolution which would change the whole meaning of the word " competition "—might entirely revise the terms of the problem?
A. It is barely conceivable—but this paper is not an accepted channel for divine revelation.

GEROID TANQUARY ROBINSON

ADVERTISING

DO I understand you to say that you do not believe in advertising? Indeed! Soon you will be telling me that you do not believe in God. Though, to be sure, in so doing you would be committing less of a crime against the tenets of modern American civilization than in doubting the existence of a power so great that overnight it can raise up in our midst gods, kings, and other potentates, creating a world which for splendour and opulence far surpasses our own poor mortal sphere—a world in which every prospect pleases and only the reluctant spender is vile.

True, we can only catch a fleeting glimpse of its many marvels. True, we have scarcely time to admire a millionth part of the joys and magnificence of one before a new and greatly improved universe floats across the horizon, and, from every corner news-stand, smilingly bids us enter its portals. True, I repeat, our inability to grasp or appreciate the full wonder of these constantly arriving creations, yet even the narrow limitations of our savage and untutored minds can hardly prevent us from acclaiming a miracle we fail to understand.

If it were only given me to live the life led by any one of the fortunate creatures that dwell in these advertising worlds, I should gladly renounce my home, my wife, and my evil ways and become the super-snob of a mock creation. All day long should I stand smartly clad in a perfectly fitting union-suit just for the sport of keeping my obsequious butler waiting painfully for me with my lounging-gown over his exhausted arm. On other days I should be found sitting in mute adoration before a bulging bowl of breakfast food, and, if any one should chance to be listening at the keyhole, they might even catch me in the act of repeating reverently and with an avid smile on my lips, "I can never stir from the table until I have completely crammed myself with Red-Blooded American Shucks," adding in a mysterious whisper, "To be had at all good grocers."

There would be other days of course, days when I should ride in a motor of unrivalled power with companions of unrivalled beauty, across canyons of unrivalled depth and mountains of unrivalled height. Then would follow still other days, the most perfect days of all, days when the snow-sheathed earth cracks in the clutches of an appalling winter and only the lower classes stir abroad. This would be the time that I should select for removing the lounging gown from my butler's arm and bask in the glowing warmth of my perfect heater, with my chair placed in such a position as to enable me to observe the miserable plight of my neighbours across the way as they strive pitifully to keep life in their bodies over the dying embers of an anæmic fire. The sight of the sobbing baby and haggard mother would only serve to intensify my satisfaction in having been so fortunate and far-sighted as to have possessed myself of a Kill Kold Liquid Heat Projector—That Keeps the Family Snug.

What days I should spend! Take the literary days, for instance. Could anything be more edifying than to dip discriminatingly into a six-inch bookshelf with the absolute assurance that a few minutes spent thus each day in dipping would, in due course of time, give me complete mastery of all the best literature of the world—and incidentally gain for me a substantial raise at the office? Nor could any of the literature of the past ages equal my hidden library of books containing Vital Secrets. In this room there would linger a never-failing thrill. Here I should retreat to learn the secret of success, the secret of salesmanship, the secret of vigour, the secret of bull-dozing one's boss, the secret of spell-binding, the secret of personality and social charm, all bearing a material value measured in dollars and cents. In time I should so seethe with secrets that, unable to bear them any longer, I should break down before my friends and give the whole game away.

But why should I lacerate my heart in the contemplation of happiness I shall never experience? Why should I dwell upon the pipe-filling days, or the days when I should send for samples? Why torture my mind with those exquisitely tailored days when, with a tennis racket in one hand and a varsity crew captain on my shoulder, I should parade across the good old campus in a suit bereft of wrinkles and a hat that destroyed the last shreds of restraint in all beholding women? No, I can go no further.

For when I consider the remarkable characters that so charmingly infest my paradise never found, I cannot help asking myself, " How do they get that way? " How do the men's legs grow so slim and long and their chins so smooth and square? Why have the women always such perfect limbs and such innocent but alluring smiles? Why are families always happy and children always good? What miracle has banished the petty irritations and deficiencies of life and smoothed out the problems of living? How and why—is there an answer? Can it all be laid at the door of advertising, or do we who read, the great, sweltering mass of us, insist upon such things and demand a world of artificial glamour and perfectly impossible people? The crime is committed by collusion, I am forced to conclude. Advertising, for the most part, makes its appeal to all that is superficial and snobbish in us, and we as a solid phalanx are only too glad to be appealed to in such a manner.

In only the most unscholarly way can I lay my reflections before you, and the first one is this: advertising is America's cruelest and most ruthless sport, religion, or profession, or whatever you choose to call it. With an accurate stroke, but with a perverted intent, it coddles and toys with all that is base and gross in our physical and spiritual compositions. The comforts and happiness it holds out to the reader are for ever contrasted with the misery and misfortune of another. Thus, if I ride in a certain make of motor, I have the satisfaction of knowing that every one who rides in a motor of another make is of a lower caste than myself and will certainly eat dust for the rest of his life. There is a real joy in this knowledge. Again, if I wear a certain advertised brand of underwear, I have the pleasure of knowing that my fellow-men not so fortunately clad are undoubtedly foolish swine who will eventually die of sunstroke, after a life devoted entirely to sweating. Here, too, is a joy of rare order. If I brush my teeth with an advertised tooth paste, my satisfaction is enhanced by the knowledge that all other persons who fail to use this particular paste will in a very short time lose all of their teeth. In this there is a savage, but authentic delight. Even if I select a certain classic from my cherished six-inch bookshelf, I shall have a buoyant feeling in knowing that all men, who, after the fatigue of the day, take comfort in the latest murder or ball-game, are of inferior intellect and will never succeed in the world of business.

This is one of the most successful weapons used in advertising, and there is no denying that a great majority of people take pleasure in being struck by it. It is a pleasure drawn from the same source that feeds so many people's sense of satisfaction when they attend a funeral, or call on a sick friend, or a friend in misfortune and disgrace. It was the same source of inner satisfaction which made it possible for many loyal citizens to bear not only with fortitude, but with bliss, the sorrows of the late war. It is the instinct of self-preservation, toned down to a spirit of complacent self-congratulation, and it responds most readily to the appeal of selfishness and snobbery. Advertising did not create this instinct, nor did it discover it, but advertising uses it for its own ends. Who is to blame, the reader or the advertiser, hardly enters in at this point. The solid fact to take into consideration is that day in and day out the susceptible public is being worked upon in an unhealthy and neurotic manner which cannot fail to effect harmful results.

At this tragic moment I purpose briefly to digress to the people who create advertisements, before returning to a consideration of the effects of their creations.

To begin with, let it never be forgotten that advertising is a red-blooded, two-fisted occupation, engaged in for the most part by upstanding Americans of the kiss-the-flag or knock-'em-down-and-drag-'em-out variety. Yet years of contact with the profession compel me for the sake of truth to temper this remark by adding that it also contains, or rather confines, within its mystic circle a group of reluctant and recalcitrant " creatures that once were men," who, moving through a phantasmagoria of perverted idealism, flabby optimism, and unexamined motives, either deaden their conscience in the twilight of the " Ad. Men's Club," or else become so blindly embittered or debauched that their usefulness is lost to all constructive movements.

Generally speaking, however, advertising is the graveyard of literary aspiration in which the spirits of the defeated aspirants, wielding a momentary power over a public that rejected their efforts, blackjack it into buying the most amazing assortment of purely useless and cheaply manufactured commodities that has ever marked the decline of culture and common sense. These men are either caught early after their flight from college, or else recruited from the newspaper world. Some—the most serious and determined—are products of correspondence schools. Others are merely robust spirits whose daily contact with their fellow-men does not give them sufficient opportunity to disgorge themselves of the abundance of misinformation that their imaginations manufacture in wholesale quantities. This advertising brotherhood is composed of a heterogeneous mass of humanity that is rapidly converted into a narrow-minded wedge of fanatics. And this wedge is continually boring into the pocketbook of the public and extracting therefrom a goodly quantity of gold and silver. Have you ever conversed with one of the more successful and important members of this vast body? If so have you been able to quit the conversation with an intelligent impression of its subject-matter? For example: do you happen to know what a visualizer is? If not, you would be completely at the mercy of a true advertising exponent. Returning to my Edisonian method of attack, do you happen to know by any chance what a rough-out man is, or what is the meaning of dealer mortality, quality appeal, class circulation, or institutional copy? Probably not, for there is at bottom very little meaning to them; nevertheless, they are terms that are sacred to a great number of advertising men, and which, if unknown, would render all intelligent communication with them quite impossible.

If you should ever attend a session of these gentlemen in full cry—and may God spare you this—you would return from it with the impression that all was not well with the world. You would have heard speeches on the idealism of meat-packing, and other kindred subjects. The idealism would be transmitted to you through the medium of a hireling of some large packing organization, a live-wire, God-bless-you, hail-fellow type. Assuming that you had been there, you would have witnessed this large fellow with a virile exhalation of cigar-smoke, heave himself from his chair; you would have observed a good-natured smile play across his lips, and then you would have suddenly been taken aback by the tenderly earnest and masterfully restrained expression that transformed our buffoon into a suffering martyr, as, flinging out his arms, he tragically exclaimed, " Gentlemen, you little know the soul of the man who has given the Dreadnought Ham to the world! " From this moment on your sense of guilt would have increased by leaps and bounds until at last you would have broken down completely and agreed with everything the prophet said, as long as he refrained from depriving you of an opportunity to make it up to the god-like man who gave Dreadnought Hams to the world.

The orator would go on to tell you about the happiness and sunlight that flood the slaughter-house in which Dreadnought Hams are made. You would hear about the lovely, whimsical old character, who, one day, when in the act of polishing off a pig, stood in a position of suspended animation with knife poised above the twitching ear of the unfortunate swine, and seizing the hand of the owner as he passed benevolently by, kissed it fervently and left on it a tear of gratitude. Perhaps you would not hear that in the ardour of loyal zeal this lovable old person practically cut the pig to ribbons, thus saving it from a nervous collapse, nor would you be permitted to hear a repetition of the imprecations the old man muttered after the departing back of the owner, for these things should not be heard,—in fact, they do not exist in the world of advertising. Nothing would be said about the red death of the pig, the control of the stock-raiser, the underpaying of the workers, the daughter who visits home when papa is out and the neighbours are not looking, the long years of service and the short shrift of age, the rottenness and hypocrisy of the whole business—no, nothing should be said about such things. But to make up for the omission, you would be told in honied words of the workers who lovingly kiss each ham as it is reverently carried from the plant to receive the partiarchal blessing of the owner before it is offered up as a sacrifice to a grateful but greedy public. The whole affair would suggest to you a sort of Passion Play in which there was neither Judas nor Pilot, but just a great, big happy family of ham producers.

This speech, as I have said, would soon appear in the principal papers of the country. It would be published in installments, each one bearing its message of peace on earth, goodwill to men, and the public—always preferring Pollyanna to Blue Beard—would be given an altogether false impression of Dreadnought Hams, and the conditions under which they were produced. But this particular speech would be only a small part of the idealism you would be permitted to absorb. There would also be a patriotic speech about Old Glory, which would somehow become entangled with the necessity for creating a wider demand for a certain brand of socks. There would perhaps be a speech on the sacredness of the home, linked cunningly with the ability of a certain type of talking-machine to keep the family in at nights and thus make the home even more sacred. There would be speeches without end, and idealism without stint, and at last every one would shake hands with every one else and the glorious occasion would come to an end only to be repeated with renewed vigour and replenished optimism on the following Friday.

But the actual work of creating advertisements is seldom done in this rarefied and rose-tinted atmosphere; it is done in the more prosaic atmosphere of the advertising agency. (And let it be said at once that although, even in the case of agencies engaging in " Honest Advertising " campaigns, many such firms indulge in the unscrupulous competitive practice of splitting their regular commission with their clients in order to keep and secure accounts, there are still honest advertising agencies.)

Now there are two important classes of workers in most agencies—the copy-writer and the solicitor—the man who writes the advertisements and the man who gets the business. This latter class contains the wolves of advertising, the restless stalkers through the forests of industry and the fields of trade. They are leather-lunged and full-throated; death alone can save their victims from hearing their stories out. Copy-writers, on the other hand, are really not bad at heart; sometimes they even possess a small saving spark of humour, and frequently they attempt to read something other than *Printer's Ink*. But the full-edged solicitor is beyond all hope. Coming in close touch with the client who usually is an industrialist, capitalist, stand-patter, and high-tariff enthusiast, the solicitor gradually becomes a small edition of the man he serves, and reflects his ideas in an even more brutal and unenlightened manner. In their minds there is no room for change, unless it be change to a new kind of automobile they are advertising, for new furniture, unless it be the collapsible table of their latest client, for spring cleaning, unless thereby one is introduced to the virtues of Germ-Destroying Soap. Things must remain as they are and the leaders of commerce and industry must be protected at all costs. To them there are no under-paid workers, no social evil, no subsidized press, no restraint of free speech, no insanitary plants, no child-labour, no infant mortality due to an absence of maternity legislation, no good strikers, and no questionable public utility corporations. Everything is as it should be, and any one who attempts to effect a change is a socialist, and that ends it all.

Advertising is very largely controlled by men of this type. Is it any wonder that it is of a reactionary and artificial nature, and that any irresponsible promoter with money to spend and an article to sell, will find a sympathetic and wily minister to execute his plans for him, regardless of their effect on the economic or social life of the nation?

Turning, for the moment, from the people who create advertisements to advertising as an institution, what is there to be said for or against it? What is there to advance in justification of its existence, or in favour of its suppression? Not knowing on which side the devil's advocate pleads his case, I shall take the liberty of representing both sides, presenting as impartially as possible the cases for the prosecution and defence and allowing the reader to bring in the verdict in accordance with the evidence.

The first charge—that the low state of the press and the magazine world is due solely to advertising—is not, I believe, wholly fair. There is no use denying that advertising is responsible for the limitation of free utterance and the nonexistence of various independent and amusing publications. However, assuming that advertising were utterly banished from the face of the earth, would the murky atmosphere be cleared thereby? Would the press become free and unafraid, and would the ideal magazine at last draw breath in the full light of day? I think not. Years before advertising had attained the importance it now· enjoys, public service corporations and other powerful vested interests had found other and equally effective methods of shaping the news and controlling editorial policies. The fact remains however, and it is a sufficiently black one, that advertising is responsible for much of the corruption of our papers and other publications, as well as for the absence of the type of periodicals that make for the culture of a people and the enjoyment of good literature. When a profiteering owner of a large department store can succeed in keeping the fact of his conviction from appearing in the news, while a number of smaller offenders are held up as horrid examples, it is not difficult to decide whether or not it pays to advertise. When any number of large but loosely conducted corporations upon which the people and the nation depend, can prevent from appearing in the press any information concerning their mismanagement, inefficiency, and extravagance, or any editorial advocating government control, one does not have to ponder deeply to determine the efficacy of advertising. When articles or stories dealing with the unholy conditions existing in certain industries, or touching on the risks of motoring, the dangers of eating canned goods, or the impossibility of receiving a dollar's value for a dollar spent in a modern department store, are rejected by many publications, regardless of their merit, one does not have to turn to the back pages of the magazine in order to discover the names and products of the advertisers paying for the space. Indeed, one of the most regrettable features of advertising is that it makes so many things possible for editors who will be good, and so many things impossible for editors who are too honest and too independent to tolerate dictation.

Another charge against advertising is that it promotes and

encourages the production of a vast quantity of costly articles many of which duplicate themselves, and that this over-production of commodities, many of them of highly questionable value, is injurious to the country and economically unsound. This charge seems to be well founded in fact, and illustrated only too convincingly in the list of our daily purchases. Admitting that a certain amount of competition creates a stimulating and healthy reaction, it still seems hardly reasonable that a nation, to appear with a clean face each morning, should require the services of a dozen producers of safety razors, and several hundred producers of soap, and that the producers of razors and soap should spend millions of dollars each year in advertising in order to remind people to wash and shave. Nor does it seem to be a well-balanced system of production when such commodities as automobiles, sewing machines, face powders, toilet accessories, food products, wearing apparel, candy, paint, furniture, rugs, tonics, machinery, and so on *ad infinitum* can exist in such lavish abundance. With so many things of the same kind to choose from, there is scarcely any reason to wonder that the purchasing public becomes addle-brained and fickle. The over-production of both the essentials and non-essentials of life is indubitably stimulated by advertising, with the result that whenever business depression threatens the country, much unnecessary unemployment and hardship arises because of an over-burdened market and an industrial world crowded with moribund manufacturing plants. " Give me a strong enough motor and I will make that table fly," an aviator once remarked. It could be said with equal truth, " Give me money enough to spend in advertising and I will make any product sell." Flying tables, however, are not nearly so objectionable as a market glutted with useless and over-priced wares, and an army of labour dependent for its existence upon an artificially stimulated demand.

The claim that advertising undermines the habits of thrift of a nation requires no defence. Products are made to be sold and it is the principal function of advertising to sell them regardless of their merits or the requirements of the people. Men and women purchase articles to-day that would have no place in any socially and economically safe civilization. As long as this condition continues, money will be drawn out of the savings accounts of the many and deposited in the commercial accounts of the few—a situation which hardly makes for happy and healthy families.

It has been asserted by many that advertising is injurious to literary style. I am far from convinced that this charge is true. In my belief it has been neither an injurious nor helpful influence. If anything, it has forced a number of writers to say a great deal in a few words, which is not in itself an undesirable accomplishment. Nor do I believe that advertising has recruited to its ranks a number of writers or potential writers who might otherwise have given pearls of faith to the world. However, if it has attracted any first-calibre writers, they have only themselves to blame and there is still an opportunity for them to scale the heights of literary eminence.

The worst has been said of advertising, I feel, when we agree that it has contributed to the corruption of the press, that it does help to endanger the economic safety of the nation, and that, to a great extent, it appeals to the public in a false and unhealthy manner. These charges certainly are sufficiently damaging. For the rest, let us admit that advertising is more or less like all other businesses, subject to the same criticisms and guilty of the same mistakes. Having admitted this, let us assume the rôle of the attorney for the defence and see what we can marshal in favour of our client.

First of all, I submit the fact that advertising has kept many artists alive—not that I am thoroughly convinced that artists should be kept alive, any more than poets or any other un-American breed; but for all that I appeal to your humanitarian instincts when I offer this fact in support of advertising, and I trust you will remember it when considering the evidence.

In the second place, advertising is largely responsible for the remarkable strides we have taken in the art of typography. If you will examine much of the literature produced by advertising, you will find there many excellent examples of what can be done with type. To-day no country in the world is producing more artistic and authentic specimens of typography than

America, and this, I repeat, is largely due to the influence of advertising.

We can also advance as an argument in favour of advertising that it has contributed materially to a greater use of the tooth-brush and a more diligent application of soap. Advertising has preached cleanliness, preached frantically, selfishly and for its own ends, no doubt, but nevertheless it has preached convincingly. It matters little what means are used to achieve the end of cleanliness as long as the end is achieved. This, advertising has helped to accomplish. The cleanliness of the body and the cleanliness of the home as desirable virtues are constantly being held up before the readers of papers and magazines. As has been said, there are altogether too many different makes of soap and other sanitary articles, but in this case permit us to modify the statement by adding that it is much better to have too many of such articles than too few. This third point in favour of advertising is no small point to consider. The profession cannot be wholly useless, if it has helped to make teeth white, faces clean, bodies healthy, homes fresh and sanitary, and people more concerned with their bodies and the way they treat them.

The fourth point in favour of advertising is that through the medium of paid space in the papers and magazines certain deserving movements have been able to reach a larger public and thus recruit from it new and valuable members. This example illustrates the value of advertising when applied to worthy ends. In all fairness we are forced to conclude, that, after all, there is much in advertising that is not totally depraved.

Now that we are about to rest the case, let us gaze once more through the magic portals of the advertising world and refresh our eyes with its beauty. On second glance we find there is something strangely pathetic and wistfully human about this World That Never Was. It is a world very much after our own creation, peopled and arranged after our own yearnings and desires. It is a world of well regulated bowels, cornless feet, and unblemished complexions, a world of perfectly fitting clothes, completely equipped kitchens, and always upright and smiling husbands. To this world of splendid country homes, humming motors, and agreeable companions, prisoners on our own poor weary world of reality may escape for a while to live a few short moments of unqualified comfort and happiness. Even if they do return from their flight with pockets empty and arms laden with a number of useless purchases, they have had at least some small reward for their folly. They have dwelt and sported with fascinating people in surroundings of unsurpassed beauty. True, it is not such a world as Rembrandt would have created, but he was a grim old realist, who, when he wanted to paint a picture of a person cutting the nails, selected for his model an old and unscrupulous woman, and cast around her such an atmosphere of reality that one can almost hear the snip of the scissors as it proceeds on its revolting business. How much better it would be done in the advertising world! Here we would be shown a young and beautiful girl sitting gracefully before her mirror and displaying just enough of her body to convince the beholder that she was neither crippled nor chicken-breasted, and all day long for ever and for ever she would sit thus smiling tenderly as she clipped the pink little moon-flecked nails from her pink little pointed fingers.

Yes, I fear it is a world of our own creation. Only a few persons would stand long before Rembrandt's crude example, while many would dwell with delight on the curves and allurements of the maid in the advertising world. Of course one might forget or never even discover what she was doing, and assuming that one did, one would hardly dwell upon such an unromantic occupation in connection with a creature so fair and refined as this ideal young woman; but for all that, one would at least have had the pleasure of contemplating her loveliness.

So many of us are poor and ill-favoured in this world of ours, so many girls are not honestly able to purchase more than one frock or one hat a year, that the occasion of the purchase takes on an importance far beyond the appreciation of the average well-to-do person. It is fun, therefore, to dwell upon the lines and features of a perfectly gowned woman and to imagine that even though poor and ill-favoured, one might possibly resemble in a modified way, the splendid model, if one could only get an extra fifteen minutes off at lunch-time in order to attend the bargain sale. There are some of us who are so very poor that from a great distance we can enjoy without hope of participation the glory and triumph of others. The advertising world supplies us with just this sort of vicarious enjoyment, and, like all other kinds of fiction, enables us to play for a moment an altogether pleasing rôle in a world of high adventure.

Therefore let us not be too uncharitable to the advertising world. While not forgetting its faults, let us also strive to remember its virtues. Some things we cannot forgive it, some things we would prefer to forget, but there are others which require less toleration and fortitude to accept when once they have been understood.

As long as the printed word is utilized and goods are bought and sold, there will be a place and a reason for advertising—not advertising as we know it to-day, but of a saner and more useful nature. He would be a doughty champion of the limitation of free speech who would deny a man the right to tell the world that he is the manufacturer of monkey-wrenches, and that he has several thousands of these same wrenches on hand, all of which he is extremely anxious to sell.

Advertising, although a precocious child, is but in its infancy. In spite of its rapid development and its robust constitution, it has not yet advanced beyond the savage and bragging age. It will appeal to our instincts of greed as quickly as to our instincts of home-building. It will make friends with the snob that is in us, as readily as it will avail itself of the companionship of our desire to be generous and well-liked. It will frighten and bulldoze us into all sorts of extravagant purchases with the same singleness of purpose that it will plead with our self-respect in urging us to live cleaner and better lives. It will use our pride and vanity for its own ends as coolly as it will use our good nature or community spirit. It will run through the whole gamut of human emotions, selecting therefrom those best suited to its immediate ends. Education alone will make the child behave—not the education of the child so much as the education of the reader.

Advertising thrives to-day in the shadows created by big

business, and, as a consequence, if it would retain its master's favour it must justify his methods, and practise his evil ways. Here it must be added that there are some honest advertising agencies which refuse to accept the business of dishonest concerns. It must also be added that there are some magazines and newspapers which will refuse to accept unscrupulous advertisements. These advertisements must be notoriously unscrupulous, however, before they meet this fate. There are even such creatures as honest manufacturers, but unfortunately for the profession they too rarely advertise. As a whole, advertising is committed to the ways of business, and as the ways of business are seldom straight and narrow, advertising perforce must follow a dubious path. We shall let it rest at that.

We have made no attempt in this article to take up the subject of out-door advertising. There is nothing to say about this branch of the profession save that it is bad beyond expression, and should be removed from sight with all possible haste. In revolting against the sign-board, direct action assumes the dignity of conservatism, and although I do not recommend an immediate assault on all sign-boards, I should be delighted if such an assault took place. Were I a judge sitting on the case of a man apprehended in the act of destroying one of these eyesores, I should give him the key to my private stock, and adjourn the court for a week.

J. THORNE SMITH

BUSINESS

MODERN business derives from three passions in this order, namely: The passion for things, the passion for
personal grandeur and the passion for power. Things are multiplied in use and possession when people exchange with each
other the products of specialized labour. Personal grandeur
may be realized in wealth. Gratification of the third passion
in this way is new. Only in recent times has business become
a means to great power, a kind of substitute for kingship,
wherein man may sate his love of conquest, practise private
vengeance, and gain dominion over people.

These passions are feeble on the Oriental side of the world,
strong in parts of Europe, powerful in America. Hence the
character of American business. It is unique, wherein it is so,
not in principle but in degree of phenomena. For natural reasons the large objects of business are most attainable in this
country. Yet this is not the essential difference. In the pursuit of them there is a characteristic American manner, as to
which one may not unreasonably prefer a romantic explanation. No white man lives on this continent who has not himself or in his ancestry the will that makes desire overt and
dynamic, the solitary strength to push his dream across seas.
Islands had been peopled before by this kind of selection,
notably England; never a continent. A reckless, egoistic, experimental spirit governs, betrays, and preserves us still.

The elemental hunger for food, warmth, and refuge gives
no direct motive to business. People may live and reproduce
without business. Civilization of a sort may exist without its
offices. The settler who disappears into the wilderness with a
wife, a gun, a few tools, and some pairs of domestic beasts,
may create him an idyllic habitation, amid orchards and fields,
self-contained in rude plenty; but he is lost to business until
he produces a money crop, that is, a surplus of the fruits of
husbandry to exchange for fancy hardware, tea, window glass,
muslin, china, and luxuries.

The American wilderness swallowed up hundreds of thousands of such hearth-bearers. Business was slow to touch them. What they had to sell was bulky. The cost of transportation was prohibitive. There were no highways, only rivers, for traffic to go upon. Food was cheap, because the earth in a simple way was bounteous; but the things for which food could be exchanged were dear. This would naturally be true in a new country, where craft industry must develop slowly. It was true also for another reason, which was that the Mother Country regarded the New World as a plantation to be exploited for the benefit of its own trade and manufactures.

Great Britain's claim to proprietary interest in America having been established against European rivals by the end of the 17th century, her struggle with the colonists began. The English wanted (1) raw materials upon which to bestow their high craft labour, (2) an exclusive market for the output of their mills and factories, and (3) a monopoly of the carrying trade. The colonists wanted industrial freedom. As long as they held themselves to chimney-corner industries, making nails, shoes, hats, and coarse cloth for their own use, there was no quarrel. But when labour even in a small way began to devote itself exclusively to handicraft, so that domestic manufactures were offered for sale in competition with imported English goods, that was business—and the British Parliament voted measures to crush it. The weaving of cloth for sale was forbidden, lest the colonists become independent of English fabrics. So was the making of beaver hats; the English were hatters. It was forbidden to set up an iron rolling-mill in America, because the English required pig iron and wished to work it themselves. To all these acts of Parliament the colonists opposed subterfuge until they were strong enough to be defiant. That impatience of legal restraints which is one of the most obstinate traits of American business was then a patriotic virtue.

Meanwhile the New England trader had appeared—that adorable, hymning, unconscious pirate who bought molasses in the French West Indies, swapped it for rum at Salem, Mass., traded the rum for Negroes on the African coast, exchanged the

Negroes for tobacco in Virginia, and sold the tobacco for money in Europe, at a profit to be settled with God. This trade brought a great deal of money to the colonies; and they needed money almost more than anything else. Then the British laid a ban on trade with the French West Indies, put a tax upon coastwise traffic between the colonies; and decreed that American tobacco should be exported nowhere but to English ports, although—or because—tobacco prices were higher everywhere else in Europe. The natural consequence of this restrictive British legislation was to make American business utterly lawless. As much as a third of it was notoriously conducted in defiance of law. Smuggling both in domestic and foreign trade became a folk custom. John Hancock, the first signer of the Declaration of Independence, was a celebrated smuggler.

During the War of Independence domestic craft industry was stimulated by necessity. But the means were crude and the products imperfect; and when, after peace, British merchants with an accumulation of goods on their hands began to offer them for sale in the United States at low prices, hoping to recover their new-world trade in competitive terms, the infant industries cried out for protection. They got it. One of the first acts of the American Congress was to erect a tariff against foreign-made goods in order that the country might become self-sufficing in manufactures. This was the beginning of our protectionist policy.

Fewer than four million unbusiness-like people coming into free possession of that part of the North American continent which is named America was a fabulous business event. We cannot even now comprehend it. They had not the dimmest notion of what it was they were possessed of, nor what it meant economically. Geography ran out at the Mississippi. The tide of Westward immigration was just beginning to break over the crest of the Alleghany mountains.

Over-seas trade grew rapidly, as there was always a surplus of food and raw materials to be exchanged abroad for things which American industry was unable to provide. Foreign commerce was an important source of group-wealth and public interest was much concerned with it. Besides, it was easier

to trade across seas than inland. Philadelphia until about
1835 was nearer London than Pittsburgh, not as the crow flies
but as freight moves. Domestic business, arising from the
internal exchange of goods, developed slowly, owing partly to
the wretched state of transportation and partly to the self-
contained nature of families and communities. The population was more than nine-tenths rural; rural habits survived
even in the towns, where people kept cows and pigs, cured
their own meats, preserved their own fruits and vegetables,
and thought ready-made garments a shocking extravagance.
Business under these conditions performed a subservient function. People's relations with it were in large measure voluntary. Its uses were more luxurious than vital. There was not
then, nor could any one at this time have imagined, that interdependence of individuals, groups, communities, and geographical sections which it is the blind aim of business increasingly
to promote, so that at length the case is reversed and people
are subservient to business.

In Southern New Jersey you may see a farm, now pros-
perously devoted to berry and fruit crops, on which, still in
good repair, are the cedar rail fences built by a farmer whose
contacts with business were six or eight trips a year over a
sand road to Trenton with surplus food to exchange for some
new tools, tea, coffee, and store luxuries. That old sand road
has become a cement pavement—a motor highway. Each
morning a New York baking corporation's motor stops at the
farm-house and the driver hands in some fresh loaves. Presently a butcher's motor stops with fresh meat, then another
one with dry groceries, and yet another from a New York department store with parcels containing ready-made garments,
stockings and shoes.

Consider what these four motors symbolize.

First is an automobile industry and a system for producing,
refining and distributing oil which together are worth as much
as the whole estimated wealth of America three generations
ago.

Back of the bakery wagon what a vista! An incorporated
baking industry, mixing, kneading, roasting, and wrapping the
loaf in paraffine paper without touch of human hands, all by

automatic machinery. Beyond the Mississippi, in a country undiscovered until 1804, the wheat fields that are ploughed, sown, reaped by power-driven machinery. In Minnesota a milling industry in which the miller has become an impersonal flour trust. A railroad system that transports first the grain and then the flour over vast distances at rates so low that the cost of two or three thousand miles of transportation in the loaf of bread delivered to the New Jersey farm-house is inexpressible. . . . Back of the butcher's motor is a meat-packing industry concentrated at Chicago. It sends fresh meat a thousand miles in iced cars and sells it to a New Jersey farmer for a price at which he can better afford to buy it than to bother about producing it for himself. . . . Back of the grocer's motor are the food products and canning industries. By means of machinery they shred, peel, hull, macerate, roll, cook, cool, and pack fruits, cereals, and vegetables in cartons and containers which are made, labelled, and sealed by other automatic machinery. . . . And back of the department store motor are the garment-making, shoe-making, textile, and knitting industries.

If one link in all this ramified scheme of business breaks there is chaos. If the State of New Jersey were suddenly cut off from the offices of business for six months, a third of her population might perish; not that the State is unable potentially to sustain her own, but that the people have formed habits of dependence upon others, as others depend upon them, for the vital products of specialized labour.

All this has happened in the life of one cedar rail fence. You say that is only fifty or sixty years. Nevertheless it is literally so. The system under which we live has been evolved since 1860. The transformation was sudden. Never in the world were the physical conditions of a nation's life altered so fast by economic means. Yet it did not happen for many years. The work of unconscious preparation occupied three-quarters of a century.

Man acts upon his environment with hands, tools, and imagination; and business requires above everything else the means of cheap and rapid transportation. In all the major particulars save one the founders were ill-equipped for their independent attack upon the American environment. At the beginning of the 19th century there were no roads, merely a few trails fit only for horseback travel. There were no canals yet. And the labour wherewith to perform heavy, monotonous tasks was dear and scarce and largely self-employed. Though the hands of the pioneer are restless they are not patiently industrious. There was need of machinery such as had already begun to revolutionize British industry, but the English jealously protected their mechanical knowledge.

There is a tradition that the Americans were marvellously inventive with labour-saving devices. That is to be qualified. Their special genius lay rather in the adaptation and enthusiastic use of such devices. The introduction of them was not resisted as in the older countries by labour unwilling to change its habits and fearful of unemployment. This was an important advantage.

The American textile industry was founded by British artisans who came to this country carrying contraband in their heads, that is, the plans of weaving, spinning, and knitting machines which the English guarded as carefully as military secrets. . . . The pre-eminence of this country in the manufacture and use of agricultural implements is set out in elementary school-books as proof of American inventiveness; yet the essential principles of the reaper were evolved in Great Britain forty years before the appearance of the historic McCormick reaper (1831) in this country, and threshing-machines were in general use in England while primitive methods of flailing, trampling, and dragging prevailed in America. As recently as 1850 the scythe and cradle reaped the American harvest and there still existed the superstition that an iron plough poisoned the soil and stimulated weeds. Of all the tools invented or adopted the one which Americans were to make the most prodigious use of was the railroad; yet the first locomotive was brought from England in 1829, the embargo on machinery having by this time been lifted—and it failed because it was too heavy!

Twenty years passed and still the possibilities of rail transportation were unperceived, which is perhaps somewhat explained by the fact that the one largest vested interest of that

time existed in canals. On the map of 1850 the railroads resemble earthworms afraid to leave water and go inland. The
notion of a railroad was that it supplemented water transportation, connecting lake, canal, and river routes, helping traffic
over the high places.

But in the next ten years—1850 to 1860—destiny surrendered. There was that rare coincidence of seed, weather, deep
ploughing, and mysterious sanction which the miracle requires.
The essential power of the American was suddenly liberated.
There was the discovery of gold in California. There was the
Crimean War, which created a high demand abroad for our
commodities. The telegraph put its indignities upon time and
space. The idea of a railroad as a tool of empire seized the
imagination. Railroads were deliriously constructed. The
map of 1860 shows a glistening steel web from the seaboard to
the Mississippi.

The gigantesque was enthroned as the national fetich. Vo-
tive offerings were mass, velocity, quantity. True cities began.
The spirit of Chicago was born. Bigness and be-damnedness.
In this decade the outlines of our economic development were
cast for good.

In the exclusive perspective of business the Civil War is an
indistinct episode. It stimulated industry in the North, shattered it in the South. The net result in a purely economic
sense is a matter of free opinion. The Morse telegraph code
probably created more wealth than the war directly destroyed.
Or the bitter sectional row over the route of the first trans-
continental railroad which postponed that project for ten years
possibly cost the country more than the struggle to preserve
the Union. But that is all forgotten.

After 1860 the momentum of growth, notwithstanding the
war and two terrible panics, was cumulative. In the next fifty
years, down to 1910, we built half as much railroad mileage
as all the rest of the world. Population trebled. This fact
stands alone in the data of vital statistics. Yet even more remarkable were the alterations of human activity. The num-
ber of city dwellers increased $3\frac{1}{2}$ times faster than the population; the number of wage-earners, 2 times faster; clerks, salesmen, and typists, $6\frac{1}{2}$ times faster; banks, 7 times faster;

corporations, 6½ times faster; miners, 3 times faster; transportation-workers, 20 times faster, and the number of independent farmers decreased. Wealth in this time increased from about $500 to more than $1,500 *per capita.*

If America in its present state of being had been revealed to the imagination of any hard-headed economist in, say, 1850, as a mirage or dream, he would have said: " There is in all the world not enough labour and capital to do it." He could not have guessed how the power of both would be multiplied.

First there was the enormous simple addition to the labour supply in the form of immigration. Then the evolution of machinery and time-saving methods incredibly increased the productivity of labour per human unit. Thirdly, the application of power to agriculture and the opening of all that virgin country west of the Mississippi to bonanza-farming so greatly increased the production of food per unit of rural labour that at length it required only half the population to feed the whole. The other half was free. Business and industry absorbed it.

Of what happened at the same time to capital, in which term we include also credit, there could have been no prescience at all. Even now when we think of building a railroad, a telephone system, or an automobile factory the thought is that it will take capital, as of course it will at first, but one should consider also how anything that increases the velocity with which goods are exchanged, or reduces the time in which a given amount of business may be transacted, adds to the functioning power of capital. To illustrate this: the merchant of 1850 did business very largely with his own capital unaided. He was obliged to invest heavily in merchandise stocks. The turn-over was slow. His margin of profit necessarily had to be large. But with the development of transportation and means of communication—the railroad, telegraph, and telephone—and with the parallel growth of banking facilities, the conditions of doing business were fundamentally changed. All the time-factors were foreshortened.

A merchant now has to lock up much less capital in merchandise, since his stocks are easily and swiftly replenished.

The turn-over is much faster because people using suburban railways and street-cars go oftener to shop. And not only is it possible for these reasons to do a larger volume of business with a given amount of capital, but the merchant now borrows two-thirds, maybe three-quarters, of his capital at the bank in the form of credit. The same is true of the manufacturer. Formerly he locked up his capital, first in raw materials and then in finished products to be sold in season as the demand was; and there was great risk of loss in this way of matching supply to an estimated demand. Now he sells his goods before he makes them, borrows credit at the bank to buy his raw materials, even to pay his labour through the processes of manufacture, and when the customer pays on delivery of the goods with credit which he also has borrowed at the bank, the manufacturer settles with *his* bank and keeps the difference. An exporter was formerly one who bought commodities with his own money, loaded them on ship, sent them on chance to a foreign market, and waited for his capital to come back with a profit. Now he first sells the goods to a foreign customer by cable, then buys them on credit, loads them on ship, sells the bill of lading to a bank, uses the proceeds to pay for the goods, and counts his profit. All large business now is transacted in this way with phantom capital, called credit; money is employed to settle differences only.

The effect of this revolution of methods upon the morals and manners of business was tremendous. It destroyed the aristocracy of business by throwing the field open to men without capital. Traders and brokers over-ran it. The man doing business on borrowed capital could out-trade one doing business on his own. The more he borrowed, the harder he could trade. Salesmanship became a specialized, conscienceless art. There was no rule but to take all the traffic would bear: let the buyer look out. Dishonesty in business became so gross that it had to be sublimated in the national sense of humour. There are many still living who remember what shopping was like even in the largest city stores when nobody dreamed of paying the price first asked and counter-higgling was a universal custom. Indeed, so ingrained it was that when A. T. Stewart in New York announced the experiment of treating all buyers alike on a one-price basis his ruin was predicted by the whole merchant community.

As credit both increases competition and enables a larger business to be done on a small base of invested capital, the margin of profit in business tends to fall. Under conditions of intense rivalry among merchants and manufacturers operating more and more with phantom capital the margin of profit did fall until it was very thin indeed. This led to the abasement of goods by adulteration and tricks of manufacture, which became at length so great an evil that the government had to interfere with pure-food acts and laws forbidding wilful misrepresentation.

There was a limit beyond which the cost of production could not be reduced by degradation of quality. It was impossible to control prices with competition so wild and spontaneous and with cheapness the touchword of success. Therefore the wages of business were low, and things apparently had come to an impasse. Yet out of this chaos arose what now we know as big business. The idea was simple—mass production of standardized foods. The small, fierce units of business began to be amalgamated. As society is integrated by steps—clan, tribe, nation, State—so big business passed through mergers, combines, and trusts toward the goal of monopoly.

When a number of competing manufacturers unite to produce standard commodities in quantity, much duplication of effort is eliminated, time-saving methods are possible as not before, the cost of production is reduced. There are other advantages. They are stronger than they were separately, not only as buyers of labour, raw materials, and transportation, but as borrowers of capital. The individual or firm is the customer of a bank. The corporation makes a partnership with finance.

Now a curious thing happens. The corporation with its mass production restores the quality of goods. It is responsible for its products and guarantees them by brands, labels and trade-marks. Sugar and oatmeal come out of the anonymous barrel behind the grocer's counter and go into attractive cartons on his shelf, bearing the name of the producer. Gloves, shirts, stockings, cutlery, furniture, meat products, jams, watches, fabrics, everything in fact becomes standardized by name and price and is advertised by the producer directly to the public over the retailer's head, so that the small retailer is no longer a merchant in the old sense but a grumbling commission-man. Big business has delivered itself from the impasse; it has recovered control of its profits; but now the retailer's margin of profit tends to become fixed. What does the retailer do? He applies the same principle to the last act of selling. Enter the chain-store. Obviously a corporation owning a chain of several hundred stores and working, like the manufacturer, with borrowed capital, is stronger than any one retailer to bargain with the powerful producers, and as the chain-store tends to displace the little retailer a balance is restored between the business of production and the business of retailing. Mass production is met by mass selling. The consumer as the last subject may resort to legislation for his protection.

Big business could not have evolved in this way without the aid of the railroads. Their dilemma was similar. Strife and competition had ruined their profits. To begin with, nobody knew what it cost to produce transportation. When a new line was opened it made rates according to circumstances. At points where it met water competition it charged very little, sometimes less than the cost of its fuel, and at points where there was no competition it charged all the traffic would stand. Then as competitive railroad-building excessively increased the high rates steadily fell. Once they got started people were obsessed to make railroads. They made them for speculative reasons, for feudal reasons, for political reasons, for any reason at all. Two men might quarrel in Wall Street, and one would build a thousand miles of railroad to spite the other—build it with the proceeds of shares sold to the public or hypothecated at the bank. Then there would be two roads to divide the business of one. Railroads under these conditions were unscientifically planned and over-built. The profit was rather in the building than in the working of them. There was scandal both ways. Quantities of fictitious capital were created and sold to the public. And when a railroad was built it became the plaything of its traffic manager, who conspired with other traffic managers to sell favours to shippers and to invent disastrous rate-wars in order to profit by the fall of shares on the stock market.

Rates could not be raised or held up, owing to the irresponsible nature of the competition. Transportation is a commodity that cannot be adulterated. How was the profit to be restored in this field of business? Why, by the same method as in industry. That is, by mass production.

Some one discovered that once you got a loaded train out of the terminal and rolling on the right-of-way it cost almost nothing to keep it moving. There was no money in hauling small lots of freight short distances at the highest rates that could be charged; but there was profit in moving large quantities of freight in full cars over long distances at very low rates. At this the railroad people went mad over the long, heavy haul. Here was industry seeking to concentrate itself in fewer places for purposes of mass production; and here were the railroads wanting masses of freight to move long distances. Their problems coincided.

Result: mass production gravitates to those far-apart long-haul points to get the benefit of low rates, there is congestion of industrial population at those points, industry at intermediate points is penalized by higher freight rates, and the railroads henceforth equip themselves with mass tonnage primarily in view. You begin now to have steel towns, meat towns, flour towns, textile towns, garment towns, and so on. That interdependence of communities and geographical sections which makes business is in full development.

However, the second state of the railroad is worse than the first. It is overwhelmed by the monster it has suckled. It is at the mercy of a few big shippers, masters of mass production, who bully it, extort lower and lower rates still, and at length secret rebates, under threat of transferring their tonnage to another railroad or in some cases of building their own railroad, which now they are powerful enough to do. The railroad yields; and whereas before only such industry as survived at intermediate points was penalized by higher freight rates, now all industry outside of big business is at a disadvantage, since big business is receiving secret benefits from the railroads.

There was no philosophy in any of this, not even a high order of intelligence. The will of business is anarchistic; its religion is fatalism. If let alone, it will seek its profit by any means that serve and then view the consequences as acts of Providence.

It has been noted that big business, going in for mass production, restored the honesty of goods. The motive was not ethical. It paid. The public's good will toward a brand or a trade-mark was an asset that could be capitalized, sometimes for more than plant and equipment, and the shares representing such capitalization could be sold to the public on the Stock Exchange. But what was gained for morality in the honesty of goods was lost again in new forms of dishonesty. Standard Oil products were always cheap and honest; its oil was never watered. But the means by which the Standard Oil Company gained its dangerous trade eminence were dishonest, and the trust was dissolved for that reason by the United States Supreme Court. It happens to be only the most notable instance. There were and are still many others—combines and trusts whose products are honest but whose tradeways are either illegal or ethically repugnant.

One cannot say that business is either honest or dishonest. It is both. Evidence of permanent gain in a kind of intrinsic commercial honesty is abundant. Wild-cat banking has disappeared. A simple book entry between merchants is as good as a promissory note. The integrity of merchandise now is a trade custom. Vulgar misrepresentations have ceased save in the slums of business. The practice of making open prices to all buyers alike, wholesale and retail, is universal. It is no longer possible to print railroad shares surreptitiously overnight and flood the Stock Exchange with them the next morning, as once happened in Erie. Nowhere is character more esteemed than in business.

And yet, in spite of all this and parallel with it, runs a bitter feud between society and business. People are continually acting upon big business through the agencies of government to make it behave. What is the explanation?

Well, in the first place, the improvement in commercial honesty has been owing not so much to ethical enlightenment as to internal necessity. Big business must do its work on credit; there is no other way. Therefore credit is a sacred thing, to be preserved by all means. Men know that unless they are scrupulous in fulfilling their obligations toward it, the system will collapse. As the use of credit increases the code of business become more rigid. It must. One who breaks faith with the code is not merely dishonest, man to man; he is an enemy of credit.

If a stock-market coterie of this day could print Erie shares without notice and sell them the public would suffer of course but Wall Street would suffer much more. Its own affairs would fall into hopeless disorder. That kind of thing cannot happen again. The code has been improved. You now may be sure that anything you buy on the Stock Exchange has been regularly issued and listed. No institution is more jealous of the integrity of its transactions—transactions as such. Purchases and sales involving millions are consummated with a nod of the head and simple dishonesty is unknown. Nevertheless, it is a notorious fact that the amount of money nowadays lost on the Stock Exchange by the unwary public is vastly greater than in Jay Gould's time. There is, you see, an important difference between formal and moral honesty.

Secondly, business morality is a term without meaning. There is no such thing. Business is neither moral nor immoral. It represents man's acquisitive instinct acting outside of humanistic motives. Morals are personal and social. Business is impersonal and unsocial.

So far we come clear. Only now, what shall be said of the man in business? He is not a race apart. He may be any of us. How then shall we account for the fact that those evils and tyrannies of big business with which the Congress, the Interstate Commerce Commission, the Department of Justice, the Federal Trade Board, and other agencies of the social will keep open war are not inhibited at the head by an innate social sense? Does the business man lose that sense? Or by reason of the material in which he works does he become an unsocial being? No. The answer is that the kind of business we now are talking about is not conducted by men. It is conducted by corporations.

A thing of policy purely, with only legal responsibilities and no personality, free from hope of heaven or fear of hell, the corporation is both a perfect instrument for the impersonal ends of business and a cave of refuge for the conscience. Business by corporations is highly responsible in all that pertains to business. Business by corporations is in all ethical respects anonymous. A corporation does many things which no one of its directors would do as an individual. The head of a corporation says: " If it were my own business, I should handle this labour problem very differently. But it isn't. I am a trustee, answerable to five thousand stockholders for the security of their dividends." Each of the five thousand stockholders says: " It isn't my business. I am merely one of a great number of stockholders. What can I do about it? "

Nobody is personally responsible.

More than two-thirds of our national wealth is owned by corporations. They control at some point every process of economic life. Their power is so great that many have wondered whether in time it might not overwhelm popular government. Yet in all this realm of power there is nowhere that sense of personal moral liability which is acknowledged between men and without which civilized human relationships would become utterly impossible. A corporation is like a State in this respect: it cannot, if it would, make moral decisions. The right to do that is not delegated by people to a State nor by stockholders to a corporation. Both therefore are limited to material decisions.

It is probably owing as much to the power-thirsty, law-baiting temperament of the American in business as to the magnitude of the work to be done that the use of the corporation, like the use of labour-saving machinery, has been carried further here than in any other country. Railroads naturally were the first great corporations. The amount of capital required to build a railroad is beyond the resources of any small group of individuals; it must be gathered from a large number, who become shareholders. The original railroads were subsidized by the government with loans of money and enormous grants of land. Industrial and trading corporations came later. For a long time America was to all corporations a Garden of Eden. They were encouraged, not precisely that they were presumed to be innocent but because they were indispensable. Then they ate of the Tree of Political Power and the feud was on. When people began really to fear them their roots were already very deep and touched nearly everything that was solid. The sinister alliance between big business and high finance was accomplished.

One of the absurdities of the case was and is that any State according to its own laws may grant corporation-charters which carry rights of eminent domain in all other states. The Standard Oil Company was once dissolved in Ohio. It took out a new charter in New Jersey, and went on as before, even in Ohio.

Every attempt to reform their oppressive ways by law they have resisted under the constitution as an attack upon the rights of property. And there has always been much confusion as to what the law was. In one case it was construed by the United States Supreme Court to mean that bigness itself, the mere power of evil, was illegal whether it had been exercised or not; in another, that each instance must be treated on its merits by a rule of reason, and, in still another, that the potential power to restrain trade in a monopolistic manner was not in itself illegal provided it had never been used.

Nevertheless the doubt as to which should control the other —the State the corporations or the corporations the State— has been resolved. Gradually the authority of the State has been asserted. The hand of the corporation in national politics is branded. The Federal Government's control over the rates and practices of the railroads is complete; so likewise is the control of many of the several separate States over the rates and practices of public-utility corporations. Federal authority over the tradeways of the great industrial and trading corporations whose operations are either so large or so essential to economic life as to become clothed with public interest is far advanced; and supervision of profits is beginning.

Now what manner of profit and loss account may we write with American business?

Given to begin with an environment superb, it has made wealth available to an aggregate extent hitherto unimaginable in the world. But in doing this it has created a conscious, implacable proletariat in revolt against private profit.

In production it has brought about a marvellous economy of human effort. At the same time it has created colossal forms of social waste. It wastes the spirit by depriving the individual of that sense of personal achievement, that feeling of participation in the final result, which is the whole joy of craftsmanship, so that the mind is bored and the heart is seared. It wastes all things prodigally in the effort to create new and extravagant wants, reserving its most dazzling rewards for him that can make two glittering baubles to sell where only one was sold before. It wastes the living machine in recurring periods of frightful and unnecessary idleness.

For the distribution of goods it has perfected a web of exchange, so elaborate that the breaking of one strand is a disaster and yet so trustworthy that we take its conveniences every day for granted and never worry. But the adjustment of supply to demand is so rude and uncontrolled that we suffer periodic economic calamities, extreme trade depression, and social distress, because there has been an over-production of some things at a price-impasse between producer and consumer.

In the field of finance and credit it has evolved a mechanism of the highest dynamic intensity known; yet the speculative abuse of credit is an unmitigated scandal, and nothing whatever has been done to eliminate or diminish those alternations of high and low prices, inflation and deflation, which produce panics and perilous political disorder. On the contrary, business continues fast in the antique superstition that such things happen in obedience to inexorable laws.

In the Great War American business amazed the world, itself included. In 1914 the United States was a debtor nation, owing Europe 3 billions of dollars. By the end of 1920 we were the largest creditor nation on earth, other nations owing us 15 billions. This means simply that in six years this country produced in excess of its own needs and sent abroad commodities amounting to 18 billions of dollars. In 1921, to the naïve astonishment of business, the foreign demand for American goods slumped because foreign countries had not the means to go on buying at any such rate. The result was an acute panic in prices here, trade prostration, unemployment, and sounds of despair. The case was stated by leaders of business and finance in these ominous terms: "America is over-equipped. It has the capacity to produce more of everything than it needs. Therefore unless we continuously sell our surplus abroad, unless the American government will lend foreign countries the credit with which to buy our excess production, prosperity is shattered. Factories will shut up, fields will lie fallow, labour will suffer for want of work. Moreover, we are threatened with a deluge of foreign goods, for presently the countries that owe us 18 billions of dollars will be trying to pay us with commodities. If we open our markets to their goods our own industries will be ruined. So we must have high tariffs to protect American producers from the competition of foreign merchandise."

Ruined by over-plenty!

We are equipped to produce more of the goods that satisfy human wants than we can use, our command over the labour of foreign countries by reason of the debt they owe us is enormous, and *business desponds*.

Attend. To keep our prosperity we must sell away our surplus, or if necessary give it away to foreign countries on credit, and then protect ourselves against their efforts to repay us! The simple absurdity of this proposition is self-evident. We mention it only for what it signifies. And it signifies that business is a blind, momentous sequence, with extravagant reflex powers of accommodation and extension and almost no faculty of original imagination.

American business despairing at over-production and the American Indian shivering on top of the Pennsylvania coalfields—these are twin ironies.

John Law's Mississippi Bubble dream three centuries ago was a phantasy of escape from the boredom of toil. The bubble itself has been captured. That is the story of American business. But who has escaped, save always a few at the expense of many? There may be in fact no other way. Still, the phantasy will not lie. And nobody knows for sure what will happen when business is no longer a feudal-minded thing, with rights and institutions apart, seeking its own profit as the consummate end, and perceives itself in the light of a subordinate human function, justified by service.

GARET GARRETT

ENGINEERING

A MERICAN engineering made its beginning almost immediately after the end of the War for Independence.
The pursuits of the colonists under British domination
were mainly agricultural. Manufacturing was systematically
thwarted in order that the Colonies might become a market
for the finished goods of England. Objection to this form of
sabotage subsequently developed into one of the main causes
of the Revolutionary War. It was but natural, therefore, as
soon as the artificial restrictions imposed upon Colonial enterprise were removed, for the new citizens of America to
devise machinery, build roads and canals, and plan cities.

The early engineers who carried on this work were seldom
formally trained. They were little more than higher types of
artisans. It was only after thirty-odd years of discussion and
agitation that the first scientific schools were established in
this country—two in number. And it was only after the enactment of the Morrill Act by Congress (1862) that formal
engineering training as we know it to-day was put on a firm
national basis. By 1870, 866 engineers had been graduated
from American technical schools and colleges. The real advent of the typical American engineer, however, has only occurred since 1870. At present he is being supplied to the industries of the country at the rate of 5,000 a year.

The coming of the formally trained technologist or scientist
of industry lagged somewhat behind the development of the
industrial revolution. This was particularly true in America. Originally all attention was centered on the training of
so-called civil engineers, i.e., canal, bridge, road, dam and
building designers and constructors. The rapid rise of the mechanical arts after the Civil War focused attention on the
training of engineers expert in manufacturing. To-day the
mechanical and electrical engineers are more numerous than
any other group and have far outstripped the civil engineers.

The original function of the engineer, especially in the first days of his systematic training, was to deal scientifically with purely mechanical problems. Thus the oft quoted definition of the British Institution of Civil Engineers that " Engineering is the art of directing the great sources of power in nature for the use and convenience of man " reveals quite clearly the legitimate field within which the engineer was supposed to operate. He was to harness the untamed energies of nature. That this conception was then sufficient, and that the careers of most engineers were shaped accordingly, is hardly to be disputed. Nor, judging from the achievement of American engineers in the last fifty years, can it be contended that their function was conceived in too narrow a light. Undoubtedly, the problems of mechanical production, power-creation and transmission, bridge and building construction, and railway and marine transportation, during this period were largely material ones, and the opportunities for their solution were especially good. To these the engineers directed their attention. Thanks to their training, technique, and accumulated experience, they became more and more successful in solving them. At the same time, their relative freedom of thought and action with 'reference to technological problems brought them into more or less coherent groups which, as time went on, began to conceive a larger function for the engineer—service to society as a whole rather than the solving of mere concrete, specific difficulties.

For while the material problems of production are undoubtedly as important as ever, the present-day industrial system has begun to reveal new problems which the engineer in America has, to a limited extent, come to realize must be faced. These new problems are not material in the old sense of the word; they concern themselves with the control and administration of the units of our producing system. Their nature is psychological and economic.

Certain groups in the American engineering profession have become quite conscious that these deeper problems are not being solved; at the same time they consider it a necessary duty to help in their solution, inasmuch as the engineer, they feel, is peculiarly fitted to see his way clearly through them. Thus is being split off from the main body of old-line engineers, a new wing not so much concerned with wringing power from nature as with adjusting power to legitimate social needs. As against the old engineer, concerned primarily with design and construction, there is to be recognized the new engineer, concerned mainly with industrial management.

Unfortunately, however, a strict evaluation of the engineer's status with reference to the influence he may have on the solution of these social and economic problems causes serious doubts to arise regarding his ultimate possibilities in this field. Despite his great value and recognized indispensability as a technologist, expert in problems of materials and processes of manufacture, he can at best but serve in an advisory capacity on questions affecting the division of the national surplus or the control of industry. Nevertheless, it is of fundamental significance that the American engineering profession has of late considerably widened the scope of the British Institution of Civil Engineers' definition of engineering, namely, to the effect that " Engineering is the science of controlling the forces and utilizing the materials of nature for the benefit of man *and the art of organizing and of directing human activities in connection therewith.*" The implications of this much broader definition, if widely accepted, will bring the American engineers sooner or later squarely before a fundamental issue.

The ideal of service is profoundly inherent in the profession of engineering. But so, also, is the ideal of creative work. The achievements of engineering enterprise are easily visualized and understood, and from them the engineer is wont to derive a great deal of satisfaction. Recently, however, the exactions of the modern complex economic system, in which the engineer finds himself relatively unimportant compared with, say, the financier, have contrived to rob him of this satisfaction. And as his creative instincts have been thwarted, he has turned upon business enterprise itself a sharp and inquiring eye. From isolated criticisms of wastes and inefficiencies in industry, for instance, he has not found it a long or difficult step to the investigation of industry on a national basis for the purpose of exposing technical and managerial shortcomings.

It appears, however, that the majority of American engineers to-day believe that their position as a class is such that they can effectively maintain an impartial position when differences which arise between large economic groups of society such as those of the merchant, the manufacturer, the labourer, the farmer, although these differences frequently lead to economic waste and loss. At all events, it is on this basis that attempts are being made to formulate a general policy for engineers as a class to pursue. It is very doubtful, however, whether a group such as the engineers, constituting the " indispensable general staff of industry," can long take an impartial attitude towards two such conflicting forces as capital and labour so long as they (the engineers) adhere to the ideal of maximum service and efficiency. The pickets of the fence may eventually prove unduly sharp.

A minority group which believes otherwise has already organized into an international federation of technicians affiliated with the standard organized labour movement of America. This group holds that the engineer is a wage-earner like all other industrial workers, and that his economic welfare in many instances is no better than that of ordinary wage-earners. In addition, this group maintains that in the last analysis it is flatly impossible for engineers to take an impartial attitude in the struggle between capital and labour. Hence they advocate the engineer affiliating with the organized labour movement like other wage earners and, in times of crisis, throwing his influence with the workers of industry.

The organized labour movement of America has indicated in clear terms its estimate of the American engineer's true value and opportunity. The American Federation of Labour in 1919 issued the following statement:

" To promote further the production of an adequate supply of the world's needs for use and higher standards of life, we urge that there be established co-operation between the scientist of industry and the representatives of the organized workers."

This conviction has also been expressed in the following terms:

" The trades-union movement of America understands fully the necessity for adequate production of the necessities of life. Ameri-

can labour understands, perhaps more fully than do American statesmen, the needs of the world in this hour, and it is exerting every
effort to see that those needs are met with intelligence and with
promptness. The question of increased productivity is not a question of putting upon the toilers a more severe strain; it is a question
of vast fundamental changes in the management of industry; a question of the elimination of outworn policies; a question of the introduction of the very best in machinery and methods of management."

The fundamental significance of these attitudes of the engineers and the organized workers of the country will perhaps
be better understood when it is realized how indispensable the
engineers have become in the conduct of industrial affairs
to-day. While virtually the product of the last fifty years,
they have already fallen heir to one of the most strategic positions in society. To them are entrusted the real " trade secrets " of industry. Only they understand how far the intricate
material processes of manufacture are interdependent, and how
they can be kept in harmony. The engineers have the skill
and the understanding which is absolutely necessary for industrial management. Without their guidance the present highly
complicated system of production would quickly tumble into
chaos.

The ownership of industry has frequently been suggested
as the key to the true emancipation of the great mass of workers of a nation. Leastwise many theoretical arguments on
the process of workers' liberation have been premised on the
necessity of eventually liquidating the institution of private
property. How futile such a programme is without recognizing the indispensable part which technical and managerial
skill plays in any system of production has been emphasized
again and again by individuals, notably in Russia and Italy,
where the experiment of securing production without the
assistance of adequate technical control has been tried. In
fact, the whole question of property control is secondary when
once the true value of engineering management is understood.
In so far as the American workers see this, and make it possible for American engineers to co-operate with them in their
struggle for liberation, will they make the task of the worker
more easy and avoid the frequent recurrence of wasteful and

often tragic conflict. The burden, however, is equally upon the shoulders of the engineer to meet labour half way in this enterprise.

It is very much to be doubted if most American engineers really have a clear understanding of the position in which they find themselves, beyond a general conception of their apparent impartiality. The progressive economic concepts and activities which have been outlined, while advanced by representatives of national associations of engineers, are not necessarily the reflection of the great mass of American engineers to-day, over 200,000 strong. Nevertheless, it is fortunate that an otherwise conservative and socially timid body of individuals, such as the engineers frequently have been in the past, should now find itself represented by a few spokesmen at least who are able to promulgate clear statements on fundamental issues. The rank and file of engineers have a long road to travel before they will be in a position to command adequate consideration for their basic ideals and purposes as expressed in their new definition of engineering, and as proposed by some of their leaders.

It is, indeed, seriously to be doubted if many engineers of America have really had the training to grasp the relation of their position to the economic developments of to-day. Conventional engineering education has been entirely too narrow in its purpose. It has succeeded in turning out good technical practitioners, not far-seeing economic statesmen. In recent years many engineering schools have placed emphasis on what has aptly been termed " The business features of engineering practice." This, while conceivably a good thing from the standpoint of the limits within which engineering enterprise must ordinarily function to-day, is bound to over-emphasize the *status quo,* and so confine the vision of the engineer.

Engineers in this country have frequently taken a sort of pharisaic attitude on the desirability—offhand—of delegating the entire running of things human to technical experts. While such experts may usually have been quite successful in operating engineering enterprises, it hardly follows that this necessarily qualifies them for the wholesale conduct of the affairs of society.

Yet the demand on the part of certain engineers for a more fundamental participation in the conduct of the larger economic and political affairs of society should be construed as a healthy sign. It is an outgrowth of an intellectual unrest among the profession, precipitated by the thwarting of a genuine desire to build and serve. This unrest, in the absence of a constructive outlet combined with the past failure of engineering education to provide a real intellectual background, has resulted from time to time in some amusing phenomena. Thus not a few engineers have developed a sort of symbolism or mysticism, expressed in the terminology of their profession, with a view to building a new heaven and a new earth whose directing head they propose to be. From this they derive a peculiar satisfaction and perhaps temporary inspiration, and incidentally they often seem to confound laymen who do not understand the meaning of their terms. Instead of deriving comfort from symbolic speculations and futurist engineering diagrams, one would rather expect engineers to be realists, especially in the larger affairs of their profession. The seriousness with which the speculations concerning " space-binding " and " time-binding " have been taken is an example of how engineers with their present one-sided intellectual development may seize upon metaphysical cobwebs for spiritual solace in their predicament.

Another aspect of the intellectual limitations of many American engineers is revealed by some of the controversies which engage the technical societies and the technical periodicals. A notable and recurring instance is the debate concerning the relative merits of steam and electrical operation of railways. The real question which underlies replacing a going system with one which is better but more costly in capital outlay is primarily economic in nature. Consequently such a change is contingent upon a revised distribution of the national surplus rather than on the comparative merits of detail parts. This fact seldom seems to get home to the engineers. They have been arguing for the last fifteen years the relative advantages of this or that detail, failing all the while to understand that the best, in the large, from an engineering standpoint, can be secured only when unrestricted, free enterprise has given way to some form of enterprise regulated principally in the interest of public service.

The profession of engineering, especially in America, is still young enough not to have become ridden with tradition and convention. It has developed rapidly along essentially pragmatic though perhaps narrow lines. Certainly it is not bound and circumscribed by precedent and convention like the legal profession, or even the medical profession. Above all, it derives its inspiration from powerful physical realities, and this constitutes its bulwark.

What the profession really lacks are two fundamentals, absolutely necessary for any group strategically located and desirous of leadership in society. These are: (1) an intellectual background based squarely upon a comprehensive study of the economic and political institutions of society, their history, growth, and function, together with a study of the larger aspects of human behaviour and rights; and, (2) the development of a facility for intelligent criticism, especially of engineering and economic enterprises. A wholesome intellectual background is necessary to interpret the new position and its prerogatives which the application of science has created for the engineer. A development of the critical faculty is desirable in order to enable him to detect the blandishments of cult, the temptations of formulas and systems expressed in indefinable abstractions, and the pitfalls of the *status quo.*

The responsibility for the American engineer's function in society rests largely upon the schools which train him. Engineering education in America has done its task relatively well considered from the simple technical point of view. Of late, progressive engineering educators have stressed the necessity for paying more attention to the humanistic studies in the engineering curriculum. The beginning made in this respect is, however, entirely too meagre to warrant much hope that younger American engineers will soon acquire either that intellectual background or genuine critical faculty which will entitle them to a larger share of responsibility for the affairs of men.

The most hopeful sign in this direction is rather the fusion of the engineers into a large federation of societies, with service to the community, State, and Nation as their motto; a growing tendency, collectively, at least, to investigate the conduct of national industrial enterprises; and, finally, an attempt at a rapprochement, in the interest of society, between labour and the engineers. Ere long these developments will reflect themselves in the schools of engineering, and then, it is reasonable to expect, will the process of developing a truly worthy class of industrial leaders in this country really make its beginning. In America to-day no such leadership exists.

O. S. BEYER, JR.

NERVES

YOUNG as America is, she is nevertheless old enough to have known the time when there were no such things as nerves. Our earliest settlers and colonists, our proverbially hardy pioneers apparently managed to get along with a very modest repertory of diseases. They died, if not from malnutrition or exposure or from Indians, then from some old-fashioned, heaven-sent seizure or sudden pain, not to mention from " old age," long a favourite diagnosis of a pious and not too inquisitive school of medicine even where the patient's age had to be entered by the coroner as of forty or thereabouts. As for the various forms of nervousness which belong to our age of indulgence and luxury, they were unknown to those sturdier times, and would undoubtedly have put their unhappy victims under the quick suspicion of having had forbidden converse with the Devil.

If, nevertheless, we feel justified in assuming that this golden age of health and disease probably hid beneath its tinsel a good many of the nervous afflictions which had already made the Middle Ages so interesting, we must bear in mind that the pioneer neurotic of those days had at his command a number of disguises and evasions to which his fellow-sufferer of to-day can no longer have recourse. One of his favourite expedients for concealing his neurotic maladjustment was to take refuge in some form of religion or rather in some new variation of religious belief or practice, for it is, of course, not claimed here that religion itself can be exhaustively explained as a manifestation of nervous maladjustment. But the colonial period was an era when it was still good form, so to speak, for a neurosis to express itself in some religious peculiarity, and as this was a country without monasteries (which had proved to be such a haven for the neurotically afflicted during the Middle Ages), the neurotic was forced to exhibit his neo-religionism in the open. Often he blossomed forth in some new form of religious segregation, which allowed him to compensate for his social defect and often gave him positive advantages.

The neurotic legacy which he thus bequeathed to the nation can still be seen all around us to-day in the extraordinary multiplicity of religious variations, not to say eccentricities, which dot the theological heavens in America. For the neurotic as a religion founder—or better, inventor—quickly gathered similarly inclined adherents, formed a sect, and moved a little further West, so that the country was rather plentifully sown with strange creeds. He was thus freed from the criticism which would have overtaken him in a more settled society and his neurotic disguise remained undetected to a degree no longer possible to-day. For if nowadays we still occasionally encounter a brand-new and crassly individual religion all registered and patented like any temperance elixir, we usually discover that its prophet is either a defective or even an illiterate person who has distorted some biblical text in favour of a bizarre interpretation, or else a psychopathic individual who already has highly systematized ideas of the delusioned type. This class of neurotic has tended to disappear by somewhat the same process through which the more flamboyant type of hysteric such as flourished in the Middle Ages has gradually succumbed to progressive exposure—an analogy to which I refer with some diffidence in the face of one of the supreme ironies of the 20th century, namely, the canonization of Joan of Arc. But that lapse into the darkness of mediævalism is probably to be explained as a by-product of the war mind.

The other great loophole for the early American neurotic was purely geographical. He could always move on. In view of the tendency towards social avoidance so characteristic of the neurotic, this was of inestimable advantage. It is, of course, generally supposed that when the embryonic American trekked Westward it was either in response to some external pressure of political oppression or religious intolerance or to the glad, free call of wider horizons and more alluring opportunities, as was the case with the earliest colonists in their flight from Europe. In both cases, however, the assumption may be challenged as a sufficient explanation. For it is extremely probable that a good many of these pioneers were, like Mr. Cohan's " Vagabond," fugitives from their own thoughts quite as much as from the tyranny of others. They felt an urge within them that made a further abidance in their social environment intolerable. This geographical flight of the neurotic has always been the most natural and the most obvious, checked though it is to-day to a large extent by the disappearance of further virgin territory and the sophistication born of the knowledge wrought by a world-wide intercommunication which says that mankind is everywhere much the same, a truth which can again be translated into an internal realization that we cannot escape from ourselves.

Certainly our pioneers have been too much romanticized. The neurotic legacy which they bequeathed to us can plainly be seen in many characteristics of our uncouth Westerners with their alternate coldness towards visitors and their undignified warmth towards the casual stranger who really cannot mean anything to them. There is something wrong about man as a social animal when he cannot live happily in a valley where he sees more than the distant smoke of his neighbour's chimney. When at last the pressure of population forces him to live socially his suspicion and distrust are likely to turn him into a zealot and reformer and make possible the domination in American life of such a sub-cultural type as Bryan or the beatitudes of a State like Kansas. The favourite Western exhortation to be able to look a man in the eye and tell him to go to Hell is worthy of an anti-social community of ex-convicts, and the maxim about minding your own business can only be understood as a defence against the prevalent tendency of everybody to mind his neighbour's business. Thus the self-isolating neurotic ends by revenging himself upon society by making it intolerable.

But this is to anticipate. It must be said that until after the Civil War America remained singularly free from " nerves." This is perhaps largely due to the fact, as I have tried to show, that they were not known as such. The only serious epidemic was the witchcraft hunting of the 17th century. It is certainly most charitable towards a religion which had so many other repellent features to characterize this as an hysterical epidemic and let it go at that, though it also freshly illustrates the time-worn truth that intolerance does not seem to make its victims any more tolerant in their turn. The passing of this epidemic also marked the last irruption of State intolerance towards religion, with the exception of later incidents in connection with the Mormon Church, though it has rarely been understood that especially in this country State tolerance of religion was compensated for by individual and social intolerance in matters that quite transcended the religious sphere. The vast importance of this phenomenon in relation to our modern nervous tension will be referred to again later on.

The first typical manifestation of American nerves on an imposing scale began to develop in the sixties and seventies of the last century in the form of neurasthenia. Until then the typical American, despite his religious obsessions and his social deficiencies, had, to a large extent, remained externally minded, a fact which is sufficiently attested by his contempt for the arts and his glorification of his purely material achievements. He had been on the make, an absorbing process while it lasts, though rather dangerous in the long run because it never comes to an end. Neurasthenia developed rapidly as soon as it had been properly labelled, and claimed a notable number of victims among our captains of industry and high-pressure men: indeed, the number might easily lead to the perhaps rather unkindly conclusion that business dishonesty, even though successful, is likely to result in nervous breakdown in a generation piously reared on the unimpeachable maxims of a Benjamin Franklin or a Herbert Smiley. More fundamentally it was, of course, the logical penalty for cultivating the purely energetic side of man at the expense of his contemplative nature. The philosophy of hurry and hustle had begun to totter.

The discoverer, expounder, and popularizer of neurasthenia was Doctor George M. Beard, under whose ægis neurasthenia came to be known as " the American disease." Dr. Beard was a sound neurologist within the limits of his generation of medicine, but with a dangerous gift of imagination. His conception of neurasthenia was truly grandiose. According to him this fascinating disease was endemic in the United States and was the result of our peculiar social conditions. Its cause, he claimed, was "modern civilization, which has these five characteristics—steam power, the periodical press, the telegraph, the sciences, the mental activity of women." Among the secondary and tertiary causes of neurasthenia or nervousness he threw in such things as climate, the dryness of our air and the extremes of heat and cold, civil and religious liberty, our institutions as a whole, inebriety, and the general indulgence of our appetites and passions. In a remarkable chapter he also assigned as one of the causes of our nervousness the remarkable beauty of American women, though he does not clearly state whether this made only the men nervous or the women as well. Such a diagnosis was to turn sociologist with a vengeance and Doctor Beard lived up to his implications by saying that the cure of neurasthenia would mean " to solve the problem of sociology itself."

The inevitable result of such a broad and confident diagnosis was to make of neurasthenia a kind of *omnium gatherum* of all the ills of mankind less obvious than a broken leg. To explain the affliction in terms of America rather than in terms of the patient and his symptoms had about the value of a foreigner's book about America written on his home-bound steamer after a six-weeks' sojourn in this country. In fact, the wildest diagnoses were made, and such perfectly well-defined medical entities as tabes, arteriosclerosis, parathyroidism, myasthenia, and incipient tumours of the brain were frequently given the neurasthenic label. Various theories of exhaustion and nervous strain were also advanced and the attempt was made to feed and strengthen the nervous system directly on the analogy of Professor Agassiz's famous assumption that the phosphates in fish could be directly absorbed as material for brain-cells, a theory which did not account for the fact that comparatively few intellectual giants have sprung from fisher-folk. This naturally opened up a wide field for quackery and ushered in the era of "nerve tonics" which are still with us to-day. The craze for sanitariums also started at about this time, and with every doctor having a little sanitarium of his own the public was pretty well fleeced both by its "medicine men" and its men of medicine.

Of course no treatment could possibly be successful in curing such a wide variety of diseases the very existence of many of which was hidden from the physician under the blanket term of neurasthenia; and in those cases where an actual neurasthenia was present the treatment as developed by Beard and his followers made only superficial progress. The S. Weir Mitchell formula, for instance, with its emphasis upon quiet, diet, and rest, remained, in the majority of cases, essentially a treatment of symptoms rather than of causes. The tired and over-wrought business man was given a pacifying vacation from his dubious labours and was then promptly sent back to them, like a dog to his vomit. The American woman, grown nervous from being insufficiently occupied, was initiated into a different form of doing nothing, whereat she felt much relieved for a time. Neurasthenia was soon moving in a vicious and ever-widening circle; the more it spread the more it had to include and thus became less and less digested medically; it played havoc especially among American women who exploited their " nervousness " much as their European sisters had exploited their " migraine " or their " vapours " in previous generations. By the nineties, however, neurasthenia had run its course as a fashionable affliction, other countries had succeeded in surviving without erecting a quarantine against it, and medical circles had begun to debate whether there was such a thing as neurasthenia at all.

But, despite the breakdown of neurasthenia and the sins that were committed in its name, it would be a mistake to be merely amused at Doctor Beard for the pretentiousness of his concept or to criticize him too severely for being too much of a medical popularizer. His insight was, after all, of considerable value. For he realized, however imperfectly, that the neuroses as a class are cultural diseases and that they cannot be properly understood without taking into account the background of modern civilization. This is a rare virtue in American medicine where the specialist is constantly in danger of isolating himself, a tendency which is particularly harmful in the study of the mental sciences. Unfortunately Doctor Beard did not follow through. He seems to have become frightened at his own diagnosis. For no sooner had he drawn the worst possible picture of American civilization as a breeder of neurasthenia than he turned around and assured the public that things were not so bad after all. He accomplished this by enriching his sociology with a philosophy which is a prodigy in itself. This philosophy of his he called the " omnistic philosophy " and claimed for it the peculiar virtue of being able to include " optimism on the one hand and pessimism on the other and make the best of both," which is undoubtedly as uplifting a piece of American metaphysics as one is likely to find on the whole Chautauqua circuit. In criticizing the slow advance of American medicine as a whole it is always well to remember the atmosphere of intellectual quackery in which our physicians no less than our early metaphysicians so confidently moved.

By the end of the 19th century the study of functional nervous disorders in America was, as I have said, pretty well strewn with the *disjecta membra* of neurasthenia which still breathed slightly under the stimulus of electro- and hydrotherapeutics and of the " health foods " industry. Meanwhile hypnotism also had come to do its turn upon the American medical stage, where it ran through a swift cycle of use and abuse. Neurology as a special department, like the rest of American medicine, had been greatly enriched by contact with continental medicine, and the works of Kraepelin had come into honour among the psychiatrists. Dr. Morton Prince had begun to publish some interesting studies of double personalities, and a number of tentative systems of psycho-therapy based on a rather mixed procedure had been set up only to be knocked down again as a beneficial exercise for the critical faculty.

But now the stage was set for the appearance of the two modern theories of the neuroses as presented in Europe by Janet and Freud. In the rivalry that immediately ensued between these two opposing theories that of Janet was soon outdistanced. His fundamental conception of hysteria as a form of degeneration was in a way quite as repugnant to American optimism as the sexual interpretation of Freud was to American prudery. Janet had indeed been of invaluable help to the hysteric by taking him seriously, but his presentation of the subject was so narrow and his theory in the end proved so static that his views have made little headway. Janet was also under the disadvantage of working as an isolated figure in a prescribed field and did not come into any revolutionary relation to psychology as a whole or find those immensely suggestive analogies in the field of psychiatry, especially in dementia præcox and paranoia, which have given the work of Freud such a wide range. He had, besides, the defects common to so much of French medicine which is often so peculiarly insular and, so to speak, not made for export. His contribution more or less began and ended with the theory of the dissociation of the personality which is not characteristic of hysteria alone and could not successfully be grafted upon the old psychology to which Janet clung.

On the other hand, Freud after an initial resistance rapidly became epidemic in America. As was the case in Europe, he enjoyed considerable vogue among the lay public while still violently opposed in medical circles. His visit to America, however, in 1909, on the occasion of the twentieth anniversary of Clark University, created a very favourable impression and brought him to the attention of such American psychologists as William James, Edwin B. Holt, Adolf Meyer, and others. His works appeared in this country in translations by Doctor A. A. Brill, and in a short while Freud was "taken up" with a vengeance.

He has had both the advantages and the handicaps of a boom. His admirers have obscured or exaggerated him and his enemies have derided his popularity as proof of a reputation based upon sensationalism. In fact, Freud met with three fates: he was either wildly embraced, or rejected in toto with an appropriate academic lynching, or else he was accepted with "improvements."

He was fortified by previous experience against the second alternative and probably resigned to the third: it was the embrace that most nearly proved fatal to him. For America was to see the most extravagant development of the so-called "wild" psychoanalysis, a danger against which Freud himself had issued a warning. In 1916, for instance, an informal canvas revealed that approximately five hundred individuals were quite willing to psychoanalyze patients in the city of New York alone, whereas there were probably not more than six properly qualified medical practitioners in the whole State. Advertisements offered to teach the psychoanalytic technique by mail and instructors in chiropractic included it in their curriculum. This gross abuse was due to the general laxness of medical law in this country which still remains to be remedied. It was not only the amateurs that offended; doctors themselves were often at fault. For it cannot be too often emphasized that a psychoanalyst must have something more than the conceit of psychological subtlety common to most of us; he must be a trained neurologist and must have had considerable experience in psychiatry if he would escape the pitfalls of differential diagnosis—a case of hysteria can be dangerously like an incipient tumour of the brain and a compulsion-neurosis may simulate a paranoid condition. These abuses are, of course, no criticism of the intrinsic value of psychoanalysis. It has been the history of so many medical discoveries that they are recommended as a cure-all; we need but recall vaccination, or the present vitamine craze. On the other hand, it is regrettable that the direct attack upon Freud in this country has rarely risen above the level of denunciation. Quite recently, for instance, one of our socially eminent neurologists allowed himself to indulge in the teleological, or rather disguised theological, argument that if the unconscious is really so full of dreadful things as Freud says, they should be left there. And yet it is just serious and sympathetic criticism of which the science of psychoanalysis stands most in need.

The attempts to assimilate Freud were of two kinds. The first of these, like Professor Holt's book on " The Freudian Wish " or Doctor Edward J. Kempf's " The Autonomic Functions and the Personality," were sincere attempts of critical dignity to relate psychoanalysis to American behaviouristic psychology on the part of men who are not altogether professed Freudians. The second were more in the nature of somewhat pompous criticisms which attempted to reconcile and soften what seemed to be the more repellent features of the Freudian theories. There is a prevalent tendency among medical men in America to indulge in criticism without any due regard to the proportions between the magnitude of a subject and their familiarity with it, somewhat after the manner of the green

theological student who is confident of his ability to subvert
the theory of evolution in a casual thesis of his own. The
scientist in many fields is constantly facing this debasement of
standards, making science not too scientific or logic not too
logical lest it should be misunderstood; it is certainly a commentary that the majority of Americans, for instance, look
upon Edison as our greatest scientist. The tendency to
sweeten and refine Freud has taken some peculiar forms, due,
in great part, to Doctor Jung who, on having re-introduced
the libido theory to American audiences with a number of
philosophical and mystical trimmings of his own, felt that he
had made Freud more palatable over here.

Ironically enough, it would have been a very simple matter
to "put over" Freud in this country with all the éclat of the
Bergsonian craze which just preceded him. It was merely
a question of the right kind of publicity, for the problem of
how to handle sex in America has been solved long ago. The
way to do it is to sentimentalize it. If Freud, instead of saying that the incestuous longing of the child for the parent of
opposite sex is a natural impulse, though normally sublimated
during the period of adolescence, had put the same idea into
the phraseology of so many of our popular songs which reiterate the theme about mother being her boy's first and last
and truest love, he would have encountered no opposition.
And if he had given his theory of the unconscious a slightly
religious setting by emphasizing the fact that the unconscious
has no sense of the passage of time and cannot conceive its
own annihilation, he would have been hailed as the latest
demonstrator of the immortality of the soul. A little personal
press-agenting to the effect that he led a chaste life and was
the father of a flourishing family would have completed the
prescription. He would have gone over with a bang, though
he probably would have been quite as amiably misunderstood
as he is now viciously misunderstood.

Freud, however, presented his case at its own value and,
aside from informing an astonished American audience that
Doctor Sanford Bell had preceded him in announcing the pre-
adolescent sexuality of children, shouldered the responsibility
for his theories. What he has said, carefully and repeatedly,

is that ever since, for a long period in our development, the difficulties of satisfying the hunger impulse have been overcome in so far as civilized man has pretty well solved the problem of nutrition; it is the sex impulse to which the individual has the greatest difficulty in adjusting himself. This difficulty increases rather than decreases with the advance of culture and at certain stages leads to the group of diseases known as the neuroses. In a normal sexual life there is no neurosis. But our civilization has in many ways become so perverse that we find something akin to an official preference for a neurosis rather than a normal sexual life, in spite of the fact that the neurosis ultimately will destroy civilization. This is the vicious circle which Freud attacked. In doing so he had first to enlarge the concept of sexuality and show its complex relation to our whole culture. In studying civilization at its breaking point he naturally had to study what was breaking it up, namely, the individual's maladjustment to his sexual impulses. But he has never attempted to sexualize the universe, as has been claimed, nor has he ever lost sight of the fact that while man as an egocentric being must put the self-regarding instincts first, man regarded as one of the processes of nature remains to be studied in terms of his reproductive instincts. Freud has been persistently oversexualized both by his admirers and his opponents, and the degree to which this has been done in America is at least some indication of how close he has come home to conditions here.

Freudian research in this country has been limited almost entirely to cases. Our physicians who practise psychoanalysis have lacked either the leisure or the culture to apply their science to wider cultural questions to which the Freudian psychology applies, and among the lay scholars using the psychoanalytic technique there has been no outstanding figure like that of Otto Rank who has done such notable work in Vienna. But the study of specific cases of hysteria and neurosis as they occur in America already permit of some general conclusions as to the character of the national matrix from which they spring. One of the most striking features of our emotional life is the exaggerated mother-love so frequently displayed by Americans. The average American, whether drunk or sober, can grow maudlin about his mother's perfections and his devotion to her in a way that must shock the European observer. Not that the European loves his mother less: it is simply that he is more reticent about expressing an emotion which he feels has a certain private sanctity; he would experience a decided constraint or αἰδώς in boasting about it, just as a woman of breeding would not parade her virtue. The American adult knows no such restraint; he will "tell the world" how much he loves his mother, will sing sentimental songs about her and cheerfully subscribe to the advice to "choose a girl like your mother if you want to be happily married," and then grows violent when the incest-complex is mentioned. This excessive mother worship has reached almost cultic proportions. It is reflected in our fiction, in our motion-pictures, in the inferior position of the American husband, and in such purely matriarchal religions as Christian Science where a form of healing is practised which is not very far removed from a mother's consolation to her boy when he has bruised his knees. All this points to a persistent sexual infantilism and an incomplete sublimation, which are such fertile breeders of hysteria. One is involuntarily reminded of Doctor Beard's rather enigmatic statement that the extraordinary beauty of our women is one of the causes of nervousness in America. In so far as they offer a maximum of enticement with a minimum of conjugal satisfaction the charge is certainly justified. It is as if they did not even know their own business in terms of their sexual function of weaning their husbands from their mothers and thus completing the necessary exogamic process. We thus have the condition where the husband, in further seeking to overcome his incest-complex, becomes everything in his business and nothing in his home, with an ultimate neurotic breakdown or a belated plunge into promiscuity. The wife, on her part, either becomes hysterical or falls a victim to religious or reformatory charlatanism.

The study of compulsion-neuroses and allied paranoid states which are so prevalent among us has given us further insights into the neurotic character of the American temperament. One of the most valuable of these is the recognition of the compulsive nature of so much of our thinking. This has also been well observed by a foreign critic like Santayana who says of America, " Though it calls itself the land of freedom, it is really the land of compulsions, and one of the greatest compulsions is that we must think and feel alike." This is a rather fatal indictment of our boasted individualism, which is, as a matter of fact, an individualism born of fear and distrust such as already marked our early pioneers. We are indeed ultra-conformists, and our fear of other-mindedness amounts almost to a phobia. But such an atmosphere constitutes a paradise for the compulsion-neurotic because he finds it easy to impose his compulsions upon the rest of society. The fact that compulsion-neurotics are constantly indulging in neo-religious formations through which they are enabled temporarily to accommodate their taboos and phobias in religious ceremonials, enables them to make use of the general religious sanctions of society in order to impose their compulsions upon their fellow-beings.

Herein probably lies a better explanation of American intolerance than in the indictment of Puritanism which furnishes such a favourite invective for our iconoclasts. Puritanism has become a literary catchword and by no means covers the case. For it must be remembered that we are dealing with offshoots of deteriorated religions which spring from a very wide range of individuals. Religion, having been cut off from direct interference with the State, and having gradually lost its primitive anthropomorphism which really was one of its sources of strength, proceeded to project itself more and more outwardly upon social questions. As the personality of God grew dim the figure of the Devil also lost its vividness and the problem between good and evil could not longer be fought out entirely in the individual's own bosom; he was no longer tempted by the figure of the Devil appearing to him in person. Christian religion in its prime saw very clearly that the soul must put its own salvation to the fore, and constantly used many apt similes, such as the beam in our own eye, to remind us that while our neighbour might also have his hands full in fighting the Devil, he probably was capable of taking care of himself. Our modern reformer has no use for any such simile;

he would have to go out of business if he could not keep pick-
ing at the mote in his neighbour's eye. He finds the equivalent
of the Devil in our social vices, in alcohol, in tobacco, in tea
and coffee, in practically all forms of amusements. He
preaches a crusade which no longer has an ideal object, and
enlists a vague religious emotion which is inaccessible to reason
and mocks intellectual criticism. The device of using religious associations as carriers of propaganda has often been
used for political purposes with consummate skill. Bryan's
famous Cross of Gold speech and Roosevelt's Armageddon
appeal are excellent examples of it.

The question has often arisen why the fanatical reformer
is so omnipotent in America. Why does he succeed so well
in imposing his compulsions upon others? Why are we so
defenceless against his blackmail? Why, in plain language,
do we stand for him? Foreign observers have frequently
commented upon the enormous docility of the American public. And it is all the more curious because ordinarily the average American prides himself upon his assertiveness and his
quickness in detecting false pretensions. Yet it is a common
occurrence to meet people with valid claims to hard-headedness
who nevertheless submit to every form of compulsion. They
do not believe in prohibition but vote for it, they smoke but
think smoking ought to be stopped, they admit the fanatical
nature of reform movements and yet continue their subscrip-
tions.

In giving what can at best be only a partial answer to this
national enigma, we may briefly consider two types which profoundly contribute to our atmosphere of compulsion: our immigrant and our native aristocrat. The first, from the very
nature of the case, becomes the victim of compulsion, while
the second imposes the compulsion and then in turn, however
unwillingly, succumbs to it himself. Our society, with its
kaleidoscopic changes of fortune and its unchannelled social
distinctions, presents a problem of adjustment with which even
those who are at home in America find it difficult to cope.
People on the make, people who are not sure of themselves
on a new social ladder, are likely to conform: we find an astonishing amount of social imitation, in its milder and more

ludicrous form, in all our pioneer communities. The immigrant faces the same problem to an intensified degree. He
comes to us in an uprooted state of mind, with many of his
emotional allegiances still lingering in his native country, and
often with an entirely alien tradition. His mind is set to conform, to obey at first without much asking. He is like a
traveller arriving in a strange town who follows the new traffic
directions even though he does not understand their purpose.
But even with the best of will he cannot entirely conform.
He finds himself in a new world where what formerly seemed
right to him is now considered wrong, his household gods have
lost their power, his conscience is no longer an infallible guide.
It is a sign of character in him to resist, to refuse to sink his
individuality entirely, to struggle somewhat against the democratic degradation which threatens to engulf him too suddenly.
But his struggle leads to a neurotic conflict which is often not
resolved until the third generation. It is thus quite permissible to talk of an immigrant's neurosis, which has considerable
sociological importance even though it does not present an
integral clinical picture. It leads either to the formation of
large segments of undigested foreigners in American society
who sullenly accept the forms we impose upon them while
remaining comparatively inarticulate in our cultural and political life, or else it produces a type of whom our melting-pot
romanticists are foolishly proud, the pseudo-American who
has sunk from individualism to the level of the mob, where he
conforms to excess in order to cover his antecedents and becomes intolerant in order that he may be tolerated.

Ordinarily, the mob tyranny which has become such an
alarming feature of our public life would be checked by the
aristocratic element in society. It is part of the aristocratic
function to foster cultural tolerance and to resist herd suggestion: the aristocratic or dominant type, in enjoying the most
privileges, is normally least subject to compulsions and taboos.
With us that is not the case. The Southerner, for instance,
our most traditional aristocrat, finds himself paralyzed by the
consciousness of a black shadow behind him who constantly
threatens both his political and his sexual superiority. He
moves in an atmosphere of taboos from which he himself

cannot escape, for it is an established fact that interdiction in one line of thought has a crippling effect upon a man's intellectual activity as a whole. Elsewhere our native aristocrat frequently finds himself in the position of a lonely outpost of a thin Anglo-Saxon tradition which he must defend against the constant onslaughts of alien civilizations, in the desperate attempt to uphold the fiction that spiritually, at least, we are still an English colony. He is in a state of tension where he himself cannot move with any of the freedom which he vaunts as one of the outstanding characteristics of the country of his fathers. In his hands his own latest hope, our war-born Americanization programme, which should really be an initiation into freedom, has quickly become little more than a forced observance of sterile rites with which to impress the alien. He already sees its failure, and, like a general who is afraid of his own army, he does not sleep very well.

ALFRED B. KUTTNER

MEDICINE

FROM time immemorial the doctor has been the object of respect and awe by the generality of mankind. It is true that he has occasionally been made the butt of the satirical humour of such dramatists as Molière and Shaw, but the majority of people have regarded these jests as amiable buffooneries, and not as penetrating criticisms. In ancient days the veneration of the medico was based upon his supposed association with gods and devils, and upon the belief that he could cure disease by wheedling propitiation of *deus,* or by the exorcism of *diabolus.* In modern times he holds sway by his supposed possession of the secrets of science.

In spite of his pretension to scientific attainment, many vestiges of his former priesthood remain, and this *mélange* of scientist and priest has produced curious contradictions and absurdities. But these absurdities must by an inexorable law remain concealed from all save a few, and the general failure to recognize them has led to a great increase in the importance and prosperity of the medical cult. In America, of all civilized nations, medical magnificence has reached its most formidable proportions. This exaggeration, characteristic of all social phenomena in the new world, makes the real importance of the doctor to society easy to inspect and to analyze.

A friend not long ago asked me to explain the co-existence, in the same city, of the elaborate installation of the Harvard Medical School and the magnificent temple of the religion of Mrs. Eddy. "What is it in our culture," said he, "that permits the symbol of such obvious quackery as that of Mrs. Eddy to flourish within a stone's throw of such an embodiment of scientific enlightenment as the medical college?"

I replied that the reason for this must be sought in the gullibility of our citizens, who are capable of entertaining most incompatible and contradictory credos. Thus, the average American can believe firmly and simultaneously in the therapeutic excellence of yeast, the salubrious cathartic effects of a famous mineral oil, the healing powers of chiropractors, and in the merits of the regimen of the Corrective Eating Society. His catholicity of belief permits him to consider such palpable frauds seriously, and at the same time to admire and respect authentic medical education and even the scientific study of disease. But the teachers, students, and alumni of medical colleges are drawn from our excessively credulous populace. So it is dangerous to consider the votaries of the profession of medicine as sceptical and open-minded *savants*, in contrast to the promulgators of the afore-mentioned imbecilities and to *Homo sapiens americanus*, who is the unconscious victim of such charlatanry. In reality the great majority of the medical profession is credulous and must always remain so, even in matters of health and disease.

The tendency to consider physicians in general as men of science is fostered by the doctors themselves. Even the most eminent among them are guilty in this respect. Thus the Director of the Hospital of the Rockefeller Institute maintains that medicine must be considered not as an applied science but as an independent science (R. Cole, *Science*, N. S., Vol. LI, p. 329). And an eminent ex-President of the American Medical Association holds a similar view, at the same time preposterously asserting that "medicine has done more for the growth of science than any other profession, and that its best representatives have been among the leaders in the advancement of knowledge. . . ." (V. C. Vaughan, *Journal*, A. M. A., 1914, Vol. LXII, p. 2003.)

Such pronunciamentoes rest upon the almost universal confusion of the *art* of the practice of medicine with the *science* of the study of disease. Science, in its modern definition, is concerned with the quantitative relationship of the factors governing natural phenomena. No favourites are to be played among these factors. They are to be weighed and measured meticulously and coldly, without enthusiasm for one, or disdain and enmity toward another. Now, in the case of relationship of doctor to patient, it is clear that such emotions must enter. The physician must entertain enthusiasm for the defensive powers of his patient, John Smith, and at the same time hate virulently the pneumococcus that attacks him. This emotional state of the soldier of health prevents the employment of what is known in the language of the laboratory as the "control." For example, a doctor wishes to test the efficacy of a serum against pneumonia. In America it is practically unknown for him to divide his cases of pneumonia into two groups of equal size, to administer his serum to group A and to leave group B untreated. He almost invariably has a *parti-pris* that the serum will work, and he reflects with horror that if he holds his remedy from group B, some members of this group will die, who might otherwise have been saved. So he injects his serum into all of his patients (A and B), and if the mortality in the entire group appears to him to be lower by statistics than that observed in previous series of cases, he concludes that the value of his nostrum is proved. This is an illustration of the fallacy of the notion that medicine is a science in the modern sense.

Modern study of disease, conducted in the laboratory upon experimental animals, has furnished medical practitioners with a few therapeutic and prophylactic weapons. In the use of these the American medico has not lagged behind his European colleague. But the great majority of the malaises that plague us are not amenable to cure, and it is with these that the doctor has since the beginning of time played his most important rôle, i.e., that of a "professional sympathizer." The encouraging conversation with the family of the sufferer; the mumbling of recondite Latin phrases; the reassuring hopeful hand on the patient's shoulder; the grave use of complicated gimcracks; the prescription of ineffective but also innocuous drugs or of water tinted to pleasing hues; all these are of incalculable value to the *ménage* stricken by disease. It is my lamentable duty to point out the danger of the decline of this essential rôle among the doctors of America. The general practitioner of the *ancien régime* was sincere in his performance of his quasi-religious function. He was unsparing of his energies, stern in his devotion to duty, deeply altruistic in sentiment, and charmingly negligent in economic matters.

But at the present time this adorable figure is disappearing from the land, to be replaced by another, more sinister type, actually less learned in the important folklore of the bedside, pseudo-scientific, given to rigidly defined office hours, and painfully exact in the extortion of his emolument. What are the factors that give rise to the appearance of this new figure on the American scene? The most important of these is to be found in the high development of the craft of surgery in the United States. Of all the dread afflictions that plague us, a few may be cured or ameliorated by the administration of remedies, and an equally small number improved or abolished by surgical interference. But in spite of the relatively few diseases to which surgery is beneficial, the number of surgeons that flourish in the land is enormous. The fundamental discoveries of Pasteur and their brilliant application by Lister were quickly seized upon in America. The names of Bull, Halstead, Murphy, the brothers Mayo, Cushing, and Finney are to be ranked with those of the best surgeons of any nation. In fact, we may be said to lead the world—to use an apt Americanism—in the production of surgeons, just as we do in that of automobiles, baby carriages, and antique furniture.

The success of these protagonists in the higher carpentry at once attracted a horde of smaller fry, imitators, men of inferior ability. The rapid advances made by the leaders resulted in the development of a diversified and complicated technic, which the ordinary surgeon was able to master in sections but not *in toto*. From this, specialization in surgery has developed rapidly and naturally, so that now certain men devote their lives exclusively to the enthusiastic and indiscriminate removal of tonsils, others are death on gall bladders, some the foes of the vermiform appendix, and yet others practise exclusively the radical cure of phimosis. It is obvious that such narrow specialization, practised in isolation, would lead to most amusing results, which may best be left to the imagination. But these absurdities were finally apparent even to the surgeons themselves, with the resulting development of what is now known as " group medicine."

In brief, surgeons with special *penchants* for the removal of various organs, form partnerships, calling to their aid the internist for the diagnosis of their prospective victims. The internist gathers about him, in turn, a group of less important fry, known as radiographers, bacteriologists, pathologists, and serologists. Frequently a dentist is added to the coterie. The entire organization is welded into a business partnership of typically American efficiency. These groups are forming over the entire nation, are appearing even in the tank-towns of the hinterland. They occupy elegant suites in important office buildings, their members are generally considered the arbiters of the medical opinion of the community. Their more or less intelligent use of the paraphernalia of pathology, bacteriology, *et cetera*, gives them an enormous advantage over their more humble brother, the general practitioner. This last, indeed, is being rapidly routed in his battle with such associations of " best minds," equipped with the armamentarium of modern science.

The remuneration required by the " super-docs " of group medicine is naturally far in excess of that demanded by the general practitioner. It is right that this should be so, if not for the results obtained, then by reason of the elaborate organization and expensive equipment that the group system demands. This increase in reward has made the profession of medicine in America what it never was before, a paying proposition—again to use an apt Americanism. The result of this entry of crass materialism into a previously free-and-easy, altruistic, anything but business-like profession is, once more, better left to the imagination than described. The brigandage of many of these medical banditti is too painful even to think about. It will be apparent that relatively few of our citizens are able to pay for group medicine. So, it is interesting to observe that the best in medical treatment and advice is accessible only to the highest and lowest castes of our plutocracy. The rich receive this at the elegant offices and private hospitals of the groups, the miserably poor at the teaching hospitals of medical colleges.

The service of the " super-doc " to such of our citizens as can afford him cannot at this time be properly estimated. It is true that he is progressive, that he leans heavily upon the subsidiary sciences of pathology, *et cetera*, that he publishes papers in medical periodicals, that he visits medical libraries, frequents medical congresses. It has just been insisted that the doctor has benefitted himself to a great extent economically by forming the group; it is for the future to divulge whether his ministrations have resulted in a perceptible reduction of human suffering or in a prolongation of human life. Certainly he has perpetrated some astounding hoaxes, the kindhearted will say unwittingly. Probably the most interesting of these is to be observed in the focal infection mania just now subsiding.

Focal infection came into prominence as the theory, so called, of a group of eminent physicians in Chicago. It is, in brief, the doctrine that many of our aches and pains whose direct etiology it is impossible to demonstrate are due to the presence in the body of foci of harmful microbes, at the roots of the teeth, in the tonsils, accessory sinuses, or the appendix. Discover the focus, remove it, and presto!—the ache disappears like the card up the sleeve of the expert American poker player. The advantages of this theory to the various specialists of a group will be obvious. To illustrate. Henry Doolittle is plagued by a persistent and annoying pain over his left shoulder-blade. He goes to the office of a group of " super-docs," is referred to the diagnostician, who makes a careful record of his *status præsens*, then orders his satellites to perform the Wassermann reaction, make the luetin test, do differential blood counts, perform the determination of his blood urea, and carry out a thorough chemical study of his basal metabolism. If the results of these tests show no departure from the normal, or if they seriously contradict each other, the cause of the pain is probably focal infection. The patient is then subjected to examination by X-ray, his teeth are pulled by the dentist, his tonsils excised by the otolaryngolist, who also takes a swipe, in passing, at his accessory sinuses, and should these mutilations fail to relieve him, his appendix is removed by the abdominal surgeon. If relief still fails to occur, the theory is not given up, but the focus is presumed to exist elsewhere. If Mr. Doolittle's patience is equal to the test, and if his purse is not by this time completely empty, additional operations are advised. These continue until all organs and appendages not actually necessary to mere existence have been removed. Henry then returns to his former mode of life, depleted and deformed, it is true, but occasionally minus his original pain. It is not the intention to deny that infected teeth and tonsils have no significance in pathology. But it is certain that their importance has been greatly exaggerated by many physicians. The question needs more investigation, with fewer preconceived ideas. The " science " underlying this astounding practice is admirably outlined in the book of Billings called " Focal Infection." It is the most striking example of medical *Ga-Ga-ism* that has appeared in our country. It is, as its author himself admits, a triumph of the new idea of team-work and co-operative research in medicine. The factors giving rise to this lamentable *Ga-Ga* are the gullibility of patient and doctor, the emotional element entering into the interpretation of all of the phenomena observed by the physician, commercialism, and, finally, the self-limiting nature of most disease.

So much for the Art of Healing as practised by the physicians of America. What of our activities in the second aim of medicine, that is, the prevention of disease? While superficial examination is enough to lay bare the many hollow pretensions of the practice of medicine, it would appear *a priori* that the work of disease prevention might at least approach the category of the applied sciences. This would seem to be so, since the greater part of this field must of necessity concern itself with infectious disease. Now the etiologic agents of the majority of infectious diseases are known. It is easy to see that the labour of their prevention rests upon an exact knowledge of the nature of the disease-producing microbes, the analysis of the delicate balance between the virulence of the microbic invader and the resistance of the human host, and, most important of all, upon the exact path by which the germ in question travels from one individual to another.

In the early days of preventive medicine, following shortly upon the fundamental researches of Pasteur, several important contributions were made by Americans. These include the brilliant investigations of Theobald Smith on the etiology and mode of transmission of the Texas fever of cattle, and, later on, the differentiation of bovine and human tuberculosis. America had again reason to be proud when, in 1901, Reed,

Carroll, Agramonte, and Lazear demonstrated that yellow fever was spread exclusively by the mosquito, *Ædes calopus*. These investigators showed a beautiful spirit of self-sacrifice and devotion to their science. The construction of the Panama Canal was made possible by the application of these researches by Gorgas. Again, the American Russell was the first to show that vaccination against typhoid• and allied infections is feasible. In the New York Board of Health, Park, Krumwiede, and their associates have made careful and valuable studies on the prevention of diphtheria. These constitute the high lights of American achievement in preventive medicine. It must be admitted that the majority of these examples are to be placed in the category of the science of the study of disease, rather than in that of its application—preventive medicine.

It is noticeable even by cursory survey of recent American work that such striking achievements have become distinctly fewer in recent years, despite an enormous increase in personnel, equipment, and money devoted to the prevention of disease. Along with this decrease in solid contributions there has been an augmentation of fatuous propaganda and windy theory. All of the judicious must view this tendency with alarm and sadness, since it seemed for a time that science was really about to remove the vestigia of witchcraft and high-priesthood from this branch of medicine at least.

What is the cause of this retrogression? It must be laid at the door of *Religio Sanitatis*, the Crusade of Health. This is one of the most striking examples of the delusion of most Americans that they are the Heaven-appointed uplifters of the human race. Just as all Baptists, Presbyterians, and Methodists deprecate the heathen happiness of the benighted Oriental, so the International Health Board seeks to mitigate his contented squalour and to eradicate his fatalistically born disease. Just as Billy Sunday rages against John Barleycorn and the Dionysians who worship him, so the Great Hygienists seek to point out the multiform malaises arising from such worship. Just as the now extinct Wilson strove to show the world that it was horrid and wrong to fight, so the Public Health Service seeks to propagate the notion that chastity and adherence to marital vows are the sole alternatives to a universal syphilization.

Thus we observe with horror the gradual replacement of those Nestors of preventive medicine who had the dispassionate view of science, and who applied its methods of cold analysis, by a group of dubious Messiahs who combine the zealous fanaticism of the missionary with the Jesuitical cynicism of the politician. For most of the organizations for the promotion of health are closely dependent upon state and municipal politics, and must become contaminated with the obscenity of political practice. Finally, it is apparent that the great privately endowed foundations are animated by the spirit of proselytism common to the majority of religions, but especially to Baptists. It will be objected that such charges are vague generalizations. It is necessary, therefore, to bring forward one or two specific instances in support of these contentions.

The soldiers of the recent successful campaign for national prohibition were supported by battalions of noted hygienists who made excellent practice with a heavy artillery of so-called scientific evidence upon the confused ranks of brewers, distillers, and their customers, the American bibuli. What is the value of their " scientific evidence "? Two charges are made against the use of alcohol as a beverage. *Primo,* that its moderate or excessive use is the direct cause of various maladies. *Secondo,* that the children of alcoholic parents are often deformed, degenerates, or imbeciles, and that such lamentable stigmata are the direct results of the imbibitions of their parents.

Now it is vain to argue that alcohol, taken in great excess, is not injurious. Mania a potu (Korsakow's disease) is without doubt its direct result, at least in some instances. On the other hand, excessive indulgence in water is also not without its harmful effects, and I, for one, would predict evil days for our Great Commoner, should he so far lose control of himself as to imbibe a gallon of grape juice *per diem.* Many enthusiastic hygienists advance the opinion that alcohol is filling our insane asylums! This generalization is a gorgeous example of *post hoc propter hoc* reasoning, and is based upon the idiotic statistical research which forms so large a part of the activity of the minions of public health. The recent careful work of Clouston and others tends more and more to indicate that chronic alcoholics do not go crazy because they drink, but become alcoholics because they already were crazy, or had the inherited tendency toward insanity. This embarrassing fact is carefully suppressed by the medico-hygienic heavy artillerists of the prohibition army. What is more, diseases with definite pathologic pictures, such as cirrhosis of the liver, have by no means been definitely proved to be caused by alcohol. Indeed, the researches of Friedenwald, who endeavoured to produce such effects by direct experiment, have led to negative results.

The second indictment, i.e., that alcoholism in parents causes degenerate offspring, rests upon still more dubious scientific foundations. The most important animal experimentation in this field is that of Stockard, who used guinea-pigs as his subjects, and of Pearl, who had recourse to chickens. Both of these researches are sound in scientific method. Unfortunately for hygienists, they lead to completely contradictory conclusions. Stockard and his collaborators found the offspring of alcoholic guinea-pigs to be fewer in number than those of his normal controls. What is more, the children of the alcoholics were frequently smaller, had a higher post-natal mortality, and were prone to suffer from epileptiform convulsions. These results brought forth *banzais* from the hygienists and were extensively quoted, though their application by analogy to the problems of human heredity is not to be made too hastily.

Pearl, on the other hand, discovered that while the number of offspring from his inebriated chickens was distinctly fewer, yet these were unquestionably superior to normal chickens in eight of the twelve hereditary characters amenable to quantitative measurement. Now if one can generalize Stockard's results to human beings, then it is equally permissible to do the same with Pearl's. Of the two, the latter generalization would be preferable, and of greater benefit to the human race, were the analogy valid. For who will not whoop for " fewer children, but better ones "? Do the votaries of preventive medicine place the results of Pearl along side of those of Stockard? Indeed, who even mentions Pearl's results at all? If satisfactory evidence is adduced that this has been done, I hereby promise to contribute one hundred dollars in cash toward the foundation of a home for inebriated prohibition agents. Again, while much is heard of the results of Bezzola in regard to the *Rauschkinder* resulting from the Swiss bacchanalia, the negative findings of Ireland in similar investigations of the seasonal debauches of Scotland are carefully avoided. Once more, Elderton and Karl Pearson have failed utterly to find increase in the stigmata of degeneracy among the children of alcoholic parents as compared with those of non-alcoholics. This research, published in a monograph of the Francis Galton Laboratory of London, is the one really careful one that has been made in the case of human beings. It was directed by Pearson, admittedly a master of biometrical science. Yet, turning to Rosenau's " Preventive Medicine and Hygiene," the bible of this branch, I find the Elderton-Pearson report relegated to a footnote in the edition of 1913, *and omitted completely from the 1920 edition.*

A discussion of the fatuity to which American preventive medicine descends cannot be terminated without touching upon the current propaganda of the syphilophobes. For just as practitioners of medicine exploit human credulity, so the preventers of disease play upon the equally universal instinct of fear. There is no intention of minimizing the seriousness of syphilis. Along with cancer, pneumonia, and tuberculosis, it is one of the major afflictions of humanity. It causes thousands of deaths yearly; it leads to great misery. Paresis, one of the important psychoses, is definitely known to be one of its manifestations. It is obvious, therefore, that its eradication is one of the major tasks of social hygiene.

But by what means? Let one of the most noted of our American syphilophobes give the answer! This gentleman, a professor of pathology in one of the most important medical schools of the Middle West, yearly lectures over the length and breadth of the land on the venereal peril. He begins his expostulation with reduction of his audiences to a state of terror by a lantern-slide display of the more loathsome manifestations of the disease. He does not state that modern treatment makes these more and more rare. He insists upon the utter impossibility of its cure, a fact by no means established. He advocates early marriage to a non-syphilitic maiden as the best means of prevention, and failing that, advises that chastity is both possible and salubrious. Then follows a master stroke of advice by innuendo—*the current belief that masturbation causes insanity is probably untrue*. Finally he denies the value of venereal prophylaxis, which was first experimentally demonstrated by Metchnikoff and Roux, and which the medical department of the Army and Navy know to be of almost perfect efficacy when applied early and thoroughly.

Lack of space prevents the display of further examples of the new phenomenon of the entrance of religion and morals into medicine. It is not my intention for a moment to adopt a nihilistic attitude toward the achievement of preventive medicine. But it is necessary to point out that its contamination by moralism, Puritanism, proselytism, in brief, *by religion,* threatens to reduce it to absurdity, and to shake its authority in instances where its functions are of unmistakable value to our republic. At present the medical profession plays a minor rôle in the more important functions of this branch. These are performed in the first place by bacteriologists who need not be doctors at all, and in the second by sanitary engineers, whose splendid achievements in water supply and sewage disposal lead those of all other nations.

It has been remarked above that one of the chief causes of the unscientific nature of medicine and the anti-scientific character of doctors lies in their innate credulity and inability to think independently. This contention is supported by the report on the intelligence of physicians recently published by the National Research Council. They are found by more or less trustworthy psychologic tests to be the lowest in intelligence of all of the professional men excepting only dentists and horse doctors. Dentists and horse doctors are ten per cent. less intelligent. But since the quantitative methods employed certainly carry an experimental error of ten per cent. or even higher, it is not certain that the members of the two more humble professions have not equal or even greater intellectual ability. It is significant that engineers head the list in intelligence.

In fact, they are rated sixty per cent. higher than doctors. This wide disparity leads to a temptation to interesting psychological probings. Is not the lamentable lack of intelligence of the doctor due to lack of necessity for rigid intellectual discipline? Many conditions conspire to make him an intellectual cheat. Fortunately for us, most diseases are self-limiting. But it is natural for the physician to turn this dispensation of nature to his advantage and to intimate that *he* has cured John Smith, when actually nature has done the trick. On the contrary, should Smith die, the good doctor can assume a pious expression and suggest that, despite his own incredible skill and tremendous effort, it was God's (or Nature's) will that John should pass beyond. Now the engineer is open to no such temptation. He builds a bridge or erects a building, and disaster is sure to follow any mis-step in calculation or fault in construction. Should such a calamity occur, he is presently discredited and disappears from view. Thus he is held up to a high mark of intellectual rigour and discipline that is utterly unknown in the world the doctor inhabits.

A survey of the present condition of American medical education offers little hope for a higher intellectual status of the medical profession or of any fundamental tendency to turn medicine as a whole from a *mélange* of religious ritual, more or less accurate folk-lore, and commercial cunning, toward the rarer heights of the applied sciences.

Such a reform depends absolutely upon the recognition that the bodies of all the fauna of the earth (including *Homo sapiens*) are essentially physico-chemical mechanisms; that disease is a derangement of one sort or another of this mechanism; and that real progress in knowledge of disease can only come from quantitatively exact investigation of such derangements.

Up to the present, the number of professors in any branch of medicine who are aware of this fact is pitifully few. The men, who, being aware of it, have the training in physics and chemistry to put their convictions into practice are less in number. So, it is vain to hope that medical students are being educated from this point of view.

This casual glance at American medicine may be thought to be an unduly pessimistic one. It has not been my intention to be pessimistic or to be impertinently critical. Indeed, turning from the art of the practice of medicine, and the religion and folk-lore of sanitation, to the science of the study of disease, we have much of which to be proud. American biochemists of the type of Van Slyke and Folin are actually in the lead of their European brothers. Their precise quantitative methods furnish invaluable tools in the exact study of the ills that afflict us.

Finally, the greatest figure of all, Jacques Loeb, working in an institution that declares its purpose to be the dubious one of *medical* research, has in the last three years published investigations which throw a flood of light upon the dark problems of the chemistry of proteins. His work is of most fundamental significance, will have far-reaching results, and is measurably in advance of that of any European in the same field. Loeb, like all men of the first rank, has no spirit of propaganda or proselytism. His exact quantitative experiments rob biology of much of its confused romantic glamour. The comprehension of his researches demands thorough knowledge of physical chemistry. However, it is encouraging to note that among a few younger investigators his point of view is being accepted with fervour and enthusiasm. But it is time to stop. We are straying from our subject which was, if I remember, American medicine.

ANONYMOUS

SPORT AND PLAY

BARTLETT does not tell us who pulled the one about all work and no play, but it probably was the man who said that the longest way round was the shortest way home. There is as much sense in one remark as in the other.

Give me an even start with George M. Cohan, who lives in Great Neck, where I also live, without his suspecting it—give us an even start in the Pennsylvania Station and route me on a Long Island train through Flushing and Bayside while he travels via San Francisco and Yokohama, and I shall undertake to beat him home, even in a blizzard. So much for "the longest way round." Now for the other. If it were your ambition to spend an evening with a dull boy, whom would you choose, H. G. Wells, whose output indicates that he doesn't even take time off to sleep, or the man that closes his desk at two o'clock every afternoon and goes to the ball-game?

You may argue that watching ball-games is not play. It is the American idea of play, which amounts to the same thing, and seventy-five per cent. of the three hundred thousand citizens who do it daily, in season, will tell you seriously that it is all the recreation they get; moreover, that deprived of it, their brain would crack under the strain of "business," that, on account of it, they are able to do more work in the forenoon, and do it better, than would be possible in two or three full days of close sticking on the job. If you believe them, inveterate baseball fans can, in a single morning, dictate as many as four or five twenty-word letters to customers or salesmen, and finish as fresh as a daisy; whereas the non-fan, the grind, is logy and torpid by the time he reaches the second "In reply to same."

But if you won't concede, in the face of the fans' own statement, that it is recreation to look on at baseball or any other sport, then let me ask you to invite to your home some evening, not a mere spectator, but an active participant in any of our popular games—say a champion or near-champion golfer,

457

or a first string pitcher on a big league baseball club. The golfer, let us say, sells insurance half the year and golfs the rest. The pitcher plays eight months of the year and loafs the other four. Bar conversation about their specialty, and you won't find two duller boys than those outside the motion-picture studios.

No, brothers, the bright minds of this or any other country are owned by the men who leave off work only to eat or go to bed. The doodles are the boys who divide their time fifty-fifty between work and play, or who play all the time and don't even pretend to work. Proper exercise undoubtedly promotes good health, but the theory that good health and an active brain are inseparable can be shot full of holes by the mention of two names—Stanislaus Zbyzsk and Robert Louis Stevenson.

It is silly, then, to propound that sport is of mental benefit. Its true, basic function is the cultivation of bodily vigour, with a view to longevity. And longevity, despite the fact that we profess belief in a post-mortem existence that makes this one look sick, is a thing we poignantly desire. Bonehead and wise guy, believer and sceptic—all of us want to postpone as long as possible the promised joy-ride to the Great Beyond. If to participate in sport helps us to do that, then there is good reason to participate in sport.

Well, how many " grown-ups " (normal human beings of twenty-two and under need not be considered; they get all the exercise they require, and then some) in this country, a country that boasts champions in nearly every branch of athletics, derive from play the physical benefit there is in it? What percentage take an active part in what the sporting editors call " the five major sports "—baseball, football, boxing, horse racing, and golf? Let us take them one by one and figure it out, beginning with " the national pastime."

Baseball. Twenty or twenty-one play. Three hundred to forty thousand look on. The latter are, for two hours, " out in the open air," and this, when the air is not so open as to give them pneumonia and when they don't catch something as bad or worse in the street-car or subway train that takes them and brings them back, is a physical benefit. Moreover, the habitual attendant at ball-games is not likely to die of brain fever. But otherwise, the only ones whose health is appreciably promoted are the twenty or twenty-one who play. And they are not doing it for their health.

Football. Thirty play. Thirty thousand look on. One or two of the thirty may be killed or suffer a broken bone, but the general health of the other twenty-nine or twenty-eight is improved by the exercise. As for the thirty thousand, all they get is the open air—usually a little too much of it—and, unless they are hardened to the present-day cheer-leader, a slight feeling of nausea.

Boxing. Eight to ten play. Five thousand to sixty thousand look on. Those of the participants who are masters of defence may profit physically by the training, though the rigorous methods sometimes employed to make an unnatural weight are certainly inimical to health. The ones not expert in defensive boxing, the ones who succeed in the game through their ability to " take punishment " (a trait that usually goes with a low mentality) die, as a rule, before reaching old age, as a result of the " gameness " that made them " successful." There is a limit to the number of punches one can " take " and retain one's health. The five or sixty thousand cannot boast that they even get the air. All but a few of the shows are given indoors, in an atmosphere as fresh and clean as that of the Gopher Prairie day-coach.

Horse Racing. Fifty horses and twenty-five jockeys play. Ten thousand people look on. I can't speak for the horses, but if a jockey wants to remain a jockey, he must, as a rule, eat a great deal less than his little stomach craves, and I don't know of any doctor who prescribes constant underfeeding as conducive to good health in a growing boy.

Racing fans, of course, are out for financial, not physical, gain. They, like the jockeys, are likely to starve to death while still young.

Golf. Here is a pastime in which the players far outnumber the lookers-on. It is a game, if it is a game, that not only takes you out in the open air, but makes you walk, and walking, the doctors say, is all the exercise you need, if you walk five miles or more a day. Golf, then, is really beneficial, and it costs you about $25.00 a week the year round.

So much for our " five major sports." We look on at four of them, and if we can support the family, and pay taxes and insurance, on $1250 a year less than we earn, we take part in the fifth.

The minor sports, as the editor will tell you, are tennis, boating, polo, track athletics, trap-shooting, archery, hockey, soccer, and so on. Not to mention games like poker, bridge, bowling, billiards, and pool (now officially known as " pocket billiards " because the Ladies' Guild thought "pool " must have something to do with betting), which we may dismiss as being of doubtful physical benefit, since they are all played indoors and in a fog of Camel smoke.

Of the outdoor " minors," tennis is unquestionably the most popular. And it is one whale of a game—if you can stand it. But what percentage of grown-ups play it? I have no statistics at hand, and must guess. The number of adult persons with whom I am acquainted, intimately or casually, is possibly two thousand. I can think of ten who play as many as five sets of tennis a year.

How many of the two thousand play polo or have ever played polo? One. How many are trap-shooters? Two. How many have boats? Six or seven. How many run foot-races or jump? None. How many are archers? None. How many play hockey, soccer, la crosse? None.

If I felt like indulging in a game of cricket, which God forbid, whom should I call up and invite to join me?

Now, how many of my two thousand acquaintances are occasional or habitual spectators at baseball games, football games, boxing matches, or horse races? All but three or four. The people I know (I do not include ball-players, boxers, and wrestlers, who make their living from sport) are average people; they are the people you know. And the overwhelming majority of them don't play.

Why not? If regular participation in a more or less interesting outdoor game is going to lengthen our lives, why don't we participate? Is it because we haven't time? It takes just as much time to look on, and we do that. Is it because we can't afford it? We can play tennis for as little as it costs to go to the ball-game and infinitely less than it costs to go to the races.

We don't play because (1) we lack imagination, and because (2) we are a nation of hero-worshippers.

When we were kids, the nurse and the minister taught us that, if we weren't good, our next stop would be hell. But, to us, there was no chance of the train's starting for seventy years. And we couldn't visualize an infernal excursion that far off. It was too vague to be scary. We kept right on swiping the old man's cigars and giggling in the choir. If they had said that misdemeanours such as those would spell death and eternal fire, not when we were old, but to-morrow, most of us would have respected father's property rights and sat through the service with a sour pan. If the family doctor were to tell us now that unless we got outdoors and exercised every afternoon this week, we should'die next Tuesday before lunch, you can bet we should get outdoors and exercise every afternoon this week. But when he tells us that, without healthful outdoor sport, we shall die in 1945 instead of 1949, why, it doesn't mean anything. It's a chimera, a myth, like the next war.

But hero-worship is the national disease that does most to keep the grandstands full and the playgrounds empty. To hell with those four extra years of life, if they are going to cut in on our afternoon at the Polo Grounds, where, in blissful asininity, we may feast our eyes on the swarthy Champion of Swat, shouting now and then in an excess of anile idolatry, " Come on, you Babe. Come on, you Baby Doll! " And if an hour of tennis is going to make us late at the Garden, perhaps keep us out of our ringside seats, so close to Dempsey's corner that (O bounteous God!) a drop of the divine perspiration may splash our undeserving snout—Hang up, liver! You're on a busy wire!

RING W. LARDNER

HUMOUR

WITH the aid of a competent bibliographer for about five days I believe I could supply the proof to any unreflecting person in need of it that there is no such thing as an American gift of humorous expression, that the sense of humour does not exist among our upper classes, especially our upper literary class, that in many respects almost every other civilized country in the world has more of it, that quiet New England humour is exceedingly loud and does not belong to New England, that British incomprehension of our jokes is as a rule commendable, the sense of humour generally beginning where our jokes leave off. And while you can prove anything about a race or about all races with the aid of a bibliographer for five days, as contemporary sociologists are now showing, I believe these things are true. Belief in American humour is a superstition that seldom outlasts youth in persons who have been exposed to American practice, and hardly ever if they know anything of the practice elsewhere. Of course I am not speaking of the sad formalism of the usual thing as we see it in newspapers and on movie screens or of the ritual of magazines wholly or in part sanctified to our solemn god of fun. I mean the best of it.

In the books and passages collated by my bibliographer the American gift of humour would be distributed over areas of time so vast and among peoples so numerous, remote, or savage, that no American would have the heart to press his claim. The quaintness, dryness, ultra-solemnity with or without the wink, exaggeration, surprise, contrast, assumption of common misunderstanding, hyperbolical innocence, quiet chuckle, upsetting of dignity, *éclat* of spontaneity with appeals to the everlasting, dislocation of elegance or familiarity, imperturbability, and twinkle—whatever the qualities may be as enumerated by the bacteriologists who alone have ever written on the subject, the most American of them would be shown in my bibliographer's report to be to a far greater degree un-American. Patriotic exultation in their ownership is like patriotic exultation in the possession of the parts of speech. Humour is no more altered by local reference than grammar is altered by being spoken through the nose. And if the bibliography is an ideal one it will not only present American humour at all times and places but will produce almost verbatim long passages of American humorous text dated at any time and place, and will show how by a few simple changes in local terms they may be made wholly verbatim and American. It will show that American humorous writing did in fact begin everywhere but only at certain periods was permitted to continue and that these periods were by no means the happiest in history. I have time to mention here only the laborious section that it will probably devote to Mark Twain in the Age of Pericles, though for the more active reader the one on Mr. Cobb, Mr. Butler, and others around the walls of Troy might be of greater contemporary interest.

Mark Twain, according to the citations in this section, would seem actually to have begun all of his longer stories, including "Pudd'nhead Wilson," and most of the shorter ones, essays, and other papers, at Athens or thereabouts during this period, but not to have finished a single one, not even the briefest of them. He started, gave a clear hint as to how the thing would naturally run, and then he stopped. The reason for this was that owing to the trained imagination of the people for whom he wrote, the beginning and the hint were sufficient, and from that point on they could amuse themselves along the line that Mark Twain indicated better than he would have amused them, had he continued. Mark Twain finally saw this and that is why he stopped, realizing that there was no need of his keeping the ball rolling when to their imaginative intelligence the ball would roll of itself. He did at first try to keep on, and being lively and observant and voluble even for a Greek he held large crowds on street-corners by the sheer repetition of a single gesture of the mind throughout long narratives of varied circumstance. In good society this was not tolerated even after supper, and there was never the slightest chance of

publication. But the streets of Athens were full of the suppressed writings of Mark Twain.

Every man of taste in Athens loved Mark Twain for the
first push of his fancy but none could endure the unmitigated
constancy of his pushing of it, and as Mark Twain went everywhere and was most persistent, the compression of his narrative flow within the limits of the good breeding of the period
was an embarrassing problem to hosts, unwilling to be down-
right rude to him. Finally he was snubbed in public by his
friends and a few of the more intimate explained to him afterwards the reason why.

The gist of their explanation was evidently this: The hypothesis of the best society in town nowadays is that the prolongation of a single posture of the mind is intolerable, no
matter how variegated the substance in which the mind re-
poses. That sort of thing belongs to an earlier day than ours,
although, as you have found, it is still much relished in the
streets. If all the slaves were writers; if readers bred like
rabbits so that the pleasing of them assured great wealth; if
the banausic element in our life should absorb all the rest of
it and if, lost in the external labour process, with the mechanism of it running in our minds, we turned only a sleepy eye
to pleasure; then we might need the single thought strung with
adventures, passions, incidents and need only that—infinitudes
of detail easily guessed but inexorably recounted; long lists of
sentiments with human countenances doing this and that;
physiological acts in millions of pages and unchanging phrase;
volumes of imaginary events without a thought among them;
invented public documents equalling the real; enormous anec-
dotes; and all in a strange reiterated gesture, caught from machines, disposing the mind to nod itself to sleep repeating the
names of what it saw while awake. But the bedside writer for
the men in bed is not desired at the present moment in our
best society.

All these things are now carried in ellipsis to the reader's
head, if the reader's head desires them; they are implied in
dots at ends of sentences. We guess long narratives merely
from a comma; we do not write them out. In this space left
free by us with deliberate aposiopesis, a literature of countless

simplicities may some day arise. At present we do not feel the
need of it. And in respect to humour the rule of the present
day is this: never do for another what he can do for himself.
A simple process of the fancy as in contrast, incongruity, exaggeration, impossibility, must be confined in public to one or
two displays. Let us take the simplest of illustrations—a cow
in the dining-room, for example—and proceed with it as simply
as we can. If by a happy stroke of fancy a cow in the dining-
room is made pleasing to the mind, never argue that the pleasure is doubled by the successive portrayal of two cows in two
dining-rooms, assuming that the stroke of fancy remains the
same. Realize rather that it diminishes, and that with the
presentation of nine cows in nine dining-rooms it has changed
to pain. Now if for cows in dining-rooms be substituted gods
in tailor shops, tailors in the houses of gods, cobblers at
king's courts, Thebans before masterpieces, one class against
another, one age against another, and so on through incalculable details, however bizarre, all in simple combination, all easily
gathered, without a shift of thought or wider imagery, the fancy
mechanistically placing the objects side by side, picked from
the world as from a catalogue—even then the situation to our
present thinking is not improved.

" Distiktos," said they, playfully turning the name of the
humourist into the argot of the street, " we find you charming
just at the turn of the tide, but when the flood comes in, *ne
Dia!* you are certainly *de trop*. And in your own private interest, Distiktos, unless you really want to lead a life totally
anexetastic and forlorn, how can you go on in that manner? "

FRANK MOORE COLBY

American Civilization from the Foreign Point of View

I. ENGLISH
II. IRISH
III. ITALIAN

I. AS AN ENGLISHMAN SEES IT

A LITTLE less than two years ago—on the 14 July, 1919, to be exact—it fell to my lot, as an officer attached to one of the many military missions in Paris, to "assist," from a reserved seat in a balcony of the Hotel Astoria, at the *défilé*, or triumphal entry of the Allied troops into Paris.

The march *à Berlin* not having eventuated owing to the upset in schedule brought about by the entry of dispassionate allies at the eleventh hour, it was felt that the French must be offered something in exchange, and this took the happy form of a sort of community march along the route once desecrated by Prussian hoof-beats—a vast military *corbeille* of the allied contingents, with flags, drums, trumpets, and all the rest of the paraphernalia that had been kept in cold storage during four years of gas, shell, and barbed wire. Such a *défilé*, it was calculated, would be something more than a frugal gratification to the French army and people. It would offer to the world at large, through the medium of a now unmuzzled press, a striking object lesson in allied good feeling and similarity of aims.

My purpose in referring to the *défilé* is merely to record one unrehearsed incident in it but I would say in passing that the affair, " for an affair," as the French say, was extraordinarily well stage-managed. A particularly happy thought was the marshalling of the allied contingents by alphabetical order. This not only obviated any international pique on what we all wanted to be France's day, but left the lead of the procession where everybody, in the rapture of delivery, was well content it should remain. Handled with a little tact, the alphabet had once more justified itself as an impartial guide:

B is for Britain, Great.
A is for America, United States of.

For impressiveness I frankly and freely allot the palm to what it was the fashion then to term the American effort. Different contingents were impressive in different ways. The Republican Guard, jack-booted, with buckskin breeches, gleaming helmets, flowing *crinières*, and sabres *au clair*, lent just the right subtle touch of the *épopée* of Austerlitz and Jena to make us feel 1871 had been an evil dream; the Highlanders, the voice of the hydra squalling and clanging from their immemorial pipes, stirred all sorts of atavistic impulses and memories. Nevertheless, had I been present that day in Paris as a newspaper man instead of as the humblest and most obscure of soldiers, neither one nor the other would have misled my journalistic instinct. I should have put the lead of my " story " where alphabetical skill had put the lead of the procession—in the American infantry.

In front the generalissimo, martial and urbane, on a bright coated horse that pranced, curvetted, " passaged " from side to side under a practised hand. At his back the band, its monster uncurved horns of brass blaring out the Broadway air before which " over there " the walls of pacifism had toppled into dust in a day. Behind them, platoon by platoon, the clean shaved, physically perfect fighting youth of the great republic. All six feet high—there was not one, it was whispered, but had earned his place in the contingent by a rigorous physical selection: moving with the alignment of pistons in some deadly machine— they had been drilled, we were told, intensively for a month back. In spotless khaki, varnished trench helmets, spick and span, scarcely touched by the withering breath of war. Whenever the procession was checked, platoon after platoon moved on to the regulation distance and marked time. When it resumed, they opened out link by link with the same almost inhuman precision, and resumed their portentous progress. How others saw them you shall hear, but to me they were no mere thousand fighting men; rather the head of a vast battering ram, the simple threat of which, aimed at the overtaxed heart of the German Empire, had ended war. A French *planton* of the Astoria staff, who had edged his way into the ticketed group was at my back. " Les voilà qui les attendaient," he almost whispered. " Look what was waiting for *them*."

The next balcony to mine had been reserved for the civil

employés of British missions, and here was gathered a little knot of average English men and women—stenographers, typists, clerks, cogs of commercialism pressed into the mechanical work of post-war settlement. As the Americans moved on after one of the impressive checks of which I have just spoken, something caught my ears that made me turn my head quickly, even from a spectacle every lost moment of which I grudged. It was, of all sounds that come from the human heart, the lowest and the most ominous—the sound that makes the unwary walker through tropical long grass look swiftly round his feet and take a firmer grasp on the stick he has been wise enough to carry.

It is impossible—it is inconceivable—and it's true. On this great day of international congratulation, one of the two branches of the Anglo-Saxon race was hissing the other.

I spoke about the matter later to a friend and former chief, whom I liked but whose position and character were no guarantee of tact or good judgment. I said I thought it rather an ominous incident, but he refused to be "rattled." With that British imperturbability which Americans have noted and filed on the card index of their impressions he dismissed the whole thing as of slight import.

"Very natural, I dare say. Fine show all the same. Perhaps your friends on the other balcony thought they were slopping over in front."

"'Slopping over . . . ?'"

"Well—going a little too far. Efficiency and all that. Bit out of step with the rest of the procession."

I have often wondered since whether this homely phrase, uttered by a simple soldier man, did not come nearer to the root of the divergence between British and American character than all the mystifying and laborious estimates which nine out of ten of our great or near-great writers seem to think is due at a certain period in their popularity.

To achieve discord, you see, it is not necessary that two instruments should play different tunes. It is quite sufficient that the tempo of one should differ from the tempo of the other. All I want to indicate in the brief space which the scope of this work leaves at my disposal are just a few of the conjunctures at which I think the beat of the national heart, here and across the Atlantic, is likely to find itself out of accord.

Englishmen do not emigrate to the United States in any large numbers, and it is many years since their arrival contributed anything but an insignificant racial element to the " melting pot." They do not come partly because their own Colonies offer a superior attraction, and partly because British labour is now aware that the economic stress is fiercer in the larger country and the material rewards proportionately no greater. Those who still come, come as a rule prepared to take executive positions, or as specialists in their several lines. Their unwillingness to assume American citizenship is notorious, and I think significant; but it is only within quite recent years that it has been made any ground of accusation—and among the class with which their activities bring them into closest contact it is, or was until a year or two ago, tacitly and tactfully ignored. During a review of the " foreign element " in Boston to which I was assigned two years before the war, I found business men of British birth not only reluctant to yield " copy " but resentful of the publicity to which the enterprise of my journal was subjecting them.

There are many reasons why eminent English writers and publicists are of little value in arriving at an estimate of " how Americans strike an Englishman." While not asserting anything so crude as that commercial motives are felt as a restraining force when the temptation arises to pass adverse judgment on the things they see and hear, it is evident that the conditions under which they come—men of achievement in their own country accredited to men of achievement here—keep them isolated from much that is restless, unstable, but vitally significant in American life. None of them, so far as I know, have had the courage or the enterprise to come to America, unheralded and anonymous, and to pay with a few months of economic struggle for an estimate that might have real value.

To this lack of real contact between the masses in America and Great Britain is due the intrinsic falsity of the language in which the racial bond is celebrated on the occasions when some political crisis calls for its reiteration. It is felt easier and safer to utter it in consecrated *clichés*—to refer to the specific gravity of blood and water, or the philological roots of the medium used by Milton and Arthur Brisbane. The banality, the insincerity, of the public utterances at the time that America's entry into the European struggle first loomed as a possible solution of the agony on the Western Front was almost unbelievable. Any one who cares to turn up the files of the great dailies between September, 1916, and March, 1918, may find them for himself.

To a mind not clouded by the will to believe, this constant invocation of common aims, this perpetual tug at the bond to ensure that it has not parted overnight, would be strong corroboration of a suspicion that the two vessels were drifting apart, borne on currents that flow in different directions. It is not upon the after-dinner banalities of wealthy and class-conscious "pilgrims" nor the sonorous platitudes of discredited laggards on the political scene, still less is it upon the sporting proclivities of titled hoydens and hawbucks to whom American sweat and dollars have arrived in a revivifying stream, that we shall have to rely should the cable really part and the two great vessels of State grope for one another on a dark and uncharted sea. It is upon the sheer and unassisted fact of how American and Englishman like or dislike one another.

It is a truism almost too stale to restate that we are standing to-day on the threshold of great changes. What is not so well realized is that many of these changes have already taken place. The passing of gold in shipment after shipment from the Eastern to the Western side of the Atlantic and the feverish hunt for new and untapped sources of exploitation are only the outward signs of a profound European impoverishment in which Britain for the first time in her history has been called upon to bear her full share. The strikes and lock-outs that have followed the peace in such rapid succession might possibly be written off as inevitable *sequelæ* of a great war. The feeble response to the call for production as a means of salvation, the general change in the English temper faced with its heavy task are far more vital and significant matters. They

seem to mark a shift in moral values—a change in the faith
by which nations, each in the sphere that character and circumstance allot, wax and flourish.

Confronted with inevitable competition by a nation more
populous, more cohesive, and richer than itself, it seems to me
that there are three courses which the older section of the
English race may elect to follow. One is war, before the
forces grow too disparate, and on the day that war is declared
one phase of our civilization will end. It will really not matter
much, to the world at large, who wins an Anglo-American
world conflict. The second, which is being preached in and
out of season by our politicians and publicists, who seldom,
however, dare to speak their full thought, is a girding up of
the national loins, a renewed consecration to the gospel of effort, a curtailment, if necessary—though this is up to now
only vaguely hinted—of political liberties bestowed in easier
and less strenuous days. The third course may easily be
guessed. It is a persistence in proclivities, always latent as I
believe in the English temperament, but which have only revealed themselves openly since the great war, a clearer questioning of values till now held as unimpeachable, a readier ear
to the muttering and murmuring of the masses in Continental
Europe, internationalism—revolution. No thoughtful man in
England to-day denies the danger. Even references to that
saving factor, the " common sense of the British workman,"
no longer allays the spectre of a problem the issues of which
have only to be stated to stand forth in all their hopeless irre-
concilability. Years ago, long before the shadow fell on the
world, in a moment of depression or inspiration, I wrote that
cravings were stirring in the human heart on the very eve of
the day when the call would be to sacrifice. That is the riddle,
nakedly stated, to which workers and rulers alike are asked
to find an answer to-day.

In this choice that lies before the British worker a great
deal may depend upon how American experiments and American achievements strike him. In England now there is no
escaping from the big transatlantic sister. Politicians use her
example as a justification; employers hold up her achievements as a reproach. A British premier dare not face the

House of Commons on an " Irish night " unequipped with artful analogies culled from the history of the war of secession. The number of bricks per hour America's bricklayers will lay or the tons of coal per week her stolid colliers will hew are the despair of the contractor face to face with the loafing and pleasure-loving native born. You will hear no more jokes to-day in high coalition places over her political machine replacing regularly and without the litter and disorder of a general election tweedledum Democrat by a tweedledee Republican. She is recognized—and this, I think, is the final value placed upon her by the entire ruling and possessing classes in my own country—as better equipped in her institutions, her character, and her population for the big economic struggle that is ahead of us.

This is the secret of the unceasing court paid to Washington by all countries, but pre-eminently by Britain. It is not fear of her power, nor hunger for her money bags and harvests, nor desire to be " on the band-wagon," as light-hearted cartoonists see it, that prompts the nervous susceptibility and the instantaneous response to anything that will offend those in high places on the banks of the Potomac. It is the sense, among all men with a strong interest in maintaining the present economic order, that the support in their own countries is crumbling under their hands, and that that fresh support, stronger and surer, is to be found in a new country with a simpler faith and a cleaner, or at any rate a shorter, record. To fight proletarianism with democracy is a method so obvious and safe that one only wonders its discovery had to wait upon to-day. Its salient characteristic is a newly aroused interest and enthusiasm in one country for the political forces that seem to make stability their watchword in the other. The coalition has become the hero of the New York *Times* and *Tribune*— the triumph of the Republican party was hailed almost as a national victory in the London *Times* and Birmingham *Post*. Intransigeance in foreign policies finds ready forgiveness in London; in return, a blind eye is turned to schemes of territorial aggrandisement at Washington.

If a flaw is to be discerned in what at first sight seems a perfectly adjusted instrument for international comity, it is that this new Anglo-American understanding seems to be founded on class rather than on national sympathy. Even offhand some inherent inconsistency would seem to be sensed from the fact that the appeal of the great republic comes most home, in the parent country, to the class that is least attached to democratic forms and the most fearful of change. References to America arouse no enthusiasm at meetings of the labour element in England, and it is still felt unwise to expose the Union Jack to possible humiliation in parades on a large scale in New York or Chicago. A sympathy that flowers into rhetoric at commercial banquets or at meetings of the archæologically inclined may have its roots in the soundest political wisdom. But to infer from such demonstrations of class solidarity any national community of thought or aim is both unwarranted and unsafe. This much is evident, that should a class subversion, always possible in a country the political fluidity of which is great, leave the destinies of Great Britain in the hands of the class that is silent or hostile to-day when the name of America is mentioned, an entire re-statement of Anglo-American unity would become necessary, in terms palatable to the average Englishman.

This average Englishman is a highly complicated being. Through the overlay which industrialism has imposed on him, he has preserved to quite an extraordinary extent the asperities, the generosities, the occasional eccentricities of the days when he was a free man in a free land. No melting process has ever subdued the sharp bright hues of his individuality into the universal, all-pervading drab that is the result of blending primary colours. No man who has employed him to useful purpose has ever succeeded in reducing his personality to the proportions of a number on a brass tag. The pirate and rover who looked upon Roman villadom and found it not good, the archer who brought the steel-clad hierarchy of France toppling from their blooded horses at Crécy and Agincourt, the churl who struck off the heads of lawyers in Westminster Palace yard survive in him.

If I am stressing this kink in the British character it is because one of its results has been to make the Englishman of all men the least impressed by scale, and the one to whom appeals made on the size of an experiment or the vastness of a vision will evoke the least response, and especially because I think I perceive a tendency to approach him in the interests of Anglo-American unity precisely from the angle that will awake antagonism where co-operation is sought. The attachment of the Englishman to little things and to hidden things, which no one except Chesterton has had the insight to perceive, or at all events which Chesterton was the first to place in its full relation to his inconsistencies, explains his strangely detached attitude to that British Empire of which his country is the core. Its discovery as an entity calling for a special quality in thought and action dates no further back than that strange interlude in history, when the personality of Roosevelt and the vision of Kipling held the imagination of the world.

This refusal to be impressed by greatness, whether his own or others', has its disadvantages, but at least it has one saving element. It leaves an Englishman quite capable of perceiving that it is possible for a thing to be grandiose in scale and mean in quality. It leaves intact his frank and childlike confidence that the little things of the world confound the strong; his implicit conviction that David will always floor Goliath, and that Jack's is the destined sword to smite off the giant's head. The grotesqueness of the Kaiser's upturned moustaches, the inadequacy of a mythical "William the Weed" to achieve results that would count, were his guiding lights to victory, the touchstones by which he tested in advance the vast machine that finally cracked and broke under its own weight. It was the "contemptible" little army of shopmen and colliers which seized his imagination and held his affection throughout, not the efficient mechanical naval machine that put out once to sea in battle array and then, appalled by the risks inherent in its own monstrousness and complexity, spent the rest of the war in Scapa Flow. I recall the comments heard at the time of Jutland in the artillery camp where fate had thrown me. They served to confirm a dawning conviction that the navy, while it still awes and impresses, lost its hold on the British heart the day wooden walls were exchanged for iron and steel. It is perhaps the "silent service" to-day because its appeal awakes so little response. It has been specialized and magnified out of the average Englishman's power to love it.

In America the contrary seems the case. The American heart appears to go out to bulk, to scale, and to efficiency. The American has neither the time nor the temperament to test and weigh. His affections, even his loyalties, seem to be at the mercy of aspects that impose and impress. I know no other country where the word "big" is used so constantly as a token of affection. Every community has its "Big Tims," "Big Bills," "Big Jacks," great hearty fellows who gambol and spout on public occasions with the abandonment of a school of whales. Gargantuan "Babe Ruth," mountainous Jack Dempsey are the idols of its sport-loving crowds. "Mammoth in character," the qualification which on the lips of the late Mr. Morgan Richards stirred laughter throughout England, is to the American no inconsequential or slipshod phrase. He does perceive a character and justification in bigness. It was perhaps to this trait in his mental make-up that the puzzling shift of allegiance tc the beginning of the great war was due. The scale and completeness of the German effort laid hold of his imagination to an extent that only those who spent the first few months of agonizing doubt in the West and the Middle West can appreciate. Something that was obscurely akin, something that transcended racial affinities and antipathies, awoke in him at the steady ordered flow of the field-grey legions Westward, so adequately pictured for him by Richard Harding Davis. He is quite merciless to defeat.

Nothing conceived on such a scale can indulge complexities. Its ideals must be ample, rugged, and primitive, adequate to the vast task. Hence the velocity, the thoroughness, the apparent ruthlessness with which American enterprises are put through. It is the fashion among a certain school of thought to call America the country of inhibitions. But there is little inhibition to be perceived on that side of his temperament, which the American has chosen to cultivate, leaving all else to those who find perverse attraction in weed and ruin. His language—and he is amazingly vocal—is as simple and direct as his thought. The appeals and admonitions of his leaders reverberate from vast and resonant lungs. They are calculated rather to carry far than to penetrate deeply. They are statements and re-statements rather than arguments. If their verbiage often aims at and sometimes seems to attain the sublime, if the American leader is forever dedicating, consecrating, inspiring something, the altitude is like the elevation given a shell in order that it may travel further. The nimble presentation of antithesis of a Lloyd George, the dagger-play of sarcasm of an Asquith, are conspicuously absent from the speeches of American leaders. There is something arrogant and ominous, like the clenching of a fist before the arm is raised, in this sonorous presentation of a faith already securely rooted in the hearts of all its hearers.

This primitiveness and single-mindedness of the American seem to intensify as his historical origins recede further and further into the past. It is idle to speculate on what might have happened had the development of his country remained normal and homogeneous, as, up to the Civil War, it admittedly did. It is an even less grateful task to look back on the literature of the Transcendental period and register all that American thought seems to have lost since in subtlety and essential catholicity. What is really important is to realize that not only the language but the essence of Occidental civilization has called for simplification, for sacrifice, year by year. It is hard to see what other choice has lain before the American, as wave after wave of immigration diluted his homogeneity, than to put his concepts into terms easily understood and quickly grasped, with the philological economy of the traveller's pocket manual and the categorical precision of the drill book. If in the very nature of things, this evangel is oftener pointed with a threat than made palatable with the honey of reason and sympathy, the task and not the taskmaster is to blame. On no other country has ever been imposed similar drudgery on a similar scale. It is idle to talk about the spiritual contribution of the foreigner when his first duty is to cast that contribution into the discard. It is futile to appeal to his traditions where the barrier of language rears itself in a few years between parents who have never learnt the new tongue and children who are unable or ashamed to speak the old.

But such a régime cannot endure for many years without a profound influence, not only on those to whom it is prescribed, but on those who administer it. The most heaven-born leader of men, put into a receiving depot to which monthly and fortnightly contingents of bemused recruits arrive, quickly deteriorates into something like a glorified and commissioned drill sergeant. The schoolmaster is notoriously a social failure in circles where intercourse must be held on the level to which the elevation of his *estrade* has dishabituated him. Exact values—visions, to use a word that misuse has made hateful—disappear under a multiplicity of minor tasks. It is one of the revenges taken by fate that those who must harass and drive become harassed and sterile in turn.

No one yet, so far as I know, has sought to place this amazing simplification in its true relation to the aridity of American life, an aridity so marked that it creates a positive thirst for softer and milder civilizations, not only in the foreigner who has tasted of them, but at a certain moment in their life in almost every one of the native born whose work lies outside the realm of material production. It is not that in England, as in every community, entire classes do not exist who seek material success by the limitation of interests and the retrenchment of sympathies. But in so doing they sacrifice to a domestic, not a national God; they follow personal not racial proclivities. There is no conscious subscription to a national ideal in their abandonment of æsthetic impulses. Side by side with them live other men whose apparent contentment with insecure and unstable lives at once redresses their pride and curtails their influence. They are conscious of the existence around them of a whole alien world, the material returns from which are negligible but in which other men somehow manage to achieve a fullness of experience and maintain self-respect. This other world reacts not only on employer but on employed. For the worker it abates the fervour and stress of his task, lends meaning and justification to his demand for leisure in the face of economic demands that threaten or deny. No one in England has yet dared to erect into an evangel the obvious

truth that poor men must work.   No compulsion sets the
mental attitude a man may choose when faced with his task.
The speeder-up and the efficiency expert is hateful and alien.
" A fair day's wage for a fair day's work " may seem a loose
and questionable phrase, but its implications go very deep.
It sets a boundary mark on the frontier between flesh and
spirit by which encroachments are registered as they occur.

In America no such frontier exists.   Here the invasion
seems to be complete.   The spirit that would disentangle material from immaterial aims wanders baffled and perplexed
through a maze of loftily conceived phrases and exhortations
each one of which holds the promise of rescue from the drudgery of visionless life, yet each one of which leads back to an
altar where production is enthroned as God.   Manuals and
primers, one had almost written psalters, pour out from the
printing presses in which such words as " inspiration," " dedi-
cation," " consecration " urge American youth not to the re-
nunciation of material aims but to their intensive pursuit.
This naïve and simple creed is quite free of self-consciousness
or hypocrisy.   In its occasional abrupt transitions from the
language of prayer to such conscience-searching questions as
" Could you hold down a $100.00 a week job? " or " Would
you hire yourself? " no lapse from the sublime to the ridiculous, far less to the squalid, is felt.   It has the childlike gravity and reverence of all religions that are held in the heart.

But its God is a jealous God.   No faltering in his service,
no divided allegiance is permitted.   His rewards are concrete
and his punishments can be overwhelming.   For open rebellion, outlawry; for secret revolt, contempt and misunderstanding are his inevitable visitations.   For this reason those who
escape into heresy not unfrequently lose their integrity and are
gibbeted or pilloried for the edification of the faithful.   The
man who will not serve because the service starves and stunts
his soul is all too likely to find himself dependent for company upon the man who will not serve because his will is too
weak or his habits too dissipated.

That this service is a hard one, its most ardent advocates
make no attempt to conceal.   Its very stringency is made the
text of appeals for ever and ever fresh efficiency, intensive

training, specialization. "The pace they must travel is so swift," one advocate of strenuousness warns his disciples, "competition has become so fierce that brains and vision are not enough. One must have the *punch* to put things through." The impression grows that the American business man, new style, is a sombre gladiator, equipped for his struggle by rigorous physical and mental discipline. The impression is helped by a host of axioms, plain and pictured, that feature a sort of new cant of virility. " Red-blooded men," " Two-fisted men," " Men who do things," " Get-there fellows," are a few headliners in this gospel of push and shove.

The service is made still more difficult by its uncertainty, since no gospel of efficiency can greatly change the proportion of rewards, though it can make the contest harder and the marking higher. Year in year out, while competition intensifies and resources are fenced off, insecurity of employment remains, an evil tradition from days when opportunity was really boundless and competition could be escaped by a move of a few score miles Westward. Continuity in one employment still remains the exception rather than the rule, and when death or retirement reveals an instance it is still thought worthy of space in local journals. " Can you use me? " remains the customary gambit for the seeker after employment. The contempt of a settled prospect, of routine work, the conception of business as something to work *up* rather than to work *at* is still latent in the imagination of atavistic and ambitious young America. Of late years this restlessness, even though in so worthy a cause as " getting on," has been felt as a hindrance to full efficiency, and the happy idea has been conceived of applying the adventurous element of competition at home. Territorial or departmental spheres are allotted within or without the " concern " to each employé; the results attained by A, B, and C are then totalled, analyzed, charted, and posted in conspicuous places where all may see, admire, and take warning. In the majority of up-to-date houses " suggestions " for the expansion or improvement of the business are not only welcomed but expected, and the employé who does not produce them in reasonable bulk and quality is slated for the " discard." When inventiveness tires, " shake-ups " on a scale unknown in England take place, and new aspirants eager to " make good " step into the shoes of the old. The business athletes strain and pant toward the goal. There is no rest for the young man " consecrated " to merchandising effort. Like the fly in the fable, he must struggle and swim until the milk around his legs is churned into the butter of executive position.

The American press, hybrid, highly coloured, and often written by men of vagrant genius who prefer the sorry wages of news writing to the commercial yoke, conveys but a partial idea of this absorption of an entire race in a single function. A far more vivid impression is to be gained from the " house organs," and publicity pamphlets which pour from the press in an unceasing stream and the production of which within recent years has become a large and lucrative industry. Here articles and symposia on such themes as " Building Character into Salesmanship," " Hidden Forces that bring Sales," and " Capitalizing Individuality," often adorned with half-tones of tense and joyless faces, recur on every page. No sanctuary is inviolable, no recess unexplored. The demand of the commercial God is for the soul, and he will be content with no less.

This demand implies a revised conception of the relation between employé and employer. The old contract under which time and effort were hired for so many hours a day at a stated remuneration, leaving life, liberty, and the pursuit of happiness outside those hours a matter of personal predilection, is now abrogated, or at least sharply questioned. It is recognized, and with entire logic, that the measure of accomplishment within working hours will depend largely on the environment amid which hours of recreation are spent; and that though detection of inefficiency is a task of keen brains that seldom fail, this detection, in the nature of things, may not take place until damage has been done the commercial structure. This is the real inwardness of a whole new gospel of " Welfare " and " Uplift," under whose dispensation employés are provided with simple and tested specifics for recreation, with the watchful and benevolent eye of department heads upon them, in which it is presumed and stated with entire candour that the physical, moral, and mental efficiency of the staffs and " salesforce " has become the concern of the organization that has allotted them a place in its economy. The organism works, plays, rests, moves on together.

Nothing is more terrifying, as that master of terror, Edgar Allan Poe, perceived, than an organism that is at once mean and colossal. Properties of efficiency and adaptation to one definite end are bestowed in an eminent degree only on the lower orders of animal life. With rigid bodies, encasing organs that are designed for simple, metabolic purposes, armed with an elaborate mechanism of claws, hinges, borers, valves, and suckers the lepidoptera are living tools that fly or creep. Absorbed in one tireless function, with all distractions of love and war delegated to specialized subspecies, they neither love, hate, nor rebel. As the scale ascends, efficiency dwindles, until in the litter and loneliness of the den, lazy domesticity with dam and cubs, the joy of prey hunt and love hunt, between the belly pinch of hunger and the sleep of repletion, the lives of the big carnivora pass in a sheer joy of living for living's sake until the gun of the hunter ends the day dream.

It has been left for man—hapless and inventive—to realize a life that touches both ends of the scale, to feel at his heart the pull of hive-life and jungle-life in turn. Something of the ant and something of the tiger lurks in every normal human creature. If he has immense powers of assertion, his faculty for abdication seems to be as limitless. It is just this dual nature in man that makes prophecy as to what " will happen the world " so difficult and unsafe. But one prophecy may be ventured on and that is, that in proportion as acquiescence or revolt seize the imaginations of separated nations will those nations coalesce or drift apart into antagonism.

If a life spent during the last twenty years between England and the United States is any title to judge, I should say that at the present moment the dominant note in America is acquiescence in, and in England revolt against the inordinate demands of commercialism. Here, to all appearances, the surrender for the moment is complete. There are revolts, but they are sporadic and misguided and their speedy suppression seems to stir no indignation and to awaken no thrill of common danger among the body of workers. Strikes confined to wage issues are treated more indulgently, but even they are generally strangled at their birth by injunctions, and a sour or hostile attitude of authority makes success difficult. In any display of opposition to established conditions, even when based on the most technical grounds, authority appears to sense a challenge to larger issues and to meet them half way with a display of force that to an Englishman appears strangely over-adequate. It is evident the ground is being tested. Interpretations of liberty that date from easier and roomier days are under revision, and where they are found at variance with a conception of society as a disciplined and productive force, they are being roughly retrenched. The prevailing character of the labour mass, at once heterogeneous and amorphous, makes it a safe and ductile medium for almost any social experiment. " If you don't like it, go back," is an argument to which no answer has been found. Native-born labour shares in the universal dis-esteem and takes refuge from it in aristocratic and doctrinaire federations whose ineffectiveness is apparent whenever a labour issue arises. For the rebel who, under these conditions, chooses to fight on, rougher methods are found. He may become *fera natura*. Tarring and feathering, ducking and rubbing with acid, and deportation from State to State may be his portion. Under any social condition conformity is the easiest course. When the prison cell and social pillory are its alternatives, to resist requires a degree of fanatical courage and interior moral resources possessed only by a handful of men in a generation.

To this conception of a disciplined community harnessed to the purpose of production, thousands of the possessing and capitalistic classes look wistfully from the other side of the Atlantic. But there are many obstacles to its realization in England. The English proletarian is no uprooted orphan, paying with docile and silent work for the citizenship of his children and grandchildren. That great going concern, the British Empire, is his personal work, built on the bones and cemented with the blood of his forebears. His enfranchisement is as complete as his disinheritance, and the impoverishment of his country, evidenced in the stream of gold that pours Westward like arterial blood, has not reached to his spirit. Even the Great

War, with its revelation to him of how ruthless and comprehensive the demands of the State on the individual can be, has only reinforced his sense of being a very deserving person and has added to the long debt which he is frankly out to collect. The promises, the appeals to national pride and tradition with which he had to be appeased while, for the first time in his history, the yoke of universal service was laid upon his neck, trip up the feet of his rulers to-day. It is difficult to tell him to go elsewhere, for he "belongs" in England. Even suggestions that he should emigrate wholesale to British colonies in order to relieve the congested labour market are received with mocking laughter in which a threat lurks. He is, I am sure, because I know him, looking on with a certain sardonic relish and enjoyment at the flurries, the perplexities of his rulers, their displays of force alternated with appeals to sweet reason, their brave words succeeded by abject denials and qualifications. He is waiting until the naked economic question, which he knows well underlies all the rhodomontade of national greatness and imperial heritage, shall be put to him. It will be a great and momentous day when the Englishman is given his choice. A choice it must be. The means to compulsion are not here.

To America just now Europeans as a whole must seem a helpless race, bewildered actors in a vast and tragic blunder. To thousands of Red Cross workers, Knights of Columbus, and welfare auxiliaries in devastated districts, the spectacle of suffering and want must have come home to reinforce impressions already gained from sights witnessed at Ellis Island or Long Wharf. None the less, it is an historical misfortune that the first real contact between the people of the two continents should have come at a time when the older was bankrupt and had little to show save the rags and tatters of its civilization. The reverse of the tenderness to the stricken European abroad has been a hardening of the heart to the immigrant at home, and it is difficult for the American, schoolmaster and lawgiver to so many alien peoples in his own country, to divest himself of a didactic character in his foreign relations. To many countries he is "saying it with flour," and those who accept the dole can do little else than swallow the sermon. Even to those countries who were his allies he does shine forth in a certain splendour of righteousness. His sacrifice was deliberate— which is, perhaps, its best excuse for being a little conscious. It was self-imposed, and fifty thousand of his dead, wrested from productive enterprises to lie in France, attest its sincerity. No Englishman, at any rate, believes in his heart that its material reward, great and inevitable as it is now seen to be, was the driving force at the time the sacrifice was accepted. There are a host of reasons, some creditable, others less so, that make Europe curb its restiveness under American homilies.

With England the case is different. No one knows just how hard Britain has been hit, but she is managing to put a good face on her wounds. No relief organization from the big sister has landed its khaki-clad apostles of hygiene and its grey-cloaked sisters of mercy on English shores. The façade is intact, the old masters in possession. With a few shifts and changes in political labelling that are a matter of domestic concern, those who steered the big concern into the bankruptcy of war are still entrusted with its extrication. No great subversion stands as a witness of a change of national faith. The destinies, the foreign relations, the aspects that attract or antagonize remain in the hands of men who secured a fresh lease of power by a clever political trick. The skeleton at the feast of racial reunion is not Ireland, nor Mesopotamia, nor Yap, nor the control of the seas. It is the emergence into political power, sooner or later, but inevitably from the very nature of British political institutions, of the British proletariat.

Frankly I do not see, when this moment arrives, who is going to put the gospel of American civilization into terms that will be, I shall not say acceptable, but even significant, to the emancipated British worker. Ruling classes in the older country who rely on a steadying force from across the Atlantic in possible political upheavals must have strange misgivings when they take account of their own stewardship. It will be an ungrateful task to preach the doctrine of salvation through work to a people that has tried it out so logically and completely that the century which has seen the commercial supremacy of their country has witnessed the progressive impoverishment and proletarization of its people. Homilies on discipline will sound strangely in the ears of those who, while America was enjoying her brief carnival of spacious and fruitful endeavour in a virgin land, went under an industrial yoke that has galled their necks and stunted their physical growth. Appeals to pride of race will have little meaning coming from a stock that has ceased through self-indulgence or economic upward pressure to resist ethnographically and whose characteristics are disappearing in the general amalgam.

The salient fact that stands out from all history is that inordinateness of any sort has never failed to act upon the English character as a challenge. His successes, whatever his libellists may seek to believe, have seldom been against the small or weak. It has been his destiny, in one recurrent crisis after another, to find himself face to face with some claimant to world power, some " cock of the walk." To use a homely phrase, it has always been " up to him." And the vision of his adversary which has nerved his arm has always been an excess in some quality easily understandable by the average man. Bigotry is not the monopoly of the Spaniard, nor commercial greed of the Hollander, nor vanity of the Frenchman, nor pomposity of the German. It would be an easy task to convict the Englishman of some share in each vice. Nevertheless history in the main has justified his instinct for proportion, his dislike for " slopping over." In something far beyond the accepted phrase, the English struggle has been a struggle for the " balance of power."

HENRY L. STUART

II. AS AN IRISHMAN SEES IT

THE application of the term " shirt-sleeve " to American diplomacy is perhaps the most concise expression of the conception we have formed in Europe of life in the United States. We imagine that it is only necessary to cross the Atlantic Ocean to find a people young and vigorous in its emancipation from ancient forms and obsolete ceremonies. The average visitor returns, after a brief tour through the more urbane centres of European imitation, and tries to startle us with a narrative in which a few picturesque crudities are supposed to indicate the democratic ease of American civilization. His mind is filled with an incoherent jumble of skyscrapers, express elevators, ice water, chewing-gum, and elevated railroads, so that his inevitable contribution to the literature relating to America becomes the mere chronicle of a tourist's experiences. Every deviation from European practice is emphasized, and in proportion to the writer's consequent personal discomfort, he will conjure up a hideous picture of uncouthness, whose effect is to confirm us in our estimate of American progress . . . or barbarism, as the case may be. If the critical stranger happens to be a well-known poet or dramatist, he will probably succeed in passing lightly over those minor inconveniences, which the generosity of wealthy admirers has prevented him from experiencing at first hand.

The consequence is that there is no subject more hopelessly involved in a cloud of voluminous complaint and banal laudation than American life as seen by the foreigner. Neither the enthusiasts nor the fault-finders have contributed much of any assistance either to Europeans or to the Americans themselves. The former accept America at its own valuation, the latter complain of precisely those things upon which the average citizen prides himself. It is not easy to decide which class of critics has helped most effectively to perpetuate the legend of American freedom; the minor commentators who hold democracy to be the cause of every offence, or the higher critics, like Viscount Bryce, who, finding no American commonwealth, proceeded to invent one. The objectors are dismissed as witnesses to the incapacity of the servile European to appreciate true liberty and equality; the well-disposed are gratefully received as evangelists of a gospel to which Americans subscribe without excessive introspection. There is something touching in the gratitude felt towards the author of " The American Commonwealth." Who would have believed that a foreigner, and a Britisher at that, could make a monument of such imposing brick with the straws of political oratory in the United States?

On one point all observers have involuntarily agreed. Whether with approval or disapproval, they have depicted for us a society which presents such marked divergencies from our own manners and customs that there is not one of us but comes to America believing that his best or worst hopes will be confirmed. It is, therefore, somewhat disconcerting to confess that neither presentment has been realized. To have passed from Continental Europe to New York, via London, is to deprive oneself of that social and intellectual shock which is responsible for the uniformly profound impression which transatlantic conditions make upon the European mind. So many continentals enjoy in the United States their first direct contact with Anglo-Saxon institutions and modes of thought that the revelation cannot fail to stimulate them. Their writings frequently testify to a naïve ignorance of the prior existence in England of what excites their dismay or admiration in America. If it be asked why, then, have Englishmen similarly reacted to the same stimuli, if acquaintance with England blunts the fine edge of perception, the reply must be: the quality of their emotion is different. The impression made upon a mind formed by purely Latin traditions necessarily differs from that received by a mind previously subjected to Anglo-Saxon influences. Consequently, the student of American life who has neither the motive of what might be called family jealousy, in the Englishman, nor the mentality, wholly innocent of alien culture, of the Latin, would seem well equipped to view the subject from another angle.

To the good European the most striking characteristic of the United States is a widespread intellectual anæmia. So far from exhibiting those traits of freedom and progress which harrow the souls of sensitive aristocrats in Europe, the American people alarm the outsider in search of stimulating ideas by their devotion to conventions and formulæ. As soon as one has learnt to discount those lesser manifestations of independence, whose perilous proximity to discourtesy gives them an exaggerated importance in the eyes of superficial critics, the conventionality of the American becomes increasingly evident. So many foreigners have been misled—mainly because of an apparent rudeness—by this show of equality, this ungraciousness in matters of service, that one hesitates at first to dismiss the unconventional American as a myth closely related to that of the " immoral Frenchman." It is only when prolonged association has revealed the timid respectability beneath this veneer of informality that it becomes possible to understand the true position of America. From questioning individuals one proceeds to an examination of the public utterances of prominent men, and the transition from the press to literature is easily made. At length comes the discovery that mentally the United States is a generation or two behind Western Europe. The rude and vigorous young democracy, cited by its admirers in extenuation of æsthetic sins of omission and commission, suddenly stands forth attired in the garment of ideas which clothed early Victorian England.

This condition is largely due to the absence of an educated class accustomed to leisure. To the American work for work's sake has a dignity unknown in Europe, where it is rare to find anybody working for mere wages if he has any means of independent subsistence, however small. In America the contrary is the case, and people who could afford to cultivate their own personalities prefer to waste their energies upon some definite business. Almost all the best that has come out of Europe has been developed in that peculiar class which sacrificed money-making for the privilege of leisure and relative independence. The only corresponding class in the United States is that of the college professors, who are an omnipresent menace to the free interplay of ideas. Terrorized by economic fears and intellectual inhibitions, they have no independence. They are despised by the plain people because of their failure to make money; and to them are relegated all matters which are considered of slight moment, namely, learning and the arts. In these fields the pedants rule unchallenged, save when some irate railroad presidents discover in their teachings the heresy of radicalism. Æsthetics is a science as incomprehensible to them as beauty, and they prefer to substitute the more homely Christian ethics. Moral preoccupations are their sole test of excellence. The views of these gentlemen and their favourite pupils fill the bookshelves and the news-stands.

The professorial guardians of Colonial precedents and traditions determine what the intellectual life of America shall be. Hence the cult of anæmia. Instead of writing out of themselves and their own lives, they aspire to nothing greater than to be classed as English. They are obsessed by the standards imposed from without, and their possible achievement is thwarted. While they are still shaking their heads over Poe, and trying to decide whether Whitman is respectable, a national literature is growing up without the guidance and help which it should expect from them. At the same time, as the official pundits have the ear of Europe, and particularly of England, American culture is known only as they reflect it. It is natural, therefore, that the European attitude should be as contemptuous as it so often is.

When the reviews publish some ignorant and patronizing dissertation on the American novel or American poetry, by an English writer, they are pained by the evident lack of appreciation. The ladies and gentlemen whose works are respectfully discussed by the professors, and warmly recommended by the reviewers, do not seem to receive the consideration due to them for their unflinching adherence to the noblest standards of academic criticism. When these torch-bearers of the purest Colonial tradition are submitted to the judgment of their " big " cousins in England, there is a noticeable condescension in those foreigners. But why should they profess to admire as the brightest stars in the American firmament what are, after all, the phosphorescent gleams of literary ghosts? Is it any wonder that the majority of Britishers can continue in the comfortable belief that there is practically no American literature worthy of serious attention?

The academic labours of American professors of literature are an easy and constant butt for English critics. Yet, they rarely think of questioning the presentation of literary America for which these gentlemen are so largely responsible. When have the Stuart Shermans and Paul Elmer Mores (and their diminutives) recognized the existence of a living American writer of genius, originality, or distinction? The only justification for their existences is their alleged capacity to estimate literary values. If they cannot do so, it is hardly surprising that their English patrons, who imagine that they are representative men, do not often penetrate the veil of Colonialism. Whatever their outward professions, the majority of Englishmen regard all other English-speaking countries as Colonies. Since they are stubborn enough when faced with undeniable proof of the contrary, as in Ireland, it is unlikely they will persuade themselves unaided that they are mistaken. When will American criticism have the courage to base the claims of contemporary literature on those works which are essentially and unmistakably American?

The mandarins, of course, have stood for reaction in all countries, and there is no intention here to acquit the European of the species. So many of his worst outrages are matters of history that it would be futile to pretend that he is untrue to type. Nevertheless, his position in Europe is measurably more human than in this country, owing to the greater freedom of intellectual intercourse. In America the mandarin is firmly established on a pedestal which rests upon the vast unculture of an immense immigrant population, enjoying for the first time the benefits of sufficient food and heat. He is obviously secure in his conviction that those qualified to challenge him —except perhaps some isolated individual—are not likely to do so, being of the same convention as himself. He belongs to the most perfect trade-union, one which has a practical monopoly of its labour. His European colleagues, on the contrary, live in constant dread of traitors from their ranks, or worse still, the advance of an opposing force manned with brains of no inferior calibre. France, for example, can boast of a remarkable roll of names which never adorned the councils of pedantry, or not until they had imposed a new tradition. The two finest minds of modern French literature, Anatole France and Rémy de Gourmont, are illustrations of this fact. France has never allowed his academic honours to restrict the daring play of his ideas; Gourmont died in the admiration of all cultivated men, although his life was a prolonged protest against the orthodox, who never succeeded in taming him.

What America requires is an unofficial *intelligentsia* as strong and as articulate as the political and literary pundits, whose purely negative attitude first exasperates, and finally sterilizes, every impulse towards originality. Only when a survey is made of the leading figures in the various departments of American life is it possible fully to realize the weight of inertia which presses upon the intellect of the country. While the spirit of enterprise and progress is stimulated and encouraged in all that relates to material advancement, the artistic and reasoning faculties are deadened. Scientific study, when directed to obviously practical ends, is the only form of mental effort which can count upon recognition and reward. It is not without its significance that the Johns Hopkins Medical School is the one learned institution in America whose fame is worldwide amongst those who appreciate original research, otherwise the names of few universities are mentioned outside academic circles. Even in the field of orthodox literary culture the mandarins have, in the main, failed to do anything positive. They have preferred to bury their talent in anæmic commentary. The reputed intellectuals are still living on a tradition bequeathed by the attenuated transcendentalism of the Bostonian era.

That tradition was, after all, but a refinement of the notorious Puritanism of New England. Having lost whatever semblance of dignity the Emersons and Thoreaus conferred upon it, its subsequent manifestations have been a decadent reversion to aboriginal barbarism. This retrograde movement, so far as it affects social life, is noticeable in the ever-increasing number of crusades and taboos, the constant probing of moral and industrial conditions, unrelated to any well-considered desire for improvement, or intelligent conception of progress. The orgies of prohibition and suppression are unbelievable to the civilized European, who has no experience of a community in which everything from alcohol to Sunday tennis has attracted the attention of the " virtuosi of vice "— to quote the phrase of a discerning critic. Innumerable commissions, committees, and boards of enquiry supplement the muck-raking of yellow journalism, and encourage espionage in social reformers. But what has the country to show for this? Probably the greatest number of bungled, unsolved, and misunderstood problems of all industrial nations of the same rank.

These debauches of virtue, however, are the direct outcome of the mental conditions fostered by those who are in a position to mould public opinion. The crowd which tolerates, or participates in, the Puritanical frenzy is merely reflecting the current political and social doctrine of the time. Occasionally the newspapers will hold a symposium, or the reviews will invite the aid of some foreign critic, to ascertain the reasons for the prevailing puerility of American fiction. Invariably it is urged, and rightly, that the novel is written by women for women. Where almost all articles of luxury are produced for female consumption, and the arts are deemed unessential to progress, the latter are naturally classed with uneconomic production destined to amuse the idle. They are left to the women, as the men explain, who have not yet understood the true dignity of leisure. They are abandoned, in other words, to the most unreal section of the community, to those centres of culture, the drama leagues and literary clubs, composed of male and female spinsters. Needless to say, any phrase or idea likely to have disturbed a mid-Victorian vicarage will be ruled out as unseemly.

The malady of intellectual anæmia is not restricted to any one department of American life. In politics, as in art and literature, there is a dread of reality. The emasculation of thought in general is such as to render colourless the ideas commonly brought to the attention of the public. Perhaps the most palpable example of this penchant for platitude is the substantial literature of a pseudo-philosophic character which encumbers the book-stores, and is read by thousands of right-thinking citizens. Namby-pamby works, it is true, exist to some extent in all Protestant countries, but their number, prevalence, and cost in America are evidence of the demand they must meet. It is not for nothing that the books of thoughtful writers are crowded from shelves amply stocked with the meditations of an Orison Swett Marden, a Henry van Dyke, or a Hamilton Wright Mabie—to mention at random some typical authors.

These moral soothsayers successfully compete with moving-picture actors, and novelists whose claim to distinction is their ability to write the best-seller of the season. If they addressed themselves only to the conventicles, the phenomenon would have less significance, but the conventicles have their own minor prophets. The conclusion, therefore, suggests itself, that these must be the leaders and moulders of American thought. The suspicion is confirmed when men of the same stamp, sometimes, indeed, the actual authors of this evangelical literature, are found holding the most important public offices. To have written a methodist-tract would appear to be an unfailing recommendation for promotion. It is rare to find the possessor of such a mentality relegated to the obscurity he deserves.

A wish to forestall the accusation of exaggeration or inaccuracy imposes the painful obligation of citing specific instances of the tendency described. Who are the leading public men of this country, and what have they written? Besides the classic volumes of Thiers and Guizot must we set such amiable puerilities as " The New Freedom," " On Being Human," and " When a Man Comes to Himself." Even the essays of Raymond Poincaré do not sound the depths indicated by the mere titles of these presidential works. But the author of "The State," for all his antiquated theories of government, writes measurably above the level of that diplomatist whose copious bibliography includes numerous variations upon such themes as " The Gospel for a World of Sin," " The First Christmas Tree," and " The Blue Flower." A search through the underworld of parish magazines in England, France, and Germany would probably reveal something to be classed with the works of Dr. Lyman Abbott, but the authors would not be entrusted with the editorship of a leading weekly review. As for the writings of his associate, the existence of his book on Shakespeare is a testimony to Anglo-Saxon indifference to the supreme genius of the race.

It is hardly necessary to dwell upon the literary labours of William Jennings Bryan, ex-Secretary of State, except to wonder that they did not alone suffice to disqualify him for such an office. They belong to the same category as those volumes of popular American philosophy whose titles are: " Character the Grandest Thing in the World," " Cheerfulness as a Life Power," and " The Miracle of Right Thought." If those quoted are to be laid to the charge of Mr. Orison Swett Marden, every department of American life contains prominent men who might say: There, but for the grace of God, speak I. The sanctimonious breath of the uplifter tarnishes the currency of ideas in almost every circle of society. Irrespective of party, Republicans, Democrats, and Socialists help to build up this monument of platitude which may one day mark the resting place of the American brain. Books, reviews, magazines, and newspapers are largely conceived in the evangelical spirit. The average contributor, when not a foreigner, suggests a Sunday-school superintendent who has (perhaps) missed his vocation. Where the subject excludes the pedantry of the professors, the tone is intensely moral, and the more it is so the surer one may be that the writer is a colonel, a rear-admiral, or a civil officer of the State or Federal government. Imagination refuses to conceive these functionaries as fulfilling their duties efficiently in any service, other than that of the Salvation Army or a revivalist campaign.

The stage of culture which these phenomena presuppose cannot but be hostile to artistic development in such as escape contamination. It has already been postulated that the just claims of ethics and æsthetics are hopelessly confounded in America, to the evident detriment of art in all its branches. To the poor quality of the current political and social philosophy corresponds an equally mediocre body of literary criticism. A recent historian of American literature accords a high place amongst contemporary critics, to the author of

" Shelburne Essays," and other works. These volumes are
dignified as " our nearest approach to those ' Causeries du
Lundi ' of an earlier age," and may well be taken as representative. Typical of the cold inhumanity which a certain
type of " cultured person " deems essential is the circumstance
related, by Mr. Paul Elmer More himself, in explanation of
the genesis of these essays. " In a secluded spot," he writes,
" in the peaceful valley of the Androscoggin I took upon myself to live two years as a hermit," and " Shelburne Essays "
was the fruit of his solitary mediations. The historian is
mightily impressed by this evidence of superiority. " In another and far more unusual way he qualified himself for his
high office of critic," says Professor Pattee, " he immured himself for two years in solitude." . . . " The period gave him
time to read leisurely, thoughtfully, with no nervous subconsciousness that the product of that reading was to be marketable."

What a revelation of combined timidity and intellectual
snobbishness there is in this attitude so fatuously endorsed
by a writer for the schools! We can imagine what the effect
of such a pose must be upon the minds of the students whom
the professor would constrain to respect. Only a young prig
could pretend to be favourably impressed by this pseudo-
Thoreau in the literary backwoods. The impulse of most
healthy young men would be to turn in contempt from an art
so unnatural as this conception of criticism implies. How are
they to know that the Taines, Sainte-Beuves, Brunetières, and
Arnolds of the world are not produced by expedients so primitive as to suggest the *mise en scène* of some latter-day Messiah,
a Dowie, or a Mrs. Baker Eddy? The heralds of new theolo-
gies may find the paraphernalia of asceticism and aloofness a
useful part of their stock in trade—neither is associated with
the great criticism of literature. The *causeries* of Sainte-Beuve
were not written in an ivory tower, yet they show no traces
of that " nervous subconsciousness " which our professor finds
inseparable from reading that is " marketable."

The suspicion of insincerity in this craving for the wilderness will be strengthened by reference to the first of Mr.
More's volumes. Whatever may have been the case of its

AS AN IRISHMAN SEES IT

successors, this work was certainly the product of his retirement. What, then, are the subjects of such a delicate nature that they could not be discussed within the sound of "the noisy jargon of the market-place"? Of the eleven essays, only four deal with writers whose proximity to the critic's own age might justify a retreat, in order that they be judged impartially, and without reference to popular enthusiasm and the prevalent fashion of the moment. The seven most substantial studies in the book are devoted to flogging horses so dead that no fear of their kicking existed. "A Hermit's Notes on Thoreau," "The Solitude of Nathaniel Hawthorne," "The Origins of Hawthorne and Poe," "The Influence of Emerson," "The Spirit of Carlyle"—these are a few of the startling topics which Mr. More could discuss only with fasting and prayer! Any European schoolmaster could have written these essays in the leisure moments of his Sunday afternoons or Easter vacation.

No more remarkable profundity or originality will be found in the critic's essays in contemporary literature. His strictures upon Lady Gregory's versions of the Irish epic, and his comments upon the Celtic Renaissance in general are the commonplaces of all hostile English criticism. "The shimmering hues of decadence rather than the strong colours of life" is the phrase in which he attempts to estimate the poetry of the Literary Revival in Ireland. In fact, for all his isolation Mr. More was obsessed by the critical cant of the hour, as witness his readiness to apply the term "decadent" to all and sundry. The work of Arthur Symons is illuminated by this appellation, as is also that of W. B. Yeats. The jargon of the literary market-place, to vary Mr. More's own *cliché*, is all that he seems to have found in that "peaceful valley of the Androscoggin." Even poor Tolstoy is branded as "a decadent with the humanitarian superimposed," an application of the word which renders its previous employment meaningless. As a crowning example of incomprehension may be cited Mr. More's opinion that the English poet, Lionel Johnson, is "the one great . . . and genuinely significant poet of the present Gaelic movement." In the circumstances, it is not surprising that he should pronounce Irishmen incapable of exploiting adequately the themes of Celtic literature. For this task he considers the Saxon genius more qualified.

With these examples before us it is unnecessary to examine the remaining volumes of " Shelburne Essays." Having started with a distorted conception of the critical office, the author naturally contributed nothing helpful to the literature of American criticism. His laborious platitudes do not help us to a better appreciation of the dead, his dogmatic hostility nullifies his judgments upon the living. Not once has he a word of discerning censure or encouragement for any rising talent. Like most of his colleagues, Mr. More prefers to exercise his faculties at the expense of reputations already established, save when he condescends to repeat the commonplaces of complaint against certain of the better known modern writers. He is so busy with Mrs. Gaskell, Charles Lamb, Milton, Plato, and Dickens that he can find time to mention only some fifteen Americans, not one of them living.

Such is the critic whom Professor Pattee salutes as " consistent " and " courageous," having " standards of criticism " which make him comparable to Sainte-Beuve. As editor of " the leading critical review of America," we are assured that Mr. More had " a dominating clientèle and a leader's authority." Alas! There can be no doubt as to this, though it is very doubtful if the fact can be regarded as " one of the most promising signs for that new literary era which already is overdue." That era will long continue overdue while criticism remains absorbed in the past, aloof from life and implacably hostile to every manifestation of originality. If the new literary generation were merely ignored its lot would be comparatively happy. But the mandarins come down periodically from their Olympic communings with George Eliot and Socrates, to fill the reviews with verbose denunciations of whatever is being written independently of their idols. The oracles having spoken, the newcomers are left with an additional obstacle in the way of their reaching the indifferent ear of the crowd. The crowd wallows in each season's literary novelties, satisfied that whatever is well advertised is good. Rather than face the subjects endorsed by the frigid enthusiasm of Mr. Paul Elmer More or Stuart Sherman, Mr. W. C. Brownell and

Professor Brander Matthews, it takes refuge in fields where the writ of pedantry does not run.   Meanwhile, the task of welcoming new talent is left to amiable journalists, whose casual recommendations, usually without any background of critical experience, are accepted as the judgments of competent experts.   The " colyumist " has to perform the true function of the critic.

Although anæmia is the dominant characteristic of intellectual life in the United States, the reaction against that condition is none the less worthy of notice.   When we remember that the fervour of righteousness is the very breath of current philosophy, we are also reminded that crudeness, sensationalism, and novelty are commonly held by Europeans to be the quintessence of America.   It might be replied, in answer to this objection, that Hearst newspapers, and the vaudeville theology of Billy Sunday, are the only alternatives to the prim conventionality of authoritative journalism, and the sanctimoniousness of popular leaders.   The man in the street obtains the illusion of strenuous cerebral activity when he contrasts the homely qualities of those prophets of democracy with the spinster-like propriety and beatific purity of prominent publicists and statesmen.   He likes to hear his master's voice, it is true, but he likes even more to hear his own, especially where his personal interests are at issue.   The æsthetic *obiter dicta* of the professors, like the language of diplomacy, are concerned with questions sufficiently remote to make sonority an acceptable substitute for thought.

In the realm of ideas, nevertheless, there is a more or less articulate expression of reaction, mainly concentrated in the larger cities of the East.   There the professional supermen and their female counterparts have come together by tacit agreement, and have attempted to shake off the incubus of respectability.   The extremists impress one as being overpowered by a sense of their own sinful identity.   In a wild burst of hysterical revolt they are plunged into a debauch of ideas from which they are emerging in a very shaken and parlous condition.   For the most part their adventures, mental and otherwise, have been in the domain of sex, with a resultant flooding of the " radical " market by varied tomes upon the subject.

What the bookstores naïvely catalogue as the literature of advanced thought is a truly wonderful *salade russe,* in which Krafft-Ebbing and Forel compete with Freud and Eugene Debs. Karl Marx, and Signora Montessori, Professor Scott Nearing, and Havelock Ellis engage the same attention as the neo-Malthusian pamphleteers, and the young ladies whose novels tell of what Flaubert called " *les souillures du mariage et les platitudes de l'adultère.*"

The natural morbidity of the Puritan mind is exasperated in advanced circles, whose interest is nothing if not catholic. Let Brieux discourse of venereal disease, or Strindberg expound his tragedies of prurience, their success is assured amongst those who would believe them geniuses, rather than risk the ignominy of agreement with the champions of orthodoxy. So long as our European pornographers are serious and inartistic, they need have no fear of America. Unbalanced by prolonged contemplation of the tedious virtues of New England, a generation has arisen whose great illusion is that the transvaluation of all values may be effected by promiscuity. Lest they should ever incur the suspicion of conservatism the emancipated have a permanent welcome for everything that is strange or new. The blush on the cheek of the vice-crusader is their criterion of excellence.

By an irony of fate, however, they are condemned to the disheartening spectacle of their moral bogies being received into a society but one removed from the Olympians themselves. In recent years it has been the practice of the latter to accept certain reputations, when they have passed through the sieve of the literary clubs and drama leagues. In fact, candidates for academic immortality frequently serve on the board of these literary filtration plants. While the mandarins execute their ritual in the cult of Longfellow and Bryant, and excommunicate heretical moderns, their servitors are engaged upon an ingenious task. They discover the more innocuous subjects of " radical " enthusiasm, deprive them of whatever sting of originality their work possesed, and then submit the result discreetly to the official pundits. When these judges have satisfied themselves as to the sterility of the innovations, their imprimatur is granted, and another mediocrity is canonized.

Ibsen is saluted because of his "message," and "Anna Karenina" becomes a masterpiece, because Tolstoy was a Christian. While remarkable talents at home are ignored or vilified, the fifth-rate European is in the process of literary naturalization. Mr. Masefield receives the benediction of Paul Elmer More, who in the same breath tries to convince us that he is qualified to pronounce "The Spoon River Anthology" a bad joke.

Nothing more clearly demonstrates the futility and disrepute of criticism in this country than the constant surrenders to the prestige of the foreigner. A cheap fashion in European literature has only to be thrust with sufficient publicity upon the women's literary clubs, and parish meeting-houses, to ensnare the uneasy wearers of the academic crown. Give them time and they will be found praising a translated French poet for precisely those qualities which offend them in the protégés of Miss Harriet Monroe. The young Englishman, Rupert Brooke, might have contributed to "Poetry" for ten years without securing any more recognition than did the American, Robert Frost. But now both reputations, made in England, are widely accepted, and the inevitable professor is found to tread respectfully where Henry James rushed in. Compare the critical essays which James wrote during a period of thirty years with the stereotyped Bostonian theses of the men he left behind him. Yet nobody will accuse James of a disregard for tradition.

The American word "standpatter" is curiously precise as a designation of the species. The conservative critic in Europe, Brunetière, for example, is never so purely negative as his counterpart on this side of the Atlantic. When Brunetière adversely criticized the Symbolist movement in French poetry he did so intelligently, not in that laboriously facetious fashion which is affected by the Stuart Shermans and W. H. Boyntons when they are moved to discuss *les jeunes*. Brunetière, in a word, was a man of education and culture, capable of defending rationally his own theories, without suggesting that the unfamiliar was necessarily bad. He condemned the excesses of the new school, not the school itself. If he had been in America, he would have denied the Symbolists even the right

to exist. Edward Dowden might also be cited as a similar
example, in English literature, of enlightened conservatism.
Dowden was partly responsible for bringing Whitman to the
favourable notice of the English public, and his work stands
as a proof that respect for the classics does not involve hostility to the moderns.   Just as he was able to write a masterpiece of Shakespearean criticism without retiring into her-
mitage, so he was qualified to appreciate original genius when
it presented itself.   He was not paralyzed, in short, by the
weight of his literary traditions and conventions.

A thousand and one reasons have been advanced to explain
the absence of a genuine American literature, and all of them
are probably true.   The country is comparatively young, and
its energies have been, are still, directed chiefly towards the
exploitation of material resources and the conquest of natural
difficulties.   Racially the nation is in an embryonic stage, and
until some homogeneity is attained the creation of a native
tradition must be slow.   Moreover, the conflict of diverse races
implies, in a broad sense, the clash of two or more civilizations, one of which must impose its culture if any organized
progress is to be made.   The language of the Hyphenated
States is English, but to what extent will the nation in being
evolve in accordance with this linguistic impulse?   Will it be
Anglo-Saxon, Teutonic, Latin, or Slav?   These are a few of
the problems which have a direct bearing upon the intellectual development of the country.   They must be solved before America can give her imprint to the arts.   They cannot
be solved by the assumption that the Anglo-Saxon hyphen is
alone authentic.   The permanent hypothesis of Colonialism
must be abandoned, if " Americanization " is ever to be more
than the silliest political cant.   Puritanism must be confined
to the conventicles, to its natural habitat.   It must not be
allowed to masquerade as art, philosophy, and statesmanship.
The evangelical tyranny exists elsewhere, but only in America
has it invaded every branch of the national life.   In the more
impatient and realistic generation which has emerged from the
world war this monstrous extension of prohibitions is arousing
a violent reaction.   It is rare now to find a young American
who does not cry out against American civilization.

To the disinterested European, this spectacle is an affecting illustration of what may be called the enchantment of distance. Evidently these disconsolate citizens imagine that there is a way of escape from the Presbyterian wilderness, an oasis in the desert of one hundred per cent. Americanism, where every prospect pleases and man is only relatively vile. One listens to the *intelligentsia,* rendered more than usually loquacious by generous potations of unconstitutional Scotch whiskey, cursing the subtle blow to the arts administered by the Volstead denial of the necessary ambrosia. Advanced thinkers revelling in the delights of a well-organized polygamy, have taken me aside to explain how the prophets of Methodism have laid waste this fair land. I have read desperate appeals to all young men of spirit to shake off the yoke of evangelistic philistinism by expatriation to more urbane centres of culture.

These are brave words, coming as they do, for the most part, from those who are in no wise incommoded by the ukases of the gospel-tent tyrants, and who have taken appropriate measures to defeat the Eighteenth Amendment. Back of all their plaints is the superstition that Europe is free from the blight which makes America intolerable in their eyes. They do not know that the war has almost destroyed the Europe of a civilized man's affections. Socially, politically, and intellectually that distracted continent is rapidly expiring in the arms of profiteers and class-conscious proletarians, who have decided between them to leave not a blade of culture upstanding. The leisured class, which was rarely the wealthiest, is being ground out of existence by the plutocracy and the proletariat. That was the class which made the old Europe possible, yet there are Americans who go on talking as if its extinction did not knock the bottom out of their utopia. Most of these disgruntled Americans are radicals, who strive to forward the designs of the plain people and their advocates.

Yet, every European knows that if prohibition is making the headway it surely is, the chief reason must be sought in the growth of radicalism. From Bernard Shaw to Trotsky, our revolutionaries are " dry." Their avowed ideal is a state of society in which the allurements of love are reduced to a eugenic operation, the mellowing influences of liquor are abolished, and compulsory labour on the Taylor efficiency plan of scientific management is substituted. In fine, by the benign workings of democratic progress Europe is moving steadily toward the state of affairs attributed here by disillusioned intellectuals to the sinister machinations of Wall Street and the evangelists.

No doubt America was a purer and happier place in 1620 than in 1920. No Sumner was needed to keep the eyes of the settlers from the dimpled knees of Ziegfeld's beauties, and the platitudes of the Wilsonian epoch were the brightest flowers of wisdom in 1776. Alas! that it should be so, and in every country of our Western World. If the Magna Charta were to be offered for signature in London now, some nasty Bolshevik would be sure to prove that the document was drawn up in a private conclave of the international financiers. If Lincoln were to make his Gettysburg speech to-day the world would snicker irreverently, and a dreadfully superior person, with a Cambridge accent (like John Maynard Keynes, C.B.), would publish the " Economic Consequences of the Civil War," full of sardonic gibes at the innocent evangelism of Springfield. As for the Declaration of Independence—well, during " the late unpleasantness " we saw what happened to such un-American sedition-mongers. In fine, things are not what they used to be; we pine for what is not, and so forth. Of this only we may be sure, that America corresponds neither more nor less than any other country to the dreams of its ancestors.

Indeed, to be more affirmative in this plea for America, it is probable that this country has followed more closely the intentions of its founders than the critics will admit. Unlike most European nations, the Americans have preserved, with an almost incomprehensible reverence, the constitution laid down to meet conditions entirely unlike those of the 20th century. Ancestor worship is the cardinal virtue of America and surpasses that of China and Japan, where revolutionary changes have been made in the whole social and political structure. America was created as a political democracy for the benefit of staunch individualists, and both these ends have been achieved to perfection. Everything against which the supersensitive revolt has come about *planmaessig,* and existed in the germ from the day when the Pilgrim Fathers first brought the blessings of Anglo-Saxon civilization to the shores of Cape Cod.

In the South alone were traces of a *Weltanschauung* which might have given an impulse in another direction, but the South went under, in obedience to the rules of democratic Darwinism. Once the dissatisfied American can bring himself to look the facts of his own history and of contemporary Europe in the face, he may be forced to relent. He will grant, at least, that it is useless to cherish the notion that the ills the American mind is heir to are spared to other peoples. He may even come to recognize the positive virtues of this country, where the stories in the *Saturday Evening Post* actually come true. Here a man can look his neighbour straight in the eye and subscribe—without a smile—to the romantic credo that all men are equal, in so far as it is possible by energy, hard work, and regular attendance at divine service, to reach the highest post in any career. Class barriers are almost unknown, and on all sides there is an endlessly generous desire to learn, to help, and to encourage. The traditional boy can still arrive from the slums of Europe and finish up in the editorial chair of a wealthy newspaper. If he ever fails to do so it can only be because he starts by reading the *Liberator,* and devotes to the deciphering of Thorstein Veblen's hieroglyphics of socialism the time which should have been given to mastering the more profitable technique of Americanism.

ERNEST BOYD

III. AS AN ITALIAN SEES IT

IN a typical form of primitive society, where institutions and ideals, collective representations and individual reactions, coincide, no distinction can be made between culture and civilization. Every element of the practical culture is a spiritual symbol, and there is no other logic or reason than that which is made manifest by the structure and habits of the social group. Life is a religion, in the two meanings of the word, that of a binding together of men, and the deeper one—of gathering the manifold activities of the individual in one compact spiritual mass. The mythical concepts, which limit and integrate the data of experience, in a sphere which is neither purely imaginative nor purely intellectual, present to the individual mind as irresistibly as to the mind of the group, a world of complementary objects which are of the same stuff as the apprehended data. Thought—practical, æsthetic, ethical—is still undifferentiated, unindividualized, as if a collective mind were an active reality, a gigantic, obscure, coherent personality, entering into definite relations with a world homogeneous with itself.

Such an abstract, ideal scheme of the life of the human spirit before it has any history, before it is even capable of history, affords, in its hypothetical indistinction (within the group, within the individual), a prefiguration of a certain higher relationship of culture with civilization, of a *humana civilitas*, in which the practical should be related to the spiritual, nature to the mind, in the full light of consciousness, with a perfect awareness of the processes of distinction and individualization. In the twilight and perspective of historical knowledge, if not in their actuality, Greece before Socrates, Rome before Christ, the Middle Ages before Saint Francis (each of them, before the apparition of the disrupting and illuminating element of growth), are successive attempts or *étapes* towards the creation of a civilization of such a kind— a human civilization.

Between these two limits—the primitive and the human—the ideal beginning and the ideal end—we can recognize, at any given moment in history, through the segmentation and aggregation of a multitude of cultures, different ages and strata of culture coexisting in the same social group; and the individual mind emerges at the confluence of the practical cultures, with science and philosophy and the ethical, non-tribal ideals, germs and *initia* of the human civilization remaining above the given society as a soul that never entirely vivifies its own body.   History begins where first the distinction between civilization and culture appears, or, to state the same fact from a different angle, where individual consciousness is born.   It ends, ideally, where the same distinction fades away into Utopia, or death, or the Kingdom of Heaven; where the highest form of individual consciousness is at no point higher than the consciousness of the group from which it originally differentiated itself.

The writer of these pages belongs, by birth, education, and election, to the civilization of Rome and to the culture, or cultures, of Italy.   The civilization of Rome, the *latina civilitas*, is a complex mind, whose successive phases of growth are the abstract humanism of ancient Greece, the civic and legal humanism of Rome, the moral and spiritual humanism of the Latin church, the æsthetic and metaphysical humanism of the Renaissance.   Each phase is an integration of the preceding one and the acquisition of a new universal principle, made independent of the particular social body in which it has partially realized itself before becoming a pure, intelligible ideal, an essential element of the human mind.   The first three phases, Greece, Rome, and the Church, are still more or less closely associated, in relation to the forms of humanism which are peculiar to each of them, with particular cultures.   But the last one, which, in its progress from the 13th century to our days, has been assimilating, purifying, and clarifying all the preceding ones, does not, at any given moment, directly connect itself with any definite social body.   In its inception, as a purely Italian Renaissance, it may appear as the spiritual form of Italian society from the 13th to the 15th century; but its apparition coincides with the natural growth of the several, sharply defined European nationalities, and very soon (and apart from the evident insufficiency of any individual nation to fulfil its spiritual exigencies) it manifests its intrinsic character of universality by overflowing the frontiers of Italy and becoming the law of the whole Western European world.

The history of Europe during the last six centuries is the history of the gradual penetration of that idea within the circle of the passively or actively resistant, or inert, local, national cultures. The Reformation, of all active resistances, is the strongest and most important. The Germanic tribes rebel against the law of Rome, because a delay of from five to ten centuries in the experience of Christianity, and an experience of Christianity to be made not on a Græco-Roman, but on an Odinic background, create in them the spiritual need of an independent elaboration of the same universal principles. Germany is practically untouched by the spirit of the Renaissance until the 18th century, and Italy herself is for two centuries reduced to spiritual and political servitude by the superior material strength which accompanies and sustains the spiritual development of the nations of the North. Through the whole continent, within the single national units, as well as between nation and nation, the contrast and collaboration of the Romanic and Germanic elements, of Renaissance and Reformation, is the actual dialectic of the development of European civilization: of the successive approximations of the single cultures, or groups of cultures, in a multitude of more or less divergent directions, with alternating accelerations and involutions, towards the common form, the *humana civilitas*.

Of all the nations of Europe, Italy is the only one that, however contingently and imperfectly, has actually realized all of the four phases of humanism in a succession of historical cultures: Magna Græcia, the Roman Empire, the Catholic Church, the Renaissance. And as each of these successive cultures was trying to embody in itself a universal, not a particular, principle, nationality in Italy is not, as for other nations, the acceptance of certain spiritual limits elaborated from within the social body, but a reaction to the pressure of adjoining nationalities, which presented themselves as obstacles and impediments, even within the life of Italy herself, to the realization of a super-national principle. This is the process through which the humanism of the Renaissance, after having received its abstract political form at the hands of the thinkers and soldiers of the French Revolution, becomes active and militant in Mazzini's principle of nationality, which is a heroic effort towards the utilization of the natural growth of European nations for the purposes of a universal civilization.

The distance between that civilization and the actual cultures of the nations of Europe can easily be measured by the observer of European events during the last seven years. To that civilization belong the ideals, to those cultures, the realities, of the Great War. And all of us who have thought and fought in it have souls which are irremediably divided between that civilization and those cultures. If we should limit ourselves to the consideration of present facts and conditions, we might well give way to despair: not for a good many years in the past have nationalities been so impervious to the voice of the common spirit as they are in Europe to-day. And the sharp contrast between ideals and realities which has been made visible even to the blind by the consequences of the war, has engendered a temper of violence and cynicism even among those rare men and parties who succeeded in keeping their ideals *au dessus de la mêlée,* and therefore did not put them to the destructive test of a promise which had to be broken.

The moral problem which every nation of Europe will have to labour at in the immediate future, is that of the relations of its historical culture or cultures with the exigencies of the *humana civilitas.* It is the problem that presents itself more or less dimly to the most earnest and thoughtful of Europeans, when they speak of the coming " death of our civilization," or of the "salvaging of civilization." To many of them, it is still a problem of institutions and technologies: its essentially spiritual quality does not seem to have been thoroughly grasped as yet. But it is also the problem that confronts, less tragically, with less urgency, but not less inevitably, this great

European Commonwealth which has created its own life on the North American continent for the space of the last three centuries.

This European Commonwealth of America owes its origin to a small number of adventurers and pilgrims, who brought the seeds of English culture to the new world. Let us very rapidly attempt a characterization of that original culture.

England holds as peculiar and distinctive a position among the nations of Europe as Italy. She is the meeting-point of the Romanic and Germanic elements in European history; and if her culture may appear as belonging to the family of mediterranean cultures (to what we have called the *latina civilitas*), to an English Catholic, like Cardinal Newman, there was a time, and not very remote, when the Protestant could be proud of its Teutonic associations. From a Catholic and Franco-Norman mediæval England, logically emerges, by a process similar to that exemplified by Italy and France and Spain, the England of Henry VIII and Elizabeth, of Shakespeare and the Cavaliers: Renaissance England. She flourishes between the suppression of the monasteries and the suppression of the theatres. She moulds, for all centuries to come, the æsthetic and political mind of the English people. But she carries the germs of a widely different culture in her womb: she borrows from them, already during the Elizabethan age, some traits that differentiate her from all other Renaissance cultures. And these germs, slowly gaining impetus through contrast and suppression, ultimately work her overthrow with the short-lived triumph of Cromwell and the Puritans.

After 1688, the law of English life is a compromise between Puritan and Cavalier, between Renaissance and Reformation, which sends the extreme representatives of each type out of the country, builders of an Empire of adventurers and pilgrims—while at home the moderate Cavalier, and the moderate Puritan, the Tory and the Whig, establish a Republic with a King, and a Parliamentary feudal régime. But the successive stages of English culture do not interest us at this point, except in so far as America has always remained closer to England than to any other European nation, and has again and again relived in her own life the social, political, spiritual experiences of the Mother Country.

It is from the two main directions of English spiritual life that America, through a double process of segmentation, Elizabethan or Cavalier in the South, Puritan in the North, draws the origins of her own life. It is in the Cavalier and the Puritan, still within the circle of English life, that the germs of American culture must be sought. The peculiar relations of the Cavalier and the Puritan to the general design of European civilization define the original attitude of this Commonwealth beyond the sea towards the other European cultures, and are the origins of the curves which, modified in their development by the addition of new elements and by the action of a new, distinctive environment, American culture has described and will describe in the future.

Puritanism is essentially a culture and not a civilization. The Puritan mind, in its quest for an original Christian experience, falls upon the Old Testament and the Ancient Law. The God of the tribes of Israel becomes its God, a God finding a complete expression in the law that rules his chosen people. A compact, immovable spiritual logic, a set of fixed standards, a rhetoric of the virtues, the identification of any element of growth and change with the power of evil, a dualistic morality, and the consequent negation of a spiritually free will, these are the characteristics of Puritanism, constituting at the same time, and with the same elements, a system of truth and a system of conduct. In both the meanings in which we have used the word religion at the beginning of this essay, Puritanism is a perfect, final religion. Transplanted to America when Europe was slowly becoming conscious of the metaphysical implications of the destruction of the old Cosmology— when the discovery of an infinite universe was depriving a purely transcendent divinity of the place it had been given beyond the limits of a finite universe—the infinite universe itself being manifest, in the words of Bruno, as *lo specchio della infinita deità*,—it gave birth to an intrinsically static culture, standing out against a background of transcendental thought.

The principles of growth in Puritanism were not specifically

Puritan: they were those universal values that Puritan discipline succeeded in rediscovering because every moral discipline,
however fettered by its premises, will inevitably be led towards
them. Quite recently, a sincere and ardent apologist of Puritanism recognized in a document which he considers as the
highest expression of that culture in America, a paraphrase of
the Roman *dulce et decorum*. The irrationality which breaks
through the most hermetically closed system of logic, in the
process of life, asserts itself by extracting from a narrowly
institutional religion values which are not dependent upon a
particular set of institutions, nor are valid for one people only.
But we might detect the germs of that irrationality already in
the very beginnings of the system, when Milton adds the whole
weight of the Roman tradition to the Puritan conception of
democracy—or in the divine words of the Gospels, through
which in all times and places every *anima naturaliter christiana*
will hear the cry of Love rebelling against the letter of the
Ancient Law.

What the Cavalier brought to America, we should have to
investigate only if we were tracing the history of divergent
directions, of local cultures: because the original soul of America is undoubtedly the Puritanic soul of New England, and
the South, even before the War of Secession, in relation to the
main direction, to the general culture, has a merely episodical
significance. Yet, though the founders of New England were
only Puritans, certain traits of the Cavalier spirit, the adventurer in the pilgrim, will inevitably reappear in their descendants, repeating the original dichotomy in the generations issu-
ing from an apparently pure stock: partly, because a difference in beliefs is not always the mark of a fundamental
difference in temperaments, and partly because those traits
correspond to some of the generally human impulses suppressed by the choice of the Puritan.

There is one element which is common to Puritan and
Cavalier in America, and which cannot be said to belong in
precisely the same fashion to their ancestors in England. It
is, in England and the rest of Europe, a mythology formed
by similar hopes and desires, by a similar necessity of giving
an imaginary body to certain thoughts and aspirations, on the

part of the spirit of the Renaissance as well as of the spirit of the Reformation: a mythology which, in the mind of the European during the centuries between the discovery of America and the French Revolution, inhabits such regions as the island of Utopia, the city of the Sun, and the continent of America. In that mythology, Utopism and American exoticism coincide. But the adventurer and the pilgrim were actually and firmly setting their feet on one of the lands mapped in that purely ideal geography, and thoughts and aspirations confined by the European to the continent of dreams, became the moral exigencies of the new Commonwealth. Thus America set herself against Europe as the ideal against the real, the land of the free, and the refuge of the oppressed; and was confirmed in such a position by her natural opportunities, by the conditions of pioneer life, by contrast to European despotism—finally, by the Revolution and the Constitution, in which she felt that the initial moral exigencies were ultimately fulfilled. It is to this myth of a Promised Land, which is neither strictly Puritan nor strictly Cavalier, and yet at times seems to coincide with the less static aspects of Puritanism, that a peculiarly American idealism, unconquerable by defeat and even by the evidence of facts, abstract, self-confident, energetic, youthful and optimistic, owes its strength and its courage: an idealism which is hardly conscious of what Europe has been taught by centuries of dire experience—the irreparable contingency and imperfection of history; and which believes, as firmly as the Puritan legislator believes it, that such institutions have been devised, or can be devised, through which the ideal law, when thought out and written, will not fail to become the law of reality for all times to come.

From two contrasting elements, a firm belief in a Law which was at the beginning, and a romantic mythology, a third characteristic of the American mind is thus engendered: a full confidence in the power of intellect conceived as a mechanism apt to contrive practical schemes for the accomplishment of ideal ends. This intellectual faith is similar in its static nature to the moral faith of the Puritan: it is the material weapon of Puritanism. Perfectibility is within its reach, but not the actual processes of evolution. The intellect that does not conceive itself as a process or function, but as a mechanism, can tend towards, and theoretically possess, a state of perfection, but will resent and condemn the gropings and failings of actual, imperfect growth and change. Not without reason, the greatest individual tragedy of the war, in a typically American mind confronted with the sins and misery of Europe, was a tragedy of intellectual pride: of the inability of a static intellect to become charitably active in the tragic flux of European life; a tragedy which a little moral and intellectual humility might well have spared to the generous hopes of America, and the childish, messianic faith which irradiated for only too short a time the bleeding soul of Europe.

If we have called Puritanism a culture, what name shall we reserve for that vast and complicated collection of mechanical contrivances which constitute the material body of American society to-day? We are in the presence of a technology, a more highly developed one, perhaps (with the possible exception of Germany before the war), than any that has ever existed in the world. Technologies have a logic of their own, and that logic is apt to take the place of higher spiritual constructions; either when conditions of life lend a miraculous character to the means of sustaining life itself and invest the practical actions of hunting or agriculture with a religious significance; or when the complexity of their organization is such that the workings of that practical logic inevitably transcend the power of observation of the individual agent, however highly placed in the machinery itself, and moral or intellectual myths are born of an imperfect knowledge. This is the case of America, and in America this technological or industrial mythology has crushed out of existence the rival myths of the farms and the prairie, allowing them a purely romantic value and decorative function, through the industrially controlled power of the press. Even pioneering, and the conquest of the West, a process in which Americans of another age found an energetic, if partly vicarious, satisfaction for certain moral and ideal yearnings, has receded, in the mind of Americans of to-day, into the shades of a fabulous and solemn background.

The industrial revolution followed in America the lines of

development of its early English model. This commonwealth
beyond the sea, agricultural and democratic, found in itself the
same elements which gave birth in the original country to an
industrial feudalism, grafting itself, without any solution of
continuity, on a feudalism of the land. The ineradicable
optimism of the American invested the whole process with
the same halo of moral romance which had coloured the age
of pioneering, and accepted as a useful substitute (or rather, as
a new content) for Puritanic moralism the philosophy of opportunity and of success constantly commensurate with true merit.
The conception of intellect as a mechanism to be used for
moral and ideal ends, gave way to a similar though more complex conception, modelled not on the methods of pure science,
from whose early conquests the revolution itself had been
started, but on those of applied science or of practical machinery.

When, in the natural course of events, the bonds which
kept together the purely economic elements of the country
became more powerful and real than any system of political
institutions, when, in fact, a financial syndicalism became the
structure underlying the apparent organs of government, all
the original ideals of America had already gathered to the
defence of the new order. Hence the extraordinary solidity of
the prevailing economic system in this country, when compared with any European country. Economic, as well as political systems, ultimately rest on convictions rather than on
sheer force, and the radical in America, in all spheres of
thought, is constantly in the necessity of fighting not mere
institutions, as in Europe, but institutionalized ideals, organisms and personalities which establish their right on the same
assumptions which prompt him in his rebellion. There is less
difference in fundamentals between a Carnegie and a Debs
than between any two individuals placed in similar positions
in Europe.

An interesting by-product of this particular development is
the myth of the captain of industry, possessed, in the popular
imagination, of all the virtues. And a consequence of this
myth is an unavoidable revision of the catalogue of virtues,
from which some were expunged that do not lead to industrial

success, and others were admitted because industrial success is thought to be impossible without them. This myth is not believed in by the aspiring multitudes only, but by a good many among the captains of industry themselves, who accept their wealth as a social trust, and conceive of their function in a manner not dissimilar from that of the old sovereign by the grace of God.

This transposition of ideals from the religious and moral field to the practical and economic, leaves only a very thin ground for personal piety and the religion of the Churches. Yet there is no country in the world (again, with the only possible exception of Northern Africa during the first centuries of the Christian Era) which has produced such a wealth and such a variety of religious movements as America. The substance of that very thin ground is diluted Puritanism, Puritanism which, in a vast majority of the population, converts itself, strangely enough, as we have seen, into social optimism, a belief sufficient to the great active masses, but not to the needs of " the heart," when the heart is given enough leisure to consider itself, through either too much wealth or too little hope: through the discovery of its emptiness, when the possession of the means makes manifest the absence of an end, or through the spasms of its hunger, when means are beyond reach, in the hands of the supposed inferior and unworthy. In this second case, even a purely sensual craving dignifies itself with the name of the Spirit. The more or less official Churches, in an attempt to retain the allegiance of their vast congregations, have followed the masses in their evolution: they pride themselves essentially on their social achievements, a little doubtfully, perhaps, knowing that their particular God has no more reason to inhabit a church than a factory, and that the highest possible embodiment of their doctrine is an orderly and paternally governed industrial organization.

To the needs of " the heart " minister the innumerable sects (and here again, the American religious history repeats, in magnified proportions, the characteristics of English religious life). But because of the gradual impoverishment of the central religious tradition of the country, because of the scanty cultural background of both apostles and neophytes, it is hard to recognize in the whole movement an intimate spiritual dialectic which might lend strength and significance to the individual sects. A vague mysticism appropriates to itself, in a haphazard and capricious fashion, shadows and ghosts of religious experiences and opinions, whose germs of truth lie in other ages and other climates. The only common feature seems to be a distrust of intellect, derived from the original divorce of the intellectual from the spiritual in the Puritan, a distrust which at times becomes active in the denunciation of the supposed crimes of science. It is this fundamental common feature which will for ever prevent any of them from becoming what all sects fail to be, a religion.

The two states of mind which are nearer to-day to being true religions are, on one side, Americanism (a religion as a common bond), and on the other, Radicalism (a religion as a personal experience). Americanism is the more or less perfect expression of the common belief that American ideals realize themselves in American society. Radicalism is the more or less spasmodic protest against such a belief, sometimes coupled with an individual attempt at realizing those ideals in one's life and actions. The sharpest contrast between the two attitudes is to be found in their ideas of political and spiritual freedom; which to one is a condition actually existing by the mere fact of the existence of American society such as it is, and to the other a dynamic principle which can never be permanently associated with any particular set of institutions.

The original spirit of Puritanism can hardly be said to be alive to-day in America. In a few intellectuals, it confuses itself with other high forms of moral discipline in the past, and reappears with a strange fidelity to form rather than substance, as Platonism, Classicism, Mediævalism, Catholicism, or any other set of fixed standards that can be accepted as a whole, and can give the soul that sense of security which is inherent in the illusion of possessing the final truth. The consequence of such a deviation is that these truly religious souls, after having satisfied themselves with a sufficiently vast and beautiful interpretation of their creed, resent any cruder and more dangerous form of intellectual experience much more keenly than they resent crudities and dangers actually present in the nature of things. They are intellectuals, but again, with no faith in intellect; they are truly isolated among their fellow-countrymen, and yet they believe in conformity, and assume the conformity of American society to be the conformity of their dreams.

Such a static apprehension of truth, such an identification of universal spiritual values with one or another particular tradition, is in fact as much an obstacle to the new life of the human spirit as the external conformity enforced by social optimism. But the polemic against the older intellectuals is carried on by younger men, many of them of recent immigrant blood, but all of them reared in the atmosphere of American culture, and who differ from them more in the objects of their preference than in the vastness or depth of their outlook. There is a way of clinging to the latest fashion in philosophy or in art which is not a progress in any sense in relation to older faiths; of combating a manifest logical fallacy by the use of the same sophism; of embracing sin with the same moral enthusiasm that in less enlightened times was kept in reserve for the highest virtues only.

More important, for their influence on certain phases of American life, than these intellectual echoes, are the moralistic remnants of Puritanism. It is always possible, for small groups of people, strongly endowed with the sense of other people's duties, to intimidate large sections of public opinion into accepting the logical consequences of certain undisputed moral assumptions, however widely they may differ from the realities of American life. It is under such circumstances that the kind-hearted, easy-going American pays the penalty for his identification of realities with ideals, by being deprived of some very dear reality in the name of an ideal which had long since ceased to have any meaning for him.

From whatever side we look at American culture, we are constantly brought face to face with a disregard or distrust, or a narrow conception, of purely intellectual values, which seems to be the common characteristic of widely divergent spiritual attitudes. The American does not, as the English-

man, glory in his capacity for muddling through: he is proud
of certain logical achievements, and has a fondness for abstract schemes, an earnest belief in their validity and efficiency; but no more than the English does he believe that
intellect is an integral part of the human personality. He
recognizes the identity of goodness and truth, provided that
truth can be found out by other means than purely intellectual: by common sense, by revelation, by instinct, by imagination, but not by intellect. It is here that even the defenders,
among Americans, of the classical tradition miss the true meaning of the message of Socrates and Plato, the foundation of
humanism.

What is peculiarly American in the opinions of American
philosophers is a clear and distinct expression of the common
attitude. The official philosophy of America has repeated for
a century the views of English empiricists and of German idealists, sometimes with very interesting and illuminating personal
variations. It has even, and it is an original achievement,
brought them to lose their peculiar accents and to coincide in
new theories of knowledge. But the heart of American philosophy is not there: it is in pragmatism, in instrumentalism,
in whatever other theory clearly establishes the purely functional character of truth, the mechanical aspect of intellect.
Having put the criterion of truth outside the intellect, and
considered intellect as the mere mechanism of belief, these
doctrines try to re-establish the dignity of intellect by making
of it a machine for the reproduction of morally or socially
useful beliefs. The operation is similar to that of an anatomist
who, having extracted the heart from a living body, would presume to reconstruct the body by artificially promoting the
movements of the heart. The doctrine of the purely pragmatic
or instrumental nature of intellect, which is the logical clarification of the popular conception, is a doctrine of radical scepticism, whatever the particular declarations of faith of the
philosophers themselves might say to the contrary: it destroys
not the objects of knowledge only, but the instrument itself.

American philosophers came to this doctrine through the
psychological and sociological approach to the problems of
the mind. Such an approach is in keeping with the general

tendency towards assuming the form of natural and mathematical sciences, which moral sciences in American universities have been obeying during the last thirty or forty years, partly under the influence of a certain kind of European positivism, and partly because of the prestige that natural and mathematical sciences gained from their practical applications. Even now it is easier to find a truly humanistic mind, a sound conception of intellectual values, among the great American scientists than among the philosophers and philologists: but pure science has become the most solitary of occupations, and the scientist the most remote of men, since his place in society has been taken by the inventor and by the popularizer. Psychology and sociology, those half-literary, half-scientific disciplines, gave as a basis to philosophy not the individual effort to understand and to think, but the positive observation of the more or less involuntary processes of thought in the multitude. Intellect was sacrificed to a democratic idea of the equality of minds: how could the philosopher presume to think, I do not say better or more efficiently than, but differently from the multitude? To European philosophy the reproach has been made again and again, and with some justice, of imposing laws upon reality which are only the laws of individual philosophic thought; and yet what else does the scientist ultimately do? But both scientist and philosopher find their justification in their faith in the validity of their instruments: in a spirit of devotion and humility, not in a gratuitous presumption. The typical American philosopher has sold his birthright, not for a pottage of lentils, but for mere love.

I am painfully aware of the fact that, through the meshes of this necessarily abstract and sketchy analysis, a good deal of the beauty and vastness, the vigour and good-humour of American life inevitably escapes. The traveller from the old countries experiences here a sense of great spaces and of practically unbounded possibilities, which reflects itself in an unparalleled gaiety and openness of heart, and freedom of social intercourse. The true meaning of the doctrine of opportunity lies much more in these individual attitudes than in any difference between the structures of American and European societies. And I do not believe that the only explanation for them is in the prosperity of America when compared to the misery of Europe, because this generosity stands in no direct relation with individual wealth.   The lumberman and the long-shoreman are as good as, if not better than, the millionaire.

These individual attitudes find their collective expression in the idea of, and readiness for, service, which is universal in this country.   Churches, political parties, movements for social reform, fraternal orders, industrial and business organi-zations, meet on this common ground.   There is no material interest or spiritual prejudice that will not yield to an appeal for service: and whenever the object of service is clearly defined, action follows the impulse, intolerant of any delay. But Service is a means and not an end: you can serve a God, or a man, or a group of men, and in that man or group of men what you conceive to be his or their need, but you cannot serve Service.   And the common end can only be given by a clear intellectual vision of the relations between a set of ideals and the realities of life.

This intrinsic generosity of the American people is the mo-tive of the song, and the substance of the ideal, of the one great poet that America has added to the small family of European poets: Walt Whitman.   In him that feeling and that impulse became a vision and a prophecy.   There is a habit on the part of American intellectuals to look with a slight contempt on the admiration of Europeans for the poetry of Walt Whit-man, as just another symptom of their ignorance of American things.   But I, for one, will confess that what I have loved passionately, as little more than a boy, in that poetry, is that same quality whose presence I have now recognized as the human flower of American culture, and which makes me love this country as passionately as I loved that poetry.

It is one of the many paradoxes of American intellectual life that even the cultural preparation of a Walt Whitman should have been deeper and more substantial, if not more systematic, than that of any professor or writer of his times. These were minds which had as fully imbibed European thought and imagination as any professor or writer in Europe: but that thought, that imagination, transplanted to the new country, stood in no real relation with the new practical and moral surroundings, and were therefore thin and sterile. Walt Whitman knew and understood the great traditions of European civilization, and tried to express them in the original idiom, moral and literary, of his America.

But *nemo propheta,* and it takes centuries to understand a poet. Walt Whitman still waits for his own generation. The modern schools of American poetry, curious of all winds of fashion, working for the day rather than for the times, have not yet fully grasped, I do not say the spirit of his message, but even, for all their free-versifying, the mystery of his magnificent rhythms. His successors are rather among some of the younger novelists, and in a few men, spiritually related to them, who approach the study of American conditions from a combined economic and psychological point of view. The novelists are busy in discovering the actual traits of the American physiognomy, with sufficient faith in the future to describe the shades with as much care as the lights, and with a deeper passion; the economists are making way for the highest and purest American ideals by revealing the contingent and merely psychological basis of the supposedly scientific axioms of classical economics.

My own experience of American life, between the autumn of 1919 and the summer of 1921, has brought me in contact with all sorts and manners of people from one end to the other of the country, from the Atlantic to the Pacific. It is from this direct intercourse with Americans, rather than from my readings of American literature, continued for a much longer time, that I have formed the opinions expressed in this paper. But as my work has brought me in closer communion with colleges and universities than with any other kind of institutions, I feel a little more assured in writing of the educational aspect of the American problem.

A university is in any case more a *universitas studentium* than a corporation of professors. I have enjoyed my life in American faculties, and I have gained a good deal from the many noble souls and intellects that I have met among them; but, whenever it has been possible to me, I have escaped from the faculties to the students and tried to understand the tendencies of the coming generations.

The students of the American college or university, from the comparatively ancient institutions of the East, to the young co-educational schools of the Middle and Far West, form a fairly homogeneous, though very widely representative, cross-section of the American community. They are, in a very precise and inclusive meaning, young America, the America of to-morrow. A good many of their intellectual and spiritual characteristics are the common traits of American culture which we have studied in the preceding paragraphs; and yet, because of the social separation of individuals according to ages, which is carried in this country much farther than in any European country, they develop also a number of independent traits, which are peculiar to each one of the " younger generations " in their turn. The life of the American boy or girl, up to the time of their entrance into college, is mainly the life of a beautiful and healthy young organism, not subject to any too strict intellectual or spiritual discipline. The High Schools seem to understand their function in a spirit which is substantially different from that of the European secondary schools, owing especially to certain prevailing educational doctrines founded on a fiction which is used also in many other fields of American life, but which in the field of education has wrought more harm than in any other one, the fiction of the public demand—in this particular case of one or another type of education. A fiction undoubtedly it is, and used to give prestige and authority to the theories of individual educationalists, since in no country and in no time there have existed educational opinions outside the circle of the educators themselves. But this fiction has unfortunately had practical consequences because American educators, subject to big business in the private institutions, and to the politicians in the State schools and universities, have not found in themselves the energy, except in a few isolated instances, to resist what came to them strengthened by such auspices. And the public itself was easily convinced that it wanted what it was told that it wanted. The students, more sinned against than sinning, enjoy the easy atmosphere of the school, and it is only when they reach college that they become aware of their absolute unpreparedness for the higher studies.

This consciousness of their inferiority manifests itself in an attitude of "low-browism," which is not contempt of that which they think is beyond them, but rather an unwillingness to pretend that they are what they know they are not. It is practically impossible for them to acquire any standards in matters of scholarship, and they are thus forcibly thrown back on that which they know very well, the sports, and social life among themselves. A Chinese friend of mine once quaintly defined an American university as an athletic association in which certain opportunities for study were provided for the feeble-bodied. Now, in athletics and social life, the student finds something that is real, and therefore is an education: there is no pretence or fraud about football, and in their institutions within the college and the university the students obey certain standards and rules which are not as clearly justified as those of athletics, but still are made by themselves, and therefore readily understood. They are standards and rules that sometimes strangely resemble those of primitive society, as it is only too natural when the ground on which they grow is a community of the very young only, and yet undoubtedly they are a preparation for a life after college in which similar features are very far from being the exception. And besides, that social life has a freedom and beauty of its own, evident in one at least of its most hallowed institutions, the dance. American dances, with those captivating and vital rhythms which American music has appropriated for itself from the Negro, are a perfect expression of the mere joy of life. The older generations are shocked and mystified by these dances, and also by many other ways and by the implicit opinions of the young; but so they have been in all ages and countries. To a curious and passionate observer, the youth of America seems to be obscurely labouring at a liberation of the sexual life from pretences and unjustified inhibitions, and, through an original experience of the elements of love, at a creation of new values, perhaps of a new morality.

But the student is an object of perplexity and wonder to the professor, who generally ends by taking very seriously, very literally, as something that cannot be changed, his attitude towards athletics and the social life of the college. Starting from such an assumption, the professor becomes shy of teaching; that is, he keeps for himself whatever true intellectual and spiritual interests he may have, and deals out to the students in the classroom rations of knowledge, which go up to form a complicated system of units and credits symbolizing the process of education. There is, to my mind, no more tragic misunderstanding in American life.

My own experience (and I give it for what it is worth) tells me that athletics and the social life are vicarious satisfactions for much deeper spiritual and intellectual needs. The student receives from the common American tradition a desire for spiritual values; from his individual reaction to that tradition, a craving for intellectual clarity. But he is handicapped by his scholastic unpreparedness, and disillusioned by the aloofness of the professor, by the intricacies and aridity of the curriculum: by the fact, only too evident to him, that what he is given is not science or thought, but their scholastic version. Whenever a man stands before him, and without trying to " put himself at his level," talks to him as one talks to a man, thinking for him as one thinks for oneself, there is no more ready and enthusiastic response to be had than from the American student. He is not afraid of the difficulties or dangers, but he must trust his guide, and know that his guide trusts him. There is evidence for this in the cases which are too frequent to be called mere exceptions, of those American professors who are truly popular in the colleges and universities. But until many more of them realize what splendid material is in their hands, what big thirst there is for them to quench, and go back to their work with this new faith, the gulf will not be bridged, and young America will have to attempt to solve her own problems without the help of the spiritual experience of the centuries.

This condition in the institutions of higher learning is a symbol and a mirror of the condition of the country. With an impoverished religious tradition, with an imperfect knowledge of the power of intellect, America is starving for religious and intellectual truth. No other country in the world has, as the phrase goes, a heart more full of service: a heart that is constantly *quaerens quem amet*. With the war, and after the war, America has wished to dedicate herself to the world, and has only withdrawn from action when she has felt that she could not trust her leaders, what was supposed to be her mind.

In a few years, the children of the recent millions of immigrants from all regions of Europe will come forward in American life and ask for their share in the common inheritance of American tradition, in the common work of American civilization. They will not have much to contribute directly from their original cultures, but they will add an unexampled variety of bloods, of intellectual and moral temperaments, to the population of America. Their Americanization, in habits and language and manners, is a natural process which, left to itself, invariably takes place in the second generation. America must clarify and intensify her tradition, the moral discipline of the Puritan, the moral enthusiasm of the Discoverers and Pioneers, for them, and they will gladly embrace her heritage; but this clarification and intensification is only possible through the revision of the original values in the light of the central humanistic tradition of European thought.

The dreams of the European founders of this Commonwealth of Utopia may yet come true, in the way in which human dreams come true, by becoming the active, all-pervading motive of spiritual effort, the substance of life. Exiles, voluntary or forced, from England and Ireland, from Russia and Italy, from Germany and Israel, children of one mother, unified in America as they will not be unified for centuries to come in Europe, will thus have a chance to anticipate, in the *civilitas americana*, the future developments of the *humana civilitas*.

And if this generation needs a motto, I would suggest one line of Dante:

luce intellettual piena d'amore:
the light of intellect, in the fulness of love.

RAFFAELLO PICCOLI

BIBLIOGRAPHICAL NOTES

BIBLIOGRAPHICAL NOTES

THE CITY

There is no adequate literature of cities in America. Some of the larger cities possess guide-books and local histories; but the most valuable illuminations on the history and development of the American city lie buried in contemporary papers, narratives of travel, and speeches. The reader who wishes to explore the ground farther should dip into volumes and papers drawn from all periods. The recent editions of " Valentine's Manual " should be interesting to those who cannot consult the original " Manual of the Common Council of New York." During the last twenty years a great many reports and surveys have been printed, by city planning commissions and other bodies: these are valuable both for showing the limitations of the established régime and for giving hints of the forces that are working, more or less, for improvement. " The Pittsburgh Survey " (Russell Sage Foundation) is the great classic in this field. A compendious summary of American city developments during the last generation is contained in Charles Zueblin's " American Municipal Progress " (Macmillan). Standing by itself in this literature is a very able book by Paul Harlan Douglass, called " The Little Town," published by Macmillan. (A book which shall deal similarly with the Great Town is badly needed.) The best general approach to the city is that of Professor Patrick Geddes in " Cities in Evolution " (Williams and Norgate, London.) Those who are acquainted with Professor Geddes's " A Study in City Development " or his contributions to " Sociological Papers " (Macmillan, 1905, 1906, 1907) will perhaps note my debt to him: I hasten heartily to acknowledge this, as well as my debt, by personal intercourse, to his colleague, Mr. Victor V. Branford. If the lay reader can learn nothing else from Professor Geddes, he can learn the utility of throwing aside the curtains of second-hand knowledge and studying cities and social institutions by direct observation. The inadequacy of American civic literature will not be altogether a handicap if it forces the reader to obtain by personal explorations impressions which he would otherwise get through the blur of the printed page. Every city and its region is in a sense an exhibition of natural and social history. Let the reader walk the streets of our cities, as through the halls of a museum, and use the books that have been suggested only as so many tickets and labels. Americans have a reputation in Europe as voracious sightseers. One wonders what might not happen if Americans started to see the sights at home—not the Grand Canyon and the Yosemite, but " Broadway," and its back alleys, and the slums and suburbs that stretch beyond. If observation led to criticism, and criticism to knowledge, where might not knowledge lead?   **L. M.**

POLITICS

The standard works on the history of American politics are so well known (and so few) that they scarcely need mention. Bryce, Ostrogorski and de Tocqueville, I assume, have been read by all serious students, as have also such personal memoirs as those of Blaine and John Sherman. Bryce's work is a favourite, but it suffers from the disingenuousness of the man. Dr. Charles A. Beard's " Economic Interpretation of the Constitution " is less a complete treatise than a prospectus of a history that is yet to be written. As far as I know, the valuable suggestions in his preface have never inspired any investigation of political origins by other American historians, most of whom are simply unintelligent school-teachers, as their current " histories " of the late war well show. All such inquiries are blocked by the timorousness and stupidity that are so characteristic of American scholarship. Our discussion of politics, like our discussion of economics, deals chiefly with superficialities. Both subjects need ventilation by psychologists not dependent upon college salaries, and hence free to speak. Certainly the influence of religious enthusiasm upon American politics deserves a careful study; nevertheless, I have never been able to find a book upon it. Again, there is the difficult question of the relations between politics and journalism. My belief is that the rising power of newspapers has tended to drive intelligent and self-respecting men out of politics, for the newspapers are chiefly operated by cads and no such man wants to be at their mercy. But that sort of thing is never studied in the United States. We even lack decent political biography, so common in England. The best light to be obtained upon current politics is in the *Congressional Record*. It costs $1.50 a month and is well worth it. Soon or late the truth gets into the *Record;* it even got there during the war. But it seldom gets into the newspapers and it never gets into books.   **H. L. M.**

JOURNALISM

I know of no quite satisfactory book on American journalism. "History of Journalism in the United States" by George Henry Payne and "History of American Journalism" by James Melvin Lee are fairly good in their treatment of the past, but neither of them shows any penetration in analyzing present conditions. The innocence of Mr. Payne may be judged by his opinion that the Kansas City *Star*, under Nelson, exemplifies a healthier kind of "reform journalism" than the *Post* under Godkin! "Liberty and the News" by Walter Lippmann is suggestive, but it does not pretend to contain any specific information. More specific in naming names and giving modern instances is a short essay by Hamilton Holt, "Commercialism and Journalism." "The Brass Check" by Upton Sinclair contains much valuable material, and perhaps what I have said of it does not do it justice; certainly it should be read by everybody interested in this subject. Will Irwin published in *Collier's Weekly* from January to July, 1911, a valuable series of articles, "The American Newspaper: A Study of Journalism." I cannot find that these articles have been reprinted in book form. There is some information in autobiographies and biographies of important journalists, such as "Recollections of a Busy Life" by Horace Greeley, "Life of Whitelaw Reid" by Royal Cortissoz, "Life and Letters of E. L. Godkin" by Rollo Ogden, "Life of Charles A. Dana" by J. H. Wilson, "Life and Letters of John Hay" by William Roscoe Thayer, "An Adventure with Genius: Recollections of Joseph Pulitzer," by Alleyne Ireland; also "The Story of the *Sun*" by Frank M. O'Brien. Biographies, however, celebrate persons and only indirectly explain institutions. A useful bibliography, which includes books and magazine articles, is "Daily Newspapers in U. S." by Wieder Callie of the Wisconsin University School of Journalism. But after all the best source of information is the daily newspaper, if one knows how to read it—and read between the lines.   J. M.

THE LAW

"Bryce's Modern Democracies," Chapter XLIII, is a recent survey of the American legal system; Raymond Fosdick, "American Police Systems," Chapter I, states the operation of criminal law. For legal proceedure, see Reginald Heber Smith, "Justice and the

Poor," published by the Carnegie Endowment for the Advancement of Teaching and dealing with legal aid societies and other methods of securing more adequate legal relief; Charles W. Eliot and others, " Efficiency in the Administration of Justice," published by the National Economic League; Moorfield Storey, " The Reform of Legal Procedure;" and many other books and articles; the reports of the American and New York Bar Associations are of especial value. John H. Wigmore, " Evidence," vol. V (1915 edition) discusses recent progress; see his " Cases on Torts, Preface," on substantive law. A very wide range of topics in American law, philosophical, historical, procedural, and substantive, is covered by the writings of Roscoe Pound, of which a list is given in " The Centennial History of the Harvard Law School." The same book deals with many phases of legal education; see also " The Case Method in American Law Schools," Josef Redlich, Carnegie Endowment. For the position of lawyers, the best book is, Charles Warren, " A History of the American Bar;" a recent discussion of their work is Simeon E. Baldwin, " The Young Man and the Law." No one interested in this field should fail to read the " Collected Legal Papers of Justice Holmes;" see also John H. Wigmore, "Justice Holmes and the Law of Torts " and Felix Frankfurter, " The Constitutional Opinions of Justice Holmes," both in the *Harvard Law Review,* April, 1916, and Roscoe Pound, " Judge Holmes's Contributions to the Science of Law," *ibid.,* March, 1921. A valuable essay on Colonial legal history is Paul S. Reinsch, "English Common Law in the Early American Colonies." A mass of material will be found in the law reviews, which are indexed through 1907 by Jones, " Index to Legal Periodicals," 3 vols., and afterwards in the *Law Library Journal,* cumulative quarterly.   Z. C., JR.

EDUCATION

The ideas contained in the article are so commonplace and of such general acceptance among educators that it is impossible to give specific authority for them. In addition to the articles mentioned, one of the latest by Dr. D. S. Miller, " The Great College Illusion " in the *New Republic* for June 22, 1921, should be referred to. For the rest the report of the Committee of Ten of the National Education Association, and the reports of President Eliot and President Lowell of Harvard, President Meiklejohn of Amherst, and President Wilson of Princeton, may be cited, with the recognition that any such selection is invidious.   R. M. L.

SCHOLARSHIP AND CRITICISM

There has been no really fundamental discussion of American scholarship or American criticism. Those who merely seek a good historical sketch of our older literary scholarship, along conventional lines, will find one in the fourth volume of the " Cambridge History of American Literature " that is at all events vastly superior to the similar chapters in the " Cambridge History of English Literature." But more illuminating than any formal treatise are the comments on our scholarly ideals and methods in Emerson's famous address on " The American Scholar," in " The Education of Henry Adams," and in the " Letters " of William James. The " Cambridge History of American Literature " contains no separate chapter on American criticism, and the treatment of individual critics is pathetically inadequate. The flavour of recent criticism may be savoured in Ludwig Lewisohn's interesting anthology, " A Modern Book of Criticism," where the most buoyant and " modern " of our younger men are set side by side with all their unacademic masters and compeers of the contemporary European world. All that can be said in favour of the faded moralism of the older American criticism is urged in an article on " The National Genius " in the *Atlantic Monthly* for January, 1921, the temper of which may be judged from this typical excerpt: " When Mr. Spingarn declares that beauty is not concerned with truth or morals or democracy, he makes a philosophical distinction which I have no doubt that Charles the Second would have understood, approved, and could, at need, have illustrated. But he says what the American schoolboy knows to be false to the history of beauty in this country. Beauty, whether we like it or not, has a heart full of service." The case against the conservative and traditional type of criticism is presented with slapdash pungency in the two volumes of H. L. Mencken's " Prejudices." But any one can make out a case for himself by reading the work of any American classical scholar side by side with a book by Gilbert Murray, or any history of literature by an American side by side with Francesco de Sanctis's " History of Italian Literature," or the work of any American critic side by side with the books of the great critics of the world.

J. E. S.

SCHOOL AND COLLEGE LIFE

The "distinguished Englishman" to whom the Martian refers is of course Viscount Bryce, whose "American Commonwealth" discusses the external aspects of our uniformity, the similarity of our buildings, cities, customs, and so on. Our spiritual unanimity has been most thoroughly examined by George Santayana, both in his earlier essays—as notably in "The Genteel Tradition"—and in his recent "Character and Opinion in the United States."

For all the welter of writing about our educational establishment, only infrequent and incidental consideration has been bestowed, either favourably or unfavourably, on its regimental effect. As custodians of a going concern, the educators have busied themselves with repairs and replacements to the machinery rather than with the right of way; and lay critics have pretty much confined themselves to selecting between machines whose slightly differing routes all lie in the same general direction. The exception that proves the rule is "Shackled Youth," by Edward Yeomans.

But undergraduate life in America has a genre of its own, the form of fiction known as "college stories." Nearly every important school has at some time had written round it a collection of tales that exploit its peculiar legends, traditions, and customs—for the most part a chafing-dish literature of pranks, patter, and athletic prowess whose murky and often distorted reflection of student attitudes is quite incidental to its business of entertaining. Owen Johnson's Lawrenceville stories—"The Prodigious Hickey," "Tennessee Shad," "The Varmint," "The Humming Bird"—are the classics of preparatory school life. Harvard has "Pepper," by H. E. Porter, "Harvard Episodes" and "The Diary of a Freshman," by Charles Flandrau, and Owen Wister's "Philosophy 4," the best of all college yarns. Yale has the books of Ralph D. Paine and of others. The Western universities have such volumes as "Ann Arbor Tales," by Karl Harriman, for Michigan, and "Maroon Tales," by W. J. Cuppy, for Chicago. George Fitch writes amusingly about life in the smaller Western colleges in "Petey Simmons at Siwash" and "At Good Old Siwash."

The catalogue of serious college fiction is brief, and most of the novels are so propagandist that they are misrepresentative. For example, Owen Johnson's "Stover at Yale," which was some years out of date when it was published, misses the essential club spirit in New Haven by almost as wide a margin as Arthur Train's "The

World and Thomas Kelly" departs from the normal club life in Cambridge; both authors set up the straw man of snobbery where snobs are an unimportant minority. Two recent novels, however, deal more faithfully with the college scene for the very reason that their authors were more interested in character than in setting: " This Side of Paradise," by Scott Fitzgerald, is true enough to have provoked endless controversy in Princeton; and " Salt: The Education of Griffith Adams," by Charles G. Norris, is a memorable appraisal of student ideals in a typical co-educational institution. Dorothy Canfield's " The Bent Twig " is also laid in a co-educational college. Booth Tarkington's " Ramsay Milholland " attends a State University; and the hero of " Gold Shod," by Newton Fuessle, is a revelatory failure of the State University regimen. To these add an autobiography—" An American in the Making, The Life Story of an Immigrant," by M. E. Ravage, whose candid report on his fellows at the Missouri State University is a masterpiece of sympathetic criticism.   C. B.

THE INTELLECTUAL LIFE

To attempt to give references to specific books on so general and inclusive a topic would be an impertinence. But one may legitimately suggest the trends of investigation one would like to see thoroughly explored. In my own case they would be: (1) a study of the pioneer from the point of view of his cultural and religious interests, correlating those interests with his general economic status; (2) a study of the revolutionary *feeling* of America (not formulas) in psychological terms and of its duration as an emotional driving force; (3) a study of the effects of the post-Civil War period and the industrial expansion upon the position of upper-class women in the United States; (4) a study of sexual maladjustment in American family life, correlated again with the economic status of the successful pioneer; (5) a very careful study of the beginnings, rise, and spread of women's clubs, and their purposes and accomplishments, correlated chronologically with the development of club life of men and the extent of vice, gambling, and drunkenness; (6) a study of American religions in more or less Freudian terms as compensations for neurotic maladjustment; (7) a study of instrumentalism in philosophy and its implications for reform; (8) a serious attempt to understand and appraise the more or less disorganized *jeunes*, with some attention to comparing the intensity of their bitterness or optimism with the places of birth and upbringing. No special study of American educational systems or of the school or college life would be necessary, it seems to me, beyond, of course, a general knowledge. The intellectual life of the nation, after all, has little relation to the academic life.

When such special studies had been finished by sympathetic investigators, probably one of several writers could synthesize the results and give us a fairly definitive essay on the intellectual life of America. Such studies, however, have not yet been done, and without them I have had to write this essay to a certain extent *en plein air*. Thus it has been impossible entirely to avoid giving the impression of stating things dogmatically or intuitively. But as a matter of fact on all the topics I have suggested for study I have already given much thought and time, and consequently, whatever its literary form, the essay is not pure impressionism.　　　　　　　　　H. E. S.

SCIENCE

There is no connected account of American achievement in science. Strangely enough, the most pretentious American book on the history of science, Sedgwick and Tyler's " Short History of Science " (New York: Macmillan, 1917), ignores the most notable figures among the author's countrymen. A useful biographical directory under the title of " American Men of Science " (New York Science Press, 1910, 2d edition), has been compiled by Professor James McKeen Cattell; a third revised edition has been prepared and issued this year prior to the appearance of the present volume.

On the tendencies manifest in the United States there are several important papers. An address by Henry A. Rowland entitled " A Plea for Pure Science " (*Popular Science Monthly*, vol. LIX, 1901, pp. 170-188), is still eminently worth reading. The external conditions under which American scientists labour have been repeatedly discussed in recent years in such journals as *Science* and *School and Society*, both edited by Professor Cattell, who has himself appended very important discussions to the above-cited biographical lexicon. Against over-organization Professor William Morton Wheeler has recently published a witty and vigorous protest (" The Organization of Research," *Science*, January 21, 1921, N. S. vol. LIII, pp. 53-67).

In order to give an understanding of the essence of scientific activity the general reader cannot do better than to trace the processes by which the master-minds of the past have brought order into the chaos that is at first blush presented by the world of reality.

In this respect the writings of the late Professor Ernst Mach are unsurpassed, and even the least mathematically trained layman can derive much insight from portions of his book " Die Mechanik " (Leipzig, 7th edition, 1912), accessible in T. J. McCormack's translation under the title of " The Science of Mechanics " (Chicago: Open Court Publishing Co.). The section on Galileo may be specially recommended. Mach's " Erkenntnis und Irrtum " (Leipzig, 1906) contains most suggestive discussions of the psychology of investigation, dealing with such questions as the nature of a scientific problem, of experimentation, of hypothetical assumptions, etc. Much may also be learned from the general sections of P. Duhem's " La theorie physique, son objet et sa structure " (Paris, 1906). E. Duclaux's " Pasteur: Histoire d'un Esprit " has fortunately been rendered accessible by Erwin F. Smith and Florence Hedges under the title " Pasteur, the History of a Mind " (Philadelphia; Saunders, 1920). It reveals in masterly fashion the methods by which a great thinker overcomes not only external opposition but the more baneful obstacles of scientific folk-lore. R. H. L.

PHILOSOPHY

The omission of Mr. Santayana's philosophy from the above account indicates no lack of appreciation of its merits. Although written at Harvard, it is hardly an American philosophy. On one hand, Mr. Santayana is free from the mystical religious longings that have given our Idealisms life, and on the other, he is too confident of the reality of culture and the value of the contemplative life to sanction that dominance of the practical which is the stronghold of instrumentalism.

The only histories of American Philosophy are those by Professor Woodbridge Riley. His " Early Schools " (Dodd, Mead & Co., 1907), is a full treatment of the period in question, but his " American Thought from Puritanism to Pragmatism " (H. Holt, 1915) is better reading and comes down to date. These are best read in connection with some history of American Literature such as Barrett Wendell's " Literary History of America " (Scribner's Sons, 1914). Royce's system is given in good condensed form in the last four chapters of his " Spirit of Modern Philosophy " (Houghton Mifflin, 1899). Its exhaustive statement is " The World and the Individual " (2 vols., Macmillan, 1900-1). The " Philosophy of Loyalty " (Macmillan, 1908) develops the ethics, and the " Problem of Christianity " (2 vols., Macmillan, 1913), relates his philosophy to

Christianity. Hocking's religious philosophy is given in his " Meaning of God in Human Experience " (Yale University Press, 1912). His general position is developed on one side in " Human Nature and Its Remaking" (Yale University Press, 1918). Anything of James is good reading. His chief work is the " Principles of Psychology " (H. Holt, 1890), but the " Talks to Teachers on Psychology and Some of Life's Ideals " (H. Holt, 1907) and the " Will to Believe " (Longmans, Green & Co., 1899), better illustrate his attitude toward life. " Pragmatism " (Longmans, Green & Co., 1907) introduces his technical philosophizing. His religious attitude can be got from the " Varieties of Religious Experience " (Longmans, Green & Co., 1902). Dewey has nowhere systematized his philosophy. Its technical points are exhibited in the " Essays in Experimental Logic " (University of Chicago Press, 1916). The " Influence of Darwin on Philosophy " (H. Holt, 1910) has two especially readable essays, one the title-essay, the other on " Intelligence and Morals." The full statement of his ethics is the " Ethics " (Dewey and Tufts, H. Holt, 1908). He is at his best in " Education and Democracy " (Macmillan, 1916). " German Philosophy and Politics " (H. Holt, 1915) is a war-time reaction giving an interesting point of view as to the significance of German Philosophy. " The New Realism " (Macmillan, 1912) is a volume of technical studies by the Six Realists. " Creative Intelligence " (H. Holt, 1917), by John Dewey and others, is a similar volume of pragmatic studies. The reviews are also announcing another co-operative volume, " Essays in Critical Realism " by Santayana, Lovejoy and others. In a technical fashion Perry has discussed the " Present Tendencies in Philosophy " (Longmans, Green & Co., 1912), but the best critical reaction to American philosophy is that of Santayana: " Character and Opinion in the United States " (Scribner's Sons, 1920). Santayana's own chief philosophic contributions are the " Sense of Beauty " (Scribner's Sons, 1896), and the " Life of Reason " (5 vols., Scribner's Sons, 1905-6). The first two chapters of his " Winds of Doctrine " (Scribner's Sons, 1913), on the " Intellectual Temper of the Age " and " Modernism and Christianity," are also relevant. Brief but excellent expositions of Royce, Dewey, James, and Santayana by Morris R. Cohen have appeared in the *New Republic*, vols. XX-XXIII.   H. C. B.

LITERATURE

Perhaps the most illuminating books for any one interested in the subject of the essay on literature are the private memorials of certain modern European writers. For a sense of everything the American literary life is *not*, one might read, for instance, the Letters of Ibsen, Dostoievsky, Chekhov, Flaubert, Taine and Leopardi—all of which have appeared, in whole or in part, in English.

V. W. B.

MUSIC

What little there is that is worth reading concerning American music is scattered through magazine articles and chapters in books upon other musical subjects. Daniel Gregory Mason has a sensible and illuminating chapter, " Music in America," in his "Contemporary Composers." The section, " America," in Chapter XVI of the Stanford-Forsyth " History of Music " contrives to be tactful and at the same time just. Two books that should be read by any one interested in native composition are Cecil Forsyth's " Music and Nationalism " and Lawrence Gilman's " Edward MacDowell." Rupert Hughes's " Contemporary American Composers " is twenty years old, but still interesting; it contains sympathetic—not to say glowing—accounts of the lives and works of an incredibly large number of Americans who do and did pursue the art of musical composition. To know what an artist means when he asks to be understood read pages 240 and 241 of Cabell's " Jurgen "—if you can get it; also the volume, " La Foire sur la Place," of " Jean Christophe."

D. T.

POETRY

Bodenheim, Maxwell: " Minna and Myself " (Pagan Publishing Co.); " Advice " (Alfred A. Knopf).

" H. D.": " Sea-Garden " (Houghton Mifflin).

Eliot, T. S.: " Poems " (Alfred A. Knopf).

Fletcher, John Gould: " Irradiations: Sand and Spray " (Houghton Mifflin); " Goblins and Pagodas " (Houghton Mifflin); " The Tree of Life " (Macmillan); " Japanese Prints " (Four Seas Co.); " Breakers and Granite " (Macmillan).

Frost, Robert: " North of Boston " (Holt); " A Boy's Will " (Holt); " Mountain Interval " (Holt).

Kreymborg, Alfred: " Plays for Poem-Mimes " (Others); " Blood of Things " (Nicholas Brown); " Plays for Merry Andrews " (Sunwise Turn).

Lindsay, Vachel: " The Congo " (Macmillan); " The Chinese Nightingale " (Macmillan).

Lowell, Amy: " Men, Women and Ghosts " (Houghton Mifflin); " Can Grande's Castle " (Houghton Mifflin); " Pictures of the Floating World " (Houghton Mifflin); " Legends " (Houghton Mifflin).

Masters, Edgar Lee: " Spoon River Anthology " (Macmillan); " The Great Valley " (Macmillan); " Domesday Book " (Macmillan).

Pound, Ezra: " Umbra " (Elkin Matthews); " Lustra " (Alfred A. Knopf).

Robinson, Edwin Arlington: " Children of the Night " (Scribners); " The Town Down the River " (Scribners); " The Man Against the Sky " (Macmillan); " Merlin " (Macmillan); " Captain Craig " (Macmillan); " The Three Taverns " (Macmillan); " Avon's Harvest " (Macmillan); " Lancelot " (Scott and Seltzer).

Sandburg, Carl: " Smoke and Steel " (Harcourt, Brace & Co.).

Stevens, Wallace: See " The New Poetry;" " Others " Anthology.

Teasdale, Sara: " Rivers to the Sea " (Macmillan).

Untermeyer, Louis: " The New Adam " (Harcourt, Brace & Co.); " Including Horace " (Harcourt, Brace & Co.).

Anthologies: " The New Poetry." Edited by Harriet Monroe and Alice Corbin Henderson (Macmillan); " An American Miscellany " (Harcourt, Brace & Co.); " Others for 1919 " edited by Alfred Kreymborg (A. A. Knopf); " Some Imagist Poets " First, Second and Third Series (Houghton Mifflin).

Criticism: Untermeyer, Louis, " The New Era in American Poetry " (Henry Holt), a comprehensive, lively, but sometimes misleading survey.   C. A.

ART

The reader may obtain most of the data on the history of American art from Samuel Isham's " History of American Painting," and Charles H. Caffin's " Story of American Painting." Very little writing of an analytical nature has been devoted to American art, and nearly all of it is devoid of a sense of perspective and of anything approaching a realization of the position that American work holds in relation to that of Europe. Outside of the writing that is only incompetent, there are the books and articles by men whose purpose is to " boost " the home product for nationalistic or commercial reasons. In contrast with all this is Mr. Roger E. Fry's essay on Ryder, in the *Burlington Magazine* for April, 1908—a masterful appreciation of the artist.   W. P.

THE THEATRE

The bibliography of this subject is extensive, but in the main unilluminating. It consists chiefly in a magnanimous waving aside of what is, and an optimistic dream of what is to be. Into this category fall most, if not all, of the many volumes written by the college professors and such of their students as have, upon graduation, carried with them into the world the college-professor manner of looking at things. Nevertheless, Professor William Lyon Phelps' " The Twentieth Century Theatre," for all its deviations from fact, and Professor Thomas H. Dickinson's " The Case of American Drama," may be looked into by the more curious. Mr. Arthur Ruhl's " Second Nights," with its penetrating humour, contains several excellent pictures of certain phases of the native theatre. Section IV of Mr. Walter Prichard Eaton's " Plays and Players," Mr. George Bronson-Howard's searching series of papers entitled, " What's Wrong with the Theatre," and perhaps even Mr. George Jean Nathan's " The Popular Theatre," " The Theatre, The Drama, The Girls," " Comedians All," and " Mr. George Jean Nathan Presents " may throw some light upon the subject. Miss Akins' " Papa " and all of Mr. O'Neill's plays are available in book form. The bulk of inferior native dramaturgy is similarly available to the curious-minded: there are hundreds of these lowly specimens on view in the nearest book store.   G. J. N.

ECONOMIC OPINION

The literature of economic opinion in America is almost as voluminous as the printed word. It ranges from the ponderous treatises of professed economists, wherein " economic laws " are printed in italics, to the sophisticated novels of the self-elect, in which economic opinion is a by-product of clever conversation. Not only can one find economic opinion to his taste, but he can have it in any form he likes. Perhaps the most human and reasonable application of the philosophy of laissez-faire to the problems of industrial society is to be found in the pages of W. G. Sumner. Of particular interest are the essays contained in the volumes entitled " Earth Hunger," " The Challenge of Facts," and " The Forgotten Man." The most subtle and articulate account of the economic order as an automatic, self-regulating mechanism is J. B. Clark, " The Distribution of Wealth." An able and readable treatise, characterized alike by a modified classical approach and by a recognition of the facts of modern industrial society, is F. W. Taussig, " The Principles of Economics." The " case for capitalism " has never been set forth as an articulate whole. The theoretical framework of the defence is to be found in any of the older treatises upon economic theory. A formal *apologia* is to be found in the last chapter of almost every text upon economics under some such title as " A Critique of the Existing Order," " Wealth and Welfare," or " Economic Progress." A defence of " what is," whatever it may chance to be, characterized alike by brilliancy and ignorance, is P. E. More's " Aristocracy and Justice." Contemporary opinion favourable to capitalism may be found, in any requisite quantity and detail, in *The Wall Street Journal, The Commercial and Financial Chronicle,* and the publications of the National Association of Manufacturers. *The Congressional Record,* a veritable treasure house of economic fallacy, presents fervent pleas both for an unqualified capitalism and for capitalism with endless modifications. The literature of the economics of " control " is beginning to be large. The essay by H. C. Adams, " The Relation of the State to Industrial Activity," elaborating the thesis that the function of the state is to regulate " the plane of competition," has become a classic. The best account of the economic opinion of organized labour is to be found in R. F. Hoxie, " Trade Unionism in the United States." Typical examples of excellent work done by men who do not profess to be economists are W. Lippmann, " Drift and Mastery," the opinions (often dissenting) delivered by Mr. Justice Holmes and Mr. Justice Brandeis, of the United States Supreme Court, and the articles frequently contributed to periodicals by T. R. Powell upon the constitutional aspects of economic questions. The appearance of such studies as the brief for the shorter working day in the case of *Bunting v. Oregon,* prepared by F. Frankfurter and J. Goldmark, and of the " Report on the Steel Strike of 1919," by the Commission of Inquiry of the Interchurch World Movement indicates that we are beginning to base our opinions and our policies upon " the facts." Among significant contributions are the articles appearing regularly in such periodicals as *The New Republic* and *The Nation.* At last the newer economics of the schools is beginning to assume the form of an articulate body of doctrine. The books of T. B. Veblen, particularly " The Theory of Business Enterprise," and " The Instinct of Workmanship," contain valuable pioneer studies. In " Personal Competition " and in the chapters upon " Valuation " in " Social Process," C. H. Cooley has shown how economic institutions are to be treated. The newer economics, however, begins with the publication in 1913 of W. C.

Mitchell, "Business Cycles." This substitutes an economics of process for one of statics and successfully merges theoretical and statistical inquiry. It marks the beginning of a new era in the study of economics. The work in general economic theory has followed the leads blazed by Veblen, Cooley, and Mitchell. W. H. Hamilton, in "Current Economic Problems," elaborates a theory of the control of industrial development, interspersed with readings from many authors. L. C. Marshal, in "Readings in Industrial Society," attempts, through selections drawn from many sources, an appraisal of the institutions which together make up the economic order. D. Friday, in "Profits, Wages, and Prices," shows how much meaning a few handfuls of figures contain and how much violence they can do to established principles. The National Bureau of Economic Research is soon to publish the results of a careful and thorough statistical inquiry into the division of income in the United States. Upon particular subjects such as trusts, tariffs, railroads, labour unions, etc., the literature is far too large to be catalogued here. There is no satisfactory history of economic opinion in the United States. T. B. Veblen's "The Place of Science in Modern Civilization" contains a series of essays which constitute the most convincing attack upon the classical system and which point the way to an institutional economics. Many articles dealing with the development of economic doctrines are to be found in the files of *The Quarterly Journal of Economics* and of *The Journal of Political Economy*. An excellent statement of the present situation in economics is an unpublished essay by W. C. Mitchell, "The Promise of Economic Science." W. H. H.

RADICALISM

For exposition of the leading radical theories the reader is urged to go, not to second-hand authorities, but to their foremost advocates. "Capital" by Karl Marx (Charles H. Kerr) is of course the chief basis of Socialism. There is nothing better on Anarchism than the article in the "Encyclopedia Britannica" by Prince Kropotkin. For revolutionary industrial unionism it is important to know "Speeches and Editorials" by Daniel de Leon (New York Labor News Co.). De Leon was one of the founders of the I.W.W., and his ideas not only influenced the separatist labour movements in the United States but the shop-steward movement in England and the Soviets of Russia. "Guild Socialism" by G. D. H. Cole is the best statement of this recent theory, while "The State and Revolution " by Nikolai Lenin (George Allen and Unwin) explains the principles and tactics of modern Communism. To these should be added another classic, " Progress and Poverty " by Henry George (Doubleday Page).

On the origins of the American government it is important to read " Economic Origins of Jeffersonian Democracy " and " Economic Interpretation of the Constitution " by Charles A. Beard (Macmillan).

The " History of Trade Unionism " by Sidney and Beatrice Webb (Longmans, Green), is an invaluable account of the growth of the British labour movement, which has many similarities to our own. " Industrial Democracy " by the same authors, issued by the same publisher, is the best statement of the theories of trade unionism. The " History of Labor in the United States " by John R. Commons and associates (Macmillan), is a scholarly work, while " Trade Unionism in the United States " by Robert F. Hoxie (Appleton), is a more analytical treatment. " The I. W. W. " by Paul F. Brissenden (Longmans, Green), is a full documentary history. Significant recent tendencies are recorded in " The New Unionism in the Clothing Industry " by Budish and Soule (Harcourt, Brace). The last chapters of " The Great Steel Strike " by William Z. Foster (B. W. Huebsch), expound his interesting interpretation of the trade unions.

For a statement of the functional attitude toward public problems one should read " Authority, Liberty and Function " by Ramiro de Maeztu (Geo. Allen and Unwin). For a brief and readable application of this attitude to economics, " The Acquisitive Society " by R. H. Tawney (Harcourt, Brace), is to be recommended.

" Modern Social Movements " by Savel Zimand (H. W. Wilson), is an authoritative guidebook to present radical movements throughout the world, and contains an excellent bibliography. And we must not forget the voluminous Report of the New York State Legislative Committee on Radicalism (the Lusk Committee), which not only collects a wealth of current radical literature, but offers an entertaining and instructive example of the current American attitude toward such matters.   G. S.

THE SMALL TOWN

Bibliography: " A Hoosier Holiday," by Theodore Dreiser. " Winesburg, Ohio," by Sherwood Anderson. " Main Street," by Sinclair Lewis.   L. R. R.

HISTORY

The late Henry Adams had much in common with Samuel Butler, that other seeker after an education. He knew that he had
written a very good book (his studies on American history were
quite as excellent in their way as " Erewhon " was in a somewhat different genre) and he was equally aware of the sad fact
that his work was not being read. In view of the general public
indifference towards history it is surprising how much excellent
work has been done. Three names suggest themselves when history in America is mentioned, Robinson, Beard, and Breasted.
Their works for the elementary schools have not been surpassed in
any country and their histories (covering the entire period from
ancient Egypt down to the present time) will undoubtedly help to
overcome the old and firmly established prejudice that " history is
dull " and will help to create a new generation which shall prefer a
good biography or history to the literature of our current periodicals.

The group of essays published last year by Professor Robinson
—the pioneer of our modern historical world—under the title of
" The New History " contains several papers of a pleasantly suggestive nature and we especially recommend " History for the Common Man " for those who want to investigate the subject in greater
detail, and " The New Allies of History " for those who want to
get an idea of the struggle that goes on between the New and the
Old Movements in our contemporary historical world.

But it is impossible to suggest a three- four- or five-foot bookshelf
for those who desire to understand the issues of the battle that is
taking place. The warfare between the forces of the official School
and University History and those who have a vision of something
quite different is merely a part of the great social and economic and
spiritual struggle that has been going on ever since, in the days of
the Encyclopedists. The scene is changing constantly. The leaders
hardly know what is happening. The soldiers who do the actual
fighting are too busy with the work at hand to waste time upon
academic discussions of the Higher Strategy. And the public will
have to do what the public did during the great war—study the
reports from all sides (the revelant and the irrevelant—the news
from Helsingfors-by-way-of-Geneva and from Copenhagen-by-way-
of Constantinople) and use its own judgment as to the probable
outcome of the conflict. H. W. V. L.

548

BIBLIOGRAPHICAL NOTES

SEX

As might be supposed, there has been little writing on sex in this country—such discussion, more or less superficial, of the social aspects as may be found in books on the family, on marriage or prostitution, some quasi-medical treatises and of late a few books along the lines of Freudian psychology, that is all. Among all the organizations of the country there is no society corresponding to the British Society for the Study of Sex. I doubt if such a society or its publications would be tolerated, since even novelists who, like Dreiser, express an interest in sex comparatively directly, run afoul of public opinion, and a book such as " Women in Love " by D. H. Lawrence, its publisher felt called upon to print without his name.

It is not surprising, therefore, that in English the most adequate discussions of sex have been made by an Englishman, Havelock Ellis —" Studies in the Psychology of Sex." Among less well known writing on the subject by Ellis I would note in particular an illuminating page or two in his essay on Casanova (" Affirmations ").

Discussion of the theories of distinguishing between mating and parenthood and of crisis psychology may be found in articles by the writer in the *International Journal of Ethics*, July, 1915, January, 1916, October, 1917, and in *The American Anthropologist*, March, 1916, and *The Journal of Philosophy, Psychology and Scientific Methods*, March, 1918.

" The Behaviour of Crowds " by E. D. Martin, and " French Ways and Their Meaning " by Edith Wharton are recent books that the reader of a comparative turn of mind will find of interest, and if he is not already familiar with the writings of the Early Christian Fathers I commend to him some browsing in the " Ante-Nicene Christian Library" and the " Nicene and Post-Nicene Fathers."

E. C. P.

THE FAMILY

For statistical facts which have a bearing on the tendencies of the family in the United States, the following group of sources has been consulted:

" Abstract of the Census, 1910;" the preliminary sheets of the " Census of 1920;" Report on " Marriage and Divorce in 1916," published by the Bureau of the Census; Bulletin of the Woman's Bureau, U. S. Department of Labour on " What Became of Women

BIBLIOGRAPHICAL NOTES 549

Who Went Into War Industries;" Bulletin of the U. S. Department
of Agriculture on " The Farm Woman;" Bulletin of the U. S. Children's Bureau on " Standards of Child Welfare." Economic aspects
of the family and income data were acquired from " Conditions of
Labour in American Industries," by Edgar Sydenstricker, and " The
Wealth and Income of the People of the United States," by Willford
I. King. For facts concerning longevity, the aid of the Census was
supplemented by " The Trend of Longevity in the United States,"
by C. H. Forsyth, in the *Journal of the American Statistical Association*, Vol. 128. For the long biological perspective to counteract the
near-sighted view of the Census, " The New Stone Age in Northern
Europe," by John M. Tyler may be commended. Psychological
aspects of family relationships are discussed in a scientific and stimulating way in the published " Proceedings of the International
Women Physicians' Conference, 1919." **K. A.**

RACIAL MINORITIES

No author or group of authors has yet attempted to treat in any
systematic and comprehensive way the position and the problem of
the several racial minorities in the United States. A perfect
bibliography of existing materials on the subject would be most
helpful, but it could not make good the existing shortage of fact,
and of thoughtful interpretation.

The anthropological phase of the subject is discussed with authority by Franz Boas in " The Mind of Primitive Man " (Macmillan, 1913), and by Robert H. Lowie in " Culture and Ethnology "
(McMurtrie, 1917). Some information on racial inter-marriage is
to be found in Drachsler's " Democracy and Assimilation—The
Blending of Immigrant Heritages in America " (Macmillan, 1920).
Among recent reports of psychological tests of race-difference, the
following are of special interest: " A Study of Race Differences in
New York City," by Katherine Murdock, (*School and Society*,
vol. XI, no. 266, p. 147, 31 January, 1920); " Racial Differences in
Mental Fatigue," by Thomas R. Garth (*Journal of Applied
Psychology*, vol. IV, nos. 2 and 3, p. 235, June-Sept. 1920); " A
Comparative Study in the Intelligence of White and Colored Chil-
dren," by R. A. Schwegler and Edith Winn (*Journal of Educational
Research*, vol. II, no. 5, p. 838, December, 1920); " The Intelli-
gence of Negro Recruits," by M. R. Trabue (*Natural History*, vol.
XIX, no. 6, p. 680, 1919); " The Intelligence of Negroes at Camp

Lee, Virginia," by George Oscar Ferguson, Jr. (*School and Society*, vol. IX, no. 233, p. 721, 14 June, 1919); and the Government's official report of all the psychological tests given in the cantonments ("Memoirs of the National Academy of Science," vol. XV, Washington, Government Printing Office, 1921).

The most important single source of information on the present status of the coloured race in the United States is "The Negro Year Book," edited by Monroe N. Work (Negro Year Book Pub. Co., Tuskegee Institute, Alabama); the edition for 1918-19 contains an extensive bibliography. Brawley's "Short History of the American Negro" (Macmillan, rev. ed., 1919) presents in text-book form a general narrative, together with supplementary chapters on such topics as religion and education among the Negroes. The Government report on "Negro Population, 1790-1915" (Washington, Bureau of the Census, Government Printing Office, 1918), is invaluable. Important recent developments are treated in "Negro Migration in 1916-17" and "The Negro at Work During the World War and During Reconstruction" (Washington, Dep't of Labour, 1919 and 1920 respectively). Some notion of the various manifestations of prejudice against the Negro may be gathered from the following sources: "Negro Education" (*U. S. Bureau of Education Bulletin*, 1916, nos. 38 and 39); "The White and the Colored Schools of Virginia as Measured by the Ayres Index," by George Oscar Ferguson, Jr. (*School and Society*, vol. XII, no. 297, p. 170, 4 Sept., 1920); "Thirty Years of Lynching in the United States, 1889-1918," and "Disfranchisement of Colored Americans in the Presidential Election of 1920" (New York, National Association for the Advancement of Coloured People, 1919 and 1921 respectively). A few representative expressions from the Negroes themselves are: "Up from Slavery, an Autobiography," by Booker T. Washington (Doubleday, 1901); "Darkwater," by W. E. Burghardt Du Bois (Harcourt, 1920); *The Messenger* (a Negro Socialist-syndicalist magazine, 2305 Seventh Avenue, New York); and the "Universal Negro Catechism" (Universal Negro Improvement Association, 56 West 135th Street, New York).

A great body of valuable information on the Indians is collected in two publications of the Government, the second of which contains a very extensive bibliography; "Indian Population in the United States and Alaska, 1910" (Washington, Bureau of the Census, Government Printing Office, 1915), and the "Handbook of American Indians North of Mexico," edited by Frederick Webb Hodge (Washington, Bureau of Ethnology, Government Printing Office, 1907-10, 2 vols.). An annual report containing current data on the status of the Indian is published by the Commissioner of Indian Affairs. Francis Ellington Leupp, who held this title from 1905 to 1909, was the author of a volume which presents in popular form the results of official experience ("The Indian and His Problem," Scribner, 1910).

The "American Jewish Year Book" (Philadelphia, Jewish Publication Society of America) is an extremely useful volume, and particularly so because one must refer to it for statistical information which in the case of the other racial minorities is available in the reports of the national census. In the *American Magazine* for April, 1921, Harry Schneiderman, the editor of the "Year Book," assembles a great many facts bearing upon the relation of the Jews to the economic, social, political, and intellectual life of the country ("The Jews of the United States," p. 24). Of special interest to students of the Semitic problem is Berkson's "Theories of Americanization; a Critical Study with Special Reference to the Jewish Group" (Teachers' College, Columbia University, 1920).

The standard works on the Oriental question are Coolidge's "Chinese Immigration" (Holt, 1909), and Millis's "Japanese Problem in the United States" (Macmillan, 1915). The Japanese problem in California is treated statistically in a booklet prepared recently by the State Board of Control ("California and the Oriental," Sacramento, State Printing Office, 1920), and in a symposium which appeared in *The Pacific Review* for December, 1920 (Seattle, University of Washington). G. T. R.

ADVERTISING

Expect from me no recommendation of the "scientific" treatises on advertising or of the professional psychological analyses of the instincts. Books, books in tons, have been written about advertising, and as far as I am concerned, every single one of them is right. Read these, if you have the hardihood, and remain mute. Read them, I should say, and be eternally damned. Read them and retire rapidly to a small room comfortably padded and securely locked. J. T. S.

BUSINESS

Within the limits of this space anything like an adequate reference to the source books of fact and thought is impossible. All that may be attempted is to suggest an arbitrary way through the whole of the subject—a thoroughfare from which the reader may take off where he will as his own interests develop. For the foundations of an economic understanding one needs only to read " Principles of Political Economy," by Simon Newcomb, the American astronomer, who in a mood of intellectual irritation inclined his mind to this mundane matter and produced the finest book of its kind in the world. For the rough physiognomy of American economic phenomena there is " A Century of Population Growth," Bureau of the Census, 1909, a splendid document prepared under the direction of S. N. D. North. Katharine Coman's " Industrial History of the United States " is an important work in itself and contains, besides, an excellent and full bibliography. " Crises and Depressions " and " Corporations and the State," by Theodore E. Burton; " Forty Years of American Finance," by Alexander D. Noyes; " Railroad Transportation, Its History and Its Laws," by A. T. Hadley; " Trusts, Pools and Corporations," by Wm. Z. Ripley; and " The Book of Wheat," by Peter Tracy Dondlinger, are books in which the separate phases indicated by title are essentially treated. For dissertation, interpretation, and universal thought every student will find himself deeply indebted to " Trade Morals, Their Origin, Growth and Province," by Edward D. Page; " The Economic Interpretation of History," by James E. Thorold Rogers; " History of the New World Called America," by E. J. Payne; " Economic Studies," by Walter Bagehot; " Essays in Finance," by R. Giffen; "Recent Economic Changes," by David A. Wells, and " The Challenge of Facts and Other Essays," by William Graham Sumner.

G. G.

ENGINEERING

Literature covering the function of the engineer in society, especially in America, is very limited compared with books of information on most subjects. Engineering activities such as are usually described cover the technical achievements of the profession. Useful material, however, will be found scattered throughout the technical literature and engineering society proceedings especially among the addresses and articles of leading engineers prepared for special occasions. A comprehensive history of engineering has never been written, although there are many treatises dealing with particular developments in this field. Among these may be mentioned Bright's " Engineering Science, 1837-1897 "; Matschoss's " Beiträge zur

Geschichte der Technik und Industrie " (" Jahrbuch des Vereines deutscher Ingenieure "); and Smiles's " Lives of the Engineers." On engineering education, the " Proceedings of the Society for the Promotion of Engineering Education " and Bulletin No. 11 of the Carnegie Foundation for the Advancement of Teaching, " A Study of Engineering Education," by Charles R. Mann, offer useful information. Concerning the status of the engineer in the economic order, Taussig's " Inventors and Money Makers," Veblen's " The Engineers and the Price System," together with Frank Watts's " An Introduction to the Psychological Factors of Industry," will be found of value. On the relation between labour and the engineer, much can be found in *The Annals of the American Academy of Political and Social Science* for September, 1920, on " Labor, Management and Production." O. S. B., JR.

NERVES

Complete works of Cotton Mather; also of Jonathan Edwards. Complete works of Dr. George M. Beard, notably his " American Nervousness," Putnam, 1881. Medical publications of Dr. S. Weir Mitchell. Dr. George M. Parker: " The Discard Heap—Neurasthenia," *N. Y. Medical Journal,* October 22, 1910. Dr. William Browning: " Is there such a thing as Neurasthenia?" *N. Y. State Medical Journal,* January, 1911. Dr. Morton Prince: " The Unconscious," Macmillan, 1914. Professor Edwin B. Holt: " The Freudian Wish." Dr. Edward J. Kempf: " The Autonomic Function and the Personality." Complete works of Professor Freud, in translation and in the original.

Files of *Journal of Abnormal Psychology,* to date. Files of *Psychoanalytic Review,* to date. Files of *Imago,* to date. Files of *Internationale Zeitschrift fuer Aerztliche Psychoanlyse,* to date. Dr. A. A. Brill, " Psychoanalysis," third edition. " Character and Opinion in the United States," by George Santayana. " Studies in American Intolerance," by Alfred B. Kuttner, *The Dial,* March 14 and 28, 1918. A. B. K.

MEDICINE

No attempt is here made to give any exhaustive, or even suggestive, bibliography. Only specific references in the text itself are here given in full, so that the reader may find them for himself, if he so desires. But on the general subject of " Professionalism," although it deals more with the profession of law than of medicine, some valuable and stimulating observations can be found in the chapter of that name in " Our Social Heritage," by Graham Wallas (Yale University Press, 1921).

Bezzola: Quoted from " Preventive Medicine and Hygiene," Rosenau, 1920, p. 340.

Clouston: " The Hygiene of the Mind," 1909.

Cole: " The University Department of Medicine," *Science*, N. S., vol. LI, No. 1318, p. 329.

Elderton and Pearson: " A First Study of the Influence of Parental Alcoholism on the Physique and Ability of the Offspring," Francis Galton Eugenics Laboratory *Memoirs*, 1910, No. 10.

Pearl: " The Effect of Parental Alcoholism upon the Progeny in the Domestic Fowl," *Proc. Nat. Acad. Sci.*, 1916, vol. II, p. 380.

Peterson: " Credulity and Cures," *Jour. Amer. Med. Assn.*, 1919, vol. LXXIII, p. 1737.

Rosenau: " Preventive Medicine and Hygiene," 1920.

Stockard: *Interstate Medical Jour.*, 1916, vol. XXIII, No. 6.

Vaughan: " The Service of Medicine to Civilization," *Jour. Amer. Med. Assn.*, 1914, vol. LXII, p. 2003.

Vincent: " Ideals and Their Function in Medical Education," *Jour. Amer. Med. Assn.*, 1920, vol. LXXIV, p. 1065.

ANON.

SPORT AND PLAY

Mr. Spalding, the well-known sporting goods manufacturer, is also the publisher of the Spalding Athletic Library, which contains, besides rule books and record books of various sports, a series of text-books, at ten cents the copy, bearing such titles as " How to Play the Outfield," " How to Catch," " How to Play Soccer," " How to Learn Golf," etc. Authorship of these works is credited to famous outfielders, catchers, soccer players, and golfers, but as the latter can field, catch, play soccer, and golf much better than they can write, the actual writing of the volumes was wisely left to persons who make their living by the pen. The books are recommended, as a cure for insomnia at least. The best sporting fiction we know of, practically the only sporting fiction an adult may read without fear of stomach trouble, is contained in the collected works of the late Charles E. Van Loan. R. W. L.

AMERICAN CIVILIZATION FROM THE FOREIGN POINT OF VIEW [1]

Frances Milton Trollope: "The Domestic Manners of the Americans," London, 1832.
                    The rest is silence . . . or repetition.

                                                    E. B.

[1] The views of foreign travellers in the United States are summarized in John Graham Brooks's "As Others See Us," New York, 1908.—*The Editor.*

WHO'S WHO
OF THE CONTRIBUTORS TO
THIS VOLUME

WHO'S WHO OF THE CONTRIBUTORS TO
THIS VOLUME

Conrad Aiken was born in Savannah, Georgia, in 1899, and was graduated from Harvard in 1912. His books include several volumes of poems, "Earth Triumphant," "Turns and Movies," "The Jig of Forslin," "Nocturne of Remembered Spring," "The Charnel Rose," "The House of Dust," and "Punch: The Immortal Liar," and one volume of critical essays, "Scepticisms: Notes on Contemporary Poetry."

Anonymous, the author of the essay on "Medicine," is an American physician who has gained distinction in the field of medical research, but who for obvious reasons desires to have his name withheld.

Katharine Anthony was born in Arkansas, and was educated at the Universities of Tennessee, Chicago, and Heidelberg. She has done research and editorial work for the Russell Sage Foundation, National Consumers' League, The National Board, Y. W. C. A., and other national reform organizations, and is the author of "Feminism in Germany and Scandinavia," "Margaret Fuller: A Psychological Biography," and other books.

O. S. Beyer, Jr., was graduated from the Stevens Institute of Technology as a mechanical engineer in 1907, and did graduate work in railway and industrial economics in the Universities of Pennsylvania and New York. After some experience as an engineering assistant and general foreman on various railways, and as research engineer in the University of Illinois, he helped organize the U. S. Army School of Military Aeronautics during the War, and later took charge of the Department of Airplanes. He was subsequently requested by the U. S. Army Ordnance Department to organize and operate schools for training ordnance specialists and officers, and in order to conduct this work, he was commissioned Captain. After the termination of the War, he helped promote, and subsequently assumed charge in the capacity of Chief, Arsenal Orders Section, of the significant industrial developments carried forward in the Army arsenals. He has contributed numerous articles to technical periodicals and proceedings of engineering and other societies.

Ernest Boyd is an Irish critic and journalist, who has lived in this country for some years, and is now on the staff of the New York *Evening Post*. He was educated in France, Germany, and Switzerland for the British Consular Service, which he entered in 1913. After having served in the United States, Spain, and Denmark, he resigned from official life in order to take up the more congenial work of literature and journalism. He has edited Standish O'Grady's "Selected Essays" for Every Irishman's Library and translated Heinrich Mann's "Der Untertan" for the European Library, and is the author of three volumes dealing with modern Anglo-Irish Literature: "Ireland's Literary Renaissance," "The Contemporary Drama of Ireland," and "Appreciations and Depreciations."

Clarence Britten was born in Pella, Iowa, in 1887, and was graduated from Harvard in 1912 as of 1910. He was Instructor of English in the Agricultural and Mechanical College of Texas, in the Department of University Extension, State of Massachusetts, and in the University of Wisconsin. He has been editor of the *Canadian Journal of Music,* and from 1918 to 1920 was an editor of the *Dial.*

Van Wyck Brooks was born in Plainfield, New Jersey, in 1886, and was graduated from Harvard in 1907, as of 1908. He was instructor in English in Leland Stanford University from 1911 to 1913, and is now associate editor of the *Freeman.* Among his books are "America's Coming-of-Age," "Letters and Leadership," and "The Ordeal of Mark Twain."

Harold Chapman Brown was born in Springfield, Mass., in 1879, and was educated at Williams and Harvard, from which he received the degree of Ph.D. in 1905. He was instructor in philosophy in Columbia University until 1914, and since then has been an instructor in Leland Stanford University. During the War he was with the American Red Cross, Home Service, at Camp Fremont. He has contributed numerous articles on philosophy to technical journals, and is co-author of "Creative Intelligence."

Zechariah Chafee, Jr., was born in Providence, R. I., in 1885, and was educated at Brown University and the Harvard Law School. After several years' practice of the law in Providence, and executive work in connection with various manufacturing industries, he became Assistant Professor of Law in Harvard University in 1916, and Professor of Law in 1919. He is the author of "Cases on Negotiable Instruments," "Freedom of Speech," and various articles in law reviews and other periodicals.

Frank M. Colby was born in Washington, D. C., in 1865, and was graduated from Columbia in 1888. He was Professor of Economics in New York University from 1895 to 1900, and has been editor of the "New International Encyclopedia" since 1900, and of the "New International Year Book" since 1907. He is the author of "Outlines of General History," "Imaginary Obligations," "Constrained Attitudes," and "The Margin of Hesitation."

Garet Garrett was born in Pana, Ill., in 1878, and from 1900 to 1912 was a financial writer on the New York *Sun,* the *Wall Street Journal,* the New York *Evening Post,* and the New York *Times.* He was the first editor of the New York *Times Annalist* in 1913-1914, and was executive editor of the New York *Tribune* from 1916 to 1919. He is the author of "The Driver," "The Blue Wound," "An Empire Beleaguered," "The Mad Dollar," and various economic and political essays.

Walton H. Hamilton was born in Tennessee in 1881, was graduated from the University of Texas in 1907, and received the degree of Ph.D. from the University of Michigan in 1913. After teaching at the Universities of Michigan and Chicago, he became Olds Professor of Economics in Amherst College in 1915. He was formerly associate editor of the *Journal of Political Economy,* and is associate editor of the series, "Materials for the Study of Economics," published by the University of Chicago Press. During the War he was on the staff of the War Labour Policies Board. He is co-editor with J. M. Clark and H. G. Moulton of "Readings in the Economics of War," and the author of "Current Economic Problems" and of various articles in economic journals.

Frederic C. Howe was born in Meadville, Pa., in 1867, and was educated at Allegheny College and Johns Hopkins University, from the latter receiving the degree of Ph.D. in 1892. After studying in the University of Maryland Law School and the New York Law School, he was admitted to the bar in 1894, and practised in Cleveland until 1909. He was director of the People's Institute of New York from 1911 to 1914, and Commissioner of Immigration in the Port of New York from 1914 to 1920. He has been a member of the Ohio State Senate, special U. S. commissioner to investigate municipal ownership in Great Britain, Professor of Law in the Cleveland College of Law, and lecturer on municipal administration and politics in the University of Wisconsin. Among his books are " The City, the Hope of Democracy," " The British City," " Privilege and Democracy in America," " Wisconsin: An Experiment in Democracy," " European Cities at Work," " Socialized Germany," " Why War? " " The High Cost of Living," and " The Land and the Soldier."

Alfred Booth Kuttner was born in 1886, and was graduated from Harvard in 1908. He was for two years dramatic critic of the *International Magazine,* and is a contributor to the *New Republic, Seven Arts, Dial,* etc. He has pursued special studies in psychology, and has translated several of the books of Sigmund Freud.

Ring W. Lardner was born in Niles, Michigan, in 1885, and was educated in the Niles High School and the Armour Institute of Technology at Chicago. He has been sporting writer on the Boston *American,* Chicago *American,* Chicago *Examiner,* and the Chicago *Tribune,* and writer for the Bell Syndicate since 1919. Among his books are " You Know Me Al," " Symptoms of Thirty-five," " Treat 'Em Rough," and " The Big Town."

Robert Morss Lovett was born in Boston in 1870, and was graduated from Harvard in 1892. He has been a teacher in the English Departments of Harvard and the University of Chicago, and dean of the Junior Colleges of the latter institution from 1907 to 1920. He was formerly editor of the *Dial,* and is at present on the staff of the *New Republic.* He is a member of the National Institute of Arts and Letters, and is the author of two novels, " Richard Gresham " and " A Winged Victory," of a play, " Cowards," and with William Vaughn Moody of " A History of English Literature."

Robert H. Lowie was born in Vienna in 1883, and came to New York at the age of ten. He was educated at the College of the City of New York and Columbia University, from which he received the degree of Ph.D. in 1908. He has made many ethnological field trips, especially to the Crow and other Plains Indians. He was associate curator of Anthropology in the American Museum of Natural History, New York, until 1921, and since then has become Associate Professor of Anthropology in the University of California. He is associate editor of the *American Anthropologist,* and was secretary of the American Ethnological Society from 1910 to 1919, and president, 1920-1921. He is the author of " Culture and Ethnology " and " Primitive Society," as well as many technical monographs dealing mainly with the sociology and mythology of North American aborigines.

John Macy was born in Detroit in 1877, and was educated at Harvard, from which he received the degree of A.B. in 1899, and A.M. in 1900. After a year as assistant in English at Harvard, he became associate editor of *Youth's Companion,* and later literary editor of the Boston *Herald.*

Among his books are "Life of Poe" (Beacon Biographies), "Guide to Reading," "The Spirit of American Literature," "Socialism in America," and "Walter James Dodd: a Biography."

H. L. Mencken was born in Baltimore in 1880, and was educated in private schools and at the Baltimore Polytechnic. He was engaged in journalism until 1916, and is now editor and part owner with George Jean Nathan of the *Smart Set Magazine,* and a contributing editor of the *Nation.* His books include "The Philosophy of Friedrich Nietzsche," "A Book of Burlesques," "A Book of Prefaces," "The American Language," and two volumes of "Prejudices." In collaboration with George Jean Nathan he has published "The American Credo," and "Heliogabalus," a play.

Lewis Mumford was born in Flushing, Long Island, in 1895. He was associate editor of the *Dial* in 1919, acting editor of the *Sociological Review* (London), a lecturer at the Summer School of Civics, High Wycombe, England, and has contributed to the *Scientific Monthly,* the *Athenaeum,* the *Nation,* the *Freeman,* the *Journal of the American Institute of Architects,* and other periodicals. He was a radio operator in the United States Navy during the War.

George Jean Nathan was born in Fort Wayne, Indiana, in 1882, and was graduated from Cornell University in 1904. He has been dramatic critic of various newspapers and periodicals, and is at present editor and part owner with H. L. Mencken of the *Smart Set Magazine.* Among his books are "The Popular Theatre," "Comedians All," "Another Book on the Theatre," "Mr. George Jean Nathan Presents," "The Theatre, the Drama, the Girls," and, with H. L. Mencken, of "The American Credo," and "Heliogabalus."

Walter Pach was born in New York in 1883, and was graduated from the College of the City of New York in 1903. He studied art under Leigh Hunt, William M. Chase, and Robert Henri, and worked during most of the eleven years before the War in Paris and other European art-centres, exhibiting both here and abroad. He was associated with the work of the International Exhibition of 1913, as well as other exhibitions of the modern masters in America, and with the founding and carrying on of the Society of Independent Artists. He is represented by paintings and etchings in various public and private collections, has lectured at the Metropolitan Museum of Art, New York, University of California, Wellesley College, and other institutions, has contributed articles on art subjects to the *Gazette des Beaux-Arts, L'Arts et les Artistes, Scribner's,* the *Century,* the *Freeman,* etc., and is the translator of Elie Faure's "History of Art."

Elsie Clews Parsons was graduated from Barnard College in 1896, and received the degree of Ph.D. from Columbia University in 1899. She has been Fellow and Lecturer in Sociology at Barnard College, Lecturer in Anthropology in the New School of Social Research, assistant editor of the *Journal of American Folk-Lore,* treasurer of the American Ethnological Society, and president of the American Folk-Lore Society. She is married and the mother of three sons and one daughter. Among her books are "The Family," "The Old-Fashioned Woman," "Fear and Conventionality," "Social Freedom," and "Social Rule."

Raffaello Piccoli, who has written the article on "American Civilization from an Italian Point of View," was born in Naples in 1886, and was educated at the Universities of Padua, Florence, and Oxford. In 1913 he was appointed Lecturer in Italian Literature in the University of Cambridge, and in 1916 was elected Foreign Correspondent of the Royal Society of Literature. During the War he was an officer in the First Regiment of Italian Grenadiers, was wounded and taken prisoner while defending a bridge-head on the Tagliamento, and spent a year of captivity in Hungary. After the Armistice he was appointed to the chair of English Literature in the University of Pisa. During the years 1919-21 he has acted as exchange professor at various American universities. He has published a number of books, including Italian translations of Oscar Wilde and of several Elizabethan dramatists.

Louis Raymond Reid was born in Warsaw, N. Y., and was graduated from Rutgers College in 1911. Since then he has been engaged in newspaper and magazine work in New York City. He was for three years the editor of the *Dramatic Mirror*.

Geroid Tanquary Robinson was born in Chase City, Virginia, in 1892, and studied at Stanford, the University of California, and Columbia. He was a member of the editorial board of the *Dial* at the time when it was appearing as a fortnightly, and is now a member of the editorial staff of the *Freeman*, and a lecturer in Modern European History at Columbia University. He served for sixteen months during the War as a First Lieutenant (Adjutant) in the American Air Service. Residence in Virginia, North Carolina, Colorado, Arizona, and California has given him the opportunity to observe at first hand some of the modes and manners of race-prejudice.

J. Thorne Smith, Jr., was born in Annapolis, Md., in 1892, and was graduated from Dartmouth College in 1914. He was Chief Boatswain's Mate in the U. S. Naval Reserve during the War, and editor of the navy paper, *The Broadside*. He is the author of " Haunts and By-Paths and Other Poems," " Biltmore Oswald," and " Out-O'-Luck."

George Soule was born in Stamford, Conn., in 1887, and was graduated from Yale in 1908. He was a member of the editorial staff of the *New Republic* from 1914 to 1918, and during 1919 editorial writer for the New York *Evening Post*. He drafted a report on the labour policy of the Industrial Service Sections, Ordnance Department and Air Service, for the War Department, and was commissioned a Second Lieutenant in the Coast Artillery Corps. He is a director of the Labour Bureau, Inc., which engages in economic research for labour organizations, and is co-author with J. M. Budish of " The New Unionism in the Clothing Industry."

J. E. Spingarn was born in New York in 1875, was educated at Columbia and Harvard, and was Professor of Comparative Literature in Columbia University until 1911. Among his other activities he has been a candidate for Congress, a delegate to state and national conventions, chairman of the board of directors of the National Association for the Advancement of Coloured People, vice-president of a publishing firm, and editor of the " European Library." During the War he was a Major of Infantry in the A. E. F. His first book, " Literary Criticism in the Renaissance," was translated into Italian in 1905, with an introduction by Benedetto Croce; he has edited three volumes of " Critical Essays of the 17th Century " for the Clarendon Press of Oxford, and contributed a chapter to the " Cambridge History of English Literature; " his selection of Goethe's " Literary Essays," with a foreword by Lord Haldane, has just appeared; and his other books include " The New Hesperides and Other Poems " and " Creative Criticism."

Harold E. Stearns was born in Barre, Mass., in 1891, and was graduated from Harvard in 1913. Since then he has been engaged in journalism in New York, and has been a contributor to the *New Republic,* the *Freeman,* the *Bookman,* and other magazines and newspapers. He was associate editor of the *Dial* during the last six months of its appearance as a fortnightly in Chicago. Among his books are " Liberalism in America" and " Collected Essays."

Henry Longan Stuart is an English author and journalist who has spent a considerable part of his life since 1901 in the United States. He served through the War as a Captain in the Royal Field Artillery, was attached to the Italian Third Army after Caporetto, and was press censor in Paris after the Armistice and during the Peace Conference. He is the author of " Weeping Cross," a study of Puritan New England, " Fenella," and a quantity of fugitive poetry and essays.

Deems Taylor was born in New York in 1885, and was graduated from New York University in 1906. He studied music with Oscar Coon from 1908 to 1911. He has been connected with the editorial staff of the " Encyclopedia Britannica," and has been assistant Sunday editor of the New York *Tribune* and associate editor of *Collier's Weekly,* and at present is a critic of the *New York World.* He has composed numerous musical works, including " The Siren Song" (symphonic poem, awarded the orchestral prize of the National Federation of Music Clubs in 1912), " The Chambered Nautilus" (cantata), " The Highwaymen" (cantata written for the MacDowell festival), and " Through the Looking Glass" (suite for symphonic orchestra).

Hendrik Willem Van Loon was born in Holland in 1882, and received his education in Dutch schools, at Cornell and Harvard, and at the University of Munich, from which he received his Ph.D., magna cum laude, in 1911. He was a correspondent of the Associated Press in various European capitals, and for some time was a lecturer on modern European history in Cornell University. He is at present Professor of the Social Sciences in Antioch College, and is the author of " The Fall of the Dutch Republic," " A Short History of Discovery," " Ancient Man," " The Story cf Mankind for Boys and Girls," " The Rise of the Dutch Kingdom," etc.

INDEX

INDEX

570

INDEX